SOCIAL PSYCHOLOGY

SOCIAL PSYCHOLOGY

The Study of Human Interaction

THEODORE M. NEWCOMB
University of Michigan

RALPH H. TURNER
Oberlin College

PHILIP E. CONVERSE
University of Michigan

LONDON
ROUTLEDGE & KEGAN PAUL LTD

First published in England 1952
by Tavistock Publications Ltd
in collaboration with
Routledge & Kegan Paul Ltd
Broadway House, 68-74 Carter Lane, London, EC4V 5EL

Reprinted 1955, 1959 and 1963
Second edition (revised) 1966
Reprinted 1967 and 1969 (twice)
First published as a paperback 1975

Printed in Great Britain
by Lowe & Brydone (Printers) Ltd, Thetford, Norfolk

© Holt, Rinehart and Winston, Inc., 1965

No part of this book may be reproduced in any form
without permission from the publisher except for
the quotation of brief passages in criticism

ISBN 0 7100 1890 8 (c)
ISBN 0 7100 8152 9 (p)

Acknowledgment is made to Stanford University Press for permission to reproduce adaptations of Figures 4 (page 41) and 5 (page 42) from *Social Pressures in Informal Groups* by L. Festinger, S. Schachter, and K. W. Back. Copyright 1950 by L. Festinger, S. Schachter, and K. W. Back.

Acknowledgment is made to Harper & Row, Publishers, for permission to reprint the following excerpts:

Figure, "The adolescent as a marginal man" and excerpts from pages 143-145, from *Field Theory in Social Science* by Kurt Lewin. Copyright 1951 by Harper & Brothers.

Figure, "Medians in groups of two subjects" from *The Psychology of Social Norms* by Muzafer Sherif. Copyright 1936 by Harper & Brothers.

PREFACE

THIS BOOK began as a revision of the senior author's *Social Psychology,* published in 1950. It has emerged as a totally new work: its organization is wholly new and so is the greater part of its content—hardly a paragraph of the earlier work reappears. After all, it can fairly be argued that the field of social psychology is moving apace. In the single area of small-group studies, according to Hare (1962), bibliographic references increased from an average of 43 a year during the ten years before 1950 to more than 150 annually during the four years beginning in 1950, with no evident slackening during the past decade. Not only do we now have far more data; we also have more substantial bases for inclusive perspectives. Such considerations led us to rebuild rather than to remodel.

Some readers with long memories will nevertheless note similarities between this and the earlier work. We have aimed at flow and continuity from chapter to chapter; it is for this reason that the almost totally new material on the measurement of individuals' attitudes and public opinion, and on interaction process analysis now appears in appendixes, rather than in chapters of the text. We have not attempted to perform the functions of handbooks and compendiums of research findings. We have tried, rather, to be selective in citing comparatively few investigations which, we hope, are not only worthy of being described at some length but are also woven into the text. We have continued the use of research illustrations like those that appeared in the opening pages of each of the 1950 chapters, now formally titling them as such and introducing a few of them in each chapter.

The present work continues, though in more explicit and formal fashion, the earlier emphasis on human interaction. Because we have taken seriously the earlier intention "to frame nearly every kind of social-psychological problem in terms of psychological processes which take their particular form from the interactional context in which they occur," we have added the subtitle, *The study of human interaction.*

Any textbook in social psychology nowadays must necessarily be selective, and our basis for inclusion and exclusion has been our conviction that most of the important notions can be organized around the phenomena of human interaction. Our sense of having omitted much is at least partially mitigated, however, by the consideration that there now exist several sets of readings, some of them modestly priced, which may serve to supplement the present work.

Whatever our biases, individual or collective, we hope that they do not include a predilection for preferring either a psychological or a sociological approach to the problems of social psychology. One of us has membership in a department of sociology, another in psychology, and a third in both. What is more important, none of us can conceive of formulating any of our central problems in terms of either discipline alone. It is no accident that we have so often resorted to schemas in which collective variables are now viewed as independent and individual ones as dependent, and a moment later the other way around. Cooley's words are as true today as they were in 1902:

> A separate individual is an abstraction unknown to experience, and so likewise is society when regarded as something apart from individuals. The real thing is Human Life, which may be considered either in an individual aspect or in a social, that is to say a general, aspect; but is always, as a matter of fact, both individual and general.

We are indebted to so many people for so many forms of aid, criticism, and stimulation that we cannot name all of them here. First, in many ways, come our students; we are all teachers, and, sometimes at least, we remember how essential is our interaction with them. Apart from the daily give and take that has provided both feedback and new ideas, several groups of students made detailed evaluations of several chapters of an early, preliminary version of this book. Members of undergraduate classes at Oberlin College, at the University of Kansas (with the help of Professor Howard Baumgartel), and of a graduate seminar at the University of Michigan were the sources of many suggestions without which this book would have been the poorer.

Messrs. Kenneth Feldman, Gerald Ginsburg, Noel McGinn, and John O'Connor, when they were teaching fellows in Social Psychology at the University of Michigan, were responsible for many improvements as a result of submitting themselves to the ordeal of trying out the preliminary version with their classes. Two of these men, Feldman and O'Connor, have prepared a *Study Guide* to accompany this book. Far from being a compendium of exercises, this publication has been designed to stimulate the student to further thought and exploration, as well as to provide self-testing devices.

Four colleagues in other universities—R. F. Bales of Harvard University, O. J. Harvey of the University of Colorado, W. J. McGuire of Columbia University, and P. J. Runkel of the University of Oregon—

have read many or most of the present chapters in an earlier version. Largely as a result of their criticisms, many chapters have been radically revised. Perhaps we had been wiser to accept all of their suggestions for revision, rather than only some of them.

For help in preparing the bibliography and the indices, and in typing successive versions of the manuscript, we have to thank Nancy Abbey, Jean Converse, Mary Newcomb, and Louise Turner.

Ann Arbor, Michigan   T.M.N.
Oberlin, Ohio   R.H.T.
Ann Arbor, Michigan   P.E.C.
November, 1964

CONTENTS

Preface   v

1. *Observing and Understanding Human Interaction*   1
   - Some Observable Forms of Interaction   3
   - Communication as Common to All Forms of Interaction   10
   - Interaction as Mediating between Individual and Group Properties   12

Part One: INDIVIDUALS' ATTITUDES   17

2. *The Organization of Psychological Activities*   19
   - The Nature of Motivation   20
   - The Acquiring of Motives   23
   - Complex Motivation and the Organization of Psychological Processes   27
   - Attitudes   40
   - Overview   45

3. *The Nature of Attitudes*   47
   - Some Formal Properties of Attitudes   48
   - Attitudes and Overt Behavior   67
   - Influence of Attitudes on Other Psychological Processes   73
   - Overview   78

4. *Attitude Change*   80
   - The Primary Conditions for Attitude Change   82
   - Attitude Properties and Attitude Change   89
   - Persuasion and Attitude Change   94
   - Strategies of Attitude Change: An Overview   110

5. *The Organization and Stability of Attitudes*   115
   - The Stable Single Attitude   118
   - Attitude Organization   121

x - CONTENTS

    The Inclusive Principle of Balance   129
    Attitude Organization and the Resistance of Attitudes to
        Change   136
    Focal Objects of Attitude Organization   138
    The Outcomes of Imbalance   149
    Overview   152

Part Two: PROCESSES OF INTERACTION   155

6. Interpersonal Perception   157
    Psychological Processes in Interpersonal Perception   158
    Accuracy in Interpersonal Perception   168
    Reciprocal Perception by Interacting Persons   182

7. Communicative Behavior   185
    The Nature of Messages   186
    Psychological Processes in Message Sending   190
    Psychological Processes in Message Receiving   204
    Interpersonal Processes   211
    Overview   219

8. The Formation of Group Norms   221
    Consensual and Shared Attitudes within Groups   222
    The Nature of Group Norms   228
    Group Norms and the Sharing Process   242
    Imperfect Sharing of Norms   250
    Overview   254

9. Interpersonal Response   256
    Interpersonal Sequences That Are Dependable   257
    Interpersonal Adaptation   264
    Predominantly Unilateral Influence   273
    Reciprocal Influence: Group Processes   281
    Overview   286

Part Three: GROUP STRUCTURES AND PROPERTIES   289

10. Structures of Interpersonal Relationships   292
    Classifications of Interpersonal Attitudes   295
    Bases of Attraction: Properties Attributed to Others   298
    Dyadic Attraction as a Basis for Group Structure   302
    Subgroup Structuring of Attraction Relationships   309
    Overview   321

CONTENTS · xi

11.	*Role Relationships*	322
	Social Positions and Role Prescriptions	324
	Positional Distance and Role Relationships	336
	Groups as Multidimensional Systems of Roles	346
	Overview	356
12.	*Group Properties*	357
	Group Size	359
	Structural Differentiation and Integration	364
	Attitudinal Uniformity	373
	Cohesiveness	380
	Group Properties as Related to Interaction: Overview	386

Part Four: INTERACTION IN GROUP SETTINGS	391
13. *Complex Role Demands*	393
Gains and Pains in Role Prescriptions	394
Role Conflict	404
The Minimizing of Role Conflict	417
Overview	426
14. *Intergroup Conflict*	428
Personal and Shared Bases of Prejudice	430
Hostility between Groups	444
The Reduction of Group Conflict	451
Overview	461
15. *Achieving Group Goals*	463
Interaction Processes in Group Problem Solving	464
Leadership Roles in Goal Achievement	473
Group Cohesiveness and Goal Achievement	486
Overview: Interaction at Work	492

APPENDIXES AND REFERENCES	495
A: *The Measurement of Attitudes*	496
Attitude Items and Attitude Scales: Early Efforts	496
General Characteristics of Measurement	500
Other Approaches to Attitude Measurement	519

B: *Survey Research and the Measurement of Public Opinion*   535

C: *Interaction Process Analysis (Bales)*   553

References   561

INDEXES   575

Index of Names   577

Index of Subjects   581

SOCIAL PSYCHOLOGY

CHAPTER 1

Observing and Understanding Human Interaction

THE STUDY OF HOW PEOPLE THINK, FEEL, AND BEHAVE TOWARD ONE ANOTHER —like the study of anything else that is both important and complex— begins to get exciting when we find that there are some general rules we can depend on to help us understand things that are not, on the surface, self-explanatory. Such rules, or principles, in their most helpful form are statements of order and regularity that go beyond mere descriptions of what can be directly observed. It is easy, on the basis of one's own experience—and with the aid of accumulated folk wisdom—to *describe* frequently observed regularities in people's behavior toward each other. For example, you have probably heard that "anger breeds anger," or that "a soft answer turneth away wrath." You may not have heard this one: people who spend a good deal of time together are apt to come to like each other. The first two of these statements are of the form: behavior X on the part of one person is likely to be followed by behavior Y on the part of another. The third is of the form: behavior X on the part of several people toward one another is likely to be followed by behavior Y on the part of those same people toward one another.

As a matter of fact, there is a good deal of truth in all three statements. Very commonly, however—as in these instances—such descriptive

2 - OBSERVING AND UNDERSTANDING

rules-of-thumb are subject to a good many exceptions. The trick is to account for what we observe in ways that will handle the exception as well as the rule. If it is often true, for example, that anger breeds anger, we need to go on and ask why—not just because we enjoy speculating but because we want to *understand* the conditions under which this particular sequence of behaviors is likely to occur, and when it is not. Answers to *why* questions generally break down into statements of conditions under which something is most or least likely to happen. And these conditions—in social psychology as in physiology or physics—often turn out not to be self-evident.

Here is an actual example of how a common observation led to some unexpected and far from self-evident statements of conditions. As described in more detail in Research Illustration 5.1 (page 122), about the time of World War II some psychologists at the University of California became interested in problems of racial, religious, and ethnic prejudice, and particularly those of anti-Semitism. They had observed, as had other students of the problem, that many Americans who were noticeably anti-Semitic also tended to be anti-Negro, anti-Mexican, anti-Turkish—in fact, quite generally prejudiced. But this generalization simply did not apply to everyone: some persons, for example, were prejudiced against Negroes but not against Jews, or vice versa. Thus it became necessary to try to understand the kinds of people who are prejudiced-in-particular, as well as those prejudiced-in-general. The California psychologists found, as others had before them, that the generally prejudiced people whom they studied felt about the same way toward certain groups regardless of whether they had had any direct contact with them, and so they pursued the hypothesis that this kind of generalized prejudice could be traced to some rather deeply ingrained personality characteristics. As reported in *The Authoritarian Personality* (Adorno et al., 1950) they found a good deal of support for this hypothesis, which we shall later report more fully.

Subsequent evidence has indicated that many cases of specialized prejudice stem from personal experience—not necessarily by direct contact with the people against whom such persons are prejudiced, but commonly the experience of being members of groups in which certain kinds of prejudice were very prevalent (such as anti-Semitism in certain large cities, and Negro prejudice in some southern communities). Very often, moreover, these "specialists" did not have the same traits of authoritarianism (as that term is used by the California psychologists) that the "generalists" did. Thus a rather commonplace observation eventually led to a two-factor explanation (that is, the personality traits labeled "authoritarian," and the sharing of prejudices common in one's own membership groups) that pretty well accounted both for the observed rule and for the exceptions to it.

As suggested by this illustration, then, we need to be alert to apparent regularities that can be observed, but these should be regarded as the beginning, not the end, of our inquiries. A keen eye for exceptions to these *descriptive* regularities, together with some curiosity as to what lies behind them, may lead to an understanding of *explanatory* regularities that account for the initial observation as well as for the exceptions. In this introductory chapter we shall present a selected sample of social-psychological observations. Our primary concern here is not with explanations but with the processes by which they are to be sought.

SOME OBSERVABLE FORMS OF INTERACTION

There are interactional processes that cannot be directly observed, but can only be inferred from what is observed—interpersonal perception, for example, as outlined in Chapter 6. But for the present we shall use the term "interaction" to refer to any set of observable behaviors on the part of two or more individuals when there is reason to assume that in some part those persons are responding to each other. What all these observable forms of interaction have in common is a *sequence of behaviors* on the part of two or more persons. That is, some observable behavior on the part of one person (such as saying "Good morning") or on the part of some group (such as a challenge by one sports team to another) is followed by some observable behavior on the part of another person or group. There are also instances, as we shall see, where people are simultaneously interacting with one another, as when two people dance together; the analysis of this kind of interaction is more complex, but it can still be regarded as a form of behavior sequence.

There follow a few examples of some important forms of observable interaction with which we shall be concerned throughout this book.

Interpersonal Influence: Unilateral Effects

In one sense, any response by one person to another—even the recognition of a casual greeting—is an instance of influence upon the responder. In this sense one may be said to be influencing a person to respond to the question "What time is it?" simply by asking the question. More extreme examples would include these: a person who is generally regarded as miserly is persuaded to make a large contribution to charity; an adolescent girl suddenly changes her makeup to resemble that of a movie actress; or a man who is ordinarily indifferent to music finds himself joining a concert audience in vigorous applause. These are all instances in which one or more persons are primarily the source of influence and another person is primarily affected by it.

One kind of such a unilateral influence process, *imitation,* has long been of interest to social psychologists, though emphasized more in earlier than in later years. Each of the first two books carrying the title *Social Psychology* (by E. A. Ross and by William McDougall, both published in 1908) offered imitation as an explanation of many forms of social or interpersonal behavior. From our present point of view, however, they seem to have confused description with explanation. At the former level, imitation may be defined quite simply as the occurrence of behavior on the part of a person that is in some way a consequence of the same behavior on the part of another person (sometimes referred to as the model). Imitative behavior may or may not be a deliberate attempt to copy another, and may even occur without the imitator's being aware that his own behavior follows and resembles another person's. Viewed simply as a descriptive label for a sequence of similar behaviors by different persons, imitation does not need to be defined in terms of intentions, awareness, or other psychological states.

It is easy to find illustrations, either from textbooks or from everyday experience, of individual behavior that follows and resembles another person's behavior. But it is also easy to find illustrations of failures to imitate—as many a parent, teacher, and supervisor has discovered. And so, if we are interested in explanation, that is, in finding a basis for orderliness and regularity in this kind of interaction, we must ask about the conditions under which one person is most likely to imitate another. One set of conditions has to do with the kinds of persons who are likely to be imitated. A summary of the characteristics of "models" (Miller and Dollard, 1941) concludes that they tend to be superior to imitators in one or more of these ways: in age, in social status, in intelligence, or in other kinds of competence. The observation that persons who are imitated often have these advantages over their imitators is common enough, but it is easy to think of exceptions. For example, school children who are closely alike in age, social status, and ability often imitate one another. Thus it is not enough to say that, behaviorally speaking, models have something that imitators want. Imitation, when it does occur, is an outcome of at least two psychological processes: wanting something, and perceiving that another's behavior points the way to getting it. And so we need to inquire about the ways in which such processes jointly operate. (Research Illustration 9.2, on page 275, points to one kind of answer.)

Both individual and social psychology, as a matter of fact, deal with what might be called rules of combination of psychological states. If we are interested in a single individual it is often useful to discover how his states of motivation, perception, thinking, and feeling are organized in relation to anything that he recognizes as important in his world. Such organizations of psychological states are known as *attitudes*. Social psychology, which deals with relationships among people, also uses attitudes as explanatory concepts, but in characteristic ways of its own. Not only the attitudes of interacting persons *toward one another* but also the relationships among *different persons' attitudes toward the same things* will be of prime concern in this book.

If we are to understand just how it is that the attitudes of interacting persons become jointly involved in a relationship, we must take a further step. One person cannot be directly influenced by another's attitudes as they "really" are, but only as he perceives them. Thus it is necessary to consider the attitudes that each of a set of interacting persons *attributes* to the others, and the relationships among these attributions. Relationships of mutual friendliness, for example, of competition, or of dominance and submission are all associated with what the interacting persons assume to be one another's attitudes. Or, to revert to our previous illustration of unilateral effects, a person who imitates another is making assumptions about the other's motives and attitudes—perhaps very general ones (such as the kinds of values he has) or specific ones about what he is trying to do and why he chooses a particular way of doing it. If the potential imitator attributes to the "model" goals that are like his own, or attitudes that he himself approves of, he is likely to become an actual imitator.

Thus it is the *relationship* between one's own and another's attitudes, as one perceives the latter, that counts. Principles of this kind, like most others designed to account for the presence or absence of an observed phenomenon, are stated in terms that are not themselves directly observable, but that have been derived from observed behavior in order to account for its variations under different conditions. In Part One, which is mostly devoted to the concept of attitudes because of its importance to social psychology, we shall find such principles emerging.

Interpersonal Influence: Reciprocal Effects

Another kind of interpersonal behavior that has intrigued social psychologists since the earliest writing on the subject has to do with the simultaneous effects of two or more persons upon each other. As early as 1895 the French sociologist Gustave Le Bon devoted a whole book— of polemical rather than scientific nature, by modern standards—to what he regarded as the unfortunate fact that groups of people ("crowds," as he called them) often thought, felt, and acted in extreme ways (mob scenes, crowd hysteria, for example, or uncritical acceptance or rejection of ideas) that would never occur if their individual members were alone. Contemporary students of such phenomena, who are more interested in understanding them than in condemning them, examine them in terms of reciprocal influence of group members upon each other.

At about the same time, an American psychologist (Triplett, 1897) reported one of the first experiments in social psychology bearing on the same problem. To forty children, ten to twelve years of age, he assigned the task of winding up fishing reels as fast as possible; each child alternately worked alone and in small groups. Triplett found that twenty of the children worked faster in groups than alone, whereas only ten of them worked more slowly, and the remaining ten did not differ in the two situations. Later, and for the most part more carefully planned experiments (e.g., Allport's and Dashiell's, pages 281–4), yielded rather similar results, which have usually been interpreted as showing that energy expended and sheer quantity of output tend to increase when people work at the same or similar task together. Quality of output may suffer, but there are a good many individual exceptions.

Allport labeled this phenomenon *social facilitation*; whatever it is called, its explanation turns out to be very complex. Allport attributed such energizing effects to "the sight and sound of others doing the same thing," with the cumulative effect of increasing the intensity of stimulation that impinges on each person. But interaction under these conditions does not necessarily have energizing effects; the continued sight and sound of others doing the same thing may, for example, become boring or distracting; or, as in the case of occasional work groups, there may be common understandings that result in restricted output (cf. Coch and French, 1948). Under "natural" as contrasted with experimental situations, perhaps the most striking instances of the energizing effects of the sight and sound of others doing the same thing are to be seen in the "spiraling" excitement of certain crowds, especially in crisislike situations (some of which are described in Chapter 14). If, as occurs at a fire in a theater, all members of the crowd have the same motive (to escape), then the observable (and, in this case, excited) expressions of the common motive are indeed likely to have energizing effects.

Another source of complexity in the phenomena of social facilitation is that, when it does occur, it often involves attitudes of rivalry, or competition. Allport attempted, in his experiments, to eliminate such effects but, as shown in later experiments by Dashiell (Research Illustration 9.3, page 279), without much success. Dashiell found that energizing effects were most pronounced when competitive attitudes were strongest, not when they were weakest, so that the effects could not be attributed merely to heightened stimulation through sights and sounds.

Thus we are led, again, to ask about the conditions under which reciprocal energizing effects occur. As our several illustrations have suggested, and as we shall further note in Chapters 9 and 14, the critical conditions include the attitudes of the interacting persons and also their attributions of attitudes to one another. These are the same conclusions to which we were led in our earlier consideration of unilateral influence. And this is as it should be: an integrated social-psychological theory does not call upon one set of principles to explain unilateral influence and a different set to explain reciprocal influence. Rather, it shows how the same set of principles works in different ways under different circumstances.

This brief consideration of one special form of reciprocal influence, labeled "social facilitation," has not, of course, yielded an all-inclusive set of principles, but has only illustrated one kind of social-psychological problem. Other forms of reciprocal influence and other explanatory principles will emerge in other chapters.

Mutual Adaptation

"Influence," as we have seen, is an inclusive term that may refer to effects that are either persisting or transitory, either unilateral or reciprocal. We shall now use "mutual adaptation" in a more limited sense, as referring to the processes by which each of two persons (or, for that matter, more than two) simultaneously affects and is affected by the other in relatively enduring ways. It often happens that different people, whether they are behaving in similar or in different ways, adapt more or less neatly to each other's behavior. You can easily think of many such instances—such as the clockwork intermeshing of throwing, catching, running on the part of the members of a professional baseball team, or the smooth integration of the movements of a pair of good dancers. Or consider this illustration.

> The following characteristic behavior was observed in a two-year-old. He would always go to the right-hand side of his high chair when ready for a meal, holding himself in a characteristic position ready to be picked up. When he had been lifted into the chair he would duck his head sideways, for the tray to be swung over his head; then he would lift his chin for the bib to be put under it, then bow his head down on the tray so the bib could be tied around his neck. He was obviously prepared for a particular sequence of actions by his mother. He was utterly confused and upset when a new baby sitter tried to lift him up from the *left* side of the high chair, and tried to put his bib on before swinging the tray into place. The little boy and his mother had learned what might have been described as *two halves of the same habit* (Maccoby, 1959, p. 244; our italics).

In this instance two individuals have become so thoroughly familiar with each other's behaviors that the latter may be considered, almost literally, "two halves of the same habit." Comparable forms of mutual adaptation may also be observed in complete strangers; for example, a salesman and a customer who have never met before may interact as if they had practiced it. In other instances interaction is awkward and uncertain—a pair of teen-agers having their first date, for example, or an African villager meeting his first anthropologist. Thus we need to inquire into the conditions under which interacting persons do or do not integrate their responses to one another so smoothly that the total exchange seems like a single multiperson habit.

One rather obvious requirement for mutual adaptation that is smooth, in this sense, is a common set of expectations on the part of the interacting persons concerning each other—including the expectations that each of them attributes to the other about himself. Smoothness presupposes predictability, both concerning what one expects of the other and what the other expects of oneself. If neither knows what to expect of the other or what the other expects of him, each of them must rely on trial and error, with resulting awkwardness, uncertainty, and perhaps anxiety. If, on the other hand, Person A's and Person B's expectations concerning both A and B are identical, then it is at least possible for them to adapt smoothly to each other. Relative similarity (though not necessarily identity) of expectations is a necessary condition but not a sufficient one, as we shall see.

Any form of mutual adaptation that is more than transitory may be described as a *role relationship,* and any particular kind of relationship describes the nature of the behavioral interdependence on the part of the persons involved in it. Thus, in our previous illustration, the mother's contribution to the relationship (her half of the joint habit) is that of providing nurturance; the child's, that of receiving it. Each has come to expect certain behaviors on the part of the other, and has learned to respond to them in certain ways, with the result that the relationship of giving and receiving nurturance is maintained. Mothers and children learn these things through direct experience with each other, but such face-to-face learning cannot explain how it happens that total strangers often adapt their behaviors smoothly to each other on their first encounter. How does it happen, for example, that almost any young man in our society has learned to take his end of role relationships with almost any teacher, or policeman, or girl of his own age? In Chapter 11 we shall approach such problems through an examination of societally recognized positions that carry with them prescriptions for role relationships between occupants of various positions.

In an investigation more fully described in Research Illustrations 6.2 and 10.1 (pages 173 and 293), the development of role relationships of varying degrees of cordiality was studied among students who in two successive years lived in a student house. There were seventeen men each year, selected as total strangers at the time of entering the house, and each of these populations included 136 different pairs of persons. Over a four-month period each man repeatedly indicated not only his own feelings toward every other man in the house, but also judged as best he could how each of the other men felt toward himself. One of the interesting things observed was the development of close mutual friendships. There follow some illustrative findings at different stages of acquaintance:

1. Both early and late, the men believed that the individuals whom they liked best (the top four, for example) in most cases reciprocated their high liking.
2. Both early and late, most of the first four individuals chosen by each man did, in fact, reciprocate his high liking.
3. These mutually high-choice pairs were very stable after several weeks of acquaintance, but not during the early weeks. During the first three weeks only one third of them persisted, as compared with nearly twice as many during the last three weeks.
4. If one of a mutual high-choice pair, as of the first week, later expressed markedly less liking for the other, chances were about two to one that the latter soon came to reciprocate the lower level of liking.

When each of two individuals considers the other a highly desirable associate, and when each of them believes that he is so considered by the other, they have adapted to each other as close friends, and their role relationship is one of mutually close friendship. It might even be said that they have a joint habit of mutual friendship, because if either of them ceases to carry his end of such a role relationship, the other is likely to drop his end of it too. That is, the tendency is for both or neither of them to continue to regard the other as a highly preferred associate. As we shall see in Chapter 10, groups are often formed on the basis of such role relationships of reciprocal trust and liking.

We return now to the question of the conditions under which interacting persons develop various kinds of role relationships. Expectations alone cannot account for their reciprocal adaptations to one another's behavior; a person may know what is expected of him without being motivated to conform to these expectations, or without being able to do so. Thus the total set of requirements for smooth mutual adaptation includes past experience that has provided opportunities for the interacting persons to become familiar with the same body of expectations and to learn how to conform with them, together with present motivation to do so. If they are to adapt to one another for more than a fleeting instant, interacting persons must continue to observe each other's responses, and thus compare expectations with actuality. Each person's behavior is not only a response on his own part but also a stimulus to the others, and this stimulus, like all others, has to be noticed, perceived in some context, and interpreted in some fashion. As long as interacting persons are able to interpret each other's behavior in terms of role relationships that they expect, they have little difficulty in adapting to one another. Deviations from expectations may lead to conflict and frustration or to new forms of reciprocal adaptation, or both. Thus in order to account for observed role relationships we must look behind them to expectations, to perceptions of others' behavior in terms of those expectations, and to processes of learning to adapt to what is perceived.

COMMUNICATION AS COMMON TO ALL FORMS OF INTERACTION

If you observe that a person is speaking heatedly and abusively to someone, you will probably infer that he is angry—though you might be wrong; he might, for example, be rehearsing his part in a play. If you should happen to listen to a street-corner speaker haranguing his audience about the virtues of vegetarianism, you are apt to conclude that he is opposed to eating meat—though it could be that he is only paying off a bet he has lost. And if a friend tells you, by word of mouth or in a letter, that he is about to get married, you are likely to conclude that he has highly favorable attitudes toward his fiancée. These instances illustrate the ways in which all of us make inferences about other people's attitudes—from their observed behavior.

The observation that one person has, so to speak, managed to see what is inside another person's head is commonplace enough, but the processes by which he does so are less self-evident. It will hardly suffice to say, "Well, he just told me, himself," because it is just this process of "telling" that we need to examine. The problem is not made easier by the fact that, in the latter two of these instances, the speaker is referring not just to himself but also to something that is not even present—meat and vegetables, in the one case, and a girl in the other. It is obviously necessary for us to think of the speaker as having some sort of psychological representation of the absent object, and as somehow transferring this representation into the psychological state of the listener. At the same time he creates in the listener a representation of the speaker himself that includes his attitudes toward the absent object.

All these notions are necessary in studying human communication. In Chapter 7 they are more formally described in terms of *symbols* that stand for objects (commonly though not necessarily absent ones); of *shared codes* that enable senders and receivers of messages to attach similar meanings to the same symbols; and of *information*, both about whatever the symbols stand for and about the message sender himself, that is contained in the message or is inferred by the receiver as being contained in it. We shall, as a matter of fact, be using the notion of information throughout this book. It is useful, for example, in seeking answers to questions such as this: Why does a particular person send a particular message to another person at a particular time? It seems to be a reasonable assumption that if one has a certain kind of information that he wants another person to have, he will communicate that information to him; or, by the same reasoning, if he wants some information that he thinks another person possesses, he will initiate a communicative exchange that is likely to result in his getting the information he wants.

We shall see that this approach to the problem helps us to understand the conditions under which communication occurs, but we shall also find that many qualifications of the underlying assumption must be introduced. Very often, for example, people convey information without intending to do so; they ask for information that they already have; and so on. In spite of such vicissitudes, however, the essential general principle that emerges is that we must take into account the *relationship* between communicators' stocks of information—especially as they themselves perceive the relationship—if we are to understand the conditions underlying their communicative exchange.

It is possible to examine the consequences as well as the preconditions of communication from this point of view. The most obvious change to be expected in the relationship between communicators, following a message exchange, is that they will have more nearly the same information about the content of the message than they did before their exchange. But this is not necessarily the case, since a message may be inaccurately received; you can probably think of other conditions under which communication may result in greater discrepancy rather than in greater similarity of information on the part of the communicators. And even in the latter case it can happen that there is in fact increased similarity of information but the communicators do not know whether or not this is so. Information is *shared* when it is not only common to two or more persons but when they also know that it is common property. Sharing is not by any means an automatic consequence of communication; it depends, among other things, upon adequate feedback—return messages concerning the reception of a previous message. One of the important themes of this book concerns the differences between discrepant information, common but unshared information, and shared information. We shall examine with special care the conditions under which each of these relationships between communicators is typically found.

Shared information, in turn, has consequences of its own. Since one's attitude toward anything depends upon one's store of information about it, the sharing of information makes possible the sharing of attitudes—although, again, this is not an inevitable consequence. The place of shared attitudes in everyday life is something like that of the air we breathe: we generally take it for granted, we miss it desperately when we notice its inadequacy, and it is possible either to underestimate or to overestimate how adequate it really is. A central set of problems in this book will therefore be to examine the ways in which discrepant attitudes, common but unshared attitudes, and shared attitudes are dependent upon conditions of communication.

Various kinds of experiments have been carried out in order to understand the preconditions and the consequences of communication. Experiments, as compared with the observation of "natural" events, have the advantage that if one has created different sets of conditions and if different consequences are observed to follow, then one can know with some precision about the exact conditions under which the behavioral variations occur. Several such experiments deal with joint problem solving, which is considered more fully in Chapter 15. One of them (as described in Research Illustration 11.3, page 342) is typical in showing that if one member of a group has opportunities to obtain more information that is essential for solving the problem than others have, then that person comes to be regarded as a leader. Such experiments commonly show, too, that unequal access of information among group members often contributes to efficiency in group problem solving, but at the same time leads to a good deal of dissatisfaction on the part of group members who have only limited information. Here, as so often in everyday life, information confers power.

You may occasionally have been curious why it is that so very much of human activity is devoted to communication. In a general way, the answer is simply that people are dependent upon one another. But there are many specific answers behind this general one, and an understanding of them will help us to look behind observable events in ways that help to account both for obvious regularities in human interaction and for exceptions to them.

INTERACTION AS MEDIATING BETWEEN INDIVIDUAL AND GROUP PROPERTIES

No one needs to be convinced that individuals differ greatly in their characteristic ways of behaving. Some years ago two psychologists (G. W. Allport and H. S. Odbert, 1936) published a list of "trait names" to be found in Webster's *New International Dictionary.* They found 17,953 of them, about 4.5 percent of all the words in the dictionary, that are used "to distinguish the behavior of one human being from another." It is almost equally obvious that groups have their distinctive characteristics, too, although no one seems to have taken the trouble to go through the dictionary and count them. In view of the fact that groups necessarily have individuals as members, this diversity of what are formally known as "properties" of individuals and of groups raises an interesting question: Can the differences among groups be attributed to the fact that they are made up of different kinds of individuals?

Differences among complex phenomena are rarely the exclusive result of one single factor, but it is easy to think of differences among groups that result primarily from differences in the selection of their members. A sandlot baseball team of ten-year-olds, for example, differs in team performance and in coordination of members' activities from a major-league professional team, and this would still be true if the members of each team had played together for the same length of time. A typical fifth-grade class in a public school acts in vastly different manner from that of a "special" class of feebleminded children of the same age. A moment's observation will show marked differences between a group whose members are selected for their interest in chess and one that is organized to take mountain hikes. The characteristics that individuals had before they became group members can contribute a great deal to the properties of those groups.

It is probable, nevertheless, that in most cases this source of group differences is far from being the most important one. This can be shown, to take an everyday illustration, by the fact that a mountain-climbing group and a chess group would still be different in many ways even if they were composed of the same individuals. It can be shown more convincingly by comparing small communities whose members, so far as is known, come from the same biological stock but which, viewed as groups, are conspicuously different, generation after generation. They differ in such characteristics as authority structure, kinship relations, or family organization, primarily as a result of cultural transmission over the generations. Exactly the same conclusion is implied by the fact that individuals of very different genetic stock—say English, Chinese, and Negro—often become indistinguishable from one another, as far as their behavior is concerned, when they become members of the same groups after two or three generations of acculturation in the same society. Another source of evidence can be found in countless experiments in which individuals, selected strictly at random, are formed into groups that, as a result of different experimental conditions, are characterized by distinctive kinds of interaction. The consequence is that the different groups develop the kinds of properties predicted by the experimenter, for reasons that had nothing to do with the properties of individual members. It has been shown, for example in Research Illustration 11.4 (page 353), that comparable sets of individuals interact in cooperative ways when group rewards but not individual ones are offered, and in competitive ways under the reverse conditions. The two modes of interaction were associated with contrasting group properties, including

14 - OBSERVING AND UNDERSTANDING

group solidarity and productivity. These diverse kinds of evidence—from informal observation and from the laboratory—all point to effects of interaction on the characteristics of groups.

Figure 1.1 illustrates how different kinds of questions related to interaction may be asked. If, to continue with the preceding illustration, we ask why it happened that interaction took cooperative forms in some groups and competitive forms in others, this figure suggests that we look at individuals' existing motives, their preexisting attitudes, and other personal characteristics (arrow 1); at the rules by which each group was instructed to act, and at the size of the group (arrow 3); and also at such aspects of the immediate situation as the materials available to work with and facilities for communication among members (arrow 5).

There are also questions to be asked about the consequences, as well as the preconditions, of interaction. Individuals' motives and attitudes are likely to be affected by their interacting experience (arrow 2); shared rules (referred to as group norms in Chapter 8) may be developed concerning the behaviors that members expect of one another (arrow 4). Arrow 5 refers to such consequences as group products, like damage done or work accomplished.

The pairs of arrows pointing in opposite directions usually refer not to simultaneous but to successive effects. Thus arrows 1 and 2 might mean that the preexisting attitudes of individual group members heavily

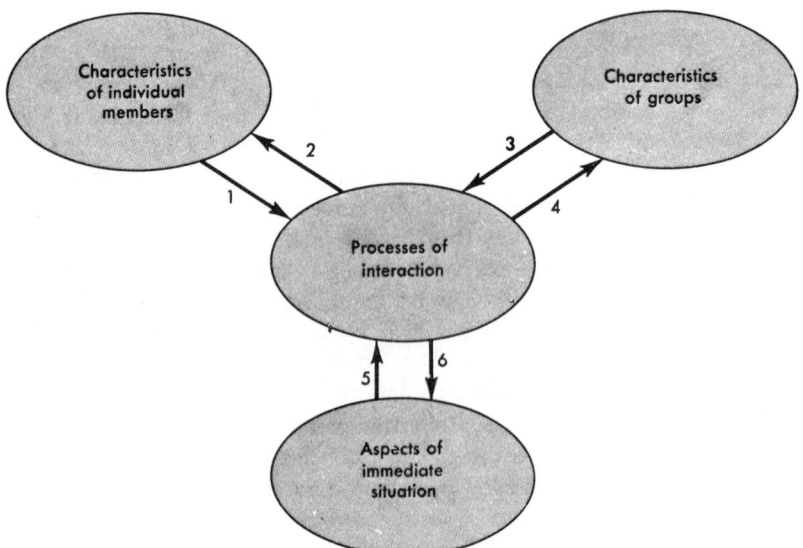

FIGURE 1.1. Schematic illustration of interaction as mediating between individual, group, and situational characteristics

influenced the manner of their interaction on first acquaintance, and that their interaction led to changes in these same attitudes, served to create new attitudes, or both. Or, in the case of arrows 3 and 4, the existing norms of an established group were in the first instance outcomes of its members' interaction.

In a general way, Figure 1.1 outlines the central problems of this book. Most of Part One is devoted to individuals' attitudes, as the peculiarly relevant properties of individuals. This concept is essential to the understanding of processes of interaction, which occupy the central place in the figure as well as in the book (Part Two, especially). Whereas the emphasis in Part One is on arrows 1 and 2, in Part Three we shall concentrate on arrows 3 and 4; here we shall present some different ways of looking at groups, and note some group properties that influence, and are influenced by, various forms of interaction. Part Four continues an examination of interaction processes, noting all the kinds of relationships that correspond to the six arrows. The last two chapters consider problems denoted by arrows 5 and 6, especially the uses of interaction in changing existing situations.

PART ONE

Individuals' Attitudes

YOU HAVE PROBABLY PARTICIPATED IN GROUPS AT A TIME WHEN SHARP differences of opinion came to the fore and led to conflict between the members. There are two rather different ways to describe such an episode. You might indicate what had happened in terms of the group as a whole—saying that the group was badly split, that it became disorganized, or something of the sort. Or, again, you might talk about the episode in terms of the behavior of individual members: Jane couldn't understand the point at all, Ralph got very angry and began to make wild accusations, and so on.

These two modes of description—group and individual—are equally "true," although one or the other way may be preferable for a specific purpose. For the study of human interaction we shall want to be comfortable with description at both levels, but it is useful to begin by looking at individuals.

This is so for the simple reason that interaction presupposes psychological activity on the part of the individuals involved. The first time you interact in any direct way with your professor—in an office appointment, perhaps—you are likely to spend a fair amount of your time trying to judge from what he says and does (or what he fails to say) what he is "really" thinking about: how hurried he is, perhaps, or—more especially—how he sizes you up. It is likely, furthermore, that at the same time he is making some guesses of his own as to what *you* are thinking. The way in which both of you act toward one another is, as you can see, vitally affected by what your respective guesses are. Even though, when you get to know each other better, both of you may be much less aware of trying to imagine what is going on in the other's mind (since it is now easier to guess), these ideas about the other continue to affect the way in which both of you interact. Indeed, it is almost as though the psychological activities on either side were themselves in interaction.

It follows, then, that human interaction is necessarily affected by the properties of individual psychological activities: these properties, whatever they may be, shape and limit the contribution of the individual to the interaction process. Hence we shall begin in Chapter 2 by examining some of the individual regularities that become most important in understanding interaction.

Since the individual is but one unit in our subject matter, we shall not spend much time dissecting the various component processes that contribute to over-all psychological activity. What we need to do instead is to put the individual together, so to speak—to see what regularities are prominent as the component processes combine to produce a total, functioning individual. Regularities emerge at this level simply because psychological activities—all the smaller contributing processes—are *organized*. We shall find that if we wish to deal with the broad and stable lines of this organization over time, it is useful to consider the individual as a complex system of attitudes.

The last three chapters of Part One will be devoted to this view of the individual. We shall be concerned primarily with the properties of attitudes in functioning individuals: what attitudes are, what they may be seen as "doing," and most importantly, the conditions that affect their stability and change.

CHAPTER 2

The Organization of Psychological Activities

WHAT DO YOU MEAN WHEN YOU SAY OF SOMEBODY, "I REALLY KNOW HIM well"? It is likely that you mean you have watched him at close range for long enough so that you are never too surprised by what he says or does, or apparently thinks. You find him predictable. You might not be able to foresee what news he will bring you about things that have happened to him, but once you know about the situations he has been in, his reactions to them are "typical." Through familiarity, you have come to detect certain characteristic lines of organization in his thought and behavior.

If you were asked to describe several people whom you know well, you would probably use a rather different set of descriptive terms for each. Joe is a happy-go-lucky guy who loves sports and loathes studies. Betty is religious and is pretty prim about a lot of things. Jack wants to get into medical school but he has a hard time keeping out of campus politics. This kind of knowledge of Joe, Betty, and Jack is very useful to you, especially if you must interact with them. But for our purposes, the information is too particular. We are tremendously interested in the fact that individuals show a high degree of psychological organization. What we need, however, are ways of describing this organization that are general enough to capture Joe, Betty, and Jack, and many others with them, in the same net.

* * *

In this chapter, then, we shall consider some very general ways of describing the psychological organization of the individual that seem most useful in understanding human interaction. In the process we shall consider a number of familiar psychological processes such as motivation, perception, learning, and cognition. We shall be less interested in these processes themselves, however, than in the way they jointly contribute to the organization of the individual. We shall see that in the short range, at least, the individual organizes his perceptions, his thoughts, his feelings, and his motor behavior so that they are directed toward a goal, and this organization is best described in terms of *motivation*. Toward the end of the chapter we shall introduce the concept of *attitude* as a means of describing the organization of individual behavior in the longer range. We shall also consider the processes of acquiring such organization of psychological activities, which are matters of learning.

Throughout, our interests may be characteristically different from those of the individual psychologist. As social psychologists we shall eventually wish to apply what we borrow from specialists in individual behavior to two problems of our own: How *within*-person processes are affected by interaction with others, and how *between*-person processes of interaction are affected by individual organization. Much of this book will be devoted to these problems. In this chapter we indicate what we find most useful to borrow from individual psychology to bring to bear on these problems.

THE NATURE OF MOTIVATION

Anyone who compares the behavior of a newborn infant with the behavior of the same individual only five years later can hardly fail to be impressed with the fact that a change has taken place. Most of the behavior observed within the few weeks after birth appears to be of a random, essentially unorganized, nature. By the age of five years, however, the behavior has become modified so that what the child does at one moment is related to the behavior seen a moment later, and this behavior, in turn, is related to the behavior that follows. He may spend the better part of an hour manipulating materials in an attempt to construct a toy. A few years later we may find that this same person spends hours, alone and with other persons, doing a variety of things all of which are consistent with each other in that they contribute to the attainment of a certain goal. When we refer to a person as "highly organized," we are commenting upon the fact that most of the things this person does make a definite contribution to a major goal or goals.

Motivation as Goal Orientation

What has happened to bring about this drastic change in behavior? This is an important question if we are to understand how we take our place in a society of interacting persons. The interpersonal behavior we shall study in social psychology is not of the random, unorganized variety. If we watch an individual interact first with one individual, then with another, and then with a group of persons, we can observe that his behavior undergoes certain changes as he moves from situation to situation. But closer examination will also reveal that in any *one* of these situations the behavior appears to be quite highly organized with reference to certain objectives or goals.

THE NATURE OF MOTIVATED BEHAVIOR. For purposes of further discussion it will be convenient to use the term "motivated behavior" to refer collectively to all the various forms of behavior in which a person engages as he strives to reach a goal. In simple terms, motivated behavior includes everything an individual notices, does, feels, and thinks in more or less integrated fashion while he is pursuing a given goal.

A student writing a term paper illustrates these aspects of motivated behavior. What he "notices" may include the insistence of the instructor that the paper should be typed, the date the paper is due, and the fact that the paper will account for half the course grade. What he "does" may include searching for relevant materials, recording information on cards, and typing the paper itself. What he "feels" may include despair at not finding a suitable topic, pleasure at suddenly discovering a subject that interests him, and frustration at failure to find sufficient material to do a thorough job. What he "thinks" may include reflections about the wisdom of having chosen the topic he did, and calculations concerning the amount of time he must devote to the paper in order to complete it on schedule.

All these processes are part of what we shall refer to as motivated behavior. This motivated behavior tends to continue until the goal is reached or until some other motivated behavior intervenes. (The term paper may have to be set aside for a few days in order to prepare for a mid-term examination.) Since the dominant characteristic of motivated behavior is the fact that it is organized around a goal, obviously we cannot fully understand it until we learn how goals and behavior come to be related to each other.

THE STATE OF MOTIVATION. In order to account for the fact that motivated behavior is directed so consistently toward a goal, it is necessary to infer the existence of a supporting state of the organism. The term "motive" will be used to refer to this state. More specifically, we shall use the term "motive" to refer to a state of the organism in which bodily energy is mobilized and directed in a selective fashion toward states of affairs, often though not necessarily in the external environment, called goals. An organism is said to be motivated only when it is characterized both by a state of energy mobilization and by the direction of behavior toward some goal that is selected in preference to all other possible goals. Motive, then, is a concept that joins together a state of energy mobilization and a goal. Without the mobilization of energy or without a goal toward which the energy is directed, there can be no motive as the term is used here. Energy and goals are thus joined in this definition. In the next section we shall see how they are joined within the organism through the process of learning.

It should be noted that "motive" refers not to the carrying out of behavior, as such, but to the state of the organism that accounts for the fact that the behavior has direction toward a certain goal. The term "motivated behavior," as previously discussed, will be used when referring to the behavior itself. It is quite proper to refer to motives by using the goals toward which the motives are directed as modifiers of the term "motive." Thus we may refer to the food motive or the water motive. In both instances from observable behavior (the person eats or drinks) we are inferring a state of the organism in which energy is mobilized and directed toward a specific goal. But since motive refers to the state of the organism and does not refer to the behavior itself, we must make observations of motivated behavior in order to achieve some understanding of underlying motive states. If we observe a stranger standing motionless on the street, we may have little basis for inferring very much about his motives. If he then springs into action, goes into a restaurant, and eats lunch, we infer from this that most of the activity we have seen was mobilized and directed toward this end by the food motive.

For purposes of clarity we have thus far restricted our examples of motivated behavior and motive states to rather simple and elementary illustrations. Later in this chapter we shall have ample opportunity to show how motives become elaborated so that they constitute a way of understanding complex human behavior of the kind found when one person interacts with another in a social setting. Before this can be done, however, it will be necessary to examine the way motives are acquired. How motives are modified and how the concept of motivation can be worked into a view of complex behavior will be more readily comprehended after a discussion of the way motives are acquired.

THE ACQUIRING OF MOTIVES

We have seen that one of the primary differences between the behavior of the newborn infant and that of an adult is that behavior gradually becomes more highly organized. Energy that originally led to quite random or diffuse behavior now becomes mobilized in a selective manner toward specific goals. In short, the individual gradually acquires motives.

Drives and the Learning Process

Since motivation involves the joining of energy states with goals, we must seek an understanding of how this comes about if we are to understand how motives are acquired.

DRIVES AS SOURCES OF ENERGY. The "energy states" we have referred to when talking about motives must be identified so that we can see how they become linked with goals. We shall use the term "drive" to refer to bodily states that initiate tendencies to general activity. These states are frequently experienced as feelings of tension or restlessness. They do not have to be learned but are aroused when the condition of the organism departs considerably from a desirable or optimum condition. The hunger drive, for example, develops when an individual is deprived of food for many hours. The resulting feelings of tension and restlessness emerge, without learning, from changes that take place when the individual goes for some time without food. In the case of the newborn infant the hunger drive leads to general activity. But in the adult the energy state associated with the hunger drive has become associated with a goal (food) and leads to highly specific activity. This comes about through the learning process.

LEARNING AND DRIVE REDUCTION. Behavior is "driven" with increasing vigor as the tension that is characteristic of a drive (hunger, thirst) becomes more acute. When appropriate behavior is finally hit upon (eating, drinking), the drive tension is reduced and the individual ceases to direct his energy toward goals relevant to that drive. Moreover, it can be shown that the appropriate behavior is hit upon more quickly as a result of this experience. After a period of further learning, the individual seeks food or drink with little or no general activity coming between the drive and whatever is needed to reduce it. The energy associated with the drive has now become linked with a specific goal and has direction. The individual no longer has just an unlearned drive; through learning he has also acquired a motive.

Repeated observations of the kind just referred to have led to the "tension-reduction theory of learning," which states that individuals learn precisely those activities that are immediately followed by tension reduction. This point of view suggests that we learn to eat because eating is followed by reduction of the hunger drive. Because of the instrumental nature of such drive-reducing acts, this kind of learning, studied by Skinner (1953) in a number of different organisms, has come to be known as "instrumental learning" or "instrumental conditioning." There is little doubt that animals and men often learn to repeat those forms of behavior that are followed by states of tension reduction, and that this is one of the ways that motives develop.

In short, then, a drive is an unlearned push from within—a push in no particular direction. A motive is based on this drive, but learning has now intervened so that the push is a specific push in the direction of whatever activity has satisfied the drive in the past. This activity centers around a goal and a goal may thus be defined as a state of affairs toward which motivated behavior is directed. Motives are thus inferred from the goal-directed character of the activity being observed.

For purposes of social psychology, it is more convenient to label any particular motive according to its goal than according to its state of drive. The reason for this preference is that the drives involved in most social behaviors are complex and usually difficult to isolate. We do not have the means, for example, for distinguishing between the drive states of a person when he is motivated to succeed on a college examination and when he is motivated to win at poker. The goals can easily be distinguished, but the drives cannot. Hence we shall speak of a *hunger drive* (the unlearned bodily state that initiates tendencies to general activity) and a *food motive* (a state of the individual in which the drive is directed in a selective fashion, through the influence of previous learning, toward a goal that satisfies the drive). It would obviously be inappropriate to speak of a food drive or a hunger motive.

LEARNING WITHOUT DRIVE REDUCTION. Harlow (1953) has repeatedly observed that monkeys can and do learn to solve mechanical puzzles without a reward that reduces an organic drive state. Since he has been unable to find any internal drive associated with this activity, he has evolved the term "curiosity-manipulation" to describe this state of affairs. These observations can be extended to human behavior. Harlow has shown that when a child has eaten and the hunger drive has already been reduced, "curiosity" emerges and the child goes out and learns without benefit of drive reduction. Similarly, an adult, who has already eaten to the point of protesting that he cannot possibly eat anything more, can often be induced to try some new food that arouses his curiosity. Harlow concludes that such behavior is not based on the reduction of drives and that the drive-reduction principle is sometimes of little importance in the learning situation.

Leuba (1955), drawing upon the work of Hebb and others, has attempted to reconcile these observations with the seemingly contradictory evidence stemming from the drive-reduction theory of learning. He suggests that we tend to learn those responses that produce a desirable or optimal level of total stimulation (or tension). If a person is exceedingly hungry, his drive state is very *high* and he tends to learn those responses (eating) that *reduce* the hunger drive because this high level of stimulation is moved toward a more satisfactory level. But if a person has satisfied all his drives, the total level of stimulation is *below* the optimal level and he seeks to *raise* it by actively seeking contacts with the environment. This would help account for the curiosity-manipulation described by Harlow. Under these circumstances, a person seems to learn those things that are accompanied by an increase rather than a decrease in the over-all level of stimulation. Leuba's suggestion, then, is that when the over-all level of stimulation is high, we tend to learn those activities that are accompanied by decreasing stimulation; when the over-all stimulation is low, we tend to learn those activities that are accompanied by increasing stimulation.

This hypothesis is an interesting one. We know that human behavior can be highly organized and directed toward goals in the areas of invention, creativity, and group action. Consequently we know that motives are acquired in these areas even though drive-reduction principles are difficult to utilize as a means of understanding their acquisition. It is possible that Leuba has suggested a way of accounting for the acquisition of motives where drive-reduction principles are difficult, if not impossible, to apply.

The Distinctive Number and Variety of Human Motives

It is not difficult to compile a short list of drives that are primary or absolutely dependable in the sense that they must be fulfilled if the organism is to survive. The familiar examples—hunger, thirst, pain, fatigue—are shared by man with most animal species. Yet much of human social behavior, and virtually all behavior that is distinctively human, has little in the way of simple one-to-one connections with such primary drives. The same drive may be involved, for example, in many different motives. Although the hunger drive usually leads directly to food-getting behavior, it may also instigate behavior directed toward injuring others (aggressiveness), toward hoarding (acquisitiveness), or toward competing or cooperating with others. Similarly, as Research Illustration 2.1 makes clear, even a simple act of motivated behavior

Research Illustration 2.1

An experiment by Blum and Miller (1952) shows that the act of eating may well satisfy more than just the hunger drive. Eighteen third-grade boys and girls were given an unlimited supply of one-ounce cups of vanilla ice cream, and records of their consumption were kept over a period of several weeks. With children eating as many as 39 cups in a 45-minute period, the experimenters doubted that the ice-cream consumption was purely a matter of hunger satisfaction. They assumed that the dispensing of food was important to the children in part as a token of personal recognition. It was hypothesized that the awarding of other tokens of recognition, such as gifts, would help to satisfy these nonhunger needs and would result in a decrease in ice-cream consumption.

Therefore on one day crayons were passed out as gifts, and fourteen out of sixteen children ate less ice cream than before. On another day the children were given some pencils they had chosen as their most desired gift on the preceding day. In this case, twelve of the fifteen children present ate less ice cream. Both differences were statistically significant.

Hence it appeared that on days when no gift was received, the act of eating satisfied not only a hunger drive but also such motives as the receiving of attention from other children. The gifts reduced some of the tensions associated with the attention motive and hence less ice cream was consumed. Similarly, any other form of behavior may satisfy more than just one drive or motive.

---

such as eating food, which seems quite directly and uniquely tied to the hunger drive, may be functioning to reduce other tensions as well.

As much as anything, the absence of simple connections between human motives and the primary drives springs from the fact that human beings have a distinctively great capacity for learning—and hence for acquiring motives. This gives man's behavior a degree of flexibility not found in other organisms. Although many of man's drives do not differ greatly from those of other primates, his motivated behavior is much more complex than that of any other animal. In the process of satisfying the hunger drive, man has learned how to make palatable a large variety of different substances from the animal, vegetable, and mineral worlds. If a substance is not edible in its natural form, man may have learned to process it so that it becomes edible.

More important still, man has learned through interaction with his fellows how to achieve goals through collective efforts that would be unattainable by individuals working alone. Some animal species have primary groups in which motives of wanting to be associated with others in approved ways are acquired, and in which collaborative behavior toward group ends does occur. But human primary groups differ in many ways from primary groups of other animal species. Our distinctive human capacities, including the use of language, make it possible for individuals to place themselves in the position of others. We thus experience vicariously what others experience directly. This fact has two important consequences. First, the individual acquires motives of being concerned about what happens to others just as truly as if the same things were happening to him. And second, the individual comes to look at himself through the eyes of others. Thus his perspective changes as he relates his own drive relief to his environment in quite different ways, and new motives are developed as a consequence.

Human motives, then, are distinctive in their number and variety. The unending possibilities of new learning experiences in complex, organized societies loosens almost beyond recognition the links between human motives and underlying primary drives. In turn, our complex social structure, with the resulting interdependence of one individual on another, is a measure of the ingenuity with which man has learned to approach the problem of satisfying his motives.

COMPLEX MOTIVATION AND THE ORGANIZATION OF PSYCHOLOGICAL PROCESSES

All of man's complex social arrangements, including his modes of interaction with his fellows, require that his behavior be very highly organized. In the following sections we shall consider how some of the familiar psychological processes, such as perception and cognition, contribute to the organization of motivated behavior.

Cognitive Organization

Man's most distinctive physiological equipment is the mind itself—an unparalleled tool for processing and storing great quantities of information. The complexity of his behavior is dependent not only on his capacity to retain much information in his memory, but also on the fact that this stored information is organized in useful ways. It has been observed that the world of the infant lacking any substantial memory must be one of "blooming, buzzing confusion." Yet an unorganized storage of information in the mind, however large, would be little improvement. If in facing new decisions we had to begin sifting at random through all of the incredibly varied pieces of information we have stored from the past in order to find something relevant to the new situation, we would certainly be crippled in our responses. And ironically, the larger our store of information, the more crippled we would be.

In point of fact, however, cognitive capacity to organize information and the sheer amount of information that can be successfully retained go hand in hand (see Research Illustration 2.2). As you may have noted in preparing for examinations, unorganized information is quickly forgotten. It is cognitive organization that permits man to store a great deal of operating information relevant to his motivated behavior.

A KEY PRINCIPLE OF COGNITIVE ORGANIZATION. The information that we store has to do with properties of objects, states, and events, and of relationships among them. Therefore it is not surprising that the main principles of cognitive organization all have to do with what we may call *object-belongingness*, or the tendency to consider certain objects (or states or relationships) as belonging together. Nor is it surprising that objects that become psychologically associated with one another do so either (1) because the environment frequently presents them together, or (2) because the individual finds it particularly useful to group them together, or (as is most common) for both reasons at the same time.

Many of the ways in which stored information is organized cognitively are reflected in what the student does with outlines and reference cards in preparing a term paper. He soon learns, for example, that it is inefficient to write information from varying sources in sequence on a sheet of paper. Instead, he writes on cards so that information can be rapidly shuffled into categories that are meaningful with respect to his purpose. Likewise, he finds it useful to construct an outline giving general headings for major categories of information, and more specific headings for more specific subclasses that the general classes embrace. An outline can also suggest the scheme which justifies the sequence in which major and minor headings are organized, and the dimensions along which the most specific elements may be ordered.

OBJECT GENERALIZATION. Although cognitive organization is not of course as explicit and self-conscious as organization for a term paper (or at least a good one!), the same modes of grouping objects and linking information about them are apparent. We shall focus here on two very general modes of object-belongingness that are important throughout this book. The first of these is *object generalization*. At the simplest level, this refers to the fact that objects that are seen to share a particular property are grouped together *with respect to that property*. Sometimes the property in question is a simple attribute that is present or absent. In such cases, the elements within classes are left undifferentiated, as when pennies, nickels, and dimes are lumped into a pile as "money." In other cases the property itself suggests an ordering of

Research Illustration 2.2

With an eye to suggesting the nature of limits on human capacity to process information, G. A. Miller (1956) has surveyed the results of a large number of experiments on human judgments, attention span, and memory capability. Studies of "absolute judgments" have dealt with the individual's ability to locate stimuli with respect to a single dimension, such as tones of various frequencies, sounds differing in loudness, samples of water differing in saltiness, and the like. Confusion increases for all these judgments as the number of stimuli presented increases. Although the point at which confusions begin—showing an approach to the limits of capacity to absorb the information accurately—is slightly different for different stimuli and different sense modalities, all experiments show a limit in distinguishable alternatives in the neighborhood of what Miller calls "the magical number seven."

There are a number of ways to increase this capacity to judge stimuli varying along a single dimension, and these involve one or another form of cognitive retention and organization of the separately presented stimuli. One such method is to proceed only with relative judgments (this tone is higher than the preceding) rather than absolute ones. Another very powerful method of increasing capacity is to organize the incoming information into more familiar units or "chunks." Thus, for example, simple tests of immediate memory requiring the subject to repeat a lengthy series of digits or other types of items often show that such a span of memory runs to about seven items. However, much larger capacities can be shown where the subject finds some cognitive device for organizing the information. Thus a lengthy series of numbers such as 19318417516615714813 . . . could easily be reproduced once the pattern or organizing principle of the series is detected. Where incoming information is nonrandom, the exercise of cognitive organization permits extreme increases in the efficiency of information processing.

---

elements within the class: interest in the mint dates of pennies would permit an ordering to be established within the pile of pennies. Similarly, it would be natural for Americans to order our larger classes of coins in terms of monetary value, placing the pile of nickels between the piles of pennies and dimes; however, a foreigner might organize such objects by size, putting the pennies in the middle.

The illustration immediately suggests a more complex aspect of object generalization: classes of specific elements may themselves take the position of elements in a still more general set of classes. Thus a penny minted in 1934 is an element in the general class of pennies; pennies are elements in the more general class of hard change; coins are elements in the more general class of money; and money is one element in a more general class of instruments of exchange. The rules that can be employed for such hierarchical organization of objects are quite various, and include such important special cases as certain part–whole relationships (carburetor and gears as elements in a car) in which elements are not left unassorted nor ordered on a single dimension, but are primarily seen as interacting parts of a larger system.

The important point is that some rather general objects subsume a number of smaller or more specific elements, and these objects themselves can be subsumed as elements in broader categories. Indeed, one means of studying cognitive organization is to present individuals with a set of elements asking what general concepts define these elements as a class, or what rules would be needed to explain a particular ordering of these elements. Such experiments are labeled "concept formation" studies, and concepts are clearly very general and abstract object categories which in one way or another subsume more specific elements.

It is hard to disengage man's unique talent for concept formation from that capacity which has so deeply impressed all students of man—the formation and manipulation of symbols (usually as language). Although man is having some success in communicating with particularly clever animals like dolphins in dolphin "language," he is unlikely to succeed in conveying to them concepts of deficit financing or the calculus. The abstract symbols that make up human language provide fine instruments not only for complex communication, but also for the classification processes that permit complex thought.

One implication of this mode of cognitive organization is that we cognize as single entities very general classes consisting of many objects at once. This is true not only of classes of physical objects, such as "metals" or "trees," but also of social objects, such as "bankers" and "Negroes," which in the very same way can be seen as large classes of elements grouped together on the basis of certain defining properties delimiting the class. Use of such mental shorthand does not mean we are unable to discriminate between elements within the class. We may say "He is not much of a banker," or "He is an unusual Negro," which suggests such differentiation. Yet such statements recognize implicitly that the general term "banker" has identifiable meaning as a single object. As we shall see, this characteristic of cognitive organization is critical in many different aspects of social behavior.

Since most objects have a wide variety of properties, the treatment of cognitive organization can become extremely complicated, for any given object may be located in rather different ways with respect to a variety of other classes of objects, according to the particular property suggested by the context. Thus a house may be considered as a temporary shelter, as an architectural creation, as real estate, as an index of status in a neighborhood, or as a home. In each case, a quite distinctive cluster of properties and judgmental standards would be called into play: comfort, cleanness of line, resale value, and the like. We shall recognize these formally as differences in *associated cognitive context,* or more simply, "cognitive context."

CAUSALITY. A second very general mode of object-belongingness important to us involves notions of *causality*. Perceptions that one event or state leads to another event or state serve to group such states together as psychological objects (Heider, 1946 and 1958).[1] Causality is itself a very general cognitive context, and a judgmental standard central to this context is the probability that one state will lead to another. Although the mathematician assigns numerical probabilities to certain events that are far more precise than those of customary thought, perceived causal relationships between states are usually modified in our thinking by cruder judgments of likelihood. The adverbs "certainly," "probably," and "likely" are familiar modifiers of common causal relationships. The perceived degree of certainty that B will follow A is itself a rough index of the "tightness" with which the two states are cognitively grouped in a particular context.

We have already seen that modes of object generalization permit more efficient use of stored information in motivated behavior. The link between causal modes of organization and motivated behavior is equally obvious once we recognize that causal perceptions include not only relatively impersonal matters (if a weight is released at a height, it will fall toward earth), but also *means-end* relationships (or *instrumentality*) that bear on the ways in which the individual can attain his goals. Since most behavior is goal-oriented, and since the environment tends to provide choices of paths that may be taken toward any particular goal, it is reasonable that means and ends are psychologically grouped together, and that this aspect of cognitive organization is crucial in motivated behavior.

As in the realm of causality more generally, such personal means-end linkages are modified by probability perceptions, often called *expectancy* in the instrumental case. Rotter (1954) has presented a social learning theory that suggests that any situation has within it possibilities for the satisfaction of many different needs. Which of these needs an individual will strive to satisfy depends on two factors: the *value* that the satisfaction of a given need has for the individual, and his *expectancy* that his behavior will actually lead to that satisfaction. According to this view, motivated behavior is more likely to persist if the indi-

---

[1] Heider (1958, pp. 177–179) notes several other "unit forming factors," or modes of object-belongingness, including proximity in space, ownership, frequency of association, "influence of the surrounding" (for example, common boundaries, or common characteristics that are distinctive).

vidual has a high expectancy that his behavior will lead to satisfaction of a valued need.

Even with lower animals, certain experiments seem most readily interpreted if it can be assumed that expectancies based on rates of past success with various behavior routes affect simple choice behavior on ensuing trials (for example, Brunswik, 1939). But human mental capacities, including large memory storage and the use of language symbols, permit means–end "maps" to attain a degree of complexity and a breadth of time perspective that nobody would attribute to lower animals. This is clear in the case of our capacity to remember physical maps that underpin extended behavior sequences: "I go to Lockport and turn left on Route 35. After about 40 miles I hit Route 18 and turn right on it until I come to Smithville," and so on. Even more abstract "maps" may link means and subgoals in elaborate chains over much of a lifetime, as in the preparation for and pursuit of a career (see Research Illustration 2.3).

PROBLEM-SOLVING VS. AUTISTIC THINKING. We may distinguish between types of thought processes according to the relative role played in means–end mapping by new information coming from the environment on one hand, and motive states on the other. At one pole is *problem-solving thought*, involving a series of processes that include selection of some features of the situation as being especially relevant to the solution, carrying out a trial performance covertly or internally by the use of symbols and language, perceiving the probable outcome, and repeating the next steps in much the same manner until the solution of each aspect of the problem has been achieved. Such "internal trial and error" is dominated by motivated behavior directed to the solution of the problem, but the thought-action sequence involves constant reality checking.

At the opposite extreme we have thought so dominated by motive states that normal reality limits—the reasonable expectancies built up through experience—are ignored. This kind of thinking, familiar to all of us as daydreaming and fantasy, has been called *autistic* from the Greek word for "self." Thinking is autistic to the degree that reality is distorted in privately motivated ways, as in making over the past or constructing an improbable future. It is not, of course, undirected or capricious, but usually represents "imaginary" progress toward a goal in line with rather strong motive states. Freud believed that the form taken by dreams is essentially this same type of motivated fantasy, although the motives involved are often so disguised as to be hard to recognize.

An interesting description of how autistic thinking may develop is given by Bergler (1957). He notes that in infancy we often experience satisfaction of our needs shortly after ardently wishing that these needs

Research Illustration 2.3

Teahan (1958) has studied differences in future time perspectives among boys in the seventh and eighth grades. He believed that although all children would have some future expectations, children who were performing at a high level of academic achievement would be more concerned with the future, and would tend more to relate their current behavior to goals that were often quite remote in time. To measure time perspectives he collected among other things the reported conversations and thoughts of the children and analyzed them for numbers of references to the future. He also gave them three ambiguous pictures (a boy with a violin, or a boy alone in front of a cabin), and asked them to write stories about the picture (Thematic Apperception Test). The stories were then rated according to the likely duration of time required for the events described to take place.

Thirty of the boys were in the top fourth of their classes in academic achievement and thirty were in the lowest fourth. The two groups were selected so that there was no difference between them in socioeconomic status. The results include the following differences:

	High achievers	Low achievers
Median number of future references	13.5	9.2
Median duration of TAT stories	6 months	14 hours

Hence high academic achievers did show significantly more extensive time perspectives, and tended to look more to the future. Teahan suggests that high achievers see school subjects as meaningful subgoals on an extended time continuum in which the final goal is vocational success. Thus it appears that superior academic achievement is associated with more extensive maps linking current motivated behavior to future goals.

---

would be satisfied. The infant thus learns that wishes can apparently bring about a satisfactory state of affairs. As infancy passes, wished-for events stop occurring when the child wishes for them, but many persons never learn to give up expecting that "wishing will make it so."

Organization and Perception

Up to this point, we have stressed the ways in which our stored cognitions are organized in the service of motives. Yet it is important to recognize that our cognitions are constantly affected by the flow of new information from the environment. The ways in which the individual handles incoming information is traditionally studied as "perception." Although it is often hard to distinguish processes that are perceptual from those that are cognitive, perception refers, literally, to the individual's organization of sensory input—that is, to what he does, psychologically, with the stimuli currently impinging upon his sense organs. Although we shall not be using the term in this literal sense, it will be worth our while to note how an experimental psychologist looks at the phenomena of perception.

> (1) These phenomena involve *organization* of peripheral, sensory events—looking about us we see patterned objects in space, not mere conglomerations of color points. (2) They manifest *holistic*, all-or-nothing properties, i.e., a pattern of dots or lines may give rise to a complete percept of a square or a cube. (3) They display *constancy* to a high degree—a white house seems to remain so despite immense variations in luminance as high noon resolves into evening, but they are (4) also broadly *transposable*—a triangular stimulus can be directed to many different parts of the retina without disturbing response. (5) They operate *selectively*—for the hungry organism, food-related objects assume figure qualities. Finally, (6) they are very *flexible* processes—the regular black-and-white pattern of a tile floor assumes a bewildering variety of temporary organizations as we watch it. What do all these characteristics taken together imply in regard to the meaning of "perception"? [It] *refers to a set of variables that intervene between stimulation and awareness* (Osgood, 1953, pp. 193–194; italics in original).

Later on (Chapter 6) we shall discuss some of these characteristics of perceptual processes in greater detail as they relate to a special case of perception: *social* perception, where the object being perceived is another person. At the moment we wish to focus on two phases of the perceptual process that illustrate most clearly the manner in which perceptual events are influenced by the motives around which behavior of the moment is organized. Since different people regarding the same objects at the same time but with different motives may "see" different things, these aspects of perception help us to understand such differences, which otherwise seem unaccountable.

PERCEPTUAL SELECTIVITY. In the initial phase—*perceptual selection*—the individual chooses for attention certain portions of the total information that the situation presents. For any complex situation (particularly a changing one), such selectivity is simply inevitable, for the sum of potential information being presented is large indeed, and as we have seen (Research Illustration 2.2), there are limits on human capacities to absorb incoming information accurately. Part of the information available will be attended to closely, some portions will be monitored with indirect attention, and other portions will escape attention entirely. The famous fable of the blind men who tried to form a concept of an elephant by feeling a part of him is an ancient recognition of perceptual selectivity. One blind man felt the elephant's trunk, and decided the elephant was like a snake; another felt his leg, and decided he was like a tree; another felt his tail, and decided he was like a rope; and so on. Even with all our senses intact, the fact remains that close attention to one aspect of a complex object or situation normally precludes close attention to all other possible aspects.

It is relatively easy to see what governs our choices for attention, since perceptual selectivity is but a part of the selective direction of energy we have attributed to motivated persons more generally. Just as the motivated person does not carry out all possible behaviors, he does not respond to all possible stimuli. His attention tends to focus on those details that provide information useful in his motivated behavior. Dearborn and Simon (1958) found this to be a troublesome matter when the executives of different departments in a large company were asked to look at problems from a company-wide rather than just a departmental point of view. They found that each executive tended to perceive only those aspects of the situation that related to the activities and goals of his department. These men were insensitive to those perceptual stimuli not closely related to their own motivated behavior in running their departments.

DECODING. A second aspect of the perceptual process can be called *decoding*. It refers to the attempt to locate incoming information with respect to one's storage of past information, thereby lending it "meaning." Such an attempt may very largely fail, as it would if you tried to make sense of a radio broadcast in Azerbaijani. However, most potential information that is important to us is rather effortlessly decoded. Indeed, we can see that perceptual selection and decoding are not entirely independent phenomena, since we are not likely to attend for long periods of time to aspects of a situation that we find impossible to decode, especially if the same situation provides other information of apparent importance to us that we can easily decode.

It is a fortunate fact of human life that much information is likely to be decoded in the same way by most of the people most of the time, for all kinds of human communication and cooperation are totally dependent on such a state of affairs. Nevertheless, important individual and situational differences do arise in the decoding process. The likelihood that such differences will arise in a given instance depends, reasonably enough, on (1) characteristics of the information, and/or (2) characteristics of the person receiving it.

The incoming information itself may be incomplete (or, as is often said, "ambiguous" or "poorly structured"), complete, or more-than-complete (*redundant*). A poorly defined form seen in dim light or a conversation partially overheard in a noisy room provides only incomplete information. Information is redundant, on the other hand, when parts of the symbolic content convey no new information beyond that which other parts of the same message have already conveyed (Shannon and Weaver, 1949).

We are indebted to modern information theorists for the insight that much of the information that comes to our attention is redundant in this sense. For example, each of the nine letter-symbols that make up the name Elizabeth conveys information. However, we would understand what word was intended even with certain of the letters missing. Thus if we encountered a page of text that was torn off two type spaces from the margin and read only "Elizabe—," we would still receive all the information that had been intended. In other words, the final "th" does not add new information at all, and hence is redundant. It turns out that languages as commonly used are quite redundant at the level of sentence structure as well as at the level of syllables and letters.

One can see immediately, however, that particular information can be called incomplete or redundant only with respect to the individual exposed to the information. Quite specifically, incoming information is more or less complete according to the storage of past information the individual holds. The remark "I've just been to Niagara Falls in New York State, in the northeastern part of the United States," would be highly redundant for most Americans, who would already know the other details of location once Niagara Falls was mentioned. For some foreigners, however, such a statement might even be incomplete.

A key principle surrounding the decoding process is that individual variation in decoding is greatest where the incoming information is most incomplete or ambiguous for the persons involved. Sometimes the incompleteness of information is recognized by the receiver, who may seek further clarifying information or, if this is difficult, may make conscious guesses as to the appropriate cognitive contexts and judgmental standards for decoding.

Sometimes information that is actually ambiguous may seem to be complete until additional information makes the receiver aware that the matter can be seen in more than one light. Where the perception of simple forms is concerned, for example, there are famous figures that can be made to appear differently according to which part of the stimulus is made to stand out and which part is perceptually left as background. One such form which can produce this "figure-ground" effect is presented in Figure 2.1. One may see either the space between the profiles as a vase *or* the two profiles themselves. Never are both figures seen simultaneously.

Analogous figure-ground ambiguity can arise in more complex perceptions. For example, a newspaperman asked Ernest Hemingway after his second airplane accident how he accounted for his run of bad luck.

FIGURE 2.1. Reversal of object and background

Hemingway replied that this was a run of good luck, not bad, and pointed out that not many persons can walk away from two such accidents unharmed! In this case the two possible interpretations, good luck or bad, stand in a figure-ground relationship.

In many instances we supplement incomplete information without realizing that we are doing so. One experimental means of keeping information incomplete is to give the subject only a split-second exposure to a stimulus object. Such studies typically show that people fill in details they expected to find, believing that they actually saw details that were not present. Thus there is an important expectancy element in perception when incoming information is incomplete. These expectancies may affect the cognitive contexts or judgmental standards against which the incoming information is located. For any given situation, expectancies vary from individual to individual, for they depend on individual experience in the past and current motive states.

We shall use the term "salient" to describe stored information that has been prompted to the forefront of the individual's conscious thought by the characteristics of the immediate situations in which he finds himself, and which he is thereby particularly disposed to relate to incoming information. The notion of saliency has an interesting counterpart in the information storage of modern "thinking machines" or large computers. It turns out that the mechanical memory capacity that is most rapidly accessible to the "thinking" or operating parts of the machine is quite limited. To extend the amount of information that can be stored for use, other storage devices are employed that can feed information into operation only at slower rates. Thus the machine storage of information is organized into "levels" of more or less rapid accessibility. Quite naturally, an efficient programming of the machine stores information that is going to be operated on most frequently in the most rapidly accessible storage level.

The immediate situation or recent experience may serve to render certain types of stored information or cognitive contexts more readily accessible or salient for the individual. When incoming information is ambiguous as to context, it is likely to be decoded into more salient contexts rather than less. If someone says to you, "I've just been to Washington," you have a choice of decoding the remark into an East-coast context of cherry blossoms and national politics, or a West-coast context of camping, boating, and mountain climbing. If one of these two contexts is particularly salient, you may choose it without recognizing the possible ambiguity. An immediate situation may render a specific context salient, as it would if the statement about "Washington" were made in the context of a conversation about the Pacific Coast. Or relevance to a state of motivation may render a context salient: the high school student who has spent six months working toward a senior class trip to the nation's capital is likely to have only one Washington in mind.

A variety of psychological tests (the Rorschach and other inkblot tests, thematic apperception tests, and the like) all capitalize on the fact that the context an individual ascribes to incomplete or ambiguous information can tell us a great deal about the sorts of cognitive contexts salient for him, and hence about his motive states. (Research Illustration 2.3 provides a good working example.) Implicitly, such tests assume that in the face of incomplete information in real life, the individual will show comparable systematic biases in perception. Since actions in a sequence of motivated behaviors tend to be checked against new incoming information relevant to the actions, any such biases will have systematic effects on the total organization of behavior.

Organization and Learning

In discussing drives and the learning process we described how the satisfaction of drive states results in learning what goals should be sought in the future when the drive state must again be satisfied. For several reasons, however, it would be incorrect to suppose that we succeed in storing information only about goals that have attained reward value in a direct way through satisfaction of a simple drive state.

In the first place, we have already seen that after complex learning has gone on for a period of time, it becomes increasingly difficult to relate most specific motives to single drives. Furthermore, we have

ORGANIZATION OF PSYCHOLOGICAL ACTIVITIES - 39

remarked upon man's great capacity for storing information concerning "what leads to what," and hence for learning complex and lengthy means–end routes. There is a good deal of evidence that perceived progress along the route is in itself gratifying, and what may be called a secondary reward value becomes associated with the steps or means, just as more direct reward value has been learned for the end or goal.

Such secondary rewards play an important role in complex social behavior, and help us to understand how a great deal of human behavior persists in highly organized form even when primary rewards do not appear to be present. Among adults, for example, we often find that a smile or a nod of approval constitutes a very potent secondary reward, sufficient to keep motivated behavior intact over a considerable period of time (cf. Research Illustration 7.4, page 214). Similarly money, which has little or no inherent worth, supports a great deal of highly organized activity as a secondary reward. Frequent accounts of deranged elderly people dying in filth and poverty amid vast hoards of money tied in rags or hidden in boxes suggest further that objects originally seen as secondary rewards may come to have primary reward value.

In general, this spreading of learned valuations from gratifying goals to many objects directly or indirectly associated with these goals is a very crucial matter for us, since it permits us to deal with a level of organization in individual behavior that the concept of motivated behavior cannot by itself illuminate. When an individual is following a particular means–end route, an understanding of motivated behavior permits predictions as to what he will think, perceive, and feel in passage, for all of these processes are organized with reference to his progress toward the goal.

Yet this is only the fine grain of behavior, so to speak. We are likely to feel, and quite justifiably, that there is a still broader consistency in an individual's behavior that is visible not only within a particular sequence of behaviors toward a goal, but also from one sequence of behaviors to others that may involve different specific motives, and that is visible as well over much longer periods of time.

This sense of broader consistency may come through most clearly as we watch friends cope with situations that are new to them, and for which choices of ends and means have not become so thoroughly learned that they are routine. A student in a predominantly white university finds herself assigned a Negro roommate. What motives, if any, does this new situation arouse? Once a particular motive is ascendant, much of what we have said in this chapter about the organization of motivated behavior becomes relevant. But until this point, we could say very little about the matter. Yet if you were well acquainted with the girl, you would probably feel that you could understand not only the organization of her behavior once a motive is aroused, but could also predict what motive is likely to be aroused! In other words, you perceive regularities in her psychological behavior over time that are more general than the organized patterns accompanying a particular motive arousal. These long-range regularities suggest that there is some psychological basis for long-range organization that we have not yet described.

Just as the organization of motivated behavior depends on the learning process, so does such long-term organization. The important fact about learning at this level has less to do, however, with specific means–end maps than with the simple and general fact that much of the information we store is not emotionally-neutral information. Very many of the objects we cognize—and by "objects" we still mean to include events, states, and relationships between objects as well—tend to be *valenced* objects. That is, they are objects accompanied by positive and negative associations.

Under certain circumstances, as we shall see in later chapters, these valences associated with cognized objects are extremely durable. In such circumstances they provide bridges between periods of relevant motive arousal, and help determine what motives new situations arouse. Hence they are central to an understanding of long-term organization and consistency in individual behavior. We shall continue to use the term "information" in its most global sense to include all material, whether stored, incoming, or ignored, whether valanced or emotionally neutral. From this point on, however, we shall refer to stored cognitions that have some positive or negative associations as *attitudes*.

ATTITUDES

From a cognitive point of view, then, an attitude represents an organization of valenced cognitions. From a motivational point of view, an attitude represents a state of readiness for motive arousal. An individual's attitude toward something is his predisposition to be motivated in relation to it. The fact that meaningful definitions of "attitude" may be made from both a cognitive and a motivational point of view is a simple reflection of the location of attitudes at a crucial intersection between cognitive processes (such as thought and memory) and motivational processes (involving emotion and striving).

In this sense, the attitude concept, like the concept of motivated behavior, is a very summary one. It is addressed to the organization of a number of component psychological processes that, for many kinds of work, we would wish to keep entirely distinct from one another. Yet the concept combines these various processes intentionally, and not through negligence. In any given sequence of motivated behavior, as we

Research Illustration 2.4

Osgood and his associates (1957; 1962) have conducted a long series of studies designed to measure the basic dimensions of meaning that individuals attribute to familiar objects. Throughout their work, these investigators have been impressed by the degree to which objects are lent meaning primarily in "good–bad" (evaluative) terms. In an early part of the study, for example, college students were given long lists of nouns and were asked to write down the first common descriptive adjective that occurred to them. The adjectives "good" and "bad" occurred more than twice as often as any other adjectives, and nearly half of the fifty most frequently mentioned were clearly evaluative in nature (such as beautiful–ugly or honest–dishonest). The same prominence of the evaluative factor emerged continually with more elegant studies of American subjects involving a technique called the *semantic differential* (see Appendix A, page 528). To check against the possibility that the findings were peculiar to the English language or to American culture, studies have now been replicated in a wide variety of language and culture areas. Although there is some variation culturally in secondary dimensions of meaning that emerge, the evaluative component is uniformly the primary one in all cultures examined, and its degree of importance from culture to culture is remarkably similar. Thus in three languages as different as English, Finnish, and Flemish the evaluative factor accounts for the meanings of a wide variety of words about as fully as do all other factors put together.

The authors have concluded that "a pervasive *evaluative factor* in human judgment" regularly appears whenever a wide sample of objects is rated. It is noteworthy that such an evaluative factor comes through clearly even in ratings of such impersonal objects as "rock" and "dawn." But it is of special interest to the social psychologist that the evaluative factor is extremely prominent—far outweighing other dimensions—whenever the object is social (a person, a group, or an institution).

have seen, we can most readily understand what is going on at the level of the component psychological processes once we know the motives of the behavior. Over the longer term, we can best understand how component psychological processes will operate if we know something about the individual as an organization of stable attitudes.

In considering what characteristics of the individual contribute to situations of human interaction, we must first understand in a more general way how the past experience of the individual interacts with the current situation to produce complex behavior. The attitude concept seems to reflect quite faithfully the primary form in which past experience is summed, stored, and organized in the individual as he approaches any new situation. Such experience is best described as a residue (but nonetheless highly organized) of cognized objects to which experience has lent affective color or valence. And, as we shall see, a knowledge of this residue helps to predict either future states of component processes (future motive arousals, future perceptions, future learning), or general trends in future behavior itself.

Although we shall spend the next several chapters exploring the nature of attitudes in much greater detail, a few introductory distinctions may be drawn here to clarify the concept.

Attitudes and Motives

An attitude is like a motive in several ways, but important differences remain. The primary difference has to do with temporal duration. The strength of a motive depends on a drive state. Hence motives appear, disappear, and reappear. An attitude is not characterized by a drive state, but merely refers to the likelihood that a given kind of motive (including its accompanying drive) can be aroused. Thus a man watching television may not at that moment be motivated to protect his family. But he may have a persistent protective attitude toward his family so that the motive is immediately aroused if, for example, a weather bulletin indicates that a tornado has been sighted in his area. The attitude persists; the motive does not, though it may recur.

Furthermore, the sorts of attitudes that are important in the long-term organization of behavior tend to involve less specific objects than motives. A persistent, general attitude of protection toward the family may facilitate the arousal of such specific motivated behavior as repairing a broken step, removing a fire hazard, or making a supply of vitamin pills available. Although these motivated acts have different specific goals, they are all related to the protective attitude of the head of the household toward his family. An attitude may thus predispose to the arousal of a whole cluster of specific motives that serve the one general attitude.

Although it is important to stress these differences, we are not implying that attitudes are not attitudes unless they are extremely stable or unless they refer to very generalized objects. Under certain interesting conditions to be spelled out later, attitudes as we have defined them may be highly unstable. Similarly, all of us have attitudes toward a great many very specific objects. You undoubtedly hold rather strong attitudes toward such specific objects as A+ grades or shells in your scrambled eggs. The point is rather that attitudes *can become* both very stable and very generalized. We have already seen that the tendency to cognize large and general classes of objects as a single entity is an important feature of cognitive organization. These generalized objects often form the core for stable and generalized attitudes. When attitudes of this sort are acquired, they may come to dominate the individual organization of behavior in durable and far-reaching ways as states of motivation cannot, since (by definition) they exist, and perhaps reappear, only when energy is being mobilized and directed toward goal attainment.

The Formation of Attitudes

How does it happen that you have developed general attitudes toward your parents, toward your education, toward the Democratic party? Such attitudes originate in specific motives. We have seen that once an object (say a candy bar) or a state (say the presence of an adult) has been associated with the satisfaction of a motive, the type of behavior that led to the satisfaction comes to be directed toward that object or event, even in the absence of the drive to which it was originally related. For example, the baby often wants the candy bar even if not hungry, and wants the presence of an adult even when he is not in need of immediate assistance in satisfying a drive. The individual has thus acquired favorable attitudes toward these objects.

Although particular attitudes may have their sources in any of a great variety of specific motives, it is possible to sketch some of the broader kinds of motivational bases on which the formation of attitudes tends to occur. Katz (1960), speaking of the functions that attitudes perform in the service of motives, has suggested the following:

1. *The adjustment function.* Essentially this function is a recognition of the fact that people strive to maximize the rewards in their external environment and to minimize the penalties. . . . Attitudes acquired in the service of the adjustment function are either the means for reaching the desired goal or avoiding the undesirable one, or are affective associations based upon experiences in attaining motive satisfactions. . . . The dynamics of attitude formation are dependent [here] upon present or past perceptions of the utility of the attitudinal object for the individual.

2. *The ego-defensive function.* The mechanisms by which the individual protects his ego from his own unacceptable impulses and from the knowledge of threatening forces from without, and the methods by which he reduces his anxieties created by such problems, are known as mechanisms of ego defense. Many of our attitudes have the function of defending our self-image. The formation of such defensive attitudes differs in essential ways from the formation of attitudes which serve the adjustment function. They proceed from within the person, and the objects and situation to which they are attached are merely convenient outlets for their expression. When no convenient target exists the individual will create one. [Adjustment] attitudes, on the other hand, are formed with

specific reference to the nature of the attitudinal object. They are thus appropriate to the nature of the social world to which they are geared.

3. *The value-expressive function.* While many attitudes have the function of preventing the individual from revealing to himself and others his true nature, other attitudes have the function of giving positive expression to his central values and to the type of person he conceives himself to be. Satisfactions accrue to the person from the expression of attitudes which reflect his cherished beliefs and his self-image.

4. *The knowledge function.* Individuals not only acquire beliefs in the interest of satisfying various specific needs; they also seek knowledge to give meaning to what would otherwise be an unorganized chaotic universe. People need standards or frames of reference for understanding their world, and attitudes help to supply such standards. [Adapted by permission.]

All these functions refer to aspects of the individual's adaptation to the environment. Attitudes that might be fitted in the first or the last of these categories are the normal consequence of cognitive adaptation to the world. The second and third have to do with the relationships of external situations to the self; they are less dependent on immediate reality than on inner motive states. What is important for us to remember at this point is that there is some variety in the kinds of motivational bases on which attitudes toward specific objects can develop, and hence attitudes toward the same object, while otherwise similar, may have developed on different bases for different people. This fact, as we shall see, becomes important in considering the ways in which a given person's attitude may be changed once it has formed.

Whatever the motivational base on which the attitude develops, the range of motivated behavior associated with the object very often enlarges itself over time. The baby's motive in desiring to be with others, for example, comes to be expressed in such various ways as crying for a person, asking for a person by name, and watching at the window for the return of someone. The motive to be with others usually grows to the point that we find college students seeking a room in a home where other students are also housed and joining a social group where membership virtually guarantees a certain amount of contact with others. In this manner very generalized attitudes are built up that affect behavior in a great variety of contexts.

VALUES AS INCLUSIVE ATTITUDES. As this process continues over a period of years even fairly general attitudes may come to be integrated into a few broad patterns. Attitudes toward certain things appear to become dominant over attitudes toward an increasing variety of other things. Thus a person may come to orient a very large part of his waking behavior around a core of religious convictions, or around the pursuit of occupational success. The term "value" is used by some social psychologists to refer to the common objects of such inclusive attitudes.

ORGANIZATION OF PSYCHOLOGICAL ACTIVITIES

VALUES — Extremely inclusive goals around which many attitude patterns may be organized.

ATTITUDES — Generalized states of readiness for motivated behavior.

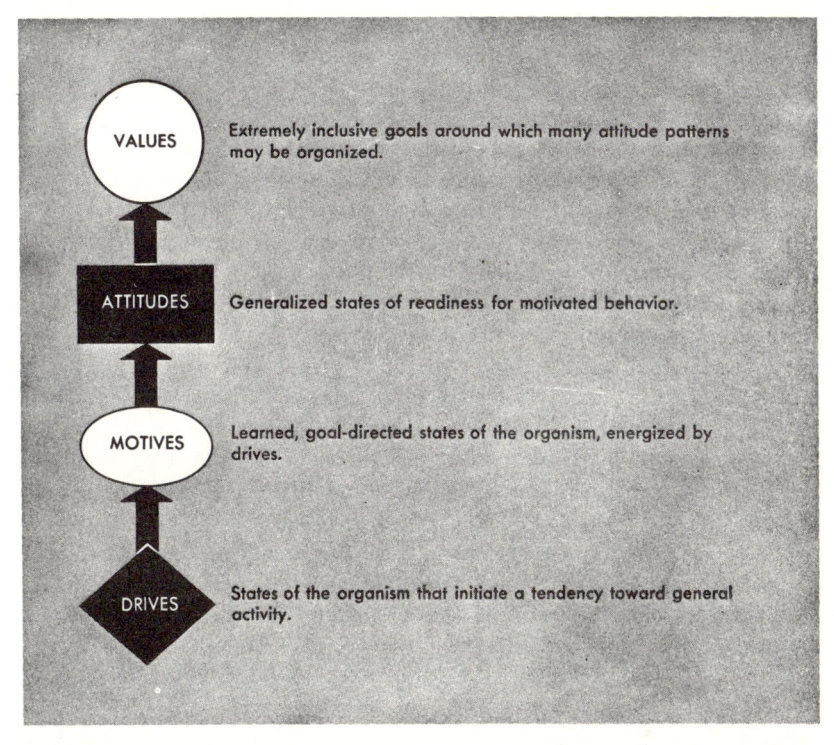

MOTIVES — Learned, goal-directed states of the organism, energized by drives.

DRIVES — States of the organism that initiate a tendency toward general activity.

FIGURE 2.2. The relationship between values, attitudes, motives, and drives

For many people, entire systems of thought and "philosophies of life" are organized around values that become, for them, more and more inclusive.

Since values are readily seen as special cases of the attitude concept, we shall not insist on any formal definition of the term here. However, we shall occasionally choose this term informally when we wish to stress the inclusiveness and importance to the individual of a particular attitude. As Figure 2.2 suggests, values can be considered as the ultimate development of those many processes of selection and generalization that produce long-range consistency and organization in individual behavior.

OVERVIEW

Since human interaction presupposes psychological activity on the part of the individuals involved, we have used this chapter to describe certain features of the psychological organization of the individual, borrowing concepts and principles of individual behavior that will be useful in considering the individual contribution to interaction.

We have been particularly interested to see how psychological organization develops in the child, and to consider how the operating organization of the adult may best be described. The key fact of the developmental process is that psychological activity, at first diffuse and unorganized, becomes more and more selectively directed toward goals. It is therefore convenient to describe this level of organization in terms of motives and motivated behavior. While a person is engaged in any activity his psychological processes of perceiving, cognizing, thinking, feeling, and performing are all directed toward a goal. The coordination of processes that such common direction requires is precisely what is meant by "organization," and the total process considered as a whole is what is meant by "motivated behavior." The most important operating characteristics of these component processes—perception, cognition, and the like—reflect their continual organization in the service of motivated behavior.

Although the motive concept is helpful in understanding the organization of sequences of behavior leading to a particular goal, the fact that man stores in his memory vast quantities of valenced information about objects means that behaviors in the longer term show high organization as well. At the close of the chapter, we introduced the concept of attitude as a useful way of describing this more durable level of organization. An attitude is a more lasting residue of affect toward an object than a motive that requires an existing state of drive: a person's attitude toward something is his predisposition *to become motivated* in relation to it.

Although we have noted briefly how attitudes develop through learning, we as yet know nothing of the formal properties of attitudes, nor of the influence they may be seen to have either on other attitudes, on component processes, or on behavior itself. It is to these considerations that we turn.

CHAPTER 3

The Nature of Attitudes

It is not hard to find examples of people who behave systematically in ways that seem contrary to their attitudes. Thus a restaurant owner who feels no personal sense of hostility toward Negroes may try to discourage service to Negroes on his premises. Or a strongly prejudiced student at a liberal university may take great pains not to show any sign of racial discrimination in his actual behavior. Observations of this sort prompted Merton (1949) to consider a sharp distinction between prejudice (*attitudes* of ethnic hostility) and discrimination (restrictive or hostile *acts* toward minority groups). In Merton's typology, there is a place for prejudiced nondiscriminators and unprejudiced discriminators. For such people, there seems to be a lack of correspondence between attitudes and behavior.

Since we have suggested that attitudes are important keys in understanding the long-range organization of behavior, any such lack of correspondence is a matter of concern to us. Although overt behavior is directly observable, attitudes are not, in the same sense. The notion of attitudes as stored dispositions is useful only in the degree that behavior can be seen as dependent in some way on such dispositions. If individuals are capable of behaving in ways that seem to correspond poorly with their attitudes, of what use is the notion of attitude at all?

* * *

In this chapter we would like to refine our view of what attitudes are and what they do. Among other things, we shall see that there is rarely any reason to expect a perfect correspondence over large numbers of people between a single attitude that we might measure and a particular behavior. Nevertheless, if our understanding of an individual's attitudes is sophisticated enough, we can indeed predict his behavior in varying situations remarkably well—better, in some instances, than he can predict it himself.

Since attitudes are seen as critical in the *total* organization of the individual, some consequences of attitudes on behavior are indirect since they are mediated through other psychological processes. We shall explore the proposition that attitudes affect not only overt behavior but such processes as learning, perception, cognition, and, most importantly, the formation of other attitudes. Before we consider what an attitude *does* as an active agent, however, it is wise first to consider what properties an attitude may be said to *have*.

SOME FORMAL PROPERTIES OF ATTITUDES

Attitudes as functioning dispositions are extremely complex. We may, however, abstract from this complexity a limited set of properties that will be particularly important to us in later chapters. Indeed, for most purposes an attitude toward a specified object can be completely described by two properties—the direction of the attitude and the degree of affect represented—and these two properties can themselves be considered as forming a single dimension.

Basic Properties of an Attitude

DIRECTION OF THE ATTITUDE. By "direction" of an attitude we mean simply that the residual affect felt toward an object can be either positive or negative. Even this statement involves a great deal of abstraction from the emotions that we feel in "real life." In the course of your life you have probably been annoyed by a mosquito, angered by a late bus, distrustful of a glib salesman, and frightened by a bat. You would have no difficulty discriminating between the emotions aroused by each of these objects, or between the vaguer residue of affect you feel toward each of these classes of objects. For our purposes, however, annoyance, anger, distrust, and fright are all shadings of negative affect, and these shadings we shall ignore. Affect toward an object can be very generally classified as either positive or negative. Positive attitudes predispose the person to some kind of approach toward the object; negative attitudes predispose to some kind of avoidance of the object. Naturally, the exact form such approach or avoidance might take, like the shadings of affect felt, need not be specified.

DEGREE OF FEELING. Since an attitude can be seen as an evaluation of some specified object in "good-bad" terms, it is obvious that the person may evaluate an object as "extremely good (desirable, appetizing, helpful)" or as "fairly good" only. In other words, there are *degrees* of goodness or badness that may be attributed to the object. In more common language, attitudes toward an object are more or less "extreme."

Sometimes a distinction is drawn between the degree of an attitude and the intensity with which the attitude is held. Suchman (1950), for example, located Army men on an attitude scale running from extremely negative to extremely positive attitudes toward the Women's Army Corps (WAC), and then asked, "How strongly do you feel about this —very strongly, or not too strongly?" Although a few soldiers held extreme views toward the WAC and yet indicated that they did not feel too strongly about it, in most cases those with extreme attitudes registered intense feeling, whereas those whose attitudes were more moderate also said that they held their opinions less strongly (Figure 3.1).

For most purposes, then, we can afford to ignore such a distinction.

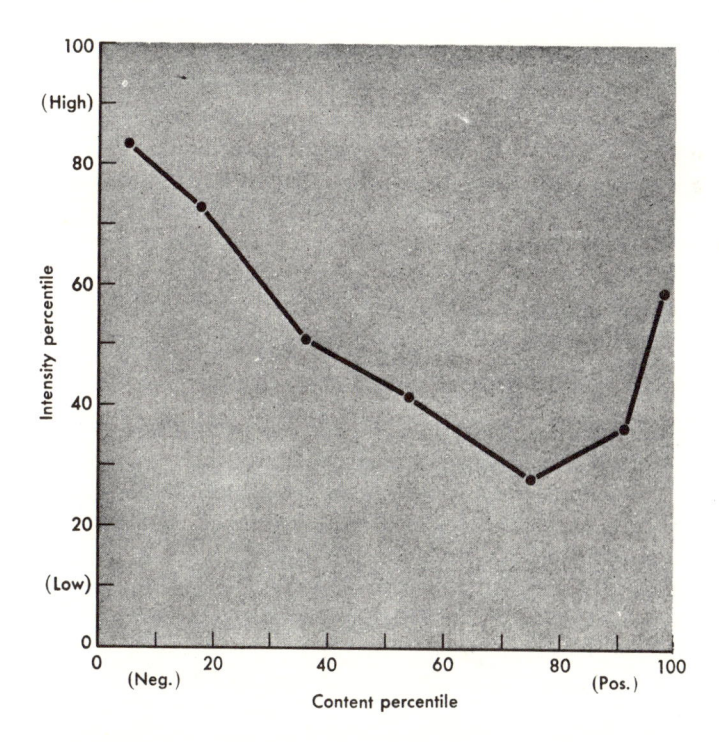

FIGURE 3.1. Enlisted men's attitudes toward the WAC (adapted from Suchman, 1950)

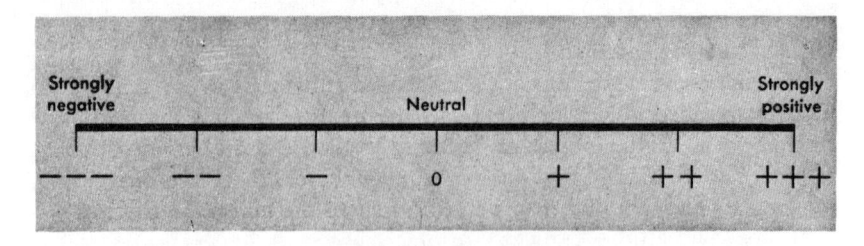

FIGURE 3.2. Representation of an attitude continuum

It is convenient to think of an attitude toward a specified object as lying at some point on a simple continuum like that of a thermometer, running from large negative values through more moderate negative values to a zero point, and then becoming increasingly positive, as illustrated in Figure 3.2.

Unfortunately, there are no simple or absolute units for measuring the degree to which an attitude is favorable or unfavorable. Nonetheless, relative locations of attitudes on such a continuum can be established with some reliability. Thus, for example, we may determine that Joe likes chemistry better than Jim does, although both may be favorably disposed to it. Or we may determine that Joe likes blondes better than he likes brunettes, although he is of course favorably disposed to both. If we can establish even relative locations such as these, we have made progress toward locating degrees of the attitude. Use of adverbs such as "strongly" and "fairly" also help to anchor the degree of affect of a particular attitude.[1] Once an attitude can be located on such a continuum, its primary description is complete. Other details may be added, but the two key properties—direction and degree of feeling—can be economically expressed in terms of this single dimension.

Characteristics of the Attitude Object

Although we can speak meaningfully about attitudes at an abstract level without taking account of characteristics of any particular attitude objects, there are certain very general characteristics of perceived or cognized objects that turn out to be important in understanding some of the more dynamic properties of attitudes.

DIMENSIONALITY OF THE COGNIZED OBJECT. We have already discussed the fact that objects vary in their inclusiveness, or the number and variety of elements or properties that they subsume (Chapter 2). Some objects we can perceive or cognize represent very simple stimuli in that

---

[1] Practical problems in attitude measurement are surveyed in some detail in Appendix A.

they have little more than a single principal property, or dimension of potential variation. A good example of such a unidimensional object is the pure tone. Two tones can be treated as differing from one another solely with respect to their greater or less frequencies, without the intrusion of any other dimensions of variation.

Psychologists have always found it extremely convenient to deal experimentally with unidimensional stimulus objects. One reason is that phenomena of discrimination and object generalization depend very heavily on degrees of object similarity. When objects vary from one another only with respect to a single property, it becomes relatively easy to make precise statements about the degree to which given objects are similar to or differ from one another. When, on the contrary, objects differ from one another in varying degrees on several dimensions at once, attempts to specify degree of difference in a summary statement become difficult indeed. Thus nobody could deny that C sharp is "closer to" or more similar to the tone C than it is to the tone F, even though the relative "psychological" distances which your ear detects may be in a different scale than the numerical relationships between physical frequencies. This is the easy case of the unidimensional tone. But now suppose you were presented with four rugs, two of which are rather large in area, and the other two rather small. Furthermore, one of the rugs of each size has a very deep three-inch pile, while the other has no pile at all. You are asked to indicate which pair of rugs is most similar. Although we have added only a second dimension of variability in this example (area and depth of pile), you can see that you might be hard pressed to answer the question of similarity without further information as to the respect in which similarity should be judged—area or depth of pile.

The basic problem is that while most psychological work is facilitated by the use of unidimensional stimulus objects, few if any objects of importance to us in real life are indeed unidimensional. And although much has been learned about psychological processes associated with unidimensional differences in stimuli, the nature of these processes with multidimensional stimuli is just beginning to be charted. This problem is perhaps most pressing for the social psychologist, since persons and groups as objects of social attitudes typically have an extremely wide range of potential properties that can be cognized.

Strategies that are now developing to handle the multidimensionality of cognized objects most frequently begin by imagining that such objects can be "located," either with physical measurements or psychologically, as points in some appropriate multidimensional space (cf. Abelson, 1954). In the relatively simple two-dimensional case of the rug, for example, any given rug could be located at some unique point in the plane of Figure 3.3. Then if we are willing to make some further

c

52 - INDIVIDUALS' ATTITUDES

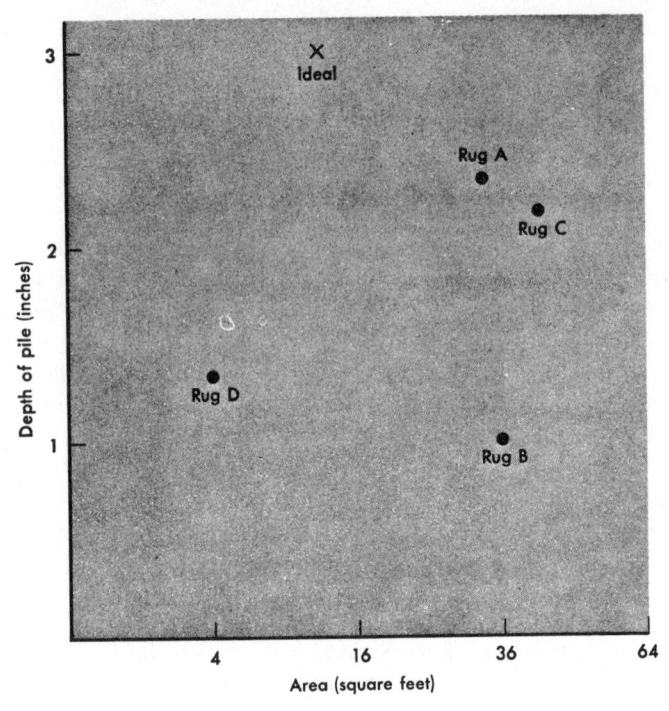

FIGURE 3.3. Location of specific objects in a two-dimensional space

assumptions about the meaningfulness and comparability of units along the two axes defining the plane, we become capable once again, as in the unidimensional case of the tones, of saying that Rug A (Figure 3.3), although almost identical with Rug B in terms of area, is in a two-dimensional sense more similar to Rug C than to Rug B. This is true because in the Euclidean space postulated, the distance between points A and C is less than that between points A and B. You may recall from analytic geometry that the Pythagorean theorem can be harnessed to calculate the distance between any two points defined in a space of any number of dimensions. Hence the reasoning can be extended from our two-dimensional case upward to cover objects located in terms of any number of dimensions at once.

The significance of such thinking for the study of attitudes toward complex objects is easy to demonstrate. Let us suppose that you need a rug to furnish your room, and that you have an ideal rug in mind, with respect to possible areas and depths of pile. This ideal rug could itself be given a location in the space of Figure 3.3. Now as the rugs a salesman shows you vary from these dimensions, it may well be that the degree of favorableness of your reaction could be predicted very neatly on the basis of the simple Euclidean distance of the given rug from the locus of your ideal rug.

Of course such efforts to deal with the multiple properties of more complex objects are still at a relatively primitive level, and beg very nearly as many questions as they answer. Even if you were clear as to an ideal rug, it is likely that you would have many more than two desirable attributes in mind, and some of these (color, fabric, and so on) do not yield easily to the kind of straightforward measurements that are presumed by our example. Furthermore, we know very little about the nature of psychological distances in multidimensional space even where measurement is more simple. If you do not care about the pile of your rug, the ordinate in Figure 3.3 would undoubtedly be greatly collapsed, and such a change might well restore Rug B to a position closer to Rug A than is Rug C. Hence the nature of psychological distances along such dimensions (and the possibility of these dimensions distorting one another when they interact) is crucial to the making of any "distance" statements at all, and our ignorance of these matters at the moment is profound.

THE INCLUSIVENESS OF THE ATTITUDE OBJECT. We have introduced the term "inclusiveness" to cover one kind of difference between attitude objects. "Degree of multidimensionality" might serve the same purpose, save that many properties of the objects that interest us are hard to conceive as neat dimensions. Furthermore, the attitude objects that interest us do not involve differences between unidimensionality and the intrusion of second or third properties. Rather, we are working in different orders of magnitude: an attitude object that is not very inclusive from the point of view of the observer might have a half-dozen or more cognized properties, whereas some of the more inclusive objects would have observed properties registering in the hundreds or conceivably the thousands. This variation is important in the study of attitudes.

Since our objects have this degree of inclusiveness, and since it would seem reasonable to expect that the individual might have different evaluative reactions ("attitudes") to each one of the dozens of properties presented by the complex object, it is fair to ask whether we are correct at all in speaking of "one" attitude toward the object.

Although we run certain risks in this kind of summary treatment (see below), there are some psychological grounds for such a procedure. That is, it is likely that we form meaningful *generalized* attitudes about any object, however complex, that we cognize as some kind of whole or unit, according to the principles of object generalization. Thus the question "Do you like war-and-flamingos?" would strike us as unanswerable because the proposed "object" of affect is nothing we would ever think of as a coherent whole. On the other hand, the question "Do you like

Brahms?" would not seem unreasonable, for the object (Brahms) is one that is seen as a whole even though it embraces a great variety of properties. We would undoubtedly evaluate this object in totally different cognitive contexts (and hence with different judgmental standards) according to whether we were neighbors of the man in 1860 or concert goers in 1960. But in either case we would be likely to have formed a generalized attitude toward the object as a whole.

Social objects in particular present us with large clusters of perceived properties. We may perceive another person as being, among other things, a good conversationalist, a sloppy dresser, and a likely target when we need to borrow money. Although we may have attitudes toward each of these perceived characteristics separately, we also form attitudes toward the person as a whole, for we cognize him as a whole. When we speak of attitudes as residues of affect from the past, this residue includes not only the subjective summation of affective experiences with the object over time, but also a summation of affective responses toward component properties of the object.

Although we do not know a great deal about the way in which attitudes toward component properties are subjectively summed, we can assume that the direction and degree of attitudes toward component properties are crucial in determining the direction and degree of the generalized attitude toward the more inclusive object. That is, if we like "everything" about someone we know, we would express a more strongly favorable generalized attitude toward him than we would if our impressions were "mixed."

The fact that we may have such mixed reactions even to an object that we perceive as a whole at one level of cognitive organization means that we may express different attitudes when the cognitive context suggests a less inclusive aspect of the object. Some attitude measurement proceeds by assessing the subject's attitudes toward a sampling of aspects of a more general object. Thus, for example, Newcomb (1943) applied to students at a small college for women a questionnaire containing fourteen items about aspects of the CIO, a labor organization that had recently come into prominence on the American scene. The subjects could express favor, disfavor, or uncertainty about each aspect. The responses of one hundred students selected at random showed that ninety-two of them gave one or more favorable *and also* one or more unfavorable replies (Table 3.1). If these subjects had been asked a more generalized question as to strength of their approval or disapproval of the CIO as a whole, it is likely that their location on the more general attitude continuum would have borne a clear relation to the mixture of favorable and unfavorable responses given to aspects of the CIO. The nine students who made 6–8 favorable replies and 0–2 unfavorable replies would probably fall toward a more extreme position of approval than the two students who likewise made 6–8 favorable replies but also gave 6–8 unfavorable replies.

TABLE 3.1. Percent of 100 subjects responding favorably to varying numbers of items in CIO questionnaire, classified according to number of unfavorable replies (Newcomb, 1943)

Number of unfavorable replies	Number of favorable replies					
	0–2	3–5	6–8	9–11	12–14	Total
0–2	0	9	9	22	17	57
3–5	0	5	18	13	0	36
6–8	1	4	2	0	0	7
Total	1	18	29	35	17	100

Furthermore, if one were to study cases in which the mixture of responses to specific aspects of the CIO did not accord well with a generalized response, one would be likely to discover that the individual had a particularly strong attitude toward some aspect not covered by the items given, yet which he considered to be of great importance. Another way of assessing attitudes that takes account of these individual differences in weighting is to ask the subjects to indicate the more important things they like and dislike about a specified complex object. It can be shown that even a simple summation of positive and negative responses places subjects in much the same order on the attitude continuum as does a more direct assessment of the generalized attitude toward the object as a whole.

Occasionally, it must be noted, a subject may have such extremely different attitudes toward different aspects of an inclusive object that he has difficulty cognizing it as a whole. He is obliged to dissociate the parts. For example, most Americans can respond comfortably to attitude questions about "the Democratic party" as a general object, even though they may have somewhat mixed reactions to certain component properties. However, a few citizens—2 or 3 percent—have such radically different reactions to the party at a national as opposed to a local level that they cannot respond meaningfully to the simple whole suggested by "the Democratic party." Instead, they feel it necessary to point out their differing reactions to *two* party-objects, the national Democratic party and the local version.

The choice whether to explore components of a general attitude or to measure the individual's natural summation of affect toward the general object depends a great deal on the research questions at hand. Except where dissociation is prevalent, however, it is often useful to deal in attitudes toward fairly generalized objects. This is true in part because more inclusive attitudes have relevance to a wider range of behaviors. Sharply mixed attitudes, moreover, for reasons to be discussed later, turn up less frequently than one might suppose.

For our current purposes, it is enough to stress the fact that attitude objects vary in their inclusiveness. This variation is both objective and subjective. Objectively, we could all agree that "America" is a more inclusive object than "this apple." But even when the object is specified, people may differ in the range of components they perceive it to include. For example, each of two men may be strongly opposed to "subversive activities." One of them may see this term as embracing only the activities of known Communists, whereas the other may apply it to a wide range of issues including group health insurance programs, the right to strike, and academic freedom.

Figure 3.4 expresses schematically a number of these differences in an attitude object, as different people might perceive and react to it. The heavy dark circle indicates what each individual sees the generalized object as embracing. Component properties or aspects of the object to which the individual has some affective reaction are symbolized by the small valenced circles. The individuals in (b) and (c) cognize the object as a less inclusive one than do the individuals in (a) and (d). Similarly, there are individual differences in the components toward which there is an affective reaction: the individual represented in (d) reacts to only one, despite the fact that he construes the object as inclusively as does the individual in (a). This may mean that he has a less differentiated set of cognitions of the object (knows less about it); or, if his cognition of the object is highly differentiated, that all but one of these cognitions lack any affective impact for him.

Below each version of the perceived object is shown the point at which the individual might locate himself on an attitude scale referring to the generalized object as a whole. The location of these check marks should be considered only as crude approximations, for any precise position supposes one or another underlying model of the way in which component reactions contribute to the general attitude, and these competing models are still the subject of research and controversy. You may note, for example, that the check mark in item (d) is entered in a position that suggests that the generalized attitude is a function of the *difference* between positive and negative components $(+1 - 0 = +1)$. Another equally plausible model suggests that the generalized attitude depends rather on a *ratio* of these components, so that the check mark

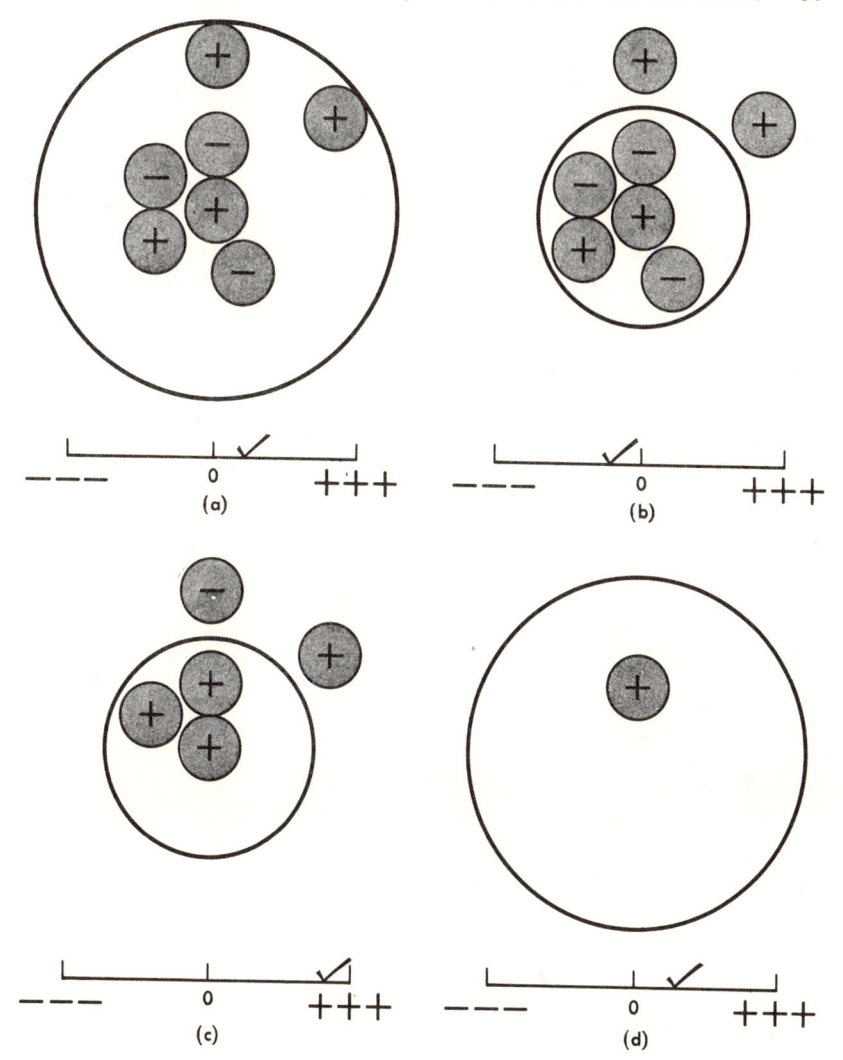

FIGURE 3.4. Differing perceptions and attitudes toward the same object

in (d) should be instead at the maximally positive extreme. Nonetheless we have given these generalized attitudes a clear relation to the component reactions; comparing (a) and (b) you can see that such general attitudes may vary according to what the object is seen to embrace.

Many objects—a person is a good example—are rather clearly

bounded. Thus there would be little variation among individuals with regard to what the person as an object includes and excludes (although there might be considerable variation in the properties drawing attention and affective reaction). For some highly inclusive and abstract objects, such as "freedom," "religion," or "human nature," variation in perceived inclusiveness among persons may occasionally become quite large. However, the necessity of communication, which is always with us, provides one constant pressure toward maintenance of at least roughly similar bounds from person to person within a language community. Hence, although we should not forget the possibility of interpersonal differences, by and large the differences in inclusiveness of attitude objects that will concern us primarily are those very large and obvious differences between types of objects: "my dog" is a much less inclusive object than "economics."

THE PSYCHOLOGICAL CENTRALITY OF THE OBJECT FOR THE INDIVIDUAL. A second prime characteristic of the attitude object is what we might call the *centrality* of the object for the individual. Some objects stay persistently in the forefront of the individual's consciousness, almost without letup, either because of external circumstance or because of internal motive states. Other objects are psychologically remote from him, and would be said to have low centrality for him. Simple geographical proximity offers a parallel that is helpful in understanding this dimension. Just as the Defense Minister of Indonesia is physically and socially remote as an object for most Americans, so he is psychologically remote for them as well. His centrality as an object is low. On the other hand, this psychological remoteness need not correspond perfectly to physical distance: for a clerk in Southeast Asian Affairs in our State Department in Washington, the Defense Minister of Indonesia may not be psychologically remote at all.

If we had a means of recording all conscious thoughts in an individual's mind, centrality would be very closely related to the simple frequency with which an object occurs to a person, either because he notes it (or a symbol for it) in the environment, or because he reflects upon it in his thought. At the remote extreme of the centrality dimension would lie objects the person does not know exist. These objects would show no incidence at all in his conscious thought, and would be of "zero" centrality. The objects that would lie at the other extreme might be more difficult to predict in advance, but we would certainly expect one of the most central objects to be that which is physically closest as well: the "self."

Research Illustration 3.1 helps to make clear the difference between the centrality of an object to an individual and the closely related matter of its *salience*. We have already (in Chapter 2) defined an object as salient if the immediate situation is such as to sensitize the individual to it. Much the same sensitivity is involved in an object that is central for the individual; but centrality refers to a durable and generalized salience. An object of low centrality may become momentarily salient for the individual when the immediate situation prompts his attention to it forcefully and explicitly enough. After its initial stages, the Stouffer interview directly introduced the possible threat of domestic Communism, and undoubtedly left the Communist question very salient momentarily in the minds of most respondents. However, responses to the opening part of the interview showed that for most people the centrality of the objects involved was extremely low. Thus salience is a short-term phenomenon that is a function of the immediate sitution; centrality refers to a much more durable interest on the part of the individual in certain objects or kinds of objects, with these objects remaining important for him through many differing specific situations.

Under what conditions does an object become very central for an individual? Perhaps the most obvious source of centrality is motivational: the goal objects of motivated behavior are highly central to the individual who pursues them. Objects associated with these goals through some perceived relevance as means toward their attainment take on added centrality as well. Furthermore, if the self as a perceived object is about as central for the individual as any object is likely to be, then other objects, states, and properties closely associated with the self have increased centrality by virtue of the fact. Indeed, the description by Katz of functions played by attitudes (Chapter 2, pages 43–44) suggests a number of mechanisms whereby objects come to be central for the individual in this motivational sense.

However, for our purposes it would not do to tie the centrality of an object too closely to current motivational states. That is, although some kind of motivation must have led the individual originally to give selective attention to one object rather than another, there are many circumstances under which objects have high centrality for an individual even though it would be hard to trace the motivational roots of his interest in them. To some degree the fact that a person devotes attention to one set of objects in his environment rather than another—to fishing rather than hunting—may be heavily determined by his history of experience in those situations; the other set of objects might have provided essentially the same gratifications as the chosen objects. More generally, many objects take on centrality for us simply because they present themselves to us persistently in the environment. These objects which through frequent contact become familiar parts of experience may take a position in our psychological worlds of a centrality hard to understand in view of their slight goal utility. Similarly, the objects of what are called "idle curiosity" and "spectator interest" may come to command a great deal of an individual's attention and hence become very central for him,

Research Illustration 3.1

> Stouffer (1955) attempted to find out how deeply concerned the American people were about the Communist threat in the cold war. The interview of a national cross section of the American population took the form of a free-flowing conversation between the interviewer and the respondent. After a few conversational questions the interviewer asked, "What kinds of things do you worry about most?" The number of persons who spontaneously brought up the threat of Communism was less than 1 percent. Even questions involving world problems, including the possibility of war, did not evoke a spontaneous reply about Communism from more than 8 percent. Such issues simply lacked the psychological proximity of issues such as personal or family economic problems or health.
>
> The lack of centrality of the Communist threat for most Americans became increasingly clear as ensuing questions became more direct. After the initial question, respondents were asked, "Are there other problems you worry or are concerned about, *especially political or world problems?*" (Italics ours.) Here there still was no specific question about Communism, but the international situation is suggested as a context. This raised the number speaking of the Communist threat from less than 1 per cent, found in the previous question, to about 6 percent. It also raised the number expressing a concern about world affairs from an initial 8 to 30 percent. Here we begin to suspect that the "concern" expressed is partially the result of the form taken by the more specific question. This suspicion is amply confirmed when we see the response to a highly specific question asked a little later in the interview: "How great a danger do you feel American Communists are to this country at the present time—a very great danger, a great danger, some danger, hardly any danger, or no danger?" Lumping together all those feeling it was a "great danger" or a "very great danger," we find that the figure has risen from 6 to 43 percent as the result of the very specific question on this point. Such a sequence of questions, from general to specific, helps to probe levels of centrality of an attitude object ("the Communist threat") as they vary from individual to individual.

despite the fact that they have very obscure motivational backgrounds. In any event, it is not necessary for us to search out these motives; it is sufficient to recognize that objects vary widely in their centrality for the individual.

The more central an object is for a person, the more likely it is that he has stored a substantial amount of information about it. The relationship is not perfect, because information costs are variable, and sometimes become prohibitive even for a relatively central object.[2] A poorly educated man may become obsessed with the notion of making money on the stock market, yet may find all information about the stock market so technical that he has trouble absorbing any information about it which is meaningful to him, and does not know where to turn to find the background information that would make it meaningful. Far more typically, however, interest and information are intertwined: attention leads to the absorption of information about an object or a set of objects, and thus the person is likely to discriminate more component properties of the object, and understand more about its relations with other neighboring objects.

It is important to know how central an object is for an individual, since this fact has a bearing on attitude formation and, as we shall see later, on attitude stability. The general rule is that we are more likely to form attitudes toward objects that have some centrality for us, and are less likely to form attitudes toward objects that are peripheral or psychologically remote. The extreme case is self-evident: we do not have opinions about objects of whose existence we are unaware. What, for instance, is *your* attitude toward hernant seeds? If you had worked in the dye industry, you would probably have one. As it is, you probably do not, if indeed such objects have been any part of your information storage at all.

The absence of attitude formation in the absence of information about an object may seem a rather trivial observation. Actually, it is not. In many realms of complex social behavior, such as politics, consumer economics, family planning, and the like, people often fail to behave as the sophisticated observer expects: he assumes that people are propelled by attitudes toward objects that are very central to his informed eye, yet are quite remote or entirely beyond the ken of less well educated people. The Stouffer study (Research Illustration 3.1) is a case in point: Although the survey was conducted to examine what was called in the early 1950s a "national hysteria" about Communism, it turned out that the objects and events involved in this hysteria were very remote or psychologically nonexistent for much of the American population. Where the objects were not remote, attitudes were intense enough. But it was easy to forget that they might be remote for many people.

[2] Information "costs" something in the sense that differing amounts of time, energy, and sometimes money must be expended to acquire it. Much information "comes our way" as we scan our environment, and its cost is negligible. For other information we might have to stir ourselves to go to a library, and the cost is higher. For still other types of information, we may not even know where to start to look, and the anticipated cost of such information is usually prohibitive.

How should we formally describe the "attitudes" of people toward objects of which they are ignorant, or that are so remote they feel only indifference about them, as you now feel toward hernant seeds? At first glance, such people would seem to fit logically at the "zero point" of our attitude continuum, since they are neither positive nor negative with regard to the object. Yet we find this zero point already occupied by those whose feelings toward the object are so mixed that they are ambivalent toward or in conflict about it! Somehow we would be hesitant to equate a person in conflict about an object with a person so remote from the object that he is indifferent to it.

This hesitation is well justified if we wish to understand the development of attitudes over time, for the remote people and the conflicted people are likely to show marked differences in development as the situation changes. One illustration that makes the point clearly is the development of attitudes toward political candidates. If we survey a cross-sectional population of American adults four months before a presidential election, we shall find the two "zero-point" types well represented. Unless the candidates are incumbents, they will be very remote objects for a large number of people. On the other hand, among those people who follow politics closely, there will be some few who know a great deal about the personalities and yet are quite conflicted in their attitudes about them. One predictable outcome of the presidential campaign is, of course, that a tremendous output of information about the candidates turns them from remote to at least moderately proximal objects for much of the population. At the end of the campaign, the people who were in dynamic conflict at the beginning are still very likely to be near the middle of the attitude continuum. Those who were originally at the zero point because of the remoteness of the objects, however, are much more likely to have shown dramatic shifts away from the zero point. Indeed, in the 1960 presidential campaign, the addition of a single piece of information—that the Democratic candidate was a Catholic— moved many voters very suddenly from the neutrality of ignorance to rather violent opinions about him. It is in this sense that we may well want to distinguish between the zero point of ignorance and that of conflict. Hence the very simple attitude continuum that appears in Figure 3.2 may now be somewhat expanded, as shown in Figure 3.5.

It is worth a reminder that what we say about properties of attitude objects also has relevance for less inclusive components (parts, aspects) of more general objects, for such components are themselves objects of less inclusive attitudes. Thus the many components of a general object may themselves vary a good deal in centrality for the individual, and there may be broad differences between individuals as to which properties of a given object are remote and which are central.

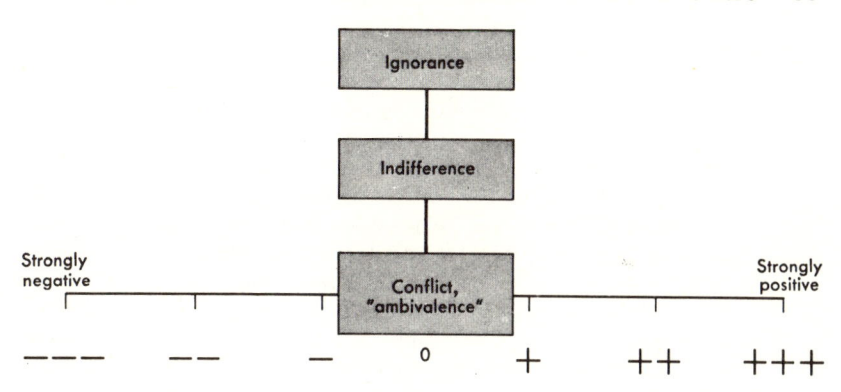

FIGURE 3.5. Expanded representation of an attitude continuum

(Such differences are suggested in Figure 3.4 by the absence of some circles for the individual in [c], and of many circles for [d].)

Once again, language and communication act in some degree to maintain interpersonal consistency in these matters. Nonetheless, differences are often large, and as Research Illustration 3.2 suggests, may become quite impressive between cultures. It is easy to see that attitudes toward the same friendly or fierce dog might vary a good deal according to which of his "use" properties is most central in one's culture.

INCLUSIVENESS, CENTRALITY, AND INFORMATION. It may have occurred to you to wonder how different inclusiveness and centrality actually are as dimensions on which attitude objects may vary. The correspondence between the two variables is far from perfect. There are some objects that have some psychological centrality in the sense defined—the desk where you work each day—to which no normal mind could attribute much inclusiveness. Similarly there are some objects—take "anarchosyndicalism," for example—that we know must be inclusive and yet are likely to be rather remote for us. However, it is true that an object is often inclusive and central for a person at the same time. The term that links the two dimensions is the amount of information the individual has stored about the object.

If an object is potentially (or objectively) an inclusive one, and if we have gone ahead to store a large mass of information about its properties or components, then it is likely that it is not only an inclusive object but a central object for us as well. As we continue to absorb additional information about an inclusive object, each new property or component cognized sets up new potential linkages with other types of information, hitherto not recognized as relevant, that we have also stored. In other words, to say that somebody has a wealth of informa-

Research Illustration 3.2

Dennis (1957) was interested in exploring cultural differences in the utility or value placed on a number of simple objects. Studies that cut across languages frequently pose difficult problems of translation. Here the investigator solved the problem by keeping his methods as simple as possible. The question "What is——for?"—with differing common nouns entered—was asked in parallel form of 900 Lebanese children (ages 5–10), of 58 Sudanese children (ages 9–10) and of 100 American children (ages 5–11) attending the American Community School in Beirut, Lebanon. This simple technique did indeed elicit large differences in response among the cultural groups. The following table shows the distributions within the three groups of the *first* response to some of the objects made by each child (and hence, presumably, the use properties that were most central for each):

Stimulus word	Use category	American	Lebanese	Sudanese
Sand	playing	41	18	2
	building	21	58	26
Gold	decorative	16	53	67
	economic	61	26	2
Birds	eating	7	37	16
	flying, singing	34	36	36
	enjoying	33	8	2
Dogs	guarding, watching	16	66	62
	barking, biting	9	19	0
	hunting	4	8	7
	pets, playing	49	4	3
Cats	catching mice	16	63	53
	meowing	6	13	2
	pets, playing	52	6	7

With these words, as with many of the others employed, the major contrast is between the American children, on one hand, and the Lebanese and Sudanese children on the other, although some of the latter differences are statistically significant as well. For American children, the central use properties of sand, birds, dogs, and cats have to do with play or enjoyment. For Lebanese and Sudanese children, more utilitarian properties are central. In the case of gold, however, it is the American children for whom utilitarian properties are most nearly central.

tion about an object is to say something at once about its inclusiveness and centrality as a perceived object for him. It also suggests that the cognitive links between this object and other objects are more likely to be more rich and numerous: the object is heavily "cross-referenced." In contrast, an object about which information is sparse is likely to be remote and isolated from other cognitions.

THE SOCIAL CHARACTER OF THE ATTITUDE OBJECT. The suggestion has been made (Research Illustration 2.4) that social objects are more likely to prompt the formation of attitudes than are other kinds of objects. There is nothing mystical in such a state of affairs; we can deduce that this should be the case from what we already know about attitudes, if we take into account as well some of the more distinctive features of social objects as objects, and of our transactions with them.

We have already seen that the attitudes a person forms toward an object depend quite directly upon the information he holds as to the properties of that object. "Good" properties are those that he has found to be rewarding. If one's experience has shown that a certain property is rewarding, either in general or in certain specific situations, the objects to which one attributes that property are considered good, or rewarding—unless those properties are outweighed by others that one has learned to consider "bad" or punishing. Where *social* objects are concerned, attitudes are readily formed because we are more likely to see such objects as mediating important rewards than is the case with physical objects.

This is true for several reasons. For example, social objects, being more complex, are usually perceived to embrace a much larger number of properties. Among all of these properties, the probability that at least some few will have affective (or reward-mediating) implications for the individual is necessarily increased. Still more fundamentally, we recognize that many of these social objects *behave toward us*, and do so with affect, either withholding or granting rewards.

It is significant that when our transactions with physical objects are similar to those with social objects, we are likely to experience similar affect. Thus some physical objects, such as food, do routinely involve gratifications and punishments, and toward such objects we tend to form clear attitudes. It is more difficult to conceive of nonsocial objects behaving toward us in an affective manner, for we no longer hold the animistic beliefs of an earlier day. However, when man supposed that rocks, trees, and other simple physical objects embodied benign and evil spirits, these objects also took on strong affective coloration for him: this tree was good, and that tree was bad, for these objects were seen as behaving toward him with good or bad intentions.

Because of the vital concern we have in others' intentions toward us and the probability that we will attribute rewarding or punishing qualities to them, it is useful to have a distinctive term to refer to these attitudes toward other persons. We shall use the term "attraction." This kind of attitude, like any other, varies not only in degree of feeling, but also in sign: that is, it can be positive or negative, favorable or unfavorable. Ordinarily, however, we shall use the term only in its positive sense, and shall refer to "aversion" rather than to negative attraction.

* * *

Thus far we have indicated the critical properties of any single attitude—direction and degree—and have considered some of the "static" properties of objects that become important in the study of attitudes: the perceived inclusiveness of the object, its centrality, and its social or nonsocial character. It is true almost by definition that the attitudes important in understanding the psychological organization of any given individual over long periods of time are those whose objects are, for him, relatively inclusive and relatively central. Attitudes toward less inclusive objects are unlikely to "govern" any very wide range of behavior; relatively remote objects—those about which the individual has stored little information—are obviously rather unimportant for him.

Once we have completed our consideration of individual attitudes and have moved to the level of interaction between individuals (Part Two), we shall put increasing emphasis on attitudes toward objects that are inclusive and central. Furthermore, we shall place increasing stress on the interpersonal attitudes of attraction and aversion, since human interaction involves an individual with another social object. For the present, however, we shall keep the total range of potential attitude objects in mind, even those that are not central, inclusive, or social. We shall do so in part because the dynamics of attitudes can be more clearly understood in this way. It is true as well, however, that less inclusive and less central attitude objects also affect interaction and are affected by it.

The communication between persons that is the stuff of human interaction may be oriented to social objects, but need not be. It may have to do with attitude objects that are quite inclusive and central for both parties. On the other hand, it need not. Indeed, we have suggested in the opening chapter that communication tends to occur when two persons hold (or suspect they hold) different amounts or kinds of information about an object. And we have now seen that the amount of information a person holds about an object has something to do with its inclusiveness and centrality as the core of an attitude.

ATTITUDES AND OVERT BEHAVIOR

Now that we have taken account of what attitudes *are* in a rather formal sense, let us replace the attitude in its natural context of the functioning individual for a more detailed consideration of what attitudes may be said to *do*. Since we have taken the position that attitudes, as stored dispositions, are central to individual psychological organization, this necessarily implies that attitudes affect not only overt behavior but the full gamut of internal psychological processes (perception, learning, and so on) as well. Nevertheless, we naturally consider overt behavior as the end product of these processes, and hence it is the "proof of the pudding."

At the beginning of the chapter we suggested that there are many instances in which people can be observed behaving in ways that seem contrary to their attitudes. Merton's "unprejudiced discriminator" and "prejudiced nondiscriminator" are merely instances from the area of ethnic relations. We do not have to search far for good illustrations in other areas as well. It is not unusual in studies of voting behavior, for example, to encounter the housewife who is loud in praise of the Republican party and indicates nothing but contempt for the Democratic party, yet who announces later in the interview that she intends to vote a straight Democratic ticket. (The two political parties can of course be reversed in this illustration.)

These attitude-behavior contradictions are less perplexing than may appear, and the attitude concept itself is useful in untangling them. However, we must refine our understanding of behavior before this is clear. Broadly speaking, we would not expect any simple and perfect correspondence between an attitude and a relevant behavior because (1) behavior is a product not only of attitudes but of the immediate situation as well; and (2) attitudes relevant to a situation are often multiple.

VARIATIONS IN BEHAVIOR AS A FUNCTION OF ATTITUDES AND SITUATION. A good deal of variation in behavior is a result of variations in the immediate situations in which the individual finds himself at different times. There is nothing surprising in this fact, of course, and we would be sadly maladjusted if our behavior had some total momentum of its own that ignored the ongoing realities of the developing situations in which the behavior was occurring. On the other hand, it is clear that human behavior is not responsive only to the direct stimuli of the immediate situation. Place a number of people in the same situation, and you are very apt to find a fair amount of variation in their behaviors.

This is least true where the "situation" involves a very limited stimulus, and where the possible responses to be observed are very restricted as well, and most true as the situation becomes more complex, and the response possibilities multiply. If you display a black card and a white one to a number of individuals, asking them to judge which is black, you should not find much variation in response. The reactions of your subjects to the broader situation (that is, to you and your "experiment"), however, may be quite varied indeed.

Although behavior is strongly shaped by the character of the immediate situation, then, people differ in what they bring to the situation and hence, within limits set by the situation, in how they respond to it. A very important part of what the individual "brings to the situation" can be summarized, of course, in terms of the stored dispositions we are calling attitudes. Thus behavior is jointly determined by individual attitudes on the one hand and by the (perceived) situation on the other. To say that attitudes help determine behavior in the situation is not to say that attitudes are "original causes" of behavior in any sense. They represent intervening conditions that have themselves been determined by the sum of past situations through which the individual has moved. These relationships are conveniently summed up in Figure 3.6.

Such a diagram is not very enlightening as to types or weightings of attitudes, situations, and behaviors, and one of our first priorities beyond this point will be to specify more precisely how past situations cumulate to current attitudes, the relative weightings of current attitudes and the current situation in the determination of behavior under varying circumstances, and the like. But the diagram does make the simple point that attitudes are not the sole determinants of behavior, or even the sole *current* determinants. When observed behavior seems at odds with known attitudes of the individual, it is worth considering the total situation he is confronting. If his behavior seems to have no relation to his attitudes, then there must be important factors in the situation inducing him to this unexpected behavior. If this behavior ac-

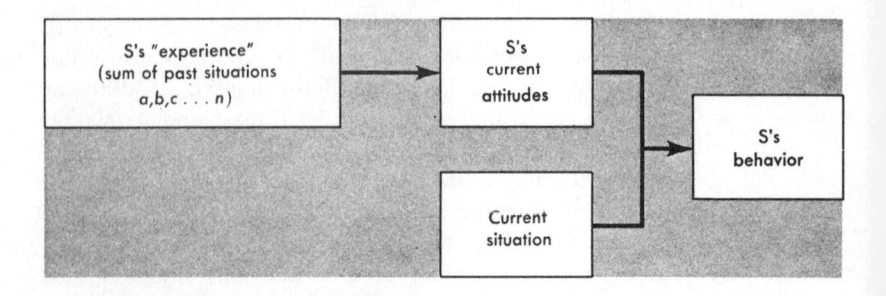

FIGURE 3.6. The role of attitudes in the determination of behavior

tually *contradicts* his most relevant attitudes, then these situational factors must be particularly powerful, for they are deflecting behavior "uphill"—against the dispositions brought to the situation that seem most relevant.

Such is the case with some of the instances of attitude-behavior discrepancy we have introduced. The unprejudiced restaurateur who discriminates against Negroes may quite truly have no negative racial feelings, but finds himself in a situation in which he feels he will lose more and more of his white clientele the more Negroes he serves. He is not prejudiced, but he perceives that some of the people necessary to his livelihood are prejudiced. Similarly, the rock-ribbed Republican housewife who takes for granted that she will vote straight Democratic invariably turns out to have a husband who is an ardent Democrat and who insists that she not cancel out his vote. Although the student may find it distressing that such people "lack the courage of their convictions," they provide the social psychologist with fascinating insights into the dynamics of complex social behavior.

BEHAVIOR AS A FUNCTION OF MULTIPLE ATTITUDES. There is a slightly different way of looking at these instances of "discrepancy" that is particularly fruitful. It springs from the simple notion that any complex object or situation to which we respond calls into play a number of attitudes at once. Once the situation is given, behavior is a resultant of the total configuration of relevant attitudes.

Research Illustration 3.3 provides a good example of behavior, as a resultant of multiple attitudes, in a political context. For this particular case, it is not surprising that attitudes toward both the candidate and his political party contribute to the determination of voting choice. However, where the housewife votes Democratic to please her husband despite her own Republican views, the additional factor (her husband) would be less likely to occur to us as relevant to the behavior choice Yet from the housewife's point of view it is not only relevant but crucial. Furthermore, this "factor," like those that seem more relevant, has its effect on the situation because of dispositions the individual (housewife) brings to the voting choice. In other words, if we represent the housewife not by a single attitude (party preference) or by a pair of attitudes (party and candidate preference) but by a larger system of attitudes (including attitudes toward her husband) then we can see that we shall gain considerable power in attempting to understand her complex reactions to complex situations. Characterizing the individual as a system of attitudes does not of course make it unnecessary to take the situation into account: the situation has an important influence on the way in which different attitudes are weighted in producing a response. Behavior is still a joint product of situation and attitudes. But we are willing to make "attitudes" quite plural.

Research Illustration 3.3

Campbell and his associates (1960) have reported on survey studies of national samples of American adults, conducted at the time of the 1952 and 1956 presidential elections, that illustrate well the influence of multiple attitudes on behavioral choices. From reactions of the respondents to the two parties and the competing presidential candidates, measurements of a system of six partisan attitudes were constructed. One of these, the attitude toward the Republican candidate Dwight D. Eisenhower, showed that he enjoyed a very marked personal popularity. Indeed, only a small proportion of the population felt negatively toward him, and if voting decisions had been based on the attitude toward Eisenhower alone, he would have won both elections by an unprecedented landslide, with two thirds to three quarters of the popular vote.

However, the actual decision situation was a complex one involving numerous components beyond Eisenhower himself. Some people who felt favorably toward Eisenhower felt even more favorably toward his opponent, Adlai Stevenson, and hence voted for him rather than for Eisenhower. Even among the people who considered Eisenhower to be a more desirable candidate than Stevenson, substantial numbers voted for Stevenson nonetheless. Most of these people had relatively strong favorable attitudes toward the Democratic party and negative attitudes toward the Republicans. Hence they were willing to vote Democratic despite the fact that they were not enchanted with the Democratic candidate.

In general, the data from the study clearly showed that the ultimate behavior of the voters was better understood as a resultant of multiple attitudes than it was if prediction was based on one of the attitudes alone. One way of measuring this predictive capacity would be in terms of a correlation between the predicting variables and the outcome. Or we could compare the proportion of individuals who were classified correctly as to expected voting behavior with a postelection report of their actual vote, on the basis of their prior attitudinal configurations. Whichever statistical criterion was used, each of the six partisan attitudes (attitude toward Eisenhower, attitude toward Stevenson, attitude toward the Democratic party, attitude toward the Republican party, and party evaluations in terms of domestic and foreign issues) made some independent contribution to predictive accuracy, and the set of six predicted the ultimate vote much more effectively than any one taken alone:

Where prediction was from:	Correlation of predictor(s) with vote	Proportion of voters incorrectly classified
Attitude toward Eisenhower only	0.52	25%
All six partisan attitudes	0.71	14%

Perhaps the most notable assessment of predictive capacity from this study, however, is one that pitted the investigators against the respondent's own ability to foresee his likely behavior. At the same time as the initial attitude measurements were gathered before the election, the respondents were asked to indicate how they intended to vote in the upcoming election, and these data amounted to the individual's prediction as to his own behavior. The statistical analysis of the six attitudes assigned correct actual votes to a larger proportion of voters than were able to predict their own votes correctly.

You would have a right to enter several objections to the argument at this point. First, if our housewife ignores her party preferences to please her husband, of what use is it to know that she has them? There is more than one answer. The first, perhaps, is a matter of tidiness. It would be rather haphazard to "explain" one person's behavior in a given situation in terms of one type of attitude (party preference) while explaining another person's response by a totally different type of attitude (feelings toward spouse). Both people have both types of attitudes, and should be represented in this way. What is to be explained is why one person weights these attitudes in one way whereas another person weights them in another. In many cases (although not always) such differences are clearly explained when the degrees of the various attitudes in the system are taken into account: when two attitudes are equally relevant in a situation and yet would tend to produce different responses, a stronger attitude "carries the day" over a weaker one.[3]

It is particularly useful to know the total system of attitudes even though some are "overruled" in a given situation, for situations are constantly changing, and we are interested in long-range trends in behavior. Thus, among all white restaurateurs who have felt a certain degree of economic threat if they serve Negroes, it may still be important to know which are personally prejudiced as well and which are not, even though all have refused to serve Negroes prior to the passage of laws prohibiting such discrimination. Following such legislation, we would expect the threatened but unprejudiced restaurateurs to be more likely to welcome, or less likely to try to get around the law, than those both threatened economically *and* personally prejudiced.

You might well object also to the freedom we have displayed in these pages in introducing "other factors" (for example, the housewife's

---

[3] For descriptive purposes, it is frequently a matter of convenience to deal in terms of a single attitude. When we do so, we are not losing sight of the person as a "system" of attitudes, but rather are saying that "other things equal" (including the character of other attitudes), a person with a positive attitude toward the single object is more disposed to behave in a particular way than is some other person less positively disposed.

attitude toward her husband) to account for behaviors that contradict the most obvious attitudes (party preference). Clearly, with such freedom of explanation after the fact we can find some reason for any behavior.

You would be entirely correct that the final test of our scientific understanding of behavior is its capacity to predict in advance, rather than its agility in *post hoc* explanation, although it is also true that we accumulate knowledge primarily by analysis of failures to predict accurately. In expressing surprise at the Republican housewife's voting Democratic we are using an expository device; actually our capacity to predict such phenomena *before* the fact is more advanced than our description may have suggested up to this point.

Sufficient knowledge has accumulated regarding some types of social behavior that in a growing number of instances it is possible to predict relatively complex individual behavior even better than the individual himself can predict how he will behave! Furthermore, such instances occur not only in laboratory situations, where many factors can be held constant and the critical aspects of the situation are being manipulated in ways the subject could not be expected to foresee, but also in "real-life" situations that are permitted to run their natural course. Research Illustration 3.3 has already provided us with one example of such prediction. In quite a different setting, Newcomb (1961) has studied the attitudes brought to a dormitory situation by a set of students who were just meeting each other for the first time (see Research Illustration 6.2). Here it was expected that friendship would develop along lines of attitudinal similarity, and analyses of such similarity did yield excellent predictions of the final stable friendship cliques that were observed to evolve many weeks later, after the students had become acquainted with one another and had tried and rejected some other tentative friendship patterns. In this instance the investigator was able to foresee the interpersonal preferences that would emerge on the basis of materials collected before the students had even started the "search" processes that would lead to friendship. Thus predictions of behavior based on a knowledge of the individual as a system of attitudes and of certain regularities in the development of complex social situations (a presidential campaign, a process of friendship formation) have attained a fair degree of power, carrying well beyond haphazard "hindsight."

Although our understanding of complex behavior is improved by taking a number of relevant and related attitudes into account at once, we should not overlook the fact that in most cases prediction can far exceed chance simply by taking one highly relevant attitude into account. This is due to the fact that attitude elements that have some logical relationship to one another tend over time to show a trend toward mutual consistency. That is, for the purposes involved in Research Illustration 3.3, it was important to recognize that not all people who preferred the Democratic party preferred the Democratic candidate in a particular election as well. However, these more or less inconsistent clusters of attitudes turn out to be exceptions. For most people, attitudes toward a party's candidates will be of the same sign as attitudes toward the party itself. This fairly high probability of consistency means that whether we happen to measure party attitude or candidate attitude by itself, we are getting some fair reflection of the other attitude as well, and hence will make rather good predictions even without measurement of all relevant attitudinal elements.

We shall examine this pressure toward consistency in greater detail in subsequent chapters. For now, we may simply observe that consistency between attitudes and decisions to behave in this way or that can be taken as one special case of psychological consistency. And just as behavior tends to follow the directions that attitudes would lead us to expect, we shall see that in the exceptional instances where there are discrepancies between the two, either may change to restore consistency.

INFLUENCE OF ATTITUDES ON OTHER PSYCHOLOGICAL PROCESSES

Up to now we have been concerned with the way in which decisions about overt behavior are shaped by the individual's attitudes. Behavior in this sense is the end product or "output" of a complex interaction of psychological processes. On the "input" side at any given point in time we have the information that the individual extracts from the situation in which he is taking part. There is a voluminous literature showing that under certain conditions, the portions of *potential* information presented by the situation that actually come to be stored away or learned by the individual can be vitally affected by the attitudes that he brings to the situation, just as it is affected by motive states (Chapter 2).

The conditions under which such effects of existing attitudes are clearest are twofold. Attitudes are more likely to play a role in shaping this "input" in the degree that

   the relevant attitudes are strong; and
   the incoming information is incomplete or ambiguous with respect to the evaluative dimension at stake.

Under such circumstances, what the individual notices, how he evaluates what is noticed, and what he is likely to remember from the situation over longer periods of time are all more likely to be influenced by existing attitudes.

Attitudes and Perception

Of many studies that could be cited to demonstrate these basic principles, we shall choose a few that highlight slightly different aspects of attitude influence on perceptual processes. Thus, for example, Hastorf and Cantril (1954) report a study of student perceptions during the viewing of a movie that had been taken of a football game between Dartmouth and Princeton. Following the game, each school had accused the other of deliberately being too rough. The movie was shown to a sample of students at each of the two colleges. Princeton students saw twice as many infractions of the rules by Dartmouth players as did Dartmouth students.

In such an instance, one can be sure that the attitudes held by the two student bodies toward their own college and the rival college were relatively strong. In the course of play, some actions would stand out as relatively unambiguous infractions of the rules. Other actions would lie in a more questionable zone: perhaps a camera shot from another angle would have provided more complete information about the legality of the action. In this zone of incomplete information, Princeton students tended to "see" Dartmouth infractions, whereas Dartmouth students did not.

Where the football movie is concerned, the visual stimuli were highly complex and were rapidly changing. It is likely that both perceptual selection and biases in the decoding of noticed actions (as legal or illegal) were involved. In other cases, the information provided by the experiment has been simpler, and hence failure to notice some part of the stimulus object has been less likely as a source of bias in perception.

In a format used by countless studies the subject is asked to judge the personality characteristics of people represented in simple photographs that can be examined at some length. It is commonly found that actual facial features and expressions make relatively little difference in such judgments if the subject can decode the person represented in the photograph into some class of social object that he commonly cognizes, and toward which he has formed some evaluative impression in the past. Thus anti-Negro subjects typically attribute personality traits to photographs of Negroes that are systematically more negative than those attributed to photographs of white people, and the effect is the more marked the more strongly anti-Negro the judge is.

In an interesting variation on such a study, Secord, Bevan, and Katz (1956) presented white subjects with white and Negro photographs, where the Negro photographs had been carefully chosen to represent a range from individuals very Negroid in appearance to very Caucasian in appearance. Although the usual differences were obtained in rating the personality characteristics of Negroes and whites, there were no differences in ratings given Negroes who were more or less Negroid. Despite objective differences in "degree of Negroeness," it seemed that these subjects typically coded the persons represented into two simple classes (Negro and white), with prior attitudes toward these classes playing a major part in estimates of personality.

The tricks of perception illustrated here create major problems in the conduct of some kinds of research in social psychology, since the capacity of observers to make objective judgments about social events and objects under study can be affected by strong prior attitudes. Thus, for example, content analysis (a form of decoding written materials that is quite explicit, with the analyst required to scan verbal materials for certain types of references that must then be located in predetermined categories) is commonly recognized to be subject to "coder bias," unless sufficient precautions are taken. A strongly Democratic coder, analyzing the same body of political material that a strongly Republican coder analyzes, is more likely than the other to "find" references favorable to the Democrats, and to see in highly ambiguous references some pro-Democratic undertones that affect the category to which such references may be assigned. Obviously, good research is possible only if such human tendencies can be kept in check.

We should not lose sight of the fact that individual differences in perceptions of the same objects become fewer as the information presented becomes less ambiguous with regard to whatever evaluation dimensions (football infractions, personality traits) are at issue. In most of our examples you can note that the ambiguity in the stimulus information is rather high. Nonetheless, social objects, states, or events (which we have said tend to arouse strong attitudes) are often highly ambiguous with respect to many customary judgmental dimensions, particularly those involving the underlying motives and intentions of persons and groups.

Attitudes and Learning

Since what an individual manages to see, and how he interprets or decodes the information that he does absorb are both influenced by existing attitudes, another logical question is whether parallel influences can be detected for success in learning and retention of information over time. Specifically, if a person sees what he finds congenial to see (given his prior attitudes), does he also remember what he finds congenial to remember and forget what he does not find congenial to remember? Once again, a large number of experiments have been addressed to this question. As Research Illustration 3.4 suggests, they show

Research Illustration 3.4

Levine and Murphy (1943) selected groups of five pro-Communist and five anti-Communist college students to participate in an experiment involving the learning of controversial material. The capacity of the two groups to learn prose materials under the experimental conditions was first tested on a neutral prose passage and was found to be essentially the same. Then two other prose passages, one sharply anti-Communist and the other moderately pro-Communist, were presented for rapid reading. Fifteen minutes after such a reading, subjects were asked to reproduce the paragraph they had read as accurately as they could. Similar tests of recall were given again after fresh

The pro-Soviet Union selection:

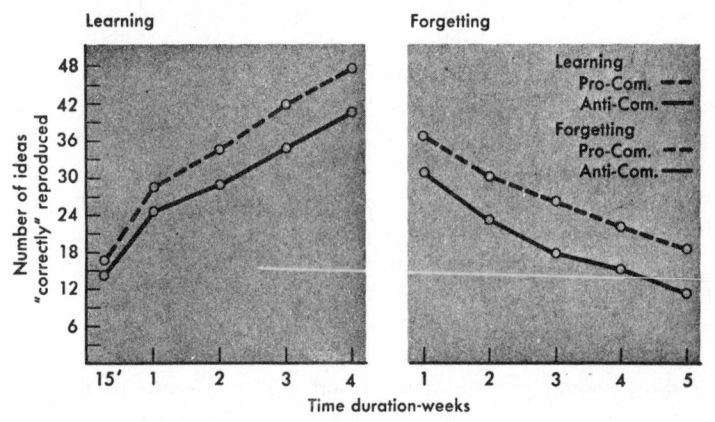

The anti-Soviet Union selection:

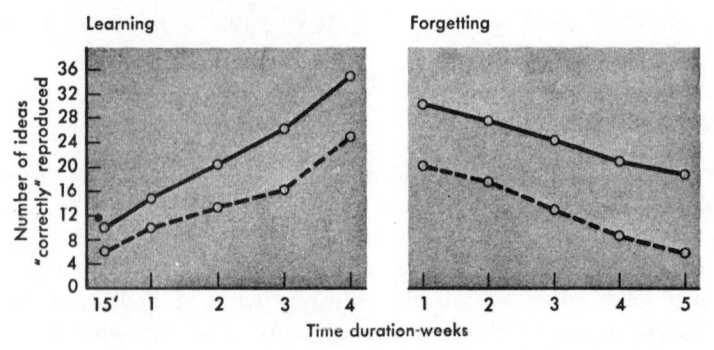

Learning and forgetting curves for "correct" responses for pro-Communist and anti-Communist groups on two opposing selections

readings at weekly intervals over a four-week "learning period." Repetitions of the reading were then dropped, and the subjects were tested again on recall at weekly intervals for a five-week "forgetting period."

To score the accuracy of recall, materials in the original paragraphs were divided into "idea groups" and the reproduced paragraphs were rated according to the number of ideas that were recaptured with reasonable accuracy. A graphing of the average scores within each of the test groups for the two types of material over the learning and forgetting periods appears in the accompanying figure.

Although not all of the test comparisons between the groups showed statistically significant differences, the results in general seemed to confirm expectations. The subjects tended to learn the passage congenial to their prior views *more* rapidly, and forgot it *less* rapidly, than did subjects for whom the passage was uncongenial.

that although reversals can be obtained under unusual conditions, this is indeed the typical effect.

* * *

There is clearly a common thread running through all of these findings regarding attitudes and the various information input processes. Certain types of new information relevant to potential attitude objects have valence implications, positive or negative. The information packaged in an act of "deliberate" roughing by a Dartmouth player holds an obvious negative valence implication for some more generalized object (such as the Dartmouth team, the college) of which the player is seen as a part. The likelihood that this or any other information with valence implications will succeed in passing through the various perceptual screens and will survive in memory storage for any substantial period is influenced by the relationship between the valence implied and the preexisting attitude of the individual, also represented as a valence. In this case (and contrary to the electrical analogy), *like valences attract, and unlike valences repel.* We are less likely to absorb information with valence implications that fail to support our prior attitudes.

The end product of these trends is, of course, that if a collection of people experiences the same flow of situations over a period of time, the shape of their perceived worlds, in the degree to which it has evolved in the time period, will show characteristic differences. These differences will be predictable in some degree from differences in attitudes held at the beginning of the common experience.

Indeed, it can well be hypothesized that when incoming information is perceived to be supportive of the individual's prior attitude, the experience itself is likely to have some reinforcing or strengthening effect on the degree of the individual's attitude. This state of affairs becomes somewhat ironic in those situations of ambiguous information where two antagonists can come away feeling equally reinforced in opposite directions. The review of the Dartmouth-Princeton movie undoubtedly "proved" to many partisan viewers of both camps that their righteous indignation at the other school had been fully warranted, and thereby strengthened their negative feelings about the other school. This, of course, despite the fact that the two groups of students were receiving identical objective information through the movie.

Since attitudes as stored dispositions have effects not only upon the key "output" side (overt behavior) but also on the various "input" processes as well, we can see more clearly why it is useful to deal with attitudes as focal points of the psychological organization of the individual. Indeed, when we say that attitudes influence behavior (in the overt sense) there is no reason why we should not include various perceptual processes, learning, and dynamic aspects of memory as "behaviors" also.

If this seems strange, consider for a moment one of the most persistent and reliable findings of research in mass communications. When arguments are presented through the mass media favoring one side of a current controversy, a person already convinced of the side being supported is more likely to tune in on (or stop and read) the argument, whereas a person convinced of the opposite side is more likely to turn the radio off (or skip the article). (See, among many examples, Hyman and Sheatsley, 1947.) Getting up to turn off the television set when a candidate of the opposing party starts a speech is, of course, "overt behavior." So are the numerous acts over time that lead to a portfolio of subscriptions to liberal political magazines in one home and conservative political magazines in another. Yet all of these overt behaviors are easy to see as being no more than special cases of perceptual selection. It is in this sense that the influence of attitudes upon component psychological processes is hard to distinguish from the influence on what is generally thought of as "behavior." In such a sense, the dividing line between implicit and explicit (or overt) behavior becomes rather inconsequential.

OVERVIEW

Our goal in this chapter has been to expand our understanding of what attitudes are and what they can be seen as doing in the total psychological organization of the individual over time.

By way of indicating what attitudes are, we have limited the key formal properties of the attitudes to the direction and the degree of feeling associated with a specified object. We have also singled out a few key properties of attitude objects, such as their inclusiveness, centrality, or status as social objects. At the same time, we have seen that attitudes have rather far-reaching effects, both on the "output" side in overt behavior and on the "input" side where the acquisition of information is concerned. Oft-cited instances in which the attitude-behavior relationship seems weak or even contradicted must generally be understood in terms of the facts that (1) behavior is a *joint* function of the situation and of the attitudes the individual brings to the situation; and (2) situations of any complexity render a number of attitudes relevant at the same time, so that once the situation is specified, behavior is some resultant of several relevant attitudes at once.

There are two propositions concerning information input which, if juxtaposed, may seem to have rather odd logical implications. The first is that where information is incomplete, the individual tends to carry away from the situation "new" information that supports his preexisting attitudes. Second, such successful input of supportive information increases the degree of his attitude in the same direction. Put together, these propositions would seem to suggest that once attitudes are even faintly formed—once there has been any movement from the zero point whatever—an inevitable spiral of "self-strengthening" occurs. We would not protest a mild reading of these propositions: that is, attitudes once formed are likely to endure. On the other hand, we would hardly want to see the strengthening of attitudes in a single direction as an irreversible process. This we know from experience is untrue. An individual's attitudes do change direction, and sometimes dramatically. We must now consider under what conditions this is so.

CHAPTER 4

Attitude Change

A GREAT DEAL OF THE HUMAN ACTIVITY DIRECTED TOWARD OTHER PEOPLE, rather than toward "things," presupposes in one way or another that people can be induced to "change their minds." The clergyman seeking converts, the salesman seeking new customers, the government official seeking to win support for his policies, or even the husband arguing with his wife are but some of the more striking examples of people endeavoring to change attitudes of others.

One real-life setting in which attitude change has special significance is that in which politicians and parties compete for the affections of voters. In this setting, many studies of attitude change have suggested that not only are occasional people "converted" from beliefs in one party to beliefs in the other, but that certain types of people seem to show a more general tendency toward "changeability" in their political beliefs. Although party loyalties are rather stable for most people most of the time, some voters show a pronounced tendency to shift from party to party over a sequence of elections; they are also likely to be the people who vacillate back and forth in their voting intentions from one side to the other during a campaign.

If these changeable people were all political "independents," they might not strike us as surprising. They would simply fall near the center of a scale of attitudes toward the two parties, and would hence cross the dividing line from one party to the other without much change in affect. But many of them express rather strong affect toward one of the parties at one time, and then are as strongly against it on another occasion. In other words, their vacillation is not a product of neutral affect: rather they simply seem more susceptible to change in attitudes than other people who tend to vote more regularly for a given party, show little vacillation in vote intention during the campaign, and the like.

There are several ways of measuring the changeability in partisan attitudes that voters manifest during a campaign. If we consider at the same time the volume of political information to which voters have exposed themselves during the same campaign, we tend to find the type of relationship shown in Figure 4.1. The form of this curve, which may strike you as surprising, reflects a number of processes at once, and all these processes will figure in our discussion of attitude change. Nonetheless, perhaps you can figure out in advance why this function behaves as it does.

We often come to understand things best by observing the conditions under which they change. Attitudes are no exception. Much of what we have already said about attitudes has been cast in the form and language we have chosen because of what has been learned about attitudes through the study of their change.

In this chapter we propose to examine some of the basic principles

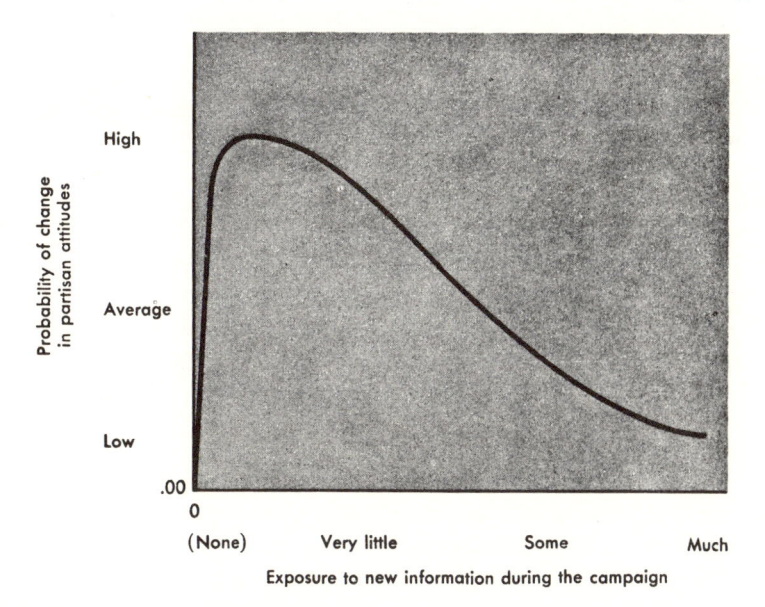

FIGURE 4.1. Hypothetical relationship between exposure to current political information and attitude change

of attitude change. There are a number of directions that might be followed. We can consider the likelihood of attitude change as a function of the affect invested in the object; or as a function of the type of object toward which attitudes have been formed (more or less inclusive, more or less central, for example); or we can hold these properties constant and consider other conditions under which attitudes of similar affect, held toward similar objects, are more or less likely to undergo change. We shall follow all these paths, and yet try to arrive at a coherent picture of what we have learned about attitudes in the process.

THE PRIMARY CONDITIONS FOR ATTITUDE CHANGE

Attitude change depends very generally on the receipt of *new information* that in some way or another is relevant to the attitude object from the point of view of the attitude holder. In some interesting special cases that we shall consider much later in the chapter, the relevance may be quite indirect. Typically, however, the new information has to do in a direct and obvious way with the properties of the attitude object. The revelation that the undistinguished-looking gentleman in the wrinkled blue serge suit is the prominent author of a series of novels you have admired represents a piece of new information that drastically changes the cognitive content of the gentleman as an object in your eyes, and is likely to change your attitude toward him as well.

Most of what we see about us as attitude change is initiated not by actual change in affect toward a particular object property, but by new information (with its own preexisting valence implications for the individual) that adds or subtracts some important property from the cognized object. That is, the gentleman in the serge suit initially embraces two negatively signed properties: (1) he lacks distinction; and (2) his suit is wrinkled. When attitude change occurs in this case, it does not occur because of any gross shift in feeling toward these properties in themselves. Instead, another property of great subjective importance and with a strong positive valence ("admired author") has been introduced. The cognitive content of the object changes, and affective change follows.

As Asch (1940) once observed, then, it is worth distinguishing change in "the object of judgment" from change in the "judgment of the object," for this distinction helps us pin down how attitudes usually change. Of course a "change in the object of judgment" that carries with it a change in affect toward the object is a legitimate case of attitude change, since attitudes have to do with the affect associated with specific objects, including complex ones. Your attitude toward the gentleman as an object has indeed undergone genuine change.

This same dependence of attitude change upon new information is, of course, the first lesson to be drawn from Figure 4.1. The general principle does not account for the total curve, and for the moment we shall postpone the question as to why change does not become increasingly probable as the volume of information input increases. But it does account for the portion of the curve at the far left. The likelihood of attitude change is higher when the individual is receiving some flow of new information about politics during the campaign. When he stands outside this flow of information (extreme left of figure), however, the probability of changes falls abruptly to zero. His attitudes are then perfectly stable, and the behavior that flows from these attitudes (in this case, voting choice) proceeds in the same direction as in the past. There is no new information to prompt attitude revision or to deflect behavior into new channels.

Since it appears clear that affective change normally follows change in cognitive content of the object, it is worth asking whether there is such a thing as affective change occurring independently of new information, and if so, whether such change in affect would lead to change in cognitive content of the object. Research Illustration 4.1 provides evidence that such change does indeed occur. Of course, Rosenberg's experiment does not contradict the generalization that in real life a change in affect normally follows, rather than precedes, a change in cognitive content. The hypnosis was an entirely unusual event. But the study does show most clearly the close interdependence of affect and cognitive content: change in either is likely to have effects on the other.

This interdependence is a prime fact in the study of attitude change. It is important in part because objects present multiple properties, and if your feeling toward the general object changes because of some new cognition of it, you may come to feel differently about some of its other properties as well. Thus after discovering that the wrinkled serge suit (which you first looked at with disdain) was inhabited by an admired author, you might thereafter react a little less negatively to wrinkled serge suits. Thus new information can touch off a chain reaction of affective changes involving associated objects.

Changes in the Perceived Properties of an Object

In the general case, then, our attitudes toward an object can change when, from our point of view, the object changes. There are two special cases of such object change. It may be that the object itself actually has changed, or merely that our information about the object has been revised, with no real change in the object.

ACTUAL OBJECT CHANGE. The more obvious case, of course, is that in which the object actually undergoes some change in its properties, and we receive the information about the change. One of the more

Research Illustration 4.1

Rosenberg (1960) conducted an interesting attempt to change affect toward an object without changing its cognitive content first. This was naturally quite difficult, and he succeeded in the enterprise only by the use of hypnotic suggestion. He first ascertained the attitudes of his subjects toward particular social objects (Negroes moving into white neighborhoods, foreign aid, federal medical insurance, and the like) along with some important aspects of the cognitive content these objects had for them. Then he hypnotized the subjects and told them that after their hypnosis they would have a different affective reaction to the attitude object. Thus a subject who felt negatively toward Negroes moving into white neighborhoods would be told, "When you awake you will be very much in favor of Negroes moving into white neighborhoods. The mere idea of Negroes moving into white neighborhoods will give you a happy, exhilarated feeling. Although you will not remember this suggestion having been made, it will strongly influence your feelings after you have awakened. Only when the signal to remember is given will you remember . . . and only then will your feelings revert to normal." By such means, affect toward the objects were changed without the injection of any new cognitive content.

In the next few days, after release from the hypnotic trance but not from the posthypnotic suggestion, the cognitive content of the attitude objects was reexamined. Changes in the cognitive content that were appropriate to the new affect had indeed occurred. Thus a subject favoring federal medical insurance before hypnosis, because he saw it as a means of permitting democratic decisions about medical care by the people affected, could see no connection between these ideas after his hypnosis. Or a subject favoring foreign aid before hypnosis on the grounds that it aided economic development in former colonies would believe after hypnosis that such a boost would be a short-range matter, and that the long-range effects of aid would be to limit the crucial development of self-reliance in the underdeveloped nations. A scoring procedure developed to measure the amount of cognitive change showed a median change score of 167 for the experimental group, with a median of only 21 for a control group submitted to all of the experimental procedures save the hypnotic suggestion. The probability that the observed difference in scores could have occurred by chance was less than .01.

At the conclusion of the experiment, of course, the subjects were released from the hypnotic suggestion and the experiment was explained.

---

dramatic large-scale examples of actual change in object properties has to do with the rapid industrialization of Russia. Until 1950 the prevalent assumptions about Russia dated from an earlier period. Russians were regarded as an illiterate people without mechanical know-how. During World War II there were many anecdotes about their inability to use the mechanical equipment we had sent them to help repel the German invasion. In 1948, reports that Russia was working on the atomic bomb were received with tolerant amusement and the American public was assured that it would take at least eight years before they could possibly succeed.

In the fall of 1949 President Truman announced that Russia had succeeded in exploding an atomic bomb. The new information was less effective in changing assumptions about the backwardness of Russian technology than it might have been, since it could be claimed that Russia succeeded only because she had stolen "the secret" of the bomb from the United States. Another important perceived property of the Russian government was that it had an efficient world-wide intelligence system. The event seemed to underscore this belief. The subsequent tightening up of penalties for subversion, the renewed interest in loyalty oaths, and the congressional investigations of leaks in our security system were all consequences of the view that if Russia had solved the problem of the bomb so quickly, her success *must* have been due to our own inefficiency in protecting our secrets. Scientists who suggested that Russia was quite capable of making the bomb herself had little impact upon attitudes, since they were already suspected of being the source of some of the leaks in vital information.

News about the Russian launching of Sputnik I in October 1957 left no doubt about the reality of rapid advances in Russian scientific knowledge and technical skill. It could no longer be claimed that Russia had achieved her success by stealing secrets from us since we had not yet achieved this capability ourselves. The new information definitively revised our estimate of certain critical properties of Russia as an object, and many abrupt attitude changes occurred. Complacency with our scientific and military development gave place to alarm. The national administration and the Defense Department became the objects of considerable aggressiveness on the part of citizens, journalists, and members of Congress. Our educational system came under attack as less rigorous than that of the Russians, and invidious comparisons were drawn between the number of engineers we were producing and the much larger number trained in Russia. Scores of American educators visited the universities and schools in Russia to learn about their methods of instruction. In this case, attitudes in a variety of directions had to be modified because the information finally penetrated that "sleeping Russia" had come very much awake.

Since interest in attitude change has tended to grow up in settings where it appears easier or more desirable to try to change attitudes than to change the properties of the attitude object, we often lose sight of the fact that a change in object properties is the surest way to change attitudes toward the object, even if it is not usually the simplest. If one were to count, as births or deaths are counted, all the instances of notable attitude change that occur within a population in a specified period, it is likely that the clear majority of such changes would have come about because the objects of the attitudes have in point of fact changed their properties, and not because of human argument or persuasion.

CHANGES IN INFORMATION ABOUT OBJECTS. Nonetheless, there is an important class of instances in which an object remains constant but attitudes change as a result of new information the individual receives about it. This is essentially the case in Research Illustration 4.2. The Negro families in the housing project had not suddenly changed character in any objective sense. What had changed was the experience with Negroes, and hence the information about them, on the part of the white housewives. The fact that housewives in relatively segregated projects were less likely to change seems to reflect less frequent contact and a weaker flow of this new and direct kind of information. If a control population of persons who had not taken up residence in a biracial housing project had been studied, one can expect with some confidence that the incidence of attitude change in the same period would have been even lower, for new information about Negroes would have been even more rare.

This study of integrated housing cannot be taken to demonstrate that the information that comes from more direct contact between ethnic groups always leads to more favorable attitudes. Other studies of group prejudice (see Chapter 14) make clear that such contact in a housing area might lead to more hostile white attitudes if the Negro families were of lower social and economic status. In such a case, their presence in the housing area would have transmitted a different kind of information—information reinforcing the negative stereotypes. For our current purposes, however, Research Illustration 4.2 provides an excellent example of extremely strong attitudes being revised on the basis of new information.

The likelihood of attitude change under these circumstances may well lead you to question our enumeration, near the close of the preceding chapter, of psychological mechanisms whereby the individual ignores or reinterprets incoming information that does not fit well with his preexisting attitudes. Much of what appears to be a difference in these accounts can be resolved by paying attention to differences in the ambiguity of incoming information in the two discussions. In illustrations in the preceding chapter, the information presented experimentally was chosen in large part for its ambiguous character, and the effects of prior attitudes on acceptance of information was at its maximum. In this chapter, the incoming information has been much less ambiguous in

Research Illustration 4.2

Deutsch and Collins (1951) have reported on a study of change in attitudes toward Negroes among white housewives who had come to live in biracial housing projects. Two of these projects were fully integrated: Negro and white families had been assigned apartments without regard to race, and so were living in relatively close physical proximity (across the hall, down the stairs, and so on) in the same building. The other two projects were relatively segregated, as Negro families had been assigned to separate buildings or to separate parts of the project from those occupied by whites. There was no evidence that white housewives in the integrated projects had been less prejudiced before coming to live in the housing area than those in the more segregated projects.

The accompanying graph below shows the incidence of change in attitudes toward Negroes reported by the housewives after a period of residence in the two types of project. Although the amount of change—much of it favorable even in the segregated project—is remarkable, attitude change was far more frequent, and almost exclu-

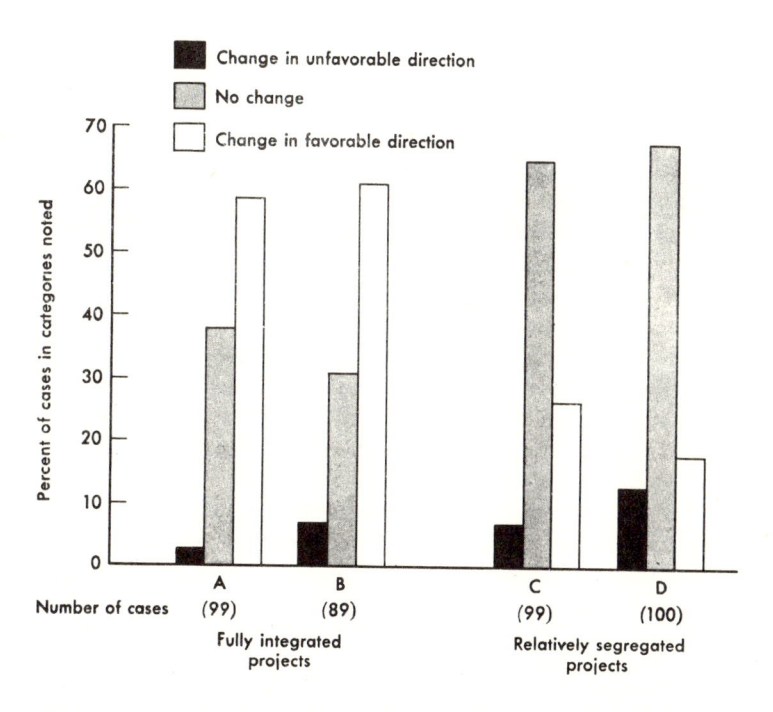

Changes in white housewives' attitudes toward Negroes following residence in biracial public housing projects (adapted from Deutsch and Collins, 1951)

sively in a positive direction, in the *integrated* project, where living contact was the closest. Some of the interviews with the housewives who had changed attitudes provide illuminating illustrations of the processes which had occurred:

> "I started to cry when my husband told me were coming to live here. I cried for three weeks. . . . I didn't want to come and live here where there were so many colored people. I didn't want to bring my children up with colored children, but we had to come. . . . Well, all that's changed. I've really come to like it. I see they're just as human as we are. They have nice apartments, they keep their children clean, and they're very friendly. I've come to like them a great deal. . . . I'd just as soon live near a colored person as a white, it makes no difference to me."

> "I thought I was moving into the heart of Africa. . . . I had always heard about how they were . . . they were dirty, drink a lot . . . were like savages. Living with them, my ideas have changed altogether. They're just people . . . they're not any different."

In this instance, circumstances were such that contact with Negro families (a new experience for most of the housewives) led to a drastic revision in properties attributed to Negroes as a social category. Marked affective changes followed the acceptance of this new information.

character. That the Russians did explode an atomic bomb in 1949, and did launch sputniks in 1957 (visible, by the way, to the naked eye), could not long have been doubted. In the housing project study, living at close range with Negroes and observing them firsthand made it increasingly difficult to fill in "expected" details concerning Negro depravity that were factually inaccurate.

Social psychologists have been deeply intrigued by distortions individuals introduce as they assimilate ambiguous information, and it is true that many crucial misunderstandings in social interaction stem directly from conflicting perceptions of the same objects on the part of interacting individuals. On the other hand, there is a danger of losing sight of the forest for the trees. Under a fair range of conditions—and unambiguous information is one of the principal of these—even strong attitudes can be readily undermined by appropriate contradictory information. Distortion effects can be intriguing and important, particularly in domains of human endeavor where information tends to be ambiguous. But they are not all, or even, normally, the "main effects."

* * *

The receipt of some kind of new information relevant to the attitude object is, then, the primary basis for attitude change. Most often, as in the cases above, such information simply serves to change the perceived properties of the objects in ways that modify attitudes toward them. However, sometimes the influential information may be somewhat less direct. Rather than changing the perception of the immediate properties of the object, it may serve instead to redefine the relationship between a given individual and the attitude object. To be effective, information of this latter kind must be more carefully tailored to the attitude systems of specific individuals, and must reflect an understanding of the more detailed conditions mediating attitude change. It is to these conditions that we turn.

ATTITUDE PROPERTIES AND ATTITUDE CHANGE

Let us now take for granted the introduction of some kind of new information, and ask why it is that some individuals faced with such information contrary to existing attitudes are more likely to be swayed in their opinions than are others. Further principles of attitude change depend on (1) variations in the characteristics of prior attitudes toward the objects about which new information is received; and on (2) variations in the characteristics of the situation in which the information is transmitted, including both the *kind* of information that is transmitted and the agent that transmits it. First we shall consider variations in attitude properties.

DEGREE OF FEELING TOWARD THE OBJECT. The first principle, linking attitude strength with attitude change, is likely to seem quite obvious. Most of us would guess that "weak" attitudes (located near the zero point of the attitude scale) would be more susceptible to change than stronger or more extreme attitudes. In one sense, at least, there is no doubt that this is true. If by "attitude change" we mean a movement across the zero point from a positive attitude to a negative one or vice versa, the generalization seems obvious, for weak attitudes are initially closer to the zero point and clearly have "less far to move" for a change in sign.

Yet this fact need not mean that new and contradictory information actually "pushes" people with weaker attitudes a greater distance (in some sense) along the attitude continuum than it would push people initially located farther toward the extremes. To find evidence for the generalization in this more pretentious form is difficult, for, as we have observed, we lack any very good units with which to gauge distance on the attitude continuum. Nonetheless, attempts have been made to test the hypothesis with techniques that involve what seem to be reasonable units.

Research Illustration 4.3

Tannenbaum (1956) gave 405 college undergraduates a pretest in which they rated legalized gambling, abstract art, and accelerated college programs on 7-point evaluation scales of the semantic differential (see Appendix A). The units employed in this technique have shown themselves, in numerous uses, to give results consistent with the supposition that they are roughly equal. If a student gave a rating of 7 (most favorable evaluation) to abstract art on all six of the evaluative scales applied he received a total score of 42 (the most favorable total score possible). But if he gave abstract art a rating of only 1 (most unfavorable) on the six scales, his total score was 6 (the most unfavorable total score possible). Both scores represent strong attitudes but differ in direction. Scores midway between these two extremes represent less intense attitudes, since a person checking the middle position of the 7-point scale has avoided saying that he has either a very favorable opinion of abstract art or a very unfavorable opinion. The strength of each student's attitude toward legalized gambling and accelerated college programs was similarly determined.

Five weeks later, the subjects were exposed to attitude change materials in the form of newspaper stories they read and then summarized in twenty-five words or less. These stories were reproduced in standard newspaper type along with appropriate headlines. Both a version favorable to the three topics and an unfavorable version were prepared so that the appropriate analysis of attitude change could be made depending on whether the student's original attitude had been predominantly favorable or unfavorable in nature. To determine whether attitudes had changed as a result of exposure to these materials, the students were then given the after-test which was identical to the attitude test taken five weeks previously.

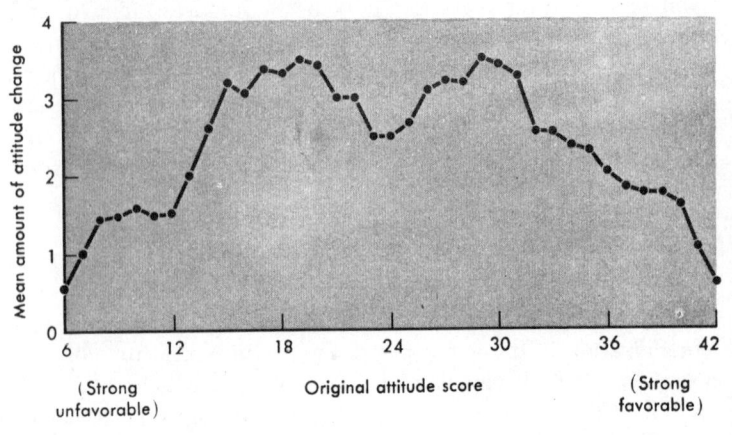

The amount of attitude change as a function of the strength of the original attitude (adapted from Tannenbaum, 1956)

In the accompanying figure is shown the amount of attitude change that occurred. It is quite apparent that those students who had very favorable attitudes (a score of 42) and very unfavorable attitudes (a score of 6) underwent the least change in attitude. As we go from the extremely favorable and the extremely unfavorable positions at the ends to the weaker attitudes in the middle, we find that attitude change was considerably greater. The authors conclude that susceptibility to attitude change is greater when the attitude is initially weak.

It would be interesting, in an experiment such as the Tannenbaum study, to know what proportion of the students who placed themselves toward the middle of the scale took such a position because they had rather conflicted reactions to different aspects of abstract art, as opposed to those "neutral" students who took center positions because they had never thought much about abstract art and did not actually care one way or another. As suggested in the preceding chapter, we would predict that attitude change upon reading the persuasive communication would be greater for the relatively indifferent than for the highly conflicted. Why this is so brings us to a principle of attitude change that is rather important, and that puts to work much of what we have learned about attitudes in preceding chapters.

THE MASS OF STORED INFORMATION ABOUT THE ATTITUDE OBJECT. If you were asked what kind of people in your experience have the least stable attitudes toward the greatest number of objects, you might well say, "Children." The susceptibility of children to rapid shifts in attitude when confronted with new information contradictory to their prior attitudes is a matter of persistent amusement to adults. Children are, as we say, "suggestible." In a vague way, we attribute this susceptibility to two sources: first, children have been trained in a variety of ways to respect the information and judgment of older people; and second, children have stored very little information about many of the objects they try to evaluate.

We are particularly interested in the latter factor because there are adults who share with children low information about certain attitude objects yet do not share with children the same pressure to respect adult judgment. And these adults show high susceptibility to attitude change under certain conditions. This is true of poorly educated people over a wide range of potential attitude objects. And in areas where they feel themselves poorly informed, highly educated people often find their own attitudes readily susceptible to revision when given new information.

The general principle is, therefore, that attitudes about an object are more subject to change through contradictory incoming information *when the existing mass of stored information about the object is smaller.*

This principle underlies the declining trend in the right side of the curve in Figure 4.1, for the axis labeled "Exposure to New Information during the Campaign" could as appropriately be labeled "Mass of Stored Information about Politics." Individuals build rather stable habits of seeking information in some areas that interest them (politics or economics or sports or religion), and of ignoring information from other areas that do not. The people in Figure 4.1 who have absorbed a great deal of information about politics during the campaign in question are also very largely the people who absorb unusual amounts of political information in *every* campaign, and between campaigns as well. They are "interested in politics" and have, over the years, accumulated a very large store of information about it. The people on the left side of the figure show very little in the way of stored political information. How they behave in any given campaign, then, depends on whether or not they become exposed to some little new information about what is going on. Those not exposed show no attitude instability; those who are exposed show a maximum likelihood of attitude change.

In the next chapter we shall discuss attitude stability, and shall attempt to show more clearly why a large mass of information *about* an object helps to stabilize attitudes *toward* that object. For now, the following formulation will serve. Let us think of incoming information as having a mass or weight (and, for the moment, we are assuming that the incoming information has valence implications contrary to the receiver's attitudes). That is, a 10-point critique of ten aspects of a foreign aid program (for example) would obviously have more mass than any one of the single points taken alone as an argument. Since stored information has mass in much the same sense, then it is not of course surprising that any given mass of incoming information will have more impact against a small mass of stored information than against a large one.

THE CENTRALITY OF THE ATTITUDE OBJECT. We have already noted that psychologically central objects are likely to be those about which the individual has stored relatively great amounts of information. Hence it follows that, on the average, attitudes toward remote objects are likely to be more susceptible to change through new information than those toward objects that are, for the individual, more central.

The instability of attitudes toward remote objects about which people have little information is a very pervasive phenomenon in public opinion research. It can be shown, for example, that attitudes concerning foreign policy are less stable for cross-section populations over time than are attitudes toward domestic policy questions, where the critical objects (employment, education, Negroes) are closer at hand and more familiar. Of course it is psychological and not geographical distance that is important here: for the expert on foreign relations, the objects of foreign policy may be more central than those of domestic policy, and we would expect him to have very stable attitudes in foreign policy areas. Furthermore, some kinds of domestic policy questions (tariffs, deficit financing) involve objects that are very remote from the daily lives of most citizens, and attitudes toward such objects are as volatile as those concerning foreign policy. Although meaningful attitudes may be formed toward relatively remote objects, these attitudes are anchored in thin reserves of information and are rather readily dislodged by small amounts of new information.

However, there is reason to believe that the sparse amounts of information that an individual is likely to hold about an object of low centrality for him is not the sole reason for potential instability of attitudes toward it. As we have observed, an object can be more or less central for the individual in a motivational sense as well, according to the degree that the object plays some helpful or hindering role in the maintenance of or progress toward prized goals. Although it is rather generally the case that greater amounts of information tend to be held about objects of greater centrality in this purely motivational sense, the correspondence is not perfect. And attitudes toward an object are more easily changed, all other things equal, if the object is less firmly imbedded in some means–end chain important to the individual (and thereby is less central in the motivational sense) than it is when it lies in a more crucial position.

Let us suppose, for instance, that you are sufficiently annoyed by one-way streets to react negatively to a proposal to change another downtown thoroughfare to one-way status. Nevertheless, a city official is likely to have an easier time convincing you that the change is desirable in the total scheme of downtown traffic flow than he is in convincing a merchant on the street who knows that the proposed change will substantially reduce the volume of his business, or even a resident on the street for whom the change will mean an extra block to drive in going to and from his home. Clearly the character of traffic flow on the street, although it stirs an affective reaction for you, is less central an object to you than for the merchant or the resident. And too, of course, your attitudes toward the one-way street proposal are likely to have been weaker in degree from the start.

More generally, we may summarize much of what we have said by observing that the following attitude and object attributes all tend to co-occur:

Affect	*Object*
Weak in degree	Low centrality (psychologically remote) Low personal goal relevance Small storage of information

We stress that these attributes only *tend* to co-occur, because if the co-occurrence were perfect we would need only one term to express the whole set. However, the distinctions are useful, for these attributes do not always co-occur. Indeed, one would judge from some of the interviews in the Deutsch-Collins housing study that Negroes had probably been rather remote objects for some of the housewives prior to their move to the housing project, although their attitudes were nonetheless extremely negative. Nevertheless, when these attributes do co-occur, we can be rather sure that we are dealing with an attitude that will be easily changed by new information.

PERSUASION AND ATTITUDE CHANGE

Up to this point we have limited the discussion to one class of factors affecting the likelihood of change in attitudes given contrary incoming information. These factors all depend on the properties of the attitude itself as it stands just prior to the receipt of new information about the object.

Most experimental work on attitude change has been forced to deal in terms of the broader situation whereby the persuasive information is transmitted to the subject. A good example of an experiment focusing on the transmission situation is provided by Research Illustration 4.4. Although many variations on this experimental design have been employed, the basic format—a "before" attitude measurement, the introduction of a source bearing a persuasive message, and an "after" measurement to register change—has been one of the classic ways in which attitude change has been studied.

We can consider these studies as a whole to be studies in *persuasion*, a special case of interpersonal influence in which one party argues a point of view to another who remains essentially a "silent partner." The typical situation in experiments on persuasion tends to be unilateral in the sense that verbal communication runs one way only. It is only one half of the two-way interchange between persons that is called social interaction.

Studies in persuasion have made clear that the likelihood of attitude change depends not only on properties of the attitudes that an individual brings to the situation in which contrary information is introduced, but also on the broader characteristics of the transmission situation itself, at least as he perceives them. In particular, two other classes of factors become important: the properties of the *persuasive message* and the properties of the agent that transmits the message, or the *source*.

Research Illustration 4.4

Kelman and Hovland (1953) measured the attitudes of several groups of high school seniors toward harshness or leniency in the treatment of criminals. Later they asked the students to listen to a recording of an educational radio program in order to judge its educational value. The program involved a guest speaker arguing for extreme leniency in the treatment of juvenile delinquents. Although the speech was the same in all experimental groups, the speaker was introduced in three different ways for different groups. Once he was represented as a judge from a juvenile court who was a highly trained, well-informed authority on delinquency. In a neutral version he was represented as a member of the studio audience, chosen at random. In a third version he was also from the studio audience, but in the introductory interview the information came out that he had been a delinquent in his youth and was currently free on bail after arrest on dope peddling charges. During the introductory interview his remarks showed a low regard for the law and a desire for lenient enforcement out of self-interest. Thus there were positive, neutral, and negative sources.

The opinion scale was applied a second time immediately after the presentation and again three weeks later. Data were also collected regarding audience evaluation of the program, and capacity to recall facts included in the presentation. There were no differences between groups in factual recall, but very large differences in evaluation, with the group that had listened to the "positive" speaker (the judge) evaluating the program most favorably, those that had listened to the "negative" speaker most negatively, and the neutral group at an intermediate position. There was evidence of attitude change immediately after the presentation, in the direction advocated by the recorded argument (favoring leniency) in all groups; however, the change was greatest in the group with the positive and least in that with the "delinquent" speaker. The mean scores for the three groups, with significance of differences between them, were as follows (a high score representing the advocated position of leniency):

Group presented	N	Mean attitude score
Positive source	97	46.7
Neutral source	56	45.7
Negative source	91	42.8

Significance of differences: positive vs. negative group: $p < .001$
positive vs. neutral group: $p < .25$
neutral vs. negative group: $p < .01$

When an alternate form of the attitude questionnaire was repeated three weeks later, however, the differences in degree of change between the groups had disappeared, although the over-all attitude change was still present. It appeared that the content of the argument had been retained but the *source* of the argument (with its positive or negative implications) had been forgotten. In some groups, however, the introductory material that had created the strong differences in evaluation of the source was played again before the final attitude questionnaire was given. This "reinstatement" or reminder of the source led to differences between experimental groups that were about the same as the initial differences between the groups, with positive-source groups showing greater attitude change than negative-source groups.

To these we might want to add a less well defined set of factors that have to do with other properties of the setting or social context in which the transmission occurs.

The Nature of the Persuasive Message

It seems reasonable that some types of persuasive messages are more effective than others in achieving attitude change. This fact has been of great interest to people who as a practical matter must find means of changing attitudes, for often the message is the only element in the persuasion situation that can be easily manipulated. The character of basic appeals in a message (to pride, to fear, to humor, and so on), the organization of the argument (presenting one side of a case only, as opposed to "both" sides), and other aspects have been examined with an eye to discovering the formal properties of messages that are most powerful in inducing change. Findings from these investigations have been sufficiently mixed for it to seem likely that no very simple set of conclusions covering a wide range of persuasive situations is likely to be reached.

There is, however, one aspect of the persuasive message that appears to be of very broad importance. This is the relationship between the content of the message and the motivational basis on which the attitude rests. In Chapter 2 we observed that across a set of individuals, all of whom have formally similar attitudes toward a given object (that is, similar merely in degree of favorableness or unfavorableness), there may be many differences in the motivational conditions under which their several attitudes were formed. For example, of three people with strong positive feelings toward the Republican party, one may have developed this attitude primarily because he sees that party as advocating a policy in which he takes great interest, and hence serving as a means to the policy goal (the instrumental or adjustment function of Chapter 2); the second person may have little cognition of the party as an instrument toward any policy goals, but may feel that his family has always been Republican, just as it has always been Methodist (perhaps the value-expressive function); and the third may know that his job and personal livelihood depend on political patronage and hence a party victory (again, a utilitarian base, but quite distinct from that of the first person). It is not hard to see that a message with persuasive information calling into question the interest of the Republican party in accomplishing the policy objective that the first person desires would stand much more chance of changing his attitude than the attitudes of either of the other two persons, for whom the argument would be largely irrelevant.

In real life, of course, attitudes toward objects as complex as these are likely to rest on quite a mixture of bases rather than on a single one. Nonetheless, the general point remains clear: attitudes toward an object of a certain degree of centrality for an individual are likely to change in response to new persuasive information in the measure that the information is relevant to the grounds on which the object has attained its centrality for that particular individual.

This principle is quite obvious and easy to apply where the attitude formation has been primarily utilitarian. For example, Carlson (1956) was able not only to measure the attitudes of subjects toward Negroes moving into white neighborhoods, but also the more general ends that such an event was seen as furthering (such as equal human rights) or threatening (the value of real estate). He then devised persuasive messages intended to change the perceived likelihood that the general ends would indeed be achieved by the event, thereby altering the strength of the cognitive bonds between means and ends, and thereby achieved change in attitudes toward the original object—residential desegregation.

However, it is important at this point to remember that attitudes can develop toward objects on grounds that are somewhat more complicated than their apparent use-properties. When this is the case, information that aims merely at changing perception of these properties may be relatively ineffectual. Thus it has become quite firmly established that some kinds of prejudice against minority groups have roots less in the properties of the groups as perceived than in pressures and frustrations from other sources that the individual cannot bring himself to recognize, or at least cannot express directly, and that hence "go underground" and are displaced to expressions of irrational hostility toward ethnic groups. The displacement mechanism here is much the same as that displayed by the office worker who cannot express his work frustrations directly to his superior, but comes home to kick the cat with special vigor after a hard day; the attitude toward the minority group in this case might be seen as having primarily an ego-defensive function (Chapter 2). Katz, Sarnoff, and McClintock (1956, 1957) have attempted with some success to show experimentally that familiarizing prejudiced subjects with "self-insight" materials designed to clarify some of the underground dynamics of prejudiced attitudes may be more effective in inducing permanent attitude change in these instances than are persuasive messages that are more directly informational in character, in the sense that they try merely to correct mistaken perceptions about properties of the groups in question.

There is undoubtedly a comparable question of the nature of the fit between message content and attitude where straight information is concerned as well. Although there has been some question as to whether persuasive messages that present all one side of an issue are more effective than "two-sided" messages that give some representation to opposing views but present counterarguments for them, it does appear to be settled that "two-sided" messages better prepare subjects to resist subsequent attempts to change their attitudes, particularly when the later persuasive message takes the tack for which a counterargument has already been presented (McGuire, 1961). Here again the mechanism seems quite clear: the better fortified the individual is with relevant counterinformation, the less effective a persuasive message is likely to be. And, too, this is one of the key reasons why individuals with a great deal of information about an object are less likely to be swayed in their attitudes by a given persuasive message than are individuals who have stored less information about it: the probability that relevant counterinformation is on hand for any given persuasive message is much greater in the former case.

In summary, then, the type of message that is likely to be most effective in inducing attitude change is one well tailored to fit the particular attitude structure, being relevant to the motivational bases of the attitude, yet involving arguments that are sufficiently novel that it is unlikely the individual is already fortified with counterinformation. The stringency of these specifications sheds light on why it is that in a persuasion experiment the same message achieves much more change in some people than in others, even with attitudes of the same strength: no single message will be equally well tailored for every subject. What the experimenter does implicitly in looking for the most effective persuasive message possible is to consider what grounds are most typical for a given attitude, and what arguments are least likely to have well-known counterarguments.

The Source of the Persuasive Message

One of the reasons why persuasion of the type studied in the typical experiments is only a special case, although an important one, of a broader class of events called attitude change is worth special emphasis.

ATTITUDE CHANGE - 99

Of course, as in other types of attitude change, persuasion occurs typically as new information relevant to the attitude object is transmitted to the listener. But this new information differs in a primary way from that which would be conveyed by direct transactions with the object itself. It is not direct information, but *socially mediated information*.

The new information we saw to be so potent in changing the attitudes of the white housewives in the biracial housing project was direct rather than socially mediated. It was based on firsthand observation of the attitude object (Negroes) itself. To imagine this information transformed into the socially mediated type, we might think of one of these housewives returning to her hometown and telling others of her experiences in the biracial project. Undoubtedly she would urge her listeners to accept her new point of view about Negroes, and she would of course be engaging in persuasion. Her listeners would receive a summary of the information she had received directly, but they would receive it second hand. Their relationship to the information is thereby complicated, for there is no longer a simple subject-object relationship, but rather a triangular relationship between subject, source, and object (see Figure 4.2).

What is important about such socially mediated information is that the subject evaluates not only the information transmitted by the source, but the source itself as well. More crucial still, as the Kelman-Hovland

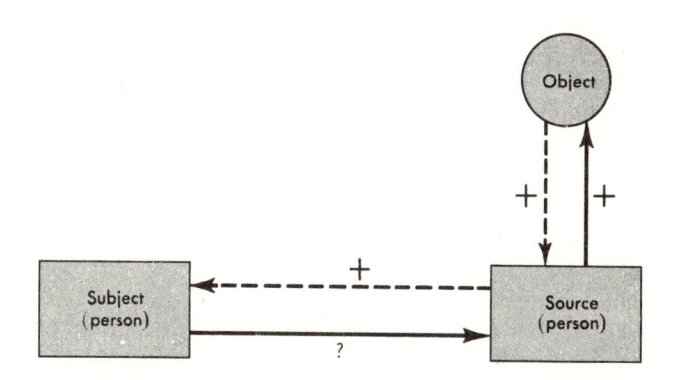

FIGURE 4.2. Direct vs. socially mediated information about an attitude object. The figure assumes that the source has a direct relationship with the object, whereas the subject is dependent on the source for such information. The broken lines represent the flow of information *from* the object or the source with the valence implications of the information indicated; the unbroken lines represent attitudes *toward* the indicated object.

study suggests, the evaluation of the source *affects* the evaluation of the persuasive message, and hence influences the likelihood of attitude change.

Although evaluation of the source of a persuasive message, like any other evaluation, may be summed up as a location on a positive-negative continuum, it is useful to consider some of the typical components of the evaluation. One such component is an implicit comparison on the part of the listener between his own pool of stored information about the object of persuasion and that which the source appears to possess. The source is more or less highly evaluated according to the ratio of source information to own information. If, for example, you detect errors in a persuasive message regarding an object on which you consider yourself well informed, it will be easy for you to discount the valence implications of the message. Normally, however, the source (in part by virtue of being a "source," either self-styled or presented by other authorities) is assumed to have above-average information regarding the object, and in many experiments the *expertise* of the source is deliberately stressed. Indeed, there was a long line of experimental work in the early days of social psychology under the rubric "prestige suggestion," which showed that when the prestige of the source suggested high *expertise*, rather remarkable information and viewpoints might be accepted by subjects whose information was sufficiently low.

Another component of source evaluation involves judgments as to how the source has selected his information. Suspicion that the source has selected information in such a way as to overplay certain valence implications lowers the listener's evaluation. Of course the listener with greater information regarding the object is more likely to be sensitive to the presence of such bias, although cues suggesting that the source has a narrow self-interest in his point of view raise comparable suspicions even on the part of the listener who has less information.

Perceptions of expertise and bias are usually lumped together and discussed as attributed *source credibility*. Such source credibility refers to the relationship between the source and the specific body of information relevant to the object of persuasion. Although it is a major component in source evaluation, it does not exhaust reactions to the source, some of which may have little logical relationship to the object of persuasion and yet "contaminate" source evaluation. How engagingly the source speaks would be one such "extraneous" but influential judgment.

Another very important factor seems to be what we might call the sense of *attitudinal* distance (or dissimilarity) the source conveys to the listener as lying between them, not only with respect to their attitudes toward the object of persuasion, but with respect to other seemingly irrelevant attitudes as well. Of course the need to persuade means that the source must make a point of *some* attitudinal distance between himself and the listener where the object of persuasion is concerned: if he were to indicate that his attitude toward this object was just the same as the listener's, the listener would be reinforced in his opinion rather than persuaded in some new direction. Furthermore, up to a point it is true that effective persuasion moves the listener to some new position partway between his original position and that of the source. And up to this point, the greater the initial discrepancy between source and listener with respect to the object of persuasion, the greater the attitude change of the listener, other things equal.

However, Hovland, Harvey, and Sherif (1957) have presented interesting evidence to suggest that there are important limits to this proposition. When the discrepancy between the listener's original position and that of the source becomes sufficiently large, attitude change becomes smaller rather than greater, or disappears altogether. The listener "writes off" the source from the start. Such categoric rejection would be likely if a doctrinaire Communist tried to persuade a chamber of commerce gathering toward a more leftist position. A liberal businessman could achieve more attitude change by presenting a milder view in such a setting.

Although a source cannot deny that his attitude differs from that of his listener with respect to the object of persuasion, he can help to minimize the listener's sense of attitudinal distance from him by making clear to the listener that they hold very similar positions in terms of many other attitudes, even ones that are quite irrelevant to the object of persuasion. Weiss (1957) has shown experimentally that a persuasion attempt preceded by expression of other opinions known to be congruent with the listeners' opinions facilitated later change in the object of persuasion. He observes that if the primary intent of a speaker is to convince a prohibitionist group to adopt a certain position on foreign policy, he might well begin his address with statements that bemoan sin and the curse of liquor!

In general, any posture taken by the source that sensitizes his listeners to attitudinal distance is likely to weaken his persuasive power. Any explicit attempt to persuade—"I'm going to set out to change your attitudes on this matter"—stresses distance, raises defenses on the part of the listener, and gives a very poor frame for any influence attempt. Allyn and Festinger (1961) have even shown that individuals are less responsive to a persuasive message if they expect in advance to disagree with it than they are to the same message when not forewarned. Similarly, the listener is *least* likely to feel that the source has any persuasive intent toward him when the message is not even addressed to him in the first place, as in the case of "overheard conversations." These appear to be particularly effective settings for attitude change, especially when the listener thinks that the source does not know he is overhearing, and when the overheard material is of some intrinsic interest to the listener in the first place (Walster and Festinger, 1962). With all these considerations in mind, it is rather clear why political campaign speeches do not achieve massive attitude change.

All these perceptions—expertise, bias, attitudinal distance, and other source traits—contribute to generalized source evaluation. The general principle implicit throughout is that where the message is held constant, attitude change through persuasion will be higher where the valence of the source is more positive.

To this general proposition Hovland, Janis, and Kelley (1953) have added an important amendment. Many studies, including the Kelman-Hovland experiment cited above, have shown that often the source of the message is forgotten even though the content appears to have been retained. As memory of the source decays, the increment in attitude change due to a positive source may decay as well, while the change in the advocated direction is increased as the negative source is forgotten. As the authors observe, the conditions under which the memory of the source decays more rapidly than memory of the content involve a complex set of further variables about which little is currently known. However, one would predict that for any situation in which the source and the content were durably attached, the effects of the source on attitude change would be more durable as well.

* * *

The interaction between attitudes toward the object of the persuasive message and attitudes toward the source of persuasion reminds us once again of the importance of considering the individual as the possessor of multiple attitudes. In the early sections of this chapter we were able to deal with simple situations and single attitudes to advance some general propositions about attitude change. However, as soon as we begin to consider the social mediation of information, the relevant objects in the situation begin to multiply, and description of attitude change rapidly becomes complicated.

One of the more complex propositions we could put together from these research findings is the following. A point of view advocated by a source could be more extremely discrepant from that of the subject *without being rejected* by the subject if *in addition* the subject knew that the source had attitudes toward other objects similar to his own. We can see that such a proposition takes into account not only the subject's position, the source's position, and the distance between them, but also subject and source attitudes toward other objects as well. In other words, in dealing with attitude change it is useful to see the subject as a system of multiple attitudes.

The Group Setting

Thus far we have largely ignored the fact that the target in many persuasion studies is not a single person who receives the message in solitude, but an audience. And there is a good deal of evidence that individuals in an audience are influenced in their reactions to the persuasive message by clues as to how others are responding.

For example, Kelley and Woodruff (1956) had different groups of students at a teachers college listen to a recording of a speech challenging the validity of modern teaching methods. The speech as recorded was punctuated seven times by applause at major points. Some of the students were told that the speech had been recorded earlier at their school, and thus were led to believe that members of their own college faculty and community had responded favorably to the speech. Another group was told that the applause came from listeners not associated with the college. Although the speech produced appropriate attitude change on the matter of methods for both groups, the change was greater where students thought members of their own college had reacted warmly.

Thus it would seem that perception of others' responses to a message not only can influence attitude change, but will do so more or less according to perceived *attitudinal similarity* between self and audience, parallel to the effects we noted between self and source. If you had strongly anti-Communist feelings and attended a Communist party meeting, it is unlikely that you would be swayed by arguments that you saw impressed those around you. Indeed, as with the very discrepant source, you might react all the more negatively to the message—what has been called a "boomerang" effect—precisely because of these perceptions. Where the audience seems similar to you in important attitudes, however, you are likely to be influenced positively by perception of its reactions.

It is likely, furthermore, that such influence was one important element that strengthened attitude change in some early experiments on "group decision" that have now become classic. Research Illustration 4.5 summarizes the original one; comparable studies have shown a parallel effectiveness for the group participation design in changing such diverse attitudes as those toward use of cod-liver oil for infants and toward the employment of older women by plant managers. A crucial factor in such studies is the recognition on the part of various participants that other people of similar attitudes and experience ("housewives like myself") *who are known to have begun the session with some aversion to the target object* (sweetbreads, cod-liver oil, employing older women) have similarly found the new information to be persuasive. This recognition must push some "waverers" over the line to accept the

Research Illustration 4.5

The late Kurt Lewin and his associates (Lewin, 1947) initiated a sequence of experiments designed to determine whether participation in a group decision might not strengthen attitude change. A World War II meat shortage had made it desirable to change food habits so that less familiar meats—beef hearts, sweetbreads, and kidneys—might be used. The persuasion attempts were made with six groups of volunteer Red Cross workers varying in size from 13 to 17 members. Only 45 minutes were available for overcoming the cultural aversion to the unfamiliar foods.

In three of the groups a lecture approach in the classic persuasion mode was used. The talk emphasized the vitamin and mineral value of the meats and linked the nutritional problem with the war effort. Recipes were distributed and the lecturer gave hints on preparing these "delicious dishes." For the other three groups, an assistant developed a group discussion about the problem. The problem was again linked to the war effort and nutrition. A discussion was started about "housewives like themselves" and led to a consideration of the obstacles they would be likely to encounter in making changes of menu toward sweetbreads, beef hearts, and kidneys. The odor during cooking, a husband's dislike of these foods, and other obstacles were examined. The same recipes were presented after the discussion. At the end of the meeting, the women were asked by a show of hands who was willing to try one of the meats within the next week. A follow-up showed that only 3 percent of the women who heard only the lecture served one of the meats never served before, whereas among the women who had participated in the group decision, 32 percent served one of them.

change, and must reinforce the tentative acceptance of all "changers" strongly enough that they are much more likely to follow through on the relevant action when released from the immediate persuasion situation. Thus group pressures are in motion toward attitude change; and once the attitude is changed, they help to support it.

Participation and Commitment

It is likely that other mechanisms are important as well in the group decision experiments. More recent discoveries suggest that attitudes of many of the participants may not be notably changed at the time of the group decision, but instead may change later, after the participants actually engage in the behavior out of a sense of having committed themselves to do so.

The findings that open this possibility may well strike you as surprising. If you consented under some pressure (as from a superior) to engage in a behavior that was basically distasteful to you (eating a food you would otherwise avoid, or administering physical punishment to another person for no good reason), you probably would not expect to have a more positive attitude toward the activity afterward than you had before. In fact, a more natural prediction might seem to be that you would develop even a heartier distaste for the activity. Yet there have been theoretical grounds for the more surprising prediction, and Research Illustration 4.6 is but one example of a large number of recent studies that have given empirical confirmation to the theory.

The theory of cognitive dissonance proposed by Festinger (1957) begins with the observation that ideas or cognitive elements are consonant with one another if one of the elements implies the other in some psychological sense, and are dissonant with one another if one implies the opposite of the other. Thus, a smoker's knowledge and acceptance of research findings that smoking is a hazard to health constitute dissonant beliefs. The theory then argues that cognitive dissonance is a state of tension of greater or less magnitude according to the importance of the elements to the individual and the degree to which they do indeed conflict. This tension has motivational force: the individual is prompted to reduce the dissonance, either by diminishing psychologically the importance of the dissonant elements, or by changing one of the elements in order to restore consonance.

In the next chapter we shall look more closely at some of the broader implications of this theory and similar recent ones having to do with psychological relationships between attitude objects. For now, one implication is of particular interest to us. This is the proposition that pressures toward a desired attitude change may be exerted by inducing the individual to commit himself to a behavior in which he would not otherwise have desired to engage. Exactly how the individual's consent is obtained is not immediately relevant. The main point is that just as attitudes influence behavior, so behavior (if at all incongruent with attitudes) can in turn exert an influence toward change in attitudes.

Among conditions that must obtain if attitude change is actually to follow the behavior, Brehm and Cohen (1962) have stressed the role of psychological commitment to engage in the behavior. That is, the expectation of attitude change need not hold for the individual who is purely and simply coerced into the undesired activity. There must be some point of consent or personal commitment to take on the activity (as there was in Research Illustration 4.6, since the students had the option to refuse both the vegetable and the reward), even though the behavior is one that the individual would never have chosen if left to his own devices. The similarities between this kind of commitment and the public commitment in the group decision studies (above) are quite

Research Illustration 4.6

Festinger's dissonance theory (1957) suggests, among other things, that commitment to engage in behavior about which one has negative attitudes sets up a dissonance or incongruence that is tension-producing for the individual, and motivates him to try to reduce the dissonance in one way or another. Of course, to have avoided the commitment at the outset would have avoided the dissonance. However, once the commitment is made, another way to reduce the tension is to decide that the attitude object "is not so bad, after all"—in other words, to undergo some favorable change in attitude.

Brehm (1960) wished to test aspects of the theory by inducing junior high school students to eat vegetables they disliked extremely. A prior questionnaire had given information as to which of 34 vegetables were disliked by each student. The students had been told to go to the homemaking room of the school to help in some "consumer research." Each student was asked questions about a vegetable supposedly chosen at random, but in actuality one of the vegetables he liked least. The student was required to report not only his reaction to the vegetable, but also to judge its vitamin content roughly in comparison with that of other vegetables.

After the questionnaire, the experimenter suggested that sometimes answers were different when the person actually ate some of the vegetable first. He said that the students need not eat the vegetable, but offered them a small reward if they would, an offer that most accepted. Some students were asked to eat only one portion of the vegetable ("low-eat" condition). Others had to return for several helpings to get their reward ("high-eat" condition). After eating, each student was shown one of two highly authoritative research reports. One said the vegetable was the best for supplying the vitamins needed in a person's diet (support condition); the other said it was the worst (nonsupport condition). Then the student was asked to fill out the initial questionnaire again.

Control subjects at another school were put through much the same procedure, save that they were only asked to imagine what it would be like to eat the disliked vegetable, and were not actually committed to eat any.

The theoretical expectations were that commitment to eat disliked food produced dissonance; and that dissonance pressures would be stronger the more of it the individual was committed to eat. Furthermore, there were at least two changes within the scope of the experiment that would help the individual to reduce dissonance: he might decide that the food was more beneficial nutritionally (greater vitamin content) than he had originally thought; or he might shift to a greater liking of the vegetable. The first possibility would be very hard for subjects who had been given the research report indicating very low nutritional value, and hence the need to reduce dissonance would have to be expressed almost entirely in terms of the second avenue: a more notable increase in liking of the vegetable.

In general, results confirmed these predictions rather well. Thus, for example, where estimates of vitamin content were concerned, subjects in the high-eat condition, who were thought to be under greater pressure to find something good about the disliked vegetable, showed less lowering of their vitamin estimate after the nonsupporting research report and greater raising of it from the supporting report than either the low-eat or the control subjects, differences too large to be reasonably attributed to chance variations between the groups.

Similarly, mean changes in units of liking for the vegetable tended to follow expectations over the six conditions:

	Research report			
	Nonsupporting	(N)	Supporting	(N)
Control	−.43	(11)	.46	(10)
Low-eat condition	.11	(8)	1.97	(7)
High-eat condition	1.33	(7)	.48	(10)

The liking changes in the control group help to indicate the effects of the research report by itself on reaction to the vegetable. Other aspects of the data would probably not have been predicted by any other theories or by common-sense expectations. An example is the great increase in favorable reaction on the part of students obliged to eat a lot of the disliked vegetable, yet who were blocked from resolving dissonance by believing in the nutritional value of the food because of the nonsupporting research report they had read. The same is true as well of the broadest finding, replicated in many settings: subjects who became committed to eat the disliked vegetable showed significantly favorable shifts in attitude toward it; their control counterparts, not so committed, did not.

obvious, and it seems likely that similar mechanisms contribute to attitude change in the two cases.

ROLE-PLAYING AND ATTITUDE CHANGE. There have also been demonstrations of attitude change in connection with another kind of commitment or participation, that involved in *role-playing*. It has been discovered that under many conditions, a subject who is induced to rehearse, justify, or debate in favor of some position quite discrepant from his own initial attitude will show real attitude change which endures after the role-play is over. There are both similarities and differences between this type of situation and that which characterizes the induced-behavior studies. From the point of view of the actor, role-playing is "just pretend" in a sense that actually eating a disliked food simply could not be. At this point it is not clear how important this difference is. Perhaps the "just-pretend" aspect becomes irrelevant, and attitude change occurs through much the same mechanisms as in the other kinds of studies; or perhaps the difference remains important and the mechanisms whereby attitude change occurs are different as well.

The evidence does seem clear that attitude change through role-playing is more likely to occur if (1) the player finds his role rewarded or rewarding; and if (2) he achieves some new insight regarding the attitude object through his role-playing efforts. Scott's experiment (Research Illustration 8.3, page 237) is relevant to the question of reward. The half of his students who had been rewarded, by the spurious information that members of their class had voted them victors in the debate, showed a significant attitude change in the direction they had been obliged to advocate, while the other half, led to believe they had lost, did not. Hence it appeared that attitude change depended on a sense of reward for the role taken.

The classical example of new insight is that of the deadlocked labor and management representatives who are induced to reverse roles, arguing the case from the other's side for several hours, after which each is more willing to "see the other's point of view." The new insights may come about in either of two ways. First, in some instances the subject taking the role is supplied with information at the start for use in arguing his case. Some of this information may actually be new to him. Putting such new information to use in an act that necessarily involves his close attention is more likely to increase its weight in his subsequent attitude toward the object. Second, he must reorganize his own store of information relevant to the object, often drawing in other information that he has not seen as relevant heretofore and in such a way as to support his new position rather than his old. "Insight" in such an instance would refer to the discovery that the reorganized information made a more comfortable and coherent whole than he would previously have suspected. King and Janis (1956) have shown that attitude change through role-playing is negligible when the role-player reads from a prepared script, but is very substantial when he departs from such a script to "improvise" arguments of his own supporting the case. It is this "improvisation" that may reflect a successful search through his storage of information for supporting material he may have failed to associate with the object in just this way before.

Social psychologists have often been interested by the fact that opinions overtly expressed in front of a group do not always correspond well with opinions the individual will express in private. Typically, as Gorden (1952) has shown, public expressions of opinion tend to represent some compromise between the individual's "real" attitude and that which he perceives to be the dominant attitude or norm of the group. Although it is easy to think of these public expressions as superficial and "expedient," they may have some of the real attitudinal effects of role-playing, for the individual is indeed constrained to play a role located somewhere between his own position and that of the group. If this is so, then repeated role-playings vis-à-vis a given group would lead us to expect a slow but real drift in underlying attitude toward the group norm over time.

* * *

Our first general principle of attitude change at the beginning of the chapter indicated that our attitudes toward objects change when new information brings change in the perceived content of the objects. Much of what we have said more recently might be boiled down to a second principle, partially derivable from the first: attitudes toward one object change as the cognitive content of other, associated objects changes.

What objects get cognitively associated with one another depends a good deal on the individual's unique experience, coupled with the general principles of object-belongingness (Chapter 2). One of these types of object-belongingness—the mode of instrumentality—has already been discussed, and we have seen that if an attitude toward some end or goal is changed, then we would not be surprised by changes in associated means-objects as well. This is a special case of the second principle.

The persuasion studies suggest another important instance of object-belongingness not hitherto mentioned: an attitude toward an object is frequently associated cognitively with other social objects (persons or groups) who hold attitudes toward the same object. Furthermore, there is a certain interdependence between the individual's attitude toward the social object on one hand, and the object toward which both have attitudes, on the other. The interdependence of source evaluation and acceptance of the message is one case in point. The influence of attitude change perceived in other members of the audience on one's own attitudes is another.

The term "reference group" has been coined to recognize this interdependence between the individual's own attitudes and the attitudes he perceives other social objects (usually "groups," but individuals as well) to hold on the matter. Many studies have shown that the individual will evaluate an attitudinal position differently according to what groups or individuals are associated with the position. If a labor union endorses a governmental policy, for example, some individuals as a result will find themselves to be more favorable and some less favorable to the policy. We would say that labor unions are functioning as a *positive* reference group for the first category of individuals and as a *negative* reference for the other.

When applied to reference groups (or persons), then, our second principle of attitude change has a double implication. It suggests on one hand that if the individual receives information indicating that a prized reference group has changed its position toward an attitude object, this fact will leave him in an incongruent (or dissonant) position, and increase the likelihood that he will change his own attitude toward that object. Or, conversely, if new information about the attitude object makes the individual change his mind about that object, he may also change his opinion of reference groups that, as he assumes, still hold his old and now discarded position. The key expectation here—that the individual will seek to maintain a congruent system of attitudes—will be examined in detail in Chapter 5.

STRATEGIES OF ATTITUDE CHANGE: AN OVERVIEW

Some practitioners who need to manipulate attitudes may take an interest in the social psychologist's principles of attitude change in order to find efficient strategies of persuasion. We have in passing seen a number of such strategies, from Carlson's manipulation of means–end links, to Weiss's strategy for minimizing the audience's sense of attitudinal distance from the source. Nevertheless, the practitioner is likely to find himself with a somewhat different point of view toward attitude change from that of the social psychologist. Understanding these differences in point of view may help to lend some shape and order to the principles of change we have discussed.

Most notably, perhaps, the practitioner is apt to find attitudes more difficult to change than our principles suggest. We have said, for example, that new information is the *sine qua non* of attitude change, and new information seems simple enough to supply. Soon after World War II a massive propaganda and education campaign, using the recognized principles of propaganda, was launched in Cincinnati as a pilot project to see how interest in and public sympathy for the United Nations might be developed. A comparison of attitude surveys concerning the United Nations after the campaign with those taken before showed very minimal increase in interest (Hyman and Sheatsley, 1947). This is a common practical experience.

The frustrations of the would-be manipulator of attitudes are less a commentary on the power of new information to change opinion than they are a reflection of two simple facts. First, the manipulator is not in a position to change the actual properties of the object; or, if he could, it would probably be self-defeating to do so. And second, the manipulator is in a scarcely better position to affect the flow of information about the object that determines its perceived properties, and hence attitudes toward it. One difference between the social psychologist and the practitioner, then, is this: the social psychologist wants to know the conditions under which attitudes change; the practitioner wants to know the conditions under which attitudes change *and over which he has some reasonable hope of control.* The irony is that the more potent modes of changing attitudes tend to be those less accessible to quick manipulation.

The normal practitioner—the propagandist, the public relations man, the politician, the clergyman—looks with some envy at the attitude change possible in the laboratory, for his "natural" means of attitude change are much weaker. Persuasion experiments are blessed with captive audiences that cannot "tune out" the message before it starts. The audience is usually made up of students, accustomed to taking with some respect information transmitted by adults. The experimenter is free to choose the attitude area he wishes, and gravitates toward attitude objects that are relatively remote for the students, of low personal goal relevance, and about which they are only moderately informed. It is very exceptional to find a persuasion experiment that depends upon such a "real" but difficult task as changing attitudes of WCTU women toward liquor, or adult Communists toward free enterprise.

Yet even the attitude change means used in the laboratory are relatively weak. In Table 4.1 we have summarized some of the principles noted in this chapter. Laboratory studies of attitude change tend to be located by and large in the upper (and "weaker") reaches of the table. Even the more powerful settings employed by the laboratory involve socially mediated information, and represent little more than a momentary intrusion in the flow of information to the individual. When the objects of attitude persuasion are psychologically remote for the individual even in his daily life, the new information represented by the persuasive message may bulk rather large in the total stream of information coming to the individual with regard to the object. On the other hand, when the object of persuasion is relatively central—and most attitudes the practitioner would like to change are of this order—then the information contained in a brief persuasive message does not compete very successfully with the rest of the daily information the subject is receiving.

Information of certain valence implications flows in channels formed by social structure. Members of social groupings communicate more with one another than they do with people in other groupings, and this is true whether the grouping is based on social class, race, religion, place of residence, occupation, or family ties. The union man who labors in the mass industry complex of Detroit tends to encounter a kind of information—direct as well as mediated through other union members—that he would not receive as a farmer in Iowa or as an industrialist even in Detroit. The Southerner receives a daily input of information about the Negro that bears little relation to that which flows sporadically in northern universities. Were we to subject either the union man or the Southerner to twenty minutes' worth of information that had contradictory valence implications, the effects on attitudes would be slight indeed.

Direct personal experience with the attitude object is a most potent setting for attitude change when the initial attitudes are based on misperceptions and inadequate information. By this we mean that even deep-seated attitudes that have developed over a considerable period of time may be rapidly revised. This is the lesson of the white housewives in the biracial project, and it is a lesson that a number of other studies of interracial contact have made clear as well. Even here, however, there are important limitations: the objects encountered in direct personal experience must actually convey information about their properties that contradicts prior expectations, or no attitude change will occur. A racially prejudiced person who believes that Negroes are ignorant and dirty will not change his mind on the basis of direct, personal contact with Negroes who are in fact ignorant and dirty.

We would deduce from all this that a "strong" measure of control over the individual's attitudes would require that the manipulator be able to designate where the subject shall live, what job he shall take, the people with whom he shall interact, and the like. Such control rarely falls to the practitioner or, for that matter, to anybody in a democratic nation.

However, there has been at least one recent instance in which control as total as this coincided with a desire to change basic attitudes of a large number of people within a relatively short period of time. American soldiers held as prisoners of war by the Chinese Communists during the Korean War were subjected to a program designed to reverse their political ideologies and turn them from enemy captives to active and willing collaborators. The effort was sufficiently successful that the American people were appalled by the number of officers and enlisted men who came to espouse the doctrines of the enemy against whom they had so recently fought. The term "brainwashing" was used to suggest the magnitude of the attitude change accomplished, and rumor had it that the Communists had developed bizarre and frightening new methods of mind control.

Later evaluations of the methods actually employed indicated that there was little that was truly new in the Communist approach, but that the total control of the prisoners' life situation had been thoroughly exploited in almost every conceivable way to try to build pressures toward defection. Life in the camp was primitive, and rewards were skillfully manipulated to encourage collaboration and punish any sign of resistance. Control of information from the outside world was complete, and censorship of any correspondence that might affect sensitive atti-

TABLE 4.1. Some conditions affecting attitude change. The conditions listed in the columns can vary independently of one another. A rough "profile" describing the attitude change setting plotted from column to column would suggest the rough level of change to be expected, however.

Nature of contact with attitude object	Information flow is	Ratio: Source info / Own info	Source bias	Intention of source	Attitudinal distance, source–listener
Socially mediated ("persuasion")	momentarily controlled	less than unity	high	to convince	DISTANCE STRESSED: ("We disagree on this and I am going to convince you I am right.")
		greater than unity	medium		DISTANCE UNRECOGNIZED: ("I would like to present some information that seems important")
	partially controlled	much greater than unity	low		DISTANCE MINIMIZED: ("You and I agree on Subject B—let's see if we can agree on A")
Direct	totally controlled			to inform	
				no intent at all toward subject	("I used to believe as you do, but then I learned that . . .")

Subject's perception of

STRONGER SURER / WEAKER LESS CERTAIN / NONE?

Assuming information being transmitted has valence implications contrary to the subject's prior attitudes, attitude change will be tudes was thorough. Most important, perhaps, were the steps taken to prevent the development of any informal group structure among the prisoners that might lend group support to the preservation of attitudes of resistance. Potential leaders were removed from the main mass of captives. Clever use of informers helped to maintain walls of distrust between inmates. Behavioral compliance in attendance at doctrinal discussions was required. Whenever prisoners did succumb to collaboration, the fact was skillfully publicized in ways that would discourage others from resisting further. In short, the effort was made to strip away every vestige of support for the prisoners' original value systems, and to replace them with new supports for new attitudes (Schein, 1957).

Although the American public was scandalized by the sequence of publicized defections, the success of the attitude change operation was somewhat more limited than the American press often implied. For one thing, it appeared that about 80 percent of the prisoners were ideologically "inert," or neutral, being rather indifferent to political indoctrination and neither actively collaborating with the captors nor resisting their propaganda in an active way. Of the remaining 20 percent, about three quarters were successfully brainwashed into active collaboration, and the other quarter (5 percent of the total) maintained their resistance throughout the experience. Without other comparable episodes, it is difficult to evaluate such figures. In view of the magnitude of the attitudinal change required for collaboration and the relative brevity of the period (compared to the total life span of the captives) in which the Communists had a chance to operate, the gross rates of attitude change appear to be dramatically high. On the other hand, it is clear that significant resistance was maintained despite the total control of information and existence wielded.

* * *

The next chapter will be devoted to an analysis of conditions that maintain attitude stability. Of course, it is self-evident that attitudes are more likely to remain stable when the conditions that facilitate change are weak or absent. We have already seen, for example, that without the input of new information, behavior proceeds under the sort of momentum one would expect of a perfectly stable system of attitudes. Hence we can deduce a good deal about the conditions for stability of attitudes simply by "reversing" our principles of attitude change. Nevertheless, there are some further relevant conditions that are more readily introduced from the side of stability than from the side of change, for they involve social and psychological anchors responsible for an "active" resistance of attitudes to change. These anchors will be our primary concern as we conclude our consideration of individual attitudes.

CHAPTER 5

The Organization and Stability of Attitudes

DYSON (1958), COMMENTING ON CREATIVITY IN PHYSICAL SCIENCE, HAS noted that very few of the established scientists of the mid-nineteenth century were able to grasp the basic revisions of Newtonian mechanics proposed by James Clerk Maxwell. Acceptance and use of Maxwell's equations had to wait for a younger generation of scientists who did not, like their elders, insist upon trying to understand Maxwell in Newtonian terms. Dyson found the same processes apparent when quantum mechanics in turn revised Maxwell's work. The older generation, quite capable of operating in Maxwell's terms, found the new concepts baffling, whereas the younger people, less experienced in the field, assimilated the new view as a matter of course. When new basic information is concerned, it is a common experience that young people are more receptive than old.

Since the attitudes we form are so intimately bound up with the information we have stored about various objects, it is not surprising that there is parallel evidence to suggest that attitudes also tend to become more stable—we might even say "rigid"—as individuals grow older. One example can be drawn from the way in which a cross section of adults evaluates the two national parties. If we construct a scale that

116 - INDIVIDUALS' ATTITUDES

runs from intensely pro-Democratic through neutral to intensely pro-Republican, we find that adults in their twenties show a distribution on the scale that is relatively bell-shaped, with fair proportions locating themselves in the central or "independent" regions of the scale. The shape of the distribution changes quite steadily as we move to older and

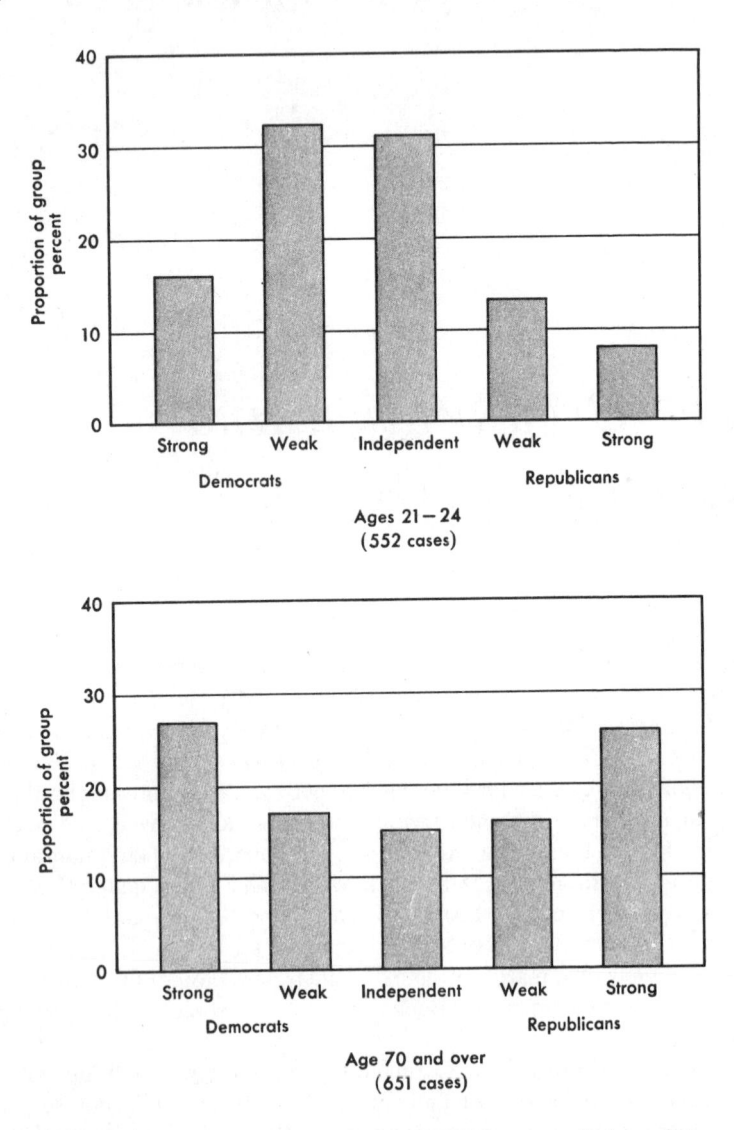

Ages 21—24
(552 cases)

Age 70 and over
(651 cases)

FIGURE 5.1. The strengthening of attitudes toward the political parties with increasing age. The data are drawn from seven national samples interviewed by the Survey Research Center between 1952 and 1957. (Adapted from Campbell *et al.*, 1960)

older slices of the population, so that the oldest generation shows a distribution which is closest to being U-shaped, with heavy proportions locating themselves at the extremes of the scale (Figure 5.1). Nor is this trend merely some quirk of expression that grows with age: these attitude extremes have behavioral consequences. Thus it can be shown, for example, that there is an actual decline in the probability that a person will be influenced to change his party—or even to defect from it momentarily—the older he gets (Campbell et al., 1960). In other words, there is reason to believe that affect toward objects often becomes stronger in significant ways with the passage of time.

* * *

In the preceding chapter we emphasized the power of new information in creating attitude change—either toward the object whose cognitive properties the information revises, or toward other objects associated with it. We have been willing to take it as axiomatic that without some input of new information, attitudes are very unlikely to change, and this proposition might be considered our first principle of attitude stability.

We cannot accept the converse of the proposition, however. It is not true that when a person's attitudes remain stable we can be sure he has been exposed to no new information on the subject. Indeed, this condition of "no-new-information," while interesting theoretically, is very unusual beyond brief spans of time, particularly where objects are not remote for the individual. In the normal course of events most of us frequently encounter ideas and beliefs in conflict with those we hold. Hence absence of new information can hardly account for the general stability that attitudes seem to show in the longer term. Such stability in the face of frequent new information suggests that our attitudes must develop some active resistance to pressures for change.

Our initial illustrations imply, furthermore, that this development of resistance is not just a phenomenon of childhood or adolescence, but seems to be a lifelong process. Intuitively, this may not seem surprising. Arteries continue to harden over the course of the life span: why should our ideas and attitudes not do likewise? And yet the biological analogy does not constitute explanation, in the scientific sense. Arteries harden as time passes not simply because time is passing, but because certain processes (which usually move rather slowly and hence take time to show their effects) are occurring to produce the hardening. If we understand the processes, we shall not be surprised now and then to discover a relatively young person with arteriosclerosis, or an elderly person with no sign of the ailment at all, for we know that peculiarities of biochemistry are the true mediating mechanisms, and not time itself.

The same may be said for attitudes: many young people have developed high resistance to attitude change in certain matters, and one could find attitudes among elderly people that turn out to be susceptible to change. Nevertheless, the conditions associated with attitude stability do tend to require time for development, and hence there is a statistical correlation between age and attitude stability.

Our purpose in this chapter is to consider the nature of these conditions, and the normal processes whereby they develop. We shall find that the key to the stabilizing of attitudes over time lies in their increasing organization over time. Attention given to the nature of attitude organization "pays off" in reducing to a few simple formulations many observations about attitude stability and change.

THE STABLE SINGLE ATTITUDE

We shall begin, as we began our discussion of attitude change, by drawing the portrait of the type of single attitude that is most likely to be highly resistant to change. This is a very simple task, for this portrait is no more than a mirror image of the one in the preceding chapter. Thus we can say that the following attributes tend to co-occur:

Affect	*Object*
Strong in degree	High centrality High personal goal relevance Large storage of information

When these attributes co-occur, one can be sure that the attitude in question is relatively resistant to change through new information. Why this is so can be understood in part by reversing some of the arguments of the preceding chapter, for of course only a single set of principles is concerned. In part, too, we are now in a position to elaborate earlier arguments. Thus, for example, we have observed that much of the new information which affects attitudes is socially mediated; that in addition the judgment of source credibility has some influence on the acceptance of such new information; and that perceived source credibility is affected by an implicit comparison between one's own information and that of the source. From these observations it follows directly that the person with a large store of information about an object (an "expert," to take the limiting case) would less often encounter socially mediated information contrary to his attitudes *which he could credit* than would someone with less information about the object. This chain of reasoning is not, of course, intended to be a total explanation of our principle that attitudes underpinned by much information are

ORGANIZATION AND STABILITY · 119

less susceptible to change. But it is one of a number of mechanisms that would contribute to such a phenomenon.

At the moment we are more interested in some other things that may be said about such a large storage of information. In Chapter 2 we proposed that large amounts of information cannot be retained in storage unless organized in some way, and we suggested a number of rules of psychological belongingness which govern the broad outlines of such organization. We also suggested that the more information held about a complex or inclusive object, the more numerous and varied are the cross-referencing ties that organize it with respect to other cognitions. These ties might be thought of as something like those that link balls in lattices, in models of the arrangement of atoms in complex molecules (see Figure 5.2). In some such way, an object about which we have large amounts of stored information is quite tightly bound into a whole latticework of cognitions.

The properties of objects (events, states, relations between states, and so on) are so varied that the specific schemes representing "con-

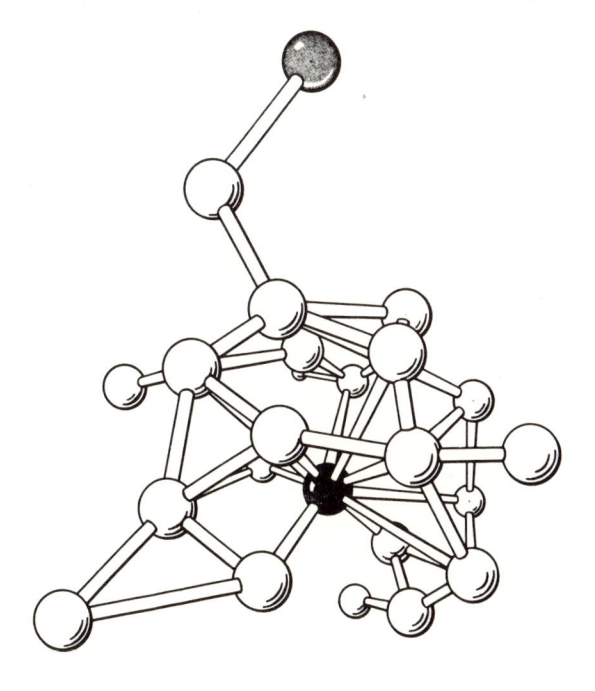

FIGURE 5.2. Elements bound together in a complex latticework. The element near the middle (black), with its multiple ties to other elements, is far more centrally embedded in the latticework than the gray element at the top of the figure.

nections" between cognitive elements are numerous almost beyond catalog, and the few we have suggested are no more than a beginning. The characteristic which all these types of connectedness share, however, is an *interdependence* between elements, which is to say that *the elements have effects on each other,* and, most particularly, that *if one element changes, something in the system of elements is likely to change as well.* Indeed, this kind of functional interdependence is what "connectedness" means, and what "organization" means as well, at least in its dynamic sense.

This interdependence for us is of course *psychological* interdependence. Thus, to crib from the famous syllogism about the mortality of Socrates, if you were to learn that Socrates is still alive, the change in one of your cognitions ("Socrates is, of course, dead") would necessitate some new doubts about one or the other of two premises linked to this cognition (for all who have been exposed to the syllogism): that "Socrates is a man" or that "all men are mortal." This cluster of cognitions is psychologically interdependent, in the sense defined. Not only does the arousal of the first cognition tend to call the others to mind, but changes in the truth-status of the first also threaten some change in the truth-status of the others. Of course we deal here with a very special type of connectedness, one associated with classical logic. Abelson and Rosenberg's happy term (1958) "psycho-logic" helps remind us of many types of psychological interdependence that fall outside the canons of pure logic. Furthermore, we must keep in mind that interdependence is a matter of degree, just as the interdependence between a man's heart and his lungs is much more intimate than that between his heart or lungs and his fingernails. But the property of interdependence remains the same, whatever the rule or degree of connectedness involved.

When we consider not simply "information" but *valenced* information, or attitudes, the questions of interdependence become more interesting still. For the presence of valences makes possible a whole new scheme of connectedness, which rests on the similarity or dissimilarity of valences between related cognitions. In other words, the organization of *attitudes,* while following the principles of *cognitive* organization more generally, has some unique characteristics as well. Especially when we begin to deal with attitude objects about which large amounts of information are stored, we can be sure that fair portions of this information have valence implications, which is to say that the generalized attitude toward the object as a whole is a summation of many "subattitudes" toward its perceived components. These subattitudes will quite naturally show signs of interdependence.

In short, then, while we can draw the portrait of a single attitude that is likely to be highly resistant to new information, *why* such an attitude resists change is another question again. And the very characteristics of such an attitude—its information underpinning in particular—

suggests that the answer lies less in the properties of the single attitude itself than in the manner in which such attitudes and subattitudes are organized. Hence it is to this problem we must turn.

ATTITUDE ORGANIZATION

When we speak of a person's attitudes being organized, we mean that they are related to one another according to an orderly arrangement, rather than haphazardly. Of course this order and interdependence is partial rather than total; not every one of a person's attitudes is systematically related to each of his other attitudes. By way of analogy, the cells in your leg muscles are arranged in orderly fashion, and so are those in the irises of your eyes, but there is little point in attempting to describe the arrangement of leg-muscle *and* iris cells. Just so, it is likely that you hold many political attitudes that are arranged in an orderly manner, and that the same thing is true of your several attitudes toward personal hobbies. Chances are that there is not much systematic arrangement between these two sets of attitudes—although they might be neatly dovetailed, in ways that we shall later examine. Our immediate purpose is to discover the general conditions under which attitudes do come to be functionally related to one another, and how this interdependence can best be described. We can make a good beginning if we work from our familiar principles of cognitive organization.

Object-Belongingness and Attitude Organization

We have already discussed several modes of object-belongingness that are crucial in cognitive organization. The general principle that links the added valence feature of attitudes with cognitive organization can be simply stated: *a person tends to have similar attitudes* (alike in sign) *toward objects that he considers to belong together.* This principle is true, as implied, whatever the mode of object-belongingness we consider.

OBJECT GENERALIZATION. As the study by Adorno *et al.* (Research Illustration 5.1) indicates, persons in our society who are prejudiced against Jews (that is, whose attitudes toward them as a class of persons are unfavorable) are very likely to be prejudiced also against other ethnic minorities of which they are not themselves members—Negroes, Mexicans, and Japanese, perhaps. The mode of object-belongingness here is that of generalization over a class of objects—ethnic outgroups. In the same way, one's attitude toward cruelty to cats tends to be associated with similar attitudes toward cruelty to dogs and horses—but not necessarily toward crickets or snakes (generalization always has its limits).

Research Illustration 5.1

In their extensive study of prejudice (see Chapter 1), Adorno et al. (1950) were interested among other things in ascertaining the degree to which people who felt hostile toward one ethnic minority or "outgroup" could be counted on to show hostility toward other ethnic minorities as well. They had initially constructed a number of attitude scales designed to measure different facets of belief and opinion concerning Jews, and had found high intercorrelations in responses to these several scales, indicating that apparently different beliefs really fell in very predictable clusters. That is, if a person saw Jews as offensive in intruding into non-Jewish groups, it could be predicted with high accuracy that he would be offended as well by their "seclusiveness" or "clannishness," even though being intrusive and being seclusive would appear to be rather opposite to one another. The person who did not attribute one specific negative trait to Jews was less likely to attribute other negative traits to them. This degree of regularity and organization in the attitudes being studied meant that the scales could be economically combined into a single scale (called the A-S scale) measuring anti-Semitism.

To see whether the cluster of anti-Semitic responses was part of a still larger cluster of attitudes, the authors constructed three other scales that avoided items about Jews but dealt with Negro-white relations, minorities other than Negroes and Jews (fringe political parties, criminals, and so on), and relative reactions to America as opposed to foreign nations. It turned out again that there were high correlations among all of these scales, so that once again they could be meaningfully combined into another more general "Ethnocentrism" or E-scale. Furthermore, each of the components of the E-scale, along with the total scale itself, correlated highly in turn with the A-S scale, as illustrated by data drawn from female students in an extension class in psychology:

Correlation with	Total E scale	E subscale "Negroes"	"Minorities"	"Patriotism"
A-S Scale	0.80	0.74	0.76	0.69

In other words, by knowing that one of these subjects felt hostile toward Jews, one could predict with fair accuracy that she would tend to feel hostile toward other outgroups as well. After attaining comparable findings on a wider range of test populations, the authors concluded that anti-Semitism was in many cases merely a part of a well-organized and much larger attitude structure.

Although more recent critics have suggested that strong similarity in the form of the questions on all these scales helps to raise their intercorrelations artificially, there seems little doubt that the measures do tap relatively coherent systems of attitudes. The evidence lies not only in data from batteries of attitude items, but also in depth clinical interviews that were held with various subjects representing "highs" and "lows" on measures of anti-Semitism and ethnocentrism as part of the larger study. Such interviews also provided strong evidence suggesting that the acceptance or rejection of these clusters of prejudiced or antidemocratic attitudes was tied in turn to the individual's overall personality structure.

The underlying theory was that persons subjected in their youth to very strict parental control, who had learned to bury their resentment and acquiesce to such control, tended to develop *authoritarian personality* structures, so that as adults they were overly obedient to strong authority while expressing their hidden hostilities toward weak objects that might be safely attacked. Since minority groups and foreign nations represented such weak or safe targets, personality development of this sort would make individuals particularly susceptible to prejudice against minorities and ethnocentric attitudes more generally.

As a partial test of this theory, a third major scale was constructed, called the Fascism or F-scale. It was designed to measure deep-seated personality trends including (1) exaggerated submission to authority and uncritical championing of ingroup values; (2) unwillingness to take a psychological, insightful view of others and oneself, avoiding examination of one's own deeper motives and conflicts; and (3) the tendency to imagine strange, evil, dangerous, and destructive forces at work in the outer world. Once again, it was found that persons with such tendencies who thereby showed high scores on the F-scale also tended to be high in Anti-Semitism and Ethnocentrism. Thus the clusters of attitudes toward outgroups seemed to form an orderly part of a still broader personality structure.

A person's attitudes toward objects he locates in the same class have effects on each other in the sense that if one of them is strengthened or weakened, then attitudes toward other objects of the same class tend to change in either of two ways. Often the changed attitude will generalize to the other objects; if, for example, an anti-vivisectionist comes to believe that, after all, cat vivisection is not so bad, then his attitudes against dog and monkey vivisection are likely to be weakened. But if, following his changed attitude toward cat vivisection, his attitudes concerning other animals do not change, then it is altogether likely that his mode of classifying animals has changed: cats are different, and just don't belong with other pets. Hence if one attitude changes in sign, some other change is likely to follow, be it (1) a change in sign for related attitudes; or (2) a psychological reorganization of the perceived class of objects, so that the object of the changed attitude is disconnected or "dissociated" from the general class of objects in which it was originally located. Where object generalization is concerned, then, the principle is that attitudes toward objects that a person classifies together —according to some dimension important to him—are functionally interdependent. This is one way in which an individual's attitudes are organized.

CAUSALITY AND INSTRUMENTALITY. Similarly, if a person views something as having caused something else, not only does he link the objects together cognitively, as we have seen, but his attitudes toward the cause and toward the effect tend to be alike. One's attitude toward lightning becomes like one's attitude toward the destruction it has caused. If a person is viewed as responsible for his acts, then a person is viewed as "good" if his acts are considered "good," or, contrariwise, an act on the part of a person considered "good" is more likely to be favorably viewed than the same act on the part of a person considered "bad."

The same principle is very obviously at work where *means–end* or *instrumental* relationships are perceived. Attitudes toward perceived means tend to resemble attitudes toward the end-states for which they are instrumental. The more you want something, the more you also want whatever it takes to get it. One's attitude toward the means may be only transitory—for example, your favorable attitude toward the dentist may last only until he has relieved your toothache. But many means–end relationships are persistent, and hence help to account for much of the persisting organization of a person's attitudes.

Attitudes toward "means" objects are of particular interest when, as is often the case, these means become desired ends in their own right. Money is a good example; submission to the dentist's drill is not. When objects initially viewed as only a means do acquire goal-value in their own right, then it often happens that the means–end relationship operates in either direction. For example, one may come to prefer a certain political party because one believes that it will further some important objective, but affiliation with that party may come to be valued intrinsically, and the original objective prized because the party stands for it. This kind of interdependence—in which two or more attitudes provide mutual support for each other—represents an instance of organization of an individual's attitudes in which the effects go in both directions, but a one-way means–end relationship also represents organization, because one attitude affects another.

Whatever the mode of object-belongingness, then, a person tends to have similar attitudes toward objects he classes together. Attitudes toward them tend to be alike in *sign,* and they also tend to be alike in *degree* of favorability or unfavorability. Attitudes that tend to become alike, and to remain alike—so that when one of them changes the others tend to change in corresponding ways—are obviously affecting each other, and hence meet our criteria for psychological interdependence.

Congruence of Own and Others' Attitudes

A special case of this general principle is so important in understanding not only attitude organization but human interaction as well that it is usefully discussed as a principle in its own right. It has to do, in the first place, with attitudes toward persons. We have earlier agreed to use the terms "attraction" and "aversion" for attitudes of this kind; and we have observed as well (Chapter 3) that a person is attractive to another person insofar as the second person perceives that his characteristics are rewarding. Now in view of the fact that any person displays many characteristics, all of which belong together because they are present in the same person, our first principle would suggest that one tends to have similar attitudes toward his various characteristics. Belongingness, in this case, has to do not with different objects like dogs and cats, but with different characteristics of the same object—a person.

More important still is a basic fact, not so far considered in any systematic way, about what we perceive as characteristics in other human beings: these characteristics include, along with such things as height or redheadedness, *the holding of attitudes*. Furthermore, it is inevitable that some of these attitudes (held by persons toward whom we have attitudes) refer to objects we ourselves have evaluated. This being the case, there are many circumstances in which one is interested in the other person's attitudes, and will compare them with one's own attitudes toward the same objects. One very special and obvious instance, already discussed, is that of persuasion: the fact of an attempt to influence in itself makes the source's attitude (as embodied in the persuasive message) one of his most salient characteristics, and the situation requires that we compare his attitude with our own toward the same object. Thus one has, in effect, an attitude toward another person's attitude.

Sometimes such comparisons are rewarding and sometimes not. One feels, naturally, that one's own attitudes are justified ("I wouldn't have them if they weren't"), and this universal tendency means that support from another person for one's own attitudes is rewarding. Under certain very common conditions, perceived similarity between one's own and another person's attitudes provides this kind of support. Given such conditions, then, the fact that the other holds attitudes congruent with one's own is seen as a rewarding characteristic of the other person; and this being so, such a person is likely to be perceived as rewarding-in-general (attractive). It is psychologically "right" that another person who is rewarding in an over-all way should also be rewarding in this particular way, but unfitting that a person who is otherwise admirable, likable, or trustworthy should have attitudes that one finds distasteful, or incongruent with one's own (see Figure 5.3).

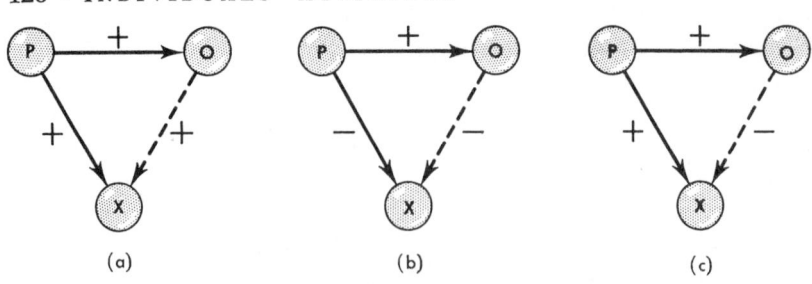

FIGURE 5.3. Two configurations (a, b) involving attitudinal congruence between a P(erson) and an O(ther person) with respect to some attitude object (X). The O → X arrow, or the attitude of O toward X, is of course his attitude *as perceived by* P. The third diagram (c) represents a situation of incongruence. Within conditions outlined in the text, the principle of self–other congruence suggests that this third configuration occurs less frequently and is less stable than the two preceding.

According to what we shall call the principle of *self–other congruence*, then, it is likely that you perceive yourself to be in basic agreement with most of the people that you feel most favorably toward—and, conversely, that you feel most favorably toward the people with whom you believe you are in basic agreement. The interdependence of these two kinds of attitudes on the part of the same individual—toward persons and toward the relationship between their attitudes and his own—has already been illustrated in a narrow way by the interaction between attitudes toward the source and toward the source's message. You are more likely to accept persuasion if you are attracted to the source; you are more likely to find the source attractive if his attitudes are more like your own. But our new principle generalizes the case considerably beyond the setting of persuasion.

If perceived self–other congruence toward an attitude object is rewarding and hence interacts with more generalized attraction to the other person, is it also true that perceptions of *in*congruence (or contradictions between own and other's attitude) are distressing, and hence tend to go with disliking the other person more generally? This certainly follows from the principle, and it is not hard to think of cases in which a sense that another person is undermining beliefs that we feel to be justified pushes us toward dislike of such a person. However, it is just as easy to oversimplify the principle on the negative side as it is to do so on the positive side (to say, for example, "If you like someone you'll agree with him"), and the conditions under which the principle operates most clearly in either direction are more limited than might appear.

These limitations can largely be deduced from other things we have said about attitudes in earlier chapters, although they are a little more complex in this setting because of the complexity of the attitudes involved. The key attitude here is that of the individual toward the *relationship* between his own and the other's attitude. This relationship is a complex object (involving, as it does, the "fit" between two other objects), and therefore we might call the attitude toward such a relationship a second-order attitude. What is important is that although second-order, this attitude, like any other, has not only a positive extreme (springing from a sense of reward) and a negative extreme (distressful), but also a point of indifference in between. When the congruence of own and other's attitude toward a given object is a matter of indifference to the individual (neither rewarding nor distressing), we would hardly expect to see any effects of the principle, even though the situation may be such that the individual cannot fail to cognize that self–other attitudes are congruent or incongruent.

The circumstances that are likely to render the question of congruence a matter of indifference to the individual are, by and large, familiar to us. Thus, for example, if the attitude object at stake is not very central for you (is neither proximal nor of high-goal relevance), your second-order attitudes toward congruence, like your first-order attitudes toward the object, tend toward indifference. Therefore when we say that you perceive yourself to be in agreement with the people you feel most favorably toward, we do not mean agreement about everything, but about the things that are relatively important to you. A parallel amendment can be made about the other person as attitude-object: when he is not very central to you (either through geographical remoteness or absence of personal goal relevance), congruence may very well be a matter of indifference to you as well. Finally, there is an indifference possibility built into the relationship you perceive to exist between the other person and the object. Some things that are central for you have no impact on the other person—perhaps because, like the three spoons of sugar you like in your coffee, they simply do not affect the other person, or perhaps because you consider something strictly a private matter and of no consequence to him.

In short, then, the importance of congruence for the individual is not likely to exceed limits set by the centrality of (1) the object; or (2) the other person; or (3) the perceived relation of the other person to the object. When centrality is absent for any of these components, attitudes toward congruence will tend toward indifference, and the general principle will be relatively inoperative. Or, to put the matter positively, the effects suggested by the principle will be most apparent when the persons involved are rather central for one another and the object in question is of mutual importance. This general set of circumstances includes a large part (although by no means all) of what we call "human interaction," and our discussions in ensuing chapters will often presuppose them as conditions.

You may have noted that at times we have spoken of the "similarity" of one's own and the other's attitudes, but that we have depended primarily on the term "congruence." Congruence (agreement, harmony, "fitting together") does not demand that the attitudes of two people toward an object be similar in direction in every case, although this is the predominant situation. It recognizes that under special and clear-cut circumstances, the "similar" attitude of another would be incompatible or incongruent. Take, for example, the case of two men, each of whom hopes to marry the same girl: if one succeeds the other does not. Under such competitive conditions it is not to be expected that either of the men will become more attracted toward the other because they are in agreement about wanting her as a wife. Indeed, it is quite likely to be the reverse, for here similar attitudes are actually incongruent.

It would do no harm, as a final refinement, to make a comparable generalization in our first principle concerning object-belongingness, for the same type of special case can crop up here. Thus, for example, we normally dissociate the Republican and Democratic parties sharply from one another, for they stand in a relationship of mutual antagonism or competition, with the triumphs of one being the griefs of the other. But it is precisely because of this mutual opposition that we might in some contexts class the two parties together, as we would if we were speaking of political as opposed to religious groups. Furthermore, attitudes toward the two parties are excellent examples of interdependence: liking one party means disliking the other, and a change in attitude toward one is usually paralleled by a change in attitude toward the other. Such a case, as well as the more frequent one of attitude similarity toward objects not in opposition to one another, can be covered by the more inclusive version of the principle: *attitudinal congruence goes with psychological belongingness*. This is the key principle of attitude organization, and, as we have seen, the self–other principle (or "subprinciple") can be readily derived from it.

* * *

These principles may seem to be "only common sense": if, psychologically, things belong together in one way they should also belong together, psychologically, in other ways. But the fact that a principle seems to be a matter of common sense is neither for nor against it; many common-sense notions turn out not to be true, and even if true not particularly useful. And the test of any principle lies in its usefulness: Does it help to explain a wide range of phenomena by describing the conditions under which they do and do not occur? Or does the principle actually seem *required* in order to explain them? If so, it is a useful principle, whether a common-sense one or not. The present principle is required only in the sense that the organization of an individual's attitudes, as revealed by evidence now available, can be explained more fully and more convincingly with than without the principle. These explanations lend shape and order to many of the things we have learned about attitude change, and permit a better understanding of the stability of attiudes as well.

THE INCLUSIVE PRINCIPLE OF BALANCE

The label *balance*[1] is commonly applied to this general principle, and the dynamics implied by this label help to indicate the usefulness of the principle. (Dynamics refers simply to the principles of change and stability.) When two or more things are in balance, their relationships to each other tend to remain stable. For example, when you first step onto weighing scales, the relationship between the tension of the scale's springs and the weight of your body is unstable, or imbalanced, as indicated by the jiggling of the pointer showing your weight. After you stand quietly, however, the pointer becomes stable, and remains so as long as there is no change either in the scales or in the pressure of your body on them. Balanced relationships remain as they are until new influences come along to upset the balance, whereas relationships that are not in balance are currently being forced toward change. The usefulness of the notion of balance is not merely that it provides a synonym for the notion of stability, but rather that it provides a challenge to seek for the *conditions* under which a relationship remains stable, or balanced. The problem of how a person's attitudes are organized is really a problem of *stable* organization, for we are not much interested in modes of organization that are only transient "halfway houses" between different states of balance.

The general conditions under which different attitudes of the same person are stably related to each other—under which, so to speak, they can peacefully coexist—are described by the principle of balance: attitudes toward objects viewed as belonging together tend to become congruent. Congruence is a balanced condition, and as long as it is maintained for an individual, his attitudes tend to remain stable. This statement, however, is the least interesting application of the principle: like our proposition that change does not tend to occur without some

---

[1] Festinger's terms *cognitive dissonance* and *consonance* (see Chapter 4, pages 106–107) refer to combinations of cognitions that are imbalanced or balanced.

input of new information, it is just about equivalent to saying that if nothing happens to induce change there will be no change. The really interesting derivations from the general principle have to do with what happens when some influence *does* induce change. The general answer is that usually some *new state of balance* will come about—not just any old change, at random, but a change that is orderly because it follows the principle of balance.

Since the notion of balance applies not to a single attitude but to *relationships* among two or more of them, there is an interesting corollary. If a certain kind of relationship between two or more things is to be maintained, a change in one of them necessarily implies a change in one or more of the others. Thus if you want to maintain the 2:1 ratio that describes the relation between the numbers 6 and 3, then if either number is changed the other must change also. Now let us apply this corollary to the principle of self-other congruence. Suppose your attitude both toward a certain friend and toward the Republican party is highly favorable, and you attribute to your friend a pro-Republican attitude. Under these conditions your favorable attitude toward your friend and your perception of congruence between your respective attitudes toward the Republican party are in balance. Now if something happens to make your attitude toward the Republican party unfavorable, these attitudes will no longer be balanced unless something else also changes. According to the balance principle, something else probably will change, and any one of these changes on your part could reestablish balance: you abandon your recently acquired anti-Republicanism (perhaps following a discussion with your friend); or you and he agree on an in-between position; or your sense of belongingness with him (that is, one or more aspects of your favorable attitude toward him) diminishes—or even disappears entirely. In all these instances, you can see that a further change in attitude toward one of the related objects can restore balance.

Attitude change is, however, only one of the two major modes of restoring balance. A second mode involves one or another kind of redefining or disconnecting operation in the individual's cognition of the situation. What these operations have in common is the fact that they restore balance without further change in the imbalanced attitudes, by breaking up the psychological bonds that made the attitudes interdependent in the first place. Thus, by way of illustration, we have pointed out that the principle of self-other congruence presupposes that the attitude object under discussion (in our example above, Republicanism) has some mutual centrality for the parties involved. One clear way, then, to maintain your newly unfavorable attitude toward Republicanism while maintaining your favorable attitude toward your friend is to begin to deny to yourself that politics is central to either either or both of you. Redefining the situation so as to destroy the bases for interdependence of the attitudes that have become imbalanced can be accomplished in a great variety of ways in any complex situation, either by dissociating the object from the others, or by differentiating some part of one of the objects and setting it aside psychologically ("compartmentalizing"). Or again, as Rosenberg and Abelson (in Rosenberg et al., 1960) have pointed out, another way of coping with imbalance is to "stop thinking" about the elements that have fallen into an imbalanced configuration.

All these responses to imbalance entail some kind of change in the psychological status of the objects involved in the situation from the point of view of the individual. What the principle of balance predicts, as far as we have developed it up to this point, is simply that when change is induced at some point in a system of attitudes, one or another of these compensatory changes in the status of the objects will occur—probably. We say "probably" because there is still another possibility: that no other changes occur, and balance is not restored.

This last possibility—of living with imbalance—is improbable, statistically speaking, because most people find it uncomfortable. Many studies—some of them experiments with "real" attitudes that are imbalanced and some involving subjective reports of imagined feelings about imbalanced combinations—support the conclusion (which had seemed necessary even before the studies had been carried out) that imbalance is experienced as uncomfortable. It may, in fact, be considered drive-like in that it serves as a goad to remove the conditions that are uncomfortable. Hence the principle of balance in the first instance alerts us to the likelihood that one change will indeed be followed by some compensating change.

We have not yet considered how we might use the principle to predict just which of the numerous possible balance-restoring changes is most likely to occur in any given instance. This is, of course, a critical question, yet one that is best postponed until we have covered more of the background issues. One of these issues involves the degree of discomfort that imbalance produces. Such discomfort varies according to a number of characteristics of the situation, the person, and the way in which his particular attitudes are organized.

Conditions Governing Degree of Discomfort at Imbalance

BALANCED SYSTEMS OF ATTITUDES. It should be made clear at the outset that the principle of balance does not apply to all of a person's attitudes, in the sense that all of them are in balance with each other. It applies only to particular sets of attitudes that show some interdependence. Indeed, the reason why we have often spoken heretofore of *systems of attitudes* rather than "many" or "sets of" is because the term "system" implies balance, as the term "set" does not.

A *system*, as we shall now formally define the term, refers to any set of entities so related to one another that (1) a change in certain states of any one of them tends to induce specifiable changes in one or more of the others, and (2) this interdependence among the entities results in certain relatively stable characteristics of the total set, viewed as a whole. This definition applies, for example, to the solar system; astronomers tell us that each of its planets affects each of the others, so that the solar system as a whole is as it is because of the interdependence of the planets and the sun. Or, to give a more homely illustration, a furnace, a thermostat with which it is connected, and the temperature of the air surrounding the thermostat all constitute a system. If the thermostat is set at 70°, then an increase in room temperature above this point shuts off the furnace until the temperature drops below 70°; whereupon it is turned on again. Thus (beginning at any point in the cycle) room temperature affects thermostat affects furnace affects room temperature, and so on; the principal characteristic of the system is the relative stability of room temperature. The bodies of warm-blooded animals are kept at relatively constant temperatures by similar, though much more complicated, systems. Attitude systems are basically like these other systems, in which the component attitudes are interdependent, and the relatively constant feature of the system as a whole is a state of balance.

It follows quite obviously that discomfort at imbalance can only arise when attitudes are indeed interdependent. This is true by definition, but it is worth stressing because there are many occasions on which a "system" of attitudes *seems* imbalanced to an outside observer, but is *not* for the individual involved. One common class of such instances includes those in which an individual has in the past successfully dissociated an object from its apparent class in order to restore balance. He may devoutly believe the dictum "thou shalt not steal," yet feel comfortable in covertly "borrowing" equipment from his place of work for personal use on grounds that such behavior is "not really theft," but a reasonable condition of employment. Other common cases include those in which the individual simply lacks one or another piece of information necessary to weld the attitudes in question into a system. Thus, for example, voting studies frequently encounter new recruits to labor unions who are strongly identified with their new union on one hand and with the Republican party on the other, even though the union in question is strongly pro-Democratic in political orientation. Naturally, such a "system" of attitudes could appear very imbalanced to an observer. However, it often turns out that the new union member (in part because of personal disinterest in politics, and in part because of faulty union communication of its position) has not (yet) learned that the union takes political positions, and much less that it is pro-Democratic. Until he does, of course, there is no imbalance and no discomfort, whatever the appearance to the outsider.

THE CREATION AND ACTIVATION OF ATTITUDE SYSTEMS. In general, one of the functions of new information in attitude change is just such creation of new connections between attitude objects not previously thought of together. You might, for example, hear a sermon that persuaded you that some practice you had always taken for granted (the manufacture of nuclear weapons, perhaps, or racial segregation) was inconsistent with your religious principles. In this case, the two attitude objects (nuclear weapons and religion) would have been dissociated prior to the persuasion, but the new information linking them forces you to consider them together, so that they constitute a system for the first time.

There is even evidence that we carry around with us in cognitive storage many imbalanced beliefs and attitudes toward objects that we ourselves would recognize (with no prompting from outside) are logically related and imbalanced, yet that cause no discomfort until something occurs to render them all salient (activated as a system) at the same time.

One deduction we might make from such findings would be that we would expect more nearly perfect internal balance in exploring systems of attitudes toward objects that are relatively central for the individual than we would toward more remote objects, for central objects by definition undergo more constant reactivation. Such reactivation should lead over time to the progressive discovery and adjustment of internal imbalances. As we shall see shortly, the proposition that attitudes toward more remote objects are likely at any point in time to be less perfectly balanced is but a short step from our earlier proposition that attitudes toward remote objects are more susceptible to change.

BALANCE AND REALITY. Of course imbalance may be experienced as being greater or less in degree, just as any given attitude may be more or less involved in a larger system of attitudes. The imbalance suggested by holding positive attitudes toward both the Republican and Democratic parties is probably greater than that suggested by liking someone faithful to an opposing party. In much the same vein, the balance principle should not be taken to mean that mixed reactions toward an object are impossible, even when reality requires that the object be cognized at some level as a whole. Thus you may have been led at some time or another to a statement like this: "I like him as a person but I hate him as a boss." The very statement suggests some effort to differentiate the person into two distinctive roles as a means of fending off imbalance, but such dissociation cannot be complete in view of

Research Illustration 5.2

McGuire (1960) has reported an experiment in which 120 student subjects were asked to rate the probable truth of a large number of propositions, and to indicate their attitude toward the desirability of the state posited in each proposition. The questionnaire was designed to contain hidden within it a number of triads of propositions that were premises and conclusions from syllogisms, so that the logical consistency of the subject's beliefs could be evaluated. Thus, for example, the following statements were dispersed through the questionnaire: "Any form of recreation that constitutes a serious health menace will be outlawed by the City Health Authority." "The increasing water pollution in this area will make swimming at the local beaches a serious health menace." "Swimming at the local beaches will be outlawed by the City Health Authority."

In the initial administration of the questionnaire (ostensibly a test to measure the effects of controversial material on reading comprehension) there was a good deal of logical inconsistency, with distortions predictable from the individual's attitudes. Thus a person who strongly opposed the closing of the beach (because he liked to swim there, for example) rated the probability that the beach would be closed at a much lower level than his estimate of the probable truth of the premises would have led one to predict.

The questionnaire was administered to the same subjects a week later. No persuasive messages had been given in the interim, and at no time had the question of belief consistency been made salient to the subjects. Nonetheless, the frequency of logical inconsistency was significantly lower in the second administration than it had been in the first. It appeared that the mere statement of related beliefs, even though widely separated in the questionnaire, sensitized the subjects to mutual inconsistencies that were adjusted before the second questionnaire.

---

reality considerations. This attitude cluster may be less stable than others more balanced, but reality may be such as to maintain the imbalance over a long period of time.

In general, the constant flow of information about the outside world constitutes a recurrent force toward imbalance. Balance itself is an inner, psychological state that is "required" not by external conditions but by dictates of the person's internal comfort. Balance can be achieved quite as well by wrongly perceiving self–other congruence, for example, as by correctly perceiving it. The force toward balance, as such, takes no account of external reality. On the other hand, continued ignoring of reality, like pride, often goeth before a fall. If you convince yourself that your father, toward whom you are attracted, agrees with you about some extravagant purchase merely because it is comfortable to experience balance, you are likely to suffer certain consequences of having ignored reality. Imbalance is painful, but so also (in the long run) are the effects of erroneous judgment.

It may be helpful to think in terms of a "strain" or "trend" toward balance, rather than of balance as a perfect and inevitable end-state. Such a modification recognizes that balance is not normally achieved at all cost to perceptions of reality. The principle merely implies that our attitude systems turn out to show somewhat more balance than the sum of the information to which we have been exposed might lead us to expect. Furthermore, when we recognize that balance is a matter of degree, and that reality constantly imposes some imbalance, it is easy to see that we may become quite accustomed to minor imbalances with little or no discomfort.

TOLERANCE FOR IMBALANCE. It is often suggested that some persons experience sharper discomfort at the same apparent degree of imbalance than do other people. That is, tolerance for imbalance may itself be a generalized aspect of personality. There are clinical observations indicating that a very common defense against strong anxiety lies in the formation of simple, unambiguous, and monolithic attitude systems. The system summed up by the cry "Anybody who isn't for us is against us" is an example of such a desperate effort toward extreme (and probably inaccurate) balance. Under emotional stress, such attitudes may be gratifying in imposing a more clear-cut order on the individual's experience. High authoritarians tend to have low tolerance for complex or ambiguous states of imbalance (cf. pages 121 and 172).

IMBALANCE, REALITY, AND OBJECT CENTRALITY. We have already seen that where one or more objects in a system of attitudes have little centrality for the individual, the balance principle cannot be expected to work very clearly, if at all. We can now understand that the reason is that the dynamic underlying the principle involves a discomfort produced by imbalance; and other things equal, this discomfort will be less strong the less central to the individual are the objects involved.

Indeed, it is by taking account of the centrality of objects that we can begin to make some predictions as to the likely outcomes of imbalance. We recall, for example, that one possible response to imbalance is to "stop thinking" about the objects in the imbalanced system. Where the objects were of low centrality to begin with, to stop thinking about them is likely to be the easiest way of coping with their imbalance. On the other hand, objects of high centrality are almost by definition quite difficult to stop thinking about, for such objects present themselves frequently in the individual's immediate environment and are important in the individual's cognitive goal structures. When reality threatens severe imbalance involving extremely central objects, and when (for reasons to be developed below) compensatory change in other attitudes is not a satisfactory alternative, the individual may succumb to some of the more dramatic distortions on reality studied in detail by the abnormal psychologist. Along with pathological forms of dissociation, these include ways of "stopping thought" about the objects that go well beyond the casual ignoring of objects not central, to the dynamic "forgetting" described by terms such as denial, repression, and amnesia.

ATTITUDE ORGANIZATION AND THE RESISTANCE OF ATTITUDES TO CHANGE

Just as the balance principle helps us to understand why other changes are likely to follow in those cases where disturbing new information must be accepted, so it helps as well to understand the general resistance to such change that attitude systems develop over time.

A person's attitude toward something is likely to be drawn into balance with not just one other attitude, but with many others. As an example, President Calvin Coolidge, according to a famous biographer (W. A. White, 1938), had favorable attitudes toward all of the following: the sanctity of private property, the competitive free-enterprise system, a minimum of government "interference," the propriety of things as they are, and the Republican party. For him, all these were linked together in a very intricate latticework, so that any one of these attitudes, if "threatened" by new information, was supported by all of the others. And the whole latticework was further supported by President Coolidge's favorable attitudes toward friends and associates—some of them remembered from his youth in Vermont, some closely affiliated with him as Republican Governor of Massachusetts or as Republican President—whom he viewed as supporting his own attitudes. Indeed, according to his biographer, most of these attitudes were, he felt, also supported by a very Protestant deity. Such a picture is one of balance on a grand design; no wonder he was viewed as a rock-ribbed President.

The key facts of attitude stability, then, are these. Insofar as a person's attitude toward something is imbedded in a larger latticework of attitudes—and such things as the amount of stored information about the object, its personal goal relevance and psychological centrality are all indicators of such imbedding—any attempt to change the attitude must come to grips with the fact that *this attitude is anchored by the other attitudes in the system.* Such an attitude does not exist in a vacuum: if *it* changes, then other compensatory changes must follow to restore balance. Hence the alternatives are either to change a number

Research Illustration 5.3

Festinger (1957) has illustrated his theory of cognitive dissonance with data concerning the reaction of people of differing smoking habits toward new medical evidence of a linkage between smoking and lung cancer. He argues that enjoyment of heavy smoking and the belief that smoking is harmful are dissonant with one another, and that individuals will be motivated to restore balance by rejecting the new information or by cutting down on smoking. The accompanying figure presents data consistent with this theory: the more an individual smokes, the more difficult it is for him to accept the information that smoking is injurious. It is the heavy smokers who experience the most dissonance and who most actively resist the pressures toward attitude change created by the medical findings. Festinger suggests more generally that mechanisms for maintaining cognitive consonance—a special case of balance—include such things as avoiding information

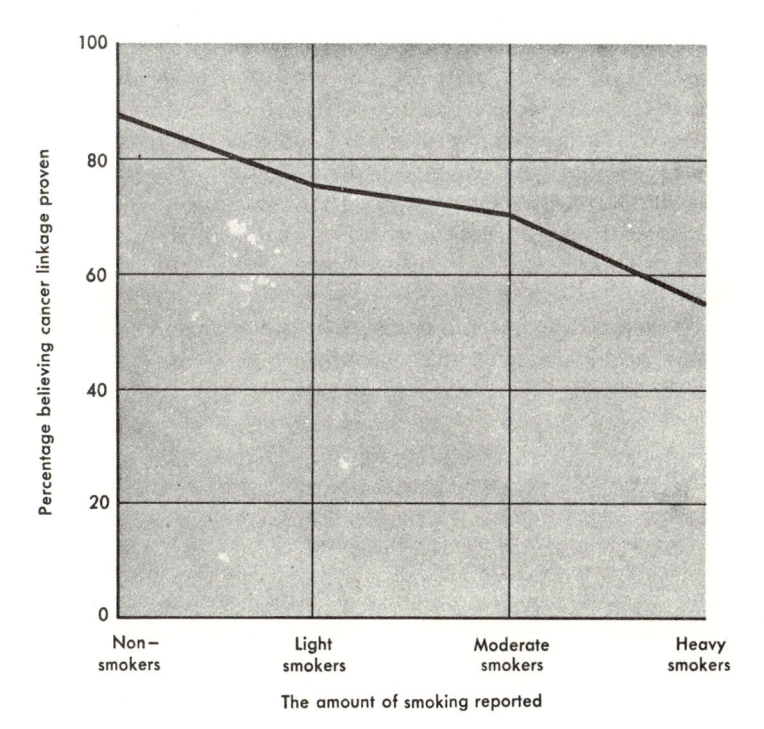

The relationship between the amount of smoking reported by individuals and the percentage who believe that a linkage between smoking and lung cancer has been established (as reported by Festinger, 1957, from the Minneapolis *Star and Tribune*, 1954)

that increases dissonance, or distorting and selecting from available information in such a way as to reduce dissonance, avoiding persons who possess attitudes or information that will increase dissonance, and seeking out persons who have attitudes or information that will decrease dissonance. All these behaviors help to "defend" attitudes from change that would create imbalance with other related attitudes, beliefs, or behaviors.

of systematically related attitudes at once, or to find a way to dissolve the anchorage between the target attitude and the rest of the system. What these alternatives have in common, of course, is that they require much more "effort" to produce some change than would be required to change an "isolated" attitude.

TIME AND ATTITUDE STABILITY. The development of large-scale, tightly balanced systems of attitudes involves a number of processes, all of which require time. The accumulation of information about an object that helps to link it with other objects obviously takes time. So do processes of selective memory whereby stored information that "does not fit" the dominant balance of the attitude system tends after some interval to be forgotten. Processes of conscious thought about an object, which serve to refine away imbalances, also are repeated sporadically over time, with cumulative effects. And as attitude systems strain toward more nearly perfect balance with the passage of time, perceptual mechanisms are increasingly likely to screen out "threatening" new information. Thus the individual imposes increasing organization on the world he perceives, and his resistance to attitude change, at least in sectors of his world involving objects that have been of some importance to him for some time, increases with it.

FOCAL OBJECTS OF ATTITUDE ORGANIZATION

An individual's many attitudes are organized in the form of many systems. Most of a person's attitude systems are interconnected, directly or indirectly, because different systems, activated at different times, include the same attitude objects as common elements. There is overlap between systems. For example, a high school boy at successive moments may be concerned with systems involving attitudes toward his father and the family car; toward his father and his own need for money; toward the costs of driving with some other boys in the family car to a distant football game; toward these friends and his father's disapproval of them; and so on. Such an interconnected set of systems is, of course, almost endless, and highly variable in content from individual to individual.

Nevertheless, the character of our experience is such that a fairly limited number of objects become so central as to figure in a great many of a person's attitude systems, and these systems tend to become integrated around such objects. For convenience we might label these few objects of greatest centrality to the individual as *focal* objects—like the mother for the child, religion for the priest, or money for the miser. The fact that focal objects are limited in number for any given individual means that we can describe his attitude organization with some economy. If, however, we are trying to describe many individuals at once, the matter is more difficult, for different people may be oriented toward rather different focal objects. The family may be a focal object for one man, fine arts for another, and political power for still a third. Nonetheless, most focal objects fall into one or more of these three categories: (1) the self; (2) other persons and groups; or (3) inclusive values. These are the primary anchors of attitude organization.

Inclusive Values

As we have seen, the more inclusive an attitude object, the more objects, events, and states can be meaningfully subsumed by it. Thus when highly inclusive objects—such as abstract ideas or ultimate values—become focal for an individual, attitudes toward these objects, by balance principles, are likely to influence a very wide range of more specific attitudes and behavior. A pacifist is likely to have a characteristic set of attitudes regarding the draft, the use of tax money for munitions, cooperating with civil defense alerts, the motives of military leaders, the rights of the individual in times of national crisis, the ethics of making a profit by selling armaments, and the importance of world government. All these attitudes, and many others associated with them, come to be organized in terms of the pacifist's dominant value—that of achieving peace in a certain way.

TYPES OF VALUE. Although the inclusive objects that can serve as focal for one person or another are certainly varied, attempts have been made to locate a limited number of basic value postures. The Allport-Vernon-Lindzey Study of Values (1951) offers an instrument for measuring six types of values suggested originally by Spranger (1928):

Theoretical: characterized by a high evaluation placed on the discovery of truth through an empirical, critical, rational approach.

Practical: emphasizing useful and practical values; conforming to the prevailing stereotype of the "average American businessman."

Aesthetic: placing the highest value on form and harmony; judging and enjoying each unique experience from the standpoint of its grace, symmetry or fitness.

Social: originally defined as love of people, this category has been narrowly limited in the revised version of the test to cover only altruism and philanthropy.

Power: primarily interested in personal power, influence, and renown; labeled originally "political," but not necessarily limited to the field of politics.

Religious: mystical, concerned with the unity of all experience, and seeking to comprehend the cosmos as a whole.

To determine an individual's "profile of values" he is asked to express his preference for a number of different situations. One item, for example, reads as follows (the answers for this item are to be rated in order of personal preference, giving 4 to the most attractive and 1 to the least attractive alternative):

In your opinion, can a man who works in business all the week best spend Sunday in—
a. trying to educate himself by reading serious books
b. trying to win at golf, or racing
c. going to an orchestral concert
d. hearing a really good sermon

By noting an individual's ratings of a large number of different items it is possible to obtain a score that expresses the relative strength of his preferences for the six value areas. The value profile for an individual is simply a line drawing showing that the preference scores differ from one value to another. Using this measure, Allport, Vernon, and Lindzey have found that a group of medical students were high in the theoretical area and relatively low in the religious area. Conversely, a group of theological students were high in the religious area and relatively low in the theoretical area. Thus medical students were not simply attracted by medicine alone, but also had positive attitudes toward a host of other activities congruent with the same general value preferences. In this sense, the theoretical value dominated a large number of more specific predispositions. The same may be said of the systems of attitudes characterizing the theological students—although the focal value was quite different.

In general, then, the attitudes that an individual holds toward many things can be expected to be in balance with a limited set of more inclusive values that he has developed, and hence such values form one important type of focal object.

The Self as Focal Object

Whatever grounds we may choose to define centrality, few objects are likely to be as central for as many persons as "the self." Even the man who has espoused the value of "selflessness" does so by making such a value a dominant and prized part of his self-image. In one degree or another, virtually all other kinds of attitudes become intertwined with attitudes toward oneself. Attempting to define what is meant by "self" here is difficult without using the word "self" in the definition. It would hardly do to say that one's self is the way in which one perceives oneself! Perhaps the best definition with which to begin is one of the simplest: "The self is the individual as known to the individual" (Murphy, 1947).

Attitudes toward the self, like attitudes toward any other objects, can be either positive or negative in varying degrees. However, it seems quite clear that one of the individual's most basic and continuing needs is for a self-image that is essentially positive. Indeed, current personality theory indicates that anything less than a positive attitude toward the self is very likely to be associated with other symptoms of emotional disorder. This does not mean, of course, that the healthy individual can tolerate no negative assessments of himself whatever. Rather, realistic recognition of shortcomings in limited areas is entirely to be desired. But it remains a basic postulate that for adequate mental health the most generalized attitude toward the self—what we shall call the individual's *self-esteem*—must remain more positive than negative.

One immediate implication of this fact is that attitudes of other persons toward this prime object (oneself) are congruent with one's own attitudes when these reactions of others are positive, and incongruent when these reactions are negative. A most obvious derivation from the self–other congruence principle, then, is that an individual will tend to have positive attitudes toward those whom he perceives to have positive attitudes toward himself (or "his self"), and negative attitudes toward those who appear to evaluate him (for "his self") negatively. If you have ever overheard two people important to you evaluating you in a conversation—positively or negatively—you can undoubtedly subscribe to this observation.

Perhaps more surprising is the fact that the operations of balance are visible even with negative sides of an individual's self-evaluation. Thus, Aronson and Carlsmith (1962) put subjects in a task situation and experimentally manipulated their expectancies as to their own probable abilities in the situation. Among subjects led to believe they lacked the particular skills necessary for the task and hence would do poorly, those informed that they had indeed performed poorly showed signs of accepting the information more readily than those who were notified that they had performed well. At least in narrow areas where performance may not be of great importance to the basic self-image, it seems that the need for balance may outweigh the need for positive self-esteem.

THE SOCIAL NATURE OF THE SELF. It may never have occurred to you to wonder how you have gone about accumulating the fund of information about yourself that makes up your self-image. Or perhaps the answer has seemed so obvious—you know about yourself because you *are* yourself—that the question hardly seems worth asking. Yet for more than seventy years sociologists and psychologists have been intrigued by the degree to which self-conceptions depend less on what we are in some absolute sense than on what we deduce that other people take us to be. Although the impression made on the self-image by images attributed to others is naturally strongest in childhood when there is little experience with standards against which one can locate oneself, our interest in others' impressions of us remains keen throughout our lifetime. In other words, then, much of what we consider ourselves to be is a product of social interaction.

No one has contributed to this point of view more clearly than Charles H. Cooley (1902). With special reference to the self, he wrote:

> In a very large and interesting class of cases the social reference takes the form of a somewhat definite imagination of how one's self . . . appears in a particular mind, and the kind of self-feeling one has is determined by the attitude toward this attributed to that other mind. A social self of this sort might be called the reflected or looking-glass self:
>
> > "Each to each a looking-glass
> > Reflects the other that doth pass."
>
> As we see our face, figure and dress in the glass, and are interested in them because they are ours, and pleased or otherwise with them according as they do or do not answer to what we should like them to be; so in imagination we perceive in another's mind some thought of our appearance, manners, aims, deeds, character, friends, and so on, and are variously affected by it.
>
> A self-idea of this sort seems to have three principal elements: the imagination of our appearance to the other person; the imagination of his judgment of that appearance, and some sort of self-feeling, such as pride or mortification.

Recent additions to this viewpoint have made much more systematic use of theories of perception and discrimination than did the earlier writers. But the original emphasis on the self as built out of social interaction has been reinforced rather than altered by the more recent investigations. We now know much more about the psychological processes by which children learn to perceive themselves, but the earlier conclusion that the self is a social product has scarcely changed at all.

A proper treatment of the development of self-attitudes and some of the emotional dynamics that surround self-conceptions could easily fill a volume. We shall limit our consideration here to a few of the details most relevant to attitude organization and attitude stability.

THE SELF AND ATTITUDE ORGANIZATION. If the self as attitude object is to serve as an anchor for other attitudes, it must show fair stability in its own right over time. Engel (1959) has reported research indicating that even during the period of adolescence, stormy as it is in our society, the self-attitudes of most persons have considerable stability. Except for those rare instances in which an individual is faced with a so-called traumatic experience, the attitudes that an individual has toward himself are sufficiently consistent from one time to the next that attitudes toward other things can be linked with these self-attitudes to form highly stable systems.

Studies such as Research Illustration 5.4 have shown that the nature of the "fit" between perceptions of one's actual self and one's self-ideals may have important ramifications in the organization of a much wider range of attitudes. Of course such a study cannot disentangle whether the attitudes held by the students toward themselves influence their other attitudes and abilities in the areas covered by the study, or whether these abilities and resultant behaviors (and the way others react to them) influence the attitudes toward the self. It is very likely, however, that these influences are flowing in both directions. As we have seen, attitudes toward self are dependent on how others react to our behavior, but further behavior and attitudes are influenced by the attitude we have acquired toward ourselves. This, in turn, has further influence on how others respond to us, and so on. Interaction, as the term implies, is a two-way street, and it is in just such an interacting state of affairs that self-attitudes take shape and finally assume a relatively stable form.

EGO-INVOLVEMENT AND RESISTANCE OF ATTITUDES TO CHANGE. Like any other form of attitude connection, the connectedness of other attitudes to the self varies in degree. Some attitudes are linked more closely with the "inner core" of the self-percept than are others. Often the term "ego" is used to describe a restricted aspect of the self, that which is a value to be protected and enhanced. Attitudes that are linked closely with the ego aspects of the self are called *ego-involved*. Typically, they are attitudes largely shaped by ego-defensive needs (see Chapter 2, pages 43–44). Alexander Hamilton, the brilliant writer, statesman, and financier, is said to have taken his many real talents rather lightly, and to have invested a great deal of pride instead in his dueling, which in fact he did rather poorly and about which he undoubtedly felt defensive. Hence positive images of dueling skill were highly ego-involved for Hamilton, a matter that had something to do with his untimely death in a duel.

Research Illustration 5.4

Since attitudes toward the self are relatively constant, one might expect that other attitudes and behavior associated with self-concepts would also show considerable stability and consistency. Turner and Vanderlippe (1958) reasoned that if this were true, persons with contrasting attitudes toward the self should also be quite different from one another in a number of other respects related to the adequacy of personal adjustment. To test this assumption, 175 undergraduate college students were given a test to measure how well each student felt he was living up to his ideal self in a number of different areas. Some students had attitudes toward the self that indicated a very good match between the perceived and ideal self. Others had self-attitudes that showed a great disparity, although this did not necessarily mean that on balance, the perceived self was negative. The 25 students who had the best match between self-attitudes and ideal self were then compared with the 25 students that had the poorest match, in order to determine whether these attitudes toward the self were related to other aspects of behavior.

It was found that there were a number of significant differences between these two groups of students. Thus, for example, the cumulative academic grades, based on the local point system, showed a mean of 1.78 for the group whose self-attitudes matched their ideal selves, and only 1.52 for the poor-match group. This stronger academic achievement—a difference in grades so large that it would not have occurred by chance one time in twenty—was particularly noteworthy in view of the fact that there were *not* significant differences between the two groups in scholastic aptitude scores. In other words, basic capacities in the two groups were similar, with differences arising in current performance. Similarly, those whose self-attitudes matched their ideal self closely engaged in significantly more extracurricular activities and received significantly higher scores on two different standard tests of personal adjustment.

Sociometric ratings on the part of close acquaintances were also obtained for each of the subjects by having groups of ten students, one of whom was always a subject in this experiment, rank each other as to organizing ability, social initiative, capacity for friendship, and so on. These groups included only the individuals that roomed most closely to the subject in the student dormitory. Once again it was found that those students whose self-attitudes matched their ideal self closely received significantly more favorable ratings than did those whose self-attitudes were at a considerable distance from their ideal self.

Ego-involved attitudes can show an extreme resistance to change. Of course any new information of contradictory valence implications creates some cognitive disturbance if there is no way in which it can be rejected. But new information that challenges one's conception of oneself and the cherished ego images have unusually strong overtones of threat, and call up very basic personality defenses. Active steps taken by the individual to preserve a positive attitude toward himself under such severe threat may lead to a rejection even of obviously accurate information, so that attitude change becomes virtually impossible. In its extreme forms, such defensiveness generalizes over a wide range of potentially disturbing information, so that the individual becomes more or less cut off from reality. These instances require the attention of the psychotherapist.

Although there are many schools of thought among psychotherapists, most of them hold in common the conviction that attitudes cannot be changed unless ways are found to reduce defensiveness. The research of Haigh (1949), for example, has shown that from earlier to later interviews, the statements made by patients in successful therapy indicate a decrease in defensive behavior. With such a decrease, as Carl Rogers (1958) has shown, attitudes become progressively more flexible, and necessary attitude changes can be produced. The success of Katz, Sarnoff, and McClintock (1956, 1957) in changing prejudiced attitudes through "self-insight" materials (Chapter 4) appears to involve a similar "loosening" of the bonds between the ego and other attitude objects as a prelude to change.

Other Persons and Groups as Focal Objects

We have already had several occasions to note that we attribute attitudes to other social objects—persons or groups. Although we may cognize many persons and groups, those that are psychologically central for us are relatively few in number, comprising such objects as one's family, a clique of close friends, or one's ethnic or religious group. Of these proximal social objects, a number that is probably still more limited are perceived to be of high personal goal relevance, although dependence on such social objects for emotional support and reward is particularly intense. These limited social objects come to serve as common elements in very many of the individual's attitude systems, and hence represent a third major class of focal objects.

In the preceding chapter we introduced the concept of the *reference group*. It should now be clear that a group is a reference group for an individual with respect to a certain object when the group and its attitude toward the object are part of the same system as the individual's own attitudes toward the object. The attitude systems of the high school boy cited above included his father at a number of points, and in such cases a reference person is playing precisely the same role as a reference group.

Reference groups need by no means coincide with membership

groups. This is most obvious when a person takes a group of which he is a nonmember as a negative reference point (the nonunion man who is predisposed to react negatively to any position a labor union takes). Similarly, if somewhat less frequently, a nonmembership group may serve as a positive reference group. For the social climber, higher-status groups of which he is not (yet) a member are likely to be taken as positive reference groups, with those of his own objective status serving as negative ones. However, reference groups would be classified as focal objects only insofar as they are central enough to figure in *many* of the individual's attitude systems. These focal groups tend to be ones in which the individual has membership.

Since much of our information about objects is socially mediated through focal persons and groups, what Festinger (1950) has called our "social reality" is largely shaped by such persons and groups. The social origin of the self is but one, though an extremely important, special case: more generally, the evaluative dimensions against which it is important to locate objects, along with the information that helps to locate them, tend to be socially defined. In some cases, such social definitions are so uncontested that the individual does not realize that assumptions could be different. Thus in one culture it may be taken for granted that work is a necessary evil, and in another that work is a desirable and ennobling activity; in one culture money earned is to be spent, and in another it is earned to be saved insofar as possible. Such assumptions, like ways of seeing the self, are socially transmitted, and in the degree that the individual fails to conceive that alternatives exist, there is no question of disagreement.

Similarly, where alternatives are apparent, the effects of persons and groups as elements in individual attitude systems are those that would be expected in view of the general principle of balance: attitudes attributed to focal persons and groups tend to be similar to one's own, and favorable attitudes toward such persons and groups are supported by assumed agreement with them—and vice versa. The net effect, if we were to consider larger and more heterogeneous populations at some point in time, should be that members of the same groupings could be found to hold similar attitudes in common, with these attitudes differing from those characteristic of other groupings.

OTHER PERSONS AND GROUPS AS ANCHORS FOR ATTITUDES. Many of the day-to-day processes of interaction and communication that sustain the focal role of others in the individual's attitude systems are the substance of ensuing chapters. For now, we need only observe that it is easy to understand that others do help to anchor a person's attitudes over time, for close friends and important membership groups tend to remain rather constant for the individual over long periods.

As a matter of fact, in the degree that focal persons and groups *do*

Research Illustration 5.5

In interviews with a national sample of the adult white male population, Centers (1949) asked six questions "designed to test conservative–radical orientations," which were expected to be different in different status groupings of the population. Respondents were also asked to describe their own occupational positions, and to answer this question: "If you were asked to use one of these four names for your social class, which would you say you belonged in: the middle class, lower class, working class, or upper class?" The question was designed to elicit the individual's class reference groups, particularly where these did not coincide with the individual's objective occupation.

Far more often than not, people of middle-class occupations—business, professional, and white-collar people—identified themselves with their objective membership group, the middle class; and manual laborers likewise identified themselves with the working class. As expected, too, higher-status respondents tended to be much more conservative in their attitudes than lower-status respondents. Nonetheless, a substantial number of people in working class occupations identified themselves as "middle class," and a substantial number of white-collar people identified themselves as "working class." Even within the same occupational groups, attitudes varied quite markedly according to the reference class chosen. Among urban business, professional, and white-collar people, for example, only 47 percent of those who considered themselves to be "working class" gave a pattern of responses to the attitude questions that were rated as "conservative," whereas among

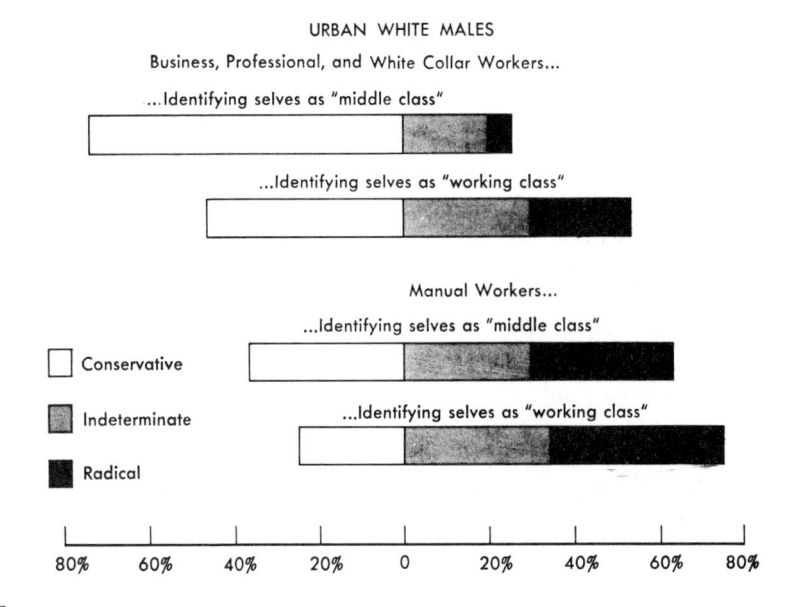

URBAN WHITE MALES

Business, Professional, and White Collar Workers...

...Identifying selves as "middle class"

...Identifying selves as "working class"

Manual Workers...

...Identifying selves as "middle class"

☐ Conservative
▨ Indeterminate
■ Radical

...Identifying selves as "working class"

80% 60% 40% 20% 0 20% 40% 60% 80%

those of the same occupations who considered themselves "middle class" the figure was 74 percent. These differences in attitude within the same occupation grouping were only slightly less than the differences between manual and nonmanual occupations, with class identification aside, as the accompanying figure suggests. This finding, together with other evidence from the study, makes clear the importance of asking, "To what groups do you refer yourself?" as well as simply, "Of what groups do other people consider you to be a member?"

One further finding is of particular interest. Respondents were asked, "In deciding whether a person belongs to your class or not, which of these other things do you think is most important to know: Who his family is; how much money he has; what sort of education he has; or how he believes and feels about certain things?" The last of these answers was by far the most common. Only about one fifth of those answering at all mentioned "family" or "money," and about one third mentioned "education." But more than one half stressed differences in attitude. Hence the majority of respondents felt that the lines between social class grouping were less clearly marked by some of the obvious objective indicators than by differential attitudes and beliefs. The respondents identified themselves positively with those whose attitudes toward common objects were believed to be like their own.

change for individuals over time (and such change is more common in mobile modern society than it once must have been), it is a social fact that the incidence of change is typically greatest in the period from early childhood through early adulthood, and thenceforth declines rather steadily over the remainder of the life span. Experiences like formal education, service in the army, and the search for an adult career niche tend to push the adolescent and young adult into more varied social settings and into close proximity with others who have not necessarily been sought out as having similar attitudes and values. Later in life, physical residence and all the informal friendships and group memberships that accompany a given residence become for many people increasingly fixed. Within such a fixed setting, there is likely to be more congruence between the attitudes of an individual and those of his focal persons and groups, as he gravitates over time toward close relationships with persons and groups supporting his attitudes, and adjusts his own attitudes toward those of the social setting.

In other words, to the various intrapsychic mechanisms that lead to an increasing stability of attitude organization with the passage of time, we may add a set of social mechanisms as well. The older person is given more reason to feel that his view of social reality is confirmed without exception by those important to him, and is less likely to encounter informally mediated information that calls his beliefs into question.

THE OUTCOMES OF IMBALANCE

We are now in a position to consider a final piece of unfinished business. At an earlier point in this chapter we noted that the principle of balance in its simplest form suggests only that when new information creates imbalance in a system of attitudes, some other compensating change is likely—but not certain—to occur. Broadly speaking, then, there are three kinds of outcomes of psychological imbalance: (1) further compensating attitude change within the system; (2) a breaking up of the system through some form of dissociation or differentiation; or (3) no change at all, with the imbalance being tolerated or the relevant attitude objects being ignored. We have also suggested that the centrality of the attitude objects to the individual may play an important part in determining whether or not some change occurs—that is, whether the third outcome or one of the other two is more likely. Where all the objects involved in the imbalanced system are of low centrality, we would predict that very little change would be prompted by that imbalance.

Now let us assume that enough of the attitude objects involved in the system have such high centrality for the individual that the third outcome is not likely to occur. A choice between the first and second outcomes may require fuller knowledge of the actual situation, for alternatives such as dissociation or differentiation might fly less in the face of reality with some configurations of complex objects than with others, and hence would be "easier" to manage psychologically. However, where reality constraints are held constant across a set of situations of imbalance, we would expect that the second outcome—some dissolution of the system—becomes more likely as the objects involved in the imbalance are more nearly equated in their centrality for the individual. Conversely, the first outcome—some further attitude change —is more likely the greater the discrepancy in the centrality of the objects involved.

Furthermore, in those cases of discrepant object centrality, we can now go on to more definite predictions as to where the compensating attitude change will occur. For other things equal, *balance-restoring change is more likely to occur in attitudes toward objects that are less rather than more central.* Thus, for example, we may imagine two people, both of whom have just become aware of an incongruence between their own attitudes toward an object and those of a person or group that is moderately central for both. Let us imagine, furthermore, that for the first of these persons, the attitude in question is a focal value (and hence involved in a large number of his attitude systems), while for the second it is not. We would predict that this first person would tend to restore balance by changing his attitude toward the person or group, and seeking other persons or groups more supportive of the focal value. The second would tend to restore balance, however, in the opposite way: by changing his attitude toward the object and retaining his positive feeling toward the person or group.

At least suggestive evidence bearing on these predictions has been noted in an experiment by Pilisuk (1962). He attempted to form a strong association in the minds of his subjects between performance on an experimental task (evaluating a case in social work) and basic self-esteem by representing the task as one requiring no special skills, yet one that measured an individual's maturity, social sensitivity, and practical intelligence. After the task was completed, purported reactions to the individual's performance on the part of several "critics" were relayed to the subject. One of these assessments was harsh and abusive. In the experimental group the sharp criticism was ultimately identified as having come from a close friend of the subject. In the control group it purported to be from a stranger. Before the source of the criticism was identified, subjects in both groups reacted negatively to the anonymous critic, thereby maintaining their positive view toward the more central object of the two (own performance, rather than the critic) and preserving balance at the same time. When the critic for the experimental subjects was identified as the close friend, it meant that prior positive attitudes toward the close friend (presumably an object of high centrality) were out of balance with the criticism and attitudes toward own performance (also of high centrality given its link with self-esteem). The typical reaction was not to change attitudes toward own performance or toward the close friend, but rather to dissolve the system through a wide range of rationalizations.

The general reasons why it is unlikely that balance will be restored by a change in attitudes toward relatively central objects can be understood in terms of the balance principle itself. For focal objects are, by definition, those involved in many of the individual's attitude systems. Hence if an attitude toward a focal object is changed to restore one system to balance, such change will throw many other systems into imbalance at the same time. The less central the object that serves to restore balance in a disturbed system, the more limited the discomfort from upheaval in other systems. In this general proposition we can recognize a simplification of many of our earlier observations, indicating

ORGANIZATION AND STABILITY - 151

that attitudes toward more remote objects of lower goal relevance were especially susceptible to change. As new information disturbs balanced systems, attitudes toward such objects are sacrificed to restore balance while protecting stable views of more focal objects.

* * *

In the last analysis, then, if we inquire about the central, solid structuring of a person's interconnected attitudes, the place to look is at the interconnections between focal objects (Figure 5.4). If both one's

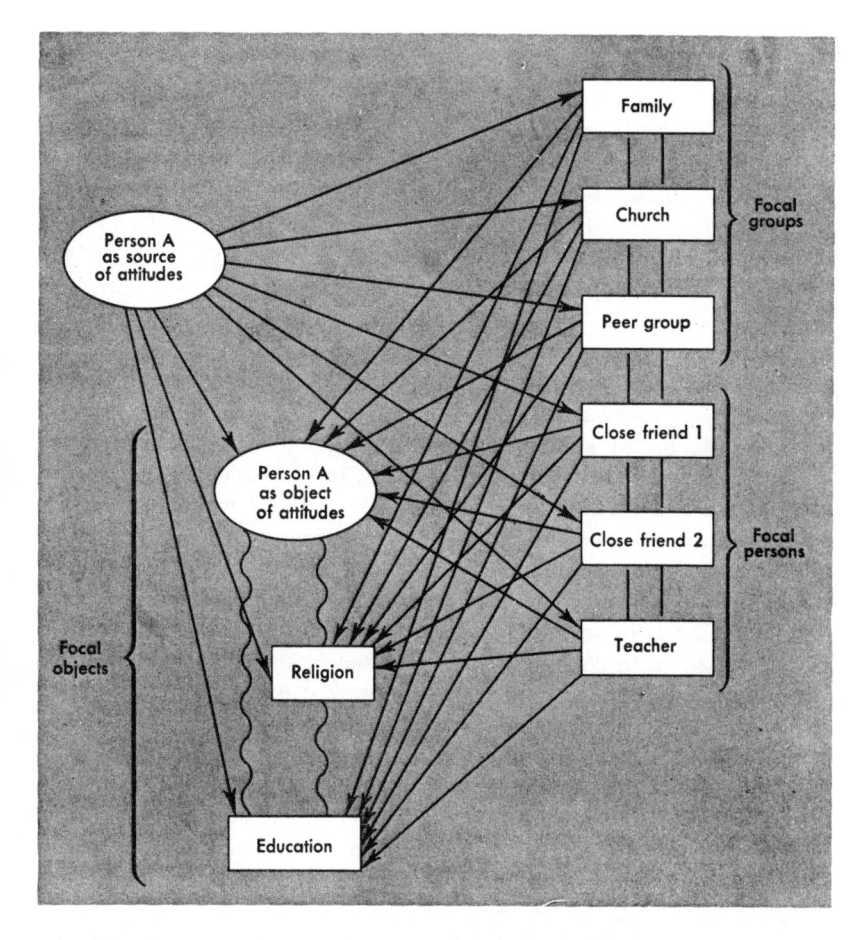

FIGURE 5.4. Schematic diagram of latticework of mutually supporting systems of attitudes in which Person A is involved. Arrows point from source to object of attitude, as held by A or as perceived by him. Wavy lines suggest belongingness between objects of attitudes.

mother and one's religion are focal objects, and if, as is likely, these are in balance (that is, her attitude and one's own are thought to be similar), then this system is structurally central to one's interconnected attitudes. Indeed, we have stressed "self-other congruence" as a principle (even though logically it is but a special case of the more inclusive principle of balance) precisely because the "self" and "others" can be counted on to be focal objects for most people most of the time, and the principle thus refers to a structurally central system of attitudes. Such focal systems are structurally central in the sense that they "do most of the work" of maintaining the organization.

OVERVIEW

Over the course of this chapter we have come to see that many observations about attitude stability (and, by implication, about attitude *change*) can be rather simply put into order through an understanding of attitude organization. We have seen that it is attitude *systems*, and not single attitudes—nor even the additive effect of many attitudes, view as isolated from each other—that are responsible for the orderly structuring of a person's attitudes. And systems, in turn, are held together by the principle of balance, which thus becomes a central feature of attitude organization.

Since balanced systems are more stable than imbalanced ones, organization based on balance tends, itself, to be stable. This fact, however, does not necessarily mean that the attitudes of which systems are composed are stable in the sense of never changing. The stable feature of a balanced system is not any single component of the system, but the *relationship* among those components. The principle of balance does not assert that attitudes in balance are impervious to change, but rather that *if* one of them changes *then* one or more other changes will probably follow, in such a manner as to restore balance.

Because we are constantly receiving new information about many of the objects of our attitudes, a fair amount of attitude change is inevitable. What the principle of balance underscores is that such changes tend *not* to occur singly; changes come in packages, or by systems. Normally, balance is restored within the system insofar as possible by adjustments in attitudes toward less rather than more focal obects. However, sometimes new information forces changes of attitude toward very focal objects themselves, and hence forces change in focal *systems*. When this occurs, what started as a change in a single attitude may spread through a pervasive network. In the extreme, such change is referred to as a conversion—as in the classical case of Saul of Tarsus, the persecutor of Christians, who became St. Paul, the prime apostle of the Christian faith.

Thus the implications of the principle of balance for the stability and change of single attitudes are conservative, in one sense; the inviolacy of any single attitude in a balanced system is protected, so to speak, by the support it receives from other attitudes in the system. But the principle also has implications for adaptability. As objects of our attitudes actually change, or as our information about them changes, our attitudes can also change. However, they tend not to do so in piecemeal fashion, but adaptively, in an *organized* manner. The opposite of organization is chaos, from which we are protected because the principle of balance permits change while maintaining organization.

* * *

For the purposes of this book, an individual will often be considered as an organization of attitudes. This, of course, is only a way of representing an individual, rather than a way of saying what an individual *is*. It is by no means a complete representation, and it is not one that is equivalent to "personality"; for example, it pretty much excludes the expressive aspects of the individual personality (cf. G. W. Allport, 1961). But in confronting the remaining problems of social psychology we shall usually allow the individual to be represented by the organization of his attitudes.

PART TWO

Processes of Interaction

THE THEME OF INTERACTION IS, AS WE INDICATED AT THE END OF CHAPTER 2, the central one in this book. If, as Figure 1.1 suggests, it is processes of interaction that mediate between many of the properties of individuals and of groups, then we need to ask about the nature of these processes. Part Two is devoted to exactly this question.

By *processes* of interaction we have in mind something more than psychological and behavioral activities on the part of single individuals. We mean to include such activities on the part of *two or more persons simultaneously*. Not in the literal sense, as if training separate cameras on different persons at the same moment, which would create a difficult problem of focusing, but in a more important sense. Our problem is to understand the ways in which the activities of interacting persons are *interdependent*, or reciprocally contingent. When persons are interacting each of them is, so to speak, controlling some portion of the other's activity. Ultimately, we are interested in interaction because it has effects both on individuals and on groups, but the understanding of these effects depends (as in chemistry or economics or any other discipline) on the processes by which they occur.

Interaction processes thus refer not just to what goes on within each of the interacting persons but also to what goes on *between* them. Take, for example, the processes by which two interacting persons perceive each other. The rather complicated things that go on within each of them, as suggested at the beginning of Chapter 6, are of course described at the individual-psychological level. But we are interested in more than just the modes by which at any given instant either of them is taking in and processing information about the other. As social psychologists, we are also interested in the continuity of their ongoing interaction. To understand this we must note the *relationships* between the perceptual content of each of them about the other. And, in particular, we must understand the changes in this relationship as they continue to interact—changes as noted either by the outside observer or by the interacting persons themselves. Thus the study of interpersonal perception in the following chapter becomes the study of changing and developing relationships in the perceptions of interacting persons—not only about each other but also about their common environment on which the relationship is dependent.

The same general points arise in Chapter 7, where communication is the particular form of interaction under scrutiny. Whether we ask about the preconditions of communication or about its consequences, in either case the answers are to be sought (as roughly outlined in Chapter 1) in relationships between the information in the possession of the interacting persons. Communication is a process by which this relationship is changed.

In the special case where information has to do with other persons' attitudes toward rules of behavior, we are dealing with the peculiarly important topic of group norms. As we shall see in Chapter 8, norms exist and exert power over group members insofar as the relationship between members' attitudes toward the rules is not only that of consensus but, in addition, that of recognized consensus, or sharing. The processes by which shared information and shared attitudes arise and change or persist are of primary concern in this chapter.

Finally, in Chapter 9 we examine some general forms of observable interaction. In our search for regularities in the ways in which persons adapt to one another's behavior we shall see that there are very few "automatic" sequences of behavior on the part of different persons. Rather, we must look behind the observed sequences in behavior to find regularities in the relationships between the ways in which one person's behavior is rewarding or punishing both to himself and to others with whom he is interacting.

Our concentration on processes of interaction in Part Two means that we shall constantly be considering more than one person. Although any set of two or more persons may be called a group if one wishes to consider them as a single entity, we shall be concerned only with groups as sets of interacting persons. In order to distinguish groups considered from this point of view from other kinds of groups, we shall refer to them as *interaction groups*. We shall not, however, be much concerned with the characteristics of groups of any size, viewed as single entities; that is the later task of Part Three.

CHAPTER 6

Interpersonal Perception

THIS CHAPTER IS DEVOTED TO A PROBLEM THAT MIGHT BE LABELED "the perception of each other by interacting persons." We shall be using the term "perception" in its extended sense, referring to what an individual does, psychologically, with his information input, as noted in Chapter 2. We can see how the general characteristics of perception apply to the particular question of perceiving persons by paraphrasing Osgood's summary statement (page 34), as follows:

> Social perception involves the *organization* of information about persons and the *attribution of properties* to them, often on the basis of only sketchy cues. These properties manifest *constancy*, in spite of observed variations, and are *selectively* attributed in the sense that they are influenced by the perceiver's psychological states. The processes by which information is organized are *flexible*; the same body of information is subject to patterning in different ways. Thus social perception refers to a set of processes that intervene between the presentation of information about a person and awareness of him.[1]

It is these processes—the selection and flexible patterning of information about persons, together with the attributing of more or less constant properties to them—that will primarily engage us in this chapter.

[1] This paraphrase omits Osgood's fourth point, to which social perception presents no direct, clear analogue.

157

Perceptual processes necessarily occur at the beginning of interaction, but they do not stop there: Continued input during the course of interaction requires the continuity of perceptual processes.

PSYCHOLOGICAL PROCESSES IN INTERPERSONAL PERCEPTION

The perception of anything involves transactional processes between the perceiver and the object of his perception: the object does something to him, and he does something to it. The perceiver-to-object part of the transaction is at a psychological level, of course; the mere process of perceiving something does not create an actual change in it, but the perceiver's representation of it is affected by his own perceptual processes, and in this sense he does something to it. We shall discuss both aspects of the transaction, with respect to persons as objects of perception.

What Is Presented by the Person Perceived

Even the simplest thing, as we noted in Chapter 2, is too complex, too many-sided, to be perceived in all respects simultaneously, and without error. Persons, which are not among the simplest things, present the perceiver with many different possibilities for selection and organization of information. And different perceivers of the same person will find still more room for variations in perceptual processes. Nevertheless, no one would deny that the perception of any object or event itself has something to do with that object or event. With respect to persons as objects of perception, we therefore confront this question: How is perception influenced by the fact that the object is a human being rather than, say, a stroke of lightning, a still-life painting, or a bowl of goldfish? This question presupposes that human beings have (or at least are commonly assumed to have) certain properties that are either absent or relatively inconspicuous in other objects of perception. The following list of person-properties is not intended to be complete, nor are we interested in arguing that they are uniquely human; we do assume, however, that they are characteristic of human beings in special ways: the perception of persons, as compared with nonhuman objects, is importantly influenced by such person-properties.

THE PERCEIVED PERSON IS HIMSELF A PERCEIVER. The existence of this property is self-evident, both in animals and in men; we may take it for granted that P, as he perceives O,[2] regards him as being, like himself, a perceiver. The general answer to the question of what P considers to be the objects of O's perception, in an interacting situation, is: more or less the same things that P himself is perceiving, together with P himself. More inclusively stated, P assumes that O perceives the salient features of the immediate situation, including P himself and anything that they are communicating about. It is as if P were saying to himself, "While we're interacting we're paying attention to the same things, and to each other."

THE PERCEIVED PERSON HAS MOTIVES AND ATTITUDES. P assumes that O, like himself, is not indifferent to what he perceives; O has motives of his own that can be gratified or frustrated in the immediate situation, and has brought to it attitudes of his own, including information and beliefs as well as affective predispositions that may be "caught up" in the situation. The objects of the motives and attitudes that he attributes to O include particularly, but not exclusively, those of concern to P—especially, as we have just indicated, P himself and whatever they are both attending to.

OTHER DISPOSITIONAL PROPERTIES OF THE PERCEIVED PERSON. Professor Fritz Heider, whose systematic contributions to the psychology of interpersonal perception are uniquely important, has suggested the phrase "dispositional properties" to refer to the relatively stable characteristics of an individual that his associates make use of and in explaining his behavior (1958). Especially when a person's behaviors seem to be inconsistent, it is convenient to account for the variations as representing different expressions of the same more or less stable characteristics that are "brought out" in varying ways by shifting circumstances. In addition to persisting attitudes, an individual's dispositional properties include his abilities and those characteristics of his personality and character that appear to be deeply ingrained and dependable. In interacting with other people, one wants to understand their participation in the interaction, and such understanding is facilitated by making assumptions about their dispositional properties.

THE PERCEIVED PERSON ATTRIBUTES ALL THE ABOVE PROPERTIES TO THE PERCEIVER. This is not merely to say that P and O are psychologically alike; after all, they are indistinguishable except that at a particular moment we are considering one of them as the perceiver and the other as

---

[2] Throughout this book we shall use the symbol P to represent a person on whom we are for the moment focusing our attention, and O to represent another person whom he is perceiving or with whom he is in some way interacting. It is sheer happenstance that the same symbols also designate, correctly, the *perceiver* and the *object* of his perception. A and B will refer to two persons *not* being distinguished in such ways.

the perceived. Our point, rather, is that P attributes to O certain psychological states that are analogous to his own. Though he may not be aware of it, it is as if P were thinking, "While we're interacting, he is attributing motives, attitudes, and other dispositional properties to me, just as I am to him." Their psychological states are analogous, rather than identical, in the sense that each is aware of both of them and of matters of immediate common interest, but not in the sense that they necessarily have similar motives, attitudes, or other dispositional properties. As a matter of fact, differences as well as similarities in their motives and attitudes are likely to be of concern to each of them; as we shall note in Chapter 8, it makes a great deal of difference whether either perceives the other as sharing his own attitudes. Meanwhile, we need only to note that P, as he perceives O, regards O's psychological processes as analogous to his own, so that the possibility of similarities or differences is present.

Psychological Processes of the Perceiver

THE PROBLEM OF THE PERCEIVER. It may never have occurred to you that whenever you really notice another person (as contrasted with the relative inattention that you give to a casual passerby) you are confronted with a problem. If you were self-conscious about the matter, as is probably not very often the case, you might formulate the problem somewhat as follows: What are the characteristics of this person that would best account for what I observe about him? This is not much of a problem, of course, if you notice nothing beyond his gross physical characteristics, such as age, sex, complexion, or body build; such properties are accepted as given, and do not need to be accounted for. But the interesting things about a person, in the long run at least, are his ways of behaving, and the behaviors of any individual are so variable from time to time that it does not make sense simply to accept each of them as given. We may "explain" the regular behavior of a squirrel in running toward a tree and climbing it by saying, "Well, that's squirrel nature," but you can hardly explain your roommate's changes in mood, in sociability, or in studying for classes by labeling every instance of his variable behavior as being "just his nature." If you have observed a stranger only once—behaving generously, let us say—you can attribute to him the property of generosity, but if you continue to observe him in varying situations you are going to have to account also for his sometimes not being generous. And if you get to know him well enough you will probably be able to account for such variations in terms of how his property of generosity fits together with his other properties, and of how some situations but not others elicit his generosity.

One's perception of a person thus includes the search for constancies in that person. The phenomena of perceptual constancy are familiar ones in psychology; Osgood's illustration of the white house at high noon and at dusk (page 34) is an illustration from visual perception. To give other examples, you know that your favorite chair in your own room is the same chair no matter from what angle you are looking at it, and you know that the man in the foreground who looks ten times bigger than the one in the distance is really about the same size. You really see the differently angled chairs and the different sized men as having constant properties, in spite of the different images on the retinas of your eyes. As applied to the perception of persons, what corresponds to constancies of color, shape, and size are the dispositional properties that we have already mentioned—especially the attitudes, capacities, and dependable personality characteristics of the person perceived. These properties may not be accurately perceived (we turn later to the problem of accuracy); what is important about them is that as attributed properties they help to account for variations in behavior. The attribution of dispositional tendencies to a person makes it possible to perceive him as the same acting person (and not just the same physical body) in spite of his different behaviors.

Strictly speaking, P gets his initial information about O not as a total person but through stimuli, or cues—visual, auditory, tactile—that O presents. P's task is to select from the available cues, to draw inferences from the information thus obtained, and to organize his inferences in such manner that he has an organized representation of the other person. As we turn to a consideration of these psychological processes on P's part, we shall proceed from the rather general treatment of cognitive organization in Chapter 2 to more specialized problems concerning the perception of persons.

STIMULUS CHARACTERISTICS THAT AFFECT THE OBSERVER'S SELECTION OF CUES. It would be quite impossible to note and to make use of all the information-yielding cues that one person presents to another, even in an encounter that is very brief. One is necessarily selective in noticing the cues that are available. We shall therefore note some of the principles that govern such selectivity, beginning with "objective" factors, external to the observer himself, that apply rather generally to stimuli presented, including person stimuli.

1. One of these principles is *primacy*: information about a person that is obtained early in one's experience with him is particularly likely to be noticed thereafter, if not clearly contradicted by later experience. Experimental demonstrations of this principle have been made by varying the order in which the same items in two verbal descriptions of a person were presented to judges (cf. Luchins, 1957). Part of the primacy effect in everyday experience may result from the fact that if a person has some particularly prominent characteristic, this is the one that is

likely to be noticed first, but controlled investigations show that experimentally contrived primacy may have lasting effects whether or not the first-observed traits are conspicuously noticeable. The noticing and remembering of relatively simple phenomena (like nonsense syllables) as well as of very complex ones have long been known to be influenced by primacy.[3]

2. Perceptual selection is often influenced by *vividness*: any cues that, for whatever reason, are striking or conspicuous are apt to be noticed, and to serve as bases for attributing properties to the persons who present the cues. For example, a person who is neatly but not meticulously groomed may be judged to have the property of concern about personal neatness if he is observed in a slum area where most people are unkempt, because the cues indicating neatness are conspicuous in that setting; but if we observe him a few minutes later in an Easter parade we may attribute to him a lack of concern about neatness, because in the latter situation a different set of cues becomes conspicuous. Such effects have been studied at length by psychologists interested in "level of adaptation" (Helson, 1948). Often, too, sheer unexpectedness conveys vividness; thus one might not even notice that a boy is whistling merrily on his way to school, but the same whistling during a church service would not escape observation, and would probably serve as a basis for attributing certain characteristics to him. The bases of conspicuousness in these illustrations are often referred to as contextual by psychologists, and as situational by sociologists, because vividness depends on the setting in which cues are presented. But vivid cues, regardless of what is responsible for their conspicuousness, are very likely to be selected.

3. *Frequency* is another common basis for the selection of cues. Cues that are frequently presented by the same person are more likely to be noticed, if other considerations are alike, than those that are only rarely repeated. One may not particularly notice a person's timidity, for example, or his wittiness (unless these qualities are very conspicuous) the first few times that he shows them, but if he continues to present cues suggesting timidity or wittiness, the perceiver is likely to attribute such characteristics to him.

CHARACTERISTICS OF THE OBSERVER THAT INFLUENCE HIS SELECTION OF CUES. The preceding principles of cue selection apply more or less universally to all perceivers, regardless of their individual histories and personal characteristics. We shall now consider some principles that are dependent on the varying characteristics of perceivers.

1. It is well known that an individual's sensitivity to certain kinds

---

[3] Cf. Hovland *et al.*, 1957, for a series of experiments on primacy effects on attitude change. These authors attribute the effects in part to learning processes (such as proactive inhibition) as well as to perceptual processes.

of perceptual cues varies with *temporary psychological states*. Sanford (1936) demonstrated long ago that subjects who had been deprived of food tended to "see" ambiguous stimuli as resembling food or food-associated objects far more frequently than when they were not hungry. In similar ways, it has been shown that various kinds of temporary motivational or emotional states affect the perceiver's selection of cues presented by other persons. For example, as part of an experiment by Feshbach and Singer (1957), sixty male undergraduates were shown a film of a young man who performed various tasks as they watched. Twenty were members of a nonshock control group; the remainder received eight painful electrical shocks, presented in the guise of distracting stimuli, while they watched the film. The subjects were then given a questionnaire regarding the personality characteristics of the young man shown in the film. It was found that the subjects who had received the electrical shocks inferred that he would be generally fearful and anxious in a variety of situations not depicted in the film. Members of the control group made these judgments significantly less often. Subjects who had been shocked also judged the filmed person to be a generally aggressive individual significantly more often than did members of the control group. Thus the emotional states of the individuals who received shocks while watching the film led them to attribute similar emotional states to the person being judged.

2. The perceiver's selection of cues is often influenced by his own well-established *attitudes*, as well as by temporary psychological states. Individuals who, for example, have strong political opinions are apt to be alert for any signs on the part of others that provide a basis for attributing political attitudes to them. The experiment by Levine and Murphy (Research Illustration 3.4, page 76) showed that both pro- and anti-Communist groups learned more items of information in the passages congenial to their preexisting attitudes than in the opposed passages. It therefore seems reasonable to assume that if they acquired more information of a certain kind, they also noticed more of it in the first place, and that they would be similarly selective of spoken cues. Several studies have also shown that individuals who have prejudices against a certain ethnic group reveal more perceptual sensitivity to real or supposed characteristics of members of that group than do nonprejudiced individuals: they indicate, in the phrasing of Bruner and Tagiuri (1954), "a heightened or vigilant awareness of cues to ethnic origin." Another example appears in Research Illustration 6.1, which shows how persons who differ in authoritarianism (which represents a broadly inclusive pattern of attitudes) perceive the same individuals in quite different terms, corresponding directly to the differences between the two sets of perceivers.

3. Most people have preconceptions to the effect that certain *per-*

Research Illustration 6.1

An experiment by Wilkins and deCharms (1962) shows how the perceiver's selection of cues presented by other persons may be influenced by his own well-established social attitudes. Eighty undergraduate college men heard one of four tape-recorded interviews that had been carefully prepared to represent four possible combinations of internal and external power cues. External power cues are defined as those that describe the individual in terms of the positions he holds and the material objects he possesses. Internal power cues are defined as those that describe the individual in terms of the individual himself and include the individual's personal mannerisms, traits, and expressed values. An example of an external power cue is the type of house a person lives in; a confident tone of voice would be an example of an internal power cue.

Each subject heard one of the following tape recordings of an interview.

1. *High internal–high external cues.* The person interviewed is highly successful and a member of the upper class. He is also forceful, vigorous, and confident and gives straightforward and direct answers.

2. *High internal–low external cues.* This person has the same forcefulness and decisiveness as the person above, but has not yet "arrived." He is of lower economic and educational background, with few advantages except his own drive.

3. *Low internal–high external cues.* This person is depicted as one who, although at the top of the heap, has gone to seed personally. He is indecisive and lacks aggressiveness, confidence, and conviction.

4. *Low internal–low external cues.* This person is a member of the lower class who lacks confidence and determination. There is some uneasiness and faltering in his speech, and he shows little interest in improving his lot.

A person with a confident, deep voice played the role of the stimulus person being interviewed in both tapes that involved the high internal power cue. For the two tapes involving the low internal power cue, the stimulus person had a high, weak voice and responded hesitantly.

In order to tap an important set of attitudes, each subject responded to a form of the California F-scale, measuring authoritarianism. As described in Research Illustration 5.1 (page 122), responses to this scale are influenced by the subject's concerns about authority, strength, and power—especially as these are associated with "the right" social groups, ethnic groups, and social classes in particular. High-authoritarians prefer a well-ordered world in which "the strong" and "the right" go together.

The purpose of the experiment was to determine whether such attitudes were related to the subject's perceptions of the stimulus person heard on the tape recording. To elicit their impressions of him, subjects were asked a number of questions about this stimulus person. It was found that high-authoritarian subjects used almost twice as many *external* cues in making descriptive statements about the stimulus person as did low-authoritarians. Similarly, those high in authoritarianism used significantly fewer *internal* cues in making their descriptive statements than did those low in authoritarianism. Although both high- and low-authoritarians showed greater acceptance for stimulus persons presenting high external power cues, this preference was more marked in the case of high-authoritarians, as shown in the table that partially summarizes the findings.

Percentage of comments used in description

	By authoritarian subjects	By nonauthoritarian subjects	Probability of chance difference
"External" comments	37.4 (N = 46)	17.1 (N = 34)	.0005
"Internal" comments	52.9 (N = 46)	78.2 (N = 34)	.0005

In general, these findings suggest that persons high in authoritarianism differ from nonauthoritarians not so much in their acceptance of others as in their bases for acceptance. The former tended to select cues to social class as the keystone for acceptance or rejection, whereas the latter used as bases for judgment cues that were more likely to be internal or psychological in nature. In a sense, those with highly authoritarian attitudes do not as often find it necessary to go "into" the persons whom they are judging.

sonal characteristics belong together. We tend to organize into categories not only objects and persons, as noted in Chapter 2, but also traits of persons. Such habits of clustering traits may be widely shared among a population of peers or compatriots, or may be individually unique. In any case, the effects of such clustering are that once the perceiver has noted a certain characteristic on the part of another person he is apt to attribute all or most of the other traits in the cluster to him. Some characteristics, however, seem to be central to the stereotype; that is, the cluster-as-a-whole may be aroused if one observes that a person has certain central traits that serve as keys to open up the whole box of traits. Intelligence is such a central trait for some individuals, as perceivers; ethnicity may also serve in this way—especially for individuals who have prejudices against certain ethnic groups.

Another characteristic that has been shown to be important for many people in this way is personal "warmth," as illustrated in an experiment by Asch (1946). He read to each of two groups of students a list of characteristics, all describing the same person. One list contained the following characteristics: intelligent, skillful, industrious, warm, determined, practical, and cautious. The other list was identical except that the word "warm" was replaced by the word "cold." The students were asked to write sketches of the individual described, and then to use a check list to describe the impressions they had formed. The "warm" and "cold" groups formed quite different impressions. Thus the "warm" group perceived the imaginary person as wise, humorous, popular, and imaginative, whereas the "cold" group formed impressions that were quite different. Asch concluded that a change in one quality produced a basic change in the entire impression. This is consistent with the Gestalt views of perception, which stress the organized nature of impressions and the fact that the entire configuration plays a part in determining how the various parts are perceived.

4. Many kinds of relatively *persistent personality characteristics* on the part of the perceiver have been shown to affect his selection among cues presented by other persons. One study (Bossom and Maslow, 1957) made use of an interesting but complex test for measuring "security–insecurity." This test, called the Maslow S-1 test, measured feelings of being liked versus feelings of rejection, feelings of belonging versus feelings of isolation, perceiving the world as friendly versus hostile, and having social interests versus egocentric interests. Each subject was given a list of 75 items that tapped these areas; he answered "Yes," "No," or "Don't know" to such statements as "Do you often have a feeling of resentment against the world?" Scores on this test were used to select 22 very secure and 22 very insecure college students from a large student group. These students then inspected 200 photographs and were asked to indicate, in each case, whether the person was "very warm," "warm," "cold," or "very cold." The secure group made a significantly greater number of "warm" judgments than did the insecure group. It appears that secure individuals more frequently perceive other persons as warm and supportive as opposed to cold and potentially hostile. These relationships are often circular: thus security, in this sense, may follow the perception of warm, supportive persons during the early years of a person's life history, and, once developed, such perceptual habits contribute to his sense of security. Such a sequence of events illustrates the "self-fulfilling prophecy" discussed on pages 265 ff.

THE ORGANIZATION OF PERCEPTUAL INPUT FROM OTHER PERSONS. We have not attempted to be complete in listing ways in which the perceiver's selection of cues is affected both by his own characteristics and by circumstances outside himself—including, of course, the object of perception. Our point is simply that, as in other psychological phenomena, there is an interplay between intra- and extrapersonal sources of influence. This interplay, as we shall now see, affects not only one's selection of cues but also one's organization of what is perceived.

We have repeatedly noted, beginning with Chapter 2, that the nature of perception is such that P does not attribute to O discrete, separate properties that have nothing to do with one another. What the perceiver first observes is an object identifiable as a person, and only afterward a person to whom certain properties are attributable. Just as we think of a person as being an organized entity, so we think of his properties—which are the perceiver's ways of representing that person— as an organized entity. It is O's properties, inferred from the cues that he presents and that P notices, that P seeks to organize into patterns.

The principles that account for the ways in which P organizes the properties that he attributes to O are essentially those that we noted in connection with the organization of an individual's cognitions and attitudes (Chapters 2 and 5, respectively). It is not surprising that the same principles should apply to all these problems, since the properties that P attributes to O correspond to cognitions, and those same properties are also objects of P's attitudes—that is, our over-all attitudes toward a person are based on our evaluations of the properties we attribute to him.

The most inclusive of these principles is very similar to object-belongingness (cf. pages 121 ff.). We have just noted that many common properties of persons seem to the perceiver to belong together, and are thus psychologically clustered; these tend to be observed, inferred, or attributed by the perceiver together—as a package, so to speak. Heider's principle of causality, as described in Chapter 2, has a good deal to do with the belonging-togetherness of associated traits. That is, if a whole set of O's characteristics is thought of as being caused by a single, *central* trait (intelligence, perhaps, or warmth, or self-centeredness) then once P has attributed that trait to O he tends also to attribute the remainder of the set to O also.

Another basis for perceived trait consistency is similarity in rewardingness to P of the properties that he attributes to O. If he has already attributed to O one or more properties that he finds rewarding —say inherently pleasant personal traits, or agreement with himself about some issue of importance—then he is likely to attribute other favorable characteristics to him also. This tendency to generalize either favorably or unfavorably about a person has long been known as "the halo effect." Research Illustration 2.2 (page 29) points to the evaluative basis for this tendency. With specific reference to perceived agreement as one source of rewardingness, we have discussed in Chapter 5 such phenomena as instances of balanced or imbalanced systems of attitudes.

An interesting problem arises in connection with the principles of consistency: What happens when O's behavior suggests to P that O has *in*consistent properties? There are several possibilities open to P in such cases, including the possibility that P will remain puzzled, or that he will attribute to O the property of being inexplicably inconsistent. Heider's principle of causality suggests another alternative: P might conclude that O was not really responsible for the particular behavior that suggests inconsistency with O's other properties. P may conclude that O was forced into a situation where the inconsistent behavior occurred, or that he did not realize what he was doing; or P might even conclude that he was mistaken in thinking that the behavior had ever occurred. What probably happens more commonly is that P simply fails to notice those behaviors on O's part that would seem inconsistent if they were noticed. Apparently it is as possible to be vigilantly unaware as to be vigilantly aware (in Bruner and Tagiuri's phrase) of cues presented by another person. By these processes or by others, P tends to obtain or to maintain a total perception of O that is characterized by a set of consistent properties.

* * *

P's psychological processes, as he perceives O, include the attribution to him of psychological states that parallel his own: he views O as also having motives, attitudes, and other dispositional properties; as being also a perceiver, especially of objects of interest to both of them and of P himself; and as regarding P, just as P regards O, as having all these characteristics. Because of this parallelism, the possibility of perceiving both similarities and differences between himself and O arises.

In perceiving O, P must not only select among the cues, especially the behavioral ones, that O presents; he must also so organize them that O becomes a locus of psychological constancies, rather than just the source of a random assortment of perceptual cues. P's manner of achieving such an organization is influenced by his own characteristics—including his habits of viewing certain personal traits as belonging together, and his own need to perceive O as consistently rewarding or consistently nonrewarding—as well as by O's objectively presented cues together with the context in which they appear.

ACCURACY IN INTERPERSONAL PERCEPTION

The perceptual processes we have been describing may result in perceptions of any degree of accuracy or inaccuracy. In everyday life one must, of course, assess people and respond to them as one perceives them, but one hopes that one's perception is reasonably accurate—for who would want to respond to things that are not really there? Common sense suggests that some people are better judges than others, and that some kinds of persons are more accurately judged than others. These are useful assumptions to begin with, but they are only partially supported by the empirical evidence. As we examine some of this evidence we shall note some of the difficulties that must be confronted in testing the assumptions.

Recognizing Others' Emotional States

Most people take it as a matter of course that they can judge the emotions of others with reasonable accuracy. The cues presented by individuals who are experiencing emotion, particularly strong emotion, seem obvious enough, and it is clear that if one is interacting with such a person it is to one's advantage to judge those cues accurately. There is a good deal of experimental evidence concerning the recognition of emotional states, but it provides only limited support for common assumptions as to everyday accuracy. Many of the experiments in this area are too limited in scope to provide complete answers to questions about accurate judgment. For example, many experiments simply present photographs or drawings of facial expressions of persons who are being subjected to various emotion-inducing conditions, without permitting the judge to see the total stimulating situation. In everyday life one rarely encounters a motionless face with no situational cues. Thus such experiments, although they have been useful in pointing to the importance of situational cues, provide very little basis for any conclusions about how well people can judge others' emotional states in everyday situations.

Despite the fact that we can make most accurate inferences about emotional states when we see the situation producing the emotion, there are certain conditions under which judges can observe a still photograph and infer the accompanying emotional state with some accuracy. Woodworth (1938) analyzed judges' responses to posed photographs and found it possible to construct a usable judgmental scale. He combined those emotions that were usually confused with each other and placed them in the same category on the scale. For example, judges could not distinguish between love, happiness, and mirth, and so these three were combined to form one category. Six categories remained after these combining operations were completed, and they formed the following scale: (1) love, happiness, and mirth, (2) surprise, (3) fear and suffering, (4) anger and determination, (5) disgust, (6) contempt. Woodworth found that the judges seldom made a mistake of more than one step on this six-point scale, and concluded that the inferences were strikingly accurate. It thus appears that when we are talking about *posed* photographs, we can achieve appreciable accuracy *if* we do not require judges to distinguish between emotional expressions that are often confused with one another.

Part of the success here must be attributed to the fact that posed photographs permit the judges to utilize stereotypes that our culture has evolved for portraying these emotional states. Movies and novels lean heavily on these agreed-upon versions of what a person looks like when he experiences this or that emotion. A posed photograph may faithfully reflect these stereotypes, and often provides more familiar cues for making a correct judgment than does an unposed photograph of a person actually experiencing a given emotional state. Landis (1924), who photographed persons while they were subjected to actual emotion-producing stimuli, found that there were no consistent expressions that were always associated with these genuine emotional states. Lacking the stereotyped expressions found in posed photographs, accurate judgments could not be made. On the other hand, it has been found that even blind children's emotional states, as expressed by laughing or crying, can be rather accurately judged by others (cf. Fulcher, 1942).

Where the judge has complete information about the situation in which the person finds himself, it could be argued that he makes this judgment solely on the basis of this situational context, and that we are no longer dealing with interpersonal perception. In some cases this may be true. Yet we find that where the *situation* is fully known, cues derived from the *behavior* of the individual may still be necessary in inferring emotional states. This can be illustrated by imagining a situation involving two college students who are exposed to identical stimuli. Both find themselves in the dean's office and both are told that their work is not satisfactory. On the basis of cues derived from the persons themselves, we might correctly infer that one student expressed penitence whereas the other expressed belligerence. There are situations, then, for which there is no universal emotional response, and in such situations we are forced to rely on the person for cues that reveal his emotional state. Even here, however, knowledge of the stimulus situation (reprimand in the dean's office) is an aid in interpreting the cues obtained from each of the individuals. Had the behaviors seen in the dean's office been observed in an entirely different situation, they might have been judged as representing something quite far removed from either belligerence or penitence.

Information about O's psychological states is not directly accessible to P, who therefore cannot judge their contribution to O's emotional expression, except by inference. But knowledge of the emotion-inducing situation is often accessible, at least potentially, to both of them. Thus the more information available to P through situational cues, as well as through cues presented in O's behavior, the more accurate his judgments of O's emotions are likely to be.

Judging Others' Attitudes

Properties of other persons are thus perceived not in a vacuum but in a context that may include any part of the objective or conceptual environment of common interest to them. The properties of O that most interest P, with respect to their common environment, are O's information and his attitudes (presumably based on his information) about common interests. Being relatively persistent, a person's attitudes are dispositional properties, in Heider's sense, and thus represent constancies that in dependable ways will affect his relationship with others. In terms of balanced and imbalanced systems of attitudes, P needs particularly to know which of O's attitudes are like or unlike his own, or congruent with them. For such reasons O's attitudes are among the most important of his properties to be perceived.

One's judgments of another's attitudes are often made on the basis of rather indirect evidence. Adults, in particular, do not always express their attitudes fully and directly, and even if they attempt to do so some ambiguity is likely to remain. Hence P is liable to many sources of error as he attributes attitudes to O, regardless of how complete the information on which he must rely. Lack of opportunity to get information about another's attitudes is the most obvious source of error, but it is not very instructive to know that one cannot be accurate without information. Given the motivation to do so, one can often find opportunities to become informed; and, conversely, it is possible to make very inaccurate judgments even with plenty of opportunity to become informed. The interesting sources of error have to do with how one uses opportunities for obtaining information, and how one uses information that one has, and we shall limit ourselves to problems of this kind.

Another common source of error is the perceiver's tendency to categorize certain kinds of attitudes as belonging together. If, for example, P has just heard a stranger express an attitude toward organized labor that P regards as conservative, then he may attribute other conservative attitudes toward him—toward taxation, perhaps, or toward the Republican party. In somewhat similar fashion, whole categories of attitudes are sometimes attributed to another person in stereotyped manner on the basis of obvious and often superficial cues. On observing that a person is male or female, young or old, or that he belongs to a certain ethnic or religious category, for example, it is tempting to infer that he has the attitudes that are typical of such persons—or are believed to be typical of them. Errors of these kinds are not universal or inevitable, but are most likely to occur under these conditions: when P's information about O is limited; when P's own attitudes—either toward the objects of O's presumed attitudes or toward groups of which O is supposed to be a member—are strong; and when P's assumptions of what attitudes tend to go together, or tend to go with membership in a certain category, are wrong or inapplicable.

One of the most pervasive sources of error is P's favorable or unfavorable attitude (his attraction or aversion) toward O. The more attractive O is to P, the more likely it is that P will attribute other favorable properties to him; attraction often invites judgments that are distorted toward agreement with oneself, for example—although there is no requirement that one accept the invitation. It is also true, on the other hand, that under conditions of freedom to associate with others as one chooses, one tends to associate most frequently with persons toward whom one is most attracted; as a result of spending more time with the more attractive persons, one has fuller information as a basis for accurate judgments of their attitudes. Each of these two kinds of effects is shown in Research Illustration 6.2.

Individuals are not all alike in their tendencies to distort others' attitudes because of personal attraction to them, and authoritarianism has been shown to be related to the tendency. Several investigators have found, as reported by Christie and Cook (1958), that nonauthoritarians estimate others' responses to the F-scale rather accurately,

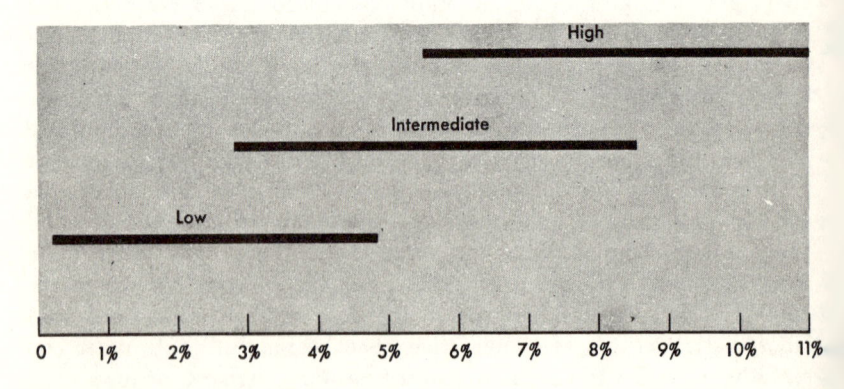

FIGURE 6.1. Range of individual contributions to the total volume of overestimating agreement with four best-liked associates, on the part of lowest five, intermediate seven, and highest five men in authoritarianism. The individual whose overestimation is lowest contributes 0.3% of the total, and the one whose overestimation is highest contributes 10.8%. None of the low authoritarians contributes more than 4.8%, and none of the high authoritarians less than 5.4%. (Adapted from Newcomb, 1961)

Research Illustration 6.2

In an attempt to study how strangers learn about each other and develop attitudes toward each other as they get acquainted (Newcomb, 1961), seventeen prospective students (sophomores and juniors who were about to transfer to the University of Michigan from other institutions) were invited to live in a campus house that had been reserved for purposes of the research. These men came from seventeen different cities in the United States, and had never known or even heard of each other before their arrival. One year later another set of seventeen men, selected in the same way, lived in the same house. During each of sixteen weeks the men answered many questions about their own and made estimates of each other's attitudes. Thus each man's accuracy could be assessed by comparing his estimates of other men with those men's actual responses.

Among other kinds of attitudes investigated during the second year was a set of six inclusive values, originally proposed by Spranger (1928) as representing many of man's most important concerns; he labeled them theoretical, economic, esthetic, social, political (referring to concern with power and influence, and not necessarily to "politics"), and religious. Each man ranked the six values in terms of their importance to him, both early and late during the semester, and at the same time estimated how each of the other men would rank them. The correlation between each man's estimate of any other man and the latter's actual response was taken as the index of the estimator's accuracy. There were in all 272 indices of accuracy (each of seventeen men estimated sixteen others). The average accuracy of all estimates increased between the third and fifteenth weeks, as would be expected, since the men had had far more opportunities to obtain information about each other at the latter time. But this general increase in accuracy was not shown in every one of the 272 estimates. In particular, there was little or no improvement in the men's estimates of their two most preferred associates—those whom they ranked first or second. The percentages of estimates at three levels of accuracy are presented in the table.

	Third week		Fifteenth week	
Accuracy level	Ranks 1–2	Ranks 3–16	Ranks 1–2	Ranks 3–16
High (0.60 or greater)	47%	21%	53%	39%
Intermediate (0.14 to 0.58)	18	41	35	35
Low (less than 0.14)	35	38	12	26
TOTAL	100%	100%	100%	100%

The important thing about this table is that at the earlier but not at the later time best-liked associates were estimated with significantly greater accuracy than were less preferred ones. The probability

> that these differences would occur by chance is less than 0.005 at the earlier time, but about 0.25 at the later time.
>
> One further fact shows why it was that, in spite of plentiful opportunity to improve their estimates of preferred associates, these men did not, on the average, do so: the errors in estimating highly attractive associates were almost entirely in the direction of *over*estimating agreement with them. (There was also a general tendency to overestimate agreement with all other men, but the frequency of doing so was significantly higher for the first two choices, for whom 86 percent of all errors were in this direction, as compared with 65 percent for less preferred associates.)
>
> In sum, all estimates tended to increase in accuracy, regardless of attraction, with increased acquaintance, but increasing acquaintance with preferred associates did not lead to superior accuracy in judging them because high attraction was accompanied by tendencies to overestimate agreement. The distorting effect of strong attraction reduced what could otherwise have been high accuracy.

whereas authoritarians do not, largely because they too often assume that others are like themselves (cf. Research Illustration 6.4, for example). A similar finding applies to the estimates described in Research Illustration 6.2. It was the authoritarians, and not the nonauthoritarians, who overestimated agreement of their preferred associates, relative to those nonpreferred. As shown in Figure 6.1, there is no overlap at all in the contribution of the highest five and the lowest five men in authoritarianism to the total volume of overestimation of agreement with attractive associates. The grounds for expecting this general finding that nonauthoritarians tend to be relatively good judges of others' attitudes lies in one of the basic meanings of the concept: authoritarians, as Adorno *et al.* have shown, find it hard to tolerate ambiguity, and the recognition of important attitudinal differences between oneself and attractive others appears to be a special case of ambiguity, or inconsistency. Authoritarians, as we have noted, tend to prefer a neat, well-ordered social world, and a person who is rewarding in some ways but not in others (as in having attitudes discrepant from one's own) does not fit the needed pattern of orderliness; hence the distortion in judging his attitudes.

Degrees of Skill in Judging Others

INDIVIDUAL DIFFERENCES IN GENERAL LEVEL OF SKILL. Most of us feel, intuitively, that some people excel in judging others, but intuition is no substitute for systematic evidence. Before asking what it is that makes some people superior judges of others (which would be begging the question), we must therefore confront the prior issue: Is there convincing evidence of individual differences in this respect?

Informal evidence, based on everyday observation, provides some basis for an affirmative answer. It is quite certain that experience, together with the learning that usually goes with it, is a necessary precondition for making accurate judgments of others. Infants and small children are not, in general, very discriminating observers, especially of older people—though they soon learn to interpret cues that are indicators of rewards and punishments to themselves. Adolescents are more skillful than small children, but they appear to be more adept at sizing up their contemporaries and their parents—with whom they have had most experience—than in assessing other categories of people. Dentists learn to be highly sensitive to signs of discomfort on the part of their patients, but otherwise they presumably have neither more nor less interpersonal sensitivity than other people. Such informal evidence suggests that there are individual differences in the accurate assessment of others that result from different opportunities for learning and, in particular, from learning in situations providing opportunities for strong rewards and punishments.

This kind of evidence indicates little more than that the wider the range of experience one has had with other people, the more likely it is that one can make accurate judgments of a wide range of persons in differing circumstances. But it does not tell us whether some individuals profit more than others from comparable experience; experience is necessary, but it is not necessarily sufficient. If there are certain personal characteristics that enable some persons to make particularly good use of their experience, and to extend what they learn from it to a wide range of situations, then we would expect to find that some individuals are good judges and others poor judges *in general,* and not just under particular sets of circumstances.

An ingenious study by Cline and Richards (Research Illustration 6.3) provides evidence directly relevant to this problem. Analysis of their data revealed both a general and a specific factor as contributing to accuracy. This two-factor analysis is particularly impressive in view of the fact that generally similar conclusions were reached by another set of experimenters (Bronfenbrenner, Harding, and Gallway, 1958), using quite different procedures.

Thus the answer to the question about general levels of skill in assessing other persons is not a simple one. At least two factors are involved—and probably more than two, as suggested by such findings as that some judges are more accurate in assessing men than women, whereas other judges are just the opposite; that some people are good judges only of others who resemble themselves; and that some people are relatively accurate only when they are judging others whom they like (cf. Bronfenbrenner *et al.,* 1958). Thus—as in the case of other abilities, such as intelligence, for example—there are both general and

Research Illustration 6.3

Cline and Richards (1960) used fifty college students as judges of adults shown in a motion picture in color and sound, who were being interviewed in a large city; these adults had been selected from a larger panel as being diverse in several ways. After seeing the movie each judge filled out several rating sheets with which he had previously been made familiar. Then a second filmed interview was shown, this procedure being continued until ratings had been made of ten persons.

The accuracy of the judges was assessed by comparing their final ratings with actual information about the persons shown in the films. These persons had previously responded to nine paper-and-pencil "tests" of intelligence, vocational interests, and various personality characteristics; information about them was also obtained through interviews with some of their close friends. Individual subjects tended to be consistent in making their judgments, as shown, first, by the fact that individuals who judged the first five films most accurately were also relatively accurate in judging the other five films; the reliability coefficients for five different "judging instruments" ranged from 0.66 to 0.79. Second, the intercorrelations of accuracy scores according to each of these five instruments, as shown below, are quite high:

	1	2	3	4	5
1. Trait rating	—				
2. Behavior postdiction	.30	—			
3. Sentence completion	.48	.47	—		
4. Opinion prediction	.52	.50	.47	—	
5. Adjective check	.65	.24	.58	.54	—
ALL JUDGING INSTRUMENTS	.63	.44	.63	.65	.66

From such evidence the investigators concluded that they had found evidence for a general, global ability to judge others accurately.

The authors were not content, however, to leave the problem at this point. Further analysis revealed two quite different bases, unrelated to each other, for the different levels of accuracy shown by the judges. They found, first, that individual judges rather consistently showed a characteristic level of "stereotype accuracy"; that is, each judge manifested a certain level of skill in judging people in general, or certain classes or categories of people. Their second factor, "differential accuracy," has to do with the judge's ability to judge a particular person, quite apart from skill stemming from general knowledgeability about people or stereotype accuracy. They found some of their judges to be high in one of these skills and, some in the other, but only those high in both factors showed consistently high accuracy.

special factors that contribute to accuracy in judging others. Some individuals can be found who combine all or most of the factors that make for accuracy, but we probably lose more than we gain by thinking of skill in assessing other people as a single, undifferentiated capacity. The more we know about what goes into a complex skill, the better we understand it.

CHARACTERISTICS OF GENERALLY SKILLFUL JUDGES. We have been at some pains to note that any particular instance of interpersonal perception, accurate or inaccurate, is influenced by situational factors, as well as by the person perceived. But the problem of individual skill has to do with the perceiver's own contributions, quite apart from situational variations. We shall mention a few categories of individual characteristics that are associated with generally skillful perception of others. These categories may be regarded as special applications of the general formulation that skill increases with interpersonal experience, the capacity to make use of it, and the motivation to make use of it.

Intelligence, which not only increases with experience (during most of the first two decades of life, as ordinarily measured) but which also governs the ability to make use of experience, should obviously have something to do with skill in judging persons. The available evidence is consistent with this expectation, although the correlations are not always high. Two kinds of capacity that are correlated with intelligence and that are relevant to social perception are the abilities to *draw inferences* about people from observations of their behavior and to account for observations in terms of general principles, or *concepts*.

A study by Gollin (1958) reports steady increases in both abilities, on the average, between the ages of about ten and sixteen. He arranged to have more than 700 boys and girls in elementary and secondary public schools observe a silent movie of a boy doing a number of things. Two scenes of this movie were designed to depict "good" and two others "bad" behavior. The children were asked to watch the movie closely, and were told that afterward they would be asked to write their opinions about the boy and what they thought of him. Their written responses were typed on separate sheets and submitted to judges, who credited each subject with an *inference* if he had attempted to go beyond the mere reporting of actions shown in the movie. A subject was credited, similarly, with the use of a *concept* if he had attempted to explain the diversity of the behavior shown by the boy in the movie—that is, if he had tried to account for both the good and the bad behavior by introducing conceptual notions. Figure 6.2 shows a steady increase in the percentages of subjects whose written statements included inferences, and similar increases (not shown in the figure) appeared for the use of concepts. At all ages girls, on the average, slightly exceeded boys in the

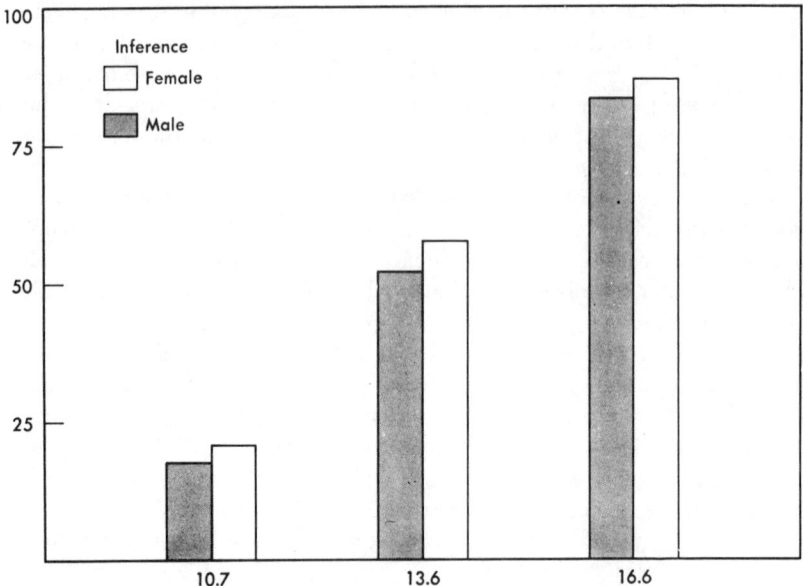

FIGURE 6.2. Percentage of Ss whose written judgments contain inference statements at three average age levels

use of inferences. Although this study presents no information about the accuracy of perception, we would surely expect greater skill on the part of older children.

A characteristic somewhat related to inference drawing and the use of concepts has been suggested by Allport (1961) as probably related to skill in interpersonal perception—*cognitive complexity*.

> As a rule, people cannot comprehend others who are more complex and subtle than they. The single-track mind has little feeling for the conflicts of a versatile mind. People who prefer simplicity of design and have no taste for the complex in their esthetic judgments are not as good judges as those with a more complex cognitive style and tastes (p. 508).

Ideally, studies like that of Gollin, which show developmental differences with increasing maturity, should be supplemented by studies showing that differences in the same capacity on the part of individuals of the same age are associated with skill in judging others. It is likely, although inadequately demonstrated, that various kinds of intellectual capacities, whether measured in terms of mental age or of IQ, are associated with such skills.

We have previously noted that persons low in authoritarianism tend to be good judges of others, in some respects at least (page 172); and that they make relatively frequent use of "internal" cues in arriving at their judgments (Research Illustration 6.1). These findings point to a component of nonauthoritarianism not mentioned heretofore, known as *intraceptiveness,* which is in many ways the opposite of projectiveness. That is, highly intraceptive persons are "open" to information from others, and thus make themselves accessible to the observation and interpretation of cues that others present. Projective individuals, low in intraceptiveness, are just the opposite in this respect: they read their own feelings into others who are considered to belong with them (in "the right" groups), and attribute the opposite of their own feelings to others about whom they have prejudiced stereotypes. In either case, authoritarians show the absence of sensitivity to what another individual is really like; instead of "taking in" the properties of the other person, the nonintraceptive person has a set of ready-made properties that he "gives out" to them. The study reported in Research Illustration 6.4, which in some ways resembles the one in Research Illustration 6.1, reveals one aspect of this general tendency.

As Allport (1961) observes, intraceptiveness presupposes a certain degree of detachment, so that one is free to observe what the other person presents: "Poor judges," he notes, "are often overly social, excessively affiliative, dependent, or nurturant. We all know the warmhearted soul who feels so much sympathy, pity, love, admiration for others that he (or she) cannot take an impartial view of their failings" (p. 509). The notion of authoritarianism, which developed out of studies of racial prejudice, is in many ways opposed to concepts like detachment and objectivity, which assume an attitude of openness to what is presented from the outside, as opposed to ready-made judgments coming from the inside, so to speak. Intraceptive persons are motivated to understand what people are like in somewhat the same way that ornithologists enjoy bird watching: they have learned to find it inherently satisfying.

It would not be surprising to find that good judges of other people have a good deal of *self-insight,* and the available evidence suggests that this is so (cf. Norman, 1953). Commonly used indicators of self-insight are a high degree of similarity between self-reports and others' reports about oneself, and awareness and nondefensiveness about one's own shortcomings. It is not necessarily true that those who are "open" to the characteristics of others are similarly open to their responses to oneself, and able to interpret the latter as reflections of oneself, but it is probably more often true than not. Objectivity and nondefensiveness contribute to both kinds of accuracy.

INDIVIDUAL HISTORY OF SOCIAL EXPERIENCE. There is abundant evidence that, other things equal, one can judge persons with whom one has a common background of experience more accurately than other persons. Members of the same age and sex categories, or of the same national, religious, or ethnic groups have an advantage in judging one

Research Illustration 6.4

Scodel and Mussen (1953) obtained responses from 54 college students to a modified version of the F-scale of authoritarianism. Each person who scored high on authoritarianism was paired with another student of the same sex who scored low on this scale. Arrangements were then made whereby members of each pair talked informally for twenty minutes about radio, television, or the movies; this gave pair members an opportunity to form impressions of each other. The purpose of the experiment was not revealed to the subjects until it had been completed.

After these casual conversations each student was taken to a separate room and was again asked to fill out this questionnaire as he thought his partner would answer it. As shown in the table below, the high authoritarians were much less accurate than were the low authoritarians. The former tended to project their own attitudes onto others, and they judged that their partners, who were all low in authoritarianism, would answer in an authoritarian manner. But the low authoritarians correctly perceived their partners as authoritarians and also more correctly estimated other personality characteristics.

	Highly accurate judgments	Moderately accurate judgments	Highly inaccurate judgments
High authoritarians ($N = 27$)	0	1	26
Low authoritarians ($N = 27$)	9	13	5

The study thus shows not only that nonauthoritarians made relatively accurate judgments concerning others, but also that individuals who were prone to *assume* that others had attitudes similar to theirs were especially likely to make inaccurate judgments of others.

---

another. This advantage may stem from sharing the same sets of norms —especially cognitive norms (as described in Chapter 8) that govern the meanings to be attached to gestures and speech mannerisms, as well as to other forms of interpersonal response. For example, an American who first-names almost anyone as soon as he meets him will probably be more fully understood by another American who recognizes him as a compatriot and who has similar habits than by, say, an Englishman to whom such habits are strange. Or the advantage may result simply from familiarity, without sharing, as in the case of an anthropologist who can interpret the behavior of the members of an obscure tribe because he has studied them and not because he accepts their norms for himself. The skill that comes from familiarity with a certain group represents not just stereotyped accuracy; familiarity also facilitates differential accuracy, because the more one knows about any set of phenomena the more sensitive one becomes to small differences within that set.

Sex differences in sensitivity to other persons present an interesting case in point. In American society, at least, both men and women appear to understand the behavior of other persons of their own sex better than that of the other sex. In all societies men and women are assigned somewhat different roles, with which are associated distinctive sets of skills, attitudes, and interests that are characteristically considered masculine or feminine. Hence persons of the same sex within the same society have a basis, in common experiences of being treated as males or as females, for judging members of their own sex with relative accuracy.

It is often alleged in our society that women are more perceptive or "intuitive" than men in making judgments of other persons. With a few exceptions, most studies do find a slight superiority for women. Such superiority as actually exists may well stem from the fact that personal relationships occupy such a central place in the lives of women. Men are preoccupied with vocational pursuits that often deal with materials, objects, mechanical matters, or abstract ideas. The woman's world is more exclusively one of people, and her role in society dictates that even a young woman must be highly sensitive to the wishes and expectations of others. Inconsiderateness and sloppiness in a young man may be excused on the grounds that "boys will be boys," but we do not dismiss this kind of behavior so lightly in girls. The same kind of double standard exists later in life and the young woman finds that she must be especially vigilant about the kinds of persons with whom she associates. It appears, then, that women are often highly motivated to make accurate judgments of others and usually have more experience along these lines. Under these conditions, it would be surprising if many women in our society did not develop habits of more accurate interpersonal perception than most men.

There are many different aspects of persons to be observed and judged. Of the many conditions that hamper or facilitate accurate judgments, some inhere in the person being judged, some in the observer himself, and some in the situation that includes one or the other or both of them. In view of these many factors that affect accuracy, it is scarcely to be expected that any person would be equally skillful at all times in judging all persons. Neither, on the other hand, is it to be expected that there will be no individual differences at all in general sensitivity to others, since some persons combine many of the factors that tend to make for accurate judging, and are able to apply their abilities in a wide variety of situations. Accuracy in the perception of others represents a complex set of skills that have been learned.

RECIPROCAL PERCEPTION BY INTERACTING PERSONS

The Mutual Field

We now return to the theme with which we opened our discussion of psychological processes in interpersonal perception: The perception of anything involves transactional processes between the perceiver and the object of his perception. This theme is of particular importance when the object of perception is another person, not only because O's perceptual processes are in fact the same[4] as P's but also because P assumes this to be the case. Asch (1952) has referred to this set of phenomena by the phrase, "the mutually shared field," which refers to the overlapping cognitive contents of two interacting persons. As schematically pictured in Figure 6.3, in which P and O are viewed as simultaneous perceivers, each of them includes in his field of awareness himself, the other person, and such aspects of their common environment as are involved in their interaction. Asch puts it this way:

> The paramount fact about social interaction is that the participants stand on common ground, that they turn *toward* one another, that their acts interpenetrate and therefore regulate each other. . . . In full interaction each participant refers his action to the other and the other's action to himself. When two people, A and B, work jointly or converse, each includes in his view, simultaneously and in their relation, the following facts: (1) A perceives the surroundings, which include B and himself; (2) A perceives that B is also oriented to the surroundings, and that B includes himself and A in the surroundings; (3) A acts toward B and notes that B is responding to his action; (4) A notes that B in responding to him sets up the expectation that A will grasp the response as an action of B directed toward A. The same ordering must exist in B. It should be noted that the field of each participant is highly objectified. The other person is not simply part of my psychological field, any more than I see myself simply as part of his field. Instead, each perceives the facts as shared by both. A conversation can proceed only when (a) the same (or a similar) context is present in the participants, *and* (b) when the context possesses for each the property of being also the context for the other. . . . It is individuals with this particular capacity to turn toward one another who in concrete action validate and consolidate in each a *mutually shared field,* one that includes both the surroundings and one another's psychological properties as the objective sphere of action (pp. 161, 162, 163; italics in original).

---

[4] Two qualifications are necessary. It is the nature of the process, not their content, that is the same for P and O; and certain classes of individuals, either as P or as O, are in some degree incapable of carrying out these processes.

INTERPERSONAL PERCEPTION - 183

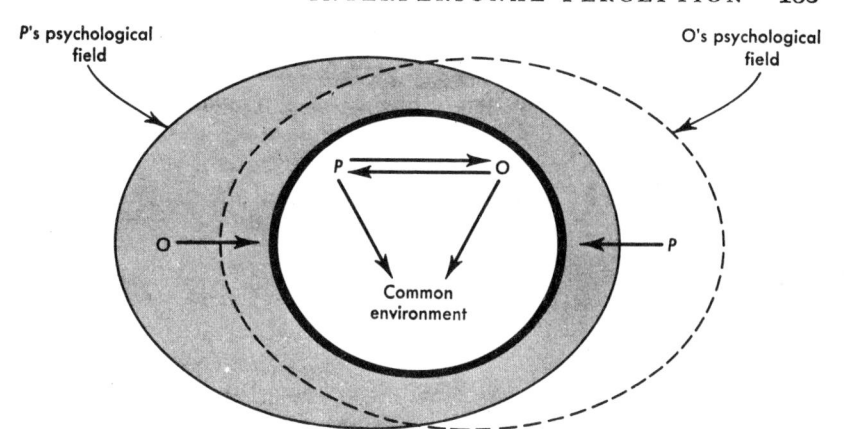

FIGURE 6.3. Schematic diagram of both *P*'s and *O*'s cognitions, including their mutually shared field, represented by the solid white ellipse. Arrows point from sources to objects of cognitions. Each one's field includes the other person as cognizer, as well as the mutual field shared by both.

Although it may be useful to obtain information from the perceiver only—*as if* there were no interdependence between him and the perceived person—one must never forget that in fact interpersonal perception in interaction situations involves at least some degree of sharing of a mutual field. If one bears this notion in mind, one is constantly reminded of the perceptual interdependence between two or more interacting persons. *P*'s view of an *O* with whom he interacts is affected, as we have noted in our discussions of balance theory, by his views of *O*'s views about *P* and about matters of common interest—which is to say that *P*'s perceptions are affected by his own involvement in the field that he shares with *O*.

Reciprocal Perception: A Gateway to the Study of Human Interaction

If we take seriously the fact that each of a pair of interacting persons is simultaneously a source of information to the other and a recipient of information from him as they perceive each other, then we face a series of other problems concerning human interaction. Each of these subsequent problems constitutes the topic of one or more of the remaining chapters of this book.

1. To say that a person is an object of perception is equivalent to saying that he is a source of information about himself. But *O* is in fact a source of information to *P* about many things other than himself; if,

for example, he is a skilled jeweler he can inform P about watch repairing, or if he has traveled widely he can tell P about places that he has visited and P has not. Such transference of information is known as communication, regardless of its content. Following a communication, say about zebras, each person (the sender and the receiver of the message) perceives the other as possessing the items of information included in the message. The study of communicative exchange is thus, in a sense, an extension of this chapter on interpersonal perception.

2. When each of two or more persons who have a favorable attitude toward some rule of behavior perceives each of the others as sharing his own attitude toward the rule (most commonly following communication about it), those persons are subscribing to a group norm. Groups and societies could not persist in stable and efficient ways if certain norms were not widely accepted by their members. Thus the processes of norm formation, involving both reciprocal perception and communication, are of central importance in social psychology.

3. Insofar as group members have accepted norms concerning the individual contributions that each of them is expected to make to group activities, the group is characterized by differing but intermeshing roles. Such a "division of labor" will not be effective, however, unless each of them perceives the other as having accepted the total system of roles—that is, each interacting person must perceive that both he, himself, and the others with whom he interacts have similar expectations concerning the behavior of each of them. The development and the smooth performance of differentiated role assignments thus depend on reciprocal perception as well as on communication and norm formation.

4. When each member of a group perceives the others as sharing some common interest of importance to all of them, and knows that he is being perceived in the same way, they have an essential ingredient for group solidarity—or cohesiveness, as we shall later term it. And if, as is likely to be the case in some degree at least, each of them not only likes, trusts, and respects the others but also perceives them as liking, trusting, and respecting him, then the group is probably a very cohesive one indeed. This and several other characteristics of groups presuppose certain kinds of reciprocal perception, of communicative processes, of norm formation, and of role expectations.

* * *

In such ways as these, interpersonal perception, especially when we view it as reciprocal on the part of interacting persons, constitutes an important gateway to other processes of human interaction, which in turn help us to understand many of the characteristics of groups.

CHAPTER 7

Communicative Behavior

As we have considered various aspects of interaction among human beings we have often made the assumption that individuals have effects upon one another *as if* there were direct contact between the psychological processes of different persons. The attitudes of each member of an interaction group are in one way or another affected by the attitudes of other members, but the process by which they do so is not direct and immediate, nor is it magical; it involves a mediating mechanism called communication. The phenomena of communication are not uniquely human; they can be readily observed in animals, for example. They are also essential to the functioning of all organized systems, including the physiological coordination of organ and tissues in living organisms, and the electronic coordination of computers. It is human beings, however, and especially their coordination in interaction groups, that interest us.

Following the introduction of a few terms that we shall need, we shall be considering the problems suggested by the schematic diagram in Figure 7.1: how do psychological states on the part of one individual give rise to a communication from him, and what do the psychological states of another person have to do with the way in which he receives the communication? Later on in the chapter we shall consider some effects of communication, both on individuals and on groups.

FIGURE 7.1. Schematic diagram of communication as mediating between the psychological states of two individuals

THE NATURE OF MESSAGES

Communication refers to the transmission of messages from one place to another. All messages have some things in common, although they differ in many ways. The principal thing that they all have in common is that the receiver's attention is called to something—as illustrated by such simple messages as "I'm hungry," or "It's five o'clock," or the still simpler one of just pointing at something. (Whether or not the receiver's attention is called to exactly the same thing that the transmitter intended is a special problem to which we shall refer later.) Whatever it is that the message calls to the receiver's notice is called the *referent* of the message. Most messages not only point at something, literally or figuratively: they also contain some kind of assertion about the referent. In general, such assertions may be considered to refer to some *property* of the referent. For example, the question "What time is it?" can usefully be translated into the assertion, "I need to know what time it is"; thus translated, the referent is the speaker, and the property of the referent is his need to know the time. The receiver's attention is called not just to the transmitter-in-general, as referent, but also to his special property of needing to know the time.

Another characteristic of messages is that they are *symbolic*. That is, the message includes something that represents, or stands for, something else. In the message "I am hungry," the transmitter does not place his own stomach pangs into the body of the receiver, but he does place into the receiver's awareness symbols that stand for the transmitter's hunger. In formal terms, the transmitter *encodes* into symbols (words, most commonly) some aspect of his own psychological state; these symbols are called to the attention of the receiver, who then *decodes* them in such manner that whatever they stand for are represented in *his* psychological state. This does not occur successfully, of course, unless there is a close correspondence between the symbol-systems of transmitter and receiver. (Shared symbol-systems, in the language of Chapter 8, are cognitive norms, or rules about what symbols stand for what.) These processes are illustrated in Figure 7.2, which is an elaborated version of Figure 7.1.

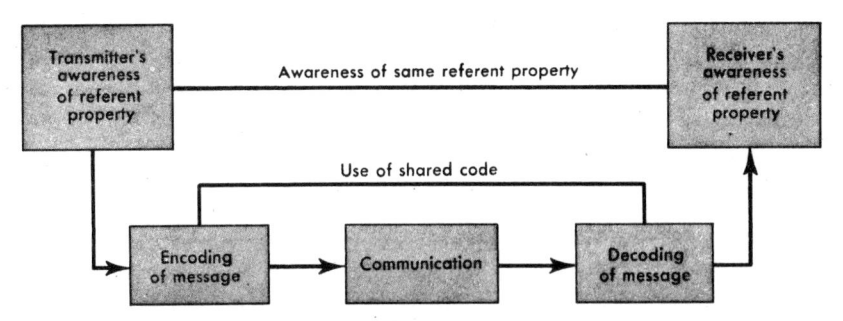

FIGURE 7.2. Elaborated schematic diagram of processes involved in communication between two individuals

Information and Uncertainty

Students of the formal theory of communication (whether of mice, men, or machines) distinguish among different messages in terms of the *information* that they contain. The meaning of this term is indicated in the following excerpt from a treatise on the subject:

> The technical meaning of "information" is not radically different from the everyday meaning; it is merely more precise. Information is something which we gain by reading or listening, or by directly observing the world about us. A statement or an observation is informative if it tells us something that we did not already know. If I hear someone say, "Eskimos live in the far North, where it is cold," my modest store of information about Eskimos is not increased. The statement may, however, give me some information about the person who makes it, or about the person to whom it is addressed. In any case, we can gain information only about matters in which we are to some degree ignorant, or uncertain: indeed, information may be defined as that which removes or reduces uncertainty (Attneave, 1959, p. 1).

Uncertainty, as used by information theorists, refers to the number of possible alternatives that a message might contain—either the possible referents or, once the referent has been determined, its possible properties. "Reducing uncertainty" is thus equivalent to "reducing the number of possible alternatives." The greater the number of alternatives that have been eliminated by a message, the greater the amount of information it contains. If, for example, you are guessing one of the ten numbers from 1 to 10 and have received the message that the correct number is divisible by 5, you have eliminated all but two alternatives (5 and 10); whereas if you have been told only that it is divisible by 2, you still have five remaining possibilities (2, 4, 6, 8, 10); the former message therefore contains more information.

Many messages, like the quoted one about Eskimos, contain no information (or, to be redundant, no new information), in this sense, about their apparent referents. It is probably true, nevertheless, that very few messages are totally devoid of information. If someone sends you exactly the same message, repeatedly and in quick succession (for example, "I mustn't forget my four o'clock appointment"), he is not reducing your uncertainty about the ostensible referent (the transmitter, whose salient property is his need to remember his appointment), but you are gaining other information about him—his state of anxiety, for example. A good analogy is the phonograph needle stuck in the same groove: the information you gain from the repetition of the same message is that the needle is stuck. You are still getting information, but the referent has changed.

Even a simple message may contain more than one possible referent. If a child tells you, for example, that the moon is made of green cheese, the moon (whose property is asserted to be green-cheesedness) is one possible referent, but a more likely one is the child himself (whose property is taken to be naïveté, or gullibility). This illustration suggests a useful criterion of what constitutes a referent in any message: anything about which uncertainty can be reduced by a message is a possible referent in that message; and anything about which the receiver's uncertainty is in fact reduced in a given message has served as a referent for him.

One particularly important kind of referent is a person who is viewed as a repository of specified information. Suppose you have just sent this message to a friend: "Okay, then, I'll meet you under the arch at noon." The special significance of this kind of message is that the transmitter is confirming a message he has received, as if to say, "I got your message, as proved by the fact that I am repeating it." In such cases an important referent is the message sender, whose relevant property is his possession of the information just received from his friend. Information about this kind of referent is known as *secondary* (cf. Miller, 1951)—that is, information about who possesses primary information, which refers to some referent in a direct, primary sense. The uncertainty that is reduced by such confirming messages concerns a person's possession of specified information, as well as the nature of that information.

Messages, in sum, convey information about one or more referents. Since the number of referents to which the receiver's attention might be called is very large, and since there are usually many properties of the selected referent that could be highlighted in the message, it is useful to think of information in terms of reducing uncertainty about referents and their properties.

The Place of Communication in Human Interaction

Interaction is of interest to us, ultimately, insofar as interacting persons have effects on each other. If we ask, What are the possible mechanisms by which effects can be mediated? the answers fall into two general classes: by transfer, from one person to another, either of *energy* or of *information*. (Both may occur together, of course, but they are conceptually distinct.) With this distinction in mind, try to think of an instance of human interaction, especially on the part of adults, that does *not* include message sending—that is, where only energy is transferred between persons. You will probably not be able to think of any such instance unless one of the persons is unconscious. If, for example, a physician is intravenously feeding an anesthetized patient he is transferring a source of energy into the patient's body but not any information that he make can use of, psychologically. If, however, the patient is aware that the doctor is feeding him intravenously, then he is receiving information ("They must think I'm pretty sick") as well as energy.

The reasons why human interaction so rarely excludes message sending lie in the facts of individual learning. That is, individuals learn that certain events serve as cues, or signs, revealing or portending some state of affairs of interest to them. Just as thunder and lightning are signs pointing to the possibility of a storm, so words, gestures, and acts on the part of other persons are signposts conveying information about their attitudes or their probable behavior. In particular (to use Heider's phrase, 1958), we learn to attribute "intentionality" to other people on the basis of the cues they provide; that is, their behavior, as well as their words, contains messages, inferred from cues, about their motives and attitudes as referents, whether or not they intend to send such messages. In sum, almost any instance of human behavior that is observable to another person carries information to him, provided only that he has learned to look for it in others' behavior, and has learned how to find it.

Not every instance of receiving information from another person can be regarded as message receiving, however. If you observe a redhaired girl on the beach who does not observe you, your information about her has been received directly through processes of perception, not through message sending; no message has been encoded, transmitted, or received. But if she waves or speaks to you in ways that you can understand, then you have received information from her not just through perception (as if you were observing the statue of the Venus of Milo) but through communication. The important differences between getting information from a person through perception and through message receiving are that the latter but not the former necessarily presupposes behavior (some form of message sending) on the part of the observed person;

and that information arrives through the use of symbols denoting the referent or its properties, rather than through direct sensory input.

The necessity of communicating indirectly, through symbols, may make it seem surprising that messages are so often sent and received with a good deal of accuracy. It is the development of codes within groups of which communicators have been members that makes such accuracy possible. Interacting persons learn together; with continuing interaction they learn that certain codes are shared; in Chapter 8 we shall refer to them as cognitive norms that embody contexts for the referents in messages. Such norms create a "common semantics," that is, similar meanings on the part of message senders and receivers, as applied to words, gestures, and other symbols. In terms of formal communication theory, sender and receiver share the same code for their respective tasks of encoding and decoding messages. Persons who share a common code can send messages with some confidence that they will be accurately decoded, and can receive them with assurance that they have been accurately encoded.

Encoding and decoding complex messages are necessarily carried out in terms of whatever cognitive structures the communicators have already developed. If we find two people paying attention to the same features or threads in a conversation—particularly if it is one that involves complexities, ambiguities, or subtleties—we can be pretty sure that they are drawing upon similar cognitive structures. If so, we would predict that the transfer of meaning from either of them to the other would occur more quickly, completely, and accurately than if their cognitive structures were dissimilar. This is the hypothesis that was pursued by Runkel in the investigation reported in Research Illustration 7.1, in which he studied the transfer of meaning from college instructors to their students.

* * *

Thus, for all practical purposes, the processes of human interaction are communicative processes. This is not to deny that persons affect each other by the transfer of energy as well as of information, but only to assert that the kinds of interpersonal effects in which we are interested, as social psychologists, are mediated by communication.

PSYCHOLOGICAL PROCESSES IN MESSAGE SENDING

A "Rational" Basis for the Occurrence of Communication

Our present task is to understand the conditions under which a particular person transmits a particular message to a particular receiver. We shall later ask a similar question about the receiver: Just what hap-

Research Illustration 7.1

Runkel (1956), in a study that examined the transmission of meaning from college instructors to their students, began by reasoning as follows. If students are to get good grades they must learn what kinds of statements about the subject matter the teacher prefers. For example, they must be able to pick out fairly accurately the statements on a multiple-choice test that the teacher himself would mark "right." The student need not *agree* with the statements that the instructor favors: he need only be able to select or recognize such statements. Presumably the instructor judges statements according to certain characteristics or "dimensions," and so also does the student. Thus Runkel's hypothesis was that meaning will get more quickly or more fully from teacher to student if the two are paying attention to the same characteristics or dimensions of the statements than when they are paying attention to different dimensions—regardless of whether teacher and student agree on which statements are best.

Runkel uses the following analogy. Suppose there is a room full of people, distributed as shown in the accompanying figure. Some are young females (YF), some are older females (OF), some young males (YM), and some older males (OM). If you were to walk into this room looking for someone of your own age with whom to talk, you would pay attention primarily to the eastern and western halves of the room because the older people are mostly in the eastern half and the younger ones in the western half. That is, you would pay attention to the "east-west dimension." If, on the other hand, your chief interest was to find someone of the opposite sex, you would pay attention primarily to the northern and southern halves of the room—the "north-south dimension."

Suppose you were in one corner of the room with a friend who

North

YF	YF	YF	YF	OF	OF	OF	OF
YF	YF	OF	YF	OF	OF	YF	OF
YF	YM	OM	YF	OF	OM	YM	OF
YF	YF	YF	YF	OF	OF	OF	OF
YM	YM	YM	YM	OM	OM	OM	OM
YM	YM	OM	YM	OM	OM	YM	OM
YM	YF	OF	YM	OM	OF	YF	OM
YM	YM	YM	YM	OM	OM	OM	OM

West ——— East

South

A field of young and old males and females

said, "I think I'll look for some more interesting people." In order to predict the direction in which he would stroll away, you would have to know the *dimension* by which he judged interestingness. But, in order to be helpful to him, you might suggest one or two persons with whom he would like to converse. If you took it for granted that he would move in the same direction you would move, and if you were right in this assumption, then he would find your suggestions good ones. If your assumption was wrong—if your cognitive structure about the interestingness of people in the room was different from his—then he would not profit much from your suggestions.

You and your friend would not need to prefer the same kind of conversationalists to comprehend each other's preferences. If you were twenty years old and he were fifty, you might suggest that he strike up a conversation with some of the people in the eastern half of the room; even though you might prefer, yourself, to talk with young people, you might readily accept the idea that he would prefer to talk with older people. But you would both be using the east-west dimension as a basis for understanding the preferences of the other person.

In planning his experiment, Runkel constructed statements about the realm of psychology which could be thought of as scattered over a field like that shown in the figure (but probably having more than two dimensions). From the preferences expressed by students and instructors among five statements, it was possible (through the use of a geometric model; cf. Coombs, 1964) to estimate whether a teacher and his student were judging the statements about psychology on the same dimensions or whether they were using different dimensions. An index of cognitive similarity or dissimilarity was thus available, according to which approximately half of the students more similar to the instructor could be distinguished from the relatively dissimilar half.

Runkel's prediction, derived from the initial hypothesis, was that the cognitively similar students would obtain higher grades on quizzes written and graded by their instructors than would be cognitively dissimilar students. The actual results, computed for all subjects who were stable in their opinions throughout the semester, were in agreement with the predictions; they are summarized in the accompanying table. Because the grading was different in level and in range from class to class, the quiz scores were converted into "standard" scores within each class. That is, they were transmuted into "z-scores," according to which the standard deviation of grade scores is the unit, the mean score is zero, and all below-average scores have a negative value; z-scores are comparable from one class to another. The mean of these scores, on the part of all "stable" students in the seven classes, was significantly higher for students with cognitive structures similar to those of their instructors than for students with dissimilar structures; the probability is less than .05 that the obtained difference could have resulted from sheer chance.

The scores for the two sets of students were as follows:

Quiz grades, transmuted into z-scores	Student-instructor relationship in cognitive structure about psychology	
	Similar ($N = 17$)	Dissimilar ($N = 19$)
Highest score	2.77	1.74
Mean score	0.60	−0.25
Lowest score	−1.16	−2.56

pens on his part, and what determines the content of the message as he receives it? These two kinds of questions need to be asked and answered in terms of the same framework, not two different ones. We shall therefore begin by presenting an initial basis, though not a complete one, for understanding the occurrence of communication.

In terms of sheerly rational considerations, we can assume that one would not need to transmit a particular message to someone who, as he believes, already possesses the information in that message. Nor would one need to ask another for information that one already possesses. These assumptions are not meant as a complete explanation, without exceptions, of the conditions under which messages are selected for transmission; they represent only a beginning. As such, these assumptions can be condensed into a briefer and a more general one: one sends a message to another person when, as a means to some form of motive satisfaction, it is useful that he and the message sender have the same information. More specifically, one sends a message when one's purposes are furthered by passing along to another person some information that one has, or by obtaining information from him—through a direct assertion in the former case, and by means of a question or a request in the latter. In either case the transmitter acts as if it were useful to him that he and the receiver should have more nearly the same information after the message has been received. Even in the case of a question, both asker and receiver will possess the information that the asker needs to have a specified item of information, whereas before the question only the asker had the former information; if the question is followed by an appropriate answer, then both have the information that only the answerer had before.

In more formal terms, the usual consequence of a communicative exchange (that is, information has been both transmitted and received) is a change in the distribution of information such that sender and receiver have more nearly equal information with regard to at least one referent of the message. This is not only the generalized consequence of a communicative exchange; it is, whether he knows it or not, a state of affairs that is desired by the transmitter. This is not to say, of course, that when a man asks his wife for lunch he is "really" motivated by the desire to equalize his and her information concerning his state of hunger. It is to say, rather, that the equalizing of relevant information is instrumental to his motive of having lunch; he is more likely to get it if she also has the information that he wants it.

Henceforth we shall be pursuing some implications of this "rational" approach, according to which communication is viewed as a process of equalizing information. As we seek to understand the conditions under which messages are sent and received we shall also be looking for instances where this approach does not seem to fit.

The Message Sender's Motives and Attitudes

Message sending, like other forms of behavior, needs to be understood in terms of motives and attitudes—in this case, on the part of the transmitter toward the intended receiver of the message or toward the referents of the message, or both. First, however, we need to note that one person may transmit information to another without any intent to do so. Such information-yielding behavior may be purely "explosive" (as in such interjections as "Ouch!"), or it may be directly consummatory—that is, providing its own gratifications, rather than being instrumental to later ones. Singing in the shower is a good example; the shower-singing husband may be informing his wife that he will soon be ready for breakfast, but if his singing is only consummatory, representing sheer *joie de vivre*, there has been no intended message sending. He has, unwittingly, provided for his wife a signal pointing to coming events, but the information that she has obtained has not resulted from decoding a message that he had encoded. Such interactional events are common enough and they may be regarded as instances of communication, even though unintended, provided that one necessary condition has been fulfilled: that the transmitter possesses the information his behavior makes available to the receiver, so that they have more nearly equal information than before. In the absence either of intent to send a particular message or of increased equalization of information, we shall regard the transaction not as a communicative one but only as one in which a person's behavior provides cues for another person. Figure 7.3 indicates, in schematic form, the possible combination of intentionality and of equalized information. Henceforth we shall be primarily concerned with intentional message sending, as depicted in the "Yes" column of this figure. Communication of this kind is instrumental, or goal-directed, and the psychology of message sending can best be understood in terms of the transmitter's goal-associated motives.

Why does the message sender want either to provide the receiver

Increased equalization of information?	Message sending intended?	
	Yes	No
Yes	Completed communication	Unintended communication
No	Attempted communication	Cue provided, but no communication

FIGURE 7.3. Possible combinations of intentionality and equalization of information, as related to communication

with information that he himself possesses or to obtain information that the receiver is believed to possess? Such motives may conveniently be classified in terms of the persons involved in communication. (1) *Self-oriented* motives refer to goals of the transmitter himself. Examples: a stamp collector asks a dealer if he will accept a certain offer; a taxi rider tells the driver where he wants to go. Giving or getting information helps the transmitter himself. (2) *Receiver-oriented* motives are perhaps no less commonplace: for example, the local citizen gives careful instructions to a stranger asking directions, or a parent asks his child what story he would like to hear. Getting or giving information is helpful to the receiver. (3) Transmitters' motives may correspond to neither of the above, alone, but rather to both; they are *jointly oriented*. A wife who reads road instructions to her driver-husband is engaged in teamwork, and so is he when he asks her about the next turnoff. Getting or giving information facilitates teamwork. A given instance of message sending may be motivated in any one of these three ways, or by any combination of them. Whatever the nature of the transmitter's motives, as these illustrations suggest, the reduction of information discrepancy between himself and the receiver is instrumental to goal attainment.

As to motives that are primarily self-oriented, the psychological uses of message sending are about as wide-ranging as a complete list of human needs and motives. We send messages, for example, to support or defend our own egos, or to maintain or enhance our own statuses. Messages designed in the interests of such motives do not, in fact, necessarily equalize information between transmitter and receiver. Their intended effect (as noted under "Apparent Exceptions" below) may be merely to influence the receiver to accept the kind of information that the transmitter wants him to have. Even so, however, the receiver, if he accepts the information, *assumes* that he and the transmitter now have similar information—which is a necessary state of affairs if the transmitter's motive is to be achieved. The equalization of information, in short, whether genuine or illusory, is not itself a goal of communicative behavior; it merely represents a necessary relationship between transmitter and receiver (generally not known to them) that is instrumental to motive satisfaction.

All messages, if they are intended, involve a particular content, among many possibilities, and such messages are usually directed to some selected receiver (one or more persons) rather than to the universe at large. Thus the psychology of message sending includes questions like, Why this particular message? Why this particular receiver? The most important thing to remember in answering these questions is that the transmitter's motives with regard to message and receiver are interdependent: the message is tailored to the receiver, or the receiver is selected to suit the message, or both. If one is alone with another person, say in a car or in a living room, then the receiver of one's messages is predetermined, and one selects one's messages as being appropriate to that receiver. If, on the other hand, the message is predetermined by some urgency on the part of the transmitter, then his problem is to find a receiver appropriate for the message. The solution of either problem—What message is appropriate for this receiver? What receiver is appropriate for this message?—involves the transmitter's motives with respect to both message and receiver.

The general principle that guides such a merging of motives in the act of message sending is that of reducing discrepancy of information in ways that are balance promoting or otherwise rewarding. The equalizing of information between transmitter and receiver is not always rewarding. If, for example, you are playing bridge, you do not want your opponents to have as much information about your hand as you yourself have, but you would like to give your partner as much information as is legitimately possible. Since message sending tends to equalize information (that is, to reduce discrepancy of information), the transmitter faces the problem of selecting his message so that information will be equalized only in particular ways that are likely to lead to the satisfaction of his present motives. In sum, a transmitter is likely to send a message about a particular referent to a particular receiver when the equalization of information between himself and the receiver about that referent is instrumental to his motive satisfaction.

APPARENT EXCEPTIONS TO THE GENERAL RULE. Doubtless you have already thought of circumstances under which the preceding generalization does not seem to apply. The apparent exceptions are of three general kinds. First, the rule that messages are so selected that information is equalized in ways that are rewarding does not apply to unintended message sending—merely expressive or explosive communications, for example, or those that are unwittingly transmitted. Principles derived from the theory of motivation can hardly apply to unintended consequences.

In the second place, a transmitter may repeatedly send the same message to the same receiver, even when he presumably knows that it has already been received; one wonders how information that has already been equalized between sender and receiver can be still further equalized between them. Most such repetitions appear to be of the following kinds. Sometimes they are not goal-directed at all, but simply expressive; children, in particular, often repeat the same message to others precisely as they repeat it in talking to themselves, with little or no concern as to whether anyone receives it. Or it often happens, particularly in the absence of feedback from the receiver, that the transmitter is uncertain whether or not his previous message has been received or inaccurately received. Under these conditions he is simply trying again, his subsequent attempts to equalize information being motivated in just the same way as the first attempt. Another kind of reason for repeating a message is more subtle: the repetition is intended to convey additional information, even though the symbols in which the message is encoded are not changed. For example, a child's second or *n*th repetition of the message "I'm hungry" may be intended to convey the new message, "I really mean it; I'm *terribly* hungry." Very often, though not necessarily, such added information is conveyed by changed inflections or emphases, which are symbols, just as words are. Under these conditions the general rule still applies: the very fact that the same message is repeated has the effect of equalizing information concerning a slightly changed referent. For all these reasons it is plausible to assume that the apparent exceptions to the general rule are not actual exceptions.

A third kind of exception involves the motivated sending of false or deceptive messages. Under competitive conditions, for example, or when one wants to avoid blame, one often deliberately sends messages that do not equalize information; they are intended, in fact, to have exactly the opposite effect in order to "throw them off the track." This is not, literally, an exception to the general rule, which merely asserts that when one regards the equalization of information as instrumental to motive satisfaction one is likely to send a message; it does not say that messages will not be sent under any other conditions. But the fact of being motivated to send deceptive messages does suggest an important extension of the rule: a transmitter is also likely to send a message about a particular referent to a particular receiver when he regards it as rewarding to have the receiver *assume* that information between them has been equalized. Thus the inclusive rule is as follows:

One is most likely to send a message when one is strongly motivated toward a goal and strongly hopeful that equalizing information about it (or leading the receiver to believe that it has been equalized) will be instrumental toward goal achievement. As we shall later note in more detail, the receiver's assumptions about the equalization of information may be quite as important to the transmitter as his own assumptions.

MESSAGE SENDING AS RELATED TO THE TRANSMITTER'S ATTITUDES. We noted long ago that motives, which serve to organize immediately present psychological processes, are influenced both by the immediate situation and by previously held attitudes. Message-sending motives are no exception; communication, like other forms of behavior, is an outcome of attitudinal and situational influences. This approach is particularly appropriate because it so frequently happens that both the referents and the receivers who are involved in message sending are objects of already existing attitudes on the part of the transmitter. Most messages are about more or less familiar referents, and are directed to more or less familiar receivers. Thus immediate situations, including receivers and referents, serve to evoke existing attitudes, which inevitably affect message sending. Just how do these effects occur?

These effects rest, in the first place, on a few commonplace facts with respect to the *referents* in messages. (1) One's information about anything affects one's attitudes toward it: if the information that one has about cabbages or kings is such as to endow them primarily with "good" properties, then one's attitudes toward them will tend to be favorable. (2) Each of us is dependent on others for information about the things that concern us, because our own time and range of experience are necessarily limited, because so many things in which we are interested are too remote for direct contact, and so on. And (3) even if we were exceedingly well informed, as of yesterday, about all the things in which we are interested, there is fresh information to be had about them today: new events happen, and things change. Thus, to bring all of these three points together, much of the information upon which our attitudes must be based has to come to us indirectly, by communication, particularly if we are interested in having a realistic base for our attitudes—and who is there who would deny such an interest?

These facts point to various ways in which the transmitter's attitudes affect his message sending. In one kind of message, it is as if the transmitter were saying to himself, "I wonder if the information on which my attitude is based is adequate. Guess I'll find out by seeking confirmation from others." The simplest illustration of such a message is the very young child's question, "Hot?" as he hesitatingly approaches a radiator. Confirmation-seeking messages on the part of an adult usually follow some disconfirming, or uncertainty-arousing experience, such as hearing an attitude different from his own expressed by someone whom he trusts as a source of information about the particular referent.

Another, quite different kind of message sending can be understood in terms of the same set of facts: the attempt to convince another person that the information on which *his* attitudes are based is inadequate (perhaps a more frequent kind of message). Such attitude-justifying messages often begin with phrases like "I disagree with you because . . ." and arguments are apt to be replete with such language. Still other kinds of message, having similar origins, lie between these extremes of reality testing and self-justification; those that are designed to test the accuracy of another's information, or to narrow down precisely the area of disagreement, or perhaps to seek an acceptable compromise. What these kinds of message have in common is, first, that attitudes stem from information (adequate or not), much of which is obtained and needs occasionally to be confirmed, not directly from the referents themselves but indirectly, from other people; and, second, that the discovery of a discrepancy between one's own information, or one's own attitudes, and those of another person tends to instigate the sending of messages that are intended to have the eventual effect either of reducing the discrepancy or of justifying it.

The effects of attitudes on message sending also rest, in the second place, on a set of facts related to the *receivers* of messages: (1) The affective components of the transmitter's attitude (that is, his attraction) toward the receiver influence his message sending. The stronger his attraction the more likely it is that his messages will tend to be helpful rather than harmful, and considerate rather than exploitative. (2) The cognitive components of the transmitter's attitude toward the receiver as a repository of information influence his message sending—particularly these properties of the receiver that are relevant to the referent of the message. Insofar as the receiver is judged to be knowledgeable as a source of information, trustworthy in reporting it, or competent as a source of help with respect to the referent, messages to him about that referent are likely to be rewarding to the transmitter. And (3) the transmitter's judgment of the receiver's attraction toward himself also influences his message sending. Insofar as he attributes to the receiver positive attraction toward himself, his messages will be based on expectations that they will be sympathetically received, will elicit sincere rather than deceptive responses, and that the receiver will not use the transmitter's information to harm him.

These statements of the relationship between attitudes and message sending are, as you may have observed, applications of the principles of balance, as outlined in Chapter 5. They also derive from the notion, developed in the same chapter, that the organization of an individual's attitudes, through mutually supporting, latticelike anchorages, tends to make his attitudes resistant to change. It is for this latter reason that so many messages seem to be defensive of the transmitter's existing attitudes: If one of his attitudes is undermined by a new supply of information, others are also threatened. Insofar as one is guided by considerations of reality testing, however, one's messages will be directed not so much toward proving that one is right as toward testing the accuracy both of one's existing information and of that which has newly arrived through communication. The latter kinds of message, being reality-oriented, are likely to lead to attitude change if the best available information requires it.

THE TRANSMITTER'S PERCEPTION OF THE RECEIVER. The essential condition of motivated message sending, as we have tried to show, is that the equalization of information between himself and a potential receiver is instrumental to a transmitter's motive satisfaction. This condition presupposes his assessment of the receiver's possession of information, both before and after he sends the message. If, as is most commonly the case, he perceives an informational discrepancy, he is likely to try to reduce the discrepancy insofar as it is rewarding to do so. Or, if he regards it as rewarding merely to give the receiver an illusion of equalized information, he may send a false message. In either case, his message will be designed to change the existing degree of similarity between his own and the receiver's information, or to reduce either his own or the receiver's degree of uncertainty about the similarity of their information. The assessment of the receiver's information that is required for such comparisons is only one of at least four ways in which the transmitter's message-sending behavior is influenced by his manner of sizing up the receiver. These assessments are typically made with little or no awareness that one is making them, but nevertheless the ways in which they are made help us to understand the psychology of the transmitter.

(1) As we have just noted, the transmitter assesses the receiver's existing information about the referent that is of interest to himself. Does he have more (or less) information than I, or different information? Message sending is more apt to be instigated by affirmative than by negative answers to these questions.

(2) Information about many kinds of referents has to do with their properties that are considered good or bad, useful or harmful in some way. Objects that are thus evaluated arouse feelings that correspond to the affective aspects of attitudes. Since it is often the desirable or undesirable properties of a referent that interest a transmitter, he is likely to be curious about the affective as well as the cognitive aspects of the receiver's attitudes.

A great deal of message sending thus follows the transmitter's assessment of another person's attitudes as affectively different from his own. Research Illustration 7.2 points to some common conditions under which communication by group members is directed toward one of them whose attitudes are considered wrong. Other investigators have also demonstrated the same tendency. Festinger and Thibaut (1951), for example, report that in one experiment 70 to 90 percent of all communications were addressed to members who held extreme opinions.

(3) The transmitter also needs to assess the receiver's competence with respect to the referent of the message. How knowledgeable is he, and how good is his judgment about the referent? One does not seriously ask for information from the village idiot, and one is not likely to give information to one who is regarded as incompetent to use it wisely or safely—as in telling a child where he will find the razor blades or the poison bottle. Message sending that is designed to equalize information is facilitated by confidence in the competence of the receiver.

(4) Finally, the transmitter almost necessarily makes a judgment as to how the receiver feels about himself. It is hard to think of any message sending that is not in some way influenced by such assessments. One hesitates to give information to someone who is considered likely to use it against oneself, and one does not confidently request information from someone who is regarded as hostile to oneself. Messages are often addressed, of course, to persons so regarded, but their content is greatly influenced by such assessments of the receiver.

* * *

Whether or not a message is intentionally sent, and if so to whom and about what, is determined by the degree to which the transmitter finds it instrumental toward motive satisfaction to increase or decrease the equalization of information between himself and a particular receiver with respect to a particular referent. Such motivations on his part, at the moment of message sending, are influenced both by his preexisting attitudes toward both referent and receiver, and by immediate situational factors concerning perceived relationships between referent and receiver. They are also influenced by his assessments of the receiver, whose information and whose attitudes as he perceives them are compared to his own—both before and, in anticipation, following the message. In such ways the relevant psychological states of the receiver are, so to speak, included—or, more accurately, represented—in the psychological states of the transmitter. Thus the transmitter simultaneously confronts a referent about which he has certain information and attitudes and also a person about whom he has information and attitudes and to whom he attributes information and attitudes concerning himself and

Research Illustration 7.2

Schachter (1951) arranged an experiment to test the hypothesis that under certain conditions communications are most frequently directed toward individuals whose attitudes are regarded as deviant. He organized thirty-two student clubs of five, six, or seven members each; eight clubs discussed the case study of a delinquent boy, eight of them magazine editorials, eight movies, and eight radio programing. Each of the thirty-two groups was composed of members who were fairly homogeneous in attitudes toward one of these activities, plus three paid assistants (assumed by the others to be regular members). One of the three assistants was instructed to take, during the forty-minute discussion period, the role of a *deviate* (that is, to take and hold a position clearly at odds with that of other members), one that of a *slider* (who initially took a deviant position and then moved toward the majority), and one to be a *middle*-man (who kept close to the central position of the true subjects).

The accompanying figure shows that, for all groups under all conditions, conspicuously more communications were indeed directed toward the deviant member, and progressively more so as he continued to be resistant to changing his position. Two additional facts illustrate the same point: fewer and fewer communications were addressed to the slider, as he came to take the majority position; and virtually none at any time were directed to the middle-man.

The experimental conditions in which Schachter was particularly interested were cohesiveness and activity-relevance. Half of the groups, in which students were assigned to clubs in which they had a high level of interest, were considered cohesive, and the other six-

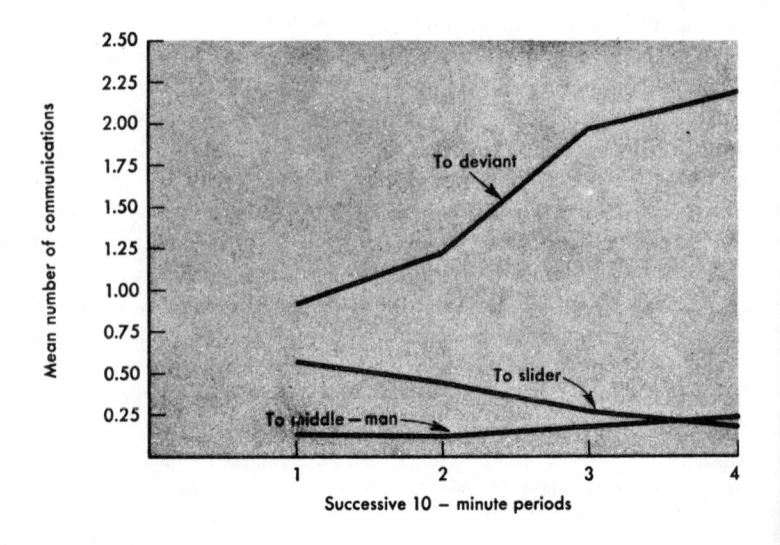

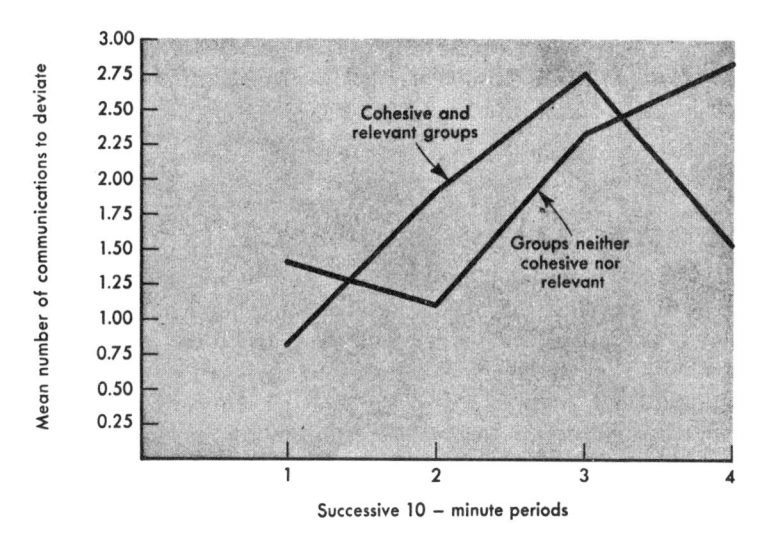

[Figure: Mean number of communications to deviate across 4 successive 10-minute periods, comparing "Cohesive and relevant groups" with "Groups neither cohesive nor relevant". Y-axis ranges from 0.25 to 3.00.]

teen groups were not. Eight of the cohesive and eight of the noncohesive groups engaged in relevant activities, in the sense that clubs did what their members expected to do, while the other sixteen groups did something entirely foreign to members' expectations. Groups that were both cohesive and activity-relevant might be expected to be more involved in the group activity than groups neither cohesive nor activity-relevant. A comparison of these sets of groups, as shown in the second figure, indicates that they did not differ greatly except during the final period, during which members of cohesive, relevant groups dropped their communications to the deviate by nearly one-half, whereas the other groups were still increasing their rate.

Data concerning the subjects' rejection of the deviate as a group member help to explain this last finding. One measure of rejection was derived from members' votes for assignments to club "committees" at the end of each meeting: votes for the "executive committee" indicated trust and confidence, whereas votes for a meaningless "correspondence committee" were equivalent to rejection. By this measure, the highly involved cohesive, relevant groups rejected the deviate whereas the noninvolved groups did not (probability of a chance difference less than .01). The conclusion seems warranted that members of the highly involved groups increasingly directed their communications to the deviate member *until* his incorrigible deviance led them to reject him as a group member, after which communications to him dropped off rapidly.

the referent. Message sending is thus a form of behavior by which the transmitter attempts to minimize conflict and maximize motive satisfaction with regard to himself, another person, and a referent.

PSYCHOLOGICAL PROCESSES IN MESSAGE RECEIVING

The reception of messages is not just a process of passive registration, like wax receiving the imprint of a seal. In his own way the receiver is just as active, psychologically, as the transmitter, and there are many parallels between them. There is a formal similarity in that the receiver's decoding processes reverse the order of the transmitter's steps in encoding; that is, the receiver translates symbols into what they stand for, just as the sender had translated what they stand for into symbols. The psychological activities of each are organized by his own attitudes and motives. Except in the case of messages that are unintended or are not in fact received, transmitter and receiver each exists, psychologically speaking, for the other. Given adequate feedback (return information), both know that a message has been sent and received. Thus there are many psychological similarities between transmitter and receiver—although, as we shall see, there are few identities.

While the transmitter, in the case of a motivated message, is presenting something (a set of symbols) for the receiver's attention, the latter is reacting to what has been presented. In psychological terms, the most prominent form of activity on the transmitter's part is performance—that is, whatever he does to make his message observable and thus receivable; and the correspondingly prominent forms on the part of the receiver are perception and cognition—that is, whatever he does to organize the information that comes his way.

Some of the differences between the psychological activities of transmitter and receiver stem from the distinction between performance and perception. Some of them spring from the fact that the transmitter's and the receiver's communicative activities are fitted into their ongoing behavior in reverse order: message sending, like other forms of performance, is the end result of a series of psychological processes that are organized by existing motivation, whereas message receiving is the beginning of a similar series, sooner or later organized around motivations of the receiver. Each of them must fit his own form of participation in the communicative exchange into his existing stream of psychological activity —after all, messages are neither sent nor received by psychologically empty organisms—but each must do it in his own, distinctive way. As in other forms of perception, the receiver's way begins with his selection of certain features of the information input as salient—that is, as primary referents. His next step is to associate in some way his freshly received information about the selected referent with his previous stock of information about it. We shall now examine both processes.

The Receiver's Selection of Referents

There is always a certain element of surprise for the receiver, in a sense that is not true of the transmitter, who was responsible for the message that he chose to send. Even if the message is a direct response to an immediately preceding inquiry by the present receiver, he was presumably not certain what the response would be; else he would not have made the inquiry. The ways in which he may be surprised are illustrated by such exclamations as these, as if the receiver were making them to himself: "So that is the answer to my question!" or "Oh, I see that he wants to call my attention to so-and-so." And, since surprise invariably arouses questions, he may ask himself such things as these: "Why did he give me that particular answer?" or "Why did he call my attention to that particular thing?" or "Why did he select me as the recipient of the message?" These "Why?" questions imply that the receiver is uncertain about the transmitter's motives, and so he may also ask himself such questions as these: "Why does he want me to believe that?" Or "Is he primarily concerned about his own welfare or mine, or both?" or "Is he telling the truth?" or "Does he really have any basis for what he is telling me?" These illustrative exclamations and questions remind us of the point with which this chapter opened: that the information contained in a message serves to reduce the receiver's uncertainty about something, in the sense that there are fewer alternatives for him to entertain about it after than before receiving the message. Also, as these illustrations suggest, a message may raise many multiple-alternative questions for the receiver, even if the message is a very simple one. There are several questions at several levels for him to be curious about.

One of the first of these questions concerns the primary referent of the message. This question turns out to be in fact a complex one, involving any or all of the following: What is the ostensible referent—that is, the immediately apparent one? What is the primary referent that the transmitter intended? What is the primary referent for the receiver—that is, the referent for which his uncertainty is primarily reduced by the message? The fact that the same receiver may give different answers to these questions illustrates the relative complexity of the receiver's problem, which arises because most messages contain more than one possible referent that he may select as the central or even the only one. Suppose, for example, that an unmarried male student, aged twenty-one, receives this message from the barber who is cutting his hair: "I hear the President is going to call up a lot more students to be drafted next month." It is as if the receiver, in selecting a major referent, asked himself, "What is it that this message tells me most about?" The main things that determine his "answer" (to a question that was never consciously asked) are (1) his degree of uncertainty, or uninformedness, concerning the several possible referents, and (2) his motivation to reduce uncertainty, or to become maximally informed about each of them. These criteria can be combined into a single principle: the greater the receiver's motivation to decrease his informational uncertainty about any possible referent in a message, the more likely he is to select it as a major referent.

This principle may be applied to our student in the barber's chair in the following illustrative ways. If he is much concerned about his own draft status, and not very clear about the President's power or other legal considerations, the referent is likely to become "possible change in draft regulations for students." If he expects to be drafted eventually but hopes to graduate first, the message is likely to be dominated by the referent "possible draft next month." If he is eager to find grounds for criticizing the political party to which the President belongs, he is likely to pounce upon "that autocratic President" as a central referent. If he regards as simply wrong the information that the message was intended to convey, he will feel that all he has learned from it is that the transmitter is an unreliable informant, and thus the barber becomes the important referent. Depending upon circumstances, there are still other possible referents, even in this comparatively simple message, each of which would be pretty well accounted for by the principle of motivation to reduce uncertainty.

A referent is something that a message contains information about, as we noted earlier, and this "information about" is best described in terms of properties assigned to the referent. Merely to know that a message contains information about draft regulations, Presidents, or barbers would not serve to reduce very much uncertainty. It is information about the properties of a referent that determines its selection as a primary referent. In the preceding illustrations, motivation to reduce uncertainty is aroused not by the bare referent, "draft regulations," but by their asserted property of change, or of their applicability to students next month; not merely by reference to the top elected official in Washington, but by his inferred property of being autocratic; not just by the fact that a haircutter is the source of the message, but by his attributed property of being an unreliable informant.

Although the receiver has no control (except partially and indirectly, if the message is a response to a question that he has just asked) over the information that is contained in a message, nevertheless he can make his own selection of primary referents. His selection is influenced not only by the message's actual content but also by his existing state of motivation just before he received the message, and by his preexisting attitude toward both referent and receiver, in ways that we shall note in the following section. Our present point is simply that premessage motives and attitudes selectively lower certain of his thresholds, so that he is predisposed to be more sensitive to information about the properties of some referents than of others. The referent that he is most eager to reduce uncertainty about is the one that he selects as primary.

Research Illustration 7.3 offers an example of how it can happen that the characteristics of a transmitter, rather than the content of the contributions he is trying to provide, become the primary referent on the part of receivers—even though he may in fact have useful or even essential information to give. In this instance it was because of experimental manipulations that the transmitter's property of untrustworthiness eventually became salient, but in everyday circumstances there are many conditions under which receivers take as their referent certain properties of the transmitter—especially those concerning his motives and his competence—rather than the referents that he had intended. "What you are speaks so loudly . . ."

Incorporating Information into Attitude Structures

Whatever the primary referent selected by the receiver, the information that he obtains about it through the message will bear some relationship to whatever information he previously had about it. His previously held information about the referent is already organized, to some degree at least, in terms of interlocking attitudes, as noted in Chapter 5. Thus one of his early responses to the freshly received information is to examine it with this kind of approach: Does it support my existing attitudes, threaten them, or is it irrelevant?

More specifically, the connection between fresh information and preexisting attitudes is as follows. One's information about the properties of a referent corresponds directly to the cognitive elements of one's attitude toward an object, and these are associated with the affective elements of the same attitude. Both cognitive and affective elements of almost any attitude are anchored in attitudes toward other objects or persons or both, after the manner of a latticework. Given this existing organization of anchorages, the receiver's problem is to fit the new information into it. If it fits smoothly, according to the principles of consistency and belongingness, as previously outlined, it is likely to be accepted—that is, incorporated into the existing structure—because it is not balance disrupting. But if the freshly received information threatens to upset the existing balance, then one or more of the balance-restoring mechanisms is brought into play. Suppose, for example, that our student at the barber's considers himself an up-to-the-minute authority on draft regulations, and that his previous information is directly contrary to that received from the barber. For him to incorporate the barber's information into his existing structure, under these conditions, would

Research Illustration 7.3

An experiment by Shaw and Penrod (1962) illustrates how information of potential usefulness in solving a problem may fail to be used because of lack of confidence in the transmitter. Subjects in one part of the experiment were 54 men and 27 women students, divided into 27 three-person groups of the same sex. Each group was given a case history as part of a human relations problem; its purpose was to evaluate five possible solutions to the problem. A rank-ordering of the five alternatives had previously been established by consensus among presumed experts.

Each group discussed three such problems under different conditions, the amount of information available being systematically varied as follows:

Condition 1: all members given only the first paragraph of the case history;

Condition 2: all members also given the second paragraph, containing four additional units of information;

Condition 3: all members also given a third paragraph, including four more units of information than in condition 2.

Qualities of decisions reached after 15 minutes of discussion were rated in terms of the previously determined criterion. As shown in the accompanying figure, there were slight improvements in decision quality with increasing information.

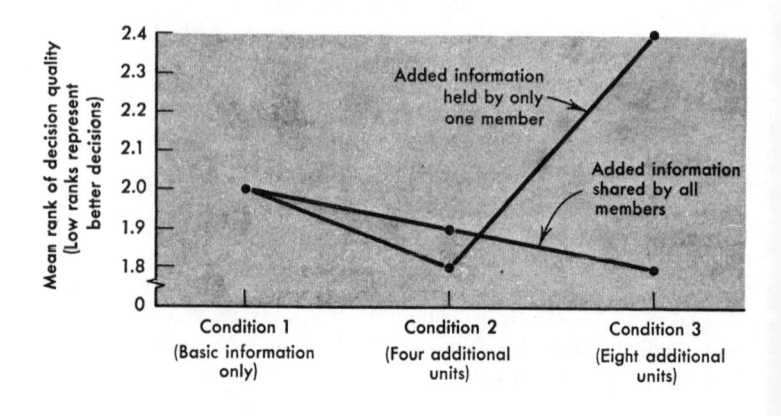

In a second part of the experiment conditions were identical except that in condition 2 only one member in each of 18 similarly arranged groups was given the second four units of information, and in condition 3 only one member was given the additional eight units. No other member of these groups knew that one of them had this additional information, and he was forbidden to inform them of this fact. Under these circumstances, as the figure shows, there was little or no difference between results of the two parts of the experiment in conditions 1 or 2. But in condition 3 the additional eight units of information resulted in relatively poor solutions when members were unaware that one of them had, so to speak, illicit extra information. In condition 3 the difference in decision quality between the two parts of the experiment was a significant one.

Basing their interpretations partly on questionnaire responses (concerning the influence of individual members, for example), the investigators conclude that this last finding was a consequence of lack of confidence in the illicitly informed member. "Moderate amounts of task-related information, even if it cannot readily be validated, may appear plausible and so be accepted and used by the group without any particular feelings about the informed member. On the other hand, when the informed person has much information which he cannot validate it may appear to other members that he is irresponsible. His information is thus seen as dogmatic, self-assertive opinions, rather than reliable, useful information. The group reacts negatively to the informed person and so rejects his contributions."

require a radical reorganization of that structure, but he can retain it intact by the balance-promoting device of disbelieving the barber. Thus the information about draft regulations is rejected rather than incorporated. But in so doing he has gained some information about the message sender, as referent: he has, rightly or wrongly, attributed to the barber the property of being an untrustworthy informant on this subject. One important principle by which the receiver organizes acquired information in messages is that he does so in ways that retain his existing structure of attitudes.

It is not always so easy, however, to adopt this solution. Suppose, for instance, that the same student saw the President himself an hour later, in a televised program from the White House, making a formal announcement of the same policy that he had heard from the barber. Now he must accept the new information if he is to remain within the bounds of what is usually considered normality. He can incorporate it into his existing attitude structure and still save his self-image of infallibility on the subject of draft regulations by reminding himself that, after all, he cannot be expected to keep up with the news moment by moment all day long, and that there was no reason to expect such a drastic revision of the rules. And he can retain a reasonably well-balanced structure of attitudes toward the draft and toward the President by blaming him for everything, since his own negative and the President's positive attitudes toward the new regulation are not imbalancing if his attitude toward the President is unfavorable.

Most commonly, however, the impact of fresh information on existing attitude structures results in the rejection neither of the information nor of the transmitter, but rather in the acceptance of both. There are two fundamental reasons why this is such a common way of processing information. First, no one can depend solely on his own, direct experience with things for information about them; particularly (but not only) in childhood we are dependent on other people as informants. We soon learn that we could not get along in our everyday experience without accepting most of the information that comes from our associates. Most of us acquire the habit, although in varying degrees we are selective in our acceptances. The second reason is that (as previously noted) most of us spend most of our time with people whose information we feel that we can generally trust—either because we have learned to be dependent on those with whom fate has thrown us into frequent association, or because we prefer to associate with those whom we trust. These two considerations—that we have to rely on information from others, and that we selectively associate with others whose information we trust—have this common consequence: provided that the information received from a trusted informant is not inconsistent with the receiver's well-anchored attitudes, it is more balance promoting for him to accept than to reject that information.

Not infrequently, however, information received from a trusted informant does conflict with the receiver's existing attitudes toward the message referent. In that case he may simply tolerate the imbalance; he may reject either information or informant, or both; or he may change his attitude toward the referent—an alternative that is very often adopted, for the reasons indicated in the preceding paragraph. Indeed, this is one of the most basic processes in attitude change. Human beings are constantly gaining experience and learning, in a world that is also constantly changing, and one requirement for adapting these two kinds of changes to each other is the capacity to modify yesterday's information in the light of today's. The consequence is that our attitudes—including both the properties that we cognitively attribute to objects and our affective evaluations of those properties—are continually subject to change as we receive new information. Insofar as the receiver trusts the informant, and insofar as the newly received information does not conflict with his existing attitude structures, attitudes toward message referents tend to change as recent information is incorporated into them.

* * *

The psychological processes of message receivers, like those of transmitters, include representations of the total communicative situation in which both of them are participating. The receiver, like the transmitter, confronts both a referent about which he has information and attitudes and another person (in this case a transmitter) about whom he also has information and attitudes, and to whom he attributes information and attitudes concerning himself and the referent. As primary referents, he selects among those in the message or related to it the ones that he is most eager to reduce uncertainty about, as determined by his existing motives and preexisting attitudes. Depending on how congruent the newly received information is with his existing attitude structures, he may accept it or reject it. Insofar as he accepts it, his existing attitudes toward the referent find additional support or are in some way changed. Insofar as he rejects it, his attitudes toward the referent will not be changed but his attitude toward the receiver will either diminish or, if already unfavorable, remain so.

INTERPERSONAL PROCESSES

We now leave the transmitter and the receiver, each viewed singly, to consider them jointly. Henceforth we shall be interested in communicative processes on the part of interacting persons, each of whom functions alternately as a transmitter and as a receiver. We shall regard them simply as communicators who are, so to speak, interchangeable; together they constitute a communicative system within which information concerning certain referents is exchanged with certain frequencies. We shall be concerned with such questions as these: Under what conditions is communication likely to occur about a given referent or about a wide range of referents, regardless of the identities of the communicators? How do communicating persons keep track of one another's changing store of information, following the exchange of messages?

In considering the phenomena of message sending and receiving, we have so far taken a psychological point of view, and necessarily so, because sending and receiving proceed from individually organized psychological states. Now that we are viewing communication as *inter*personal, however, we shall shift our emphasis to *relationships* among individuals. That is, we shall relate communication within a group to similarities and differences in members' information and attitudes.

The Nature of Feedback

Since both the sending and the receiving of messages are forms of motivated behavior, communicators are pretty sure to be interested in how successfully they are moving toward their goals. Motive satisfaction through communication depends to a considerable extent on *accurate* exchange of information, which corresponds to equalizing it. That is, if the conveying of certain information is instrumental to one's motive satisfaction, one is likely to be frustrated if the message has not been received as intended. By the same token, the receiver is sooner or later apt to find himself frustrated if he discovers that the information he has received is quite different from what the transmitter had intended to convey. Thus it is to the communicator's advantage to be as sure as he can that he is both transmitting and receiving with relative accuracy. The best way of making sure of this is to note various cues presented by fellow communicators following the exchange of messages. Each communicator thus needs secondary information (about the other's information) in order to assess his own success as he participates in the equalizing of primary information, both as transmitter and as receiver.

The information that one gets by noting the effects of one's own behavior is known as *feedback*. A noted authority on this kind of problem, in a book devoted to certain similarities in the regulation of machines and of human behavior, puts it this way:

> For any machine subject to a varied external environment to act effectively it is necessary that information concerning the results of its own action be furnished to it as part of the information on which it must continue to act. For example, if we are running an elevator, it is not enough to open the outside door because the orders we have given should make the elevator be at that door at the time we open it. It is important that the release for opening the door be dependent on the fact that the elevator is actually at the door; otherwise something might have detained it, and the passenger might step into the empty shaft. The control of a machine on the basis of its *actual* performance rather than its *expected* performance is known as feedback. . . . Similarly, when I drive a car, I do not follow out a series of commands dependent simply on a mental image of the road and the task I am doing. If I find the car swerving too much to the right, that causes me to pull it to the left. This depends on the actual performance of the car, and not simply on the road; and it allows me to drive with nearly equal efficiency a light Austin or a heavy truck, without having formed separate habits for the driving of the two. . . . In both the animal and the machine . . . their *performed* action on the outer world, and not merely their *intended* action is reported back to the central regulatory apparatus (Wiener, 1954, pp. 24, 27; italics in original).

In the case of the driver, feedback comes from his own observation of car and road, which are inanimate objects, but the basic principles are the same in the case of another person, O, with whom P is interacting. If, for example, P's interaction with O consists of giving him orders, according to a prearranged schedule he slavishly follows, then O as a source of feedback to P will not differ much from the feel of the car and the sight of the road as a source of feedback; in either case P is getting information about the immediate success of his own efforts, and very little other information. But there are many other kinds of return information that are possible from persons, under ordinary conditions of interaction. These additional kinds of information stem from the fact that P is pretty sure to be interested in getting information about O, viewed as the *locus of psychological activities that are closely related to those of* P *himself.*

These matters are further discussed in Chapter 9; meanwhile we need only to note that one's success in communicating must be judged not merely by whether fellow communicators make overt responses in expected ways, but also in terms of their dispositional properties, in Heider's phrase—their more enduring characteristics that, in the long run, determine overt responses—as these may have been elicited or inferred through the exchange of messages. In particular, P needs to observe cues that serve as feedback concerning similarities and discrepancies between his own and O's cognitions, motives, and attitudes.

In Research Illustration 7.4, one kind of feedback, involving minimal awareness, is described. The experimenter, under conditions of reinforcement, provided feedback to the subject by letting him know, in various ways, that he took the latter's opinions seriously. At other times the subject received no information concerning the experimenter's acceptance of his opinions. The feedback, presumably of rewarding nature, resulted in increased rates of stating opinions. Verplanck, noting that these findings make both psychological and scientific sense, points out that "people like to talk to people who are interested in what they are saying," and it seems likely that most subjects felt this way about the experimenter during the reinforcement period. If so, the feedback provided the subjects with information to the effect that their contributions were interesting to the person with whom they were conversing. In this sense, feedback from O enabled P to attribute psychological characteristics to him—characteristics that were directly related to something P was interested in doing, namely, expressing his own opinions.

Not all the information that P can obtain from O while he interacts with him is feedback in the literal sense. If, for example, he notes that O replies to his question in a deep bass voice, this item of information is not a consequence of P's own behavior. Even though it is information that P has obtained as a result of his own behavior, he has learned nothing about the *consequences of his own behavior* in noting the quality of O's voice. The distinctive thing about feedback is not P's intentions in eliciting it, but simply the fact that the return information provides some kind of basis for evaluating his own contribution to the interaction.

Communication on a Given Topic

Suppose that you knew nothing about a group of a dozen men except that they are present in the same room for a few hours, speak the same language, are free to talk about anything or nothing, and are in complete agreement about referent X. In view of the general proposi-

Research Illustration 7.4

Verplanck (1955), a psychologist who has long been interested in operant conditioning, has reported an experiment in which twenty men and four women, most of them students, served as unwitting subjects. Seventeen students of psychology served as experimenters, each of whom engaged one or more subjects in "ordinary conversations"; most of the subjects were friends or roommates of the experimenters, and they had no idea that they were participating in an experiment. The settings of the experimental conversations were so selected that the experimenter could, in natural and inconspicuous manner, record the necessary observations—for example, by making innocent-appearing doodles during the conversations.

The experiment had to do with the effects of reinforcing responses made by the experimenter in response to the expression of opinions by subjects. Once the conversation had got started, the experimenter took pains to make *no response* to the subject's expressed opinions for the first ten minutes; this made it possible to determine under control conditions each subject's individual "basic level" of stating opinions. During the second ten minutes, the experimenter reinforced every expressed opinion, either by such phrases as "That's so," "Yes, you're right," or by paraphrasing, aloud, the opinion that the subject had just expressed. The final ten minutes constituted an "extinction period"; that is, no reinforcement was given, with the expectation that the effects of the just-previous reinforcement would tend to disappear. (This division of time actually applied to only seventeen of the twenty-four subjects; for the remaining seven, the first and third periods were used for reinforcement and the second for extinction, in order to make sure that the observed effects were consequences of reinforcement and extinction, rather than merely of chronological sequence.)

The findings may be summarized as follows: (1) No subject showed any indication of being aware that he was serving as an experimental subject, though a few of them showed irritation at the experimenter during the extinction period, sometimes accusing him of "lack of interest." (2) The rates of making statements—that is, *any* statements, including opinions—were quite unrelated to reinforcement. (3) Both the group of seventeen and the group of seven made about twice as many statements of opinion during the reinforcement periods as during other periods, this difference being highly significant. The median percentages of opinions (out of all statements) were as follows:

Before reinforcement	32 ($N = 17$)	
During reinforcement	56 ($N = 17$)	57 and 60 ($N = 7$)
During extinction	33 ($N = 17$)	30 ($N = 7$)

Every one of the twenty-four subjects increased his rate of expressing opinions with reinforcement, whether by agreement or by paraphrase on the experimenter's part; and twenty-one of them showed a decreased rate with nonreinforcement. Since these findings are completely in accord with predictions, it may be concluded that under these experimental conditions the expression of opinions was not merely self-determined but was also a response to the experimenter's behavior, which in turn was a response to the subjects' preceding behavior.

tion that communication results from the existence rather than the absence of informational or attitudinal discrepancy, you might conclude that there would not be much communication about X within this group. If the men were aware of their agreement, this conclusion would be justified, but if they were complete strangers to one another, they would have no way of realizing that they were in agreement. One or more of them might, however, be curious about what the others knew or felt about X, in which case we would predict, according to the principle of reducing uncertainty, that someone in the group would initiate communication about it.

We are thus led to another question: under what conditions is communication about a particular referent likely to arise out of sheer uncertainty concerning others' information or attitudes? The general answer to this question, as we noted on page 193, is that the likelihood of sending such a message depends on the instrumental usefulness to the transmitter of equalizing information between himself and a receiver. As applied to the initiation of communication among strangers, this would mean that the greater such instrumental value on the part of one or more group members, and the greater the number of members for whom it has such value (for whatever reasons), the more probable it is that someone in the group will initiate communication about X. These motives toward which communication is instrumental might be as diverse as wanting to find out whether others agree with oneself, to show off one's knowledge, to gain more information, or merely to talk about something rather than remain silent. All of these reflect some degree of interest in or concern about X, and so we can conclude that the greater the number of group members for whom X is an object of importance, and the greater the degree of this importance, the more likely it is (all other things being equal) that communication about X will occur within the group.

This principle would also apply to groups whose members are well acquainted, but in such groups there would be other factors to consider. Suppose that a group of ten good friends, businessmen engaged in various enterprises, are listening to the same newscast, which includes the unexpected announcement that the firm to which some of them belong has been indicted for illegal procedures. They now share this information, since each one knows that all of them have heard the announcement. Although there is no informational discrepancy with regard to the announcement, you would probably expect some communication among them about it. This might be because the men belonging to the indicted firm have a wider store of other information related to the announcement than the other men do, or because some of them might be uncertain about others' attitudes toward the indictment, or both. But now let us broaden the extent of their sharing by considering a group of executives from the indicted firm, all of whom share the same body of relevant information and the same relevant attitudes. Even with all these areas of discrepancy removed, you would still expect communication to be centered around the indictment, because there is some planning to be done. If all of them knew exactly what should be done; if there were complete sharing about these plans; and, in particular, if they knew what the outcome was to be—under these conditions one would not expect much communication on this subject: there would be neither discrepancy nor uncertainty to be removed by communication.

In such ways it is possible to estimate how probable it is that within any group communication about any topic will occur, provided one knows (1) how many members have how much interest in that topic; (2) how much informational discrepancy there is within the group about matters relevant to that topic; (3) how much agreement exists within the group; (4) the degree to which members are aware of their agreement; and (5) the degree to which members are uncertain about future events relevant to the topic. These conditions are based on the principles of the transmitting and receiving behavior of individuals, but they are stated in terms of the total group membership. The relationship between the psychology of transmitting and receiving, on the one hand, and the probability of exchanging messages within a group, on the other, is a very simple one. It depends on only two things: How many group members are there whose interests are such that they are likely to seek motive satisfaction through equalizing information about the particular topic? And, second, How strong will their motivation be, once it is aroused? The more of them whose motivation is likely to be strong, the more probable it is that one or more of them will initiate communication about it, and that one or more others will continue it.

Some Effects of Continuing Communication

Many "natural" groups—families, friendship groups, or work groups, for example—continue over long periods of time, so that their members have repeated opportunities for communicating with one another about matters both old and new. It is to be expected that groups whose members have had long-continued communication with one another would develop certain characteristics that newly formed groups do not have. Such a history of continued communication among the same set of persons is likely to have two kinds of effects on communication content. First, over a period of time messages are likely to include a wider range of referents than in the case of group members less well known to one another. This is predictable partly because of the amount of time they have spent together. With regard to some topics, at least, relative equalization of information becomes established rather early in the life of the group; hence there are likely to be periods of time during which there is little information to be exchanged about such topics, so that conversation turns in other directions.

As group members' association with one another continues over longer periods of time, furthermore, more new and different events occur that are of common interest to them. As the children in a family grow up, for example, there is an increasing range of things that interest the whole family, so that communication about them is required. Or, to give another example, the members of a continuing work group will meet new kinds of obstacles and make contacts with a wider range of persons as time goes on. It also happens very commonly (though with certain exceptions) that what were at first matters of interest only to one or a few group members tend to enter the common domain, as association and communication continue. The principal exceptions have to do with matters considered private, or with situations that are highly formal or bureaucratic, or with interpersonal relationships that continue to be characterized by mistrust or hostility. Particularly in groups whose members are free to leave if they wish, the general tendency is that among those who have continued opportunity for communication the range of communicable topics comes to include most matters that are of interest to any of its members, as well as those that are demanded by group tasks and by the problems presented by a common environment.

A second outcome of long-continued communication is the development of favorite topics: a large proportion of messages continue, over a long period of time, to deal with the same referents. These common themes are of two kinds, particularly: the members themselves, and their common environment. Members of a continuing work group will communicate with one another on the nth day, as on the first day of their association, about their work and also (though perhaps guardedly at first) about themselves. Members of both new and old families communicate about the tasks associated with maintaining their homes and the things they do in them—and about one another. Long-continued association means that certain common concerns that are inherent in living or working together in a common environment become continued topics of communication.

In the following chapter we shall note why it is that still other kinds of effects so often follow long-continuing communication. Not only do frequently associating group members usually develop uniformities with respect to cognitions, attitudes, and overt behavior; they also influence one another to maintain many of these uniformities. Group norms and groups' power over their members are the central themes of that chapter, which in a way is a continuation of this one. Sometimes, as we shall note, such effects of continuing communication are particularly strong and sometimes hardly noticeable at all, and so we shall also point to the particular conditions under which these outcomes typically occur.

The General Rewardingness of Communication

Most of these outcomes of communication depend, directly or indirectly, on the fact that communication tends to be rewarding—especially accurate communication. Such is our dependence on one another from the very beginnings of communicative experience, and such is our indebtedness to culture, which is transmitted by communication, that success in the enterprise of becoming socialized depends on success in transmitting and receiving messages. Most of us enjoy being not only the bearer but also the recipient of news. In spite of important exceptions—especially mistrust or dislike of potential communicators, and situations regarded as competitive—most people, most of the time, find it rewarding both to send and to receive messages. Not only do most people talk more than they really need to; most of us also create opportunities for listening, by associating with others who like to talk, and even by asking questions. One of the interesting and important things about communication is that so often the same message rewards both transmitter and receiver.

Communication is not always rewarding: there are many messages —for example, "I hate you"—the accurate receipt of which is unpleasant, and others—such as the confession of shortcomings—that it may be painful to transmit. But insofar as it is rewarding to either transmitter or receiver, its reward value tends to become attached to the other. Thus, typically though not universally, the bonds of attraction tend to be strengthened in both directions by successful communication; *mutual* attraction tends to increase. Perhaps the most common example of this is the fact that adults generally have strongest attraction toward those children, and children toward those adults, with whom they are in most frequent communication—which is to say, their own children and their own parents (in spite of the circumstance that neither parents nor children choose each other). And so the relationship between frequency of communication and attraction becomes circular: we communicate most frequently (if we can) with those toward whom we are most strongly attracted, and are most strongly attracted toward those with whom we communicate most frequently. As Homans (1950) puts it, "If the frequency of interaction between two or more persons increases, the degree of their liking for one another will increase, and vice versa" (p. 112).

Everyone knows that there are many exceptions to this well-established generalization. Family members, work associates, and roommates often continue to communicate with each other, though perhaps angrily, sullenly, or suspiciously, in spite of strong aversions. It is usually the case that when communication continues in spite of such feelings there are strong constraints on group members to continue their association with each other: they are not free to leave the group. Communication nevertheless continues, either because it is required in the course of daily activities (as in the case of families and work groups) or because it brings some kind of reward to one of the communicators, though probably not to both. An example of unilateral rewards would be any injurious remark or gesture, on the part of one person toward another, that may make the transmitter feel better but certainly does not lead to mutual rewards. One common development within a group whose members are not free to leave it even though some of them have strong negative feelings toward one another is a splitting of the group. That is, the group remains intact, formally, but communication and mutual attraction are to be found mostly within rather than between the divided subgroups. Or, under such conditions of restraint, mutually hostile members may simply restrict their communication to a minimum, both in frequency and in range of referents. If, on the other hand, members are free to leave the group, their departure results in reduced communication with the remaining members. All these modes of adapting to within-group hostility—subgroup formation, restricted communication, or leaving the group—reveal the same general tendency: reduced attraction and reduced communication go together, just as attraction and communication, under other conditions, increase together.

OVERVIEW

Communication is the form of interpersonal exchange through which, figuratively speaking, persons can come into contact with each other's minds. The mechanism of communication includes the encoding, through symbols, of information; the behavioral transmission and the perceptual reception of those symbols; and their decoding. Following the exchange of a message, if the exchange has been sincere and reasonably accurate, transmitter and sender have more nearly the same information about one or more referents of the message than before. Such equalization of information is not the goal of communication; it is only a relationship between the participants, usually not recognized by them, through which the motive satisfaction to which communication is instrumental can be attained.

Communicators test the success of their exchanges through feedback, that is, by noticing each other's behavioral cues that show the effects on the receiver of a previous message, thus helping the transmitter to judge whether it has been received as intended. Just as the cognitions, motives, and attitudes of transmitter and receiver affect their respective performances, so each of them tends to be alert to the other's cues that suggest how his cognitions, motives, and attitudes have been affected by their exchange.

None of us could lead anything but drab and impoverished lives if we were each totally dependent on our own direct contacts with persons, things, and ideas that we need information about. This fact of interdependence has the result that each of us has been repeatedly rewarded by communication. Thus both the giving and the receiving of messages come to be satisfying in their own right. The initial means becomes an end in itself, under many conditions, though communication never loses its instrumental usefulness.

CHAPTER 8

The Formation of Group Norms

THE MEMBERS OF ANY GROUP WHO HAVE HAD A HISTORY OF INTERACTING with one another may be said to constitute an *interaction group,* by way of distinguishing it from other sets of persons whom one wishes, for whatever reason, to consider as a single entity. It is instructive to pose the question, What is it that distinguishes these persons from others who are not members of that group? If this question is taken as a very general one, applying to any and all kinds of interaction groups, probably the most general answer is that members of the same group have something in common, that they are alike in certain ways. If we then ask in what ways they resemble one another, the first answer that is likely to come to mind is that they share some common interest—whether it be maintaining a home, getting a job done, pursuing some sport, worshiping at the same church, or electing a slate of political candidates. And in many instances, though not all, one might go on and answer that they have similar attitudes, or that they behave in similar ways. In any case, there is no more adequate single answer to the general question than that of relative similarity, or uniformity, in some or all of these ways.

If we now go on and ask about the sources of uniformities among members of interaction groups, there is probably no single answer that will suffice. It may be that the members have been selected because of already existing similarities—perhaps by employers, because they are skilled at a certain kind of work; or perhaps they have selected themselves on the basis of existing interests, such as surfboarding, or a particular religious belief. Another common basis for many kinds of similarities is simply exposure to similar influences. Thus brothers and sisters may use similar mannerisms of speech because they have been taught by the same parents, or neighboring shore dwellers have common apprehensions about tidal waves because of similar experiences with them. It is usually the case, in fact, that individuals who have already come to be members of an interaction group are subject to many common influences that intensify or extend whatever similarities may have brought them together in the first place.

A third source of uniformities within interaction groups will be of primary interest in this chapter: the reciprocal influence that group members have on one another as they interact. This kind of influence is often so great, as we shall see, that it seems appropriate to speak of a group's power over its members, as expressed through norms that are developed through interaction. Research Illustration 8.1 describes some effects of this kind of power. Though this experiment happened to deal with young children, the group-norm effects that resulted from their interaction can readily be paralleled in older people. This experiment does not, of course, *explain* these effects very fully; that is the task of the remainder of this chapter.

Even though every interaction group is characterized by uniformities that are in some way relevant to its reasons for existence, the power of the group, as expressed through its norms, is not limited to creating or enforcing uniformities. Its norms may, in fact, prescribe differentiations and dissimilarities, some of which are considered in Chapter 10 as role differentiations. Even so, however, there are underlying similarities in attitudes that support such differentiations. Much of this chapter will therefore deal with uniformities and with group power, and how they are related to each other.

CONSENSUAL AND SHARED ATTITUDES WITHIN GROUPS

The Nature of Consensus and Sharing

Insofar as members of a group hold similar attitudes toward the same object, its members are consensual with respect to that attitude. Most groups within the same society are consensual in many of their

Research Illustration 8.1

Merei (1949) carried out an experiment with children in two Czechoslovakian day nurseries that neatly demonstrates the power of group norms. He began by observing the children's behavior for several hours during a two-week period. His research design made it necessary to identify children who were especially influential with their peers, whom he labeled "leaders." Boys and girls were thus selected as being relatively dominant, aggressive, tending to initiate activities, and tending to be imitated by other children. From the remainder of the population, about 50 children ("who were *not* leaders") were selected as having the following characteristics:

> they followed orders from peers much more often than they gave orders;
> they imitated more frequently than they were imitated;
> they were about average in frequency of participating in group play, in "degree of cooperation," and in "acts of attacking, crying, telling on each other."

These children were then assigned to twelve different groups, each homogeneous in age (some from four to seven, others eight to eleven) and in sex. The children's preferences for one another were ignored in making group assignments. Each group then spent a half hour or more together on each of several days, in the same room and using the same furniture and equipment, continuing until its "habits and traditions appeared to become lasting." Habits were considered to have become traditions only if they had developed during the experimental period and had not previously been observed in the day nurseries.

Following each group's establishment of "fixed traditions," a child who had been identified as a leader was added to the group, no other changes being made. Observations were continued as before, with special attention to the continuation of the group's traditions, which were, of course, unknown to the newly introduced child. The important finding was that the newly added child, although he had previously exhibited leaderlike characteristics, almost never modified the group's customary ways of doing things, which members had come to consider right and proper. This finding is best shown by noting contrasts between the new child's behavior in the day nursery, prior to the experiment, and after his introduction into the established group. The following table shows frequencies of selected behavior incidents on the part of one ex-leader:

	In day nursery	*During experiment*
Giving orders	12	11
Following orders	2	3
Being imitated	6	5
Imitating	3	11

Typically, the new member gave many orders but was rarely followed. Merei summarizes and interprets his findings as follows:

> In the overwhelming majority of our cases the leader was forced to accept the group traditions—that is, he proved weaker than the group but still managed to play the role of leader. . . . His roundabout road to leadership is clear here:
>
> 1. He tries to do away with the group traditions and lead it on to new ones.
> 2. He is rejected.
> 3. He accepts the traditions and quickly learns them.
> 4. Within the frame of these traditions he soon assumes leadership, and, though reluctantly, the group follows him because he does a good job.
> 5. He introduces insignificant variations, loosening the tradition.
> 6. He then introduces new elements into the ritual already weakened by variation.
>
> Thus the curious situation obtains where the order-giver imitates, while the [other group members] follow the orders of their imitator.

attitudes; the members of almost any group of Americans that you can think of are in general agreement that stealing is reprehensible, that family life is a good thing, that nuclear warfare should be avoided, and so on. But group consensus about such matters merely reflects a general, society-wide state of affairs; it does not distinguish one group from another. Consensus that is distinctive of some particular group or class of groups is known as *group-relevant*. Thus the members of the Grand Lake Sailing Club may be completely consensual in taking both a dim view of murder and a rosy view of sailing; the latter attitude is highly group-relevant but the former not at all. Group-relevant attitudes are distinctive of a particular group not in the sense that no other group is consensual about those same attitudes, but rather in the sense that the group's members are more like one another in respect to those particular attitudes than they are like the members of other groups to which they belong.

Consensus, insofar as it stems from members' interaction, is a consequence of reciprocal influence—not necessarily by deliberate efforts to persuade but, more commonly, simply by expressing one kind of attitude rather than its opposite. When you hear only one kind of attitude expressed by most of the people who, like yourself, are concerned, your own attitudes are likely to be influenced. And insofar as this happens to many or most members of a group their consensus is increased, through communication among members about the objects of the consensual attitudes, particularly when communication includes members' expressions of their own attitudes.

A sailing-club member, for example, not only reports to fellow members that he has seen some motorboats on the lake; if he adds, perhaps with some vehemence, that one of them nearly capsized him, that motorboats are in general noisy and dirty, or that their owners are inconsiderate so-and-sos, he hardly leaves his listener in doubt as to his own attitudes. Now let us assume that the listener was already of the same unfavorable opinion about motorboats; in that case he is not only in fact consensual with his fellow member, but he also knows it. And let us assume, further, that the listener indicates in some way, perhaps casually or even unwittingly, that he feels the same way about motorboats; the result is that both of them know that they are consensual. We shall refer to this state of affairs as *sharing*.

Sharing thus refers to consensus on the part of two or more individuals who are aware of being consensual. It is consensual perception of consensus—a second-order consensus. Sharing is not a concept that can be applied to a single individual, though he may perceive that a state of sharing exists between himself and one or more others. It is, rather, a collective or a group concept, referring to a state of affairs on the part of at least two individuals considered as a single entity.

It may happen that some or even many members of a group erroneously perceive group consensus; this would constitute not sharing, as we have defined it, but only misperceived consensus. An instance of this is offered in a study made a good many years ago by a young social psychologist (Schanck, 1932), who settled down in a small, rural community in New York in order to study its people, their customs, institutions, and their attitudes. Soon after arriving, he discovered, through questionnaires and interviews, that nearly everyone expressed attitudes in opposition to cardplaying and to the use of tobacco and liquor. These attitudes, as he also soon discovered, were in conformity with those prescribed by officials of the local Methodist Church, to which most of the influential citizens belonged. During his two years' stay in the community he became well acquainted with many people there, a good many of whom invited him to their homes and talked informally and confidentially to him. Before he left, he had several times participated in card games, drinking hard cider and smoking—but always behind locked doors and drawn blinds—with individuals who had previously expressed the prevailing and "proper" attitudes. Nearly all these individuals, he discovered, believed themselves to be the only ones in the community who would think of engaging in such activities.

In this community, attitudes toward drinking, smoking, and cardplaying were group-relevant: community members expressed attitudes concerning these activities, but because of strong pressures toward conformity, in many persons these expressions were not consistent with their privately held attitudes. Thus, as a result of interaction, a state of misperceived sharing, or pluralistic ignorance, developed. Assumptions about sharing must necessarily rest on observations of others' expressions of their attitudes, but if the latter are not valid indicators of privately held attitudes, the assumptions are bound to be erroneous.

Sources of accurately perceived consensus, or sharing, can be rather simply described. Given an actual state of consensus about group-relevant attitudes, the conditions that give rise to individuals' expressions of those attitudes will determine, at the same time, the degree to which the actual state of consensus is accurately perceived. Insofar as group members feel it necessary to conceal their own attitudes, this very concealment gives the impression that "silence gives consent"; behavioral conformity, which is a form of communication, carries the message, whether or not it is intended, "You may judge my attitudes from my behavior." Such are the sources of misperceived consensus. But in the absence of common influences to inhibit the expression of their own attitudes, group members express them more or less directly, by word or action; the existing state of consensus is recognized, and a state of sharing exists. The two preconditions of sharing, in sum, are actual consensus and relatively uninhibited expression of members' actual attitudes as they interact with one another.

Consequences of Consensus and Sharing

Sharing, by definition, presupposes consensus, which is thus a necessary condition for sharing. But it is not a sufficient condition: sharing also presupposes communication, in the form of expressing one's attitudes in some manner that is observable to others. These two conditions, together, are for practical purposes both necessary and sufficient.[1] Thus one possible consequence of consensus (and, under the proper conditions of communication, a predictable consequence) is sharing.

The consequences of sharing are neither so obvious nor so simple, though they may be profound. They include effects both on the individuals' attitudes that are consensual and that they express, and on their attitudes toward one another. That is, to continue our illustration, the discovery by two or more members of a sailing club that they have consensual attitudes toward motorboats may affect their attitudes toward motorboats and also toward each other. In later parts of this chapter we

[1] We ignore, for present purposes, instances of sharing that are based on "accidentally" correct inferences rather than on any expression of attitudes. Thus if each of two strangers in a foreign country observes that the other has an American passport, each may infer that the other has many attitudes like his own that he assumes to be held by practically all American citizens. If each attributes to the other in this manner the same attitudes, and if the two individuals are in fact consensual, their attitudes would also be shared, without any expression of attitudes on the part of either. Under such conditions, the mere fact that persons perceive each other can result in sharing, without direct communication.

shall consider the psychological processes by which the consequences of sharing come about; meanwhile let us look at the general nature of the attitudinal changes that are involved.

SOCIAL SUPPORT FOR THE ATTITUDE THAT IS SHARED. We noted in Chapters 4 and 5 that one of the confirming experiences by which individuals' attitudes are supported is the discovery that others' attitudes are like their own, particularly if those others are trusted, admired, or respected. The fact of sharing an attitude with such kinds of people thus provides additional support for each of the sharers' attitudes. The principal consequence of this additional support is that each individual's attitude becomes more resistant to change *provided that the sharing is maintained*. But it is also true that an attitude that is supported by sharing becomes more vulnerable to change if that support is removed; that is, if an individual discovers that a trusted person no longer holds an attitude the two of them had been sharing, his own attitude is likely to become more susceptible to change.

WIDENING COGNITIVE RANGE OF THE ATTITUDE. It is not likely that different individuals who share the same feelings toward something will have exactly the same range of direct experience with it, nor exactly the same range of information about it. It is therefore likely that, as the sharers communicate with each other about it, each of them will learn from the others such things as arguments in support of the attitude, areas of experience that are affected by the attitude, and so on. The total pool of experience and information relevant to that attitude tends to become available to all the sharers, with the result that the cognitive content of the attitude tends to be extended for each of them.

INCREASED ATTRACTION AMONG SHARERS. In general, as we have seen in Chapter 5, the perception of agreement with other persons about matters of importance is accompanied by positive attraction toward them. It is as if one said to oneself, "Someone who agrees with me about such an important thing is likely to have other good qualities too." This common effect of sharing must, however, be understood in the light of other sources of interpersonal attraction. One may share an important attitude with a person who on other grounds is so offensive that the fact of sharing has little effect on one's attraction toward him. The proper generalization is not that one is always attracted toward those with whom one shares an important attitude, but that the effects of sharing—whether they be great or too small to be noticed—are usually in the direction of increased attraction.

GROUP SOLIDARITY. So far we have been discussing the effects on individuals of sharing their attitudes, but the effects on all the sharers *as a group*, viewed as a single entity, are no less pronounced. Pending a fuller discussion of group properties in Chapter 12 we shall stop only to note some rather general characteristics of groups whose members share both positive attraction toward all or most other members and similar attitudes toward group-relevant matters. Groups characterized by such sharing tend to mobilize themselves quickly and effectively for collective action, because members trust one anothers' motives and intentions. For similar reasons, such a group can tolerate disagreement among its members, especially concerning means toward shared ends, and even profit by its expression. It can delegate specialized activities and responsibilities to individual members or committees, since members who share group-relevant attitudes are in many respects substitutable for one another and even for the group as a whole. And the general level of member satisfaction tends to be high in such a group, because the mutual confidence that goes with sharing makes it easy for dissatisfactions to be confronted and dealt with.

Such characteristics tend to go along with the group property of cohesiveness (cf. pages 380–386). Sharing of attitudes toward group-relevant matters (including group members themselves) facilitates cohesiveness, in its literal sense of "sticking together," because sharing means that members know that they can speak and act as one.

* * *

Although members of most groups in the same society are consensual with respect to many aspects of their own culture, it is consensus with respect to group-relevant matters that distinguishes one group from another. When consensuality exists for two or more individuals who are aware of their consensuality we have a state of affairs known as sharing. Sharing requires not only consensus but also sufficient communication with others to make the consensus visible. Sharing serves to provide mutual support for attitudes shared, to widen the cognitive range of the attitudes involved, to increase attraction among individual sharers, and to increase group solidarity.

THE NATURE OF GROUP NORMS

Human life would be chaotic indeed if there were not certain regularities that people could count on. Regularities may apply to almost any kind of events, on the part of atoms or clouds, bacteria or giraffes, stopwatches or bulldozers. We shall be interested, however, only in those that apply to what human beings do—not only their overt behavior but also their thinking, their feelings, their motives, and so on. Such regularities may apply to only one person ("You can depend on Mr. McElroy to walk past this corner at five every afternoon"), or to many ("We always drive on the right-hand side of the street"). If a regularity applies only to one person, it may guide the behavior of no one but himself (a purely private regularity rule) or it may guide the behavior of many: other people might set their watches when Mr. McElroy appears. The regularities of primary social-psychological interest are those that are recognized by two or more individuals who in some way, directly or indirectly, interact with one another and who are in some way affected by them.

Some regularities of this kind are society-wide and some apply only to a single pair of individuals who have worked out an agreement for themselves alone. Some are formally legalized and some quite informal. They may be very general or highly specific. They may or may not have the force of moral rules, in the sense that notions like "ought," "should," or "right and wrong" are applied to them. It is even possible that they are never formulated in words. In spite of these and other variations, all these regularities have the following things in common: they describe a situation, or a set of circumstances in which the regularity applies; they include specifications of what people think, feel, or do in that situation; and they define the persons to whom these specifications apply.

Regularities, including all their specifications, become objects of attitudes; one may approve or disapprove of them with any degree of intensity. A *group norm* exists[2] insofar as a set of group members share favorable attitudes toward such a regularity—insofar, that is, as they agree and are aware that they agree that the regularity should be regarded as a *rule* that properly applies to the specified persons in the specified situations. The principal characteristic of group norms as distinct from other shared attitudes is that they represent shared acceptance of a rule, which is a prescription for ways of perceiving, thinking, feeling, or acting.

The psychological counterpart of an observed regularity is the expectation, with some degree of certainty, that an event will occur: the sun will rise tomorrow morning, for example, or the driver of a car will stop when the traffic light is red. When, as in the latter case, we are dealing with a regularity that is also a rule concerning human behavior, its psychological counterpart includes not just the expectation that the rule will probably be observed but also the anticipation of consequences of observing it, or of violating it. Such consequences are sometimes automatic, in the sense that other people's intervention is not needed to make them occur; if, for example, one does not accept the rule that the bus leaves the terminal precisely at noon, one suffers the consequence of missing it. Or, to give a different kind of illustration, all human societies

[2] This formulation has been heavily influenced by that of Kelley and Thibaut (1959), especially Chapters 8 and 13.

have rules concerning the use of words; the consequence of not accepting such rules is that one will have difficulty in understanding others and in making oneself understood.

We shall be mainly concerned, however, with consequences in the form of behaviors by other people that presumably encourage the observing of rules and discourage their violation. The very existence of any explicitly formulated rule suggests that the prescribed behavior is not dependable without the application of *sanctions*—either positive, in the form of some sort of reward, or negative, in the form of punishment. To accept such a rule, in fact, is to accept not only the probability but also the *legitimacy* (or the propriety) of sanctions on the part of others who observe whether and how one conforms to it.

Group norms exist, in short, whenever interacting persons share the acceptance of a rule that affects their relationships with one another. If the norms persist, it is because they are believed to encourage relationships that are considered desirable. And the less probable it is that they will be self-enforcing, the more likely that sanctions will be applied. In the following pages we first consider norms concerning psychological processes (perception and cognition) and then go on to norms about publicly expressed attitudes and overt behavior, to which sanctions are likely to be applied in quite direct ways.

Psychological Processes Affected by Group Norms

PERCEPTUAL NORMS. The first experiment dealing with group-norm effects on immediate visual perception (and in many respects still the standard one) was carried out by Sherif in 1935, and is reported in Research Illustration 8.2. A particularly neat part of this experiment is its answer to the question whether subjects might have been "only conforming" rather than "really seeing" different amounts of movement of the light. The fact is that the subjects who initially worked in groups continued, later working alone, to report the same extent of movement that they had previously reported in the group situation; and this fact strongly suggests that their perceptual processes, and not merely their verbal responses, had actually been affected by their earlier experiences in the group situation.

Under the conditions of this experiment, each group of subjects developed a perceptual norm: judgments of the extent of apparent movement of the light were affected by their acceptance of a rule. As to whether the subjects *shared* acceptance of the rule, however, we have no direct evidence, unfortunately: no subject was asked how he thought other subjects perceived the movement of the light. But the indirect evidence almost forces us to conclude that judgments were based on sharing, and not on mere consensuality. Judgments were expressed

Research Illustration 8.2

Sherif (1935) made use of the fact that a stationary pinpoint of light, if observed under proper laboratory conditions, is perceived as moving. This effect, known as "the autokinetic phenomenon," is not dependent on anticipatory expectations aroused by the experimenter. The stimulus is a thoroughly ambiguous one, since the experimental subjects are in a completely dark room, seated at an unknown distance from the pinpoint of light; thus there are at first no standards by which to judge the extent of the apparent movement of the light.

In the first part of the experiment subjects worked *alone*, making successive judgments of the extent of the apparent movement of the light for 100 separate trials. Under these conditions, each subject's estimates of movement gradually settled down to a very restricted range (for example, between 2 and 3 inches, or between 8 and 10 inches). When a further series of 100 judgments was made, each individual persisted in making estimates of movement within the range characteristic of his own previous behavior. The range of perceived movement established by each individual is peculiar to himself when he is experimented on alone. Such standards of judgment, developed by a person alone, represent individual regularities (or, in Sherif's terminology, individual norms).

Sherif also had his subjects work in groups of two and three. As in the first part of the experiment, there were 100 consecutive exposures of the light, each one lasting exactly 2 seconds. Each subject announced aloud his own judgment of the extent of movement of the light, which all had observed together. Each subject also heard each of the others make his judgment after each exposure. Members of half of the groups had no previous individual experience with the autokinetic phenomenon whereas the other half had already built up their individual norms, as described previously. In the group situation both sets of subjects gradually developed *group norms*; that is, the members of each group came to make their judgments within a restricted range characteristic of that group. Within each group the individual norms were very much alike but these norms differed a great deal from group to group.

The figure on page 232 shows some of these group results. Note that the subjects who first worked alone (extreme left of the figure) had built up rather divergent individual norms. These norms came to be much alike soon after they began to make their judgments together and stayed that way through the remaining three group sessions. This is shown in the funnel-shaped figures made by the converging lines in the left half of the chart. Note also that when subjects began by making judgments together (as shown at the extreme right of the chart), they kept their group norms when later making judgments alone. Group norms persist in the individual situation, but the individually developed behavior does not persist in the group situation; rather, it is superseded by the group norm that arises as group members express judgments to others and hear others express their judgments.

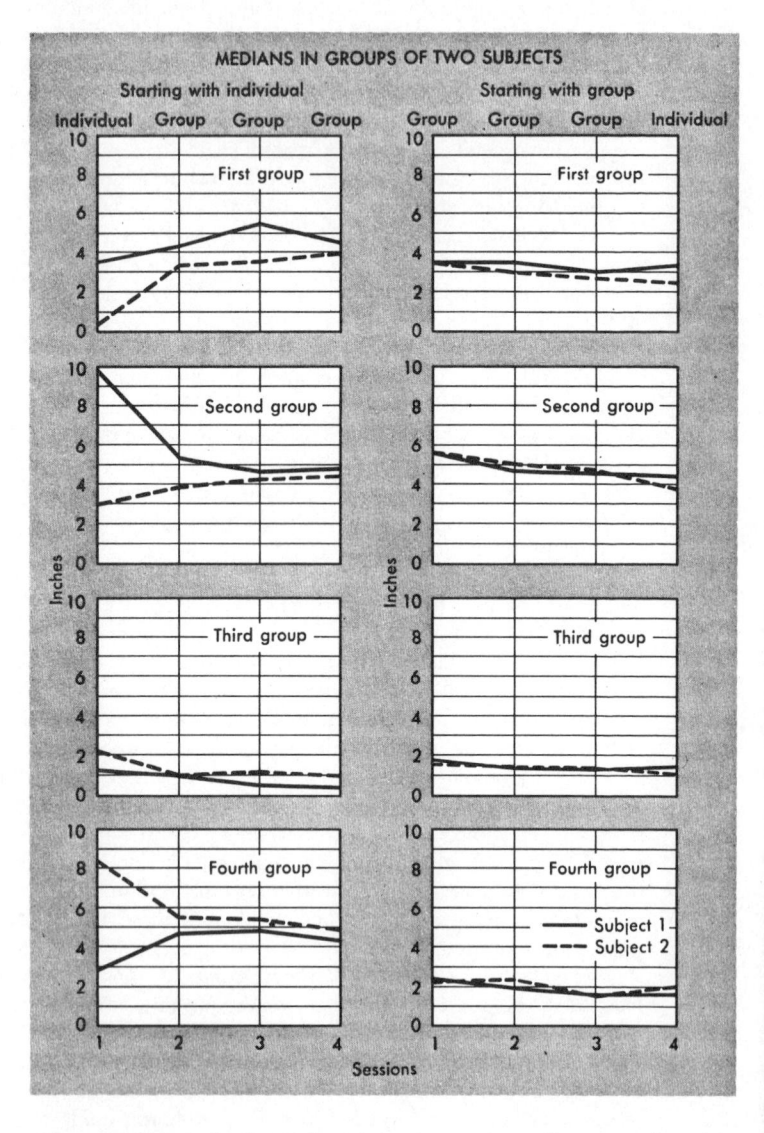

Amount of perceived autokinetic movement on the part of various groups, showing "funnel" effect on the part of subjects who first develop individual norms and then make their judgments in the group situation (from Sherif, 1936)

aloud, and no subject could have failed to observe, after several rounds of responses to exposures of the light, that he and the other subject(s) were making very similar judgments. We can therefore infer with considerable confidence that each subject knew that each other subject in the same group knew that both (or all three) of them were accepting more or less the same standard of judgment. The conditions of this experiment made sharing inevitable, and so we conclude both that a perceptual norm developed in each group of subjects and that group members' judgments were affected by it. It is not just that each member was influenced by the other; rather, each of them was influenced by something they had jointly, through their interaction, created—a norm.

The interaction that takes place in the kind of situation described by Sherif is influenced by the previous experiences an individual has had in the process of interacting with others. Certain predispositions created by these former interactions have measurable outcomes in the Sherif type of experiment. Vidulich and Kaiman (1961), for example, have demonstrated that when persons high in authoritarianism are placed in the autokinetic situation, they are influenced significantly more by a high-status individual than by a low-status individual. This finding did not hold for persons low in authoritarianism. High and low authoritarianism, as we have noted previously, represent the residuals of previous interaction in situations where fairly definite shared norms emerged. It is not surprising that we must take the past history of previous interaction into account as we watch standards of judgment emerge in any specific situation that involves shared experiences.

COGNITIVE NORMS. The cognitive aspects of an attitude include beliefs about the attitude object, and the attribution of properties to it—knives are sharp, the universe is peopled with spirits, big-eared people are generous. Thus a cognitive norm is a rule, the acceptance of which is shared by group members, as to what they expect one another to believe about something.

Most attitudes, as we noted in Chapter 5, do not exist in isolation from other attitudes. One tends to organize objects as belonging together in one way or another, and thus to have similar attitudes toward objects that belong together. It is possible for a person to cognize each one in a set of attitude objects that belong together as having its own properties, but in fact cognitions about belonging-together objects are not insulated from each other. Thus an attitude that a person brings with him to a situation includes not only beliefs about that specific attitude object but also beliefs about other objects that belong with it. The specific attitude functions in an *extended* cognitive context, and group norms have something to say about this context. That is, groups have their rules about appropriate contexts. For example, different groups within the same university may have divergent norms about the appropriate context for college football: A group of administrators views a successful football season as helpful in raising money; a fraternity group thinks about how much its own members contribute to victory; a group of faculty members is concerned about football's interference with academic pursuits. Each group has its own shared rules about other attitude objects that belong with football, and this total, extended cognitive context comes to be included in the group's cognitive norms.

We are all so familiar with cognitive norms that most of the time we simply take them for granted. There are many beliefs that we share with most members of our own society, and additional ones that we share with members of our families, friendship groups, communities, interest groups, and so on. The importance of sharing them, as opposed to merely holding such beliefs privately, is that we can count on the support of others for our own beliefs. This is no mere matter of personal egotism ("I like to be right"); it is, rather, a matter of being able to count on other people for the kinds of behavior that presuppose common beliefs. For example, each of us counts on others' holding the belief that unsupported objects will fall, or that cars will be wrecked and their occupants injured if they collide at sixty miles an hour. There are matters of physical reality that each of us has personally observed, but our everyday behavior is based on assumptions that others share our beliefs about gravity and about traffic safety. Such shared beliefs are rules, in the sense that they are conventions (in these instances buttressed by physical reality) about what people are expected to believe. They represent the cognitive aspects of attitudes, and they are normative because they represent shared acceptance of the same rules.

There are many other cognitive rules that are grounded only in convention, with no buttressing at all from physical reality. In most countries of the West we expect others to believe that the right side of the road is made to drive on. If we are playing baseball we expect everyone to believe that the team with the higher score at the end of the ninth inning is the victor. If one is a native of a certain African society one expects others to share one's belief that illness results from sorcery. Such shared beliefs are cognitive norms; they are based on shared acceptance of rules about what to believe, just as perceptual norms are based on shared acceptance of rules about perceiving. Cognitive norms that do not correspond to any physical reality have effects that are just as real as those that do. Insofar as they are generally shared they come to constitute a kind of reality known as *social reality*. They differ principally from those corresponding to physical reality in that they depend exclusively upon sharing. That is, individuals would not, except by chance, adopt the rules in the first place except by a process of sharing; and the norms would lose some or all of their effectiveness if those who at one time shared them should discover that they are no longer shared.

The fact that norms tend to lose their effectiveness if not sustained by shared experience is nicely illustrated in the experiment by Maccoby and others (1961). A number of women were exposed to a communication advocating later toilet training for children than most of them initially supported. It was found that conversations following exposure to this communication were selective, so that those most influenced tended to converse with other women supporting this new position and vice versa. The major effect of conversations was to prevent backsliding on the part of those women who had initially been influenced by the communication. The women who did not engage in these change-supporting conversations tended to revert to their initial position.

EVALUATIVE NORMS. Societies and smaller groups also have rules about the goodness or desirability of objects (using the term "objects" in the broad sense of any distinguishable entity toward which one can have an attitude). An evaluative norm is thus a shared acceptance of a rule according to which group members are expected to consider something good in some degree or bad in some degree. Such norms might also be labeled "affective," since they are often thought of as referring to people's feelings about them: we feel favorably toward things we evaluate as good, and unfavorably toward those we consider bad.

Evaluative norms are conceptually distinct from cognitive ones, but there is usually a close relationship between them. Merely cognitive norms have to do with *un*evaluated beliefs, or attributions of properties. For example, such bald and merely definitional statements as the following refer merely to cognitions, without evaluations: murder involves the death of one person by intention of another; theft involves the transfer of one person's belongings to another without mutual consent. But it is virtually impossible to think of murder or theft without becoming evaluative: both are bad. The general principle is that most of us, most of the time, evaluate objects in terms of their properties, and their properties are rarely altogether neutral. There is adaptive value in this tendency to evaluate everything: we need to know whether it is likely to help us or harm us. But our tendencies to evaluate things are often so strong that we do so prematurely—that is, before we have calmly and objectively examined them in more than one extended context. Because it is useful to evaluate what one cognizes, and necessary to cognize what one values, the two kinds of norms are often closely associated.

Most measures of attitudes are made in terms of the evaluative, or affective, aspects of attitudes. That is, the scores yielded by these measures represent answers to such questions as, To what degree are you favorable or opposed to this object? How strongly do you feel about it? But answers to such questions, alone, from group members will tell us nothing about the group's norms. If all members give similar answers we know only that the group is consensual. We cannot infer that there is shared acceptance of a rule unless we also know that all or most of the group's members attribute to one another the same attitudes that they themselves hold. In Chapter 12 we shall refer to some ways of measuring degrees of sharing, without which norms do not exist.

The shared acceptance of evaluative norms is furthered by the administration of punishments and rewards (often in subtle ways) as individuals interact with one another. Under such pressures it is common to find considerable parent-child consensus on a large number of issues. It can also be shown that adults are not immune to these influences, as in Research Illustration 8.3, which describes some conditions under which individuals internalized attitudes with group approval, even though not initially holding those attitudes. In this experiment, positive reinforcement brought with it an attitude change that survived beyond the brief period when the individual complied with the behavior suggested by another person. Since a change in the same direction was not found for the group that received negative reinforcement for similar compliance, it appears that internalization of the attitude was not a matter of mere compliance but of compliance that was rewarded.

Findings like those reported in Research Illustrations 8.3 and 4.6 (page 106) are predictable in terms of dissonance theory, as previously noted. That is, it is distressing to find oneself saying or doing something in which one does not really believe, and hence one changes one's attitudes in ways that are more consonant with what one has actually done. This kind of attitude change has the effect of changing self-punishment to self-reward. But such processes are often more complicated than a simple approach to dissonance theory would suggest. The circumstances that induce overt compliance also instigate cognitive explorations that may lead to new ideas, or new ways of viewing familiar ones.

Such processes are illustrated by another study (Janis and King, 1954) that somewhat resembles the one described in Research Illustration 8.3. One set of subjects merely read to an audience a prepared script advocating a certain position concerning military service, whereas a second set improvised speeches of their own, taking the same position as convincingly as they could. Both sets of subjects took positions opposed to their own attitudes. The script-reading subjects reported more satisfaction with their own performance, but it was the speechmakers who showed the greater attitude change; following their performances the latter group had changed significantly toward the position they had advocated. These findings suggest that the experience of thinking up new arguments to convince other people was an important factor in their attitude change. The investigators consider it plausible that "there is a

Research Illustration 8.3

In an interesting study by Scott (1957), all students in twenty-nine general psychology classes were administered questions to determine their attitudes toward universal military training, night hours for women students, and de-emphasis of football. These three issues had been the subject of considerable controversy. Two weeks later, fifty-eight of these students who had expressed clear opinions served as subjects in an experiment in which they were persuaded to engage in classroom debates on these issues. Each of them was asked to debate on the side opposed to his own attitude, as previously expressed. Half of them were rewarded with a purported "vote" by members of the class that led them to believe that they had been proclaimed the better debaters. The other half were punished by receiving information that they had lost the debate.

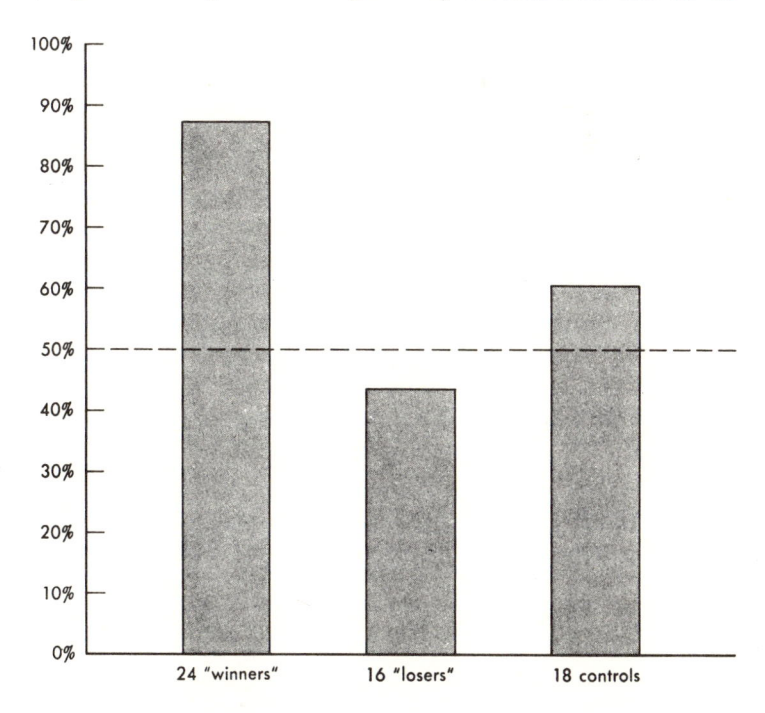

When the attitudes of the participants in the debate were then measured again, it was found that the "winners" had undergone a significant attitude change in the direction of the argument they had supported while debating, and away from their previously held attitudes. "Losers" underwent an attitude change in the other direction, that is, their previous attitudes tended to become even stronger, although this change was not significantly different from that on the part of a control group whose members did not participate in the debate. Among those who changed, the percentages of those whose change was away from their original position appear in the figure on page 237. The probability that 21 of 24 changes by the "winners" (87 percent of them) would all be in the same direction is less than .001, but for the other two groups the obtained frequencies are well within chance expectations.

lowering of psychological resistance whenever a person regards the persuasive arguments emanating from others as his 'own' ideas."

BEHAVIORAL NORMS. It is possible for a set of group members to have perceptual, cognitive, and evaluative norms about something but not to have any shared acceptance of rules about observable behavior with respect to it. Or, conversely, group members may subscribe to a behavioral norm without sharing cognitive or evaluative norms that are associated with it. Although the general rule is that, with regard to group-relevant matters, behavioral as well as the other kinds of norms are shared by group members, it is well to keep the conceptual distinctions clearly in mind.

Checking answers to an attitude scale is, of course, a form of behavior; the existence of behavioral norms is not inferred, however, from such answers, but rather from what group members do in ways that are observable to one another. The observance of shared rules about such behavior is often referred to as *conformity*, but we must be careful not to conclude that the fact of behavioral conformity necessarily presupposes sharing in cognitive or evaluative rules; one may conform externally in order to conceal the fact that one does not share cognitive or evaluative rules with others. Both possibilities are illustrated in Asch's experiment on the effects of "group pressure" on individuals' judgments (see Research Illustration 8.4). While all Asch's "critical subjects" must have assumed that all group members except themselves were guided by the same perceptual norms, only "a very few" of them claimed that they themselves came to accept those norms. Nearly all the fifteen "yielders" conformed outwardly, but only outwardly; it was only the behavioral norms that they shared with others.

Perceptual, cognitive, evaluative, and behavioral norms are in no sense mutually exclusive. Everyday interaction that is related to everyday things—movies, perhaps, or meals—would typically involve all these kinds of norms. The psychological processes of perception, cognition, affect, and performance (as we have already noted, especially in Part One) go on simultaneously and interdependently. Norms tend to develop concerning anything that is important to members of an interaction group, and to involve all these psychological processes.

Research Illustration 8.4

In a pioneering attempt to determine the effects of confronting an individual with what was experimentally made to appear to the subject like a perceptual norm held by all other subjects, Asch (1951) brought together several different groups of eight male college students. Each group was instructed to match the length of a given line with one of three clearly unequal lines. Each member of the group announced his judgments aloud. All but one member (the "critical subject") had previously received instructions to respond unanimously at certain times with the same wrong judgment. One individual thus found himself suddenly contradicted by the entire group, and this experience was repeated again and again. The critical subject thus faced, possibly for the first time in his life, a situation in which a group unanimously contradicted the clear evidence of his own senses.

Among fifty critical subjects there was a marked shift toward the majority responses. Approximately one third of all their judgments were errors identical with or in the direction of the planned errors of the majority. Since control groups showed virtually no error in this situation, it was clear that the errors resulted primarily from the unanimous majority. At the same time, the influence of the majority was far from complete, since about two thirds of all estimates were correct despite the majority verdict. There were also interesting individual differences: some subjects remained independent of the majority without exception, whereas others were almost always influenced to conform.

In a variation of this experiment, one individual was instructed by the experimenter to make correct responses in every instance. When the critical subject thus found himself joined by a partner who agreed with him, his independence was markedly increased. The frequency of errors made in the direction of the majority dropped to 5.5 percent, as compared with the original 32 percent. It is clear that the presence of even one other individual who responded correctly was sufficient to diminish and sometimes to destroy the power of the majority.

In a special analysis of the thirty-seven (out of fifty) critical subjects who were influenced by the majority in at least one of the twelve trials, Asch considered the fifteen of them who conformed to the majority judgment half or more of the time (that is, on six or more trials) as "yielders." On the basis of interviews with these fifteen subjects, Asch concluded that three different kinds of psychological processes were responsible for yielding. A very few of them appeared to have undergone a "distortion of perception"; these subjects reported that they came to perceive the majority estimates as correct, and that they were not aware of being influenced by the majority. A majority of the fifteen yielders reported what seems to be a "distortion of judgment." They reported that, for some reason unknown to them, they were forced to conclude that their own perceptions were inaccurate whereas the majority judgment must be correct. Lacking confidence in their own perceptions, they reported not what they saw but what they felt must be right. And there were also a few yielders who clearly experienced "distortion of action." They frankly admitted that they did not report what they saw, and that they never came to the conclusion that their own perceptions were inaccurate. They yielded simply because they did not want to appear different or defective in the eyes of other group members. These subjects suppressed their own observations and voiced the majority position with full awareness of what they were doing.

The Functions of Group Norms

A group norm is not likely to endure unless it is in some way advantageous both to the group as a whole and to a significant number of its individual members (a minority of individuals who exercise power in one or more ways may constitute a significant number). We shall therefore consider some of the ways in which norms are advantageous, or functional in the sense of facilitating something of importance.

Most obvious, perhaps, is the function of providing the stability and orderliness that go with predictability. In the total absence of norms, group life would simply be chaotic, the relationships among individuals being as unpredictable as those among single grains of sand in a windstorm, or among molecules of water in a raging surf. Such total disorganization would be equivalent to no stability of group life, and no persistence of any particular group. There is a kind of Darwinian principle at work: either a group develops norms that provide adaptability of members to one another and to their common environment, or it disappears as a group. And predictability is equally necessary to group members, as individuals—not just because of the anxiety that accompanies uncertainty but also, more importantly, because of man's never-ending dependence on other men. The cooperative ventures that are so necessary for human beings—as in family life, in maintaining subsistence, or in finding security against external dangers—presuppose common understandings about one another and about the common environment. Even individualistic enterprises, or success in competitive ones, are not very likely to be successful without some basis for predicting the behavior of others. Thus motive satisfaction of almost every kind, among interdependent persons, is facilitated by the sharing of norms.

Group norms have a very special place, moreover, in the understanding of human interaction—the central problem of this book. Although norms could not develop apart from the interactional processes of perceiving and communicating with other people, the reverse is equally true. The mutually shared field (pages 182 ff.), as the matrix within which interpersonal perception occurs, presupposes perceptual and cognitive norms at the very least, if there is to be correspondence between the perceptual fields of the interacting persons. That is, if they are to interact realistically they must put similar content into the mutual field, and to do this they must have a common body of norms in terms of which they can organize their perceptions and cognitions. In particular, if each of them is to attribute attitudes to the other with some degree of accuracy, they must draw on some common source with which both are familiar; otherwise they would have no more success than the proverbial man from Mars on first encountering the man from Jupiter.

Successful communication, too, presupposes shared norms about symbols and their referents. Learning to speak or to use gestures, or to read and write, is quite literally a process of becoming familiar with and internalizing norms concerning the use of symbols, grammar, and syntax. And so it is with virtually all processes of interaction. Norms arise out of interaction and, at whatever stage of development they may be at a particular moment, also make possible more intricate, more realistic, and more satisfying interaction than could possibly occur in their absence.

Individual Motivation to Conform

Why do people conform to the rules embodied in norms—that is, if and when they do conform? We cannot answer that it is because they have motives to conform; this would be to reason, in circular manner, that people conform because they are motivated to conform. In view of the fact that no one is always a conformist, we face again the problem of *conditions*: When are people most likely and when least likely to want to conform to norms?

Incorporated in many rules are shared sanctions; that is, the rules specify not only who is supposed to do what under what circumstances, but also how one is to be rewarded for conforming, or punished for failing to. Thus it would be surprising if motives for conforming did not include expectations of being rewarded (say, by approval or praise) or of avoiding punishment. The "yielding" of Asch's subjects who conformed was in most cases motivated in just such ways, even though sanctions had in no way been mentioned. This kind of motivation to conform because of external incentives may be labeled compliance (cf. Kelman, 1958). Purely compliant conformity does not occur in private, but only when it is observable to others who might apply sanctions.

A very great deal of conformity to norms occurs, however, quite apart from such external incentives. This is shown by the fact that (like Sherif's subjects who acquired perceptual norms in groups but maintained them when alone) we so often conform to norms even in strict privacy—when there is no possibility that other people will reward or punish us for conformity or nonconformity. The norms have, so to speak, become *internalized*; they now function not only as a shared rule but also as an individual rule. This phenomenon is closely related to the processes by which attitudes become shared, and we turn next to a consideration of these processes.

* * *

A group norm exists when a group's members share favorable attitudes toward a rule that applies to specified persons in specified situations. Norms may have to do with ways of perceiving, with cognitions and beliefs, with the evaluation of the objects of attitudes on a good–bad continuum, or with overt behavior. Most group norms are enforced either through sanctions applied by other people or through individuals' internalization of the rules, or through both together. Group norms tend to persist to the degree that the observing of the rules is functional either for the group as a whole or for significant numbers of its individual members.

GROUP NORMS AND THE SHARING PROCESS

We have noted in this chapter some of the consequences, for individuals and for groups, of sharing under theoretically ideal conditions. But we have not considered the mechanisms by which these consequences occur, nor have we looked at the more true-to-life situations in which attitudes are only partially shared by group members. We now turn to these problems.

Processes That Make Sharing Possible

The degree to which any group member can participate in the shared acceptance of a rule is limited by three conditions: he must recognize the existence of the rule, in the sense of seeing that others accept it; he must accept it himself; and both he and they must recognize that all of them accept it. These limiting conditions, imposed by our definition of group norms, are all necessary. We must therefore ask what it is that determines whether each of these conditions will be met. It will help us to understand the mechanisms by which the consequences of sharing are brought about if we first understand the processes by which sharing occurs.

RECOGNIZING THE EXISTENCE OF RULES. If a sixth-grade child is shown by his teacher just how to extract the square root of a number, he has, insofar as he understands it, recognized a rule. By hearing instructions from older people a small child learns about rules concerning crossing busy streets. Later on he may hear, in Sunday school, about the Golden Rule. In all these cases he has been presented with verbal formulations, but these are not always necessary. Children may become familiar with rules about wearing clothes, for example, with little or no verbal instructions, and they often imitate other people (especially bigger ones) as if on the assumption that a rule is called for and the person to be imitated knows what it is. Learning to conform to the rule is a different matter; our present point is that, as these illustrations suggest, one learns to recognize it by observing or inferring that other people accept it. The basis for shared acceptance of rules—though not the certainty of it— is present in the same interactional processes by which rules first come to be recognized.

ACCEPTING RULES. Favorable attitudes toward a rule are acquired in basically the same ways as are other attitudes: insofar as one's previous experience with something has been associated with motive satisfaction, one's attitudes toward it are favorable. Although attitudes toward rules are often complicated by the fact that one may feel differently about their application to oneself and to others, this consideration is often outweighed by the advantages of predictability. That is, the satisfactions of knowing what to expect from others, and what others expect of oneself, may be greater than whatever dissatisfactions are involved in abiding by the rule oneself. For example, most of us accept traffic regulations in spite of having to wait for red lights because they make possible the kind of predictability without which we ourselves might become involved in traffic accidents. At the same time we are more favorable to rules if they benefit ourselves in direct ways than if they do not; thus most businessmen do not favor rules enforcing high corporate taxes, even though they realize that there must be a body of rules about taxation.

We are all familiar with the ways in which we can, while in general accepting a rule, rationalize our own nonconformity to it: "If other people were familiar with all the circumstances they would understand how the rule really doesn't apply to me this time." There may well be special situations in which the nonapplicability of a rule to oneself or to others is justified, but a person who regularly practices such evasion cannot be said to have accepted the rule. Acceptance means adopting a favorable attitude toward it, including all its specifications, whether or not these apply to oneself. Insofar as a person's experience with a rule, and in particular its application to himself, has been frustrating rather than motive satisfying, his attitudes toward it will be unfavorable and he therefore cannot share its acceptance with others.

The kinds of motives commonly satisfied by experience with a rule, including its application to oneself, include not only those of predictability but also many others. One class of motives is associated with rules that result from accumulated human experience, and represent "the best way of doing things"—ways that have been discovered by trial and error in the past, and that individuals are not likely to discover easily for themselves. There are "established" ways of making bread or stone walls or airplanes that are more effective than other ways; some ways of treating sick people or of writing clear English simply work better than others. Anyone who is interested in doing these things is more likely to find motive satisfaction by following the rules than by starting from scratch, on his own. In the case of rules that are no more than conventions (social reality), their observance brings social commendation and their violation disapproval or punishment. The process of learning to accept rules of either kind is like that of acquiring any other attitudes, as described in Chapter 2, with the additional feature that the rewards and punishments that were at first externally administered by other people, come to be self-administered—that is, the expectation of future reward or punishment becomes presently rewarding or punishing. In this sense the group norms have then been internalized; they have become one's own. When the rule has been thus fully accepted, one feels that this way of doing things is the right way, the way in which one wants to do it, the way in which one has now learned to find motive satisfaction.

SHARED ACCEPTANCE OF THE RULE. Once a person has recognized the existence of a rule and has accepted it, full sharing requires two more steps: recognition by others that he has accepted the rule that they also accept, and awareness by him of this recognition on their part. These two steps are apt to occur more or less simultaneously, and may therefore be considered together. The reason for this simultaneity is as follows: the individual's acceptance is indicated by behavior on his part that is observable to others, and thus they know that he shares their own acceptance of the rule; and the individual's awareness that he has been observed by them, together with probable indications of their approval, assures him that they know of his acceptance of the rule. Although these last two steps are almost inevitable consequences of the previous ones, they are necessary for full sharing, and should not be lost sight of.

Processes That Result from Sharing

Assume now that all the members of a certain group fully share one of its norms—say, about etiquette, or a religious belief. Insofar as attitudes toward the rule are concerned, that is, not only are all members alike but each of them considers that all are alike. There is thus a relationship among members that might be described as psychological *substitutability*; each of them assumes that each of the others is predisposed to apply the same rule that he himself would apply. This means that, apart from the considerations mentioned in the following paragraphs, the Golden Rule is spontaneously applied within the specified limits of the norm: Do unto others as you would have them do unto you. Within those limits, each member feels that each of the others can act for him; since their attitudes are similar, any one of them can substitute for any other.

This kind of substitutability refers only to attitudes, however, and not necessarily to overt behavior, which is always a function both of preexisting attitudes and of immediate, situational factors. A given situation may or may not have the same impact on different individuals, even though they subscribe to the same norms that are relevant to the same situation. One member may take account of certain aspects of a situation that another does not even notice; or a situation may include elements that have some special meaning for one member. For example, a young man's behavior may be inhibited by the presence of his prospective father-in-law, but his friends would probably not feel the same kind of inhibition. For such reasons substitutability does not necessarily apply to observable behavior.

There is another partial exception to the principle of substitutability. Norms very often prescribe differentiation among members of the same group. Perhaps a shared rule explicitly specifies a division of labor: husbands and wives do not expect each other to share their own attitudes toward washing diapers or toward shoveling sidewalks; what they share is acceptance of the rule according to which the wife is responsible for one of these and the husband for the other. There is substitutability with respect to accepting the rule, but not with respect to the differentiated prescriptions of the rule.

Within these limitations, however, the existence of a group norm implies substitutability, and this concept helps us to understand the power that a group's norms exert upon its members. Substitutability means, in the first place, that any group member can trust another as fully as he can trust himself to be guided by the rule. Thus no enforcement, in the form of constraints or sanctions, is needed: the rule is self-administered by each member. Since we are not interested in merely private rules, but only in group-shared ones, it therefore makes sense to speak of the norms as being *internalized* by each member. Internalization presupposes sharing, however, if it is to be more than transitory; each group member must be able to observe both that he is trusted by others and that they trust him to be guided by the rule. Internalization is not likely to persist, moreover, in the face of evidence that important reference persons or groups no longer share one's norms. It is not so much that one continually needs to be approved, or otherwise rewarded, by fellow norm sharers, for internalization implies that rewards are self-administered. The persistence of an internalized norm depends, rather, on at least occasional evidence that there is still a basis for substitutability—that the norm still represents something shared. One may continue to accept a rule while feeling that one is now alone in doing so, but this would no longer represent internalization of a norm, in the absence of sharing; there is no longer a basis for substitutability.

Because substitutability implies *mutual trust*, in norm-related matters, it has consequences for groups as well as for individuals. The group as a whole can delegate tasks to its individual members, since any one of them can stand for all of them. A single member can speak or act in behalf of the group even without being delegated to do so, in confident assurance that he represents the other members and that they trust him to do so. Assuming only that group members share acceptance of rules concerning differentiated role assignments, they can work smoothly toward the same objectives whether they are together or separated. Thus group effectiveness is maximized by reason of the substitutability that accompanies sharing of norms. Effective communication would appear to be an essential ingredient in developing the shared acceptance that is the basis for mutual trust and cooperative behavior. This assumption was tested in an experiment summarized in Research Illustration 8.5, which epitomizes many of the processes and characteristics of sharing.

Group solidarity, or cohesiveness (more fully described in Chapter 12), is also enhanced by the sharing of norms—partly, though not exclusively, as a result of shared attitudes of pride in group effectiveness. Another factor making for cohesiveness is reciprocal attraction of members, as persons, to one another. We tend to feel rewarded by, and thus to be attracted to, a person who is perceived as supporting our values and working toward shared goals that we have internalized as our own. In such ways sharing contributes to group cohesiveness, if indeed it is not indispensable.

A Group's Power over Its Members

Members of a group who, by such processes of sharing, subscribe to its norms are powerfully influenced by those norms, and thus the group may be said to have power over its members. This phrase may sound paradoxical, since the notions of submission to power and of willing acceptance may seem contradictory. The fact is, however, that no influence is more powerful than one willingly accepted. If sharing is viewed in terms of intermember substitutability, the reasons for this become evident. As he conforms to a group's norms, a member finds it satisfying because other members' approval is substitutable by his own. He rewards himself—even if his conformity has taken private, outwardly

Research Illustration 8.5

Loomis (1959), utilizing concepts developed by Deutsch (1957), has suggested that an individual will have cooperative intentions and expectations if he and another person share the knowledge of their mutual interdependence. It was hypothesized that this shared knowledge may come into being in two-person situations when an individual wishes to reach some goal, when he knows that the other person also wishes to reach a similar goal, when he is aware that he will reach his goal and that the other person will reach his goal only if they cooperate with each other, and when he is convinced that the other person's motivation, knowledge, and awareness are similar to his own. These conditions would appear to depend on effective communication between the two persons.

One hundred ninety-eight men and women college students were placed in what appeared to them to be a two-person "game" where the object was for each person to win as much money as he could for himself. The nature of this complex game was described fully, and it was emphasized that this was not a competitive nor a cooperative game since both could win, both could lose, or one could win and the other could lose. Mutual dependence existed, however, since the other person's move was never revealed until the subject's own move was stated, and the players could, therefore, engage in either cooperative behavior or in double-crossing tactics. Each S was seated alone in a booth and played the game against the other person (actually the experimenter) by using electrical switches to indicate his moves.

In order to control precisely the amount of communication between the two persons, one of five levels of communication was permitted in the form of five standard notes prepared by the experimenter. Some pairs communicated at level 1 (the least information regarding proposed game behavior), others at levels 2, 3, 4, or 5 (the most information regarding proposed game behavior). Before a subject made his move he was asked to guess the behavior and expectations of his partner, and this permitted calculating the amount of mutual trust that the subject perceived to exist between himself and the partner at that moment.

It was found, as hypothesized, that the development of perceived mutual trust was a function of the amount of communication permitted. The percentage of Ss who perceived trust increased progressively with each communication level from 50 percent at communication level 1 (least information) to 83 percent at communication level 5 (most information). Perceived trust, in turn, correlated +.56 with actual cooperative behavior as observed in the game situation. The increased sharing of information regarding mutual problem-solving activities resulted in an increase in shared acceptance of rules and in mutual trust.

unobservable forms—because he approves of himself in the same way that other members would approve. This process can be overdone, of course: a person can, by reversing the direction of substitutability, self-righteously assume that all his own attitudes and behaviors are automatically approved by others, and therefore justified. But the fact remains that a group whose members share acceptance of a rule has such power over its members, with respect to that rule, that external sanctions are not needed. The power is, so to speak, self-imposed, and for that reason all the more effective.

Group norms are important precisely because they have such power over group members—power that is both external and internal. It is the sharing process that melds the external and the internal. Each of the two sources of influence is supported by and anchored in the other.

Common Elements among Different Kinds of Norms

This way of looking at group norms suggests something that various kinds of norms, apparently quite different, have in common. Insofar as conformity to rules is approved by others and internalized as self-approval, issues of conformity and nonconformity are imbued with a "sense of oughtness" (see Angell, 1958) that is characteristic of *moral* norms. But there are other rules, shared acceptance of which is very common, that do not include social sanctions and that, as they are internalized, are not accompanied by any sense of oughtness. Take Sherif's perceptual norms, for instance: it seems like stretching things to say that his experimental subjects felt that they *ought* to judge the light to have moved about three inches; it is almost certain that they felt, on the contrary, that the light really did move about that far. There are many instances of cognitive norms that correspond quite directly to reality, whether physical or social, and conformity to them seems to be based on reality rather than on conscience.

Or, to take another kind of illustration, many norms represent nothing more than routinized regularity, as when all family members expect Father to sit at one end of the table, Sonny at his right, Sissie at his left, and Mother at the other end. Such regularity cannot be said to represent only four persons' individual habits, because their habits are interdependent; if one of them takes the place of someone else, that person is displaced. It is a norm, in the sense of shared expectations, but individual conformity to it is maintained not by conscience but by simple expectations. There is internalization of the norm, but there is no necessary sense of oughtness about it.

What these two categories of norms—those based on reality, and those on mere routinization—have in common with moral norms, based on internalization of sanctions, is shared expectations. They differ in respect to the consequences of flouting the norms. In the case of moral norms, the consequences are disapproval of others and self-disapproval (or guilt). In the case of reality-based and routine-based norms, the consequences are little more than surprise on the part of others. But the fact that norms are shared, with the consequent implication of substitutability, means that he who flouts them—even though they be "nonmoral"—anticipates his fellows' surprise. It is sometimes fun to be surprised (as on receiving a birthday present) but sometimes it is not. Insofar as there is complete sharing and complete substitutability, the would-be flouter of norms has internalized the same feelings of pleasure, indifference, or annoyance (as the case may be) that his fellows will experience on being surprised. In this manner conformity to any kind of norm—even those based merely on reality or on routinization—may have a moral component of oughtness. The crucial matter is the shared anticipation of the consequences of flouting the norm; whether or not approvals and disapprovals are involved, norms exist insofar as there is shared acceptance of the rule, whatever the nature of shared anticipations about flouting it.

There is no absolute distinction, finally, between moral and nonmoral norms. As we have previously noted (page 39), there is a very common psychological tendency for what were initially only behavioral means toward goals to become satisfying in their own right: means become ends. Thibaut and Kelley (1959) summarize the matter as follows:

> . . . as Waller and Hill (1951, p. 49) so aptly put it, "The *usual* quickly becomes the *right.* . . ." The rule is likely to take on the characteristics of a moral obligation (or even to have them from the start). This means, in brief, that conformity to agreements becomes rewarding in and of itself (p. 128).

Insofar, then, as there are shared attitudes to the effect that "the usual . . . becomes the right," it may be said that all group norms have a moral component.

* * *

Shared acceptance of rules is dependent on motive satisfaction that comes to be associated with the rules; such satisfaction is a necessary but not a sufficient condition for sharing. Rule acceptance brings with it the advantage of being able to predict the attitudes and behavior of others. It also serves as a guide to behavior, so that the individual need not repeat the errors of others.

A consequence of rule sharing is psychological substitutability. This makes it possible for a group member to trust another as fully as he can trust himself to be guided by the rule. The internalization of norms rests on continued evidence that such substitutability is a mutually accepted and expected state of affairs. Because of others' expectations of behavior that is "due" them, conformity to norms is thus often judged to be morally appropriate behavior.

IMPERFECT SHARING OF NORMS

Our reasons for considering norms as "perfectly" shared, till now, have been simply those of clarity in describing the nature of the sharing process. In everyday life imperfect sharing is the rule, rather than the exception, and we shall now consider some of the reasons for this. We shall also inquire how it happens that group norms are so often effective, even when sharing is imperfect.

Conflicting Forces: Balance and Reality

The actual degree of sharing that characterizes two or more group members is an outcome of two kinds of forces that are often opposed. Forces toward sharing may be treated as balance-promoting forces: it is psychologically rewarding to perceive oneself as sharing group-relevant attitudes with attractive group members. Such a state of affairs represents psychological balance. But it is also psychologically rewarding to assess things—including other people's attitudes—as they really are; to act on erroneous assumptions is often to invite trouble. This kind of rewardingness may be referred to as a force toward reality, or toward accuracy in assessing things. Whenever two or more group members do not in fact have the same attitudes toward some group-relevant matter, these two forces are in opposition. And the fact is that different individuals—even members of the same group—rarely have exactly the same attitudes, even toward group-relevant matters. Hence most of us are constantly subject to some conflict from these opposed forces. Only if group members' attitudes are in fact alike (or, strictly speaking, congruent; cf. pages 125–128), can there be complete sharing, and absence of conflict.

Research Illustration 8.6 points to some of the conditions under which people commonly perceive consensus, whether it actually exists or not. These data show that most of the respondents tended to perceive other groups as agreeing with themselves, though the effects of reality forces are also evident, especially on the part of high-status respondents.

Overperceptions of consensus sometimes result from another kind of process, too, especially when there is direct, face-to-face interaction. When one person, P, suspects that O's attitudes differ a good deal from his own, he may have reasons for not wanting to appear as different as

Research Illustration 8.6

Prior to the 1948 presidential election a thousand or so voters were intensively interviewed on several occasions and information was obtained on a wide range of topics (Kitt and Gleicher, 1950). When these prospective voters were asked to estimate the votes of other groups, it was found that people tended to "pull" the group whose vote was being estimated in the direction of their own vote intention, even though this was contrary to the way the group actually voted. Whatever group was under discussion, it was found that Republicans were more likely to expect the group to vote Republican, whereas Democrats more frequently expected the group to vote Democratic. This distortion in estimating the voting intentions of others was found to be greater the more strongly the voter felt about his own party choice. It was as if everyone tended to "universalize" his own opinions.

When a respondent was asked to estimate the voting intentions of other groups, the distortion in the direction of his own voting intention tended to be greater when the group was close to himself than when the group was at a considerable social distance. For example, when estimating how most poor people would vote, those at the

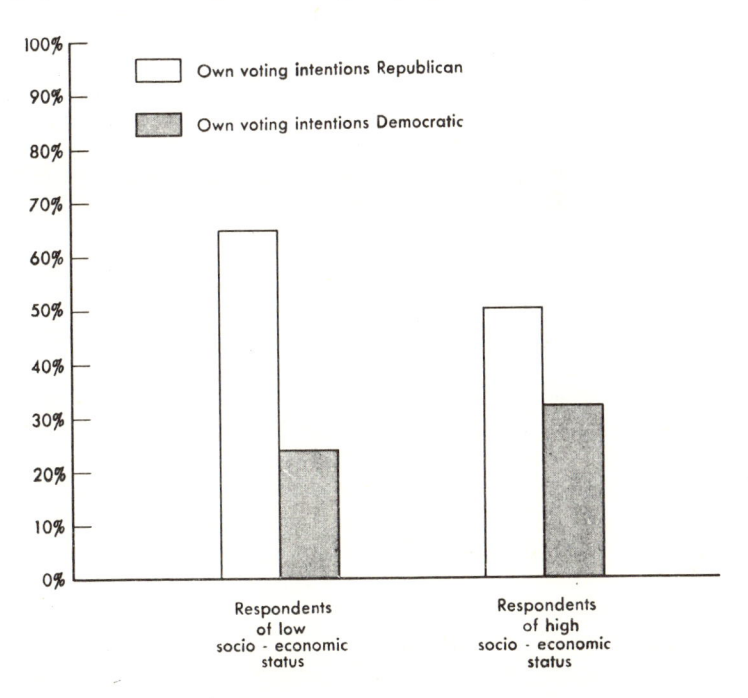

Percentages of four categories of respondents who estimate the "party preference of poor people" as being Republican rather than Democratic

lower socioeconomic levels tended to distort their estimates in the direction of their own preferences, whether Republican or Democratic, more than did those at the higher socioeconomic levels, as shown in the accompanying figure. Only 23 percent of low-status Democrats, as compared with 65 percent of low-status Republicans, thought that most poor people would vote Republican. This is a difference of 42 percent, but the comparable difference for high-status estimators is only 18 percent.

he really is. If so, he is likely to express those aspects of his own position that are least divergent from O's, and to soft-pedal the more extreme differences. What he says and does "halves the difference," so to speak, between his own attitude and O's as he perceives it. This kind of communication, not surprisingly, leads O to perceive P's attitudes in ways that are not very accurate, and to perceive greater consensus than actually exists. If O is much admired by P, or is of higher status or exerts power over him, then to be perceived by O as disagreeing with him may be threatening to P. Hence he provides O with a basis for overperceiving consensus.

Nonconformity to group norms is often threatening, in similar ways. Evidence for this is provided in a study by Hoffman (1957), who asked each of several college students to indicate in writing his agreement or disagreement with a series of statements dealing with social attitudes. Six weeks later each student was asked to indicate aloud his attitude toward each of the same items, after hearing the experimenter present bogus norms for each item that alternately agreed and disagreed with the responses he had previously written. Each subject's galvanic skin response (GSR) was measured immediately after he expressed his agreement or disagreement with the bogus group norms. The GSR index was taken as a measure of the anxiety induced by expressing an opinion at variance with an alleged group norm.

It was found that where the bogus group norm agreed with the subject's original response, the GSR anxiety scores were lowest. Under these conditions there was no conflict between forces toward balance and toward reality, as reality was described to the subjects. When the bogus norms disagreed with the subject's original responses and he altered his position in order to conform to this divergent norm, his GSR scores were only slightly higher. But when the subjects did not alter their original responses, and thus failed to conform to the divergent norms, the anxiety level was significantly higher than under other conditions. It was particularly high, in fact, for subjects who had made high scores on a set of questions designed to measure conformity needs.

The most common reason for imperfect sharing is the rather obvious one that there is imperfect consensus. The general reason for the latter is that no two individuals have had exactly the same experiences with the objects of their imperfectly shared attitudes. And one very frequent reason for such differential experience is the fact of multiple-group membership. That is, all of us belong to many different groups, each of which has its own area of group-relevant matters. But there is often some overlap in the content of the norms of the different groups—and often, too, some actual opposition. Thus it happens that if one is to share a certain set of norms with the members of one attractive group one cannot share them with another attractive group. A common solution to this kind of conflict is to compromise so that there is partial sharing with both groups. These matters are considered more fully in Chapter 13.

It frequently happens, moreover, as we noted in Chapter 4, that one has what might be called psychological membership in groups that one does not actually belong to, as well as in those in which one's membership is commonly recognized. Such groups, regardless of one's actual membership in them, are reference groups for persons who have a sense of psychological membership in them. The would-be fraternity pledge, for example, or the religious devotee who thinks of himself as "really belonging" with the community of saints, is often influenced by the norms he attributes to those groups quite as much as if he were a formal member of them. If one is not recognized by other members of a group as belonging to it, and cannot communicate with its members, one cannot, of course, genuinely share their norms. But such illusory, or one-way sharing, may nevertheless have profound effects.

Self-Perceptions of Conformity and Autonomy

Although it is often threatening to perceive oneself as a nonconformist, it appears to be no less so to perceive oneself as being merely a conformist. Most of us like to believe that we conform to group norms only because they are correct, rather than because we do not like to be different; the latter motivation suggests weakness and lack of independence. We feel prouder in saying "I call 'em the way I see 'em" than in saying "I call 'em the way they see 'em." The fact seems to be that contemporary college students in America (from whom most of our data come) are more strongly influenced toward conforming with many kinds of group norms than they themselves like to believe.

Many individuals achieve some sort of compromise between the threats posed by perceiving oneself as a conformist and as a nonconformist. Such processes are illustrated in a study by Tuddenham and McBride (1959), who analyzed the subjective reports of persons who yielded appreciably to group pressures in a modified Asch type of experiment. Responses to a questionnaire and to open-end questions revealed the interesting fact that many of the same subjects who yielded substantially also expressed attitudes of independence. These subjective feelings of independence from the group persisted even though their judgments had shifted toward the group norm. A study of the subjects' responses suggests that if the individual perceives a number of attitudes or positions intermediate between his own attitude and that of the group, he can move an appreciable distance in the direction of the group norm but still be aware of not moving the entire distance. If he selectively emphasizes the fact that he has *not* moved the *entire* distance toward the group attitude, rather than the fact that he *has* moved appreciably in this direction, he may be able to adapt to the group norm while still retaining a belief in his own independence.

There are strong theoretical reasons for thinking that originality and creativity are more closely associated with personal needs for autonomy than for conformity. How can one be creative if one mistrusts one's own ideas—if one kills them at birth, so to speak, on observing that they are deviant, rather than letting them grow up? At the same time, human beings are so interdependent that a great deal of conformity to norms is essential. The dilemma is a particularly sharp one for college students, but is by no means limited to them; it is, in fact, as old as civilization. The major outlines of the many possible solutions to the dilemma are reasonably clear, however. If a group or a society is to provide both reasonable stability and reasonable opportunity for effective and creative change, it must make clear distinctions between two classes of norms. Collective life breaks down without rather close conformity to certain norms, the outlines of which need to be clear and unambiguous. Other kinds of norms, however, need to be recognized with equal clarity as little more than temporary expedients that might well be improved upon. The long-range solution to the dilemma consists in the development of a master set of norms that support "the right to deviate" and that not only embody this distinction but also provide positive rewards for effective creativity.

OVERVIEW

Observed regularities of any kind may be stated as rules; for human beings who are members of the same group, rules are efficacious only insofar as they are accepted, and only insofar as group members know that they are accepted by others as well as by themselves. Under these conditions there exists a group norm, defined as *shared acceptance of a rule*. Since sharing represents individuals' awareness of existing agreement, or consensus, between themselves and other members, our understanding of group norms must begin with consensus.

Members of a group are often selected as being already consensual about group-relevant matters, and once they have interacted with one another as group members they are likely to influence one another toward further consensus. To the degree that members have similar attitudes that they express to one another, they come to share those attitudes. When such sharing represents acceptance of group-relevant rules, group norms exist. The necessary mechanism by which they come into existence is communication among members, whether intentional or not, to this general effect: "You can see by my behavior that I accept the rule, and in the same way I can see that you accept it."

The general consequences of a relatively high degree of sharing any attitude among group members are that individuals' attitudes are supported, and that attraction among the sharers is increased; as a consequence, group solidarity also increases. With specific reference to shared acceptance of rules, important consequences are that individuals internalize the rules so that they become self-enforcing; thus one member becomes substitutable for another, or for the group as a whole. In view of all these consequences, the existence of group norms means that groups can exert great power over their members.

CHAPTER 9

Interpersonal Response

IN THE OPENING PARAGRAPHS OF THIS BOOK WE RAISED A QUESTION ABOUT the universality of the Biblical observation, "A soft answer turneth away wrath" (Proverbs 15:1): Under what conditions is this sequence of interpersonal events most or least likely to occur? An equally important question would be: Under what conditions is a person most likely to give a soft answer to a wrathful person? You would probably mention, as one such condition, the degree to which the answerer considers it important to avoid or to quiet the other person's anger. This might lead to the further question, Are there other kinds of response to an angry person that are likely to alleviate his anger? William Blake, the mystic poet, proposes one answer in the following quatrain:

> I was angry with my friend:
> I told my wrath, my wrath did end.
> I was angry with my foe:
> I told him not, my wrath did grow.
> —*A Poison Tree,* Stanza 1.

Blake's lines imply that a certain kind of communication from P to O, following behavior by O that is annoying to P, will lead to a reduction in P's anger, and that this is particularly likely to happen if P considers O his friend.

Interpersonal behavior does not necessarily have to be studied in terms of sequences of individuals' responses to one another; such responses may also go on simultaneously. In either case, the major conditions that determine the nature of interpersonal response can be very complex, particularly because of *reciprocal* effects that interacting persons have on each other. Even when one person seems to be doing all the initiating and the other merely responding to him—as is the case of a patient in the dentist's chair, or of a boy who is yelling while his father spanks him—there are pretty sure to be ways in which the initiator is also responding to the other person. The dentist slows his pace, for example, if the patient indicates that the pain is intolerable, or the spanking father may increase his pace if the boy does not seem to be adequately affected. It is because of such interdependence between interacting persons that the phenomena of interpersonal behavior are rather complex. Interacting persons are simultaneously dependent on one another.

In this chapter (as contrasted with Chapter 11, where persisting role relationships are considered), we shall examine immediate, ongoing behavior from the point of view of *behavioral contingency*. This term refers simply to the fact that each behaver is influenced by, and thus, to some degree at least, is dependent on, the behavior of his interacting partners. Thus we can speak of the degree of contingency that characterizes each of them, that is, the degree of dependence of each person's behavior on the behavior of one or more others.[1] We shall later make a distinction between contingency that is approximately equal, or symmetric, and that which is heavily one-sided, or asymmetric. These are roughly equivalent to reciprocal and unilateral influence, respectively, since we use the term "influence" to refer only to effects and not necessarily to intentions.

INTERPERSONAL SEQUENCES THAT ARE DEPENDABLE

Interpersonal Reflexes?

If it could be demonstrated that "turning off wrath" is a standard, "automatic" response to a soft answer, this sequence could be considered reflexlike. A reflex—an eyeblink, a hiccough, or a knee jerk, for example—is defined as "a very simple act in which there is no element of choice or premeditation and no variability save in intensity or time" (English and English, 1958). Usually, moreover, a reflex-eliciting stimulus is phys-

[1] For our treatment of this problem we are especially indebted to E. E. Jones and J. W. Thibaut (1958).

iologically specific—such as irritation in the nostrils, or a sharp blow just below the kneecap. Given the required stimulation, the reflex response is "automatically" elicited, in some cases following learning after birth and in some (like swallowing) natively. The commonly recognized reflexes are responses to such stimuli as light, pressure, or physical irritation, but it is not inappropriate to ask whether there are stimuli from other persons' behavior that elicit reflexlike responses. If it is true that certain kinds of uniquely human behavior on the part of O "automatically" elicit certain responses with no variability on P's part, the study of interpersonal response should surely begin with this fact. Strictly speaking, however, it is not true; although there are *classes* of stimuli presented by O that with high probability elicit specified *classes* of response by P, the variability of both stimulus and response is so great as to preclude the use of the term "reflex" in any literal sense.

It is nevertheless useful to examine the evidence concerning reflex-*like* responses of P to O. Response to pain or injury inflicted by another person is perhaps the simplest case; the young infant's response to pain is indeed reflexlike, consisting especially of withdrawal or crying—but these reflexes are identical regardless of whether or not the pain is person-induced. With subsequent learning on the child's part, the range both of adequate stimuli and of responses to them becomes greatly extended. For example, the mere threat of pain, or psychological frustration without physical pain, may elicit either withdrawal or crying or any of a very large class of responses, including aggression (cf. Dollard *et al.*, 1938). In view of such extensions both of stimuli and of responses to them, it is no longer the case that the response is necessarily "very simple" or that there is "no element of choice . . . and no variability." The term "reflex" is hardly applicable.

Emotional responses are in some ways like reflexes. The term "emotion" is itself "virtually impossible to define" (English and English, 1958), because it has come to include so much, even as used technically by psychologists; nevertheless, a good deal is known about certain kinds of emotional responses. Typically, they are characterized by heightened states of feeling that accompany certain visceral states, and also by characteristic forms of motor response—laughing or sobbing, for example. Many such responses are patterned in rather standard ways, with relatively no variability, because their forms are determined by "built-in" neural and muscular patterns. Smiling is a good example: several sets of muscles and nerves are called on to produce a smile. Thus, a smile may be considered an individual reflex, but it is not an interpersonal one unless it can be demonstrated that it regularly occurs in response to specific responses from other persons. Actually, this cannot be demonstrated. Bruner and Tagiuri (1954), quoting from various studies of infant behavior, conclude as follows:

... There is a striking lack of specificity in the stimuli capable of evoking a smile in the young baby (even scolding may evoke a smile).... Up to two months of age, a human face does not produce a smiling response in the baby. From about two to six months, the presence of any human face in full frontal view evokes a smiling response—whether the presented face is smiling or threatening. Even a mask will provoke the response, as well as a strange face the infant has not encountered before. After six months, the smiling response becomes increasingly discriminative and only a familiar face has the capacity to elicit a smile (p. 638).

Later on, of course, the smiling response comes to be elicited by a very wide range of stimulus patterns. One of these is the sight of another person's smile. Under a fairly limited set of circumstances, one smile rather dependably elicits another. The necessary conditions do not ordinarily include the *mere* sight of a smiling person—as in a picture, for example, or the mere observation of a smiling person with whom one is not engaged in interaction. But when O's smile is, so to speak, directed at P, it is quite likely to elicit a smile from him. This phenomenon appears not to have been studied systematically, but we examine certain aspects of it a few pages later.

Strictly speaking, then, there are no interpersonal reflexes, in the literal sense, that are dependable. There is nothing surprising in this conclusion. The interesting and important forms of human behavior are too complex to be reflexlike, largely because they are so heavily influenced by individuals' learning experiences. Individuals who have been brought up in the same cultural background, or who have had long experience with one another, are likely, however, to develop some reasonably dependable response *sequences,* because they are familiar with one another's habits and attitudes. We therefore turn from interpersonal reflexes to a consideration of two general classes of response sequences that seem to be rather dependably learned.

Reward–Reward Sequences

EXPERIMENTS IN "MINIMAL SOCIAL SITUATIONS." The experiments described in Research Illustration 9.1 provide a plausible explanation of the learning processes involved in the development of reward–reward sequences—that is, being rewarded by another person and following it by a response that is rewarding to him. The only assumptions that need to be made in these experimental situations—that were strange to the subjects—are that a person who has just made a certain response that is accompanied or followed by a reward will tend to repeat that response; this is the central hypothesis of reinforcement theory (cf. Skinner, 1953). One tends also not to repeat responses associated with punishment. Kelley *et al.* refer to these two tendencies as the "win-stay, lose-change"

Research Illustration 9.1

Sidowsky (1957; and, with associates, 1956) began a series of experiments, later pursued by Kelley et al. (1962), concerning the learning of reward–reward sequences. Sidowsky viewed such phenomena "entirely within the framework of conditioning theory." Each of his forty subjects was in fact one of a pair, though assuming himself to be the only one. Each was attached to laboratory apparatus and confronted with two buttons, either of which he was to press, one at a time, for an instant, in any sequence and at any rate. Instructions were "to make as many points as you can," and that each success would be indicated by a red light. He soon discovered, also, that when the red light did not appear he received an electric shock. What neither subject knew was that he was hitched to another person in such manner that whenever either of them pressed the left button, the other received a red light and a point; when either pushed the button at the right the other received a shock.

The experimenters' principal objective was to discover whether, by sheer trial and error, subjects would learn how to get points rather than shocks. Learning to do so would require the discovery by each of them that it was necessary to follow a success by pressing the left button. To earn points consistently thus made it necessary for each (however unwittingly) to reward the other. Thus success presupposed the development of a reward–reward sequence.

Most dyads did learn to do just this, during the first thirty-minute experiment (though with many exceptions when only a weak shock was received). No individual, moreover, indicated awareness of being hooked up with another—having assumed that some automatic mechanism determined lights and shocks. In a second experiment, using only the stronger shock, half of the subjects were told that they were paired with a similarly instructed subject. Results now were about the same; subjects learned to reward each other, whether or not they knew they were doing so.

Kelley and his associates later pursued the question of learning a reward–reward sequence without awareness of its interpersonal nature. They modified the above procedure so that the two dyad members responded simultaneously (rather than at each one's whim, as in Sidowsky's experiments). A detailed analysis of their data showed that each of two comparable groups, as a whole, showed a significant increase in scoring points during the course of the experiment—as should be the case, of course, if most of them were learning how to get rewarded. Only twenty of their thirty-seven dyads, however (combining both groups), showed such an increase. It was thus possible to show that the members of the twenty dyads had hit upon enough successful sequences to learn the rule and to continue it in spite of occasional "misses," while the members of the other seventeen dyads failed, for one reason or another, to experience early reward–reward sequences, and thus were not reinforced as the other twenty were.

These experimenters also informed each member of one set of subjects that he was interacting with another person, not with a machine, and took pains (as Sidowsky had not) to show exactly how he was dependent on his partner, and vice versa, though not indicating which button had which effects. They found that in nearly all of their twenty "learning" dyads (but not in the other seventeen dyads) one or both subjects reported having used this information; many of them pointed out that their partners could be expected to be most dependable when most constantly rewarded. Thus we may conclude that understanding of the partners' interdependence, while not essential for learning the rules, facilitated the learning of reward–reward sequences.

pattern. Provided only that the simultaneity or sequentiality of response and reward or punishment is discoverable, they show that (under their experimental conditions) any initial combination of responses on the part of two persons eventually leads to a dependable reward–reward sequence.

Suppose, for example, that to begin with person A rewards B and, simultaneously or soon after, B punishes A. By the win-stay, lose-change principle, B would then repeat his response (punishing to A) while A would shift from a rewarding to a punishing response; they are punishing each other. Since each of them has been punished, each will shift, at the next "turn," to a rewarding response, after which both follow the win-stay policy. (This is an abbreviated and idealized account, of course; in practice, it may take a good many repetitions of each possible combination before the win-stay rule is learned.)

What we can learn from these "minimal social situations" is thus that, if there are enough reward–reward combinations, by sheer chance, to permit subjects to distinguish them from reward–punishment or punishment–punishment combinations, then reward–reward combinations will eventually "take over." As Kelley and his associates put it, the win-stay rule can "be learned by virtue of the fact that if the members' early responses are such that one person's adherence to the rule is reinforced, the other's adherence is also reinforced."

SEQUENCES INVOLVING RECIPROCAL OBSERVATION. Under everyday conditions, people can quite directly observe others' behavior and often, also, their own effects on others, as they could not in the foregoing experiments. We shall begin a consideration of reward–reward sequences under these conditions by returning to smile–smile sequences.

Students of the smiling response are in general agreement that most commonly it accompanies a state of felt well-being or euphoria. According to one review of the subject,

> Primitive laughter and smiling express contentment, pleasure, joy—whether the satisfaction is due to a general state of euphoria or to the effect of some special pleasing stimulus or situation (social or otherwise). . . . Darwin remarked that in apes the expressions of pleasure and affection are often indistinguishable. Much the same thing is true of humans, and this is not astonishing, since when we love a person we derive pleasure from that person's presence (Flugel, 1954, p. 712).

If the receiver of a smile makes this same assumption (that smiling tends to express euphoria), under conditions that lead him to believe that a smile is being directed at him, then he is likely to feel rewarded and to express his own gratification by a return smile. This is particularly true when, as appears to be the general rule, one likes to be liked.

In many ways the relatively dependable smile–smile sequence is typical of a large class of sequences of interpersonal behavior. We may therefore ask what are the *general* conditions under which the expression of gratification by O is rewarding to P, who observes O's behavior. Since the same conditions apply both to P and O, they will help to account for reciprocally rewarding behavior, or, in the term proposed by Homans (1961), the exchange of rewards.

It turns out that these conditions vary, depending on the degree to which P is favorably disposed to O. Given existing attitudes that are favorable[2] to O, then the mere observation by P that O feels rewarded (no matter what the source of O's feeling, unless P disapproves of it) is rewarding to P. If so, then P in turn is likely to express his gratification to O, who in turn is rewarded. The general principle here is simply that it is usually rewarding to observe that a liked or trusted person has been rewarded, and the observer is likely to express in observable ways his own sense of being rewarded.

Given a state of relative indifference on P's part to O (they are strangers, perhaps, or casual acquaintances), then P is rewarded by O's expression of gratification to the extent that he interprets it as stemming from O's motivation to reward P himself, perhaps as a response to his own preceding behavior. The general principle, in everyday language, is that it is nice to be appreciated, and that one is likely to express one's gratification in ways that can be observed by the appreciator.

Regardless of existing interpersonal attitudes, there are apparently universal norms that prescribe approximate equality in the exchange of rewards. The "norm of reciprocity" has been described as follows:

---

[2] Such interpersonal attitudes are more formally considered in Chapter 10 as attraction and aversion.

... It can be hypothesized that a norm of reciprocity is universal. As Westermarck states, "to requite a benefit, or to be grateful to him who bestows it, is probably everywhere, at least under certain conditions, regarded as a duty." ... Specifically, I suggest that a norm of reciprocity, in its universal form, makes two interrelated, minimal demands: (1) people should help those who have helped them, and (2) people should not injure those who have helped them (Gouldner, 1960, p. 170).

This very general norm is best exemplified, perhaps, in assumptions concerning gift giving (cf., for example, Mauss, 1954); the rules usually require that if one accepts a gift one must give one in return, and that the return gift (allowing for situational circumstances such as status differences, abilities, and opportunities) should be of value comparable with the initial gift. This same norm applies to simple, everyday courtesies—smiling, for example. Both the offering and the reciprocating of presumed rewards, in almost any form, may result in purely formal exchanges, which may not in fact be very rewarding to either party, particularly if they are regarded as being formal rather than spontaneous offerings. In a certain sense, such exchanges are nevertheless apt to be rewarding: to receive even a formally bestowed offering is preferable to being snubbed by not receiving it.

Distress–Distress Sequences

As we noted in discussing the experiments in "minimal social situations," punishment–punishment sequences tended (though not always) to drop out, eventually to be replaced by reward–reward sequences. And, in everyday situations, it is not necessarily the case that P, on perceiving that O is in some way displeased, will respond in similar fashion. In general, this kind of sequence is elicited under conditions like those appropriate for reward–reward sequences. Distress is often expressed in such reflexlike ways as frowning or crying, just as gratification is often expressed by smiling or laughing. Both the conditions that elicit such responses and the manner of expressing them tend to be extended and elaborated—in verbal expletives, for example—just as in the case of gratification. To observe distress on the part of a person toward whom one is attracted is distressful, but one does not necessarily respond by demonstrating distress. Expressions of sympathy by the observer imply that he is distressed, but attempts to distract the distressed person (as in the case of a child who has just had a bump) or to cheer him up may seem more like indifference than sympathetic distress. The observation that a person whom one dislikes is in distress often invites actual indifference—which may, of course, be interpreted as hostility.

P is especially apt to respond to O's expression of displeasure in the same manner when he interprets O's behavior as a response to himself. Just as a smile directed at oneself is likely to evoke a responding smile, so an expression of criticism or hostility is apt to be answered in kind. The general principle, applying both to reward–reward and to distress–distress sequences, is that like begets like when P perceives O's response as being an implied evaluation of himself or of his cherished values. What lies behind this principle is the same pair of commonsense notions: it is pleasant to be appreciated but unpleasant to be disapproved, and the usual tendency is to express such feelings.

* * *

The most general classes of interpersonal behavior, viewed either as stimulus or as response, are those that are expressions of reward or distress, or are so perceived. It is a fairly dependable principle that behavior expressing either gratification or distress will, if interpreted as an evaluation of himself by the perceiver, evoke a similar response.

In Chapter 1 we offered an illustration of behavioral sequences on the part of a mother and child that were so dependable as to be described as two halves of the same habit, and in Chapter 11 we shall describe them as role relationships of a certain kind. All role relationships, including those that are characterized by far more behavioral variability than our illustrative mother and child, involve some degree of habit formation in the sense that individuals have learned to respond in fairly dependable ways to role partners, often including total strangers. This is particularly true of members of continuing interaction groups, and generally true of persons brought up in the same cultural environment. Such response–response sequences, however, are matters of habit rather than reflexes. Habits, as Dewey long ago pointed out (1922), must be considered potentially flexible and adaptable rather than necessarily reflexlike. Role partners (such as teachers and children, or salesclerks and customers) do not ordinarily respond to one another in completely preordained ways, but rather in varying ways that take account of the immediate situation, the preceding behavior of other persons, and the general nature of the existing role relationship. The sequential regularities of interacting role partners are thus matters of general attitudes and general expectations rather than specific reflexes. For such reasons, we shall henceforth consider behavioral regularities on the part of interacting persons as matters of adaptation to one another.

INTERPERSONAL ADAPTATION

While persons are interacting with one another, each of them is in some sense adapting himself to the others. Even the elementary fact of noticing other persons and perceiving their behavior is a form of adaptation; responding to behavior that one has perceived is another form of it. Such adaptation on the part of interacting persons is reciprocal, not only because each of them is behaving and being observed, either in turn or simultaneously, but also because in the more fundamental sense each of them is adapting to something that he himself has helped to produce. That is, the behavior of O that P perceives was very likely affected by P's previous behavior to which O was responding. Thus, except perhaps in the most fleeting episodes of interaction, both P and O are adapting to events that both of them have helped to create. There is a sequential quality in interaction—not only between different persons but also on the part of each of them, because each has contributed something to the behavior of the person to whom he is now responding. What he is responding to is in part a product of his own earlier behavior.

Obvious instances of what might be termed individual sequentiality through the mediation of other people are those in which P contrives to make O respond in such ways that P can then respond to him in some desired manner. Thus a skillful lawyer traps his opponent's witness into saying something that can be used against him, or a wife asks her husband to do an errand so that during his absence she may prepare a pleasant surprise to show him on his return. The "self-fulfilling prophecy" illustrates such sequentiality in still other ways, often not realized by the behavers themselves. As defined by Merton (1957, p. 423), this refers to a "false definition of a situation evoking a new behavior which makes the originally false conception come true." A standard illustration of this phenomenon begins with rumors of an impending bank failure; those who act on the assumption that it is true by drawing out their money may, even though the rumor was initially without foundation, cause the bank to fail. At the level of simple, person-to-person interaction, a generally surly person often invites hostile behavior, and then wonders why people are so unfriendly, or a person who exudes good cheer finds a world full of good-natured people. These, too, are self-fulfilling prophecies in the sense that one's own behavior helps to make the kind of social world that one has come to expect. The fact of one's own contribution to another's behavior to which one is now responding is one reason for the inadequacy of any simple doctrine of interpersonal response.

Individual Adaptation

A good way to approach the processes of reciprocal adaptation is to look first at the ways in which a single individual adapts his behavior to some aspect of his nonhuman environment. Suppose a boy is attempting for the first time to chop down a tree. The essential processes by which he learns to become more or less efficient at it are as follows. (1) He begins **by being** *motivated*: his goal is to sever the tree trunk.

(2) Using whatever skills he has already acquired, he *behaves* in ways that are directed toward that goal; he applies ax to tree as best he can. (3) He *observes* the consequences of his own behavior; sometimes the ax glances to one side, making no impression on the tree, and at other times it cuts deeply, or perhaps gets stuck in the wood. (4) He *relates* variable consequences to variations in his own behavior, though he may have little or no awareness of doing so; he notes, for example, that a stroke at a certain angle is more effective than other kinds of strokes. (5) In the light of these observed relationships, he *modifies* his subsequent behaviors in such ways that they lead more effectively toward his goal. Even an experienced woodcutter goes through the same processes; the principal differences between him and the beginner are that he is more expert at all of these processes, and in particular he can better anticipate the consequences of his behavior under varying circumstances, and thus is less dependent on trial and error. These processes—behaving, observing, relating what one observes to what one has done, and adapting one's later behaviors accordingly—provide a model for examining any particular instance of an individual's behavioral adaptation, whether by beginner or by expert. They do not, of course, necessarily describe what actually happens in any particular instance; there may be no observable consequences of one's own behavior, or, if so, one may fail to observe them, or to relate them to one's own behavior. Our point is simply that the nature of adaptive behavior, if it occurs at all, is determined by the way in which these processes occur.

Though we shall note many differences between behaving toward persons and toward objects like trees, the individual processes of adaptation are in principle much the same. In either case a person behaves in some way that causes a change in his environment, and this change— whether on the part of a person or a physical object—may be regarded as a response to his behavior. Insofar as such a response is rewarding, his behavior tends to be reinforced; otherwise it tends to be modified in ways that are more successful. We shall now apply these basic principles of individual adaptation to the particular instances in which it is another person to whom one is adapting.

FEEDBACK CONCERNING OTHERS' EVALUATION OF ONESELF. One thing that is pretty sure to influence a person's adaptation to someone with whom he is interacting is his own set of assumptions as to how the other person evaluates him. Such assumptions (that is, P's perceptions of O's attraction toward P) may in fact be treated as variables that intervene between O's actual behavior toward P and P's adaptation to that behavior. Verplanck's interpretation of his findings, as we noted in our discussion of the feedback processes that occurred in his experiment (Research Illustration 7.4), makes use of such assumptions on the part of the experimental subjects.

As shown by a good deal of other evidence, a person's attraction toward another varies quite directly with the former's perception of the other's attraction toward him. This relationship is quite a constant one, regardless of the interactional history between P and O, as illustrated by Table 9.1 for high-attraction choices on the part of P. The interesting thing about this table from the study described in Research Illustrations 6.2 (page 173) and 10.1 (page 293) is that the relationship persists throughout four months of acquaintance in spite of the fact that high-attraction choices change a good deal during this period. That is, no matter whether one's most preferred choice among housemates continues to be the same person, this chosen person, whoever he is, is perceived as rather closely reciprocating one's own high attraction. This constant relationship of reciprocating "in kind" has been widely reported not only for first-choice preferences but also for other, lower-preference choices and even for negative ones (cf. Tagiuri, 1958). It is not possible to say that either of these variables necessarily has a causal relationship to the other, but only that if either of them changes the other is likely to change too.

TABLE 9.1. Relationship between giving highest attraction and perception of receiving high attraction from same persons, on the part of seventeen initial strangers (Newcomb, 1963)

Estimated rank of reciprocated attraction	Number of persons estimating reciprocal attraction from their own highest choices at level indicated		
	Week 1	Week 5	Week 15
1– 2 (very high)	14	14	12
3– 4 (high)	3	2	2
5– 8 (2nd quarter)	0	1	3
9–16 (lower half)	0	0	0
TOTAL	17	17	17

The relationship between O's *actual* attraction toward P and P's judgment thereof is not, however, a constant one regardless of the degree of their acquaintance. The accuracy of P's judgment will depend on the amount of information available to him, and this is likely to increase as they continue to interact. One general effect of these two relationships together (similarity between P's attraction toward O and his perception of O's attraction toward P, together with increasing accuracy of the latter) is that P tends, increasingly, to adapt to O by

268 - PROCESSES OF INTERACTION

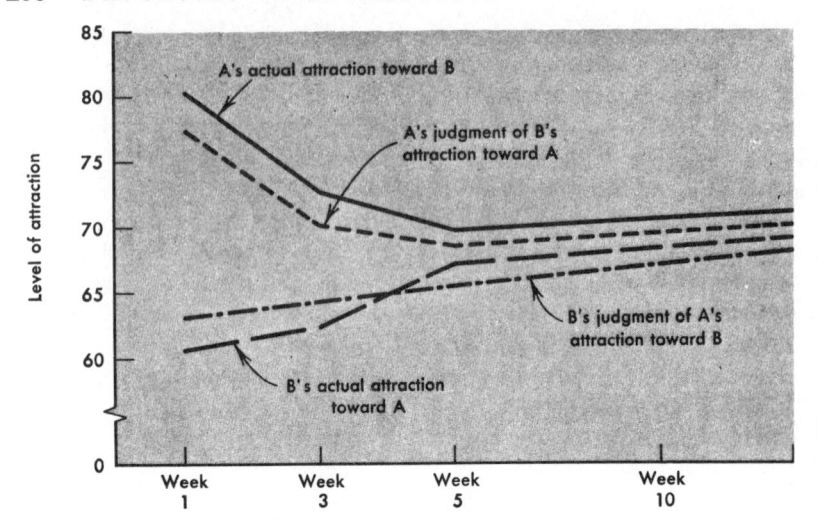

FIGURE 9.1. Illustrative set of attraction scores on the part of two initial strangers, after increasing periods of acquaintance. Scores are ratings on a 100-point scale, on which high scores indicate high levels of attraction. (Adapted from Newcomb, 1961)

feeling toward him very much as O in fact feels toward P.[3] Another effect, though less prominent, is that over time P's estimates of reciprocated attraction become more realistic, even at the cost of perfect reciprocity. Figure 9.1 presents some actual data that illustrate these kinds of effects. This kind of adaptation usually results in part from the fact that O is also adapting to P, and thus P has some effects on O. Our present concern, however, is with processes of adaptation on the part of one person at a time; central to any individual's adaptation is the way in which he perceives others as adapting to and evaluating himself. Information of this kind represents feedback because it concerns the effects of his own performance.

Feedback from another person, as compared with objects like axes and trees, is distinctive in that the other person adds something of his own. O, of course, is "the other person" only from P's point of view; and from our point of view he is different from P only for the temporary purposes of examining interactional processes. O feeds back to P not only information about his own adaptive processes to P; a tree yielding to

---

[3] This statement refers, of course, to statistical probabilities which allow for many individual exceptions. Prominent exceptions include highly popular or highly unpopular individuals, who are not likely to adapt to *all* of their admirers or detractors by reciprocating the same degrees of very high or low attraction that the latter accord to them.

P's stroke of the ax is doing that. What O feeds back to P, that sticks and stones do not, is information about his own psychological processes in adapting to P. Thus interpersonal feedback is, in a sense, a contaminated rather than a "pure" report from O to P about P's performance; it is a report that represents an amalgam of two persons' adaptive processes, and not only P's. It is part of P's task to disentangle these two strands in O's report.

ADAPTATION TO OTHERS' ATTITUDES. As we noted in our discussion of balanced and imbalanced systems of attitudes (pages 129–138), P's attraction toward O varies also with his perceptions of O's attitudes toward objects of concern to himself. This relationship is illustrated in Table 9.2, in which the common objects for each pair of subjects were all the remaining subjects in a population of seventeen men who were initially strangers to one another. What this table shows is that if a man's attraction to another man remained very high between weeks 1 and 5, then at the latter time he was very likely to continue to perceive close agreement with him about the relative attractiveness of the other men; but the more his attraction toward those same men declined during this period, the lower his perceived agreement with them became. Declining attraction is paralleled by the perception of declining agreement.

TABLE 9.2. Perceived agreement by seventeen men about other house members, after five weeks of acquaintance, with two men who had been their highest attraction choices at end of first week (adapted from Newcomb, 1961)

Rank of attraction at week 5	N of recipients of attraction	Mean perceived self–other correlation
1– 2 (very high)	16	.73
3– 8	9	.54
9–16 (low)	9	.31
ALL RANKS	34	.57

These and other data that might be cited indicate that one way of adapting to other persons is by comparing them with oneself. It is not necessarily rewarding to perceive others as resembling oneself—they may have different hobbies, for example, or different complexions and still be highly attractive; but insofar as self–other similarity in certain respects is rewarding, one tends to adapt to persons considered similar to oneself by viewing them as generally attractive. And, conversely, one adapts to generally attractive others by viewing them as similar to oneself in ways that are rewarding. Both kinds of perceptual adaptation go on together, in consistent ways, accompanied by behavioral adaptation that takes such forms as cordiality, friendliness, and trying to provide rewards for others. In similar ways, when the perception of self-other similarity or, more commonly, of dissimilarity is distressing, adaptation takes the form of declining attraction, together with the appropriate behavioral manifestations.

Reciprocal Adaptation: Dyadic Processes

We now examine more fully the consequences of the fact that while P and O are interacting, both of them (and not just P as we have been assuming) are going through experiences of adaptation. Since both are adapting to each other, we shall regard the dyad rather than its two individual members as our object of study. That is, we shall be interested in *relationships* between dyad members, which are characteristics of the dyad as a unit, rather than in the characteristics of either member, singly.

INDIVIDUAL REWARDS AND COSTS. Each participant brings to an interaction situation a set of attitudes, some of which will become engaged in the situation. He may bring to it certain present motives (as when he arranges an appointment for a certain purpose), and other motives may be aroused during the interaction (he may discover, for example, that he is being considered for a desirable position). Like any other living organism, he has a set of potentialities for being rewarded and also for being injured; he is susceptible to both gains and pains. As Thibaut and Kelley (1959) have shown in considerable detail, the processes and the outcomes of interaction can usefully be examined from the point of view of the costs and rewards incurred by participants.

From this point of view, any meaningful unit of behavior on the part of any participant can result in any combination of costs and rewards both to the behaver and to observers of it. To take a simple illustration, a guest at a party yawns; physiologically, he finds it more satisfying to yawn than to stifle the impulse, but in interpersonal terms he suffers some embarrassment. His host may be dismayed ("Is my party that dull?") but at the same time a little amused. Under these conditions both guest and host have experienced both costs and rewards. Let us assume that, on balance, the costs have exceeded the rewards for each of them. If so, the *individual* consequences might be that the guest subsequently learns to stifle his yawns at parties, and that the host does not invite the yawning guest again. Consequences for the relationship between guest and host—that is, for the dyad as a unit—might be a lower level of mutual attraction and decreased frequency of association; these matters are discussed more fully in a later section. Such consequences are brought about, as we have already noted, partly through internal rewards (like the inherent satisfaction of yawning, or of doing the right thing in the right way whether or not others appreciate it) or through self-administered penalties, like regret or guilt; and partly through the rewarding or punishing nature of others' responses to one's own behavior.

BASIC FORMS OF REWARD–COST EXPERIENCES IN THE DYAD. Simultaneous adaptations on the part of interacting members of a dyad may now be examined in the light of these individual processes. If for each member we view the possibilities as consisting primarily of rewards or primarily of costs (algebraically plus and minus, respectively), then there are three basic combinations: primarily rewarding for each (++), primarily distressing to each (− −), or rewarding for one and distressing for the other (+−). These three forms, the first two of which are symmetric, are illustrated in Figure 9.2.

Most if not all the properties of dyads and larger groups, as described throughout this book, can be better understood with than without cost–reward analysis. For example, dyads are most likely to be stable, as suggested in Chapter 10, when they provide primarily symmetrical rewards (A, in Figure 9.2) rather than when they are symmetrically penalizing or asymmetrical. Among the many forms that mutually rewarding behavior can take, those of sharing norms concerning important values (intellectual, esthetic, religious, or political, for instance) are of great importance in holding groups together, as we noted in Chapter 8. Whatever the forms of mutually rewarding behavior, the general principle is this: insofar as both members of a dyad find that rewards outweigh costs as they interact with each other, and insofar as each observes that his interaction partner is also being rewarded, the dyad tends to be stable.

As a corollary of this principle, the particular *ways* in which dyad members develop relations that are more rewarding than distressing determine the dyadic interactional patterns. For a certain pair of spouses, for example, a complementary relationship of dominance and submis-

A. Symmetrically rewarding   B. Symmetrically penalizing   C. Asymmetrical

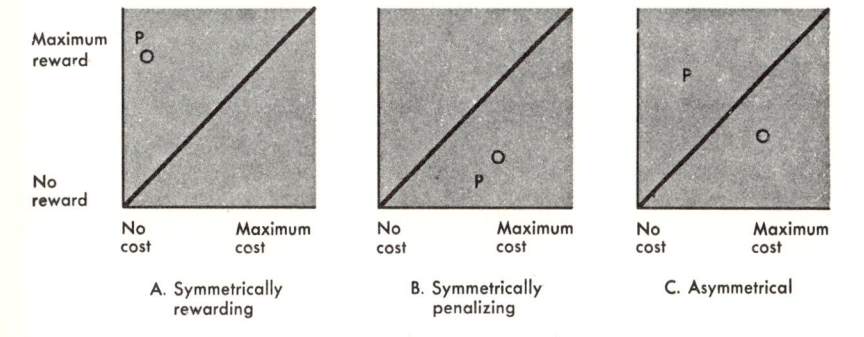

FIGURE 9.2. Schematic diagrams of three basic forms of cost–reward outcomes of interaction on the part of a dyad. The diagonal line represents points at which costs and rewards are equal; points above the line are predominantly rewarding, and those below the line predominantly penalizing.

sion may prove maximally rewarding to both (cf. page 301). A division of labor ("you put up the tent while I start a fire") may provide the maximally satisfying reward–cost ratio to both members. Such distinctions frequently involve personal costs, but these are often accepted in the interests of shared attitudes toward task completion.

It is not always the case, of course, that dyads or larger groups develop interactional patterns that provide a generally favorable reward–cost ratio for each member. The greater the degree to which costs outweigh rewards, the greater the likelihood that the group will disband or change its membership (some members dropping out or new ones being introduced, or both). Particularly in the case of groups that face strong forces to continue in spite of an unfavorable reward–cost ratio for many members (families, for example, or work groups that are necessary in a larger organization), there are various devices by which costs can be kept to a tolerable limit. Thibaut and Kelley (1959) analyze these possibilities in the following terms:

> A person often cannot do two things at the same time and do them efficiently and well. This is the phenomenon referred to as *response interference,* by which is meant that the performance of one response (or even the existence of a tendency to make that response) may be incompatible with the performance of another. Response interference is important in the analysis of dyadic interaction because for each individual the behaviors of the other constitute powerful instigations to responses. These may be incompatible with other responses which, by virtue of other instigations (events in the social or physical environment or internal events such as need or drive stimuli), the individual happens to be performing at the moment (pp. 51–52).

O's responses, in short, may be the source of costs to P by arousing conflict in him, or by thwarting him. O's criticism of P, for example, or his monopolizing of resources that P needs, may arouse incompatible responses on P's part: to continue what he was engaged in doing or to respond to O. Such conflict is apt to be experienced as a cost rather than as a reward.

The stability of a group depends on eliminating as far as possible the costs of response interference arising from interaction. In a work setting this can sometimes be done by rearranging role assignments so that persons who are likely to arouse such interferences in each other are no longer in close contact, or so that neither can monopolize resources needed by both. Many people have through experience in "training groups" gained new insight into ways in which they themselves, unwittingly, have provided response interference for other group members (cf. Lippitt *et al.*, 1959; Miles, 1959). Such insights, when attained as a member of a supportive training group, and when accompanied by the experiencing of the rewards of more satisfying interpersonal relations, can be associated with significant changes in behavior.

Adaptation as a Triple Confrontation

These several considerations suggest that one adapts not just to others with whom one is interacting but to a total situation that also includes oneself. It also includes certain aspects of the world beyond the interacting persons; there is very little interaction that does not include communication about something (objects, events, persons, or ideas) in the common environment of the interacting persons. And so any interaction situation may be said to present each participant with a triple confrontation; he must somehow come to terms, simultaneously, with each of the following:

1. His own preferences, needs, and attitudes, insofar as he considers them relevant to the situation; the preference for cognitive consistency and balance is of particular importance.
2. The other persons in the situation, including their demands and their preferences, needs, and attitudes as he perceives them.
3. Aspects of the world, apart from the interacting persons themselves, that are common to them and that are relevant in some way to the situation.

To the adapting person these are not three separate problems but a single one, though a complex one having interdependent aspects. One's mode of adaptation—compliance, for example, or defiance or withdrawal—represents a way of coming to terms with the total confrontation.

PREDOMINANTLY UNILATERAL INFLUENCE

In its most general sense, the term "influence" refers to any kinds of effects that one or more persons exert upon one or more others. Thus widely interpreted, however, the term sometimes becomes almost synonymous with "contingency," which we have used to refer to the fact that the behavior of interacting persons is in some way dependent upon one another's behavior. And so we shall use the former term in the everyday sense of pointing to readily observable effects that are clearly traceable to the behavior of others. To exert influence, in this sense, means that in some direct sense one or more persons so affect the psychological processes of one or more others as to control, in some part, their behavior or their attitudes. Thus predominantly unilateral influence, with which this section deals, refers to many of the same phenomena that we have previously described as asymmetric contingency. Reciprocal influence, to which the section following this one is devoted, has much in common, similarly, with symmetric contingency.

The first textbooks ever to appear in social psychology, by E. A. Ross and by William McDougall (both in 1908), made a great deal of use of imitation and suggestion as forms of interpersonal behavior. Infants and children often repeat actions of their elders, and so it was no wonder that McDougall, who was one of the most persuasive defenders of the doctrine of instincts, felt that tendencies to imitate and to be suggestible must be inborn. Fads and fashions do sweep through communities or even whole societies, and Ross was following an already established tradition, led by the French sociologists Tarde (1890) and Le Bon (1895), when he accounted for such collective phenomena in terms of "the suggestibility of human nature," especially as seen in the tendency to do what others are doing. Since all these men took for granted the instinctive basis for the processes that they described so well, they had little reason to inquire into the conditions of social interaction under which imitative or "suggestible" behavior might be learned. Even though we no longer accept their instinct-based explanations for such behavior, the fact remains that they first called attention, in systematic manner, to some important forms of interpersonal response. After all, people often do copy what others are doing, and they not infrequently comply with the suggestions of others—sometimes in extreme and "irrational" ways. For us, if not for them, the problem is to understand the conditions under which people do not respond to one another in such ways, as well as the conditions under which they do.

Imitative Behavior

The objective *description* of imitation is simple enough: any behavior is imitative insofar as it resembles another person's behavior to which it is a response. It is often difficult, under everyday conditions, to be sure that P's behavior, which is observed to resemble and to follow O's, is in fact a response to O's behavior. Under laboratory conditions, however, it is easy to arrange things so that we can be sure of this. Research Illustration 9.2 provides a good example of how this may be done. The findings of this experiment also support conclusions that are now generally accepted concerning the psychological processes involved in imitation. These conclusions are, first, that imitative behavior is selective. No one imitates all the time; one imitates some persons more than others, some kinds of behavior more than others, in some situations rather than others. Thus imitation is not a generalized tendency; rather, it is like other kinds of response that it is possible to make to other people in that it is one way of satisfying motives and expressing attitudes in certain situations. In the case of Miller and Dollard's experiment, children imitated as a way of getting candy.

Second, imitative behavior is like nearly all other behavior in that it involves the "standard" psychological processes of motivation, perception, and learning. If one is *motivated* to get candy (or almost anything else) but is not sure just how to do it, and if one *perceives* another

Research Illustration 9.2

The first few of a series of experiments by Miller and Dollard (1941) on imitation demonstrated that both rats and six-year-old children could rather easily be taught either to imitate other rats and other children or not to. The basic procedures were very simple. In one experiment, a certain child was previously trained always to go to whichever of two positions was indicated by the experimenter. Then another child, the experimental subject, was brought into the room and was instructed as follows: "Here are two boxes, there and there.... You are to find the candy. He gets the first turn. Then you get a turn. If you don't find it the first time, you will get another turn." Under conditions designed to teach a child to imitate, he always found candy in the same box to which the previous child had gone; under the other experimental conditions he found candy only in the box to which the previous child had not gone. After a very few trials, some of which were generally successful and some not, every one of twenty children learned to imitate the other child if he had been rewarded by finding candy in the same box, and every one of another twenty children learned not to imitate if he had found his candy in the other box. In the very first trial, incidentally, only nine of the forty children imitated the first child, the probable reasons for which you can readily guess.

In a later experiment with the same forty children, certain modifications were introduced. Candy could now be obtained only by choosing whichever box contained a visible though not a conspicuous light. Children who had learned either to imitate or not to imitate the previous child's behavior were now rewarded only if their previous habits happened to take them to the box in which the light, as the relevant cue, had been placed (this had been arranged in half the cases). The children whose previous habits led them to the unlighted box had no opportunity to discover that the light was the relevant cue; thus their previous habits were of no use in learning how to get the candy in the new situation. Of the twenty experimental subjects whose previous habits resulted in their choosing the box that had the light, nineteen learned to choose the correct box in the absence of any other child to imitate or not to imitate. Of the other twenty children, whose previous habits resulted in their not seeing the light, only seven learned to solve the problem. The experimenters' conclusion is that "the degree to which responses of imitation or non-imitation hinder exposure to the relevant cue is a crucial factor in determining the extent to which they will facilitate or hinder the course of learning to respond independently"—that is, in the absence of any other person whose behavior points either to the right or to the wrong solution to the problem.

person as being able to show the way to do it, then one tends to *learn* what persons, or kinds of persons, to imitate in what kinds of situations in order to satisfy the motivation. In terms of individual psychology, the phenomena of imitation do not set any new problems; they merely describe situations in which rather well known psychological processes operate with the consequence that one person's behavior resembles another's.

PERCEIVING AND REPEATING ONE'S OWN RESPONSES. One rather special psychological process, however, is directly relevant to the phenomena of imitation. It refers to what is sometimes called iterative, or repetitive, behavior by an individual. There are good theoretical grounds for believing that such behaviors—repetitive babbling on the part of a small child, for example—represent responses to self-stimulation. On uttering a sound, one stimulates oneself not only proprioceptively but also auditorily. Insofar as a child finds it satisfying (for whatever reasons) to hear a sound that he has just made, he is likely to make it again. Such repetitiveness might be considered to be self-imitation; whatever one calls it, it is a form of *circular* behavior; there is a reverberative process on the part of a single organism, according to which it makes a response that at the same time stimulates itself to repeat the same response. (In case you are wondering whatever stops such a process, the probable answer is that it is some combination of fatigue, of boredom, and of the greater attractiveness of alternative stimuli that sooner or later come along.) One way in which such processes are relevant to the imitation of other people is simply that an individual who has already learned to imitate himself in a certain way is likely to imitate the same behavior on the part of another person, when he perceives it. And, as we shall note later in this chapter, there are circular processes between two or more people that are quite analogous to these intra-individual circularities.

PERCEIVING AND IMITATING ANOTHER'S BEHAVIOR. One person's imitation of another (known as the model) sometimes occurs while he is already motivated to achieve some goal; observation of the model suggests a way of doing something that he already wants to do. Sometimes his perception of the model's behavior arouses a motive that he did not previously have, in which case he may imitate either in ways that he has already learned or in new ways that he copies from the model. In any case, imitation is initiated by his perception of one or more other persons who are behaving. Thus we may expect that many of the processes occurring in interpersonal perception (cf. Chapter 6) will be involved in imitation.

The content of P's perception of O may be described, as we have already indicated, in terms of the properties he attributes to O. Those that are especially relevant to P as a potential imitator of O include some or all of the following: O's motives (what he is trying to do, or what satisfaction he finds in what he is doing); O's competence (his skill, his familiarity with the situation, his probable success in achieving his goal); and O's trustworthiness (the degree to which he is sincere or trying to be misleading). Insofar as the properties he attributes to O add up to the conclusion (whether impulsively or intuitively or deliberately reached by P) that O has "got something" that P wants, he is likely to imitate him.

In some situations these interpersonal aspects of imitation are of minimal importance. In the case of a theater fire, for example, many people follow others toward a hoped-for exit without stopping to attribute any properties to them except their desire to get out. Or, especially in the case of children, another person's behavior is copied simply because that behavior seems inherently attractive, regardless of the other's properties. But in most everyday cases of imitation on the part of adolescents and adults, at least, imitators are selective not only as to what they imitate but also as to whom. For most of us, most of the time, imitation is a matter of perceiving persons and their several properties and not just a matter of perceiving disembodied behavior that seems to be worth trying.

Miller and Dollard conclude (as we noted on page 4) that imitative behavior is most likely to occur under "the social conditions . . . of hierarchy or rank with regard to specific skills and social statuses. It is true of learning in general, as well as of imitation in particular," they continue, "that the superordinated teach the subordinated and the latter learn from the former." In terms of interpersonal relationships rather than of "social conditions," a person is likely to imitate another insofar as he attributes to him not only superior skill or sophistication but also attitudes that are sufficiently similar to his own to make him, for the moment at least, a trustworthy model.

Compliant Behavior

Compliance, like imitation, refers to interpersonal response sequences in which contingency is primarily unilateral: O's behavior is more influenced by P's than P's by O's, in both cases. Compliance differs from imitation in that it is not necessarily shown by duplicating the behavior of the other person—typically, in fact, this is not the case. Rather, as the term itself implies, it involves complying with the perceived wishes of another person; P may have directly communicated his wishes, or O may only be making certain assumptions about them. Compliance probably corresponds roughly to the older term "suggestion," a term whose meanings have been so diffuse that it is hard to be sure of this.[4] Extreme forms of compliance are illustrated by persons under

___
[4] McDougall defines suggestion as "a process of communication resulting in the acceptance with conviction of the communicated proposition in the absence of logically adequate grounds for its acceptance" (1908, p. 97). Ross defines "suggestions" as "the abrupt entrance from without into consciousness of an idea or image which becomes a part of the stream of thought and tends to produce the muscular and volitional effects which ordinarily follow upon its presence" (1908, p. 12). The first of these suffers from the impossibility of objectively defining "logically adequate grounds," and both definitions could be so interpreted as to include too much to be very useful.

hypnosis, who often act out in quite uncritical manner even the most absurd instructions given to them by the hypnotist. Everyday examples would include common courtesies, such as closing the door when one is asked to do so. We shall have more to learn from such "normal" instances than from the more bizarre ones.

CONDITIONS OF "SUGGESTIBLE" COMPLIANCE. Experiments on "suggestibility" have a long history and a voluminous literature. From the very first, they have shown two conditions, as noted in Chapter 4, under which compliance is most pronounced: relatively little sophistication on the part of the complying person, and relatively high prestige on the part of the person who is the source of the proposals to be complied with. One very early series of experiments, which is described in Research Illustration 9.3, shows the effects of both these conditions: under these circumstances (including a hint by the experimenter that "the next line will be a little longer") compliance decreased between the ages of 7 and 12. The effects of the suggester's prestige are very much the same as in the case of imitation: compliance is most likely to occur in response to a person to whom such properties as skill, experience, and sophistication are attributed. The effects of age upon compliance are, in part at least, similar: the younger the child, the greater the gap between his own and an adult's sophistication, and the less experience he has probably had with older persons whose assertions need to be questioned. Such skepticism usually takes years to learn.

More recent experiments in this area have dealt with more complex variables. Coffin, for example, found (as shown in Figure 9.3) that

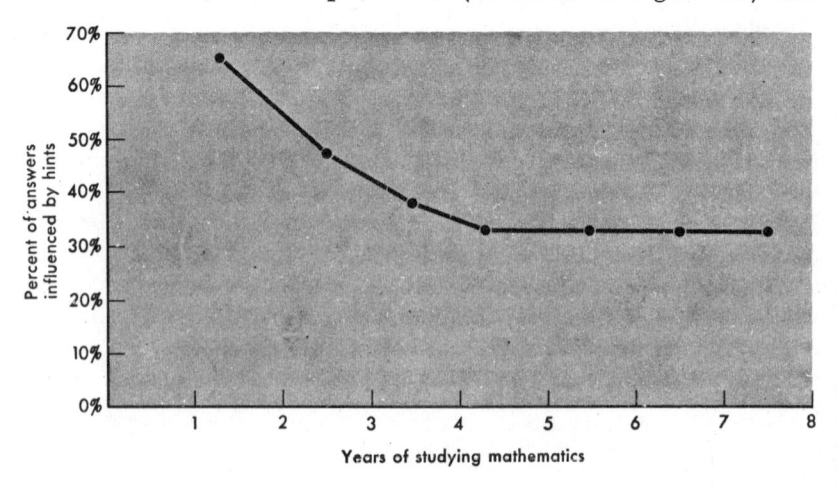

FIGURE 9.3. Relationship between years of mathematics studied and percent of answers judged to have been influenced by hints (adapted from Coffin, 1941)

Research Illustration 9.3

Alfred Binet (1900), the famous progenitor of individual tests of intelligence, devoted much of his professional life to the study of children. During the 1890s he became interested in what he called their suggestibility, and devised various kinds of experimental conditions under which he could observe it. In one of these, known as the "progressive lines" experiment, he arranged to have a schoolmaster show a five-centimeter line to a group of children, after which he asked them to reproduce it from memory. He then told them that he would show them another line that would be a little longer, which they were then to reproduce from memory. Although the second line was only four centimeters long, seventy-seven of eighty-six children drew longer lines the second time than they had at first. This seemed clearly to demonstrate that an adult in a position of authority could exert a good deal of influence on such responses by children. The next step was to ascertain whether, as might be expected, such influence would be greater for younger than for older children. A follow-up study by Giroud (1911), one of Binet's associates, indicates that this was indeed the case. Presenting the same line fifteen times, she found the average numbers of times that reproductions of it showed increases to be as follows:

for ten children aged 7	10.7
for ten children aged 8	8.2
for ten children aged 9 or 10	4.5
for five children aged 12	1.0

These results presumably show the effects both of the prestige attributed by subjects to the source of the suggestion, and of the subjects' ages.

among students who were taking an alleged test of mathematical aptitude, those who had the least background in mathematics were most willing to accept convenient "hints" (most of them misleading) that the experimenter had written in the margins of the test. The problems were of course more difficult for them than for advanced students in mathematics. In a related experiment, Coffin also showed that the more ambiguous the situation subjects were asked to interpret, the more likely they were to perceive it in ways proffered by the experimenter. Difficulty and ambiguity are probably very closely related, in these instances: the more difficult a problem for an individual, the more ambiguous for him is the method of its solution. The general principle involved is perhaps self-evident: the more helpless one feels when confronted with a situation that someone has presented, the more ready one is to accept any kind of suggestions that he may offer—especially if he appears to be more familiar with the situation than oneself.

It is hardly exaggerating to say that everyday compliance is the stuff of which social life is made; one can scarcely imagine a society in which compliance with requests like "Please pass the butter" or with invitations like "C'mon, let's go swimmin'" was the exception rather than the rule. But its commonplace occurrence does not mean that there is no need to search for the conditions under which it is most likely to occur. These conditions, together with those that facilitate imitation, are summarized below.

Unilateral Influence: General Considerations

The social-psychological processes involved in imitation and compliance are, for the most part, already familiar to us. Of special importance are existing understandings such that interacting persons share expectations that one of them will provide and the other will receive help or protection, for example, or that one of them is to accord and the other to receive manifestations of differences in status, power, or prestige. Such understandings are characteristic of established role relationships, as we shall see in Chapter 11. Interpersonal relationships of this kind, insofar as they are free from enforced constraints, involve the internalization of norms, so that there are shared expectations and acceptance of rules corresponding to the predominantly unilateral influence: both influencer and influencee desire, or at least accept, the unilateral relationship. No less important are relationships of interpersonal attraction. Influence is most likely to be accepted from a person toward whom one is positively attracted; indeed, to be attracted toward someone is almost equivalent to ceding to him some power over oneself. For similar reasons, influence of the kind that is likely to be accepted is most likely to be offered by someone who is attracted toward the person being influenced. Thus mutual attraction facilitates the combination of being offered help and accepting it.

Unilateral influence is sometimes facilitated, also, by attitudes on the part of the person influenced that are described by the term "identification." Insofar as one person wants to resemble another—say a small boy who admires his father or the local baseball hero, or a girl who "worships" a movie actress—he is said to be identifying with him. Such an attitudinal state obviously opens the identifier to influence by the admired person. Not all extreme susceptibility to another person's influence involves identification, however; one may eagerly accept another's influence without wanting to be like him.

In general, the principles that account for predominantly unilateral influence also apply to reciprocal influence, as we shall see. Indeed, influence is rarely unilateral, strictly speaking. Perhaps the only exceptions are those instances where the person influenced is totally unknown to the influencer. Any behavior on the part of the person being influenced that indicates to the influencer that he is having such effects serves to influence him, and therefore reciprocal influence in some degree is the rule in interaction situations.

The conditions under which unilateral influence is most likely to occur can be pretty well summarized under the following categories: (1) Inherent attractiveness, in the existing situation, of the behavior toward which the influencer points—one needs the kind of help that he is able to provide, for example, or one is bored and ready for almost anything new. (2) Degree and nature of one's attraction to the potential influencer—including especially his perceived competence and trustworthiness, as well as one's own eagerness to please him. (3) Requirements of one's existing role relationships with the potential influencer —for example, deference to be accorded to a superior, or learning the requirements of a task. If any of these conditions is present in extreme degree, acceptance of the influence is likely regardless of the others; and the more so if all of them are present. By the same token, its acceptance in the absence of all these conditions is not at all likely.

RECIPROCAL INFLUENCE: GROUP PROCESSES

Whenever people are engaged in interaction they are, so to speak, exchanging influence, even though the visible effects of the exchange may seem to be heavily one-sided. We shall now consider some problems of reciprocal influence, without regard to questions of equality or inequality of visible effects. We shall consider instances in which two or more persons influence one another in the same way; for example, members of a group of singers respond to one another by keeping together in tempo and pitch. In other instances persons influence each other to do different things: a husband may respond to his wife's nagging by staying away from home, to which she responds by further nagging. Our first concern will be with the processes that underlie such effects, rather than with their similarities or differences. We shall henceforth be considering dyads less frequently than larger groups.

Social Facilitation

Just after World War I, F. H. Allport (1920, 1924) carried out a series of experiments in which subjects were assigned a series of tasks under two conditions: alone, and in the presence of three or four other co-working subjects. He found that in several different tasks a majority of subjects—sometimes a very large majority—worked faster and turned out more work, though often less accurately, in the group situation than when working alone. He had tried to eliminate any possible effects of rivalry by assuring his subjects that their scores would not be compared; he therefore concluded that it was the presence of other people —especially the sights and sounds of others doing the same things—that stimulated his subjects to a greater output of energy. This is what he meant by "social facilitation"; as used by him, the term refers to purely quantitative increases in stimulation, followed by quantitative increases in work output.

A few years later another American psychologist, Dashiell (1930, 1935), repeated many of the same experiments, with some modifications; some of his findings are presented in Research Illustration 9.4. Based on larger groups of subjects and more exacting experimental controls, they suggest that competitive attitudes have more effect in arousing energetic production than does social facilitation, in the strict sense in which Allport used it, in the case of tasks like multiplication or reasoning tests. It seems likely, however, that processes like those which Allport described as social facilitation do have a good deal to do with the heightening, spiraling effects that sometimes occur under conditions of group excitement; such processes are noted in Chapter 14. With respect to such crowd phenomena, Allport's doctrine is very explicit: "Nothing new or different [is] added by the crowd situation except an intensification of the feeling already present, and the possibility of concerted action. The individual in the crowd behaves just as he would behave alone, *only more so*" (1924, p. 295). Taken literally, this statement is open to question, for reasons that we shall now indicate.

Group Reinforcement

The nature of group members' behavior, as well as its intensity, is often influenced by their interaction with one another; many studies cited in this book testify to this.[5] Insofar as the norms of any group affect its members' behavior, in fact, reciprocal influence is at work. Such effects on the content or the quality of behavior may be attributed to group reinforcement. This term refers to interactional processes whereby norms are developed, shared, internalized, and reinvigorated among persons as group members. Social facilitation, on the other hand, refers to processes whereby individuals who, for whatever reasons, are doing the same thing together, collectively exert intensifying effects upon whatever that behavior happens to be. Our problem is to understand the

[5] Cf. Asch (pages 239–240), Sherif (pages 458–461), Schanck (pages 225–226), Merei (pages 223–224).

Research Illustration 9.4

Dashiell (1930), impressed by F. H. Allport's findings that most individuals were stimulated to greater productivity when working at the same tasks in close proximity to others, as compared to working in separate cubicles in the same room at the same time, decided to repeat some of those experiments. In particular, Dashiell felt that Allport's findings were not clear in regard to the respective effects of social facilitation and rivalry. He therefore introduced varying degrees of competitiveness as an experimental variable. His major experimental conditions were as follows:

1. *Competing in groups.* Subjects were seated around two large tables and were explicitly told that their scores would be compared.

2. *In groups, with instructions not to compete.* Subjects were seated around two large tables and were explicitly and repeatedly told not to compete, as their results would never be compared.

3. *In separate rooms in the same building at the same time.* Subjects could neither see nor hear each other but began and stopped work on signals from buzzers sounded simultaneously; they knew that other subjects were working on the same tasks in adjacent rooms. Nothing was said about competing.

4. *Under close supervision of others.* Three students were seated at a small table; one was a subject while the other two watched his work closely and intently. Nothing was said about competing.

As the following table shows, productivity was far greater in the first and fourth of these situations than in the other two:

Experimental condition	Speed of multiplication	Speed of analogies	Speed of serial association
1	31%	36%	43%
2	17	8	3
3	20	18	11
4	32	38	43
ALL CONDITIONS	100%	100%	100%

Nature of task

Numbers in this table refer to percentages of subjects who did best or second-best rather than third- or fourth-best in each task under the experimental condition noted—in terms of number of responses, without regard to accuracy. More than fifty subjects participated in each task under each condition.

In a later experiment, sixteen subjects worked both under condition 3, above, and alone, by individual appointment, receiving starting and stopping signals from an automatic device. In two of the three tasks, twelve of the sixteen showed greater productivity under condition 3 than when in the laboratory alone, suggesting that merely the known presence of other subjects who were not seen had competition-like effects; no such differences appeared in the third task. Altogether, the data show that under the presumably "purest" conditions of social facilitation without rivalry (condition 2) production tended to be lower, not higher, than under other conditions. Condition 4 (close supervision) does not directly test the effects either of competition or of the "sights and sounds of others doing the same thing." Apart from this condition, effects were greatest when competition was greatest (condition 1). Thus the findings provide very little support for the hypothesis that social facilitation, apart from rivalry, contributes significantly to increased production in tasks of this kind.

processes of reciprocal influence: Just how does interaction among group members have the effect that they simultaneously influence one another and are themselves influenced to adopt new norms or to strengthen existing ones?

These effects may be viewed as involving communication and interpersonal perception under three sets of circumstances. The first of these is an existing relationship of *reciprocal influenceability* on the part of two or more individuals. That is, they have communicative access to one another, they perceive one another as potential communicators, and they are motivated to exchange information about some common (or potentially common) interest. Merely to initiate a communication is, of course, to expose oneself to the possibility of being influenced by the other person's response. If, in addition, P is positively attracted to O, he is predisposed to be influenced by him, at least in ways that are related to his attraction. (This is necessarily the case, because being attracted toward a person means that one attributes rewarding characteristics to him, and to be rewarded is to be influenced.) And if, furthermore, P needs O's help or his participation in some joint enterprise, then he is all the more subject to O's influence, because O may "control" P by withholding his help, or by giving it in various degrees or various ways. A relationship of reciprocal influenceability exists insofar as two or more persons have such attitudes toward one another.

A second condition that is necessary for group reinforcement is *communication that implies consensus*. If two or more persons know that they are going to be associating with one another—in a work crew, for example, or in a club—each of them will have some uncertainty, or even anxiety, in the absence of any indications of common understandings. The more important it is for them to pool their efforts—in working, in planning, or even in playing—the more essential is an awareness of consensus about matters relevant to their association. Consensus is needed regarding whatever it is that brings them together for a period of time, and the discovery of consensus is therefore rewarding. Hence each of them is likely to be alert to any expressions on the part of others that indicate common understandings among them. And insofar as members follow their perceptions of agreement by feedback messages, indicating that they perceive and accept agreement, consensus is followed by sharing. The process of developing shared attitudes and expectations is usually accompanied by a good deal of trial and error; eventually, however, through processes both of attitude change and of sheer discovery of mutual consensus, some degree of sharing group-relevant attitudes develops through continued association.

As we suggested in Chapter 8, shared attitudes tend to become normative; this occurs under a third condition, involving communication that may be labeled *testing and reconfirming*. The essence of this kind of communication, which need not involve the use of words, is that group members indicate to one another by their behavior not only what they themselves consider proper but also what they take to be the group's norms of proper behavior. Rommetveit's phrase, "norm-sending" (1955), expresses this notion neatly. If, for example, members of a certain fraternity nearly always dress in a certain way whereas members of a folk singers' group almost invariably dress in quite a different way, they are not only wearing certain kinds of clothes but also informing others that their group norms prescribe that manner of dress. If any form of "standard" behavior is admired, or even just taken for granted by group members, or if some less common form of behavior meets with disapproval, no matter how subtly expressed, such behaviors convey information about norms. Everyone who conforms to the norms—especially if he does so in confident, assured manner without subsequent disapprobation—is thereby reinforcing them. By the same token, every expression of disapproval at some behavioral deviation from the norms serves also to reinforce them.

During all these stages group reinforcement depends heavily on an interactional process of special interest to social psychologists: it may be labeled *simultaneous reinforcement of self and others*. Insofar as a group member finds it rewarding to be approved by fellow members, his own norm-conforming behavior is likely to be reinforced—either by their approbation or, if he has pretty well internalized the norms, by self-approbation. The same act of conforming also provides, in ways that we have just noted, reinforcing effects for other members who observe it. Apart from these simultaneous effects on the behaver and the observers of his behavior, it is doubtful that group norms would ever develop in dependable, continuing ways. That is, if a member's behavior were rewarding, and thus reinforcing, only to himself, it would simply be idiosyncratic and unrelated to group norms; and if it were rewarding only to others and not to himself, then he would not be likely to repeat it, and it might be expected that he would, if possible, drop out of the group. Although it is not uncommon that some members conform only in perfunctory manner to some of their groups' normative expectations, group stability depends in very basic ways on the principle of simultaneous reinforcement of self and others. In the absence of members' behavior that is simultaneously rewarding to themselves and to others, group norms could never develop and there could be little group stability. Thus the principle of simultaneous reinforcement is crucial to continued group life: each member's behavior has effects both on himself and on others, and the sum total of such normative effects is what is meant by group reinforcement, as an almost universal kind of reciprocal influence.

OVERVIEW

There are regularities in response–response sequences on the part of two or more interacting persons, but they are often not self-apparent, in merely descriptive terms. The regularities have to do, in any case, with the expression and the perception of psychological states of being rewarded and punished, and with learned coordination as in interdependent role behaviors. Individuals learn to adapt to one another's behavior through the receipt of return information, or feedback, especially concerning oneself; and also by comparing others' attitudes and values with one's own. Dyads and larger groups are most likely to remain stable when members provide maximal rewards and minimal costs for one another; this state of affairs usually presupposes adaptive processes on the part of members. Such adaptation confronts each individual with a threefold set of demands: he must simultaneously come to terms with his own needs, with the requirements of his interaction partners, and with aspects of their common world that are relevant to the interaction situation.

Although there is mutual contingency, or interdependence, in all interaction, it is useful to distinguish between symmetric and asymmetric contingency. The latter may be analyzed in terms of predominantly unilateral influence, of which imitation and compliance are examples; such influence is most readily accepted from persons who are liked and trusted, who are thought to "have something" that one wants, and who are thought to share one's own norms and values that are immediately relevant. Reciprocal influence is illustrated by social facilitation, a process by which sights and sounds resulting from group members' doing the same thing serve to intensify the doing of it on the part of all of them. Group reinforcement, consisting of processes by which observable conformity with norms results in reinforcement of the norms, also illustrates reciprocal influence: each individual's acts of conforming with the norms simultaneously reinforce them in himself and in other group members.

PART THREE

Group Structures and Properties

PERHAPS IT HAS NEVER OCCURRED TO YOU TO WONDER WHETHER A MOLECULE, which is composed of two or more atoms, "exists" in the same sense that an atom "exists." Most of us have no trouble at all with the notion that matter and energy can appear in either form, one of which includes the other. A good many people, however, who have no doubts about the "reality" of human individuals wonder just how "real" groups of such individuals are. As we shall see, there are understandable grounds for such misgivings, but we shall take the position that the "reality" of any entity has nothing to do with whether or not it is composed of subentities (as molecules are composed of atoms, and groups are composed of individual persons). It has to do, rather, with whether or not it can be shown that the entity—at whatever level of inclusiveness—has characteristics of its own that can be distinguished from the characteristics of any of its constituent parts. And, since there are many borderline cases where there is a good deal of uncertainty (for example, a few specks of dust that happen to be floating around in the same room at the same time, or some casual passersby on a busy street corner), we shall add a further stipulation: we shall not be much interested in the characteristics of human groups, as entities composed of constituent parts, unless it can be shown that these characteristics have some degree of stability, and that they vary in orderly ways.

It is easy to show that some human groups do meet these conditions. A family, for example, may have such characteristics as intimacy or divisiveness that simply do not apply to any single one of its members—because it takes at least two of them to be intimate or divisive. Sometimes groups of fraternity members, or of workmates, or of basketball teammates, or of community neighbors have a great deal of solidarity (or cohesiveness, as we shall later term it), and sometimes not; in either case, these are characteristics that do not apply to individual members of such groups. Since such group characteristics, or properties, are often rather stable, and since we know something about the conditions under which they vary, it is clear that some groups meet our criteria of "really existing."

The fact remains, however, that it is harder to identify human groups than individuals, each of whom remains within his skin and has persisting physical characteristics by which he may be recognized. In the case of groups, such awkward questions as these arise: If there is a change in the membership of a group—say the United States Senate, or a local chapter of the Lambda Chi Alpha fraternity—is it still the same group? Does a group persist even though its members are dispersed? Does a local group of the American Automobile Workers include members who have joined only because they were legally required to do so? Such questions obviously suggest that there may be many different criteria for group membership, and this fact represents one of the important differences between individuals and groups: there are relatively simple criteria for identifying any individual, but not for identifying any group. For different purposes, such diverse criteria as these may be used: formal, enrolled membership; individuals' feeling that they belong; the possession of certain skin color or physiognomic traits; or the frequency with which members of a group of persons interact with one another.

The fact that there are different kinds of groups, and that some kinds have little in common with other kinds except that two or more individuals are being referred to as a single entity, means that we shall need to distinguish one kind from another, but it does not mean that groups are necessarily figments of the imagination rather than being "real." And it also means that we shall need to be careful about definitions. There is, unfortunately, no standard usage. The only unambiguous meaning of the single word group is "a set of persons considered as a single entity"; without any further qualification, the term thus means little more than that the speaker wishes to view two or more persons in this manner. When we wish to refer to some special kind of group we shall therefore indicate that this is the case, by such phrases as *formal membership* group, *ethnic* or *residential* group, *family* group, and so on. For most purposes we shall be primarily interested in groups of persons who have face-to-face interaction with one another over a continued period of time. We have referred to these as "interaction groups," although if the context is clear we sometimes use only the term "group."

In Chapter 10 we shall regard an interaction group in terms of specific persons' attitudes toward one another, whereas in Chapter 11 a group is considered in terms of shared expectations among its members concerning their behavior; these reciprocal ways of behaving, viewed jointly, are known as role relationships. The conditions that lead to various kinds of commonly recognized role relationships are independent of particular persons, and so this way of looking at interaction groups is complementary to the preceding one. Since role relationships are maintained through group norms, this chapter is in a way a continuation of Chapter 8.

Chapter 12 is devoted to some of the more important properties of groups, and ways in which they can be objectively described. Such properties, as we shall see, are on the one hand outcomes of the ways in which group members have interacted with one another in the past; on the other hand, the same properties, as they exist at any given moment, help to determine the nature of subsequent interaction on the part of the same group members.

CHAPTER 10

Structures of Interpersonal Relationships

IF AN INTERACTION GROUP IS TO BE STABLE AND EFFECTIVE, THERE IS probably no more important requirement than that its members have favorable attitudes toward one another. This does not necessarily mean that all or most of its members must like each other, personally, though this is apt to be the case in informal, voluntary, social groups. In groups that are primarily task-oriented, on the other hand, respect of its members for one another as working associates is usually a more significant form of favorable attitude. Sometimes group members are forced by external constraints to remain together in spite of their negative feelings toward one another, but under most other circumstances favorable attitudes form an indispensable cement for holding them together.

In this chapter we shall regard an interaction group as one particular kind of structure among several possible kinds—namely, as an attraction structure. The structure of anything refers to the relationships among its parts, and the attraction structure of a group is thus a description of interpersonal relationships of attraction and aversion among its members. Research Illustration 10.1 portrays four such structures. This chapter is devoted to the description and explanation of characteristics of interaction groups, viewed as structures of interpersonal attraction.

Research Illustration 10.1

Throughout their four-month period of living together, each subject in the two seventeen-man populations described in Research Illustration 6.2 (page 173) repeatedly answered questions about interpersonal attraction. Degrees of it were indicated (each man toward every other man, and estimates of each other man's attraction toward the estimator

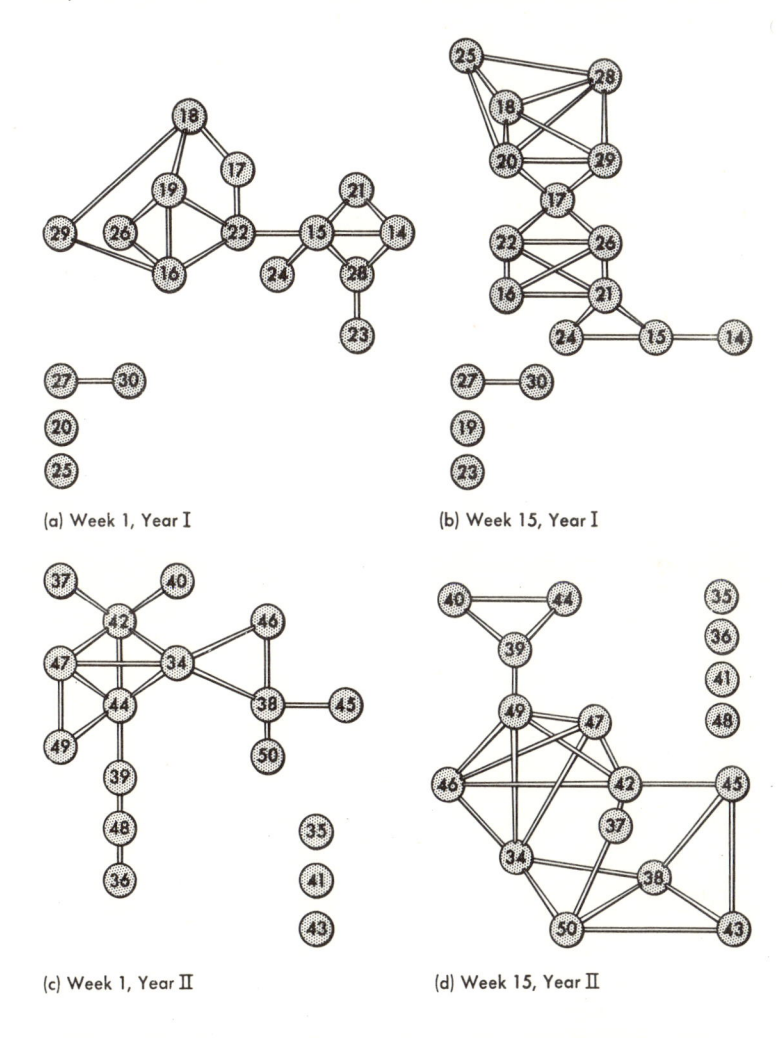

(a) Week 1, Year I

(b) Week 15, Year I

(c) Week 1, Year II

(d) Week 15, Year II

Sociograms showing all pairs and larger sets of individuals whose relationships reach a high level of mutual attraction. Unconnected individuals have no such relationships. Each circle represents an individual whose code number appears within the circle.

himself) on a 100-point scale ranging from "feeling as favorably toward him as I could toward any man of my own age" to "feeling as unfavorably . . . as I could. . . ." One of the ways in which these ratings were used was to construct an index of mutual attraction that characterized every pair of men (altogether there were 136 such dyads). The accompanying figure shows all the pairs whose mutual attraction was very high, according to a predetermined cutting point; these are dyads each of whose members chose the other as being highly attractive. These same pairs, with few exceptions, were also frequently mentioned by men other than the dyad members themselves as belonging together.

The visual illustrations in the figure on page 293 (known as sociograms) represent the structuring of the two groups in terms of mutually high attraction, on early and on late acquaintance. Several things can be seen merely by inspecting the figure: (1) Comparatively few (about 40 percent) of the early high-attraction pairs (or dyads) persist throughout the fifteen weeks. Early mutual attraction at high levels is not very stable. (2) There are many more triads (three-man groups) composed entirely of high-attraction pairs at week 15 than at week 1; they increase from 4 to 13 in Year I and from 6 to 14 in Year II. The structuring of high mutual attraction tends to become more complex with increasing acquaintance. (3) The Year I population seems to be more divisively structured than the Year II population, both early and late. Continuing acquaintance does not necessarily result in similar kinds of structuring. (4) In each population, at both times, there are two to four individuals who are not included in the high-attraction structure at all; none of them is included even in one mutually high-attraction pair. They would be included in a structure of mutual aversion, but for various reasons this kind of structure is much less interesting. Thus certain kinds of structures do not necessarily include every member of an interaction group.

As we noted in Chapter 2, the attitudes a person forms toward an object depend quite directly on the information he holds as to the properties of that object. "Good" properties are those that he has found to be rewarding. If a person's experience has shown that a certain property is rewarding, either in general or in certain specific situations, the objects to which he attributes that property are considered good, or rewarding—unless those properties are outweighed by others that he has learned to consider "bad," or punishing. Very few objects have exclusively rewarding or punishing properties, of course: one learns to weigh the good and the bad properties as best one can. Thus an object may elicit a good deal of conflict, or ambivalence, but in a particular situation most objects tend, on balance, to be regarded as mostly rewarding or mostly punishing.

With respect to interpersonal attraction, as with other kinds of attitudes, this means that processes of feeling and of cognizing go together. Being positively or negatively attracted toward a person is paralleled by endowing him, cognitively, with properties that one regards as rewarding or punishing, respectively. Attraction and aversion thus go with reward value, and may be defined as one person's attitude toward another person, characterized by the attribution of reward value, positive or negative, to him.

The particular ways in which one person can regard another as rewarding are numerous and varied, but our main concerns in this chapter stem from two general sources of these variations. Persons, viewed as objects of others' attraction, differ from one another, so that they have different kinds of rewards to offer to others; viewed as persons who are attracted to others, they also differ, so that they are interested in finding different kinds of rewards. Thus the nature and degree of any person's attraction toward another is necessarily an affair involving both of them. We cannot possibly indicate all the conceivable combinations of reward possibilities that one person has to offer and of possibilities that another person has for being rewarded, but we can at least illustrate the general principle that attraction is influenced by the characteristics of both persons involved.

CLASSIFICATIONS OF INTERPERSONAL ATTITUDES

A Psychiatric Classification

There could hardly be a simpler classification of generalized attitudes toward other persons than that employed by the psychiatrist Karen Horney, who distinguished between the tendencies of her neurotic patients to move toward, against, or away from other people.[1] The following excerpts from her descriptions of these types of neurotics illustrate how individuals who need certain kinds of interpersonal rewards tend to seek out others who can provide them and to avoid those who threaten to deprive them of the needed rewards.

[1] Horney regarded each of these tendencies as a strategy for coping with "basic anxiety," which she described (1945) as "an insidiously increasing, all-pervading feeling of being alone and helpless in a hostile world," and which, she believed, had its origins in repressed hostility. Our present interest is not in the individual psychodynamics of neurosis, but the interested reader will find in her book, *Our Inner Conflicts*, a theory that is in many ways congruent with contemporary social-psychological notions.

Persons whose dominant attitude is one of moving toward people are described by Horney as "compliant." Such a person

> shows a marked need for affection and approval and an especial need for a "partner"—that is, a friend, lover, husband or wife who is to fulfill all expectations of life. . . . He needs to be liked, wanted, desired, loved; to feel accepted, welcomed, approved of, appreciated; to be needed, to be of importance to others, especially to one particular person; to be helped, protected, taken care of, guided (1945, pp. 50, 51).

Individuals whose dominant characteristic is one of moving against people are above all interested in being "tough," or "aggressive." They regard themselves as "realistic" in recognizing that they live in a world of "every man for himself." They are apt to regard doctrines of humility and brotherly love as confessions of weakness, or as hypocritical pretensions. Such a person feels that

> the world is an arena where, in the Darwinian sense, only the fittest survive and the strong annihilate the weak. . . . Hence his primary need becomes one of control over others. . . . He needs to excel, to achieve success, prestige, or recognition in any form. . . . In contrast to the compliant type, who is afraid to win a game, he is a bad loser. . . . A strong need to exploit others, to outsmart them, to make them of use to himself, is part of the picture (pp. 64, 66).

"Detached" persons, whose general attitude is that of moving away from people, are described by Horney as follows:

> What is crucial is their inner need to put emotional distance between themselves and others . . . not to get emotionally involved with others in any way, whether in love, fight, cooperation or competition. . . . Self-sufficiency and privacy both serve his outstanding need, the need for independence which has a negative orientation: it is aimed at *not* being influenced, coerced, tied, obligated. . . . To conform with accepted rules of behavior or traditional sets of values is repellent to him. . . . The need to feel superior . . . must be stressed. . . . Abhorring competitive struggle, he does not want to excel through consistent effort. He feels rather that the treasures within him should be recognized without any effort on his part. . . . He may liken himself to a tree standing alone on a hilltop, while the trees in the forest below are stunted by those about them.
>
> Where the compliant type looks at his fellow men with the silent question, "Will he like me?"—and the aggressive type wants to know, "How strong an adversary is he?" or "Can he be useful to me?"—the detached person's first concern is, "Will he interfere with me? Will he want to influence me or leave me alone?" (pp. 75, 77, 78, 79, 80).

These excerpts are not meant to suggest that people are divided into these three "pure types," but rather to illustrate differences in the kinds of interpersonal response that different people find rewarding—and, correspondingly, differences in the kinds of properties in other persons to which they are sensitive.

A Social-Psychological Classification

Leary, a psychologist, has proposed (1957) a set of categories of interpersonal behaviors, derived from a systematic ordering of many thousands of observations of several scores of individuals. It eventually became clear that all of an initial list of several hundred terms referring to interpersonal behavior could be classified as involving more or less of two basic kinds of relationship: power (dominance–submission) and affiliation (hostility–affection). Different combinations of these two basic forms of relationship gradually merge into one another, so that Leary found it useful to portray them as different sectors of a circle, as shown in Figure 10.1. Thus dominating and submissive behavior, as opposites

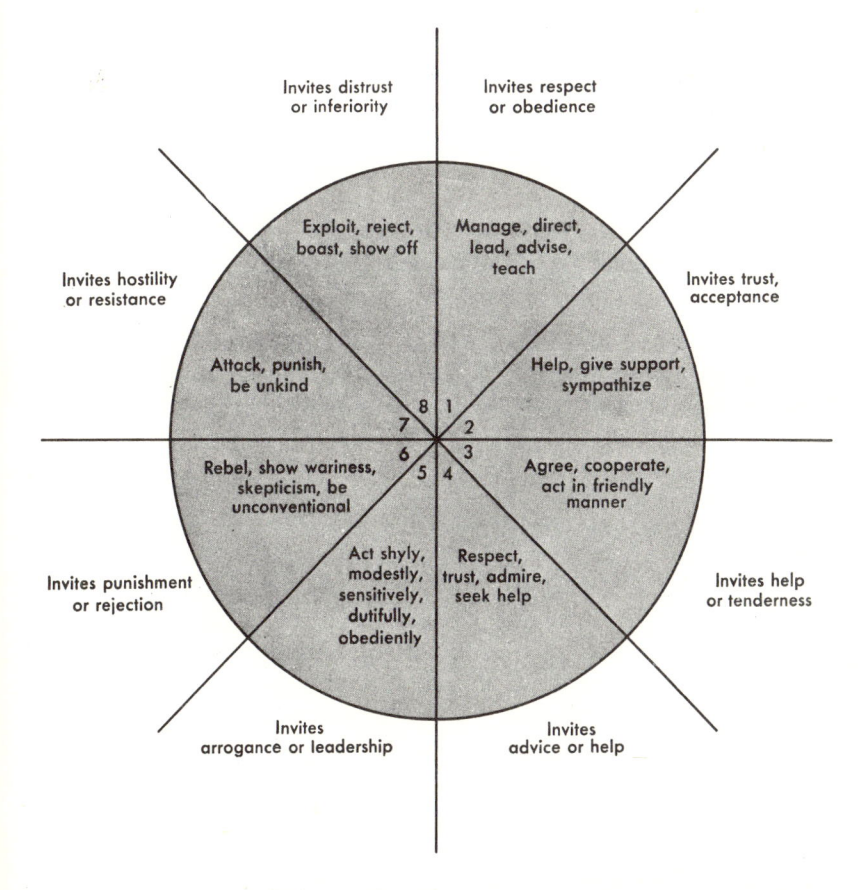

FIGURE 10.1. Eightfold classification of forms of interpersonal behavior (within the circle) together with corresponding forms of behavior (outside the sectors) likely to be evoked by each (adapted from Leary, 1957)

along the same dimension, appear on opposite sides of the circle, as do hostility and affection.

If we view such forms of behavior as potentially rewarding or punishing to others, then they provide bases for attraction or aversion. Leary and his associates have therefore indicated the nature of attitudes or behavior that tends to be evoked on the part of others by each kind of behavior, as indicated by the phrases just outside each sector of the circle. The relationships between initiating and responding behaviors (inside and outside the circle, respectively) will suggest forms of reward and punishment. Sectors 7 and 8, for example, include behaviors that are likely to be punishing and that invite responses that are also likely to be punishing, whereas the behaviors noted in sectors 2, 3, and 4 are primarily rewarding and tend to invite responses that are rewarding. There are few if any forms of behavior that are always rewarding or always punishing to everyone under all circumstances; we are referring to most probable evaluations, not inevitable ones, of these various kinds of behavior as bases of attraction or aversion.

BASES OF ATTRACTION: PROPERTIES ATTRIBUTED TO OTHERS

The ways in which one person may be attractive to another may also be classified in terms of the characteristics that the one attributes to the other. In principle, the same could be said about the attractiveness of nonhuman objects, but some of the characteristics of persons are uniquely human; hence it is to be expected that some of the sources of rewards offered by human beings will be unique to them. Among the three general bases of attraction (that is, sources of reward) listed below, the first two are distinctively human: they presuppose the attribution of attitudes to another person—attitudes that are strictly comparable to those held by the attributor himself. So far as we can tell, this kind of relationship does not exist except among human beings; that is, even the "higher" animals probably do not attribute to one another attitudes that correspond to their own. Thus the basic nature of interpersonal attraction is in important ways different from all other attitudes, because people attribute properties to one another that are, with minor exceptions, attributed only by and only to human beings.

Reciprocated Attraction

Most people like to be liked, trusted, admired, or respected. If another's behavior toward oneself is interpreted as meaning that his attitudes toward oneself are favorable, one feels rewarded and tends to reciprocate the other's attraction toward oneself. This tendency is consistent with the general principles of balance, as outlined in Chapter 5. If one's attitudes toward oneself are primarily favorable, then it is balance-promoting to be attracted toward another person who provides support for this important attitude.

The evidence concerning this basis of attraction is particularly clear. Degree of attraction toward other persons is closely associated with degree of perceived attraction on the part of those persons toward oneself. Within the first of the two populations described in Research Illustration 10.1, for example, none of the 17 men at any time estimated that the reciprocated attraction of the individual toward whom his own attraction was strongest was in the lower half of all ratings made by that individual. Table 9.1 (page 267) shows that 12 to 14 of the 17 men believed that their own highest-attraction choices were reciprocated either at the highest or the second-highest of 16 ranks. Similar estimates were made by the second population, with almost identical results. The exceptions, who did not estimate high-attraction reciprocation by their highest-attraction choices, were relatively unpopular individuals who, after several weeks, recognized that the highly popular men whom they chose did not reciprocate their choices at very high levels. (These almost uniform estimates that one's own high attraction is reciprocated at the same level were often exaggerations of the real facts, according to which reciprocation was in many cases lower than estimated.)

Although this and other evidence (cf. Tagiuri *et al.*, 1953) indicate that the relationship between one's own attraction to others and one's judgment of their attraction to oneself is very close under conditions of face-to-face interaction, it does not prove that one's own attraction is the dependent and perceived reciprocation the independent variable. It might equally well be the other way, and probably the cause-and-effect relationship operates in both directions. It seems safe to conclude, however, that—except under relatively infrequent conditions such as those just noted—the attribution to others of high attraction toward oneself is one basis for high attraction toward them in the sense that it almost universally accompanies high attraction. But it is not, apparently, a sufficient basis, since all the available evidence indicates that high attraction almost always has more than one basis.

Perceived Attitudinal Support

One is apt to be attracted toward other persons if one believes that their interests are likely to lead to forms of behavioral collaboration that one finds rewarding (such as playing chess or sharing a task); or that their knowledgeability in a certain area is likely to prove instructive or authoritative (as in the case of a student's admiration for a renowned professor); or that their values (religious, perhaps, or political) provide support for one's own. All these attributed attitudes have in common the associated expectation that the persons to whom they are attributed will provide some kind of support—as collaborators in interesting activities, as authorities about matters that demand expertness, as reinforcers of beliefs that are not universally held—that is rewarding.

An illustrative set of data, from the same students just described, appears in Table 10.1. Each of the 17 men first ranked the six Spranger Values (labeled theoretical, economic, aesthetic, social, political, religious; cf. pages 139–140 ff.) in terms of their relative importance to themselves. Then each of the 17 men estimated how each of the other 16 would rank-order the same values in importance; there were thus 272 estimates in all. By comparing the 16 estimates made by each individual with his own responses, it was possible to note which of the other men he considered to be most closely in agreement with himself, which second closest, and so on. In Table 10.1 the levels of attraction (based on each man's ranks, from 1 to 16) are shown to be much higher toward those individuals with whom the estimators consider themselves in close agreement (ranks 1-2) than toward those at lower levels of estimated agreement.

TABLE 10.1. Relationship between attraction toward other men and perceived agreement with them about Spranger Values

	Numbers of persons estimated by each of 17 men to be highest or second highest in agreement with themselves	
Ranks of attraction	*Actual responses*	*Chance expectations*
1– 4 (high)	19	8.5
5– 8	6	8.5
9–12	7	8.5
13–16 (low)	2	8.5
TOTAL	34	34

These and other similar data show quite clearly that high attraction toward others tends to be associated with the attribution to them of values like one's own. But this fact, again, tells us nothing as to which of the variables is the independent and the other the dependent one. We do, however, obtain some enlightenment about this from the following facts: (1) the responses in Table 10.1 were obtained after only two weeks of acquaintance on the part of these men, who had been total strangers before; and (2) the relationships shown in this table are almost exactly the same after three additional months of acquaintance.

It seems reasonable to assume that, although the men may have been quite sure of how much they were attracted to other men after knowing them for two weeks, they could scarcely have known much about the relative importance of these six values to each of the other men, whom they had never seen until recently. At first, then, it seems likely that perceived agreement was influenced by existing attraction more than the other way around. After nearly four months of close acquaintance, however, the situation was different. At that time it is known that they estimated each other's values more accurately, and by then they had changed their attraction preferences in such ways that, in general, they were attracted toward those individuals whom they *accurately* perceived to be in agreement with them. Hence we must conclude that, particularly at the later time, attraction was also influenced by the perception of value support. Thus we see once more that it is necessary to think in terms of systems of attitudes rather than in terms of separate ones.

Role support, which has to do with the rewards of behavioral interaction, is quite as important as value support. A small child's attraction to its mother is largely the outgrowth of interaction during which he receives help, physical comfort, consolation, and so on. Individuals who find that they play well together at tennis or in musical performance, or who merely enjoy conversational bantering, are providing role support for each other. These last illustrations are forms of reciprocal role support; that is, the interacting persons provide very similar forms of reward for each other. The interacting mother and small child, on the other hand, who reward each other in quite different ways, provide an instance of asymmetrical role support. One interesting series of studies of married couples has been made to test a theory of "complementary needs," the following examples of which are offered:

> If A is highly ascendant, we should expect A to be more attracted maritally to B, who is submissive, than to C who, like A, is ascendant. If A is somewhat sadistic, we should expect A to be more attracted maritally to B, who is somewhat masochistic, than to C who is sadistic. If A is a succorant person [having needs to be helped or protected] we should expect A to be attracted to nurturant B [having needs to give help or protection] rather than to succorant C. And in each of these cases B should be reciprocally attracted to A (Winch, Ktsanes, and Ktsanes, 1954, p. 242).

Their intensive study of twenty-five recently married couples, involving long interviews and many kinds of psychological tests, indicated that (particularly as inferred from interview responses) there were indeed a good many couples who were characterized by such opposite needs as succorance and nurturance, or dominance and submission. Each member of such a couple would be rewarded by receiving the very kinds of behavior that the other member found it rewarding to make:

both are rewarded by the same behavior. There is of course no general reason why reciprocal rewards should necessarily correspond to complementary needs rather than to similar ones. The important thing, from the point of view of maintaining a continuing interpersonal relationship, is that both (or all) of the interacting persons find role support in rewarding ways.

Nonattitudinal Characteristics

There are many personal characteristics that may be regarded as rewarding or annoying but that do not depend on the attribution of attitudes. One may find another person good-looking, jovial, intelligent, or pleasant-voiced and thus be attracted to him for the same kinds of reasons, psychologically, that one likes gay waltz music or flavorful oranges. Since it takes time to obtain evidence concerning another person's attitudes, first impressions of others are apt to be based pretty much on such personal characteristics of nonattitudinal nature. The effects of such characteristics are not limited to first impressions, but with increasing acquaintance it becomes more difficult to disentangle the several bases of attraction.

The data reported in Research Illustration 10.2 suggest that impressions obtained from very limited observation refer more frequently to physical and behavioral characteristics (such as being quiet, dark, foreign-born) than to motives or attitudes (like modesty, enjoyment of the occasion, or congeniality). And yet the judges' reports show that their impressions are not limited to objective observations: they include attitudes that are inferred from what is observed, and nearly all the judges attribute to Mr. X such attitudes as friendliness, warmth, shyness, sensitivity, open-mindedness. From these and other data we may conclude that one's feelings of attraction toward a person are based both on his personal characteristics, as directly perceived, and also on the attitudes that one infers from those characteristics or that one otherwise attributes to him. Interpersonal attraction, in any particular instance, is a resultant of the rewardingness to the perceiver of all the characteristics that he attributes to the other person.

DYADIC ATTRACTION AS A BASIS FOR GROUP STRUCTURE

The smallest possible group is a dyad, composed of two persons. We shall consider its attraction structure as being composed of two attitudes—each person's toward the other; these two attitudes, consid-

Research Illustration 10.2

G. W. Allport (1961) has reported a demonstration in which an instructor invited a friend to come into the classroom and join him on the platform. The friend, a stranger to the students, was asked by the instructor, "What do you think of the weather?" The stranger made some neutral comments and left the room after about one minute. The students then wrote for three minutes in response to this request: "Will you please write down your impression of Mr. X? Anything that has come to your mind about him. Just list your first impressions."

On the average, the students wrote down 5.6 separate impressions during the three minutes allowed. In all, 259 impressions were noted, distributed as follows:

	Percentage of total impressions
Personal traits (quiet, humorous, cultivated, modest and so on)	56
Physical characteristics (dark, angular, well-dressed)	14
Situational judgments (trying to please, enjoys occasion, unaccustomed to group)	12
Ethnic characteristics (foreign-born, Jewish, European)	7
Status and role (may be a photographer, teaches science, belongs to wealthy class)	7
Effect on judge's feelings (nice guy, congenial, disconcerting)	4
TOTAL	100

These results are fairly typical of studies of first impressions in showing that reports usually include a number of personal characteristics on the basis of very little information, and that nevertheless there is considerable agreement among the judges concerning some characteristics. In this case, nearly all judges agreed that Mr. X was intelligent, friendly, warm, shy, sensitive, well-mannered, and not opinionated. These judgments were not necessarily correct, but the agreement does indicate that persons raised in the same culture often tend to utilize the same cues in similar ways in forming impressions of other persons.

---

ered together, constitute a relationship. A group of three (a triad) is more complex, since its structure is made up of three person-to-person relationships. There are six pair relationships within a four-person group, ten of them in a five-person group, fifteen for six persons, and so on. The complexities of group structuring increase rapidly with group size.

Any pair, triad, or larger set of persons could be characterized by the numbers and the kinds of person-to-person attractions included in it. But the complexities of describing every individual's attitudes toward every other individual, especially in larger groups, are so great that we shall resort to a simpler, two-step procedure. First, since the dyad is the only set that is included in all groups of two or more, we shall consider every larger set as made up of dyadic relationships, which are properties of the dyad, not of single persons. Thus a triad includes the relationships between members A and B, A and C, and B and C. Second, we shall here deal with only two categories of individual attraction: positive and negative.[2] Thus any dyad can be described as ++, +−, or −− (reciprocal positive, mixed, reciprocal negative), and any triad or larger set can be described as made of so many dyads of any one, any two, or all three kinds. For many purposes, of course, larger groups should be looked at as wholes having various characteristics of their own, but the analysis of their internal dyadic structure is a good way to approach their study.

Characteristics of the Three Basic Kinds of Dyads

Dyads vary in some obvious and some not-so-obvious ways. We shall first consider the kinds of interpersonal behavior that are characteristic of the three kinds of dyads, and then compare them with regard to stability—that is, the tendency for dyad members who at any given time have a ++, a +−, or a −− relationship to retain the same relationship over a period of time.

BEHAVIORAL CHARACTERISTICS. Members of ++ dyads tend to associate freely and to communicate with each other with relatively few restraints, and to behave cordially toward each other—as might be expected. Members of −− dyads tend to do none of these things, except as situationally required. The behavior of +− dyad members is often restrained, and tends to resemble that of −− dyads. It seems reasonable to conclude that, given higher attraction from A to B than from B to A, the attraction level of the dyad as a unit is closer to B's level of attraction toward A than to A's toward B—that is, closer to the lower of the two levels. Thus the frequencies of behavioral variables that are relevant to attraction—association, communication, and expressed cordiality—tend to increase as the dyadic level of positive attraction becomes more extreme, and to decrease as the dyadic level of negative attraction (or aversion) becomes more extreme.

STABILITY. The general principle here is quite different: the more nearly A's attraction toward B and B's toward A are the same, the more stable the dyadic level of attraction. We have already noted that a per-

---

[2] This is, of course, a gross oversimplification, justified only by the fact that our purposes are to illustrate general principles, not to present all of the technical complexities. For many purposes a third, "neutral" category of attraction should be added, but even this complication would result in six possible combinations of attractions in a single pair relationship. For two quite different quantitative approaches to the problem, see Harary and Ross (1957) and Newcomb (1961).

son, A, who is positively attracted to another, B, tends to see B as attracted toward himself; what we are now adding to this statement is that, following adequate opportunity for acquaintance, such perceptions tend either to be justified or to be recognized as unjustified and corrected accordingly. Thus if A perceives that his positive attraction toward B is reciprocated, and if he is right about it, then each of them is being rewarded by the other and the dyad tends to remain stable at a ++ level. Such relative stability is illustrated by the data in Table 10.2, from the two populations of students who were initial strangers (cf. Research Illustration 10.1). The table shows that of the twenty-nine dyads that had developed a ++ relationship during their first five weeks of acquaintance, eighteen (or 62 percent) retained the same relationship nearly three months later, and only one of them became either +− or −−. Of the initially +− dyads, 21 percent remained the same, as did 46 percent of the initially −− dyads.

TABLE 10.2. Subsequent stability of ++, +−, and −− dyads, as of fifth week of acquaintance

| Relationship at week 5 | Number of dyads at week 15 that are ||||||||
| | ++ || +− || −− || other ||
	act.	exp.	act.	exp.	act.	exp.	act.	exp.
++ (N = 29)	18	1.8	1	3.6	0	1.8	10	21.8
+− (N = 14)	1	0.9	3	1.8	4	0.9	6	10.4
−− (N = 26)	0	1.6	0	3.2	12	1.6	14	19.6

In this table, + indicates the highest quarter of an individual's attraction choices, and − indicates the lowest quarter; "act." and "exp." stand for actual frequencies and those to be expected by chance, respectively. The 69 dyads reported in the table constitute about one fourth of all dyads in both populations; each of the remaining dyads included at least one attraction choice at intermediate levels, that is, neither + nor − by this criterion. By reading across the rows of the table, the "fate" of each kind of dyad can be observed.

Aversion (negative attraction) that is reciprocated in kind tends also to result in stable dyads, and for similar reasons. Each member of a −− dyad is negatively rewarded ("punished"), and is thus motivated to avoid association, spontaneous communication, and cordial behavior vis-à-vis the other. The more they avoid each other, the less opportunity they have to modify their hostile attitudes—a condition sometimes known as "autistic hostility." Thus the dyadic level of attraction tends to remain stably negative, as shown in Table 10.2, according to which not one of

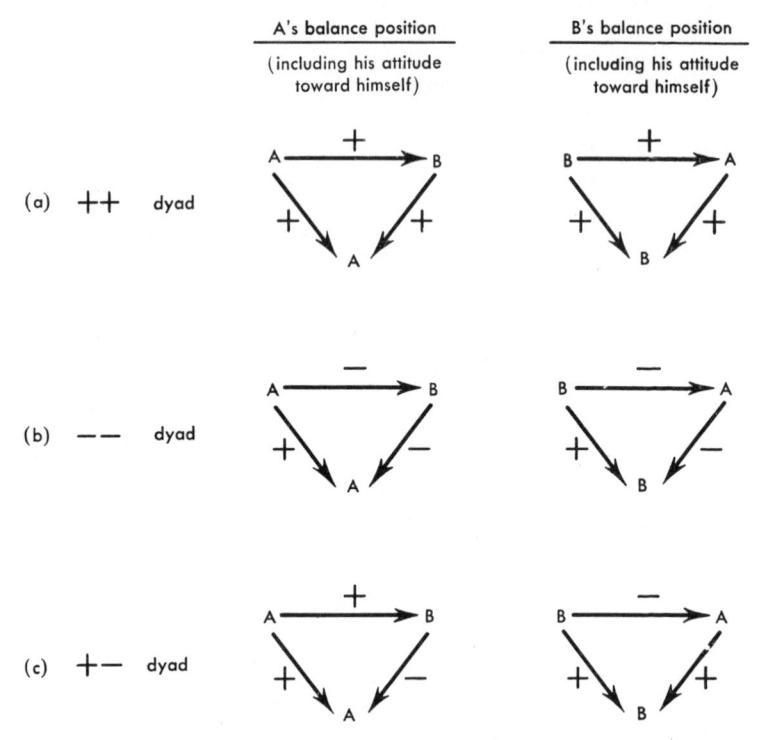

	A's balance position (including his attitude toward himself)	B's balance position (including his attitude toward himself)
(a) ++ dyad	A →+→ B, A→+, +→B (to self A)	B →+→ A, B→+, +→A (to self B)
(b) —— dyad	A →−→ B, A→+, −→B	B →−→ A, B→+, −→A
(c) +− dyad	A →+→ B, A→+, −→B	B →−→ A, B→+, +→A

FIGURE 10.2. Dyadic relations of balance (a), of absence of imbalance (b), and of imbalance (c), as experienced by each dyad member with respect to himself. Each arrow represents attraction or aversion from one member to the other.

twenty-six —— dyads at week 5 later became either ++ or +−, and the proportion of those that remained —— very greatly exceeds chance expectations.

Mixed dyads (+− pairs) tend to be unstable and therefore infrequent under conditions of continuing interaction. They tend to move either in a ++ or a —— direction, depending in part on how overtly one member shows his cordiality and the other his avoidance or hostility. Among the fourteen dyads of this kind at week 5, ten weeks later the —— combination is the only one that significantly exceeds chance expectations.

These findings concerning dyad stability are consistent with what we would expect in view of the general principle of mutual rewardingness. Balanced systems of attitudes tend to be stable because they are rewarding and thus there is little motivation to change them, whereas imbalanced ones are dissatisfying and lead to attempts to reduce the dissatisfaction. Balance with respect to himself is of special importance to each dyad member; that is, if his generally favorable self-attitudes are thought to be matched by favorable attitudes on the part of the other member toward himself, then for him the relationship is a balanced one. If this is true for both members, neither of them is motivated to change it, and thus a ++ relationship is balanced for both persons. This state of affairs is illustrated in Figure 10.2(a). A −− relationship, as illustrated in Figure 10.2(b), is at least not imbalanced, since for each person self–other discrepancy in attitudes toward himself is not accompanied by positive attraction. A +− relationship is necessarily imbalanced for the person toward whom the other person's attraction is negative (Fig. 10.2[c], at the left), and is thus imbalanced for the dyad as a whole.

Psychological balance, whether with respect to oneself or any other attitude object of importance, is of course only one of the ways in which dyad members may reward each other, or fail to do so. The basic principle is that a dyad relationship tends to be stable (that is, resistant to change) as long as it is rewarding, in whatever ways, to both members.

The Mutually Attractive Dyad as the Core of Larger Groups

Triads and larger groups can also be described as balanced or imbalanced. A triad is balanced, and thus relatively stable, if it is characterized exclusively by positive attraction—that is, it is composed of three ++ pairs. Any pair that is +− tends not to be stable, as we have seen, since it is itself not balanced. A triad that includes one −− dyad is imbalanced since, as illustrated in Figure 10.3(a), each of its three members will be positively attracted to another who does not share his own attitudes. (B's attraction to A, for example, is not shared by C, and his + attraction to C is not shared by A.) And a triad that includes two −− dyads will not remain stable since person C, as shown in Figure 10.3(b), whose relationships with both A and B are negative, will tend to break away from the other two if he can. Thus, in terms of attraction structure, the all-positive triad is the most stable.

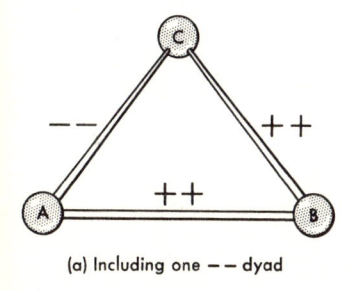

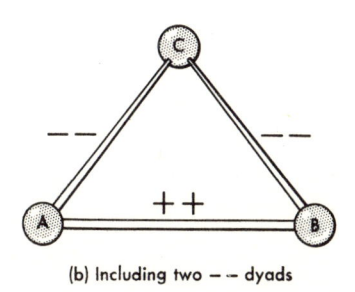

(a) Including one −− dyad

(b) Including two −− dyads

FIGURE 10.3. Illustrations of imbalanced triads

In a population large enough and diverse enough to afford some individual choices of attraction preferences, a ++ dyad will tend to "build up" into an all-positive triad. The reasons for this are simply that the members of a ++ dyad can achieve balance with regard to any other member of the population only if their attraction toward him is shared—whether it be positive or negative—and in at least some cases it is likely to be positive. Since, furthermore, positive attraction is likely to continue only if reciprocated, when both members of a ++ dyad are positively attracted to some other person, then that person is likely to become positively attracted to both of them—a constellation that describes an all-positive triad.

Such "building up" of ++ dyads into all-positive triads did in fact occur in the population of initial strangers that we have previously described. As shown in Table 10.3, there was comparatively little increase, between the end of the first and the fifteenth weeks of acquaintance, in the number of ++ dyads, but the number of all-positive triads during the same interval increased dramatically, in both populations. Another way of showing the same trend is the fact that (combining the two populations) at the earlier time twenty-one of thirty-seven pairs, or 57 percent of the ++ pairs, were in one or more all-positive triads, as compared with forty-four of forty-nine, or 90 percent, at the later time. (There is no analogous reason why −− dyads should be expected to "grow" into all-negative triads, and our data show no consistent tendency for this to occur.)

TABLE 10.3. Numbers of balanced dyads and triads among seventeen men, on early and late acquaintance

	Year I		Year II	
	Dyads	Triads	Dyads	Triads
Week 1	19	4	18	6
Week 15	24	13	25	14

This tendency for positive attraction toward another person to be reciprocated, and for the resulting ++ dyad to "grow" into an all-positive triad, appears to be very common in interaction groups that are large enough to permit both dyad members to find a third person who is congenial, provided that all of them are free to associate with whom they please. If, however, for some reason (like having to work or to live closely together) a set of three persons is forced into close association, there is a much lesser probability that the members will form an all-positive triad. It is likely, under these circumstances, that the mutual attraction on the part of one of the triad's three dyads (A-B) will be higher than that of either of the other two (A-C and B-C). If so, then A and B are likely to discover that they share a lesser degree of attraction toward C, and the resulting state of balance on the part of A and B with respect to C is likely to increase both their own mutual attraction and their relatively low attraction toward C. This is one of the processes involved in the formation of coalitions within triads, as noted long ago by Simmel (translated in 1950). Particularly under conditions that are competitive, or conditions that force three individuals into continued association, two-person coalitions "against" the third member have often been observed. Triads that include coalitions tend not to be stable, however, especially since the isolated member is likely to "escape" if he can, or to break up the existing coalition by striking a bargain with one of the other two members. In formal terms, the instability of such a triad is based on the fact that it necessarily includes imbalanced dyads. The general principle is that, other things being equal, triad stability varies inversely with the number of imbalanced dyads in the triad.

All-positive triads often "grow," just as dyads do, into larger groups made up of ++ dyads. Such a triad typically expands into a tetrad when both of two triad members, A and B, develop ++ relationships with a fourth person, D, according to processes just described. If, subsequently, D and C also develop a ++ relationship, then the new tetrad becomes an all-positive one, like the one made up of individuals 18, 20, 28, 29 in Sociogram (b) on page 293. If not, the result is a tetrad composed of two all-positive triads having two members in common; in Sociogram (d) individuals 38 and 43 are the two common members, along with individuals 45 and 50, in such a tetrad. In general, the larger an existing all-positive group the less likely it is that another person having ++ relationships with all its existing members will be added, because with increasing size the probability increases that at least one member will not find the additional person congenial.

SUBGROUP STRUCTURING OF ATTRACTION RELATIONSHIPS

Even groups as small as triads may, as we have seen, include a smaller subgroup, or clique, in the form of a ++ dyad that has the characteristics of stability although the triad as a whole is not very stable. As the size of interaction groups increases, it becomes more and more likely that they will become differentiated into two or more subgroups, each of which, in itself, forms a stable, high-attraction group but between the members of which there may be many +− or −− relationships. In addition, there may be individuals known as isolates who have no stable relationships at all, even in dyads. Thus a population of a dozen or more may include dyads, triads, or even larger subgroups whose internal relations are all positive, as well as individuals who are involved in no ++ relationships at all. All these possibilities, including an all-positive subgroup of five in Sociogram (d) and isolates in all four sociograms, appear in Research Illustration 10.1. Another sociogram (page 313), concerns a group described in Research Illustration 10.3.

For several reasons it is more useful to describe subgroup structuring in terms of *positive* dyad relationships (and the absence thereof, in the case of isolates) than in terms of negative ones. First, members of all-positive subgroups tend to spend time together, to interact with one another, and to develop consensual attitudes that function as group norms. It is by such means that groups influence their members. Second, cliques of this kind are visible; the fact that clique members associate frequently with one another and have a set of norms of their own is noted by others, who will react to the clique in various ways: some "outsiders" may wish to be included in it, while others may be members of an opposed, all-positive clique. And, finally, every member of an interaction group either is or is not a member of at least one all-positive clique, and thus each one can be described either as a clique member or as an isolate. One may also take note of dyads and larger subgroups that are not all-positive.

Thus the structuring of a total population can be described in terms of the numbers of all-positive cliques of various sizes, the nature of the connections (if any) between different cliques, and the number of isolates included in that population. In the sociogram included in Research Illustration 10.3, for example, there are two isolates and two substructures with no positive connections between them; the seven-person substructure includes two all-positive triads connected both by an all-positive dyad and by a partially positive dyad, and a partially positive triad; the four-person substructure includes two all-positive dyads and one that is partially positive, linked together in a chain.

Propinquity as a Determinant of Clique Structure

The effects of spatial arrangements, as shown in Research Illustration 10.3, start with the simple fact that one's attraction relationships are necessarily limited to the people whom one has encountered. But they also depend on an interesting and well-documented relationship between attraction and frequency of interaction. Paraphrasing the first formal statement of this relationship (by Homans, cf. page 219), the

Research Illustration 10.3

Just after World War II, in the face of a sudden influx of married veteran students, a twin housing project was set up for such students by the Massachusetts Institute of Technology. One unit, Westgate, consisted of 100 single-family houses, arranged in nine courts; the other, Westgate West, included 17 buildings of 10 apartments each, five on each floor. The layout of one of these courts is shown in the accompanying diagram. The housing project was relatively isolated, geographically, so that its 270 families constituted a relatively self-contained community. The population was a homogeneous one, composed of married students and their young families. Applicants for housing were treated on a first-come, first-served basis, and had no choice whatever as to residential location; assignments were, from their point of view, simply made at random.

In this setting the investigators (Festinger *et al.*, 1950) launched a study of spontaneous group formation. All wives (as representatives of families) at Westgate and nearly all at Westgate West answered the question, "What three people in Westgate or Westgate West do you see most of socially?" Responses showed that there was a direct relationship between frequency of social contact and residential closeness, as shown in the diagram on page 312. (In this figure the "units of physical distance" differ for the same floor, between floors, and between apartments, but in relative terms they are comparable, and may be thought of as quarters of maximum distance. For each of the three lines in the figure, the number of possible choices is constant, regardless of distance.) As shown in this figure, the farther people lived from each other, the less frequently they saw each other socially, and this was as true at Westgate, where most residents had lived for a good many months together, as at Westgate West, where most of them had lived for not more than several weeks. The investigators

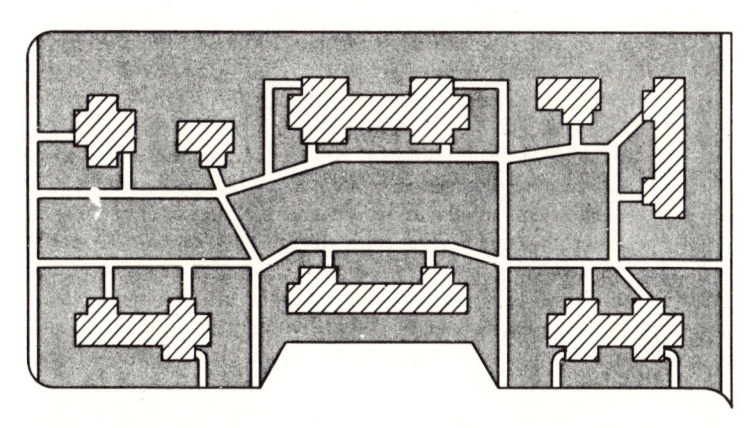

Schematic diagram of the arrangement of the Westgate West courts

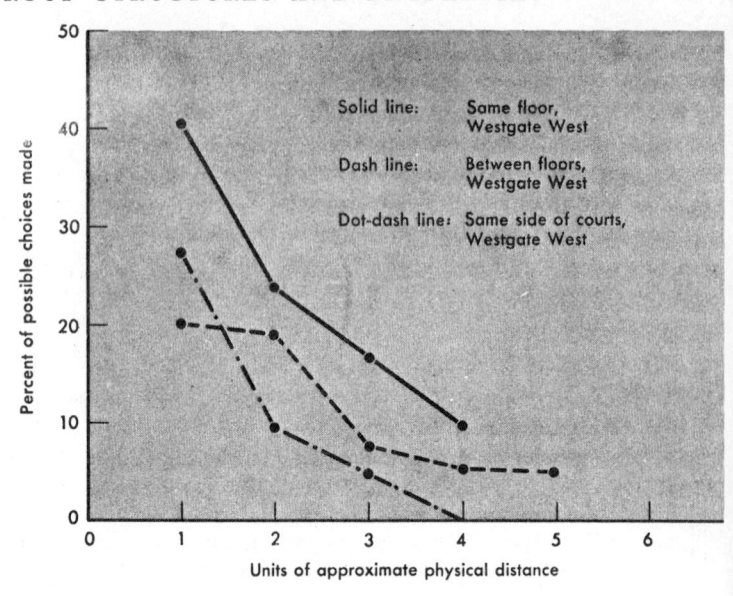

Relationship between physical distance and choices of social contact

show that in most cases physical distance is closely related to "functional distance," that is, distance as it affects the frequency of actual social encounters, but the exceptions are particularly interesting. For example, there were "end houses" at Westgate which were immediately adjacent to another house but whose entrances were onto the street rather than onto the court. The average number of choices received by people in these end houses was only about one third of those received by people living in the inner courts. At Westgate West, people who had to use the same stairways and the same utility rooms saw more of each other socially than did people who used different ones, even though their apartments were very close together.

Clique structure (especially but not always within houses or courts) is shown by the investigators to be directly related to certain forms of behavior. For example, a rumor that they themselves planted for experimental purposes was quickly passed along within cliques, but only rarely from members of one clique to members of another. As another example, an issue about the formation of a Tenants' Organization became quite controversial at Westgate. Opposition to the proposed organization was pretty much concentrated in two courts, and these two were the ones in which a large proportion of the residents were involved in all-positive cliques. The accompanying sociogram shows the clique structure in one of these, Howe Court, in which only three of the thirteen wives were favorable to the organization.

The investigators conclude that group life is greatly influenced by the presence or absence and the nature of the cliques within larger

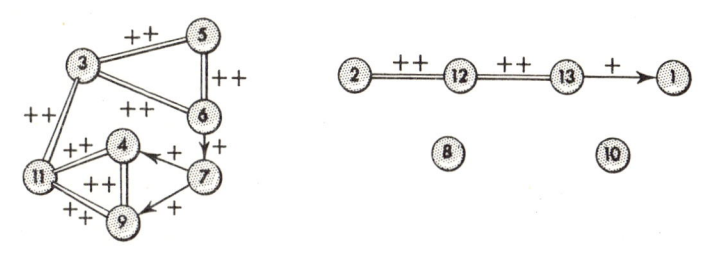

Clique structure of Howe Court, Westgate West. Arrows represent unreciprocated choices. (Festinger, Schachter, & Back, 1950)

groups, and by their number and size, if any. Group cohesiveness and group norms, in particular, are affected by cliques within larger groups. For example, they found courts with large cliques to be relatively cohesive and to be in general agreement about the Tenants' Organization, whereas courts with several small cliques had little esprit de corps and relatively little agreement. "When cliques existed they seemed to become major determinants of the total effectiveness of the group" (p. 148).

higher the attraction among two or more persons the more frequently they will interact with one another, and vice versa—that is, the more frequently they interact the higher their attraction. The first half of this proposition is self-evident, assuming opportunity for voluntary association. The second half is not self-evident but is true in a statistical sense: all of us can think of many exceptions but, again assuming relative freedom of action, it turns out to be true more often than not. Just for example, parents and children do not ordinarily select each other, but they do interact frequently, and more often than not they develop positive attraction toward each other (perhaps combined, ambivalently, with some hostility). Homans's own evidence (1950) is taken from a famous early study of workers in an electric manufacturing firm (Roethlisberger and Dickson, 1939): the "bank wiremen," assigned by management to work together, "interacting with one another frequently, also became friendly. . . . The relationship between association and friendliness is one of those commonly observed facts that we use all the time as a guide for action" (p. 111).

Another kind of evidence comes from Whyte's study (1956) of parties held in a suburban residential development known as Park Forest. "I have read every single one of the social notes in the *Park Forest Reporter* for a three-and-one-half-year period," he writes; and summarizes the evidence as follows: "the guests at any one party come

▲ Valentine costume party
𝄁𝄁𝄁𝄁 Suprise baby shower
△ P.T.A. Bunco party
■ Hosts at progressive dinner party
▨ Picnic at Sauk Trail Forest Preserve
≡ Christmas - gift - exchange party
◆ New once - a - month bridge club
◇ New Year's Eve party
⋯ Fishhouse punch party
■ Meeting of "the Homemakers"

FIGURE 10.4. Residential layout in suburban development, at various social gatherings

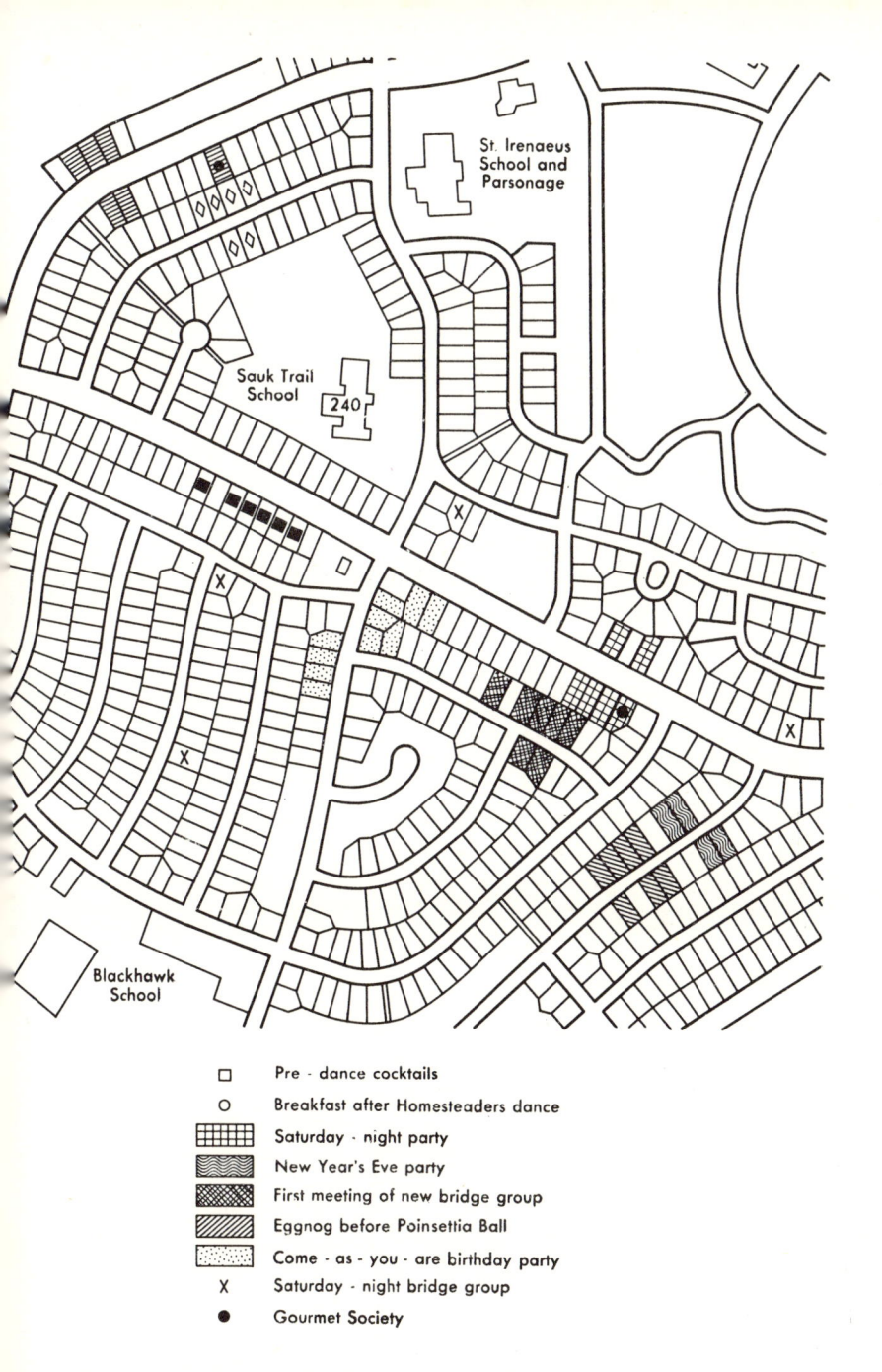

	Pre - dance cocktails
○	Breakfast after Homesteaders dance
▦	Saturday - night party
≋	New Year's Eve party
▩	First meeting of new bridge group
▨	Eggnog before Poinsettia Ball
░	Come - as - you - are birthday party
X	Saturday - night bridge group
●	Gourmet Society

showing effects of propinquity on the selection of participants (from Whyte, 1956) from a fairly circumscribed geographic area. . . . the groups usually formed along and across streets; rarely did the groupings include people on the other side of the back yard. . . . Three years later, new people have moved in, others have moved out, yet the basic patterns are unchanged." These findings are pictorially illustrated in Figure 10.4. Still another kind of evidence shows that within large cities marriages occur most frequently between men and women who live close together, and least frequently between those who live at great distances.[3]

The important fact illustrated by Homans's proposition is that interaction with other persons tends, on balance, to be rewarding; we tend to become attracted toward those with whom we interact, even when we have not chosen to interact with them because we already find them attractive. The investigation by Festinger, Schachter, and Back documents this proposition particularly well because families were randomly assigned to their living quarters, and had no opportunity to choose neighbors whom they already liked. Students in the two populations of initial strangers (Research Illustration 10.1) were assigned to rooms in arbitrary fashion, but in this case relationships of attraction were not affected, except to a slight degree during the first week or two, by spatial arrangements. Distances in the house occupied by these populations were small; all the men used the same stairways, the same living room, and ate in the same dining room, so that differences of a few feet in distance between their rooms had no effects. Thus the general principle is that insofar as spatial arrangements affect frequency of interaction they will tend to affect relationships of attraction, and thereby affect the attraction structuring of a population.

Demographic Variables

Perhaps you have been thinking that if the populations of married students described in Research Illustration 10.3 had not been so homogeneous in age and interests, residential proximity would not have had so much to do with attraction. This is probably the case: if the population had been more diverse in demographic characteristics (such as age, religious affiliation, and nationality) these factors might have had much more influence on attraction than did proximity. On the other hand, within the two 17-man populations of male students, which were no less homogeneous in most respects, there were significant relationships between attraction and certain demographic variables. Following several weeks of acquaintance, men who were alike in age, in urban or rural background, and in college enrollment (all were either in Liberal Arts or in Engineering) were more likely to be highly attracted to one

[3] Cf. Gouldner and Gouldner (1963, pp. 328–355) for a treatment of these and other "determinants of friendship."

another than were men who were different in these respects. (Comparable analyses were not made in the study of married students.)

Insofar as similarities in age, religious affiliation, and urban or rural background are associated with high interpersonal attraction in any population that is somewhat diverse in these respects, the reasons are not hard to discern. The relationship is mediated by similar attitudes. That is, age peers, members of the same religious sects, and urban or rural residents tend to have certain values and interests in common; and we have already noted that attitudinal similarity often serves to promote attraction. In the two 17-man populations, for example, older men tended to be attracted toward one another, as did large-city residents, small-town residents, Arts College students, and Engineering students. Most of the older men shared certain attitudes toward "immaturity"; most of the city residents shared attitudes toward "sophisticated" vs. "corn-fed" ways of behaving; most of the small-town men shared more conventional values; and so on. Thus the attraction structure of populations may be influenced by demographic variables, but indirectly rather than directly.

The Distribution of Members' Attitudes

Attitudinally speaking, birds of a feather tend to flock together, and we would therefore expect that subgroup structuring would to some degree parallel the differences among group members in certain interests and values. If all members of an interaction group share some common value—such as the religious beliefs common to the members of a monastery—then this value will not provide a basis for differentiation. If, on the other hand, the population members are divided into opposed camps about some issue of importance to them, we may expect that attraction structuring will parallel this division. These two illustrations are somewhat extreme; typically one finds neither complete unanimity nor complete divisiveness but rather a range or distribution of attitudes.

It should thus be possible to predict from attitudinal similarity on the part of group members what the clique structuring will be like. Furthermore, if we have reason to believe that members' attitudes have not changed following interaction with each other, it should be possible to predict postacquaintance structuring from preacquaintance attitudes. In the case of the populations of initial strangers (Research Illustrations 6.2, page 173, and 10.1), clique formations after four months of acquaintance quite closely followed the predictions. For example, using batteries of miscellaneous attitude items, 26 (or 62 percent) of the dyads in the two populations that were in close agreement before getting acquainted were in the same high-attraction cliques four months

318 - GROUP STRUCTURES AND PROPERTIES

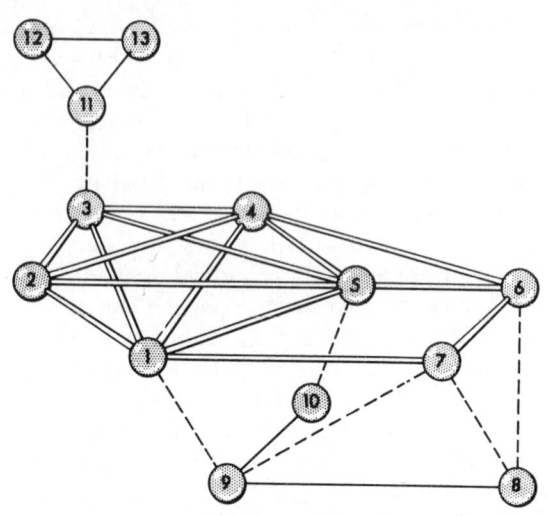

FIGURE 10.5. High-attraction clique structure after four months of acquaintance, as related to preacquaintance preferences among six values

later. Among the remaining 230 dyads not in close agreement initially, only 24 percent were later in the same cliques.

In the second of these populations, early responses concerning the relative importance of the six Spranger Values indicated that nine of the men ranked theoretical and esthetic values rather high and religious values low. Nearly four months later two of these men were in no ++ dyads at all, but each of the remaining seven had ++ relationships with at least two of the other six. In Figure 10.5 (which corresponds closely to Sociogram [d] on page 293), ++ connections among these men (who are numbered from 1 to 7) are shown by double lines. The other eight men ranked theoretical and esthetic values relatively low and religious values high. Four months later two of these were in no ++ dyads, whereas each of the remaining six had ++ relationships with at least two of the other men, as shown by the single lines connecting circles numbered from 8 to 13 in the figure. The broken lines show ++ relationships between initially disagreeing men. The actual as compared with the possible numbers of ++ relationships within and between the two subpopulations are as follows:

Number of ++ relationships

	Actual	Possible	Percent
Among agreeing Ss Nos. 1–7	14	21	67
Among agreeing Ss Nos. 8–13	5	15	33
Between the two sets	6	42	14

There were 19 of a possible 36 ++ relationships, or 53 percent, among initially agreeing men, as compared with only 14 percent among initially disagreeing men; these 19 represented 76 percent of all ++ relationships, as compared with a chance expectation of 46 percent.

Thus information concerning the men's attitudes, after short acquaintance (or none at all, in the case of the second population), predicted with high dependability which individuals would and which would not be attracted to one another four months later. (The significance level is beyond .001.) Preferences among values of such importance that they showed very little change over a period of months provided a basis for predicting, at a time when the men themselves could not have done so, which individuals would eventually form themselves into high-attraction cliques. In these populations, as presumably in others having a similar distribution of initial attitudes, preacquaintance attitudes do not provide a basis for knowing which individuals will be isolates, but they can tell us a good deal about the later structuring of high-attraction relationships among persons who develop them.

Personal Characteristics

Most groups, other than tiny ones, contain one or more individuals who are extreme with respect to characteristics that are generally liked or disliked by group members, with the result that some of them are more popular than others. Most sociograms, like those shown in Research Illustrations 10.1 and 10.3, contain one or more "stars" and one or more isolates. Male student groups, for example, usually regard such characteristics as dependability, friendliness, intelligence, masculinity, and maturity as desirable in their companions, and hence rewarding. By the same token, the opposites of such characteristics are considered undesirable or, if extreme, offensive. The substructuring within any group is bound to be influenced by the combinations of favorable and unfavorable characteristics that its individual members are generally perceived to have.

The two sociograms (b) and (d) in Research Illustration 10.1 appear, visually, to be quite differently structured after four months of acquaintance: the second population seems to be centrally structured, as contrasted with a divisive structure within the first one. An index of "structural centrality" (cf. Newcomb, 1961) shows that this is indeed the case. In a search for reasons for this difference, the following facts came to light: There was not much difference between the two populations with respect to high or low popularity: in each one there were three or four conspicuously popular members and about as many isolates. What did distinguish the two populations was the nature of the relationships among the very popular individuals. In the second population, individuals 34, 42, 47, and 49 were, without exception, mutually attracted to each other; thus all of the many ++ dyads in which the popular men were involved were clustered around those individuals in a central structure. Since nearly every member had a ++ relationship with at least one of these popular men, and since these men had ++ relationships with each other, the inevitable result was a central structure. In the first population, on the other hand, the very popular men (18, 20, 21, 22) were not generally attracted to each other, and in some cases were actually hostile. The result was a divisive structure, since the popular men who were not attracted to each other became the centers of quite different cliques.

The explanation of these two different structures requires one further step: Why should popular members be attracted to one another in one population but not in the other? The answer is the "accidental" fact that in the second year, but not in the first, the popular men "happened" to share many interests and values, some of which we have just described. It was only happenstance that the two sets of popular men differed in this way, but the facts lead to this general principle of substructuring: the greater the number of ++ relationships among the most popular members in a group the more centrally it will be structured. Since popularity depends in part on personal characteristics, the latter contribute a good deal to the internal structuring of a group.

Attraction Mediates Other Determinants of Structure

This chapter has dealt with interpersonal attitudes as one of several bases of group structuring. We have tried to show that interpersonal attraction does not "just happen"; it follows lawful regularities according to which particular individuals in specific situations are rewarded by particular other persons. Different individuals are interested in different kinds of rewards, and other persons have different kinds of rewards to offer; a good fit between getting and giving rewards is more likely to be found under certain conditions than under others. A really good fit presupposes a continued period of interaction, so that persons can try each other out and discover that they are both giving and receiving rewards; group structuring is a consequence of such trying-out processes. Structural forms depend, on the one hand, on the distribution of members' attitudes and personal characteristics and the ways in which these are combined in the same persons; on the other hand, they also depend on situational conditions, such as propinquity or the nature of the problems that confront a group. Situational conditions determine the opportunities that members will have to try each other out, as well as the nature of their rewards.

We have not, in this chapter, dealt very fully with situational determinants of attraction, which may be regarded as sets of conditions that tend to have the same effects on the development of interpersonal attraction, regardless of individuals' personal characteristics. In later chapters these matters are discussed at some length. In particular, we shall note that attraction may be based on the satisfactions associated with working together on a common task, as well as on sheerly interpersonal rewards, and that in many situations group structuring is determined by task-relevant rather than person-relevant rewards. We shall also consider the phenomena of leadership and how leaders' task-relevant relationships with other members affect their relationships of attraction, and thus determine group structure.

Interpersonal attraction is thus only an immediate source of group structuring. It is platitudinous to say that people will prefer to associate with each other insofar as they find it rewarding to do so. What is interesting is to see the situational conditions under which certain combinations of persons do and others do not develop reciprocal rewardingness—that is, the underlying conditions, both personal and situational, that determine attraction which in turn affects group structuring. In this sense, attraction mediates between the underlying conditions and the developing group structure.

OVERVIEW

Any set of persons viewed as a single entity constitutes a group, but we are primarily interested in interaction groups, and in their relatively stable characteristics. Group members' relationships of attraction toward one another tend to become stable following adequate opportunity for acquaintance.

Attraction is like other attitudes in that it is based on the perceived rewardingness of objects, but it differs from attitudes toward most nonperson objects in presupposing that individuals attribute attitudes to one another. Insofar as persons have similar attitudes toward things of importance to both or all of them, and discover that this is so, they have shared attitudes; under most conditions the experience of sharing such attitudes is rewarding, and thus provides a basis for mutual attraction. Attraction relationships are most stable when characterized by mutual, positive attraction.

Structure varies with respect to the number of high-attraction subgroups, their size, the relationships of attraction among them, and the number of isolates. Because they mediate intermember attraction, the conditions that account for different structures include the distribution of members' interests and values, their personal characteristics, and various situational factors that determine the frequency and the nature of their interaction.

CHAPTER 11

Role Relationships

MOST OF US HABITUALLY REGARD A GROUP AS A SET OF PERSONS, AND SO it is—but any group whose members have a history of interaction is more than that. If we view a group only as a set of unique individuals, we cannot generalize from one group to another. This book began with the usual scientific assumption that if one wants to understand things in more than a commonsense way one must discover the general, recurrent aspects of phenomena that, on the surface, may not be evident at all. And so this chapter will indicate some general characteristics of interaction groups, regardless of who their members are. The problem is to describe the ways in which group members interact, and to account for regularities in interaction in terms of group influences rather than in terms of unique individual characteristics.

There is an enormous difference between viewing individuals as unique persons and as group members who are responding to influences that groups bring to bear on them. From the former point of view we would account for a person's behavior in a group in terms of what he brings to the group situation—especially his personality characteristics and his attitudes. In Part One we took this view, but now that we have seen how groups exert power over their members through group norms (Chapter 8), we are in a position to examine this second point of view. Looked at in this way, group members' behavior is to be understood in terms not of who the members are but in terms of influences exerted or mediated by other persons with whom they are interacting.

In any interaction group there are role relationships, that is, behavioral and attitudinal relationships, among its members. For example, a military squad composed of eight men and an officer could be described in terms of role relationships of equality among the men and of giving and receiving orders, as between the men and the officer. These role relationships are pretty much the same in any squad, regardless of the individual personalities of the members. The role relationship between a mother and her child is one in which the mother gives and the child receives nurturance, particularly in such forms as care, protection, and training. We can understand a great deal about such a two-person group merely by knowing that mother and child have this kind of role relationship, whether or not we know much about their personalities, and whether or not we know the specific ways in which the mother gives and the child receives nurturance.

The relationship between any two things depends on what each of them contributes to it, and a person's contribution to a role relationship—that is, what he does to create and maintain the relationship—may be regarded as his own role. It often happens that in order to maintain a particular role relationship—say on the part of a mother toward her child—one must also maintain somewhat different relationships with several other people. Her *general* role as mother is dominated by her nurturant relationship to her child, but in order to maintain this relationship she also has *specific* roles in relation to such other persons as neighboring children, the child's teacher, and the child's doctor. Whether general or specific, the mother's *role* refers to her behavioral contribution to her relationships with other people, insofar as these involve her child in some way.

The term is in fact used in a rather extended sense. Very commonly it refers to widely shared norms concerning what an individual's contribution to a behavioral relationship should be; thus affection, helpfulness, and sexual fidelity are expected of a husband in our society. This usage refers to an *idealized*, or prescribed role. The term may also refer simply to *actual* behavioral regularity on the part of interacting persons; for example, two friends work out a smooth relationship according to which one takes a dominant and the other a submissive role. The mother and child described on page 7 as presenting "two halves of the same habit" present a picture of rather extreme regularity in interacting with each other. In these cases, too, there come to be normative expectations, but they are not regarded as normative except by the interacting persons themselves. These are not socially prescribed but rather *emergent* roles. *Role*, in all these senses—ideal or actual, general or specific, prescribed or emergent—refers to the behavioral consistencies on the part of one person as he contributes to a more or less stable relationship with one or more others. The persons involved in the relationship may be either specific, named individuals or, more commonly, representatives of categories—like mothers, policemen, students.

In order to understand clearly the role relationships that make up the ongoing life of a group, we must first examine the nature of the influence that group members bring to bear on one another. The impact of such influence on an individual is related to the position he occupies in the group. And so this chapter begins with an analysis of position-related influence and ends with an examination of the network of role relationships that characterizes a group of interacting persons.

SOCIAL POSITIONS AND ROLE PRESCRIPTIONS

Societies and Groups as Networks of Interrelated Positions

Each human being is born into a society that is not formless but organized. Both society as a whole and its subparts—the large and small groups, the social classes, institutions, and organizations, for example— are organized into a complex structure. The structures of all societies —even the small, preliterate ones that seem "simple" to us—have been shown by anthropologists to have rather elaborate form and structure. If we are to understand the social norms in terms of which people perceive and interact with one another, it is necessary to examine the organization of groups and societies as providing norms for perceiving their own members and the behavior of their own members.

The members of a society, like other common objects such as rocks or birds, are classified. Just as pebbles are distinguished from boulders, and sparrows from eagles, so different kinds of people are distinguished from one another. Just as sparrows are expected to behave differently from eagles, so different behaviors are expected from different kinds of people—men and women, for example. But there is an obvious difference between people's norms about birds and about themselves. A person, unlike a rock or a bird, is capable of responding to others' anticipations of his own behavior. Partly for this reason, people who are classified differently behave differently. Teen-age boys, for example, behave differently from teen-age girls in the same society because, to begin with, they know that they are boys and are expected to act like boys, not girls; sooner or later, of course, most of them come to want to act like boys.

THE NATURE OF SOCIAL POSITIONS. For social-psychological purposes, the manner in which a society is organized is best described in terms of the *positions* that exist in that society for people to fill. Every individual in any society occupies at least one position; even the newborn child occupies the position of an infant. Most individuals beyond the age of infancy occupy several positions: the same adolescent girl is daughter, sister, and secretary of her high school class; the same man may be a husband, a father, a deacon, and a councilman. No one, however, occupies all the positions that are recognized by his society. No one individual, in fact, participates in all of a culture. It is his positions in his society that determine the parts of the culture in which he will or will not participate. Thus small children do not participate in the political aspects of American culture; and employers play a part in the affairs of management associations but not in labor unions.

In viewing societies as consisting of a complex organization of positions, the scientist disregards the particular individuals who happen to occupy the positions; from this point of view, the personal identity of the occupants is irrelevant. When the people are subtracted in this particular way from a society, what is left is a great network of positions, all the elements of which are more or less related to and consistent with one another. Our society, for example, provides such positions as those of father, bishop, housewife, mayor, railroad engineer, and many hundreds of others.

Every position that continues to be recognized by the members of a group contributes in some way to the purposes of the group; this contribution represents its *function*. Associated with every position is a body of common beliefs concerning its function; these beliefs represent one part of the group's system of norms. The functions of a position, as understood by group members who recognize it, do not necessarily correspond to its functions as they would be seen by an outsider—by a sociologist, for example, who is especially interested in the ways in which a position contributes to group survival. But this objective function—that is, the function seen by the sociologist—is dependent on some shared assumptions on the part of group members concerning the contribution made by the occupant of a position. Thus, to certain Indian tribes of the southwestern regions of the United States the function of a priest may be generally accepted as that of bringing rain. As viewed by a sociologist, however, the service performed by the priest might be that of promoting group solidarity. His objective function thus differs from his accepted function, but the former could not be performed without this or some other accepted function, as provided for in group norms. Positions exist, then, because they correspond to functions as commonly understood according to group norms, whether or not there is a close correspondence between "real" and commonly understood functions.

Thus the positions, which are the smallest element—the construction blocks—of societies and organized groups, are interrelated and consistent because they are organized to common ends. From this point of view societies and organized groups are structures of positions that are organized to meet certain goals. Since every position is a part of an inclusive system of positions, no one of them has any meaning apart from the others to which it is related. The position of mother cannot exist without the position of child, for example, nor that of leader without that of follower. Every position points to one or more others related to it.

SOME POSITIONS COMMON TO ALL SOCIETIES. Societies vary considerably in degree of organization of positions—or, as sociologists say, in the extent of their division of labor. Some societies provide very complicated systems of positions, whereas others provide only relatively few. Even the simplest societies, however, provide at least five different kinds of positions (Linton, 1945):

1. age-sex: at least seven of these are apparently identified by all societies—infant, boy, girl, young man, young woman, old man, old woman;
2. occupational: for some individuals, at least, in every society;
3. prestige: some sort of ranking, such as chief or slave, in a hierarchy of prestige;
4. family, clan, or household group: for example, a member of the John Smith family;
5. association groups: membership in interest groups, cliques, and so on, established on the basis of congeniality and/or common interests.

The functions of these various positions vary enormously, and even positions that look alike to outsiders—such as that of priest, for example—may be regarded as having very different functions in different societies. Among some societies the function of the child's position is merely that of preparation for adulthood, whereas in other societies it is that of providing a period of carefree life before adult responsibilities begin. For some positions, such as that of carpenter, the actual contribution made corresponds closely to that which is commonly recognized by members of the group. For others—many "prestige" positions, for example—the actual contribution to group life, as understood by a sociologist, bears little relationship to the function as perceived by group members.

HOW INDIVIDUALS ARE ASSIGNED TO POSITIONS. Individuals are assigned to some positions on the basis of factors over which they do not have any control, such as their age or sex (for example, the position of boy or old woman). Other positions (for example, bishop or mayor in our society) are accorded largely on the basis of individual achievement. The former are technically known as *ascribed positions* and the latter as *achieved*. Some are matters of preference ("He belongs to the country-club set") and some are very largely matters of "good luck" and "bad luck." Different societies vary enormously as to the ways in which individuals are assigned to different positions. Among an African people named the BaThonga, for example, factors of achievement and preference have little to do with the matter. An individual's position is largely determined by sex, age, and (in the case of men) by succession in the age-hierarchy among brothers; cattle and wives of a deceased man are inherited by the oldest living brother. Among the BaThonga, position cannot be changed or improved by competition. Among the Kwakiutl Indians of North America, on the other hand, some men are born into "noble" positions, but cannot maintain the positions acquired by birth without competing for them. In other societies many kinds of positions are determined by age and sex alone, but a good deal also depends on how much "luck" or success the individual has in contriving a favorable marriage. No two societies are just alike in the ways in which they combine all these and other factors in assigning individuals to positions.

Not all positions are enduring ones; some of them, like that of best man at a wedding, may be briefly held. The position of mourner at one's mother's funeral can be held but once during a lifetime. Other positions, such as that of receiving public support while unemployed, may be held for indeterminate periods or intermittently. Such positions, however, have the same basic characteristics as those more persistently held. They correspond to functions (actual or assumed) in the society, and they carry with them prescriptions for behaving toward other persons in related positions.

THE SIGNIFICANCE OF SOCIAL POSITION. Position, like motion, is a relative matter: it has meaning only in relation to other positions. This meaning lies in the role relationships that a group or society prescribes between two or more positions. Although it is possible to concentrate on just one of two interrelated things, highlighting it against the other as ground, the fact remains that *reciprocal* relationships are always implied by any position. The significance of a husband's position, for example, lies not only in the prescriptions for his behavior toward his wife, but also in hers toward him. Thus a social position is a placement of an individual in a group or society in respect to his prescribed contribution to a relationship with one or more other persons who also have placements.

Role Prescriptions Attached to Positions

Role prescriptions are normative descriptions of ways of carrying out the functions for which positions exist—ways that are generally agreed upon within whatever group recognizes the particular position. For social-psychological purposes, as we have noted, the functions of a position have to do mainly with the maintaining of certain kinds of relationships between the occupant and other persons. Not all the things the occupants of any particular position do are essential in carrying out the functions of that position. Some of their behavior is simply irrelevant, and some may actually interfere with the supposed functions. For example, treating ill patients is a necessary part of the physician's prescribed role; wearing a goatee or a white coat is a permitted but not a necessary part of it; poisoning patients is forbidden, and thus totally excluded from the role prescription. As indicated in Figure 11.1, the ways in which it is possible for the occupant of a position (in this case a mother in American society) to maintain relationships with another person may be thought of as extending along a continuum. At one extreme are behaviors that it forbids; at the other are behaviors that are demanded. Intermediate between these extremes are various behaviors that are permitted but not demanded—permitted to some mothers but not to others, perhaps, or to all mothers under certain conditions, or left to the personal choice of any mother.

If you are interested in drawing a line between what is and is not included in the role prescription for a mother in a specific society you would need to obtain the following kinds of information from a representative sample of all the people in that society who recognize the position: (1) an inclusive list of behaviors potentially to be included in the prescription (drawn, ideally, from preliminary investigations); and (2) information as to how many respondents regard each behavior on the list as required or merely permitted. A criterion of 50 percent agreement that any given behavior on the list is required of all mothers might be established. In that case, the role prescription would include all

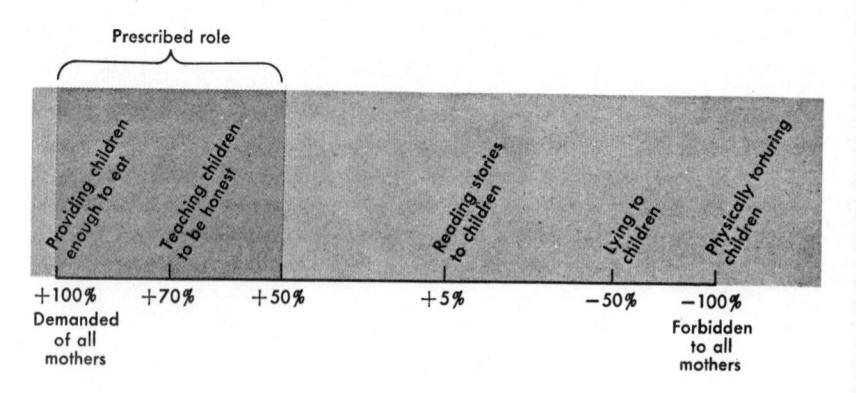

FIGURE 11.1. Combination of behaviors associated with mother's role in contemporary American society. Numbers preceded by + or by − refer to hypothetical percentages of informants who consider the indicated behavior to be demanded or forbidden, respectively. Behaviors included in the area of darker gray make up the prescribed role, according to criterion of agreement by at least 50 percent of informants that the indicated behavior is demanded.

behaviors considered by at least half of all respondents to be demanded of all mothers. But the important thing about any role prescription is to be found not in any list of behaviors but rather in the elements that such behaviors have in common. These elements, which can be inferred from the list of required, permitted, and forbidden behaviors, describe the relationships that the group norms prescribe between the occupant of the position in question and occupants of related positions.

INTERLOCKING ROLES. Any role prescription thus necessarily implies one or more others. A mother cannot perform her role except in relation to a child, or an employer his except in relation to an employee. A professor's role as lecturer and a student's as listener are dependent upon one another. The interdependence of related roles is shown in the fact that any position involves rights as well as obligations: there are obligations *to* the occupant of a position, as well as obligations *on* him. The obligations of a wife to her husband, for example, correspond directly to the rights that he expects from her, and vice versa. There could be neither rights nor obligations unless every role were defined in relation to one or more others. The same group norms provide prescriptions for each one in a set of interlocking roles.

This means that the occupant of any position learns, more or less at the same time, the prescriptions for his own and for closely related roles. Prospective brides and grooms are likely to be almost as familiar with each other's role prescriptions as with their own. If the marriage of any particular couple "fails," it is not likely to be merely because of unfamiliarity of either spouse with the other's role prescription. Rather, as Burgess and Cottrell long ago showed (1939), it is apt to be because the personality of one or both of them is such that special demands, not necessarily included in the role prescriptions, are made in ways that the other spouse is unable or unwilling to meet.

Very few roles are defined in relation to only one other role. As illustrated by Figure 11.2, the mother's general role is at the center of a network of specific roles, each of which also includes prescriptions in relation to the child. Many roles, unlike that of mother or employer, are defined with reference to several others, rather than a single other one. Such prescriptions as that of the mayor of a city do not have primary reference to any single other role; his role is defined in relation to councilmen, administrative chiefs, party officials, and constituents, among others, and all or most of these are also related to one another.

Thus any role is necessarily a part of a system of interdependent roles, and can be modified by changes in other parts of the system. A mother's role changes as her son becomes an adolescent and (particularly as his relationships with peers change) his role changes; if he sees the relationship as changing and she does not, role conflict ensues. The system as a whole is supported by a set of norms that prescribes relation-

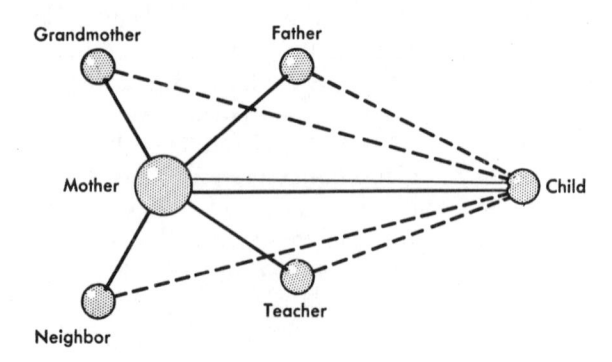

FIGURE 11.2. Representation of mother's role in relation to other roles

ships among all the roles included in it. Each one of them is unique in having its own position—its own point of intersection with all the others in the system. What all of them have in common is the fact of being prescribed by an inclusive set of norms. Thus it happens that individuals who occupy different positions behave in different ways but nevertheless share common understandings about one another's behavior. And thus, in turn, it happens that interaction among them so often continues in relatively smooth and predictable manner—predictable, that is, not in terms of specific behaviors but in terms of role relationships.

Role Prescriptions and Role Behavior

Anyone who occupies a position is bound to be influenced by its accompanying role prescription, but his actual behavior is also influenced in many other ways: one often faces conflicting kinds of influence. Personal preferences, abilities, and various kinds of personality characteristics may be quite incompatible with role prescriptions, particularly those associated with a prescribed position—like those associated with sex or age or membership in a racial group—over which one has no control. For such reasons a person's actual behavior, as occupant of a position, may conform only partially to the prescription, or may even deviate radically from it. And, whether he conforms to the prescription or violates it, he will in any case adapt to the prescription in his own way, as dictated by some compromise between what is desirable and what is possible.

Thus the actual behavior of the occupant of a position will not correspond exactly to the role prescription, because it will be affected by other influences, too. This means that in our search for regularities in the behavioral relationships of one person to another we must also take account of these other influences. As shown in the following illustration, there are two quite different kinds of determinants of the regularities that are found in actual role behavior.

> At eleven o'clock of a certain Tuesday morning we observe John Doe sitting in an office while he is being interviewed by the president of his company. Twenty minutes later he is dictating to his stenographer; two hours after that he is entertaining a prospective customer at lunch; and that same evening he may be observed dancing with his wife at the local country club. In each of these situations he is involved in a behavioral relationship with another person. The four situations call for quite different sets of activities on his part, and yet a close observer would note certain characteristics in Mr. Doe's behavior that reappear in all the situations. Such forms of order and regularity in his behavior are commonly referred to as aspects of his personality.
>
> Tom Coe, who lives in a neighboring city, occupies a professional position very much like that of John Doe. He too might be observed, perhaps on the same day, in exactly the same kinds of situations—behaving as employee, employer, host, and husband, respectively. Some of his behaviors are similar to those of John Doe in the comparable situations, but in many ways they are quite different: his manner of participating in the interview, the ways in which he interacts with his stenographer, his hostmanship, and his style of dancing are distinctive, his own. Yet in spite of the differences between the two men—and between each of them and Richard Roe, who lives in a third city and who also behaves as employee, employer, host, and husband on the same day—most of us would immediately recognize the similarities in the behavior of the three men in each one of the situations. Order and regularity can be observed both in the behavior of each man in different situations and in that of all the men in the same situation.

These two kinds of behavioral regularity are illustrated in Figure 11.3, which shows that the twelve episodes of behavior on the part of the three men can be examined either for individual consistency regardless of role relationships or for role consistency regardless of individuals. Although we are concerned, in this chapter, with the latter, we need to note in passing that the actual behavior of anyone in a given position also has regularities of the former kind. As schematically illustrated in Figure 11.4, actual role behavior may vary from forms that are almost totally determined by personal factors to those that are almost totally determined by positional prescriptions. An instance of the latter would be the well-rehearsed, stylized performance of the bride in a formal wedding ceremony; a well-known illustration of the former would be Napoleon's way of being crowned emperor by the Pope: he insisted on placing the crown upon his head himself.

The principal reason why most of us, most of the time, conform

332 - GROUP STRUCTURES AND PROPERTIES

	As employee	As employer	As host	As husband
John Doe	X	X	X	X
Tom Coe	X	X	X	X
Richard Roe	X	X	X	X

FIGURE 11.3. Different kinds of common elements in role behavior. Ellipse 1 refers to regularities on the part of different persons taking the same role; ellipse 2, to regularities on the part of the same person taking different roles. Each X refers to a behavior episode on the part of the person named at the left.

reasonably well to role prescriptions is that groups provide prescriptions not only for the occupant of any position but also for persons in related positions as they respond to his role behavior. The latter prescriptions include sanctions for conforming or markedly deviating behavior. Insofar as sanctioning norms are internalized, one comes to reward oneself for role conformity: one has become motivated to enact the role properly, so that role behavior corresponds more or less closely to role prescription.

One of the major reasons for failure to conform to role prescriptions is the fact of belonging, simultaneously, to different groups whose prescriptions are different from or even in conflict with each other. Even small children may be caught in such a dilemma—between, for example, a family group whose language and culture are foreign and a "typically American" school or playground group. Adolescents in our society are notoriously squeezed between conflicting prescriptions of their parents and their peers. In Chapter 13, where conflicting role prescriptions are considered more fully, we shall note that such conflicts do not neces-

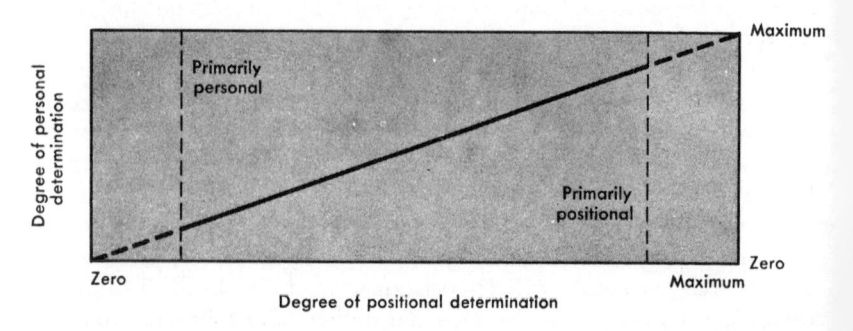

FIGURE 11.4. Schematic diagram of possible combinations of personal and positional determinants of role behavior. Areas beyond the broken lines indicate extremes that are rarely if ever found. (Adapted from Rommetveit, 1955)

sarily result in deviant role behavior. It is possible, for example, to work out compromises, or to conform to quite different prescriptions of different groups when associating only with members of those groups. The opposing pulls of multiple-group membership represent a special case of the general principle that influences upon a person by reason of a particular role assignment are often in conflict with other influences upon him. Unless counterinfluences outweigh them, he will tend to conform to them. As long as he holds a given position in a given group he must adapt in some way to that group's prescriptions for maintaining relationships with specified role partners; his manner of adapting, whether conforming or not, represents his role behavior.

Changed Role Behavior Follows Change in Position

If the effects of holding a position on one's actual behavioral relationships with one's associates are as great as we have indicated, it should follow that a change in the one should be followed by a corresponding change in the other. Everyday observation provides many illustrative instances: the boy who has been elected president of his high school class takes on new dignity; the young man turned husband forsakes many of his former ways: "The role makes the man." From this belief it is sometimes derived that the way to turn an irresponsible group member into a responsible one is to place him in a position (a committee chairmanship, perhaps) that will impose inescapable responsibilities on him. The trouble with such selected illustrations is, of course, that others might illustrate exactly the opposite: newly appointed committee chairmen are sometimes just as irresponsible as they were before.

For such reasons an experimental study, like that described in Research Illustration 11.1, is a more trustworthy source of evidence. Lieberman's experiment took advantage of a natural setting in which he knew that a certain number of men would change their positions during the ensuing year, though no one knew which men they would be. His findings were in no sense preordained; indeed, it could have been the case that foremen's attitudes are different from those of rank-and-file workers because foremen are *selected* as already having "the right" attitudes for foremen to have, and not because the men's attitudes changed with their changing positions. Although the foremen's and the stewards' role relationships to management and union were measured only indirectly, through their expressed attitudes, we know from other evidence that these attitudes correspond fairly well to actual behavior as reported by others than the foremen and the stewards themselves. We may therefore conclude that changes in role behavior followed changes in position, in opposite ways for foremen and for stewards

Research Illustration 11.1

Lieberman (1956) carried out a study designed to test the assumption that a person's attitudes are influenced by his position in a social system. He began by obtaining attitude responses from 2354 rank-and-file workers in a factory. These responses were to be used as background data, to be compared with later ones of men who had meanwhile changed positions—specifically, who had become either foremen or union stewards; there was no way of knowing, in advance, which individuals would be involved in such changes. About fifteen months later, the same questionnaires were answered by 23 of the earlier respondents who had meanwhile been appointed by the management as foremen, and by 35 who had been elected by their work groups as stewards. For purposes of comparison, responses were also obtained at the later time from 46 of the original group who had not become foremen meanwhile, although they closely resembled the 23 who had, both in original attitudes and in several demographic characteristics. A control group of 35 of the original respondents who had not meanwhile become stewards was also selected as originally similar to the 35 who later became stewards.

The data were analyzed in terms of changes during the fifteen-month period, comparisons being made between initially similar groups. The attitude questions were so constructed that responses could indicate any degree of favorable or unfavorable attitude either toward management or toward unions. Sample questions, together with percentages of respondents who did or did not show changes during the interval, are as follows:

How much do management officers care about workers?	Percent becoming more favorable to management	Percent showing no change	Percent becoming more critical of management	Total
New foremen	48	52	0	100
Control group	15	76	9	100
New stewards	29	62	9	100
Control group	20	80	0	100

How much say should the union have in setting standards?	Percent becoming more favorable to the union	Percent showing no change	Percent becoming more critical of the union	Total
New foremen	0	26	74	100
Control group	22	54	24	100
New stewards	31	66	3	100
Control group	20	60	20	100

How much should seniority count in moving to better jobs?	Percent becoming more favorable to seniority system	Percent showing no change	Percent becoming more critical of seniority system	Total
New foremen	17	44	39	100
Control group	20	54	26	100
New stewards	34	46	20	100
Control group	17	34	49	100

Differences between the responses of experimental and control groups are not, in the case of every item taken singly, statistically significant, but the total set of sixteen items shows highly significant differences in the predicted directions. Individuals whose attitudes were the same before they changed positions showed quite consistent changes in attitudes toward specified groups: changes were of exactly the kinds expected in view of their new positions.

Another finding is equally important. It happened, two years later, that fewer foremen were needed in the plant, so that eight of them were demoted to their former positions. These eight were therefore compared with twelve other foremen who continued in that role. The interesting finding is that the changed attitudes of the continuing foremen remained as they were after the fifteen-month interval, whereas the eight who returned to rank-and-file status "reverted" to their attitudes of three years earlier. Here are the percentages of the two sets of foremen, at three different times, who felt that the union "should not have more say in setting labor standards":

	Initially	After 15 months	After 3 years
Twelve continuing foremen	33	100	100
Eight demoted foremen	13	63	13

(exactly as predicted), as a result of being subjected to new influences in the new positions. To be recognized as occupying a position is to invite such influences.

* * *

Social position determines role behavior—not in the sense of being the only determinant but of being an inescapable one. To occupy a social position means, in fact, to be subject to normative influences toward role conformity. A position is thus a *locus of influences* that impinge on whatever persons are recognized as occupying it; the direction of such influence is toward the maintenance of prescribed relationships with role partners.

POSITIONAL DISTANCE AND ROLE RELATIONSHIPS

If an individual's occupancy of a position influences his role behavior, then it should also be true that *relationships* between different persons' positions should influence their role *relationships*. But to examine our problem in this way requires that we be more precise about relationships. It is easy to describe a pair of social positions—say those of teacher and student—in terms of the role prescriptions associated with each one, separately. And it is not particularly difficult to describe the essential features of their relationship, in terms like the giving and receiving of instruction, just as we have described the mother-child relationship as one of giving and receiving nurturance. The difficulty begins with the fact that there are countless numbers of named positions in groups and societies around the world, each of which has relationships with one or more other positions. We shall not get beyond the sheerly descriptive level if we have to find a new term for every possible relationship between positions. All scientific disciplines involve the reducing of a multiplicity of observed phenomena to a comparatively few principles that apply to all of them, and we therefore confront this problem: What kinds of characteristics are there, if any, that recur in the relationships between *many* pairs of positions and their associated roles? Insofar as we succeed in finding *common dimensions* that apply to many relationships, we shall no longer have to treat each one of them as unique but can more adequately develop scientific generalizations.

We shall approach this problem by describing positional and role relationships in terms of *relative distance along a dimension*. Beginning with our assumption that positional relationships should influence role relationships, we shall regard the former as independent and the latter as dependent. That is, we shall inquire into the behavioral relationships between position holders whose relative locations along specified dimensions are known. We shall not attempt to be complete, but only to illustrate an approach. No relationship between any pair of positions can be fully described in terms of a single dimension; husband-wife relationships, for example, are far too complex to be fully described so simply. And we shall select only a very few of the dimensions that might be considered, concentrating on a few that, according to available research evidence, appear to be both common and important. The first of these is hierarchical status.

Relationships of Status and Hierarchy

In groups both large and small whose members continue to interact with one another over a period of time, distinctions among members are likely to appear such that we refer to some of them as being

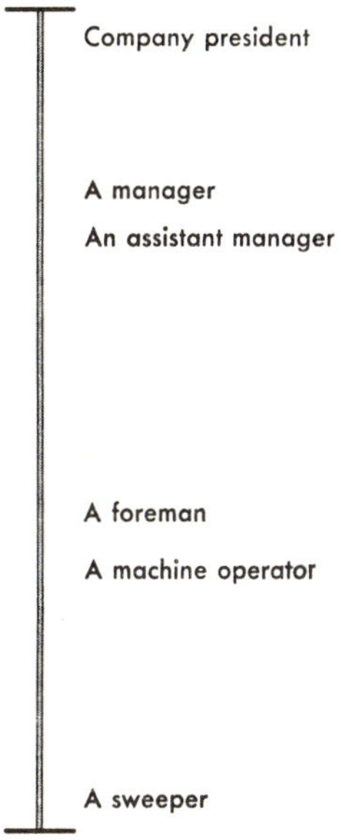

ROLE RELATIONSHIPS - 337

Company president

A manager
An assistant manager

A foreman
A machine operator

A sweeper

FIGURE 11.5. Illustration of distances along the dimension of authority

"above," "lower than," or "superior to" others. Insofar as these distinctions are generally recognized by group members they correspond to positions, with their associated roles. There are various ways in which distinctions come about, and there are many characteristics—such as skill, wealth, power, popularity—with respect to which members are classified as higher or lower, but nevertheless the distinctions all have something in common. We shall therefore consider them together as instances of *status differentiation*.[1]

Suppose we have observed that status differentiation exists within a group or organization, as illustrated in Figure 11.5. What does this imply about the role relationships between higher and lower members, and between members of more or less equal status? Such observations have been made in many kinds of groups characterized by all sorts of status distinctions, and we shall cite a few examples.

PROFESSIONAL PRESTIGE. In our society there are many familiar examples of prestige hierarchies; an example appears in Research Illustration 11.2. The kinds of relationships reported in this study are much like those found in many quite different settings. They suggest behavioral relationships of deference on the part of low-status members toward those of high status, and expected deference from the former on the part of high-status members, under conditions of generally recognized differences with respect to power and prestige. Relationships among equals, according to this study and others, vary with status when members of all status levels are in the same situation: high-level members tend to like and to communicate frequently with each other, whereas low-level members neither like nor communicate with each other as much under these conditions. We shall comment more fully on these findings after looking at some other examples.

POPULARITY STATUS. In the two populations of students who, beginning as strangers, lived closely together for several months (Research Illustrations 6.2, page 173, and 10.1, page 293) there were wide differences in personal popularity. (The index of popularity status is the

[1] Some sociologists and anthropologists (for example, Linton, 1945) use *status* in the sense in which we have used *position*. Since the literal meaning of the former term is "standing," and, by extension, "standing higher or lower than," we shall consider *status* as a special case of the more general concept of position.

Research Illustration 11.2

Some years ago forty-two persons—social workers, psychologists, psychiatrists, nurses, and guidance counselors working in the general area of mental health—met for a one-day conference. Though they did not realize it at first, they had been so selected that about half of them had high and the other half low prestige in the eyes of fellow professionals. During the day each person was a member of four entirely different groups of about six members each for a half hour or so, to discuss a specified problem of interest to all of them. Before these meetings began, each person indicated how much influence he thought each of the other persons with whom he was to meet would have on his own opinions and judgments: a seven-point scale ranging from "none at all" to "very much" was used for this purpose. Then, just after each discussion, everyone indicated how much he liked each of the persons with whom he had just met, how much he thought these same individuals liked him, and how much each of them had participated in the discussion; again, seven-point scales were used. In addition, the investigators kept records of how much each person actually participated in the discussions.

Results show, first, that persons perceived as highly influential actually did most of the talking, and that they talked mainly to other high-influentials. Low-influentials also directed most of their communications to high-influentials, so that there was comparatively little communication among low-influentials. Second, all members, regardless of their influence status, tended to overestimate the amount of participation by low-influentials; these distortions of judgment are interpreted by the investigators as indicating that there was general expectation that low-influentials would not participate much, so that their actual participation, though relatively small, was seen as more than expected. Third, high-influentials were in general better liked than low-influentials, but both lows and highs tended to estimate that they were better liked by highs than by lows—a judgmental distortion suggesting that "group members *need* to see the *highs* as liking them."

The total set of findings is interpreted as indicating that low-status persons "perceive and behave toward high-status members in . . . ego-defensive manner," that is, in ways that serve "to reduce the feeling of uneasiness experienced in their relations with highs." This interpretation is consistent with nearly all of the findings (Hurwitz, Zander, and Hymovitch, 1960).

average rank order of preference expressed toward each individual by all others.) We shall examine these data in order to answer this question: What is the relationship between the popularity statuses of any two men and the frequency of their voluntary association with each other? Figure 11.6 indicates the popularity status of each of seventeen male students, after they had lived together in the same house for about

ROLE RELATIONSHIPS - 339

5 individuals highest in popularity

7 of 10 pairs (70%) reported by other men as frequently associating pairs

7 individuals intermediate in popularity

9 of 21 pairs (43%) reported by other men as frequently associating pairs

5 individuals lowest in popularity

2 of 6 pairs (33%) reported by other men as frequently associating pairs

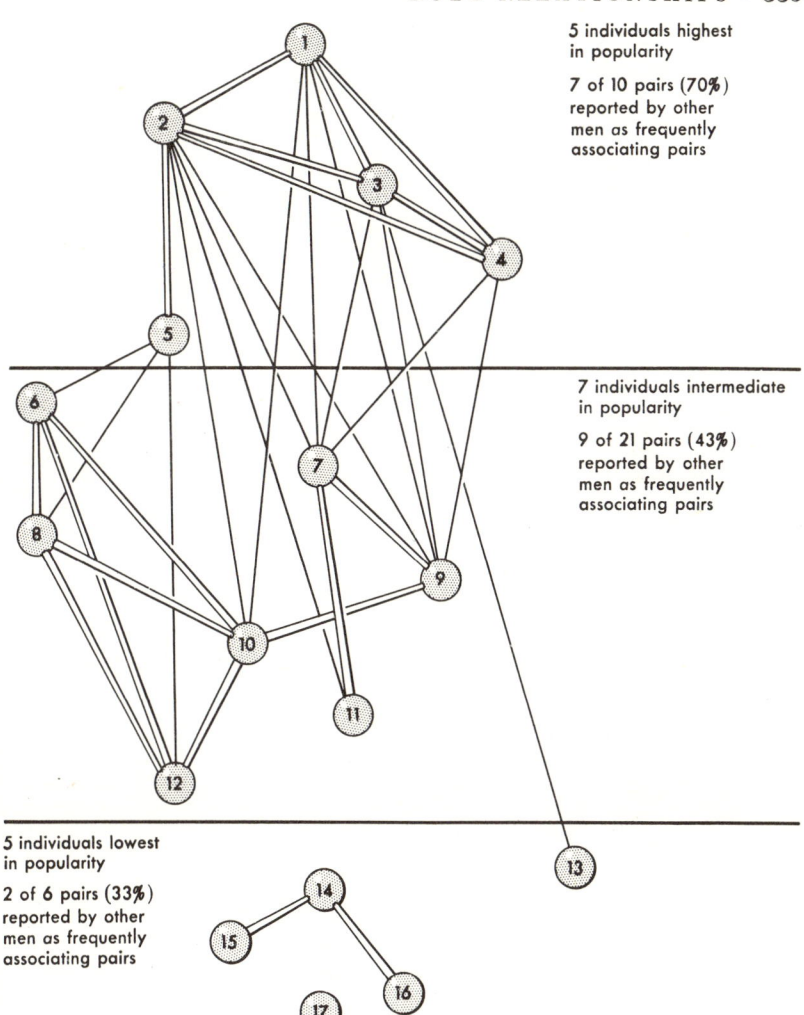

FIGURE 11.6. Popularity status-structuring as related to frequency of association after four months of acquaintance. Double lines represent frequently associating dyads within the same status category, and single lines those in different categories. Numbers in circles represent each individual's rank in popularity. (Adapted from Newcomb, 1961)

four months. Each man is represented by a circle, and numbered according to his rank in popularity; and the pairs of men represented by connecting lines indicate pairs that were reported by the fifteen men other than themselves to be in frequent association with each other. The seventeen individuals are divided as nearly as possible into equal thirds according to popularity status, and the double lines indicate frequently associating pairs within the same one of the three status levels.[2]

Figure 11.6 shows (1) that the men highest in popularity status tend to associate frequently with each other (among the four most popular individuals, all possible pairs are frequently associating ones); (2) that those intermediate in popularity are also intermediate in numbers of pairs in frequent association; and (3) that those lowest in popularity show relatively little tendency toward frequent association with each other (none at all, in the case of the lowest three). High-status men are found in frequently associating pairs with intermediate-status men in 14 of 35, or 40 percent of all possible cases—less frequently than high-status men associate with each other; and with one exception (number 13, paired with high-status man 3) none of the low-status men is in frequent association with any of the others. Thus within this group status relationships in popularity are closely associated with actual role relationships: one can predict fairly well from status relationships of popularity what the behavioral relationships of association will be. Or, to put it somewhat differently, status distances between individuals tell us a good deal about the closeness of their interpersonal relationships: the less the *status* distance between any two individuals the less the *behavioral* distance, in terms of close association.

This last finding—that low-status men do not associate frequently with one another—obviously does not apply to the larger scene of total communities: we know from studies of social-class membership in small cities, for example, that members of the same class associate with one another as frequently at the lower as at the higher levels (cf. Warner et al., 1949). The contradiction probably stems from the fact that in the student group the unpopular men could seek frequent association with people outside it, whereas in total communities the lower-status people have no one but each other. Thus the generalization still holds that status distance determines frequency of association; but the effects of small distances at low-level positions do not differ from small distances at higher levels in a relatively "closed" society like a total community.

* * *

We have chosen only two examples of the many kinds of differential status that have been observed in human groups. In addition to positions and roles that are differentiated according to prestige and popularity, we might have mentioned differentiations of power and authority (within families or organizations, for example); knowledge, skill,

---

[2] The data from which indices of popularity were derived are independent from those from which indices of frequency of association were computed, though obtained during the same week (cf. Newcomb, 1961).

or other kinds of expertness (especially within occupational groups); social class; and caste (often, though not necessarily, associated with racial differences). Each of these kinds of differentiation is unique in some ways, but an important thing they have in common is that behavioral relationships vary with status distances. The greater the status distance between persons, the greater the behavioral distance between them on such dimensions as deference or the kinds of intimate behavior that are associated with high mutual attraction. If the giving and receiving of deferential behavior may be assumed to represent distance, and intimate behavior closeness, then behavioral distance tends to parallel status distance.

Relationships of Communicative Accessibility

Except in the very smallest groups, there is almost sure to be more communication on the part of some dyads than others. In a group of ten persons, for example, there are forty-five dyads, among which uneven distribution of dyadic communication is the rule. There are many possible reasons for this, including the personality characteristics of individuals, but it also has a great deal to do with positions in a group's communicative structure. Distance along the dimension of communicative access may be determined by the physical nearness or remoteness of position holders, or by role prescriptions according to which specified position holders are required or are forbidden to communicate freely with each other. In any case we would expect role relationships to be influenced by the ways in which positional distances affect the nature and frequency of communication.

In Research Illustration 11.3 experiments designed to discover some consequences of different kinds of communication networks are described. In all but one of the four networks shown there is one position of high communicative centrality; that is, the average distance between this and all other positions is small. Other positions have greater or less peripherality, or relatively great distance, on the average, from all other positions. (The peripherality of any position can be directly measured, and its centrality inversely measured, by the minimum number of messages that need to be sent in order to get all the necessary information to that position; the fewer the required messages, the greater the centrality. For certain purposes the time required to get the necessary messages to a given position provides a second index.) These experiments showed that occupants of the peripheral positions felt that their relations with the central position holder were like those between follower and leader; they felt dependent on the central person, as indeed they were. Persons in peripheral positions also felt less satisfied than the central persons with their own contributions; evidently they did not like being on the dependent end of a relationship with the central person.

Research Illustration 11.3

A pair of experiments reported by Leavitt (1951) took off from the obvious fact that the possibilities of communication among five group members are different in Pattern I and in Pattern II, as shown in the accompanying figure, in which circles represent individuals and lines indicate that the connected individuals could communicate with each other. Subjects in this experiment were placed in enclosed cubicles, close together, and they exchanged written messages (which could later be studied by the experimenter) that were placed in slots. For each individual, in Pattern I, only two slots were open, whereas in Pattern II two slots were available to each of three individuals; for the other two subjects only one slot was open. A task was assigned to the group: to discover as quickly as possible which of six symbols (+, *, O, ◊, △, □) was included on all the different cards supplied to the five group members; each subject's card contained only five symbols, and one symbol (its identity being unknown) was common to all the cards. The task was considered complete when all five men had the right answer. What they had to do, of course, was to exchange messages something like "My card does *not* have the square; what is your missing one," or "D is missing the circle and I am missing the square."

One of the interesting results of the experiment had to do with members' answers to the question, "Did your group have a leader? If so, who?" The numbers appearing in each circle in the accompanying figure show the numbers of times that each person in that position was reported by group members to be the leader. Not surprisingly, there is little differentiation among the five positions in Pattern I; after all, the positions do not differ, though the individuals occupying them probably did. But in spite of individual differences there was almost unanimous agreement among those who thought the

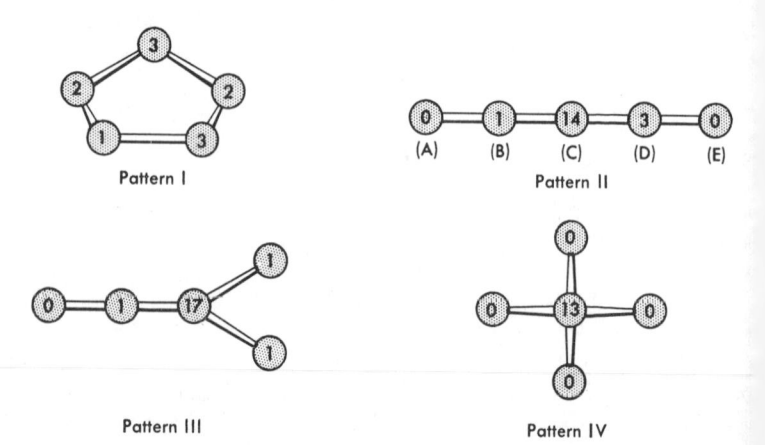

Pattern I

Pattern II

Pattern III

Pattern IV

group had any leader that the *central* person in Pattern II was the leader, and in Pattern I only eleven subjects named anyone as leader. (The experiment was repeated four times with each pattern, so that altogether there were twenty responses for each pattern.)

In a later and somewhat extended experiment, Leavitt obtained very similar results for these two patterns, and even more dramatic ones when the degree of "centrality" was increased as in Patterns III and IV. Leavitt also found that in all three patterns having differentiated positions (that is, all except Pattern I) there was a strong tendency for individuals in central positions to feel better about the experience than did those in peripheral positions, as indicated by their answers to these questions: "How much did you like your job?" and "How satisfied are you with the job done?" This finding suggests that centrality is associated with independence of action, which in turn is associated with satisfaction. General level of satisfaction within a group, however, tended to be higher in the less efficient patterns, like Pattern I—presumably because there were no peripheral members whose independence was limited by their restricted access to information.

Why, in Pattern II, should the central person be considered the leader? The answer, almost certainly, is that whoever was in this place in the network had complete information earlier than anyone else. And the reason why the person in this place got complete information first is not hard to see. The end man at place A, for example, in order to have complete information, would have had to wait (1) for D to get information from E, (2) for D to inform C both about his own and E's missing symbol, (3) for C to inform B about his and D's and E's missing symbol, and (4) for B to pass along to A all this information, together with the identity of his own missing symbol. Unless all these steps occurred in exactly this order, moreover, still more messages would have to be transmitted. And (still assuming that A was the first to obtain full information) the task would not be completed until these same steps had been reversed, from A to B to C to D to E, in order that all five subjects might have the right answer. The central place, in contrast, is more favorable for two reasons: first, less complicated messages are required, since C needs to learn from B only B's and A's missing symbols, and from D only D's and E's; second, the exchange of messages on either side of him can be going on simultaneously, both in getting information to C and in getting the right answer from C to all the others.°

° In quantitative terms, 10 items of information must be passed from one man to another (1 item from E to D, 2 from D to C, 3 from C to B, and 4 from B to A) if A is to get complete information, and an additional 4 to get the right answer back to every man. To get complete information to C, however, requires only 6 item transmissions from one man to another (1 each from A to B and from E to D, and 2 each from B and D to C), and another 4 to get the right answers back in two directions simultaneously. See Bavelas (1950) and Leavitt (1949) for suggestions about the measurement of centrality.

Positions of centrality and peripherality represent not just abstract distances between sources and destinations of messages but also points where persons are sending and receiving them. Distances refer not to inches or miles but to degrees of difficulty or delay in getting messages transmitted; they may in fact be regarded as barriers to direct communication. Thus the distance between any two persons has direct effects on their behavioral relationship. These relationships, in turn, are satisfying or frustrating in varying degrees. Insofar as the sharing of information with another person is rewarding, the relationship between centrally and peripherally situated persons will be more satisfying for the former than for the latter. For the same reason relationships between peripheral persons will be rewarding to neither.

Quite apart from the matter of personal satisfyingness, varying degrees of information sharing have other consequences, some of which we noted in the previous chapter. As interacting persons exchange more and more information, they tend increasingly to share the same attitudes, to subscribe to the same norms, and to have higher levels of attraction toward one another. Increasing frequency of information is not necessarily the independent variable in these relationships; it often follows increasing attraction, for example. Nor is it a sufficient condition, because it often happens that the more contact one has with a person the less one likes or respects him. But it is, with rare exceptions, a necessary condition; shared attitudes and mutual high attraction tend not to persist without continuing communication of some kind.

In Chapter 10 we gave some instances of how interpersonal attraction is influenced by residential propinquity; such findings may, of course, be interpreted in terms of communicative access. Another example, of rather extreme nature, may now be given. In one of the 17-man populations previously described, the students (sophomores and juniors who had attended this university for only three months) were asked the following question:

"Suppose that you were going to live in this house next semester. Suppose, also, that you personally were permitted to select the other 16 men to live in the house. You may select any male undergraduate in the United States, including those now living here, whom you personally know. What 16 men would you most prefer to live with in the house?"

The 272 names mentioned by these 17 men, all of whom had previously spent one or two years on some other campus, were classifiable as follows:

Men from other campuses	151
Men from the same house	102
Other men, same campus	19

Among all choices on the same campus, 84 percent were thus concentrated among the 17 members of their own house, in spite of the fact that they had had ample opportunity to meet many other men during their three months on the campus. There were, of course, rather special reasons why they had all spent very large proportions of their time with each other: they had entered the house simultaneously, as total strangers; they had been invited to live there, and had looked forward to the experience; not only had they lived and taken their meals there; they had also engaged in many common enterprises as part of the research project. All these considerations highlight our present point: the less the distance, in terms of communicative access, among group members as compared with their distance to other persons, the greater the probability that they will develop role relationships characterized both by shared interests and interpersonal attraction—especially when, as in this instance, the circumstances making for ready communicative access are voluntarily accepted.

Dimensional Descriptions of Role Relationships

To describe a role relationship like that between a mother and her child in terms of distances between them on such dimensions as status superiority and communicative access may seem to take the heart out of it: one gets a better "feel" for roles by descriptions that are rich in concrete detail. Thus a description of a trail of summer moonlight across a pine-sheltered lake in terms of candlepower, inches, and stability of illumination seems totally inadequate. Our problem, however, is a scientific one and it is no more required that our descriptions of role relationships resemble everyday appearances than that the physicist's description of sticks and stones *look* like sticks and stones, rather than looking like clouds of tiny particles. All that is required, either of the social psychologist or of the physicist, is that his descriptive devices correspond to something that can be objectively reported, and that they help to account for observable events (role behavior, in our case).

One important advantage of approaching role relationships through dimensions and distances is that it becomes possible to make comparisons of roles—either similar ones in different societies or different ones in the same society—in systematic ways. For example, it might be shown that in some societies mother-child relationships resemble husband-wife relationships on the dimension of hierarchical status, whereas in other societies they do not. It might even be possible to show that in some societies nearly all role relationships are characterized by considerable distance on the status dimension. The systematic study of role relationships would not be very useful if such comparisons could not be made.

Nor is it sufficient merely to compare concrete, photographic events (like role behaviors) without comparing them on some specified dimensions; by way of analogy, one cannot compare carrots and oranges as totalities, but one can meaningfully compare them regarding such variables as size, shape, color, or vitamin content.

Perhaps you are wondering how one knows on what dimensions to compare different role relationships. The answer is that one selects role dimensions in the same way that one selects relevant variables in any other kind of study. Using either informal evidence ("I have a hunch that . . .") or research evidence that has already been obtained ("I have a hypothesis that . . ."), one categorizes concrete instances of behavior in terms of different degrees of the hypothetical dimension. Some of the dimensions that are thus "tried out" will turn out to be consistent and widely generalizable—like hierarchical status or communicative access: these are the ones that make comparisons possible.

The dimensional approach, finally, is only a way of describing role relationships, not a way of accounting for them. The latter problem, as we have tried to show, has to do with positional and personal determinants of norms that are known as role prescriptions.

GROUPS AS MULTIDIMENSIONAL SYSTEMS OF ROLES

All groups have structures that may be described in terms of more than one dimension. It can always be said, for example, that every member of an interaction group has *both* a status relationship with every other member either of equality, on the one hand, or of subordination or superordination on the other, and also a relationship of communicative accessibility. Thus, any interaction group has a status structure, a communication structure, an attraction structure (as noted in Chapter 10), and doubtless many others. Our final problems, in this chapter, are to examine the notion of structure as applied to a total group of several persons; and to consider how various kinds of structuring, on the part of the same group, fit together.

The Role Structure of a Total Group

If one has a particular dimension in mind, together with an index of distance on that dimension, it is not difficult to describe the structure of a group. The simplest way is to select some criterion (even if an arbitrary one) of distance, and then to indicate the number of pairs that meet the criterion. Figure 11.7, representing the communicative structure of two 17-man groups of students after four months of ac-

Population I

Population II

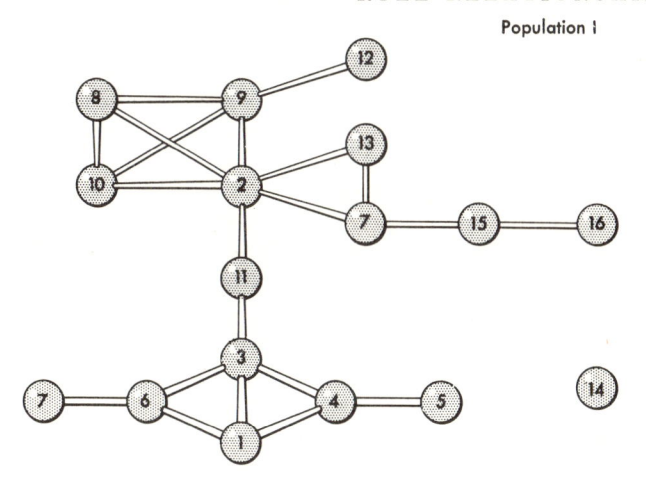

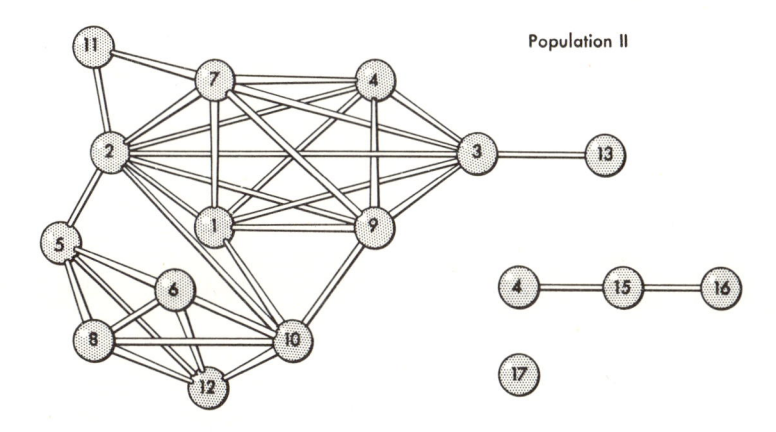

FIGURE 11.7. Frequently associating pairs of individuals in two populations, after four months of acquaintance. Connecting lines refer to frequently associating pairs, as reported by individuals other than themselves. Numbers in circles refer to rank in popularity status.

quaintance, illustrates this procedure. According to a criterion of rather frequent association, in the first population there are two subgroups that are unconnected except for person 11, plus one isolated individual; in the second population, however, a larger and a smaller subgroup are connected by several pairs, together with a separate chain of three individuals, and one isolate. These graphic representations of communicative structure suggest a rather limited range of communicative access for most individuals in the first population, in which there is a total of 21

348 - GROUP STRUCTURES AND PROPERTIES

communicative links, as compared with 33 in the other population. This is also indicated by the fact that in the second population there are seven men who are in frequent communication with five or more others, whereas there are no men in the first population who communicate frequently with so many others. Thus we may conclude that the communicative structure of the second population shows more accessibility of members to one another than does that of the first population.

A somewhat different way of portraying group structure appears in Figure 11.8, which shows status structure in terms of individual popularity. In the first population only one person holds an extreme position in unpopularity, and no one is extreme in popularity; the other sixteen men in this population are intermediate in status. In the second population, however, five men hold extreme positions; only twelve hold intermediate ones. Thus there was greater differentiation in popularity status in the second than in the first population; the extreme individuals in this population were farther apart on this dimension than in the first population. This is one way of comparing the status structures of the total populations.

We shall not stop to illustrate other forms of group structuring. Regardless of the particular dimension in which you are interested, if you know the distribution of distances—how many positional relationships are close to and remote from how many others—you have a general idea of the group's role structure according to that dimension. Summary statements about role structure will take such forms as these: In a certain office staff there are few role relationships of equality, and many that are characterized by varying degrees of status barriers. In a small sorority, nearly all members communicate easily and frequently with all other members. The role structure of a cliquish ladies' club includes

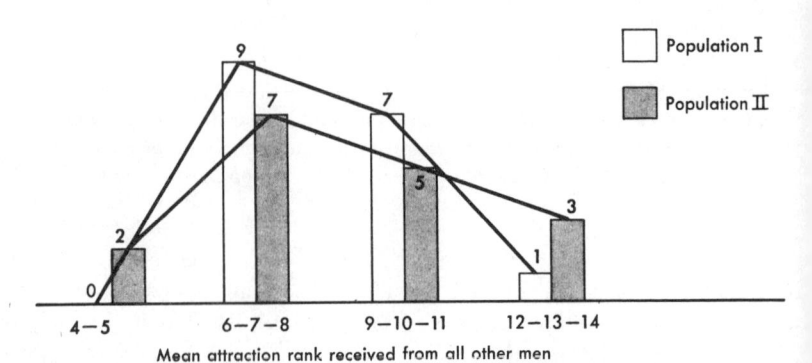

FIGURE 11.8. Numbers of individuals in two populations at four levels of popularity status (adapted from Newcomb, 1961)

many relationships of close interpersonal attraction and still more of personal antagonism.

Perhaps it has occurred to you that these very general summary statements about role structures of groups are of such commonsense nature that any member of any one of these groups could have made them, and without such cumbersome notions as role structures. Our reason for presenting such statements has not been to document, in a technical way, what is already known in an informal way about some particular group. Rather, we have attempted to present some notions and some procedures that have wide generality; they can be applied to *any* interaction group—including groups about which we do not have advance information, or those about which conflicting opinions are held. Insofar as our concepts and procedures can be applied to many and diverse groups, we have a common basis for comparison among them.

Multidimensional Structures within the Same Group

Since any interaction group has a number of structures that may be described in terms of different dimensions, the question naturally arises as to how the several dimensions fit together. Considering almost any American family, for example, as a group, father-son relationships are typically characterized by relationships of subordination, of fairly close (but still limited) communicative accessibility, and of rather strong attraction. Since all these relationships exist at the same time between the same persons, it is reasonable to ask whether they affect one another or whether they are quite independent. The answer is that they are all very likely to be interrelated, but there are many exceptions to the general rule.

Take, for example, communicative accessibility and attraction. In general, the closer the accessibility the higher the positive attraction—for two reasons. First, communicative exchange tends to be rewarding, and without it close interpersonal attraction is not likely to develop; it is usually a necessary though not a sufficient condition for the development of attraction. And, second, persons who are already attracted to one another are likely to find ways of circumventing barriers to communication. Thus closeness on either dimension tends to bring about closeness on the other.

Communicative accessibility between role participants tends also to be associated with their relative equality in status—in respect to popularity, professional prestige, or social class, for example. Status differences usually impose barriers to communication—particularly in the "upward" direction. This may occur because the higher-status persons seek protection by making themselves inaccessible, or perhaps because a relatively few high-status persons cannot in fact be accessible to relatively many of the lower status, or simply because the gulf between high- and low-status persons is assumed to be too wide ("we wouldn't have anything in common"). And it may also work the other way around: that is, existing barriers to communication (such as differences in language or vocabulary, or sheer infrequency of encounter) may lead to beliefs of superiority on either side to attribute feelings of superiority to the other side. Insofar as such beliefs are shared on both sides, actual status differences arise.

The interesting thing about these and other relationships among different role dimensions is that the dimension of communicative accessibility particularly affects each of the others. If you stop to ask, for example, why there is apt to be higher mutual attraction between persons at similar than at remote status levels, you will sooner or later come back to the fact that both mutual attraction and similar status levels tend to be associated with ready communicative access. Thus, role relationships characterized by ready communication tend either to result from or to lead to role relationships characterized by high attraction and by closeness of status.

Groups as Systems of Roles

What distinguishes one group from others is its members' behavior, and not just who its members are—that is, their names, faces, and personal idiosyncrasies. And any member's behavior, as we have seen, is strongly influenced by the positions as centers of influence both from and upon the occupants of related positions—that he occupies. Thus the role relationships within a group represent the ways in which its members adapt to their positional relationships with each other. From this it follows that if different persons, as members of different groups, have similar positions in their own groups, then we would expect role relationships to be similar in the different groups. And so it happens that role relationships between husbands and wives or between employers and employees have much in common the world around. And so it happens, also, that even though there is a complete turnover of individual members, as in the case of the United States Senate every forty years or so, the role relationships of its members remain much the same. It is for this reason that we feel justified in saying that the Senate remains the same body even though its members change.

Since, in this sense, a group *is* what its role relationships are, our descriptions and explanations of any group as a whole must be stated in terms of its entire network of role relationships. The most effective way of doing this is to regard a total set of roles as a *system*. This term refers to any set of things that continue to interact with each other in such ways that the total set, viewed as a single entity, maintains relatively constant properties. Some simple systems—an ordinary pin, for example, or a boulder—are relatively uninteresting because their constancy results from the fact that their parts (the molecules of which they are constructed) continue to interact in the *same* ways over long periods of time. Others, like the human body, are more complex and more interesting because system constancy is maintained by *changing* relationships among its parts. Take, for example, the whole set of organs—including heart, lungs, arm and leg muscles, nerves, sweat glands—that in a human body interact in ways that keep bodily temperature relatively constant. Constancy on the part of the total system, as it encounters changes in the environment, is maintained by changed behavior on the part of its constituent organs.

In Chapter 5 we considered, from just this point of view, that a set of attitudes can constitute a system that tends to retain the constant property of balance while its constituent attitudes change. This is a social-psychological example of interacting parts in more or less stable systems. We shall now look at roles in the same way, that is, as constituents whose interaction with each other helps to maintain constant properties of groups.

As we shall see in the following chapter, there are many different properties of groups that are of considerable importance—including group size, normativeness, and cohesiveness. When we speak of these or other properties as remaining relatively constant, we do not mean that they never change, but simply that they normally fluctuate only within certain limits, like those within which your body temperature usually varies. When these limits are exceeded, the group will either correct the excess, become a very different kind of group, or cease to exist at all. Such "group death" means that members have ceased to interact with one another, without transmitting their modes of interaction to other group members as their successors.

Role Relationships of Cooperation and Competition

The role system within a sports team, say in basketball, is a cooperative one. Any two members of the team are likely, at any moment during a game, to share the same goals as outcomes of their interaction. If one of them aims the ball at the basket, all members want it to be successful, and each of them knows that the others want the same thing. All members of the competing team want it to be unsuccessful, and all members of both teams know it. From a social-psychological point of view, a system of role relationships is a cooperative one insofar as the behavior of any one of the interacting persons, or any combination of them, affects all members in the same way with respect to goal attainment.

By the same token, a role system is competitive to the degree that behavior on the part of any interacting person which brings him closer to his goal necessarily moves one or more others farther from their goals. A cooperative role relationship presupposes shared goals, and a competitive one opposed goals. Without regard to the particular behaviors by which one group member brings himself closer to his goal, and in so doing brings others closer to it, the essence of cooperative role relationships is mutually facilitative behavior induced by the recognition of a "common fate" desired by all. Competitive role relationships are characterized by mutually opposed behavior, since fates are believed to be opposed.

The group properties of integration and cohesiveness (cf. Chapter 12) are among those that tend to be maintained by role relationships which are cooperative. It has been possible, through experiments like the one by Deutsch described in Research Illustration 11.4, to show that such group properties are indeed the outcome of cooperative role relationships, because the latter were created by manipulations in the laboratory. Deutsch's findings are not to be interpreted, of course, as indicating that cooperation is in general "as good as" or "better than" competition. But the following general conclusions do seem justified. First, complex and more or less new problems are likely to get solved more efficiently and at higher qualitative levels, when time is limited, under conditions that facilitate interdependence. These conditions, as created in the experiment, were such that goals, and rewards stemming from goal attainment, were shared. And second, the providing of such conditions tends to bring about, as by-products, friendliness, sense of group membership, mutual helpfulness, and openness to suggestions from others.

GENERALIZING FROM COOPERATIVE AND COMPETITIVE ROLE SYSTEMS. The persisting properties of these groups were maintained by each group's role system, and this fact raises two final questions for consideration in this chapter. First, what can be said about the role systems within cooperative and within competitive groups? Such descriptive phrases as "friendly," "mutually helpful," "open to suggestion," and "differentiated task assignments" suggest role relationships that can be described in terms of the three dimensions previously considered in this chapter. In the cooperative groups, mutually high attraction was the rule; status differences were slight, in spite of the fact that tasks were divided up; and members had ready communicative access to one another. In the competitive groups, on the other hand, mutual attraction was relatively low; status differences tended to be created by the fact that some individuals appeared to be achieving more success than others; and communicative access was limited by the fact that each member was motivated to offer his best ideas as his own rather than as contributions to a group product. Although these three dimensions are by no

Research Illustration 11.4

Ten groups of students were organized, each composed of four or five men from a large class in psychology at the Massachusetts Institute of Technology. These small groups met weekly, in lieu of regular class attendance. It was planned by the experimenter (Deutsch, 1949), though not known to the students, that five of the groups were to be assigned cooperative and the other five competitive tasks, and that each cooperative group was to be compared with a certain competitive group, so selected that the members of the two groups were as nearly alike as possible in skills related to their tasks. Here are excerpts from the sets of instructions given to the two kinds of groups:

Cooperative. "Every week you will be given a puzzle to solve as a group . . . Your effectiveness in handling the problem will be evaluated by ranking you as a group in comparison with four other groups that will handle the same problems. . . . The group that comes out with the best average (at the end of five weeks) will be excused from one term paper and every member of that group will receive an *H* (the highest possible grade) for that paper. You are to come out with one solution as a group. . . . Your grade for this course will also be influenced by the discussions in this class of the human relations problems. All members of the group whose discussions and recommendations are best . . . will get the highest grade. . . ."

Competitive. "Every week you will be given a puzzle to solve as a group. . . . The person who contributes most to the solution will receive a rank of 1, the one who contributes next most will receive a rank of 2, and so on. The ranks that each of you receive on the weekly problems will be averaged. . . . We will have a reward for the individual who comes out with the best individual average. He will be excused from one term paper, and will receive an automatic *H* for that paper. You are to come out with one solution as a group. . . . Your grade for this course will also be influenced by your discussions in this class of the human relations problems. Each week the individual who contributes most will receive a rank of 1, the individual contributing next most will get a 2, and so on. . . ."

In all sessions, puzzles were first presented, and then the human relations problems. The investigators repeated the same instructions at each of the five group meetings, and solicited the students' cooperation in not discussing problems and procedures outside the group meetings. They also ascertained that in fact all subjects in all groups clearly understood the procedures by which grades in the course would be assigned. At the end of each of five sessions, and also following the completion of the entire experiment, all subjects answered questionnaires concerning interest, "group feeling," amount of group cooperation, group productivity, individual productivity, and related matters. Four observers were present at experimental sessions, at the end of which they made ratings of both individual and group behaviors of various kinds.

From the rather complex set of findings, the following may be selected as of special interest: (1) There was more "group-centeredness" and "group feeling" in the cooperative than in the competitive groups, and more "desire to excel others" in the competitive groups. (2) According to subjects' own questionnaire responses or observers' ratings, or both, the cooperative groups excelled the competitive ones in "working together," in "degree of coordination," and in "group cooperation." (3) There was more division of labor in the cooperative groups; that is, cooperative members organized themselves, as competitive ones did not, so that different parts of the tasks were carried out simultaneously by different individuals, with resulting increases in group efficiency. (4) There were almost no differences between the two kinds of groups in degree of motivation, interest, or involvement in the tasks. (5) There were fewer difficulties of communication and understanding each other within the cooperative groups. (6) Acceptance of each other's ideas and expressions of agreement were more frequent within cooperative than within competitive groups. "Cooperative groups solve the puzzle problems more rapidly . . . and also produce more on human relations problems." (8) The cooperative groups also showed qualitative superiority: "According to observer ratings, the discussions of the cooperative groups not only came out with more fruitful ideas . . . but also their group discussions showed more insight and understanding of the nature of the problem." (9) There was more friendliness within the cooperative than within the competitive groups, as well as more appreciation of others' contributions. They even learned each other's last names more rapidly.

means the only ones that can be used to describe important role relationships, they go pretty far toward describing the differences between the two kinds of groups.

Just how, in the second place, did these different kinds of role relationships in the two kinds of groups contribute to their different group properties? Take, for example, productivity as a group property; we know that individuals in the two kinds of groups did not differ in motivation, interest, or task involvement (finding 4, above). Hence we conclude that the differences lay not in simple, additive effects of individual productivity; they had something to do, rather, with the *organization of individuals' contributions*—their patterning, their ways of fitting together so that certain effects are produced. And these modes of organization refer, basically, to role relationships. That is, a set of role relationships characterized by ready communicative accessibility is a more effective way of organizing information within a group than one characterized by barriers to communication. Role relationships of mutual at-

ROLE RELATIONSHIPS · 355

Group Norms, in the form of role prescriptions

Role System, composed of interrelated roles, as acted out by members

Group Properties

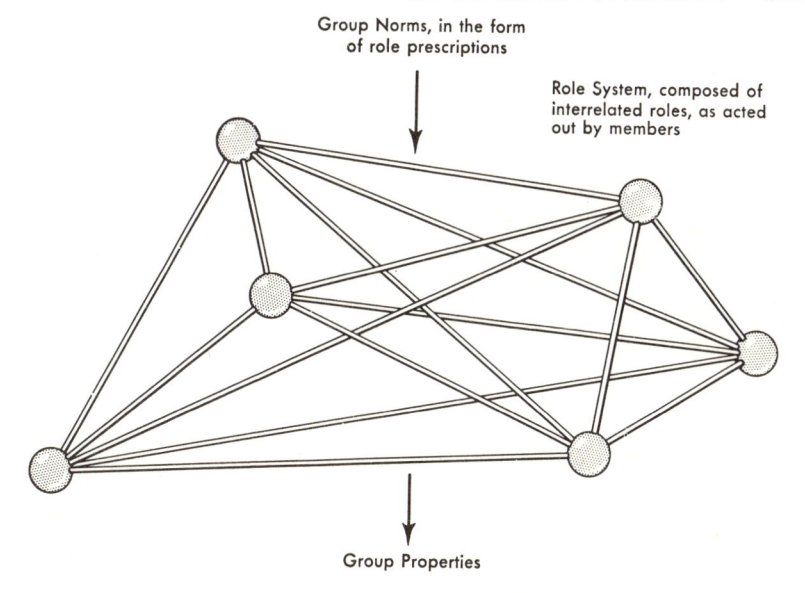

FIGURE 11.9. Schematic diagram illustrating how a group's role system mediates between its norms and its behavioral properties. Circles represent behavioral enactment of role prescriptions and lines represent role relationships. Arrows refer to direction of influence.

traction result (commonly, but not necessarily) in better organization of interpersonal response than, for example, those of mutual aversion (some partial exceptions are noted in Chapter 9). The general principle, apparently applicable to any kind of relatively stable role system, is that the ways in which group resources are mobilized and organized through role relationships determine the group's properties.[3]

It is well to remember, finally, that role prescriptions are norms, either potentially or actually. They are rules for the behavior of occupants of positions, whether the latter are described in commonly recognized terms in the form of social positions or in the social scientist's terms of locations on specified dimensions. In either case, the rules are effective insofar as there is shared acceptance of them by interacting persons. And a role system corresponds directly to the whole set of norms that apply to all the role relationships within a given group. Just as group properties are maintained by role relationships, the latter are maintained by group norms. As schematically illustrated in Figure 11.9, it is the group's system of role relationships, as expressed in interpersonal behavior, that mediates between its norms and its behavioral properties.

[3] This principle applies to behavioral properties of the group, and not to such properties as size; cf. Chapter 12, pages 359–364.

OVERVIEW

Insofar as groups maintain more or less stable characteristics, they do so because of regularities in the behaviors of their members toward one another. Such regularities can best be understood in terms of member-to-member relationships, rather than in terms of members' specific behaviors. What each individual does by way of contributing to such a relationship constitutes the behavioral aspect of his role, which in the case of the dyadic relationship may be thought of as one half of a dyadic habit.

Any society recognizes many common roles for which there exist more or less standard prescriptions, or norms, concerning the nature of the relationship between the occupants of specified positions. In the case of any particular set of interacting persons there exist, moreover, normative prescriptions that they have developed in their own history of interacting with each other. Any concrete instance of a role relationship has both positional and personal determinants.

Since we need to go beyond intuitive notions about interpersonal relationships, we have attempted to describe them in terms of individuals' relative locations on specified dimensions. Thus role relationships can be described in terms of individuals' distances from each other along the dimensions of hierarchical status, of communicative accessibility, and of mutual attraction, among other dimensions. One advantage of this approach is that comparisons among different roles can be made in systematic ways.

Any particular role, describing an individual's actual or prescribed contributions to a behavioral relationship with one or more other persons, is necessarily interdependent with the roles of others with whom that individual interacts. One role cannot exist apart from one or more other roles, and a change in any one of them is likely to induce change in one or more of the others. Such interdependence is characteristic of systems, and interaction groups may thus be viewed as systems of roles.

CHAPTER 12

Group Properties

MOST PEOPLE DEVELOP A GOOD DEAL OF SENSITIVITY TO THE CHARACTERISTICS of other persons. We may not always be right in our judgments of them, but at least we notice their characteristics, and we generally have a pretty good notion as to the kinds of things that it is important to take note of as we observe other people. We are likely to be less sensitive, however, and less skillful in judging the characteristics of groups. The latter task is surely the more difficult one, and it is not made easier by the fact that our language, which contains many thousands of words applicable to individuals, is relatively poor in words that describe groups *as groups*. It might amuse you, in fact, to see how many such terms you can think of in two minutes. But it is the demonstrable characteristics, or properties, of groups that will concern us in this chapter, rather than our existing familiarity with them, or our ability to judge them. Group properties—like the properties of atoms or of cells in our bodies—may affect our lives whether or not we are aware of them or can identify and judge them.

If there are important group properties that are not necessarily self-evident, how are they to be identified? Pursuing our discussion of human groups on pages 289–290, we shall suggest three criteria. First, a group property is a characteristic that applies to the *group as a single entity*, and not to any single member. Thus it would make sense to say that a basketball team has the property of smooth intermember

357

coordination, or that the average height of its members is 76.27 inches, but no single member has the property of smooth intermember coordination, and average height is not a property of a single individual. These, of course, are totally different kinds of group properties. Each member contributes to average height simply as an individual, alone, whereas each contributes to team coordination only in relation to the others, by interacting with them.

Second, a group property is a *variable*: that is, it varies in degree, either on the part of the same group or by way of comparison among groups. This criterion is important because it is only by observing the conditions with which the property varies—either the antecedent, independent conditions or the dependent conditions, as consequences—that the study of group properties contributes to our understanding of social psychology.

And, finally, a group property, if it is to be considered a variable, must be susceptible to *objective indexing*, or measurement. The emphasis here is on objectivity—that is, confirmability by independent observers—rather than on quantitative exactness. If it can be repeatedly shown that trained observers, each working independently, display high agreement in making similar distinctions between different groups with respect to some specified group property, then it may be said that that property is susceptible to objective indexing, whether or not the observers have made use of numbers.

In this chapter we shall consider a few group properties that can be shown to meet these criteria, and that are known to affect or to be affected by interaction among group members.

A Classification of Group Properties

Group properties, like plants or animals or people, can be classified in numberless ways. We shall not attempt a complete classification, but shall make a distinction that is based on the fact that many but not all properties have to do with uniformity and differentiation among members, in some way. This distinction results in three general categories: (1) *intermember* properties, which are based on similarities and differences among members; (2) *member-irrelevant* properties, which have nothing to do with intermember similarities and differences; and (3) *very inclusive* properties that are resultants of both kinds of properties. We shall begin with a member-irrelevant property, group size; this is a variable that ignores all intermember comparisons, every member being simply counted as one. We shall then consider two kinds of intermember properties, based on similarities and differences with respect, first, to structural position and, second, with respect to members' attitudes.

Finally, we shall use group cohesiveness as an example of a very inclusive, general property.

These four are not, of course, all-inclusive; they are selected only as important and illustrative for the purposes of this chapter, which are to show that groups having different properties invite or discourage different kinds or degrees of interaction among their members, with varying consequences both for groups and for their individual members.

GROUP SIZE

An interaction group may number as few as two members or as many as several hundreds. The size of a group is, as we shall see, a property that can have important effects on other properties because it affects interaction among members. It is also true, in indirect ways, that group size may be affected by member interaction (as a result of which additional members may be recruited, or some members may drop out), but we shall be concerned with size as an independent variable only. We shall assume, in short, that this particular property affects other properties only as it influences interaction, which in turn affects other properties.

A good many comparative studies have been made of larger and smaller groups, most of them involving groups of twenty or less; and many different characteristics of groups and of individual members have been observed, as dependent variables. We shall not discuss all these characteristics, but shall include only those that seem rather clearly to be outcomes of member interaction as affected by group size. Our treatment of this property is therefore organized in terms of three fairly common kinds of effects of group size on interaction.[1]

Interaction as Affected by Resource Input

Resource input, which is of particular importance in problem-solving groups, refers to members' knowledge, intellectual or physical capacities, or any kinds of skills in interacting with others that are relevant to the group's immediate situation. Since such resources are considered to be brought into the group situation by individual members, they are referred to as "input." For many kinds of problem solving, the total volume of resources possessed by the group tends to increase with

[1] For these ideas we are heavily indebted to our colleagues Edwin J. Thomas and Clinton F. Fink, from whose summary and interpretation of the relevant literature (1963) we have drawn freely.

the number of members, simply because with each added member there is increased probability that at least one of them will have some special skill or capacity that is helpful or even essential for solving the problem. This is particularly true of what are sometimes referred to as Eureka types of problem, in which a sudden insight or a bright and relevant idea quickly moves the problem toward solution. It does not necessarily follow, of course, that because one member offers just the right idea then other group members will accept it, but in many cases they do, so that the likelihood of a quick and correct solution is increased by the presence of at least one person who has an unusual capacity to propose such an idea. And such a person is more likely to be present in a larger than in a smaller group. It may also be the case that interaction between two or more such persons greatly contributes to the problem's solution. We would therefore expect better solutions to be found more frequently by larger than by smaller groups—provided that the problems are fairly difficult ones in the sense that they demand greater resources than the "typical" member of the group can command. As noted in Chapter 15, this expectation tends to be supported by the available research findings.

The ways in which member interaction mediates between input resources and group problem solving have to do primarily with the responses by others to solutions proffered by an individual. A satisfactory group solution requires other members not only to recognize the usefulness of the good idea proposed by one member but also, by communications to that effect, to show each other that they accept the idea. And this presupposes sufficient resource input on the part of the total group so that most members can recognize a useful idea presented by one of them, whether or not they are themselves able to originate it. In sum, resource input tends to *be increased* by larger numbers in the group, and this in turn tends to *cause an increase* in the kinds of communication (both proffering and responding favorably to a useful suggestion) that facilitate good solutions.

But what about suggestions that are not useful, or even downright wrong? Research Illustration 12.1, though it does not make use of group size as a variable, shows how increased resource input can make it easier to shunt aside such "wrong" solutions. The mediating effects of member interaction between group size and group success in problem solving depended, in this case, on the fact that a member other than the originator of a suggestion provides a kind of critical resource that is often necessary. And the larger the number of persons who can provide such a resource, the greater the likelihood that the appropriate criticisms will be made. This is but a special case of the generalization that—within limits soon to be considered—increase in group size tends to result in increases of whatever kinds of communication contribute to a good solution.

Research Illustration 12.1

An early study by Marjorie Shaw (1932) was concerned with the relative abilities of individuals, working alone, and of four-person, like-sex groups to solve very difficult problems—so difficult, as it turned out, that even the most successful individuals managed to solve only one of the four problems. One of these problems was presented as follows:

> On the A-side of the river [a diagram of which was provided by the experimenter] are three wives (W1, W2, W3) and their husbands (H1, H2, H3). All of the men but none of the women can row. Get them across to the B-side of the river by means of a boat carrying only three of them at a time. No man will allow his wife to be in the presence of another man unless he is also there. Use the discs marked H1, W2, etc.

Discussions among group members, as they attacked the problems, were recorded, so that the fate of useless suggestions as well as of useful ones could be traced for each group. As illustrated by the following excerpt from one of the group records, one kind of interaction that frequently occurred in successful groups involved the recognition by one member, at an early stage, that the strategy then being followed would not be successful. (A, B, C, and D, in this excerpt, refer to group members.)

> B: Let's move W1, H1, H2 and take them all in the boat to the other side. Then bring H2 back.
>
> D: Then take H2, W2, H3 across. And bring back H3 with the boat. And then H3 takes W3 across.
>
> A: That seems too easy; read the instructions over again.
>
> B: We'll try it over again and check. (They work through the solution again.)
>
> D: Oh, but it works too simply. I believe we ought to try it all over again.
>
> A: The first move is wrong. W2 is with H3 when H2 is not present. No wonder it was so simple before. . . . Just let H1 and W1 go over. No one else can go.
>
> C: All right, now let H1 come back and leave W1 on the B-side alone.
>
> D: Now try this. H1, H2, W2 go across. That's O.K., isn't it?
>
> C: Bring the two husbands back. H1, H2 back.
>
> A: Now all three husbands will have to go over. Don't you see? And leave W3 on the A-side. H3 can take the two over.
>
> D: Oh sure, and then he comes back for his own wife.
>
> B: Now work it through again while we watch.
>
> A: It checks now. Let's call it solved.

The experimenter concluded that one reason why there were so few successful solutions by individuals (only 5 of a possible 63) as compared with groups (8 of a possible 15) was that individuals were slow to criticize their own early strategies, and thus they continued along blind alleys, sometimes indefinitely.

Interaction as Affected by Demand Input

A second way in which group size may be expected to affect member interaction has to do with the needs and motives (rather than the capacities) that members bring to the situation—like motives of being recognized, of being liked, or of wanting to participate in group activities. Since each member is likely to have some such motives, the totality of individual "demands" increases with the size of the group. In one study of member satisfactions (Slater, 1958), groups of two to seven members discussed a human-relations problem for a period of forty minutes, after which they were asked (by variously worded questionnaire items) how they felt about the size of their group, and why. Members of groups of five, six, and seven persons agreed with all the following items significantly more often than did persons in groups of two, three, or four members:

> There wasn't enough time.
> The group didn't make the best use of its time.
> The group didn't stay on the track.
> The group needed a more definite leader.
> There was too much competition, and not an equal chance for everyone to talk.

There tended to be an "inner circle" and an "outer fringe." Members of smaller groups, on the other hand, more often felt that there was no need for a leader, and were satisfied with their own participation. Some members of two- and three-person groups felt that their groups were too small; groups of about five members were in general considered to be just about right.

In sum, the larger the totality of demand input in a group—which, we have assumed, varies directly with the size—the larger the number, and also the proportion, of individuals who are likely to be unsatisfied because their "demands" have not been met. This is particularly true under two conditions: insofar as group activities remain organized and focused, and insofar as the time available for group activity is limited. These effects are mediated by member interaction not merely in the sense that some individuals feel that they have not had enough of it, but rather in this more general sense: while some members are responding to others' participation by feeling disappointed or frustrated, the more active members are responding to their relative silence and nonparticipation more by taking advantage of it than by modifying their own participation accordingly.

Interaction as Affected by Networks of Interpersonal Relationships

As the size of a group increases, the number of possible person-to-person relationships rapidly mounts. Only one pair relationship is possible between two persons, but there are 3 among three group members, 6 among four members, 10 among five members—and 190 with twenty members. This fact affects interaction among group members in various ways, but especially because most people have some "demands" for satisfying personal relationships as well as a strictly limited capacity for establishing close relationships with others. According to a study of several hundred girls in an industrial training school (Jennings, 1950), twelve such relationships per individual was a typical limit, even when a wide variety of work and leisure-time situations was included. The consequence of this latter fact is that in groups larger than a dozen or so (and often, for that matter, in smaller groups) continued interaction of a personal nature occurs for the most part in relatively small subgroups.

The consequence of all these facts, together—that is, demand input, limited capacity, and increasing numbers of possible relationships in larger groups—is that many potential relationships will not be developed. Thus in smaller but not in larger groups there can be a single network of more or less close interpersonal relationships that pervades all or nearly all the group. In this sense, a larger group cannot have the degree of unity that a smaller one can.

Various Effects of Group Size Mediated by Communication

The effects of increasing group size that we have considered may be simply summarized as increased resources for problem solving, lesser satisfaction on the part of some group members, and lesser unity on the part of the total group. Some of these are effects on individuals, others on the total group. But in either case they are mediated by communication, through which available resources are made effective, dissatisfactions incurred, and subgroups formed at the expense of total-group unity.

These very general statements are probabilistic: the effects noted are likely to occur, but not necessarily in all cases, because they are also influenced by factors other than sheer size. And another warning is also in order: these effects do not necessarily appear in direct proportion to the sizes of groups. We do not know the exact ranges of group size within which they are most likely to occur, because most of the available studies have concerned a small range of sizes. Because most studies have involved such a small range, we shall mention one of them that covers a very wide range indeed.

In an investigation of voluntary organizations (Indik, 1961), ranging in membership between 15 and 2983, various indices of member participation were related to group size. Not surprisingly, it was found that the larger the membership the less the tendency of members to participate in its activities. Among several possible explanations for this finding, the investigator shows that the following is the most satisfactory. The general level of intermember communication was highest in small organizations, and lowest in the larger ones. And frequency of communication, in turn, was closely associated with feelings of loyalty to and involvement in the organization. What this seems to mean is that smallness facilitates intermember communication, which in turn leads to a strong sense of group membership.

STRUCTURAL DIFFERENTIATION AND INTEGRATION

We have previously described (especially in Chapters 10 and 11) various ways in which groups may be structured, but we have not dealt with structuring as a group property—that is, as a variable. In what ways does it make sense to refer to structuring, whatever its nature (for example, of interpersonal attraction, of communicative access, or of hierarchical status), as something that different groups have more or less of? We shall approach this problem, which has by no means been solved by social scientists, through the notion of *differentiation*—since the concept of structuring presupposes differentiated parts that are somehow interrelated. Two kinds of questions thus suggest themselves: To what extent are parts differentiated? How are the parts interrelated?

Structural Elaboration

In asking about degrees of differentiation within any group, one would first want to know *how many* parts can be distinguished. The more there are of them (roles, that is, not persons), the more elaborated the differentiation of that group may be considered to be. If, for example, we consider a professor and 18 students with whom he is conducting a discussion to constitute an interaction group, then the group's role differentiation is very simple, since only two roles are recognized: teacher and student. Another group of equal size might be highly elaborated; for example, a group consisting of the President of the United States, ten Cabinet members, and three specialized assistants contains as many differentiated roles as there are persons in the group. As indices of this variable we could use either absolute numbers (2 in the case of the classroom group and 14 in the case of the Cabinet group); or we could use the ratio of persons to roles (18:2, or 9.0, for the classroom group and 14:14, or 1.0, for the Cabinet).

Or, for a different purpose, we could compute the ratios of specified kinds of distinguishable roles; thus a group of 10 men playing volleyball would have a team ratio of 5:5, or 1.0, indicating equal numbers on each team; and our classroom group would have a teacher-student ratio of 18:1, or 18.0, indicating a highly unequal distribution of role assignments.

For some purposes there is no sharp dividing line among parts that we nevertheless want to differentiate in some manner—as, for example, in the case of popularity statuses among the two 17-man populations described in Research Illustrations 6.2 and 10.1 (pages 173 and 293, respectively). We can make arbitrary distinctions that will have no absolute meaning but that are nevertheless legitimate for comparative purposes. Or we can forego the literal question of how many parts there are and ask, instead, about the extent of the differentiation, in terms of the range, or *distribution*. Figure 12.1 shows, for these two populations, the num-

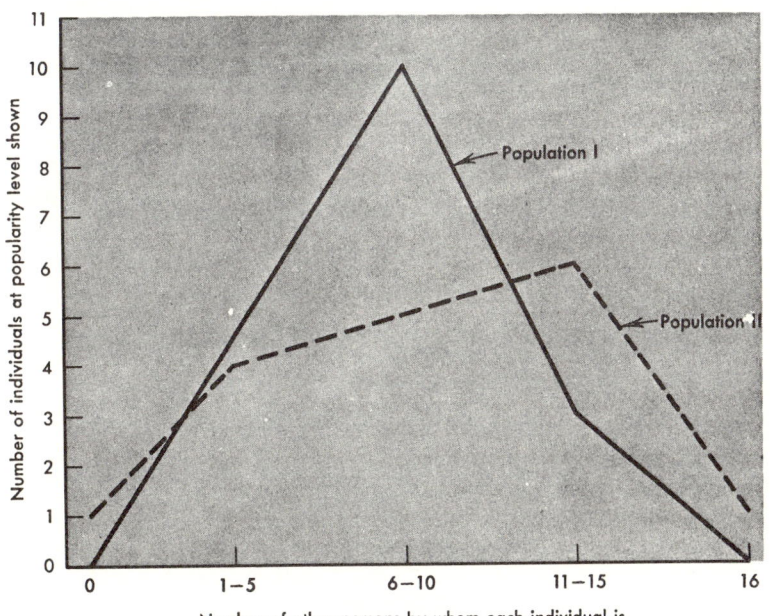

FIGURE 12.1. Distribution of popularity statuses among two populations, after four months of acquaintance (adapted from Newcomb, 1961)

bers of individuals at five levels of popularity. This figure shows, first, that the range of popularity statuses is greater in the second population; second, that there is greater concentration at one level (the middle) in the first population than at any level for the other population; and, third, that there are more individuals who are very popular and who are very unpopular in the second than in the first population. Thus it is clear that there is greater differentiation of popularity statuses in the second population: more individuals are "spread out" at greater extremes of popularity and unpopularity.

Indices of the number of *parts*, in Figure 12.1 are as follows: in Population I there are only three popularity statuses (1–5, 6–10, 11–15), whereas in Population II there are two additional ones (0 and 16, the maximum possible). Indices of the *range* are: in Population II, 17 (from 0 through 16), and in Population I, 12 (from 1 through 12; the exact details do not appear in the figure). These indices confirm the visual impressions made by the figure.

Many kinds of structuring (like that of the Cabinet group) do not involve differentiated parts that can be thought of as extended along a continuum from more to less (as in Figure 12.1); the several Cabinet roles, though different, may be considered equal. In such instances the ratio index (cf. page 365) can tell us the average number of persons in each position, but this is not very useful since it would not distinguish between, for example, two groups, one of which contains a lecturer and 99 undifferentiated listeners and the other of which consists of 50 fraternity and 50 nonfraternity men who are discussing the merits of fraternities. In order to distinguish between these two groups we need an index of distribution. When there are only two differentiated parts, this is very simple: the ratios of 99:1 and 50:50, yielding values of 99 and 1, will serve as indices. But when several different positions are represented in a group—say a college committee consisting of five faculty members, three administrators, one fraternity and one sorority representative, and three other students—a single index not only is difficult to construct but also is not very informative. Under these conditions several simple indices, each chosen for a particular purpose—like the proportions of students and nonstudents, or the number of distinguishable interests represented—would be most useful. Thus different but comparable groups (say on different campuses) could be shown to be similar or contrasting in various ways—for example, one is more faculty-dominated than another, or one represents a wider range of interests than another.

ELABORATION AS A DEPENDENT VARIABLE. The preconditions that invite increasing elaboration are not particularly surprising. Foremost among them are group size and complexity of activities. The nature of the effects of group size has been discussed in the preceding section in terms of resource input, demand input, and networks of interpersonal relationships. The general rule is that degree of elaboration increases as group size increases, but the relationship between these two variables is not linear: that is, they do not remain strictly proportional at all degrees of either variable. Thus an increase from three to four members, or even from three to ten, may have little or no effect on degree of differentiation, but an increase from thirty to forty or to one hundred may have very pronounced effects: the rate of increase tends to be geometric, or exponential.

The reasons why the curve tends to be exponential instead of linear are essentially as follows. At the lower limits of size, efficiency may be increased rather than decreased by adding more members, and the individual needs represented by demand input can equally well (or even better) be met by small increases in size. When numbers become very large, however, the benefits of added resource input becomes less probable, individual demands become less and less likely to be met, and the proportion of close personal relationships rapidly declines. Hence both efficiency and personal satisfaction tend to be increased by increasing the numbers of subgroups of moderate size. But as the number of subgroups increases, mechanisms are required for integrating them, and with still further increases in size the integrators (supervisors, branch chiefs, department heads, and so on) themselves have to be integrated. Perhaps you have heard of Parkinson's law, which states, in effect, that any increase in size in one part of an organization leads to other increases. This "law," which appears to be pretty well supported by evidence, is really based on the kinds of social-psychological considerations we have been describing. Being based on solid facts of group life, its effects can be observed in any large organization—whether in government, in industry, in churches, or in universities.

By complexity of activity we refer to the number of separable subactivities into which an enterprise can be divided. The job of mowing ten acres of lawn cannot be divided into very many different assignments (though any number of people might be given the same one), but the job of manufacturing an automobile literally requires thousands of distinguishable jobs; given enough time, one man might conceivably perform all of them, but at the cost of efficiency. The more cars there are to be made, and the greater the demands for efficiency, the more probable it is that the total activity will be subdivided into many different jobs, most of them quite limited. Even from the point of view of efficiency, however, the process of subdividing can be carried too far if it results in excessive boredom or other kinds of dissatisfaction.

ELABORATION AS AN INDEPENDENT VARIABLE. Insofar as increased elaboration is associated with increasing group size, some of its effects have been considered in the preceding section. Groups of comparable size may, however (unless they are very small), have different degrees of elaboration, the effects of which have to do with communication, and hence with sharing, among the differentiated parts of the group. These are matters of group integration, which are discussed in the following section, but meanwhile there is a special point to be noted.

Among groups of comparable size, communication does not necessarily occur less freely, nor is sharing necessarily more limited, in those groups that are most fully elaborated. Take, for example, a secretarial pool of ten girls who, together with their supervisor, constitute an administrative unit in a large organization; and compare this group with another eleven-person group including a research director, four research assistants, three interviewers, a statistician, and two secretaries, all of whom are concerned with the same research problem. The latter group is the more elaborated: it includes five different role assignments as compared with two in the former. It is likely, nevertheless, that there will be more communication and more sharing in the research group—in spite of its greater elaboration—than in the secretarial pool, in which no two of the secretaries may be working with the same materials. Communication and sharing tend to follow from common concerns, not just from similar role assignments. Apart from matters of size, then, communication and sharing depend more on role interdependence than on sheer amount of elaboration.

There are, however, limits to the number of differentiated role-takers among whom a high degree of communication and sharing is possible. No one can familiarize himself very fully with a hundred different roles, nor could he carry on very frequent communication with that many different role-takers. Among groups of this size, or even a good deal smaller, subgroups tend to form, either formally or informally or both—partly for reasons of efficiency and partly because of demand inputs, as we have already seen. And once this has occurred, we have elaboration in terms of individuals or roles. The consequences of elaboration at this level involve a somewhat different level of principles, known as organization theory, which we shall not further pursue, since our principal concern is with interaction groups. (See Kahn, Wolfe, *et al.*, 1964.)

The effects of structural elaboration thus have to do largely with group integration, to the direct consideration of which we now turn.

Structural Integration

The other half of the problem of the structural properties of groups has to do with *relationships* among differentiated parts. In a general sense we shall think of these relationships in terms of degree of integration, as a single variable, although there are, of course, many different forms of integration. For example, two contesting tennis players, or four of them playing doubles, may for certain purposes be considered as a single group whose level of integration is very high, even though the forms of integration for team members and for opponents are different. More specifically, both or all four players are integrated behaviorally, but their goal orientations differ. As these illustrations imply, we are using the term "integration" to refer to regularity of *behavioral interdependence that is coordinated*. This property of a group, as it may have occurred to you, has a good deal in common with a role relationship, which we have considered (pages 323-324 ff.) as a behavioral relationship between one individual and one or more others that is characterized by regularity. The only important difference between the two notions is that *role* is defined with reference to a single behaving person (even though he may be any one of a large category), whereas integration is a property of the entire group. (These would, of course, be the same in a two-person group.) Whatever the level of integration of a particular group, it has to do with the role relationships of *all* the group's members with one another. The more closely interdependent the role relationships, the more integrated the group.

INTEGRATION AS A DEPENDENT VARIABLE. There are two important preconditions of group integration, the first of which presupposes the second. In the first place there must be some degree of sharing among group members as to each other's behavior—in particular, shared expectations as to what probably will occur under given circumstances, especially in response to one another. In the case of cooperative but not of competitive intermember relationships, motivations as well as expectations must be shared if there is to be a high degree of integration; that is, each group member must want, as well as expect, the same kind of behavior from each member, including himself, and each must know that all want it, under a given set of circumstances. There is one way, incidentally, in which it is possible for a cooperating group to be more highly integrated than one whose members are in competition: one of the common stratagems in competition but not in cooperation is concealment and surprise, which is the opposite of sharing and which tends to reduce, momentarily at least, the level of integration between competitors.

In any case, continued regularity of interdependence presupposes sharing and this, in turn, is a consequence of previous communication. The communicative processes from which sharing emerges need not be verbal; indeed, the communicators need not be fully aware that they are constantly giving and receiving cues to and from each other. The emitting of the cue by one person (a gesture, or muscular stance, or tone of voice, for example) is a kind of signal to himself that other group members will now expect a certain kind of behavior on his part, and the receiving of the same cue represents the same signal to them—whether or not any of them are fully aware of what is going on. It is through a previous history of learning to recognize such communicative cues that shared expectations, and also shared motives, are acquired.

Indices of integration may be constructed more readily from attitudinal data than from direct observations of behavior. Suppose that all members of a group indicate, by verbal statements, that they expect the same kinds of behaviors from the same role-takers (e.g., secretarylike behaviors from secretaries, and treasurerlike behaviors from treasurers, and so on for other differentiated roles) under specified circumstances. Insofar as they also attribute the same expectations to others, we have an attitudinal basis for considering the group highly integrated. For example, in one of the 17-man populations previously described, each man was asked, during the second week of acquaintance, to indicate which of the following alternatives he thought each of the 17 men, including himself, would choose:

> How should this group set up its cooking and eating arrangements?
>   A. Everyone eat out; use dining room as a lounge.
>   B. Hire someone to cook, serve, and clean up.
>   C. Hire a cook, and all members pitch in and serve and clean up.
>   D. Members cook and eat in groups of three or four, working separately.
>   E. Members all eat together; groups of three or four take turns cooking, serving, and cleaning up.

Following a good deal of informal discussion, but before a formal decision had been made, written responses to this question showed that nearly all of the men believed that alternative C was generally preferred by the group. (A formal vote, an hour or so later, confirmed their estimates.) Figure 12.2 shows that 16 of the 17 men estimated that nine or more of the group (a majority) favored alternative C—as compared to 13 of the 17 who actually expressed that preference. Since 12 of the 17 both preferred this alternative and correctly believed that a majority of the others also preferred it, we may take 12/17, or 70.6 percent, as an index of shared preference for alternative C. (See page 375 for other indices of degree of sharing.) Three months later, after this alternative had been in practice during most of the interval, the index had risen to 94 percent.

Another set of responses by the same population, after only two days of acquaintance, reveals a much lower degree of sharing. Eleven of the 17 men chose A, B, or C (all of which have in common a certain degree of stand-offishness) among the following alternatives:

To what extent should a person try to become close friends with others?

    A. Be self-sufficient and don't form close ties with anyone; one doesn't get hurt that way.
    B. Form close ties with only a few people who are really understanding and can be trusted.
    C. Become close friends with anyone you trust; a lot of people can be trusted but a lot cannot.
    D. Try to become close friends with all the people you know; most people will be loyal friends if they know they are trusted, though a few may take advantage of such trust.
    E. Let people know you trust them and want to be close friends with them; they will respond in kind.

Only 4 of the 11, however, believed that a majority of the 17 men would choose one of these same alternatives; thus the index of sharedness is only 23.5 percent. This represents a state of *pluralistic ignorance,* according to which common attitudes are not recognized as common, and therefore are not widely shared. This state of affairs later gave way to a much higher level of sharing; the early inaccuracy almost certainly resulted from the fact that, during the early days of acquaintance, most of the men tried to appear cordial, and their only way of judging the others was based on this apparent cordiality. Here, as commonly, pluralistic ignorance represents a state of restricted communication, and

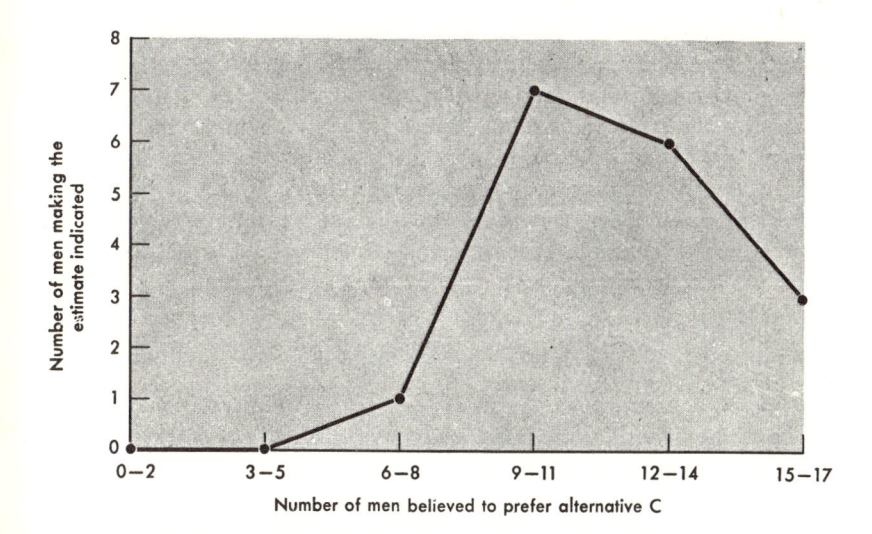

FIGURE 12.2. Numbers of men in a seventeen-man population who attribute varying degrees of consensus to the group (adapted from Newcomb, 1961)

disappears with reasonably adequate communication. Additional considerations involved in constructing an index of sharing will be discussed later in this chapter.

INTEGRATION AS AN INDEPENDENT VARIABLE. The outcomes of group integration are, in general, consequences of accurate communication and shared motivation. Behaviorally, they are to be seen in such forms as efficiency in a group task; smooth and coordinated performance on the part of a troupe of dancers, acrobats, or parading soldiers; or success on the part of a competing team. Indices based on such observable outcomes are likely, however, to be confounded with other factors. For example, the number of runs or of errors on the part of a baseball team in nine innings of play may be influenced by individual skill as well as by intermember coordination. The number of units processed by an assembly line, as an index, might be contaminated by quality of materials and other extragroup factors. Such indices, alone, may be useful but they need to be interpreted with caution.

The attitudinal outcomes of group integration often include shared pride in group performance—sometimes identified with the loosely used term "morale." Shared interpersonal attitudes are also likely outcomes—including not only personal attraction but also dependence on certain individuals for special contributions, respect for skill or personal qualities, and indulgence or irritation concerning other personal qualities. It may strike you as strange that sharing, which we have considered a precondition for group integration, is now mentioned as an outcome of it. Such circularity, however, is the rule and not the exception. Group activity necessarily includes intermember communication, and some degree of sharing by at least some members almost inevitably follows. Insofar as dissatisfactions rather than satisfactions come to be shared, or insofar as different subgroups share opposing attitudes, the group is likely to dissolve. But insofar as satisfactions are shared by all or most group members, the circularity is maintained: sharing makes possible integration, which enhances further sharing. This is one characteristic of what we shall later term a cohesive group.

* * *

When a group possesses many degrees of differentiation, it is said to have considerable structural elaboration. Such elaboration may be viewed as either a dependent or an independent variable in the study of interaction groups. It is possible to differentiate between two groups by noting differences in the distribution of structural properties. Various methods have been devised to express these differences in quantitative terms.

Structural integration has to do with regularity of coordinated behavioral interdependence and, unlike the concept of a role relationship, is the property of an entire group. Since it influences group interaction and is also influenced by such interaction, it functions both as an independent variable and as a dependent variable.

ATTITUDINAL UNIFORMITY

Groups may readily be described in terms of the degree to which their members are similar. We now turn from the consideration of similarities and differences of positions and roles to group members themselves—with respect, first, to their attitudes and then, in the following section, to their observable behavior. We have already considered (in Chapter 8) the general nature of consensus, sharing, and group norms as forms of attitudinal uniformity; here we shall be interested in different degrees of these forms of uniformity, as variables.

Consensus

Maximum similarity of attitudes, as a group property, is easy to describe: all members are just alike. Minimal similarity is a more complex matter, because there are different ways in which a set of individuals may show attitudinal disparity. With respect, for example, to degree of favoring the Republican party, we might find any of the distributions represented in c, d, or e in Figure 12.3, all of which show, in different ways, a good deal of variation in members' attitudes. In this figure, a shows the probable distribution of attitudes toward the Republican party among a group of devoted party workers; in a group whose members were selected in ways unrelated to political preferences (the clerical staff, say, in a large organization), we would expect to find a normal distribution, as in c; if a group were deliberately selected in order to represent equally all shades of political-party preferences, we would find the rectangular distribution in d; and if a group were composed equally of active workers in both parties, we would expect to find the bimodal distribution in e. In terms of the standard deviation (a statistical measure commonly used as an index of dispersion), a and e would have the smallest and the largest values, respectively, showing the most and the least similarity. Both d and e, however, are rather unusual; most distributions are more like c, though they are often lopsided (asymmetrical, or skewed), as in b. Distributions like b often occur if the attitude represented is one that is highly relevant to group members, but not the sole basis for their selection—like "socialized medicine" among members of the American Medical Association, or belief in immortality among

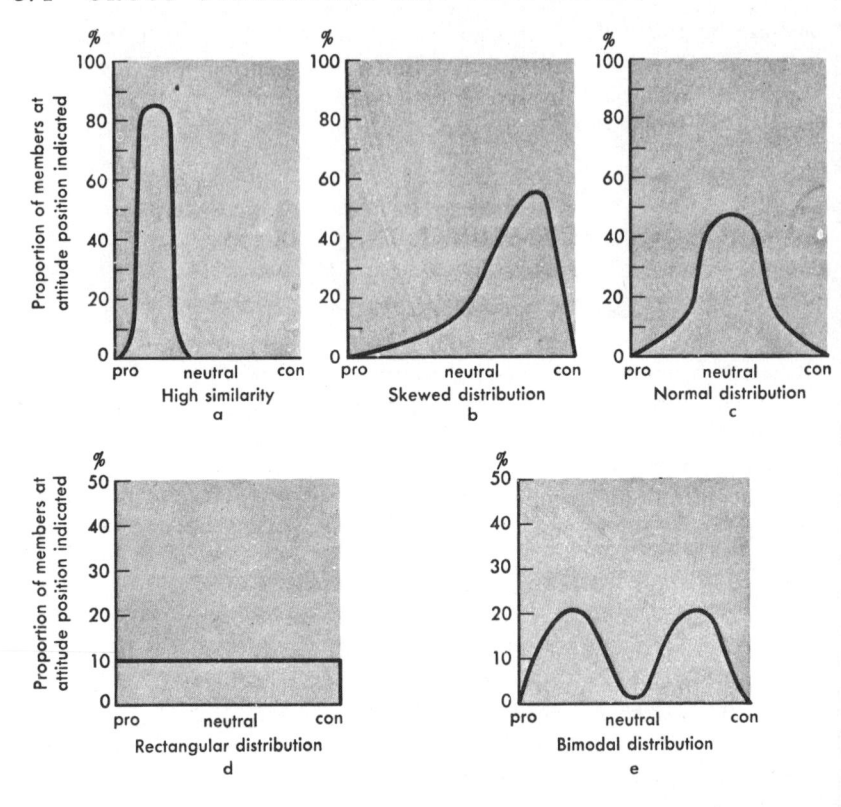

FIGURE 12.3. Some varieties of distributions of group members' attitudes

Protestant church members; under these conditions most members are clustered rather closely together while a few take deviant positions.

Degree of consensus, as a dependent variable, is likely to be greatest when attitudinal uniformity is a requirement for group membership, when members have predominantly similar experiences with the objects of their attitudes, and when members influence one another to take similar attitudes. If some but not all of these conditions prevail, or if they are present only in limited degree, we would expect to find lesser degrees of consensus—that is, increased dispersion of attitudes, as in *b* in Figure 12.3. If none of these conditions is present—which is to say that the attitude has little or no group relevance—the distribution of attitudes would probably resemble the distribution in the larger population from which members are drawn, perhaps as in *c*. The perfectly rectangular distribution in *d* is highly improbable except as a result of deliberate selection of members; and bimodal distributions, like that in *e*, usually result either from special processes of selection or from a split within the group such that members of either faction develop exaggerated attitudes in reaction to the other faction.

The effects of varying degrees of consensus, as an independent variable, are for the most part mediated by the degree of sharing that a given degree of consensus makes possible. The degree of sharing cannot, by definition, exceed the degree of consensus; the existing degree of the latter places a ceiling on the possible degree of the former. And the general principle that individuals respond to situations not as they "really are" but as they are perceived applies here as elsewhere: group members respond to whatever degree of consensus they recognize, not to some actual degree of it that they do not recognize. Hence we turn now to a consideration of varying degrees of sharing.

Sharing

One kind of index of sharing, perhaps the most useful, is based on the number of dyads in a group both of whose members are in agreement and are aware of it. (Agreement is defined by some criterion that is appropriate to the data and to the purpose for which the index is being constructed.) Take, for example, the rank-order preferences expressed by each man for all the others in one of the 17-man populations previously described. Of the 136 dyads in the total group 28 were made up of 8 individuals all of whom were actually in close agreement with one another and with the over-all popularity ranking of the 17 men. Of these 28 dyads there were 15 whose members were not only in close agreement but who were also aware of it, as indicated by their estimates of each other's rankings. Two different indices of sharing may be derived from these data. (1) There were 15 of 136 dyads whose members were in close agreement and knew it—or 11.0 percent. (2) There were 15 of 28 actually agreeing dyads whose members were aware of their agreement—or 55.5 percent. The first of these indices indicates a rather small degree of sharing about the relative attractiveness of all the men (this was the "divisively structured" population described on pages 319–320). The second index indicates a relatively high degree of awareness of agreement among those who were in fact in agreement—that is, a high degree of sharing among them.

The principal conditions under which the index of sharing, as a dependent variable, tends to be high relative to actual consensus are those of communication. Insofar as group members interact frequently, express to one another the attitudes about which they are consensual, observe one another's expressions of those attitudes, and interpret them correctly, the index of sharing will tend to be high. The conditions that tend to restrict such interaction, and thus reduce the level of sharing that would otherwise be possible, are limited contact and such forms of negative interpersonal attraction as mistrust, dislike, or hostility. These latter conditions tend to reduce both members' motivation to communicate to one another and their credence in the information that is communicated.[2]

Normativeness

The degree of power that any group exerts over its members by reason of its norms may be referred to as its normativeness. Groups surely differ in this respect, but it is difficult to apply any single index of normativeness, because group members usually share acceptance of many rules, rather than just one. Thus a group's normativeness-in-general cannot be measured without knowledge of *all* the group's norms, or without combining all this information in some arbitrary way. Hence we shall consider normativeness from the point of view of a single norm. Even if we accept this limitation, normativeness turns out to be a complex matter, because at least two dimensions of it must be taken into account.[3]

One of these dimensions may be labeled range of *latitude*, which refers to the fact that most rules permit some variation in the degree or the manner of meeting their specifications. Thus, for example, a rule of punctuality does not mean that any member who arrives at a group meeting one second after the announced time is a nonconformist, nor that the member who arrives one hour early is conforming more satisfactorily than one who comes exactly on time. Latitude thus refers to the content of the rule: what is the range of behaviors that, according to the group's norms, constitute conformity to the rule? The range may vary between very small and very great latitude.

Acceptability refers to the degree to which specified behaviors within this range are approved, or disapproved outside that range, by group members—commonly, though not necessarily, through sanctions. Acceptability is also a variable; there are many degrees of it, and the rule upon which any norm is based always includes, implicitly at least, varying degrees of acceptability that are accorded to varying ways of adhering to the norm. Thus the two dimensions are not unrelated. Latitude, or the range of conformity, may be thought of as having a certain region of high acceptability (like arriving within five minutes of the announced time, in the case of a norm concerning punctuality), and the more any behavior deviates from this region the greater its unacceptability.

---

[2] The effects of varying degrees of sharing, viewed as an independent variable, are discussed on pages 226–228.

[3] We are indebted to Professor J. M. Jackson (1960) for the following analysis of the dimensions of normativeness.

GROUP PROPERTIES - 377

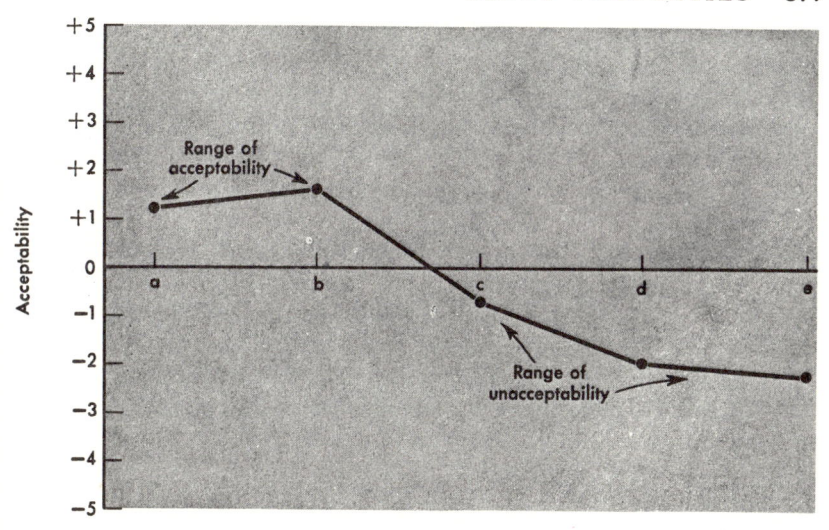

[Figure: graph with y-axis "Acceptability" ranging from -5 to +5, x-axis labeled "Range of latitude" with points a, b, c, d, e. Points approximately: a at +1, b at +1.5 (Range of acceptability), c at -1, d at -2, e at -2.5 (Range of unacceptability).]

FIGURE 12.4. Mean degrees of acceptance of five alternatives concerning dancing, on the part of students in a small sectarian college (adapted from Jackson, 1960)

Figure 12.4 illustrates how the relationship between these two dimensions may be described. The *a*-to-*e* dimension is range of latitude; it represents these five ways of responding to rules about dancing, on the part of students in a small, sectarian college:

a. refuses to participate in any form of dancing whatsoever
b. participates in folk games and square dancing on campus
c. engages in social dancing in private parties off campus
d. occasionally engages in dancing in nightclubs or public dance halls
e. frequently engages in dancing in nightclubs or public dance halls

The dimension of acceptability is represented by 5 degrees of acceptance (from +1 to +5) and 5 degrees of rejection (−1 to −5). The mean scores of accepting the five alternatives correspond to values between +5 and −5 at the left, opposite the five dots shown in the figure.[4] The figure shows that in this group the region around alternative *b* is most acceptable, and that *a* is also acceptable, *c* slightly beyond the bounds, and both *d* and *e* are intolerable to typical group members. These data represent true normativeness only if we assume a high

[4] The curve shown in Figure 12.4 is referred to by Jackson (1960) as a "reward potential curve," so named because it shows the alternatives that are most and least rewarded by group members.

degree of shared acceptance of rules about dancing. Only if we assume that there was free expression of attitudes toward dancing, together with reasonably accurate interpretation of the expressed attitudes on the part of most group members, can Figure 12.4 be taken as a description of normativeness in this group. Otherwise there is likely to be a good deal of pluralistic ignorance, as in the community described by Schanck (page 225).

Data that do permit the examination of shared attitudes were obtained from one of the populations described in Research Illustrations 6.2 (page 173) and 10.1 (page 293). Each of the 17 men was asked the following question at several different times: "If you had the choice to make over again, do you think you would volunteer for this project?" (that is, volunteer to live in the same house with the same men). Responses during the tenth week of the semester were as follows:

10 "Would definitely volunteer" (a)
5 "Would probably volunteer" (b)
1 "Would have mixed feelings, and would have a hard time deciding" (c)
1 "Would probably not volunteer" (d)
0 "Would definitely not volunteer" (e)

These responses suggest a high degree of consensus for the first two alternatives; 13 of the 15 men who chose either of these as his first alternative made the other their second choice. Each man also estimated how each other man would answer the same question, and from these responses it is possible to compute the degree of sharing among the 15 men who themselves chose one of the first two alternatives. Among the 105 dyads in this set of 15 men in actual agreement, there were 90 (or 83 percent of them) both of whose members were aware of their agreement—a high index of sharing among these 15 men, who are thus known to be highly normative in the literal sense.

The two dimensions of normativeness are shown in Figure 12.5, in which the average rank-order choice for each of the five alternatives, by the 15 men who share favorable attitudes, is plotted against each of the alternatives, so that the figure resembles Figure 12.4. In terms of latitude, the range of shared acceptance includes the first two alternatives, and the range of acceptability just barely includes the third. Acceptability is greatest for the first alternative, almost as great for the second, but definitely negative for the fourth and especially the fifth. The figure thus graphically portrays the high degree of normativeness among these 15 men, who share acceptance of the rule that the men in this house like to live in it. (Incidentally, the remaining two men, viewed as a group, showed equal normativeness to the opposite effect: both were aware of their consensus in not being willing to volunteer

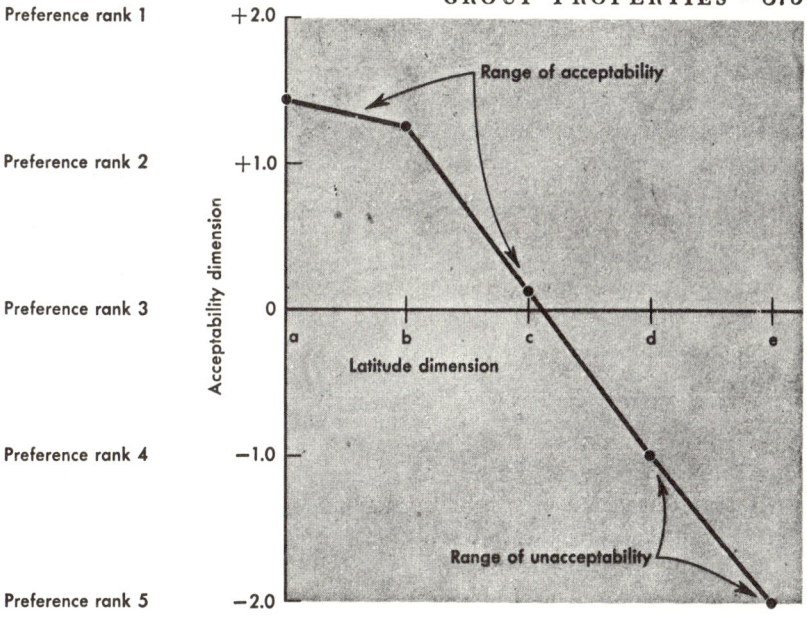

[Figure 12.5: A graph with "Acceptability dimension" on the y-axis ranging from -2.0 to +2.0, labeled with Preference ranks 1 through 5. The x-axis is "Latitude dimension" with points a, b, c, d, e. A line descends from upper left (Range of acceptability) through the middle to lower right (Range of unacceptability).]

FIGURE 12.5. Mean degrees of shared acceptance by fifteen men of five alternatives concerning volunteering to live in a project house (adapted from Newcomb, 1961)

again. One of them was a good deal older than most of the others, and remained somewhat aloof, and the other was the most unpopular man in the group. Their attraction toward each other was extremely low; their reasons for preferring not to live in the house were too divergent to provide a basis for mutual attraction.)

Latitude and acceptability contribute to normativeness in opposite ways. That is, the degree of power that any group exerts over its members, by reason of a norm, *de*creases with latitude, since the group exerts very little power if almost anything is acceptable; and it *in*creases with acceptability, because the greater the rewards and punishments associated with certain ways of adhering to the rule the greater the group's power. In terms of curves like those shown in Figures 12.4 and 12.5, this means that the narrower the width of latitude and the greater the elevation of acceptability, the greater the normativeness. Indices of these two variables can be combined into a single index of normativeness by some measure of dispersion, as suggested in the previous discussion of consensus as a group variable. Curves showing a high, narrow distribution yield small dispersions, and this is exactly what high normativeness refers to: a high degree of shared acceptance for a narrow range of ways of adhering to a rule.

All of the following are necessary, finally, in order to draw some conclusions about any group's normativeness. (1) One must limit oneself to a single norm at a time, as we have already noted. (2) One must be able to compare that group with others; indices of latitude, acceptability, or normativeness are so dependent on the particular data employed that they have no absolute meaning. (3) Data from the several groups must be strictly comparable—from identical questionnaires, for example. Bearing in mind these precautions, the conclusions that can be drawn about a group's normativeness are of particular importance, because normativeness has so much to do with the effects that a group has on its members.

* * *

Degree of consensus is a group property that may be depicted as a distribution of relevant attitudes possessed by members of the group. Such a measure of consensus does not indicate the extent of sharing, since members' perceptions of consensus may not be accurate. For this reason an index of sharing must be devised that measures the percentage of accurate estimates of agreement among members of the group. This index has proven a useful tool for studying sharing and the factors associated with it.

Normativeness refers to the degree of power that any group exerts over its members by reason of its norms, and is a complex concept because it is a function of all the norms found in the group. For analytical purposes normativeness may be considered from the standpoint of a single norm. Even a single norm has at least two dimensions, including the dimension of latitude (variation permitted in conforming to a rule) and acceptability (the degree to which specified behaviors within the range of latitude are approved or disapproved).

Latitude and acceptability make different contributions to normativeness. The power over members of a group decreases with latitude and increases with acceptability. Thus a high degree of acceptance for a relatively few ways of conforming to a rule is associated with high normativeness.

COHESIVENESS

We turn now to a property of groups that is very inclusive—so much so, in fact, that if it is not carefully defined, it can become a catchall term that includes almost everything that can be said about a group. We must avoid such looseness as is suggested by descriptions like "groupiness"; although this term does have some intuitive meaning, to say that one group is more "groupy" than another is somewhat like saying that one orange is "more orangey" than another. The trouble with such statements is that both groups and oranges have many properties, and it is not likely that any group or any orange will be high in all of them. We need to be more precise about the properties that we have in mind, whether we are considering oranges or groups, if we are to communicate clearly.

The term "cohesive" means, literally, "sticking together," and we shall attempt to use it in exactly this sense: that is, it means the degree to which members stick together, in any or all of several possible ways, so that the group has unity. The reasons why the term tends to become so inclusive are that cohesiveness can manifest itself in so many ways, and so many different factors can contribute to the same end result. In short, cohesiveness is a very complex property of groups, but it is not everything. In this respect, it is somewhat like individual intelligence: this property of individuals can be conceptualized as a single entity—the ability to learn, for example, or to solve problems. But it has long been known that it can be broken down into several measurable sub-entities, like word fluency, ability to use numbers, perceptual speed, and reasoning (cf. Thurstone, 1938), that are objectively distinguishable and yet have something in common. Complex though it is, it is only one of the many properties that individuals have.

Since both individual intelligence and group cohesiveness are complex, it is clear that no single index of either of them can reveal all the complexities. Single indices, like standard intelligence test scores, represent some sort of weighting of many components but they do not tell us which of them any particular individual or group has most or least of. In the case of group cohesiveness, which is probably more complex than individual intelligence, we can therefore choose either of the following alternatives in constructing indices. We can somehow combine separate indices of the different factors that go to make up cohesiveness, or we can select some form of behavior that appears to be influenced by all these factors. The latter alternative, which is both simpler and cruder than the former, rests on the assumption that certain behaviors are influenced in similar ways by all the distinguishable factors that go to make up cohesiveness, viewed as a single, unitary property of groups.

Back's experiment (Research Illustration 12.2) was designed to test the hypothesis that highly cohesive groups will, *regardless of the sources of cohesiveness*, exert more influence on their members than less cohesive ones will. He did not attempt to construct indices of degrees of cohesiveness; rather, by his experimental procedures he created conditions such that one group had more of some characteristic presumably contributing to high cohesiveness than another, making use of three such characteristics in three pairs of groups. Since his findings tended to support the hypothesis, we conclude that under the conditions of his study there was something unitary about cohesiveness, in the sense that its effects were about the same regardless of variations in its components.

Research Illustration 12.2

If groups that have different bases for cohesiveness show the same consequences, in the sense that they all differ in the same predictable ways from noncohesive groups, then it would seem necessary to consider cohesiveness as a property in its own right. Back (1950, 1951) planned an experiment to test the "if" clause in the preceding statement. He used, as an indicator of the effects of cohesiveness, the development of agreement on the part of group members with respect to a newly presented problem. His groups consisted of two persons, and in all cases they were strangers to one another. Each subject was asked to write a story that would "connect" a set of three pictures—first before and then after the pairs of subjects discussed the pictures. The subjects were not told that there were slight differences in the sets of pictures presented individually to the two group members, differences that might lead to quite different interpretations; and they were not allowed to see the pictures again after writing their first stories. Subjects were told that the purpose of the discussions was to help them improve their initial stories, and that it was not necessary to "conclude with a common story."

Six sets of ten groups each were used for comparing high and low cohesiveness. Each set received a special kind of treatment in order to create a particular basis for cohesiveness, as follows:

High *interpersonal attraction* was created in Set I, by methods previously found to be effective; individuals were told that the experimenter had been able to match them with "almost exactly the person you described" as ideal persons to work with, in previously submitted statements. Subjects in Set II were told that it had been impossible to pair them with individuals who would be congenial; interpersonal attraction in these groups was relatively low.

In Set III high *motivation for task success* was created by announcing a $5 award for "the two members of the group in which the best story is produced." No such promise was mentioned to members of Set IV, whose motivation would presumably be low, relative to Set III.

Group prestige was enhanced in Set V by telling its members, "You two should be about the best group we have had," judging from information supplied from the lab instructor. Members of Set VI were merely told, "We are trying to compare good groups and bad groups"; pride in group membership was thus relatively low.

In general, lumping together all low-cohesive and all high-cohesive groups, regardless of the nature of the basis for their cohesiveness, there was more active engagement in the discussion on the part of the highs than of the lows; the latter tended to withdraw from active discussions. Also, regardless of the basis for cohesiveness, there were more changes between initial and postdiscussion stories, on the part of each pair member whose stories showed the greater

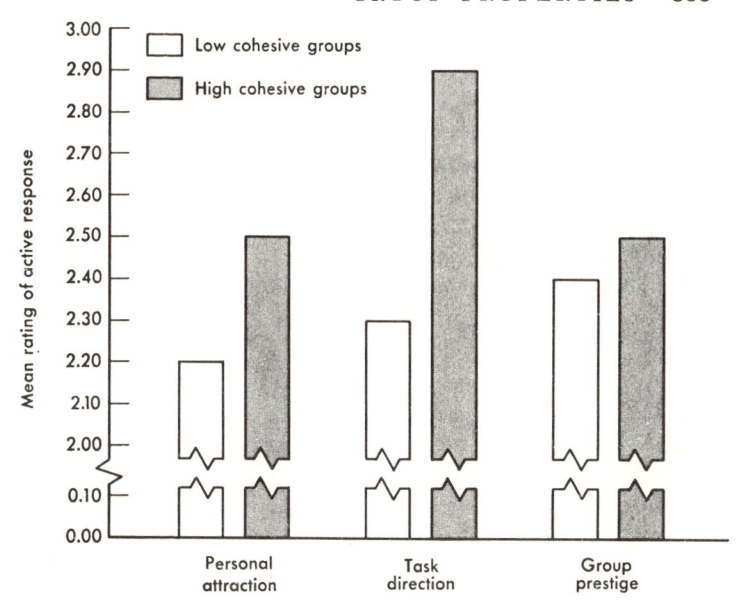

[Bar chart showing mean rating of active response for Low cohesive groups vs High cohesive groups across three conditions: Personal attraction (≈2.20 vs ≈2.50), Task direction (≈2.30 vs ≈2.90), Group prestige (≈2.40 vs ≈2.50).]

Mean ratings of degree of active response to influence attempts under three conditions of attempted influence (adapted from Back, 1950)

change, in the cohesive than in the noncohesive groups—that is, more influence was actually effected in the cohesive groups.

These findings show that cohesiveness, without regard to its sources, had effects, but what about the different bases for cohesiveness? As shown in the accompanying figure, each of the three bases of cohesiveness produced the same kind of response on the part of one group member to influence attempts on the part of the other. In the more cohesive groups of all three kinds there was more active reaction—for example, arguing back or outrightly rejecting an idea—than in the less cohesive ones. In the latter groups there were more instances of passively accepting the partner's story, or of expressing doubts about one's own story. Judging from such evidence, the effects of cohesiveness are about the same regardless of what is responsible for it.

In addition to the factors just explored (interpersonal attraction, individual motivation to succeed in the group task, and pride in group membership), most of the group properties already discussed in this chapter are also related to cohesiveness in some way. These latter relationships are summarized below.

1. The effects of *group size* are indirect, being mediated through intermember communication and participation. That is, members of

smaller groups tend to participate more in group-relevant tasks than do members of larger groups, and such kinds of interaction contribute to cohesiveness.

2. *Structural elaboration* in groups of comparable size does not seem to be related to cohesiveness, unless elaboration takes such forms as to restrict communication among members.

3. *Structural integration* contributes directly to cohesiveness. Integration facilitates efficiency and smooth, coordinated performance that are likely to be experienced as rewarding by group members; thus their attraction to the group is reinforced or increased.

4. We have no evidence to suggest that degree of *consensus* contributes to cohesiveness, apart from the fact that consensus makes sharing possible.

5. *Sharing*, on the other hand, appears to be a necessary precondition for cohesiveness. In the absence of group-relevant attitudes that are shared, individuals either do not know what other members' attitudes are or they assume that others' attitudes are different from their own. Neither of these conditions is conducive to cohesiveness; each of them, on the contrary, is associated with a member's sense of being alone and uncertain as to what he can count on from other group members. Shared attitudes toward group-relevant objects, toward the group itself, or toward its goals presuppose adequate communication among group members. Schachter's study (Research Illustration 7.2, page 202) shows how persuasive communication may be directed toward a deviant (non-sharing) member and how, when he persists in not sharing others' attitudes, group cohesiveness is maintained by rejecting him.

6. Some degree of *normativeness*, as a special case of sharing, is also essential to cohesiveness. The more important it is to a group to complete a task successfully, the more essential task-relevant rules become, together with shared acceptance of them. Even in groups that are primarily person-oriented, rather than task-oriented, shared acceptance of rules about interpersonal behavior contributes to cohesiveness, because of greater predictability under these conditions. In this kind of group, however (and perhaps in most others, also), too much normativeness ("the rules are too strict") can detract from cohesiveness. Relatively high but not maximally high normativeness thus appears to be associated with high cohesiveness. Adequate communication, including the expression of attitudes that members really hold, tends to prevent the development of excessive normativeness.

Other bases of cohesiveness might also be considered, but the important ones seem to be included under these three categories: structural integration, interpersonal attraction, and shared attitudes (including normativeness). The problem of combining indices of these three kinds of group properties into a single index of cohesiveness is, in general, probably insoluble—because any one of them, alone, may under certain conditions be responsible for very high or very low cohesiveness. Thus there is no way in which they can safely be combined that will apply to all groups. If we assume, as Back's experiment suggests, that there are some more or less "standard" consequences of high cohesiveness, regardless of its sources, then the degree of a group's cohesiveness can best be indexed in terms of its consequences rather than its sources. Back's main hypothesis—that "with increase in cohesiveness there will be an increase in pressure toward uniformity within a group"—suggests one important consequence, and we shall mention some others.

Lippitt and White (1943, 1958) made use of the relative frequency with which the pronouns "I" and "we" were used, in their well-known studies of behavior on the part of boys in clubs whose leaders manifested quite different sorts of behavior. In one of their experiments they found that in an "autocratic" group 82 percent of all first-person pronouns were "I" as compared with 64 percent in a "democratic" group, the difference being statistically significant. In a later experiment this index was extended to include a wide range of "group-minded" remarks, with similar results: in "democratic" groups 18 percent of all remarks were coded as "group-minded," as compared with 7 percent in one type of "autocratic" group and 4 percent in another. Thus, as might be expected in view of many other differences between "autocratic" and "democratic" groups, the latter were significantly more cohesive by this index.

Most single indices that have been employed to measure cohesiveness are less than ideal. Many investigators (Festinger, Schachter, and Back, 1950; Dimock, 1937) have used as an index the proportion of sociometric choices within a group when members are free to mention nonmembers if they choose. The shortcoming of this index is that a group may be highly cohesive even if many members have nonmembers as their preferred associates; work groups, in particular, may be very cohesive even though few of their members consider themselves best friends. An index that is even more dubious is the productivity of a work group; its dubiousness lies in the fact that cohesive groups may have norms according to which productivity should be curtailed rather than increased (cf. Coch and French, 1948; Schachter *et al.*, 1951). To mention another example, Libo (1953) used as an index the number of references that group members made to the group in writing projective stories about pictures while present at a group meeting. This index distinguished fairly well between members who, when they were free to remain in a group or to leave it, chose to stay, but the validity of this index is probably reduced by the fact that some individuals are much more affected than are others by influences in the immediate environment. Finally, indices may be derived from responses to direct statements, like "Our crew is better than others at sticking together" (Mann and Baumgartel, 1952). The investigators who used this last question found that only 21 percent of employees in groups with high absence rates, in a large industrial concern, gave this answer, as compared with 62 percent of employees in groups having low absence rates. Absenteeism is not in itself a very good index of cohesiveness, however, and so we have no way of evaluating the index based upon responses to this direct statement.

All in all, therefore, we conclude that the group property of cohesiveness is most useful as a conceptual framework bringing together various properties that are less inclusive, rather than as a single property that can be directly and validly measured. The use of this inclusive concept helps to remind us that there are many sources of unity within a group, whether or not we have a single index of their combined effects. Indeed, it is probably true that we will better understand a group when we have indices of several of the sources of its cohesiveness than if we put our confidence in a single index.

GROUP PROPERTIES AS RELATED TO INTERACTION: OVERVIEW

It is not possible to know everything about groups—not even about one very small group. And it would be impossible to handle so much information if one did try to assemble every possible fact about a group. In our attempts to understand groups for social-psychological purposes we must therefore concentrate on comparatively few of their characteristics. We have attempted, in this chapter, to select characteristics that we have some reason to believe will apply to most or all interaction groups and are important, in the sense that they really make a difference. In particular, we have referred to *group properties* as those characteristics that refer to the total group as a single entity; that vary, either quantitatively or qualitatively; and to which some sort of objective index can be applied. Groups can best be understood in terms of such properties, and these, in turn, can best be understood by viewing them alternately as dependent and as independent. That is, the more we know about how a property varies with antecedent conditions, and how consequent conditions vary with that property, the better our understanding of groups.

The kinds of covarying conditions of most interest to us are those that have to do with interaction among members. There follows a partial summary of conditions associated with variations in the group properties considered in this chapter, as they are related to interaction.

As *group size* increases, resource input tends also to increase, but the potentially greater input does not become available for group problem solving unless there is a corresponding increase in certain kinds of interaction—specifically, in the form of communications that either propose solutions or evaluate proposals previously made. Demand input also tends to increase with group size, with the usual consequence that the level of member satisfaction decreases because participation on the part of some members usually precludes participation on the part of others. Thus the effects of group size—both on finding good solutions and on member satisfaction—are mediated by the kinds and the amounts of interaction that are facilitated or discouraged by the size of the group.

Structural elaboration tends to increase with the complexity of a group's activities. With this increase there often follow increases both in task efficiency and in member satisfaction, but these depend partly or even wholly on the forms of interaction among members that result from increased complexity. Efficiency in a group setting is rarely an exclusive matter of handling materials without reference to other persons; it usually involves transactions among group members—perhaps passing materials from one pair of hands to another or perhaps communicating about the task. Increased elaboration in the form of a division of labor yields increased efficiency partly because there is a limit to the number of persons with whom one can carry out the necessary transactions. And insofar as member satisfaction increases with elaboration, it is for similar reasons: it is more nearly possible within each of a number of rather small groups for members to develop role relationships that provide satisfying modes of interaction than for the same number of individuals to do so in a single, larger, and less elaborated group. Thus the effects of elaboration, like those of group size, are mediated through interaction.

Structural integration tends to increase as a consequence of communication among differentiated parts about shared interests. Its increase tends to result in greater efficiency, smoother coordination among parts, and the extension of the range of persons with whom common interests are shared. In circular fashion, moreover, increased integration tends to enhance the very conditions of communication and sharing that, in some degree at least, are preconditions for integration. Thus communication is an essential form of interaction both for the development of integration and for its consequences.

Consensus tends to be greatest when attitudinal uniformity is a condition for group membership, when group members continue to have similar experiences that are relevant to those attitudes, and when members influence one another toward attitudinal similarity. All these conditions involve interaction: the circumstances attending the joining or the forming of a group require it; members are likely to tell one another about their similar experience; and intermember influence obviously involves interaction. The most important consequence of consensuality is that it makes *sharing* possible; given high consensus, sharing results almost automatically insofar as members express their actual attitudes to one another. Sharing, in turn, makes possible normativeness; as group members observe one another's behavior and other members' responses to it, they have repeated opportunities to learn the range of behavior within which acceptance of the rules is shared.

Cohesiveness is a complex group property, influenced by several different kinds of conditions and having varied consequences, and no single index of it is altogether satisfactory. Its diverse sources have to do, directly or indirectly, with members' interaction, by which they manifest to one another attitudes that are conducive to group unity. Its consequences are also expressed interactionally, especially in those forms of coordinated activity that spring from members' awareness that they belong to a cohesive group—or, in the opposite case, in poorly coordinated activity or perhaps even in conflict.

All these properties, finally (with the partial exception of group size), are both preconditions and outcomes of communicative processes. Varying degrees of each group property now maintain or change, now are maintained or changed by, the frequency and the content of communicative exchanges among group members.

PART FOUR

Interaction in Group Settings

THE TASK WE SET FOR OURSELVES IN THE OPENING PAGES OF THIS BOOK WAS to discover some of the conditions that underlie varying forms of human interaction. Our reasons for wanting to understand these conditions include not only the scientific ones of intellectual curiosity but also more practical ones. The better we understand how and why things happen, the more effectively we can control them, in the sense of making them happen more closely to the heart's desire.

Part Four therefore deals, though not exclusively, with such practical concerns. Taking off from the principles that have so far emerged as underlying various forms of interaction, we shall ask about the ways in which they operate in everyday group settings. We shall also inquire into the possibilities of applying the relevant principles in useful ways.

In Chapter 13 we shall note the complexities of the role demands that confront nearly all of us. We shall see that these complexities take several distinguishable forms, and that under certain conditions the conflicts commonly associated with each of them are either alleviated or exacerbated.

Intergroup conflict, which has existed from prehistoric times but which in contemporary American society is prominent in certain special ways, will concern us in Chapter 14. Here we shall note not only some of the conditions that underlie it, but shall also point to some general considerations that make possible its reduction.

Finally, in Chapter 15, we shall look at the interactional processes that characterize group members as they jointly confront problems that they need to solve together. We shall see that the challenge of achieving group goals is, on the one hand, a source of complexity as individuals meet their role demands. But it also provides a possible solution to problems of intergroup conflict, as well as being an everyday necessity, quite apart from considerations of role conflict and intergroup conflict.

Although the problems of Part Four are, in a sense, very practical ones, their consideration will also enable us to extend the principles of interaction that have already been presented. By applying these principles in everyday group settings, we can also extend our understanding of them.

CHAPTER 13

Complex Role Demands

As we pursue our daily round of activities we are called on to take a remarkable succession of roles. Within a very few hours we are likely to be called on to switch back and forth between the different role behaviors required as students, as roommates, as sons or daughters, as church members, as "dates," as discussion group leaders, and the like. Behavior appropriate to one of these relationships may well be inappropriate to one of the others.

That we do not get more mixed up than we do in shifting from role to role is a fortunate consequence of our capacity for broad social learning. The variety of roles we must juggle reflects the fact that complex social systems are compounded of a great variety of subsystems such as families, friendship groups, working groups, and other more or less organized collectivities of persons. Although none of us participates in anything like all the specific groups about us, the fact remains that all of us are required to participate in a substantial number. In each of such kinds of groups, one or more roles are prescribed for us. And each of them, taken as a system of roles, presupposes that its members can indeed manage to engage in behaviors appropriate to that particular system when the situation warrants.

Far more often than not, of course, these system requirements are fulfilled. Nevertheless, problems can easily arise. If you have ever had four professors, each of whom seems to forget that he is not the only person requiring homework of you, then you may have experienced one type of role difficulty that has been called "role overload." Or when you have encountered behaviors expected by your friends that you know would be forbidden by your parents, you have suffered another type of difficulty known as role conflict. Such problems are of particular interest because they have consequences in two directions. They affect both the individuals who experience the role difficulties, and the functioning of the group or groups that depends on role fulfillment.

In this chapter, then, we shall consider some of the general problems that arise from the necessity of meeting complex role demands, with special emphasis on the fact that individuals are called on to fulfill multiple roles. We have already seen in earlier chapters that a role refers to regularities in one person's behavioral relationship to another, and that these regularities are governed by norms, or shared acceptance of the same rules prescribing appropriate behavior.

Our focus here will be on the relationship between such role prescriptions and the individual who is trying to meet his end of a behavioral relationship. Many of the problems that arise in systems of roles can be classified according to whether the role prescriptions facing the individual are (1) unclear, (2) too numerous, or (3) mutually contradictory. In the course of the chapter we shall explore each of these cases. At the outset, however, we need to be clear as to the kind of choices individuals make in the initial selection of roles.

GAINS AND PAINS IN ROLE PRESCRIPTIONS

Once the individual has become accustomed to a certain pattern of behaviors toward another person, we may say that he has added a role to his repertoire of behaviors. After acquiring familiarity with the role, the fact that the individual begins to perform behaviors relevant to it at one moment in time and stops performing them at some later point is very heavily determined by the immediate situation: he behaves as a husband when he is with his wife at breakfast, but stops behaving as husband when he leaves her presence and goes off to work.

A more challenging question has to do with the circumstances under which a person adds one type of role rather than another to his repertoire in the first place. Of course he does not always have much choice in the matter. Many roles are taken, as we noted in Chapter 11, because they are prescribed for certain positions or niches in the society that are simply ascribed to an individual on the basis of characteristics (age, sex, race, ethnic background) over which he has no control. When there is no real choice of position, our question has to do with the degree to which the individual accepts his position and roles.

Nevertheless, individuals do make systematic and recurring decisions that they will enter one social position rather than another. One of the more important of these decisions is occupational choice. The decision to enter one occupation rather than another is based largely on information as to the role prescriptions that are typically associated with the positions being considered. If a person becomes a doctor, in this occupational capacity he will establish role relations with a variety of other persons. Even his role relations with his many clients will show a certain amount of variety. However, there will be many common threads in these role relations, and a limited, distinctive set of goals to be achieved by them, the curing of illness being the primary one. These common elements in prescriptions for the role make up in effect much of the "job description," and to the degree that they are perceived by the aspirant are major bases for occupational choice.

The Attractiveness of Positions and Their Associated Roles

Much of what is known concerning the selection of certain positions, or the acceptability of roles associated with positions into which a person is thrust without choice, is easily understood in terms of some of our earlier propositions. The most general proposition is, of course, that insofar as possible, positions are chosen or accepted that involve rewarding role relationships.

PERSONAL FACTORS: ABILITIES. As we watch individuals engage in various activities, they seem to be seeking out positions that permit them to demonstrate their special abilities. For most of us it is rewarding to do those things in which we excel, and distressing to do those things in which others persistently surpass us. Students who do well in mathematics are encouraged to think seriously of an ultimate position as an engineer or as a professor of mathematics. Those who do well in a variety of athletics often give serious thought to the role of coach or recreation director. People gravitate toward those positions consistent with their abilities.

Some of the mechanisms underlying this trend are apparent in a study by Jackson (1959) of the staff members of a child welfare agency in a midwestern state. A measure was obtained of how much each person valued every other person on the staff in terms of the **contribution** made toward the organization's goals. Each staff member was also asked to select from a list of the entire staff the teṅ persons he considered most valuable. Similar information was obtained from the individual's smaller work group. Attraction to the organization was determined by a scale designed to measure the amount of benefit the staff member felt he was receiving by belonging to the group. Finally, each staff member indicated the frequency with which he had contact with each other staff member.

If it is true that a person is rewarded by interacting with others who have a high regard for his contribution to the group, it should follow that a person's attraction to membership in the group will be stronger if he comes in *frequent* contact with those who have this high regard for him. Both expectations were confirmed for the professional staff members of the organization. An individual is most attracted to those organization roles in which his worth is given a high rating by a number of individuals, and is least attracted to those roles in which his efforts are least valued by others.

The fact that a person's attraction to certain organizational roles was dependent on frequent contact with those who had high regard for his contribution provides important supplementary information. In view of such results, it becomes hard to argue that initial preference for a role leads to higher achievement and hence higher ratings, rather than that higher ratings increase the attractiveness of the role. This is so simply because the individual's attraction to the role appeared to await the rewarding approval of others. It is concluded that the level of gratification an individual experiences in connection with a given role often depends on the kind of evaluation he receives in interaction with other persons in a role structure.

Higher-status positions that provide the occupant with the superior rather than the subordinate end of a maximal number of role relationships similarly tend to be experienced as rewarding and are selected insofar as possible. There have been frequent demonstrations of a correlation between occupancy of higher-status positions and expressed satisfaction with the role relationships entailed, as well as greater satisfaction with the group that encompasses these role relationships. Thus, for example, officers tend to have more favorable attitudes toward the Army than do enlisted men.

THE COMPATIBILITY OF SECONDARY VALUES. With other things equal (such as the status of a position and the specific skills required), there is a good deal of research evidence to indicate that individuals find more attractive those positions that involve them in close role relations with others of similar tastes and values *not only* regarding specific objects central to a position (such as pain or socialized medicine among doctors), but of similar values with respect to a broader range of objects as well. Indeed, a number of tests designed to aid young people in the selection of a vocation hinge on the fact that certain more general outlooks, side interests, hobbies, and minor tastes are distinctively characteristic of members of various occupational groupings. Subjects are counseled toward occupations whose members have value and interest profiles that most closely match their own. Underlying these diagnostic procedures are assumptions that are closely related to some of our earlier propositions, such as the principle that interaction is most rewarding with others who share many values with us. The success of these vocational tests in predicting occupational role compatibility is in itself some indication of the importance of this proposition.

Although individuals are likely to fit more comfortably in positions where others around them share similar attitudes, anticipation of shared attitudes is not of much importance where the assignment of position is involuntary or where the chooser lacks prior information about such common values. In these instances, individuals often show remarkable ability to adapt their attitudes to the demands associated with their roles. Such effects are most impressive within a set of complementary roles involving some antagonistic interdependence. One illustration of such roles might be the parent-child relationship as the child moves toward the latter stages of adolescence: although strong elements of facilitative interdependence remain, goals diverge increasingly as the parent attempts to limit and protect the child while the child seeks increasing liberation and independence. Another good example is provided by labor-management relations in industrial organizations, where there are some basic common goals (production of goods and services), and yet important elements of antagonism and competition over some aspects of the venture (working conditions, distribution of rewards, and so on). The effects of role-taking in reshaping attitudes come through most clearly when a given person moves from one side of such a complementary relationship to the "other side of the fence." Since attitudes on certain key matters are antithetical at the two ends of the role, individuals who make such a shift are likely to undergo a rather major attitude change. Most students would attest to the suspicion that their parents must have undergone such change. Research Illustration 11.1 (page 334) provides evidence of similar changes in an industrial setting.

In general, then, it appears that a fairly high degree of "fit" occurs between role prescriptions and the abilities, attitudes, and personality characteristics of position occupants. Such a fit comes about both through the selection of roles that are compatible in these terms, when choice of position is possible, and by the development of more appropriate individual characteristics over time to fit roles and positions that have been imposed.

In part because a good fit between individual characteristics and role prescriptions seems rewarding and motivating to the role-taker, and in part on more general grounds, it has often been hypothesized that groups as systems of roles function most effectively when this person-to-position fit is maximized. In an experiment demonstrating this point, Smelser (1961) measured subjects on a dominant-submissive scale, and then assigned pairs of subjects to a cooperative task of operating two model railroad trains. The task was structured so that one half of the role relationship was naturally dominant over the other in the performance of the job. The most productive groups were those in which a dominant subject was assigned the dominant role and a submissive subject was assigned the submissive role. The least productive were those groups in which the pairing was directly reversed.

Although such an individual-role fit seems desirable both in terms of individual adjustment and in terms of group performance, in larger social systems this degree of fit is only imperfectly achieved. Let us turn to some of the difficulties that can arise in the role-taking process.

Inadequate Role Prescriptions

Up to this point we have assumed that persons have no difficulty knowing what is expected of them as they engage in role behavior. This is not always the case, however. Role prescriptions covering various situations differ a great deal in the range of behaviors they cover and in the detail of their specification. When role prescriptions cover a wide range of contingencies in a detailed way, we may say that they are highly structured. Interaction requiring complex or rapid coordination between persons tends to be governed by role prescriptions that are relatively highly structured. Clear-cut prescriptions also apply in formalized rituals like weddings, funerals, or initiations.

It is apparent, however, that few situations involve role prescriptions as highly structured as those surrounding teamwork and ritual. Even many committees are so loosely organized that almost anyone is free to behave in a variety of different ways toward others. Role relations involving such figures as the chairman and the secretary are usually more clearly defined, but nonetheless prescriptions often remain very vague. The purpose of such formal codes as "parliamentary rules" and a set of "bylaws" is to give clarification as to how one should behave in such situations. Nevertheless, these ground rules cannot cover every situation that may arise and committee chairmen often find it necessary to improvise.

Least structured of all are role prescriptions governing informal interaction where no particular task achievement is required, as when one chats with a friend. This is not to say that latitude for behavior choice is complete in such informal relations. For one thing, of course, there are many improper or bizarre behaviors that by shared understanding would lie "beyond the pale." More significant, perhaps, is the fact that as individuals become acquainted with one another, they are likely to fall into certain styles of interaction that, at a very personalized level, form a coherent set of shared understandings about mutual behavior. Indeed, you probably recognize that in your own behavior you display a variety of more or less distinctive patterns toward different persons: perhaps, for example, you tend to wisecrack with Joe and Jim, to exchange emotional confidences with Bob, and to be aloof and proper with Jane. After some familiarity, you take your end of these role relationships with ease, and although they lack some of the external imperative quality of more formal role prescriptions, they are likely to circumscribe your behavior in important ways. You know, for example, that if you acted toward Jim as you do toward Jane, he would at least wonder what was wrong with you, and might very likely become offended with you.

Within certain limits, we undoubtedly find gratification in interaction that is not closely circumscribed by highly structured prescriptions, and hence leaves considerable latitude for more spontaneous individual expression. There are certain recurrent situations, however, where we are likely to feel that the culture provides us with inadequate guidelines for role behavior. There are other situations in which the individual may recognize that relevant prescriptions exist, but that he is unfamiliar with them. In either case, the situation is likely to produce a sense of insecurity in the individual, not only because he is unsure as to what behavior is appropriate, but also because he is uncertain as to what behavior to expect of others toward him, or how such behavior is to be interpreted.

OBJECTIVELY INADEQUATE ROLE PRESCRIPTIONS. Role relations between certain positions in a society are often ambiguous in an objective sense. An excellent example within American society is provided by relations between in-laws. In some societies, the interaction between a young man and his wife's mother is sufficiently ritualized that there is little room for doubt or insecurity about appropriate patterns of interaction. In other societies, there is a cultural understanding that a man and his mother-in-law formally avoid each other, which is, of course, a role prescription in itself. In the United States, however, there is a good deal of ambiguity surrounding the "proper" form of the relationship, even on such concrete points as forms of address. Does this unfamiliar elderly woman want to be called "Mother," "Mrs. Jones," "Ann," or what?

Such an objective absence of sufficient role prescriptions characterizes many situations of interpersonal contact where there is objective reason for familiarity (in-laws have become part of the same "family"; new residents next door have become part of the neighborhood) but still without adequate contact for the establishment of shared norms about role relationships. With sufficient contact, such norms naturally develop and the awkwardness or insecurity experienced by the participants is remedied.

INADEQUATE SOCIALIZATION INTO ROLE BEHAVIORS. The consequences of perceived role ambiguity are most commonly seen, however, when people feel themselves to be novices in certain interaction situations. They have not as yet fully assimilated the relevant role prescriptions and are aware that they have not. Such an awareness may be intensified in a variety of ways. For example, the more formal the interaction setting, the more aware the novice is of the likelihood of highly structured role prescriptions, and hence the more uncertainty he will suffer if these prescriptions are largely unfamiliar. The traveler in a foreign land can anticipate more torment to be suffered at a formal dinner party than in a chance conversation on the train. Similarly, unexpected behavior from others toward himself that a person has difficulty in interpreting will serve as a strong cue to emphasize the unfamiliarity of the role relation, and will increase his anxiety.

The classic example of such experienced ambiguity in role prescriptions is that of the adolescent in an adult gathering. He is old enough to be aware that there are distinctive adult role relations he would like to mimic, yet his exposure to them has been too slight for any mastery. As a result he is awkward, insecure, and self-conscious. Certain aspects of this predicament are referred to in the following section as "marginality." Much the same kind of inadequacy is experienced by any individual who is a newcomer to an ongoing group, unless he has had very thorough prior practice in the role patterns that have become characteristic of the group.

COPING WITH AMBIGUOUS ROLE PRESCRIPTIONS. What determines a person's selection among available behaviors in highly ambiguous situations? A tentative answer consistent with considerable clinical and some experimental evidence is the following: When a person experiences ambiguity as to his role behavior, he will tend to respond with whatever behavior he anticipates will best combine maximum personal motive satisfaction and minimal uncertainty of response (a source of anxiety) from others. In other words, the more strongly he is motivated to make a particular response, the less his behavior will be influenced by the uncertainty of others' responses to him. Conversely, the weaker his motivation to make any particular response, the greater the likelihood that his behavior will reflect attempts to reduce uncertainty as to how others will act toward him.

This formulation helps account for the commonly observed ways in which people respond to ambiguous situations. People who suffer general feelings of insecurity may well respond to the additional insecurity of the ambiguous situation by withdrawing from it entirely if possible. Persons who can tolerate some of the situational insecurity or who cannot escape from the situation will take other steps to reduce the uncertainty of others' responses to them. This often takes the form of extreme conformity to whatever norms the person *does* recognize, and especially to certain norms that he believes are held by others whose favorable responses he seeks. The new second lieutenant, fresh from Officers Candidate School, often finds himself placed in an Army situation where he recognizes that his familiarity with "going" prescriptions is spotty. His dominant personal motive is to be successful in his first leadership role. He may achieve a minimum uncertainty of response from his higher-ranking fellow officers if he adheres rigidly to what he can guess will be their notions of the proper role of a second lieutenant. He may achieve a minimum uncertainty of response from the enlisted men under his command if he insists on strict adherence to every formal requirement of Army regulations so that everything is done "through channels" and thereby becomes more predictable. It is probably for the latter reason that new second lieutenants are reputed to be more "G.I" than seasoned officers who feel more secure in their expectations concerning the behavior of others under their command..

Role Overload

At the opposite extreme from the dearth of perceived role prescriptions that can plague the individual in some situations are instances in which the burdens of role demands become too heavy for him to fulfill. Such "role overload" seems to be a persistent difficulty in many task-oriented formal organizations. Each formal position in such an organization has some specified connection to other positions above it, below it, or at the same level in the hierarchy. The occupant of such a position thus has role relations with a variety of others around him, and these involve principally a set of expectations as to the work he should be accomplishing. Such expectations from any other person in a related job can readily be thought of as constituting "role pressure." When a large number of surrounding positions are converging on the individual with pressures for behavior at the same time, he may well have difficulty coping with the demands. Research Illustration 13.1 portrays some of these complex role demands.

It is likely that varying distances between persons in large and complex role structures are systematically related to the strength or unreasonableness of role pressures. In connection with the study reported in Research Illustration 13.1, for example, Wolfe and Snoek (1962) found that role partners exerting the most unrealistic demands on any given individual were those located at greater rather than lesser distances from him. That is, they varied in the degree to which they were dependent on the individual for material, services, and the like; where this dependence was less (and hence the goal distance greater, although not necessarily to the point of antagonism mentioned in Chapter 11), these

Research Illustration 13.1

Kahn and Wolfe (1961) have studied role pressures on the occupants of certain positions in the management hierarchy of an industrial organization. An initial interview with a selected number of individuals in the organization produced information concerning the responsibilities of each (called henceforth the "star," for reasons apparent from the accompanying figure), and an indication of his most important work associates—superiors, subordinates, co-workers both in his own and other departments—who could be expected to have relevant opinions about what he should do in his job.

A second round of interviews was then held with all these role-sending "satellites" (work associates) of the 57 stars. The satellites were asked to describe the star's responsibilities and their view of his relationship to them. In addition, the satellites were shown a list made by the star of his role specifications, and were asked to agree or disagree with each item, specifying in what way the list should be different. From these materials a measure of the amount of role pressure placed on the star was developed. (See accompanying table.)

A final round of interviews was taken once again with the stars themselves, inquiring about the nature and kinds of pressure they felt

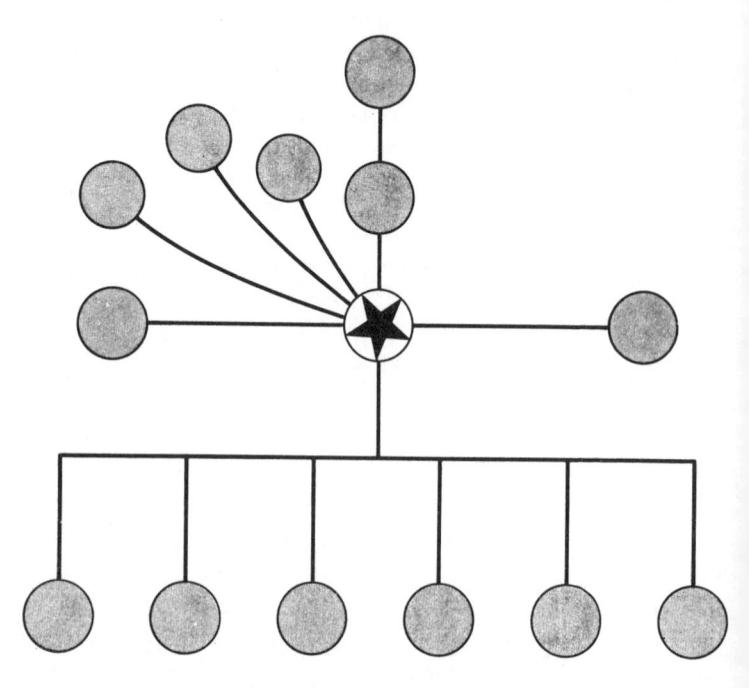

The numerous role relationships associated with a given position (starred) in a formal organization

they were experiencing from their colleagues. Various measures were taken that helped to assess the way in which the stars were responding to role stresses.

The broad results made clear what a central problem role overload was in the functioning of the organization. None of the satellites knew the totality of demands on the star's time. When they were asked how much time they felt the star should spend on his itemized job prescriptions, they tended to be indifferent to items that were not involved in their role relations with him, and indicated that the star was spending a proper amount of time on that item. When they were concerned about an item, they indicated that the star should spend more time on it. They almost never indicated that the star should spend *less* time on a given job!

Although the objective estimates of role pressure varied in some degree from star to star, most were subject to more demands than they could reasonably fulfill. And where the pressures were relatively strong, the data showed that the stars experienced significantly more on-the-job tension, less job satisfaction, and less confidence in the organization:

| | *Mean score of role pressures* ||
	Strong	*Weak*
Tension	5.04	3.96
Job satisfaction	4.23	5.13
Confidence in superiors	5.62	6.96

Other reports from the same general study make clear the ways in which personality factors can modify both the degree of overload experienced, and the means of coping with such overload (see Wolfe and Snoek, 1962). Thus, for example, a measure of flexibility-rigidity in star personality showed that the flexible star was more sensitive to objective pressures than was the rigid person, who felt moderate pressure regardless of the pressures actually exerted. When pressures built up on the rigid person he was more likely to cut off communication with his associates than were the flexible stars. The associates in turn appeared to recognize these differences in their interaction with the stars: more flexible stars were more likely to be made the target of strong pressures than were the more rigid ones.

individuals produced an increased sense of tension in the person on whom they were dependent. Similarly, where communicative distance was greater (as measured by the frequency of communication between them) the pressures produced were greater as well. Probably with increasing distance in any role system there is a less realistic understanding of the totality of role expectations bearing on a person: those who have positions closer to him are better able to anticipate that pressures on him may become too heavy.

Many of the difficulties of role ambiguity decrease through continued interaction between persons over time, however; and there is at least presumptive evidence that problems of role overload are ironed out over time if stable interaction continues. In the study described in Research Illustration 13.1, for example, the most unreasonable expectations were held by relative newcomers to the organization; individuals who dealt mainly with "old hands" suffered less role overload. This is, in one sense, another aspect of the distance dimension, although it refers to distance in the temporal sense. The longer members of a group work together, the greater the likelihood that they will arrive at more satisfactory solutions to the problems created by the complexity of their multiple interdependencies.

* * *

Because we live in a complex society, we find it necessary—and often desirable, too—to interact with many different kinds of people whose role expectations of us are often quite diverse. Some of the role relationships that we are thus expected to maintain are difficult or frustrating and others are highly attractive, depending on such factors as our existing habits and preferences, our abilities, and the compatibility of our values with those of the persons with whom we interact. To some degree it is possible to achieve a reasonably good fit between our patterns of preferences and abilities and the role demands that are made on us. There are sometimes opportunities for choice among different alternatives, and our capacities for learning and changing our attitudes usually enable us to make some viable adaptations when we have no choice. Among the sources of limited success in adapting to role demands are inadequacies of role prescriptions, inadequate experience or opportunity to become familiar with role demands, and overheavy or overcomplex role assignments. There are characteristic ways of coping both with role ambiguities and with role overload.

ROLE CONFLICT

There are many reasons why a role relationship that a person is expected to maintain may be a source of conflict to him. Most obvious, perhaps, is that the relationship is simply unwelcome: a servant does not like to be subservient to a master, or a child may resent having to be polite to guests. Such conflict is not, in principle, different from having to do anything else that one prefers not to do, and is essentially a problem of individual psychology. Our present problem is a more clearly social-psychological one: conflict stemming from contradictory sets of role expectations. It often happens, as we shall see, that a person finds one of two conflicting sets of role expectations more objectionable than the other, or that one is welcome and the other is not. In such cases both kinds of conflict are involved: that of being expected to do things that he does not want to do, and that of facing incompatible expectations at the same time.

Contradictory role expectations are usually a consequence of membership in different groups: an adolescent is a member both of his family and of his peer group, for example. There are two general ways in which the norms of different membership groups impinge simultaneously on a person. He may find himself present with members of both groups, so that whatever he does is observed by people who expect him to do different things. Or, to the extent that he has internalized the norms of both groups, he finds himself in conflict, whether or not he is observed by members of either of them. The first of these may result in conflict, but it tends to be of immediate, transitory nature, whereas conflict of the second kind is more persistent, perhaps pervading many different kinds of situations. As we now consider individuals' conflicts that stem from their membership in multiple groups, we shall bear in mind all these kinds and sources of conflict.

Marginal Man

Whenever an individual has membership in different groups whose norms are in important ways opposed to each other, he may find it impossible to be regarded, or to regard himself, as a full-fledged member of either. If he also finds it impossible to relinquish membership in either group—perhaps because he does not wish to, perhaps because circumstances make it impossible—he is said to be *marginal* to both groups. Such persons are neither fish nor fowl, since they are not recognized as 100 percent members of either group. Their marginality usually results, in part, from the fact that they are recognized as outsiders by one group or the other by reason of their physical appearance, language, dress, or customs. And if, as is commonly the case, one of the groups is higher than the other in the societal hierarchy of privilege, power, and prestige, the marginal person is often thought of by one group as disloyal because he is trying to escape, and by the other as trying to intrude where he does not belong. Such attributions of motives, insofar as they become known to the marginal person, only serve to intensify his conflict.

In a society of such recently heterogeneous origins as our own, there are many possible sources of marginality. We shall describe a few of these to illustrate the general problem.

Ethnic origins have long served as a source of marginality the world around. During and following a half century or so of large-scale immigration into this country, millions of immigrants and especially their children faced marginal conflicts. Research Illustration 13.2 describes and analyzes the conflicts of second-generation Italian-Americans as a fairly recent example.

There are two principal conditions under which the marginality of immigrants tends to be limited to one or two generations. It is less likely to persist through successive generations when the earmarks of being an outsider are merely behavioral, as in the case of Irish immigrants, rather than visibly anatomical, as in the case of Chinese immigrants. And, second, marginality is less likely to persist when there is strong motivation to achieve full membership in the new group and to abandon the old. The absence of such motivation seems largely responsible for the continued marginality of many Jews, in many countries over a period of centuries—as illustrated, for example, by Shakespeare's Merchant of Venice. The severity of their conflicts, like those of all marginals, is measured by the degree to which they can neither live in two worlds nor abandon either of them.

Similar problems are typically faced by persons of "mixed blood," especially those who are descended from conspicuously different racial groups. When one racial group is subordinate to another, and the lines between them are tightly drawn, individuals of mixed ancestry often occupy a position intermediate between the two groups. Mulattoes in the United States, for example, are more favorably treated in some ways by both white and Negro groups than are full-blooded Negroes. They may or may not have full membership in Negro groups, but rarely do in white groups. In general, they are most likely to face role conflict when membership in either group is available to them; if so, there are strong motivations in both directions. Loyalties to Negro family and friends pull them in one direction and the advantages of membership in the more privileged white groups pull them in the other. Since they cannot have both, conflict is inevitable.

The term "passing" has long been applied to individuals whose appearance, even though they have grown up as Negroes, is such that they successfully mingle with whites and are accepted by them as such. One report of Negro life in a northern city describes their plight as follows:

> For a Negro to pass socially means sociological death and rebirth. . . . People well established in the Negro world and older people seldom pass socially and completely. There is too much to lose and too little to be gained. For one who is not firmly anchored in the Negro community emotionally, there is much temptation to take such a step.
>
> At first he finds that the color line . . . seems to disappear for him. There is no close scrutiny by his new-found white working companions and

Research Illustration 13.2

After living for several months as a "participant observer" in the Italian section of a New England city, Child (1943) interviewed at some length each of fifty young men who were second-generation Italian-Americans, concerning their views about their problems of dual allegiance and their preferred solutions to them. The nature of their dilemma can be seen in the following excerpts from his report.

> The structure of the Italian family denotes a secure and reasonably tranquil family life for the member of the second generation. Although conformity with the Italian custom of the son's handing over all his wages to his parents may result in less pocket money for the son, it is rewarded on the other hand by the family's assuming a greater financial responsibility for him, and, negatively, by the prevention of considerable conflict within the family. Membership in the Italian group permits enjoyment of participation in social functions with people who may accept one more completely as an equal than will any group of mixed nationality. . . . Rewards offered by the Italian group rather than the non-Italian [include] acceptance as a perfect equal in status; freedom from attack, in social intercourse, as a member of a national group of low status; and the security of feeling oneself to be a part of a national and cultural group which has displayed great power and achievement.
>
> [On the other hand] due to the widespread prejudice against Italians, those who are considered more nearly "American" find it easier to obtain the more desirable jobs. . . . The American family custom of a young man's managing his own finances generally permits the individual a variety of enjoyments which cost more money than his parents might be willing to grant him; in particular, it allows many second-generation Italians to compete for attention of the opposite sex more successfully than they could if dependent upon their parents for pocket money. . . . [In many schools] rewards and punishments are administered by persons who are thoroughly American in background and whose behavior is determined by a deliberate policy of encouraging him to act like an American. . . . The achievement of the goal of rising in status in the community is dependent, in large part, upon the individual's acceptance by non-Italians. It is the general American community, or its representatives in small groups, that can offer the reward of accepted rise in status. . . . The second-generation Italian cannot escape from being a member of American society and from constantly being shown that he will be punished, or will not be rewarded, by his fellow Americans for behaving like an Italian. (pp. 57–61, *passim*)
>
> Child notes three major types of solutions that these men made to such conflicts. Those who showed the *rebel* reaction did everything they could to establish themselves as Americans. They tried to get away from the Italian label, though never with complete success. The *ingroup* reaction was just the opposite. Those who tried this solution wanted to be known as Italians, and were in many ways hostile

to Americans and to symbols of America. They continued, however, to feel threatened by the various barriers against them as Italians. Those who tried the *apathetic* solution appeared to have the most difficult time of all; they sought to avoid being known either as Italians or as Americans. They preferred to keep out of situations in which their uncertain nationality aroused their conflicts, while attempting to deny that there were any real differences of importance between the two groups. The author makes it clear that these three solutions do not represent "pure types": they are, nevertheless, distinguishable kinds of solutions, even though some individuals attempted two or even all three of them at one time or another.

friends. There is no fear of any more reprisal than being fired or losing some new acquaintances. Then more and more difficulties begin to arise. He begins to dread meeting old Negro friends while out with the new ones. There are cases where daughters have refused to speak to their mothers on the street and sons have looked the other way, when accompanied by whites, upon encountering their Negro fathers. As the new job and the new friends become of more emotional importance, the individual has a constant, haunting fear of being discovered. There is the possibility that an old Negro enemy may turn him in, or that some white person may accidentally discover him and work vengeance on him (Drake and Cayton, 1945).

Adolescents, in our own society at least, often present many of the characteristics of marginality. Lewin, a social psychologist who liked to look at problems that appeared to be quite different in terms of general principles that brought them all under the same tent, viewed the situation of racial minorities, criminals, and adolescents, for example, as having in common an ambiguous and divided "life space." This term he defined as "consisting of the person and the psychological environment as it exists for him" (1951, p. xi). In a much-quoted passage, he had this to say about adolescents.

The transition from childhood to adulthood may be a rather sudden shift (for instance, in some of the primitive societies), or it may occur gradually in a setting where children and adults are not sharply separated groups. In case of "adolescence difficulties," however, a third state of affairs is often prevalent: children and adults constitute clearly defined groups; the adolescent does not wish to belong any longer to the children's group and, at the same time, knows that he is not really accepted in the adult group. In this case he has a position similar to what is called in sociology the "marginal man."

The marginal man is a person who stands on the boundary [see Figure 13.1] between two groups, A and B. He does not belong to either of them, or at least he is not certain about his belongingness. Not infrequently this situation occurs for members of an underprivileged minority group,

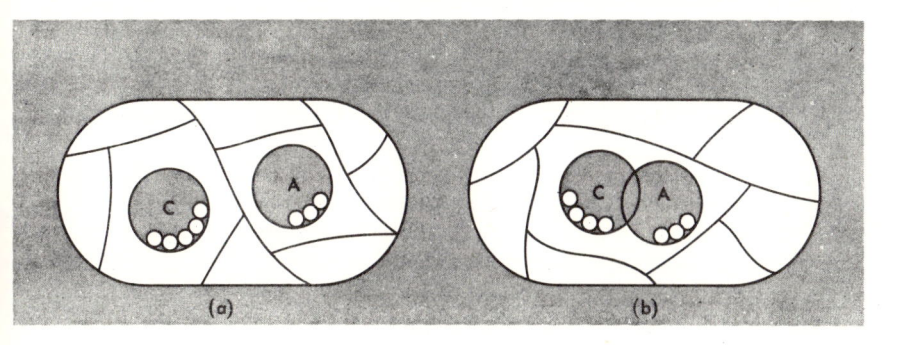

FIGURE 13.1. The adolescent as a marginal man. (a) During childhood and adulthood the adults (A) and the children (C) are viewed as relatively separated groups, the individual child (represented by small circles within C) and the individual adult (represented by small circles within A) being sure of their belongingness to their respective groups. (b) The adolescent belongs to a group that can be viewed as an overlapping region of the children's or the adults' group belonging to both of them, or standing between them and not belonging to either one. (Lewin, 1951)

particularly for the more privileged members within this group. . . . The fact of being located in a social "no man's land" can be observed in very different types of minority groups—for instance, racial groups or the hard-of-hearing, which is a marginal group between the deaf and the normal group.

Characteristic symptoms of the behavior of marginal men are emotional instability and sensitivity. They tend to unbalanced behavior, to either boisterousness or shyness, exhibiting too much tension, and a frequent shift between extremes of contradictory behavior. The marginal man shows a typical aversion to the less privileged members of his own group. This can be noted in the hostile attitude of some subgroups of the Negroes or other races against members of their own race, and the hard-of-hearing against the deaf. . . . [The adolescent] too is oversensitive, easily shifted from one extreme to the other, and particularly sensitive to the shortcomings of his younger fellows. . . . The similarities between' the position of the members of the underprivileged minority and the adolescent, and between their behavior, seem to me so great that one might characterize the behavior of the marginal members of the minority group as that of permanent adolescence.

We might sum up our discussion of the adolescent in the following manner. (a) The basic fact . . . can be represented as the position of a person during [change] from one region to another. This includes the widening of the life space (geographically, socially, and in time perspective), and the cognitively unstructured character of the new situation. (b) Somewhat more specifically, the adolescent has a social position "between" the adult and the child, similar to a marginal member of an underprivileged minority group. (c) There are still more specific factors . . . such as the new experiences with one's own body, which can be represented as the baffling change of a central region of the established life space.

Only the procedure [of characterizing] events and objects by their interdependence, rather than by their similarity or dissimilarity of appearance, made possible the linking of such divergent factors as group belongingness, bodily changes, and attitudes (Lewin, 1951, pp. 143–145).

Dual Membership in Society and in Distinctive Groups within It

We shall present here a few illustrations of multiple memberships that, like those of marginal people, involve incompatible role behaviors. The dual memberships with which we shall deal here, however, are different. The marginal man is pulled toward two groups, in *neither* of which he has full membership. Here we shall be dealing with conflicting role demands of two groups in *one or both* of which the individual has full membership. Specifically, they are common role prescriptions made by the society at large and those made by some smaller group within the society. Many of the conflicts to which we shall call attention apply also to marginals, but the nature of the conflicts is somewhat different.

MEMBERSHIP IN DISTINCTIVE RACIAL GROUPS. There are in this country many minority groups whose members do not necessarily occupy a marginal position. If—like Child's "ingroup" subjects—they make no attempt to participate in other groups, they are not, strictly speaking, marginal, because they have full membership in one group. Many Negroes belong to this category, and we shall take them as an example.

We have no way of knowing how many American Negroes participate only in all-Negro groups, but they must be extremely numerous. They avoid the conflicts of marginality insofar as they are not motivated toward membership in non-Negro groups, but there are other conflicts, perhaps even more poignant, to which they are subject. They do not escape the role demands of the society at large by limiting themselves to ingroup associations. There are in any society common role prescriptions that apply to many of its members, or even to all of them, regardless of the distinctive positions they hold. Many of the common role prescriptions that in our society apply to whites and Negroes alike are embodied in laws—concerning theft, payment of taxes, truancy, and support of children, for example. In addition to such role demands, common to members of both majority and minority groups, there is for American Negroes an additional body of role demands made on Negroes but not on whites. In those parts of America where Negroes are most numerous, their lives go on (or have until recently) under conditions like these: they must be willing to accept menial work, sometimes for less money than whites are paid for similar work; they must live, travel, and find their recreation in segregated quarters; they must be willing to be addressed by whites by their first names, but must not address whites by their first names, and so on.

Any role prescription includes a set of obligations made on any person who takes that role and also a set of rights he is entitled to demand from other persons. Much of the conflict to which Negroes in America are subject stems from what they feel to be incompatible sets of obligations and rights. Many of them feel that in terms of obligations they are expected to take the role of "Americans"—they are members of society at large, just as white people are. But they also feel that in terms of rights they are expected to take the role of Negro—a role whose rights seem to them distinctly limited. They point out, for example, that Negroes are selected for military service as Americans, but that many of them have traditionally been assigned certain types of military service as Negroes.

Psychologically speaking, the plight of the American Negro is inevitably one of frustration to some degree. He cannot help wishing for the privileges that go with membership in the majority group, but they are not fully open to him. And he cannot help resenting a situation in which, as he sees it, white people expect him to act like an American when it is to their advantage and to act like a Negro when it is to their advantage. (This, of course, is not necessarily an objective picture. Moreover, many white people feel that Negroes are apt to claim the rights that go with being Americans but to consider only the obligations that are theirs as Negroes. Our present concern is not with the validity of either view but with the impact of dual membership upon Negroes.) Whether he likes it or not, the American Negro is a member of both groups, but he cannot enjoy all the rights of membership in both groups.

Modes of adaptation similar to those noted by Child on the part of Italian-Americans (Research Illustration 13.2) may be found among contemporary American Negroes. Because of Negroes' distinctive physiognomic features, genetically transmitted across the generations, however, they show these three patterns in their own distinctive ways. The "rebel reaction" (getting away from the Negro label) is not available to them, save for the few who find it possible to "pass." The "apathetic" solution (trying to avoid being known either as Negro or white) is not, strictly speaking, available to them either. But something that resembles it—an attitude of hopeless resignation to the fate of one who is born a visible Negro—has, until recently at least, been the dominant mode of adaptation, usually involving seclusion within Negro society as far as possible. The "ingroup" reaction (wanting to be known as Negroes and manifesting hostility to whites, or at least to their enforcement of discrimination) has in recent years become much more conspicuous. Negroes are not likely again to be quiescent in the face of what they regard as enforced inferiority of opportunity while, at the same time, they cannot erase the visible marks of their racial identity. On the part of coming generations of Negroes, therefore, the modes of adaptation to an always potential conflict of roles are likely to be profoundly influenced by the systematic efforts during the 1960s, on the part of both whites and Negroes, to eradicate some of the sources of the conflict of roles that Negroes now face. (These and other ways of minimizing role conflict are further considered in the final section of this chapter.)

MEMBERSHIP IN NONCONFORMING GROUPS. It has long been known that a large proportion of young males, especially in cities, who have been convicted of criminal acts are members of groups, usually known as gangs; their norms support kinds of behavior that are outlawed by the rest of society. Indeed, it has been shown that many gangs have an almost total way of life that has many elements of a self-sufficient culture (cf. Shaw, 1938; Barron, 1954). This fact in itself, however, does not adequately account for the phenomena of juvenile delinquency because, after all, gangs exist within a larger society from which they are not completely insulated. Gang members are reasonably familiar with the more "respectable" norms of the society that surrounds them, and are in fact dependent on that society.

It also appears, according to evidence reported in part in Research Illustration 13.3, that many delinquents have spent all or most of their young lives as members of marginal families, and that a large proportion of male "criminals" in their twenties could have been predicted, when they were still preadolescent, to be foredoomed to criminal careers. According to these data, the effects of being reared in a crime-prone area in a home where both parents were criminal or otherwise deviant, as compared to the effects of being reared in such an area but in a home not known to include adult deviants, were such that 88 percent of the former but only 34 percent of the latter had subsequent careers of crime.

Sutherland's classic *The Professional Thief* (1937) vividly describes both the nature of group membership in the "honorific" society of thieves and the role conflicts to which its members are subject. The following excerpts are illustrative.

> The professional thief has a complex of abilities and skills, just as do physicians, lawyers or bricklayers. . . . The division between professional and nonprofessional thieves in regard to this complex of techniques is relatively sharp. This is because these techniques are developed to a high point only by education, and the education can be secured only in association with professional thieves; . . . these techniques generally call for cooperation which can be secured only in association with professional thieves. . . . Professional thieves are contemptuous of amateur thieves

Research Illustration 13.3

McCord and McCord (1958) carried out a study of some effects of being reared in a home including one or more adults known to have criminal or otherwise deviant records. Their procedures included two stages. First, they obtained voluminous information concerning 253 boys in lower- and middle-class families in two cities in Massachusetts. The boys' average age at that time was about seven years. During the next few years the investigators continued to gather systematic information about these boys and their families. Then, when the boys had become young men whose average age was twenty-seven, their records, according to the Massachusetts Board of Probation, were examined for references to them or to their parents.

Almost without exception, these boys had all come from relatively disorganized urban areas, and had been exposed to subcultures known to be characteristic of delinquent behavior, although they had not been selected as already delinquent. In respect to urban background, individuals who later had delinquent careers were thus like those who did not. What did distinguish them, as shown in the following table, was the status of their parents as criminal or otherwise deviant (including alcoholism or known sexual promiscuity).

Parental records	Percentage of all young men in category at the left who had been convicted of crimes
Mother criminal or deviant, father criminal	88
Mother criminal or deviant, father deviant	59
Mother criminal or deviant, father neither	42
Neither parent criminal or deviant	34

and have many epithets which they apply to the amateurs. . . . They will have no dealings with thieves who are unable to use the correct methods . . . there is pride in one's own position in the group.

One of the most heinous offenses that a thief can commit against another thief is to inform, "squeal," or "squawk." . . . Many thieves will submit to severe punishment rather than inform. Two factors enter into this behavior. One is the injury that would result to himself in the form of loss of prestige, inability to find companions among thieves in the future, and reprisals if he should inform. The other is loyalty and identification of self with other thieves. . . . Consensus is the basis of both of these reactions, and the two together explain how the rule against informing grows out of the common experiences of the thieves. Consensus means, also, that thieves have a system of values and an *esprit de corps* which support the individual thief in his criminal career.

The group defines its own membership. A person who is received within the group and recognized as a professional thief is a professional thief. One who is not so received and recognized is not a professional thief, regardless of his methods of making a living. . . . Professional theft is a group-way of life. One can get into the group and remain in it only by the consent of those previously in the group. Recognition as a professional thief by other professional thieves is the absolutely necessary, universal and definitive characteristic of the professional thief. . . . A professional thief is a person who has the status of a professional thief in the differential association of professional thieves (pp. 197–211, *passim*).

The common role prescriptions of the larger society are clearly at odds with those of the society of thieves, particularly in regard to honesty and "respect for the law." The professional thief therefore cannot avoid role conflict. Sutherland describes his conflicts as follows:

The professional thief in America feels that he is a social outcast. This is especially true of the professional thieves who originated in middle-class society, as many of them did. He feels that he is a renegade when he becomes a thief. Chic Conwell stated that the thief is looking for arguments to ease his conscience and that he blocks off considerations about the effects of his crimes upon the victims and about the ultimate end of his career. When he is alone in prison, he cannot refrain from thought about such things, and then he shudders at the prospect of returning to his professional activities. Once he is back in his group, he assumes the "bravado" attitude of the other thieves, his shuddering ceases, and everything seems to be all right. Under the circumstances he cannot develop an integrated personality, but the distress is mitigated, his isolation reduced, and his professional life made possible because he has a group of his own in which he carries on a social existence as a thief, with a culture and values held in common by many thieves (pp. 205–206).

Most of us feel, quite naturally, that "it serves him right" if the professional thief is tortured by such conflicts. Our purpose, however, is not to render moral judgments but to add to our understanding of how incompatible role prescriptions lead to personal conflict. And so we are led to ask how it happens that thieves and members of other nonconformist groups get themselves into a position where they face incompatible role demands.

There are two major sources of motivation to enter such nonconforming groups. The first, though the less frequent, is a "rebel reaction" against conforming groups. The young man or postadolescent who feels himself too severely restricted, or unjustly punished, or otherwise getting a "raw deal" may turn against the standards of conforming groups in which he has been reared. The lure of excitement, together with his need to rebel, may lead him to join in the activities of criminals whom he "happens" to meet. Once he has shared in their activities, the need for protection, together with the "good fellowship" of companions who are not highly critical of his morals, gradually leads him into full membership in a criminal group.

The more common source of motivation toward membership in such groups is quite different. It springs from childhood membership in relatively nonprivileged groups. Most criminals in our society come not from middle-class backgrounds but from backgrounds of poverty. As adolescents, the only forms of recreation available to them, in crowded tenements and street-corner "playgrounds," almost inevitably lead to acts of delinquency. The only groups of their own age in which they can have membership are groups in which acts of delinquency are common. Such acts—stealing by boys and sex delinquency by girls, for example—are not begun just as acts of rebellion. Rather, they are conforming acts, or at least tolerated acts, according to the norms of the groups available to them.

If they are not aware of it at first, members of such adolescent groups soon learn that many of their behaviors are disapproved by the larger society—particularly in the person of the local policeman. They are, however, not averse to some degree of rebellion against the standards personified by the policeman. Not surprisingly, their frustrations—which are very much like those we described as inevitable for most Negroes in America—lead to aggression in this form. Many members of such underprivileged groups come to feel, as most Negroes do, that society imposes on them obligations which outweigh the rights it confers. They cannot help noticing the greater privileges of those higher in the social scale than themselves—privileges such as pleasant homes, automobiles, and spending money, which are in sharp contrast to what they can afford. Many of them come to sense, perhaps only half-consciously, that they are expected to live up to middle-class standards of cleanliness, ambition, and morality without the means of doing so. They are apt to feel, moreover, that there is little likelihood of reward even if they try to live up to such standards. The rewards of participation in relatively nonconforming groups are immediately available and much more certain than the remote rewards of participating in groups that in any case seem inaccessible.

Personal frustration, then, is one of the factors that leads people to take on or to continue membership in nonconforming groups. In some cases it is frustration felt by individuals and not shared with other members of their face-to-face groups. More commonly it is group-shared frustration that leads to the acceptance of norms known to be at odds with those of the larger society. In either case the norms of the larger and of the smaller group are incompatible, and conflict inevitably results. Membership in the nonconforming group usually offers the satisfactions of uncritical, personal acceptance, together with the satisfaction of expressing aggression. But it also offers the threats of punishment and of ostracism by more favored groups into which the individual might eventually gain membership. Membership in the society at large cannot be avoided, but conformity to its norms carries with it freedom from fear of detection and punishment, together with some hope, however remote, of being rewarded for "good" behavior. Conformity to its norms also presents threats, which take the form of ostracism by other members of the nonconforming group, together with having to give up practices that, though nonconforming, are very satisfying, and the fear of not being rewarded after all for such self-denial.

Thus there are both threats and rewards for taking either role. There is ordinarily no way of taking both roles, of gaining the advantages of both without the disadvantages of either.

Findings like those reported in Research Illustration 13.3 and reports like those of Sutherland must be viewed in the light of the fact that members of families, neighborhood groups, or "professional" groups characterized by criminal behavior are inevitably familiar with the norms and the general way of life of what they regard as a more privileged society-at-large. Such a viewpoint has led Merton (1957) and other sociologists to account for much criminal behavior as a consequence of role conflict of a special kind. The inclusive society, most of whose members are more privileged than members of criminal subsocieties, presents the latter with a set of desirable goals (financial comfort, respectability, freedom from harassment by the law). But it does not present them with ready-made means toward the achievement of the attractive goals. The very society that "preaches respectability" denies them the means of becoming respectable—or so many of them feel, at any rate. Many of them, by way of analogy, manage to "pass," eventually, but in some cases, at least, the dangers of attempting to do so are like those that face the Negro who has tried to do so.

These, of course, are not the only sources of delinquency and crime. Individuals' personal characteristics have something to do with it, and help to determine whether, to use the three kinds of solutions observed by Child, they rebel against the minority group of which they have become members, identify themselves completely with it, or become apathetic. There is some evidence to indicate that serious delinquents are deficient in the ability to learn proper discriminations between the requirements of different kinds of role relationships; Baker and Sarbin (1956) present experimental evidence to this effect. Personality differences of these and other kinds are rarely if ever the sole precondition of delinquency, however. Rather, they operate in combination with environmental influences, among which multiple-group membership, with its possible consequences of role conflict, is particularly important.

* * *

Severe conflict involving contradictory sets of role demands on the same person usually stems from his having or wanting membership in different groups. If such a person feels that he is not fully accepted by either group, he is considered to be marginal. Common examples of marginality in our society include many adolescents who feel that they are neither children nor adults, and members of ethnic minorities who have some possibility of achieving full membership in the majority group. Since his minority membership group is apt to be the less privileged one, a marginal person tends to be sensitive about his status in that group, and perhaps even hostile to other members of it. His mode of adaptation to this predicament may include various combinations of rebellion against the minority group, hostile defensiveness of it, or apathy.

Many persons who belong to two groups, in one or both of which he has full membership, face similar conflicts. We have taken as one example of such dual membership American Negroes, for whom there is no escape from membership in the less favored group; delinquent gangs and criminal groups serve as another example of memberships from which it is often difficult to escape. Their conflicts are often rationalized, and are in part to be understood, in terms of their belief that the larger society expects conformity from them while at the same time denying them many of the customary means of achieving it.

THE MINIMIZING OF ROLE CONFLICT

In view of the many different kinds of role demands that each of us faces, you may be wondering how it happens that most of us, most of the time, succeed rather well in avoiding serious conflict even though we are involved in many quite different kinds of role relationships. The fact that a person does something rather well does not necessarily mean, of course, that he understands how he does it, and so we turn to an examination of the conditions under which the pains of potentially contradictory role demands are most successfully minimized.

Role conflict arises not just because of doing different or opposite things in assuming different role relationships—like talking vs. not talking, giving vs. receiving orders, and so on; after all, there is nothing contradictory about carrying out different activities at different times, even within a single role relationship. The crux of the matter lies, rather, in the fact that any role relationship involves at least two persons, each of whom has a set of expectations concerning each of them. Role conflict stems from these expectations—either because role partners have contradictory ones or because those of one partner are unwelcome to the other. Conflict of any kind presupposes being subjected to opposed forces at the same time; if it happens to be difficult or painful to cope with both opposed forces, conflict becomes troublesome. These are the considerations to bear in mind as we try to understand why it is that an individual who is involved in multiple role relationships sometimes finds himself in conflict and sometimes does not; and also to understand some of the ways in which it is possible to circumvent, or at least to minimize, conflict when he does experience it.

Shared Expectations of Differentiated Role Relationships

In our society a man may be living in a household that includes wife, son, daughter and perhaps his brother, sister, or his own or his wife's parents. His role prescriptions for these several relationships are somewhat different, and certain of them—that of being father and husband, for example—are very different indeed. Although instances of conflict among these relationships do occur, relatively few men in our society develop intense or prolonged conflict as they assume these different family roles in rapid succession. Such absence of conflict is for the most part not the result of concealment; a man's quite different behaviors toward different family members are open for all to see. His relative freedom from conflict is, so to speak, guaranteed at the outset because of the ways in which his different positions are defined. His several role relationships are *prescribed* as different; a shared system of norms requires that he maintain different relationships with different family members. Identical relationships with all of them would, in fact, result in more conflict for him than properly differentiated ones because failure to differentiate would violate the shared expectations of other group members.

Thus the general principle is as follows: Insofar as a person shares with various role partners the same normative expectations concerning his own differentiated role relationships with them, the fact that the behavioral relationships are different will not be a source of conflict to him. The principle of substitutability among persons who share the same norms comes into play: "This is what they want me to do, and what each of them would do in my place." Under these conditions, not much conflict is to be expected.

The importance of things that we take for granted—whether fresh air or shared role expectations—is apt to be more fully appreciated when they are absent than when they are present. An American anthropologist, Ruth Benedict (1938), gives a vivid illustration of a pair of parents who did not share a common set of norms with respect to differential treatment, by adults, of children as distinguished from adults. The following incident involves a Mohave Indian father:

> The child's mother was white, and protested to its father that he must take action when the child disobeyed and struck him. "But why?" the

father said, "he is little. He cannot possibly injure me." He did not know of any dichotomy according to which an adult expects obedience and a child must accord it. If his child had been docile he would simply have judged that it would become a docile man—an eventuality of which he would not have approved.

This Mohave father expected no more docility from a child than from a man, whereas his wife did; they did not share a set of differentiated role expectations according to which, with respect to docility, one maintains different role relationships with children and with adults. We would expect, therefore, that each of these parents would experience more conflict in role relationships toward their child than if both had been Mohaves, or both whites of similar backgrounds.

We have so far been discussing shared expectations of differentiated role relationships within the same group, as a condition that minimizes role conflict. Does the same principle apply to persons who face potential conflict because of their membership in different groups that have conflicting norms? Consider adolescents, for example; though they are often "marginal men" in our society, they rather commonly adapt themselves fairly comfortably to quite different sets of norms on the part of peers and of parents concerning their own behavior. Parental norms may prescribe more cleanliness, for example, earlier hours for retirement, or less noisiness than do peer-group norms.

A slight modification of the principle of shared expectations does seem to account for the fact that many adolescents experience only minimal conflict between their roles as members of families and of peer groups. This modification is exemplified in the common adult saying, "Boys will be boys," which implies that there is understanding, though perhaps with less than full approval, of behavior that does not meet adult standards. Insofar as parents make it clear that their own role expectations concerning their adolescent children *include* the latters' conformity with peer-group norms in certain situations, the parents' contribution to their children's role conflict is minimized. And, by the same token, insofar as peer-group norms *include* expectations that individual members will conform to parental norms in certain situations, peer groups serve as only minimal sources of role conflict. A combination of these two conditions suggests the following corollary to the general principle: Membership in different groups whose role prescriptions are opposed to each other involves minimal conflict when the different norms are alike in specifying situations in which one set of role expectations takes precedence over the other. This area of intergroup consensus, if it is effective in minimizing conflict, has the effect of presenting a single set of norms that says, "Everybody expects you to be peer-group-like in these and these situations and to be family-like in those and those. It's like churches and circuses: church people expect you to be rowdy at circuses and sober at church, and so do circus crowds. No sweat."

Selective Association with Resulting Insulation

Perhaps you know of some people who obviously subscribe to norms that are prevalent in our society concerning democracy, neighborliness, and respect for other people's values—but for certain people only, excluding certain class, ethnic, or racial groups. Perhaps such persons are proud members of a religious group that stresses doctrines of the brotherhood of man. Though distinctions between different categories of men may seem inconsistent to others, such persons often reveal no signs of conflict as they maintain quite different role relationships—say toward Negroes and toward whites.

Research Illustration 13.4 indicates that distinctions are indeed made in these ways in our society. In terms of individual psychology, the processes by which such apparently contradictory role relationships are reconciled are sometimes referred to as erecting "logic-tight compartments." In less figurative language, the processes are those of contrasting rather than assimilating different classes of objects in cognitive structuring. Assimilation of different ethnic or racial groups as belonging together (as far as role relationships with their members are concerned) would be consistent with doctrines of the universal brotherhood of man, whereas the contrasting of role relationships appropriate for favored and disfavored groups would not. Since, as we noted in Chapter 5, it is not inconsistent to have different attitudes toward things that do not belong together, this kind of cognitive structuring almost invariably underlines the acceptance without conflict of what seem to other people to be incompatible role relationships.

Such psychological processes are probably necessary conditions for avoiding role conflict of this kind, but from a social-psychological point of view they are not sufficient conditions. We need to inquire also about the environmental conditions—especially those of social interaction—that serve to support and maintain these psychological processes. These conditions almost universally include distinctive ways of interacting with members of more and of less favored groups. The latter are kept at a distance. In terms of two of the dimensions described in Chapter 11, there is little communicative access to them, and considerable status difference between them. One not only associates more frequently and intimately with members of the favored groups, but one also communicates more freely and fully with them. Thus one daily reinforces one's own norms, according to which discriminating role relationships are

Research Illustration 13.4

A study by Kelly, Ferson, and Holtzman (1958) illustrates the extent to which many students in a southern university entertained views that were apparently supported by their association with other churchgoers. More than 500 students, most of them Christians, responded to a scale of attitudes toward Negroes that included twenty-six items like these: "I would not object to participating in athletics with Negroes," "I would not object to dancing with a good Negro dancer." Each response was made on a five-point scale ranging from "strongly agree" through "undecided" to "strongly disagree." An overall attitude score was computed from each student's twenty-six re-

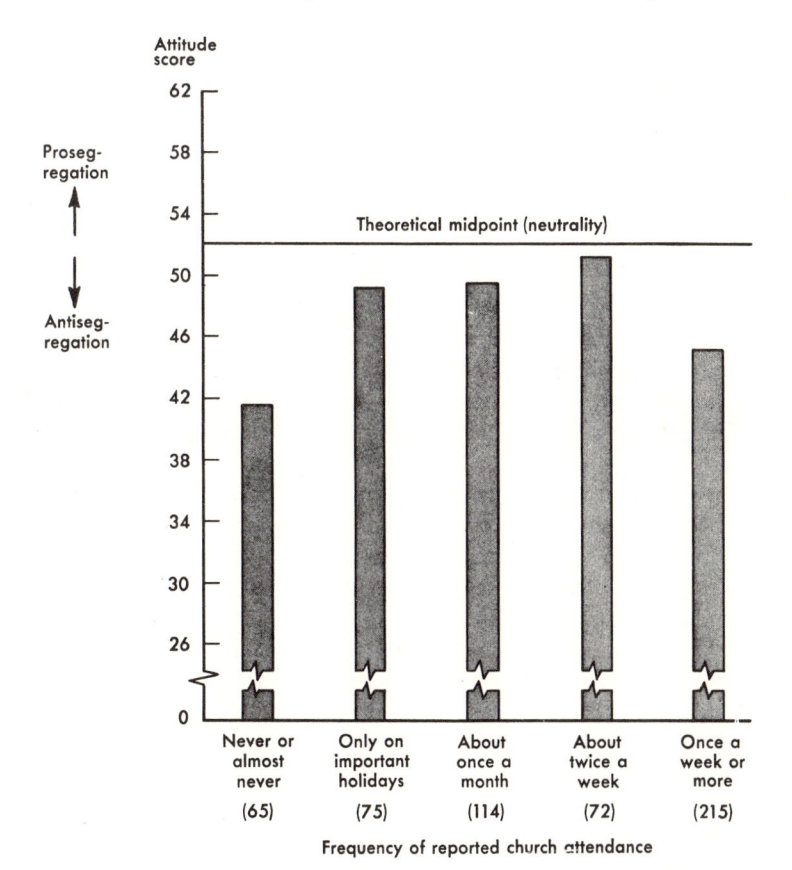

	Never or almost never (65)	Only on important holidays (75)	About once a month (114)	About twice a week (72)	Once a week or more (215)
Attitude score	~41	~49	~49	~51	~45

Frequency of reported church attendance

Proseg-regation ↑
↓ Antiseg-regation

Theoretical midpoint (neutrality) = 52

Mean degree of favoring segregation of Negroes, for categories of students reporting differing frequencies of attending church. Numbers of respondents in each category appear in parentheses.

sponses, in such manner that the higher the score the greater the respondent's intolerance toward Negroes. The same students also responded to a questionnaire about church attendance.

The figure on page 421 shows the relationship (a statistically significant one) between intolerance and reported frequency of church attendance. Those who reported virtually no attendance at all showed most tolerance, whereas reported attendance every other week or so was associated with least tolerance. The reasons for this relationship probably have more to do with the norms of these students' families than with any direct indoctrination during church services. Evidence from other sources indicates that most students agree rather closely with their parents in both religious and racial attitudes. It is also known that adult membership in various religious sects is closely related to social class, to attitudes toward segregation, and to degree of religious involvement. Thus it seems likely that these students shared whole patterns of attitudes with their families and their families' circles—patterns which included norms concerning both segregation and church attendance. Thus the students' own attitude patterns would be consequences of their both interacting with and being influenced by somewhat restricted family and neighborhood circles.

approved and supported, and at the same time insulates oneself against influences that might modify those norms.

The findings reported in Research Illustration 13.4 are not, of course, intended to imply that there is any necessary connection between attendance at Christian churches and racial prejudice. What they do show is that it is possible for faithful adherents of a doctrine that includes the brotherhood of man to accept a set of norms according to which some categories of men are more completely included in the brotherhood than others. The findings also suggest that the social support which church attendants provided for one another helped them to maintain such attitudes, presumably with minimal conflict.

Restricted association and communication within homogeneous groups whose members share the same set of norms is often accompanied by "the illusion of universality" (F. H. Allport, 1924). This phenomenon is well illustrated by the small community studied by Schanck (page 225). If one assumes that "everybody knows" that distinctive kinds of role relationships between different categories of people are appropriate, then one will experience little conflict in making such role distinctions. One form of the illusion of universality is characteristic of highly authoritarian individuals (cf. pages 121–123), for whom "everyone" really means "all those who count." The more authoritarian a person is, the more likely it is that he will limit his reference groups and, if possible, also his membership groups to those who are not only "strong" but also whose norms are "right." Insofar as he is successful in doing so, the universality that he perceives is, for him, not illusory at all—since he never meets anyone who disagrees with him. He is like the little old lady in New England who is reported to have protested, following the presidential election in 1936 in which the Republican candidate carried only two states (Maine and Vermont) that the election could not have been an honest one: "Why, I never even *met* anyone who was not going to vote Republican!" Such insulation is not necessarily associated with authoritarianism, but the effects of authoritarianism are in many ways similar to those of geographic insulation.

Insulating Effects of Barriers between Social Classes

If distinctions are made in any society that tend not only to distinguish between persons and groups in terms of hierarchic levels but also to separate them from one another, we would expect to find that such class distinctions would affect the nature of role conflicts in that society. As *between* different class levels—especially adjacent levels, and especially if there are some possibilities of mobility across class lines—role conflict is likely to be increased by class distinctions, as we shall note in the following chapter. But *within* any class level—especially if there are few opportunities for crossing class lines—there are reasons to expect that role conflict will be minimized. We shall now examine some of the ways in which this occurs.

There are many ways of defining social classes, and many different kinds of data than can be assembled to provide indices of class differences. Nearly all recent studies of the problem in the United States find that indices based on the following criteria are positively, though not perfectly, correlated: income, occupation, education, and area or cost of residence. According to a series of studies by W. L. Warner and his associates (1941, 1949), moreover, all these kinds of class distinctions are closely associated with another kind of distinction with which social psychologists are directly concerned: frequency of association and interaction.[1]

Adopting, for our purposes, the criterion of the ways in which people actually associate with one another, we may think in terms of *social distance*, which is considered to be close when people associate freely with one another, or would feel free to do so, and remote when they do not. Warner's findings indicate that individuals between whom there is little social distance may be considered to belong to the same social

[1] Most of Warner's data were obtained during the 1930s and 1940s; it is possible that more recently class distinctions in this country are less conspicuous. Our present concern is not with present-day facts about social classes in America, but with the ways in which class distinctions at any time or in any society affect social interaction.

class, since freely associating persons tend to be similar by the other criteria of class membership (income, occupational and educational level, and so on). Figure 13.2 illustrates this neatly; it shows that actual membership in the organizations listed, in a midwestern town studied by Warner, tends to be concentrated among people at a single class level, or in two adjacent ones. Since membership in such organizations necessarily involves association and interaction among members, it is clear that in this community there was a good deal more interaction within a limited range of class levels than across high and low levels.

Warner's methods of assigning individuals to one or another social class are based on intensive interviewing of a wide range of people from the same community. People from gold coast and slum, as well as from sections intermediate in wealth, are asked about persons with whom they associate freely and about those with whom they do not, and why. Respondents' use of such phrases as "top crowd" or "slum folks" often point to barriers of a higher-lower nature that prevent free association. After interviewing a sizable proportion of members of a community that is not too large, it becomes possible to identify groups within which there is much but between which there is little free association. The higher-lower relationship between groups of freely associating people can usually be ascertained with considerable certainty. This is possible because a set of freely associating individuals (tentatively identified as "lower middle," for example) are in general agreement that they are "lower in the scale" than another set of freely associating individuals who, in turn, designate themselves as "higher in the scale" than the former. The method, in sum, is basically that of across-class consensus concerning association and higher-lower barriers to it.

There can be little doubt that—except perhaps in the smallest and newest of American communities—the everyday lives of Americans of different social classes (by almost any of the criteria that we have mentioned) differ in many ways. Not only do they have different kinds of housing in different parts of town and different kinds of jobs with different incomes, but they show many other differences that are associated with these higher-lower distinctions. Their recreational preferences are typically different; they have different patterns of reading books, magazines, and newspapers and of selecting television programs. Their religious memberships, beliefs, and practices differ, except at immediately adjacent class levels, and they rarely worship together. Their attitudes toward many public issues differ considerably, and they tend to prefer different kinds of food and drink.

In addition to these and other typical differences among adults, their children are trained in different ways. One such difference is summarized in a review of many studies during the 1930s, 1940s, and 1950s, as follows: "We have clear confirmation that, over the entire 25-year

	Upper	Upper-middle	Lower-middle	Upper-lower	Lower-lower
Monday club	50%	50%			
Rotary	16.7%	80.6%		2.7%	
D.A.R.	57.1%	14.3%	28.6%		
Hospital aide	51.6%	32.8%	15.6%		
Country club	29.9%	27.8%	42.3%		
Masons	14.7%	19%	65.3%		
Lions	4.8%	23.8%	71.4%		
Odd fellows	2.2%	20%	42.2%	35.6%	
American legion auxiliary	1.6%	11.1%	63.5%	22.2%	1.6%
Eastern star		8.3%	91.7%		
Girl scout mothers		9.3%	50%	35.2%	5.5%
Royal neighbors			69%	28.2%	2.8%
Polish national alliance			8.3%	83.4%	8.3%
Free methodists				100%	
Gospel tabernacle				87.5%	12.5%

FIGURE 13.2. Class distributions of selected associations. The size of membership in each case is indicated by the shaded areas. (From Warner *et al.*, 1949)

period, middle-class parents have had a more acceptant, equalitarian relationship [than have working-class parents] with their children" (Bronfenbrenner, 1958). And, finally, because of different interests, different resources, different ambitions, and restricted associations, people tend to marry at or near their own class levels. Thus class distinctions tend to be maintained as distinctive ways of living are acquired by another generation.

Class distinctions, like other sources of restricted association, often serve to reduce role conflict, but there is nothing inevitable about this consequence. The more nearly class barriers have the effect of total insulation, the more probably they will be conflict-reducing for the individuals within each class, because within the insulating walls there is apt to be considerable homogeneity of norms and role expectations. At the same time, however, such barriers potentially invite more intense interclass conflict. The classic but now waning caste system in India is a good illustration. The walls themselves are apt to invite inspection, and as it becomes obvious to the people inside them that they bar the way to privileges regarded as part of a better life, the barriers come to enhance rather than to reduce role conflict.

OVERVIEW

Problems of role adaptation arise when an individual is confronted with role prescriptions that are personally unwelcome; when the nature of the demands is either unclear to him or too complex and overburdensome; and when different sets of demands are mutually contradictory. The goodness of the fit between his own personal characteristics and the demands of his role assignments depends in large part on his own willingness and capacity to learn what the prescriptions are and how to adapt to them, as well as on the objective nature of the role system to which he is expected to adapt. An understanding of this system can sometimes make it possible to change it.

Actual conflict between different role demands may arise from contradictory demands on the part of different members of a single group of which one is a member, but serious and continued conflict is more commonly a result of simultaneous membership in different groups. Borderline membership in two groups is considered marginal if it results in one's being a full member of neither. The consequences of marginality are especially difficult to bear when one membership group is more privileged than the other and when, at the same time, it is impossible to escape from the less attractive one. Even when marginality is only temporary, as in the case of adolescents who are in the midst of "escaping" from childhood into adulthood, its consequences often pervade many areas of behavior, attitudes, and personality.

Dual membership in society-at-large and in smaller groups from which it is difficult to escape may have similar consequences. The nature of such dual membership is different from that of marginality, however, since most Negroes and gang delinquents, for example, have full membership in the smaller if not in the larger group, whereas marginals have full membership in neither group. Both the sources of conflict and the means of coping with it, in the case of such dual memberships, include feelings on the part of members of minority and of nonconforming groups that they are expected to comply with the norms of the larger society without having access to the means of doing so.

Multiple role relationships on the part of the same individual involve minimal conflict for him to the extent that he shares expectations with different role partners that he will maintain distinctive kinds of relationships with them. Conflict is thus minimized by the fact of group support for what might otherwise be incompatible ways of behaving. If different groups are in disagreement about the propriety of behaving in one way toward some people and in other ways toward others, conflict can be minimized by limiting one's associations and one's reference groups to those from which one can find group support for one's own distinctions among different role relationships. Insofar as social-class barriers result in insulation of class groups from one another, so that each group lives within a homogeneous world of consensual role expectations, conflict may be reduced. In today's world of increasing mobility and ready availability of mass communications, however, barriers among social classes are becoming increasingly permeable, so that in the long run class distinctions are likely to increase rather than to reduce the intensity of role conflict.

CHAPTER 14

Intergroup Conflict

IF IN ANY SOCIETY IT IS A GENERAL PRACTICE TO LABEL INDIVIDUALS ON the basis of their membership in ethnic, religious, or other groups, it is altogether likely that there are correspondingly widespread attitudes on the part of those sets of people toward one another. Research Illustration 14.1 provides a case in point. As this and many other comparable sets of data show, the attitudes of white Americans toward various national and ethnic groups are marked by sharp distinctions. Although the degree of favor and disfavor they show toward particular groups varies from region to region, and to a lesser extent from generation to generation, the order of preference is remarkably constant. Insofar as members of one group communicate to one another their similar attitudes toward other groups, they become aware of their similarities, and those attitudes are shared.

In this chapter we shall be concerned not with distributions of group members' different attitudes toward other groups, but with shared attitudes within groups; not with all shared attitudes but primarily with those that represent antagonism, hostility, and prejudice; and in particular with ethnic prejudice, research data concerning which are relatively abundant. We shall attempt not only to show how shared attitudes of antagonism are maintained through interaction within groups, but also to point to the conditions under which prejudice and hostility are expressed in action between groups, sometimes violently. And, as a further

Research Illustration 14.1

A few years after the conclusion of World War II, Prothro and Miles (1953) administered an attitude scale to five hundred middle-class adults from thirty towns and cities in Louisiana, Mississippi, Alabama, and Georgia. Each person was asked to indicate the degree of social distance that he felt toward seventeen recognized groups. The scale was a revision of the original Bogardus scale (1925) and included the following statements, which had been constructed by the method of equal-appearing intervals (see Appendix A).

1. I would accept a member of this group as my husband (or wife).
2. I would accept a member of this group as a personal chum in my club.
3. I would accept a member of this group as one of my business friends.
4. I would share a taxi with a member of this group.
5. I would accept a member of this group as a house servant.
6. I would grant citizenship only to members of this group who adopt our customs and mores.

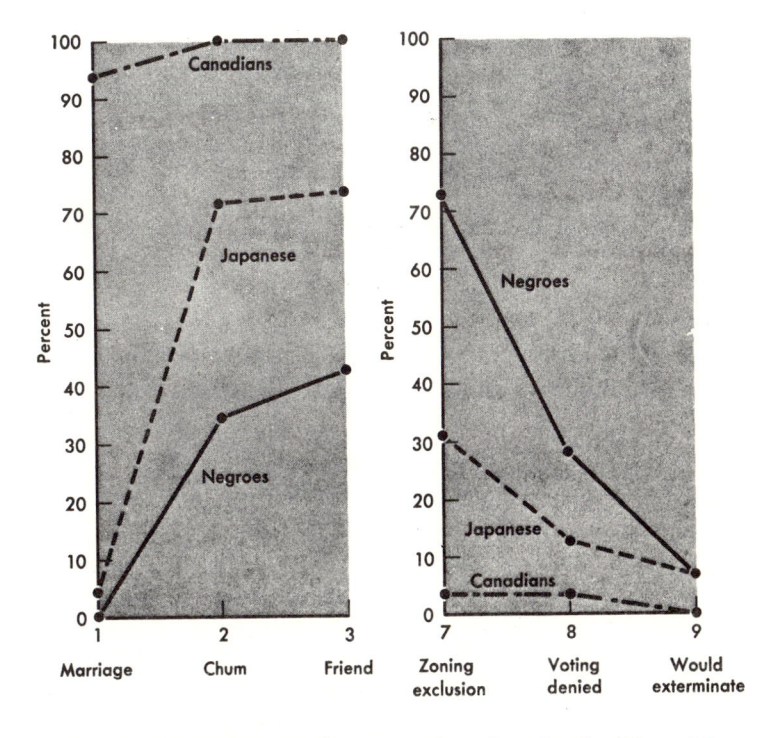

Percentages of 500 white Southerners making three kinds of favorable and three kinds of unfavorable responses to three selected ethnic groups

7. I would eliminate members of this group from my neighborhood by zoning laws.
8. I would prohibit members of this group from voting.
9. I would exterminate all members of this group.

The figure on page 429 shows percentages of responses to the three items at each end of the scale, with respect to three selected ethnic groups (responses to the middle three items are about the same for all three groups). Attitudes toward Canadians are representative of those toward English, French, Germans, and white Americans; those toward Japanese closely resemble those toward Chinese and Hindus; there was little distinction between Negroes and mulattoes; other ethnic groups fell between the first and second of these sets of ethnic groups. Thus, in general, preference was shown for North European groups, with South Europeans, Orientals, and "African" groups following in that order.

When an over-all rank was computed for each group and compared with the rank order reported by Bogardus in 1928, it was found that there was a fairly high correlation between the rankings (.84), despite the fact that more than twenty years had elapsed since the original responses had been made by quite different populations in other areas of the United States. The consistency of the order of preference within this southern region of the United States is shown by the fact that the correlation between respondents from Louisiana and from the tristate area of Mississippi, Alabama, and Georgia was +.98.

way of gaining understanding about the place of interaction in group conflict, we shall consider some of the ways in which hostilities may be reduced.

PERSONAL AND SHARED BASES OF PREJUDICE

The term "prejudice" is sometimes used to refer to any kind of prejudgment. This usage would suggest that we are all prejudiced in favor of our friends and our preferred membership groups. To avoid this kind of interpretation we shall use the term in the more limited and usual sense of "prejudice against." A prejudice is thus an unfavorable attitude, and may be thought of as a predisposition to perceive, think, feel, and act in ways that are "against" or "away from" rather than "for" or "toward" other persons, especially as members of groups.

Prejudice is not an all-or-none affair but includes the entire range of attitudes shown in the right-hand half of Figure 14.1. Attitudes of prejudice toward others differ from favorable attitudes in two principal

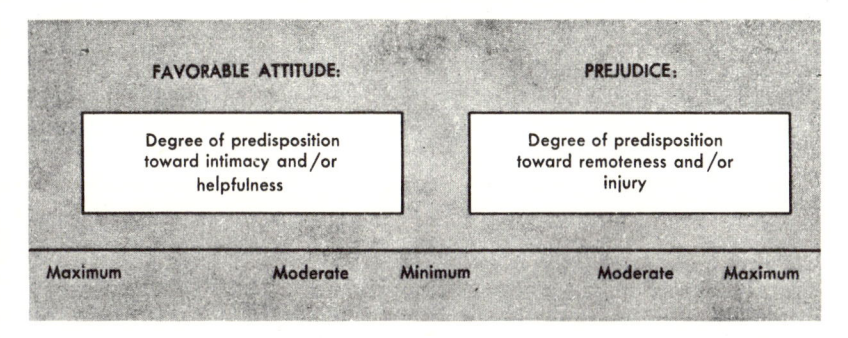

FIGURE 14.1. Schematic illustration of the concept of prejudice as the unfavorable half of an attitude continuum

respects: they involve the tendency to keep people at a distance rather than to have close relations with them, and the tendency to injure rather than to help them. Although these two tendencies often go together, this is not always the case. For this reason prejudice often includes varying and often unknown combinations of these two tendencies. We shall limit ourselves in this chapter to prejudice toward groups or toward individuals as representatives of groups. The primary focus is not on the individual characteristics of the outgroup as a basis for prejudice but on the prejudice that arises when individuals are not distinguished from one another and are placed together in a category that is unfavorably regarded.

Prejudice against Groups as an Acquired Attitude

THE GENERAL NATURE OF THE EVIDENCE. Very few informed persons hold the belief that there is a specific "instinct" to feel hostility toward members of specified groups. Yet we must be clear as to the reasons for concluding that group prejudice is *acquired* by individuals in the course of interacting with other persons.

One of the few generalizations that can be made about "human nature" is that normal human beings are capable of learning from their environment. This basic capacity has no inherent direction; what "kind" of learning will take place is primarily an environmental matter: whether a person learns tolerance or prejudice toward a group of persons depends on a variety of environmental circumstances. Whatever a person's tendencies to feel hostile in general, he does not direct hostility toward any particular person or group until he has learned to do so, as we would expect in view of the acquired nature of motives and attitudes. On theoretical grounds alone, therefore, we should expect that any specific example of prejudice would have to be learned. In short, the capacity for learning to be hostile is present early in life (perhaps in different degrees on the part of different persons), but whether prejudice against a given group is actually learned depends on whether or not circumstances make such learning likely.

In support of this theoretical position it can be shown that young children the world over play indiscriminately with children of other ethnic groups. Prejudice comes with further learning opportunities as they grow older. It might be objected that children of three or four show no prejudice only because they cannot yet discriminate between such groups as whites, Negroes, and Chinese. This objection must be rejected: infants a few months old can distinguish between persons, even when those persons are in the *same* ethnic group; and, judging from findings reported by Clark and Clark (1947), nearly all Negro children as young as three distinguish accurately between Negro and white dolls. Despite this, very young children show no prejudice against other ethnic groups.

If learning is the basis for prejudice, we should expect to find some fairly systematic teaching process at work in groups where prejudice is common. This is precisely what is found, although the teaching may be of a very informal nature. Horowitz and Horowitz (1938) interviewed most of the young white children in a southern community concerning their attitudes and behavior toward Negroes. They found that teaching went on in both subtle and explicit ways. The younger children, either because they were less inhibited or because the events were closer in time, were more apt to mention specific instances of being punished for not maintaining the proper distance toward Negro children. But many children were scarcely aware of the more subtle means employed, and the older children had either forgotten or preferred not to discuss the disciplinary methods employed by their parents.

Still another line of evidence supports the conclusion that the directing of prejudice toward specific groups is learned. It has been found in study after study that children raised in one culture usually develop very little prejudice toward certain particular groups, whereas children in other societies commonly develop considerable prejudice toward specified groups. French, Scandinavian, and Russian children, for example, develop little prejudice toward those with colored skin but generation after generation of white children in South Africa develop strong prejudices against Negroes. Such geographic variations in prejudice are hard to account for in terms of "instinctive" behavior. And so we conclude that although all children have the capacity to develop prejudice, some of them acquire it more readily than others and all must learn what groups to select as targets.

PROCESSES OF LEARNING TO MAKE DISTINCTIONS. For some persons the differences between Jews and gentiles or Negroes and whites are quite important; others do not appear to notice any difference. A few years ago many Americans neither knew nor cared about the distinctions among Koreans, Chinese, and Japanese. The march of world events has since led many Americans to make these distinctions. Learning to notice such differences between groups is one of the steps involved in the process of developing a prejudice. Evidence that the ability to distinguish between groups is more highly developed in persons who are known to have considerable prejudice appears in Research Illustration 14.2. If prejudice is habitually related to the making of distinctions between groups of persons, this is exactly what we would expect. The findings of this study are consistent with the commonsense observation that it makes little difference to persons who have no prejudice against Jews whether another person is Jewish or not, and so they do not have much incentive to learn to tell the difference. The prejudiced person appears to be particularly vigilant or alert to stimuli that will permit him to make such distinctions. Since he tends to regard Jews as a threat, he is motivated to make proper identification, and obtains the practice that makes for greater accuracy. The fact that prejudiced persons label more subjects of photographs as Jewish than do the nonprejudiced may be thought of as an attempt to come to grips with a possibly threatening situation. The prejudiced person has a set of responses he can utilize in his defense once a person is identified as a Jew. It is the unidentified Jew that represents the greater threat. Classifying as Jews persons who are in a doubtful category amounts to "playing it safe" from the prejudiced person's point of view; hence the tendency to label more persons as Jews. These interpretations are in keeping with the theoretical position that any attitude includes a predisposition to perceive things in ways appropriate to that attitude. Learning plays a very important part, of course, in acquiring such perceptual predispositions.

One aspect of learning to be prejudiced, in many societies, is a direct consequence of observing socially enforced differences between groups. Thus compulsory segregation of Negroes is a way of calling color differences to a child's attention, without even discussing the issue. If the growing child finds that segregation is practiced in certain areas in housing, hospitals, and eating establishments, these ethnic differences are forcibly called to his attention. And if Negroes who commit crimes are referred to in the press as Negroes while whites who commit crimes are not identified as white, a kind of selective perception is encouraged that works to the disadvantage of the Negro.

Perhaps one of the most effective ways of bringing ethnic distinctions forcibly to the attention of children is through the application of a double standard in determining what constitutes proper behavior toward others. The child may learn that it is not proper to cheat, lie to, or make disparaging comments concerning members of his own groups

Research Illustration 14.2

Lindzey and Rogolsky (1950) selected from the yearbook of a large state university approximately 200 photographs of male undergraduate students. Half of these students were members of Jewish organizations and half belonged to organizations known to exclude Jews. A group of judges rated separately the pictures of Jewish and non-Jewish students in terms of how Jewish-looking they were. The judges' ratings made it possible to select ten pictures from each group in such a way that the pictures represented different degrees of Jewish appearance. The pictures were projected on a large screen, and more than 600 students from two eastern colleges were asked to identify the photographs as Jewish, non-Jewish, or to indicate that they did not know. They were also asked to indicate, on a four-point scale, how much certainty they felt in making these judgments. Following this they filled out a standard scale of prejudice, and anti-Semitism scores were computed for each person.

The responses of the more anti-Semitic and the less anti-Semitic students who themselves were not Jewish differed in several important ways. Those high in anti-Semitism were somewhat more accurate in identifying Jewish and non-Jewish photographs; they labeled many more faces as Jewish than did those low in prejudice; and they were very much more confident of their judgments of Jewish and non-Jewish faces. All these differences are significant at or beyond the .05 level.

but that these forms of behavior are acceptable when dealing with certain ethnic groups. The observant child thus learns that such people are "outsiders" who are not entitled to the same standards of good treatment that apply to "insiders." Acts of prejudice are facilitated by also learning that outsiders can be treated, without disapproval, in ways that would bring punishment if applied to members of one's own group. The outsiders thus become relatively safe targets for prejudicial behavior. Where the outsiders are perceived as a positive or a potential threat to one's own group, such prejudicial behavior often comes to be defended as a means of self-protection.

Prejudice against Outgroups as Shared by Ingroup Members

Prejudice is typically learned through processes of interacting with members of one's own groups; after all, these provide the loci of most interaction. Hence we shall emphasize that both kinds of learning—that a particular group is a "fair target" and that certain kinds of behavior toward its members are approved by one's own groups—consist in large part of internalizing the social norms of one's own groups.

PREVALENT NORMS CONCERNING ETHNIC GROUPS IN AMERICA. As we noted at the beginning of this chapter, the preferences of Americans for various ethnic groups, expressed in average tendencies, are remarkably widespread and stable. Not only do they vary only slightly, geographically, but they have undergone only moderate change over a period of many years. Ever since Bogardus started to use his social-distance scale, similar responses have been obtained by scores of investigators from hundreds of groups. Aside from the fact that any particular group has a tendency to place itself at the top, members of various ethnic groups are inclined to place other groups in about the same order.

There must be a reason for this stability in attitudes toward others. It suggests that there may be a set of widely distributed group norms that result in highly similar responses as we go from group to group—except, of course, when a group describes its own position. Even in this latter case, however, there is accumulating evidence that members of the less-favored groups are not entirely uninfluenced by widely shared norms, even when the norms apply to their own group. Thus Bayton (1941) found that Negro college students possessed stereotypes concerning Negroes that were surprisingly similar to those found among white students from Princeton. For example, although Negroes avoided the terms "lazy" and "ignorant," which had been frequently applied by Princeton students, the five adjectives they applied most frequently to their own group were "superstitious," "very religious," "musical," "happy-go-lucky," and "loud." To a certain extent these Negro subjects subscribed to the same norms concerning Negroes as did white subjects. Similarly, Engel and associates (1958) have found that a group of Jewish college students, members of their own campus religious organization, showed many of the same kinds of negative attitudes toward their own ethnic group that are commonly found among prejudiced gentiles.

One reason why the order of preference for various ethnic groups in America is so nearly standard is that there is a more or less closely corresponding order of privilege. The more privileged groups—which are not always majority groups—tend to set the standards by which the various groups are judged. Such deprivation often leads persons to be, in part at least, ashamed of their group membership and to be attracted to the symbols associated with groups in which they are denied membership. These standards come to be widely accepted, even to the extent that some members of groups low in the order of preference accept the general verdict concerning their own groups. They are acquired through adopting the norms of the larger or more privileged-groups, with whose members they interact more or less frequently and who serve as attractive reference groups.

PERSONAL CONTACT AS A FACTOR IN PREJUDICE. Most of us like to feel that we have arrived at our own attitudes independently of others. Prejudiced persons are no exception, and they are reluctant to believe that they are merely reflecting the attitudes of others when they emphasize distinctions between ethnic groups. When questioned about their beliefs, prejudiced persons often cite some unfortunate experience with a member of the minority group to prove the point. There is little doubt that such incidents occur, but there are strong reasons for doubting that they create the unfavorable attitudes or even play the most important part in their development.

One reason for doubting the importance of personal incidents as major sources of prejudice is the fact that degree of prejudice against various groups is not correlated with opportunity for contact with them. It has been shown in a number of studies that the groups against which college students have the greatest prejudice include *both* those with whom they have much contact and those with whom they have little contact. The same can be said about groups for whom they have the least prejudice. For at least thirty years quite diverse American groups have consistently expressed the least social distance toward Canadians and English, who are relatively familiar, and toward French and Norwegians, who are less familiar. With similar consistency, persons in all parts of the country have expressed the greatest social distance toward Turks, who are relatively unfamiliar to most, and toward Negroes, who are familiar to nearly all. These facts make it difficult to attribute either favorable or unfavorable attitudes to firsthand contact or to the lack of such contact.

Another reason for doubting that personal contact is essential in the development of prejudice stems from the fact that people have selective perception and selective memories. A person tends to note and to remember those contacts with an individual that confirm a prejudice he already has against the group to which that individual belongs. And a person tends to forget those instances in which a member of the group did not behave in such a way as to confirm his prejudices. In this way selective perception and memory serve to verify a preexisting attitude toward another group. Psychiatrists as well as psychologists have often observed that such distortions are particularly common in those areas of our lives characterized by sensitivity to threat and where hostility arises as a defense against it.

Yet a third reason for suspecting that personal contact is not a main ingredient in the development of prejudice is that persons who have prejudices against one minority group are predisposed to have prejudices against others. For example, Lindzey and Rogolsky (Research Illustration 14.2) found that if a person is prejudiced against Jews, he is likely also to be prejudiced against Catholics and Negroes. They interpret this to mean that in accounting for prejudice we should place more emphasis on the behavior and characteristics of prejudiced persons and less on the behavior of the minority group. This conclusion is consistent with the belief that contact with minority group members is not usually the basis for prejudice.

UNDESIRABLE CHARACTERISTICS AS AN ALLEGED BASIS FOR PREJUDICE. Although we have indicated that personal contact is not usually an important factor in the development of prejudice, we have avoided the question as to whether there may be some truth to such beliefs as that Jews are shrewd bargainers and that Negroes are often ignorant. By the standards of middle-class Americans who are not Jews or Negroes there is often a certain amount of truth to these descriptions. Prejudiced persons, however, are apt to regard such tendencies as biologically determined, and to underestimate the degree to which they are the result of social environments and group norms. A prejudiced person is also likely to forget that the environment of a specific disliked group may be restricted by the pressures of members of his own group—for example, by making it difficult for members of underprivileged groups to obtain adequate housing or adequate schooling.

When a person insists that disliked traits are *inherent and unchangeable,* he may be rationalizing his own feelings of threat and hostility. The readily available stereotypes, which are part of the norms of his group, make it easy for such a person to perceive differences he believes to exist. The acceptance of these views by other members of his group protects him from the realization that he is rationalizing or being defensive in his attitudes. In the context of the group norms, the prejudiced person learns to interpret many differences between his own group and the outgroup as opportunities for invidious comparisons. He comes to have little use for the notion that there can be group situations in which "differences make no difference."

PREJUDICE AS INCLUDED IN ROLE PRESCRIPTIONS. Such considerations point to a major source of prejudice against groups: with certain exceptions to be noted later, most prejudices against other groups are shared within one's own group. In fact, they are generally prescribed by one's own group norms. Prejudiced behavior is permitted, or perhaps even prescribed in the role relationships between one's own and certain other groups. If so, group norms stipulate that members shall maintain relationships of avoidance, or even outright hostility, toward members of the outgroup, and shall express to one another attitudes consistent with such outgroup relationships.

Support for this point of view is to be found by studying the development of prejudice with increasing age. One of the most revealing of such studies is summarized in Research Illustration 14.3. It is quite evident that the three tests used by Horowitz show the development of quite different levels of prejudice. The *Ranks* test may represent little more than sheer ability to discriminate; at any rate it represents no more than a general preference for white faces that is apparently well estab-

Research Illustration 14.3

Horowitz (1936), in a developmental study of white children's attitudes toward Negroes, used three measures of prejudice. Several groups of boys, some northern and some southern, were tested at every age from five through fourteen. Two of these tests made use of photographs of the faces of four white and eight Negro boys that had been carefully selected to make sure that all faces were "racially typical" and "generally pleasant." In the *Ranks* test, boys were simply asked to pick out "The one you like best, next best, next best," and so on until all twelve faces had been picked. The greater the degree of preference for white faces, the greater the prejudice score. In the *Show Me* test, the boys were asked to select as many of the faces as they wanted, as companions for a variety of imagined situations: "Show me all those that you want to sit next to you on a street car . . . that you would want to play ball with," and so on through a number of situations. Again, the greater the percentage of white faces chosen, the greater the prejudice score.

The *Social Situations* test was designed to find out how frequently white boys would refuse participation in an activity because of the presence of a Negro boy. Fifteen posed situations were photographed twice. One of the photos showed four white boys and another was identical except that a Negro boy replaced one of the white boys. The photographed situations included playing marbles, choosing sides for baseball, eating dinner at home, and so on. Each boy could answer either yes or no when asked whether he wanted "to join in with them and do what they're doing along with them." The greater the frequency with which the boys chose to participate exclusively with the white groups, the greater the prejudice score.

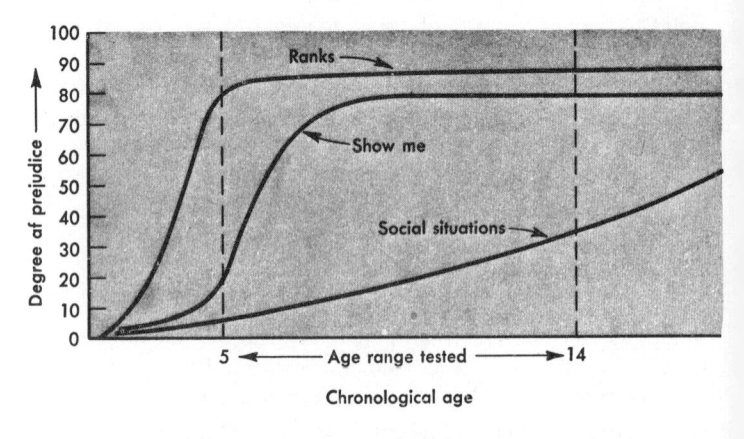

Theoretical (smoothed) curves showing increase of prejudice with age, according to each of three tests

In the accompanying figure we can observe the development of prejudice from ages five to fourteen. For the *Ranks* test, the youngest boys already showed almost as much prejudice as the oldest. For the *Show Me* test, there is a sharp increase between five and eight or nine years of age but no increase after that. But for the *Social Situations* test, there was virtually no prejudice at age five and only a slow and gradual increase up to age fourteen.

lished in practically all boys by the age of five. The *Show Me* test represents, in addition to mere general preference, the presence or absence of willingness to have Negro boys join in with white boys in attractive activities. This test thus provides more opportunity for actual exclusion of Negroes, and attitudes of exclusion apparently develop a little later than attitudes of general preference. The *Social Situations* test affords still more definite opportunities for exclusion. It is more of a definite yes-or-no test, and also one in which the sheer attractiveness of the activity might easily outweigh mildly unfavorable attitudes toward Negroes. Prejudice strong enough to outweigh such activities was found to be almost nonexistent in the younger boys, and increased very slowly with age.

To the question, then, of how prejudice develops with age, Horowitz's data suggest quite clearly that its development is gradual. It is also clear that there is no single answer to the question of how early or how late it develops, since the rate of development depends on the competing attractions of specific situations. In general, however, the older the boy, the fewer the situations attractive enough to overcome the preference to avoid Negro boys.

Horowitz's data also provide an answer to the question as to how important personal contact is in the development of these attitudes. He found that children in the North and in the South, in mixed schools and in all-white schools, showed the same course in developing attitudes toward Negroes. The three tests showed no differences between these groups of boys, despite the fact that the opportunity for contact with Negroes was quite different in these situations. Even a comparison of boys from urban and rural areas turned up no difference. What these findings mean is that the amount of a child's daily contact with Negroes has little to do with the development of his prejudice as measured by these three tests (which, of course, did not take account of some of the issues that divide adults on such matters as civil rights). As a result of these and other findings it seems fair to conclude that emerging attitudes toward Negroes are "now chiefly determined not by contact with Negroes, but by contact with the prevalent attitude toward Negroes."

We may thus conclude that such prejudices develop insofar as they are included in the role prescriptions common to all members of the group—regardless of the nature of one's personal contacts with Negroes.

This conclusion is further supported by Horowitz's findings concerning a group of children of Communist parents. (During these years of economic depression there were groups of avowed Communists in many American cities.) These children showed, in general, no prejudice at all —in fact, some slight "negative prejudice." The fact that distinguished them from other boys was that they and their parents belonged to left-wing groups in which it was a cardinal point not to indulge in prejudice on racial grounds. Thus the one group whose norms specifically prescribed "no prejudice" was the one group among which prejudice was not found. Prejudice, or lack of it, can thus be related to role prescription much more easily than it can be related to personal contact.

Personality Variables Affect Susceptibility to Prejudice

Despite the tremendous importance of social norms, it is not always possible to predict an individual's attitude toward an ethnic group merely from a knowledge of his group memberships. The highly individual tendencies referred to as "personality factors" also have a part to play in determining one's attitudes toward these groups.

AUTHORITARIANISM AS A PERVASIVE PERSONALITY CHARACTERISTIC. A central hypothesis of *The Authoritarian Personality* was that individuals are most receptive to ideologies that are most compatible with their over-all personality structures (cf. Research Illustration 5.1, page 122). If a person is highly receptive to antidemocratic ideologies, such as anti-Semitism and ethnocentrism, it is possible that the reason is that they express pervasive personality characteristics predisposing him to acquire prejudiced attitudes. The early work of Adorno *et al.* provided a good deal of support for this hypothesis. They also found evidence that the major factors influencing such personality development arise in the course of child training as carried forward in a family setting.

Typical of later studies that have tried to relate authoritarian tendencies to child-rearing practices is a study by Hart (1957). He interviewed 126 mothers of preschool children to determine what kind of decisions they made in a number of critical problem areas involving feeding, cleanliness, toilet training, sex, aggression, dependence, and so on. When the mothers had indicated how they handled problems in these areas, independent raters were asked to classify the answers into three categories as "love-oriented," "nonlove-oriented," or "ambiguous." It was found that the mothers' scores of authoritarianism were inversely related to the numbers of love-oriented responses they reported: the fewer such responses, the more authoritarian they tended to be.

The assumptions of *The Authoritarian Personality* are that highly authoritarian persons have been subjected to strict parental control, that as children they have learned to acquiesce in this authoritarian control and to depend on it, and that they retain some resentment (often without recognizing or accepting it) against such control, which is expressed in the form of hostility toward those who can be safely attacked. Hart's study is consistent with these assumptions in showing that authoritarian parents quite consistently adopt child-rearing practices that are likely to bring about the tendencies described by Adorno *et al.* Further careful work in this area will be necessary before it can be said that the relationship has been established beyond question.

The Interplay of Personality and Group Norms

We have noted two conditions under which individuals are likely to show prejudice against ethnic groups: membership in a sector of society whose norms prescribe prejudice toward specified groups; and a high degree of authoritarianism. We shall now inquire whether both or either of these conditions, alone, increases the likelihood of being prejudiced, and whether a combination of both conditions increases that likelihood.

Pettigrew's findings, as reported in Research Illustration 14.4, show very little difference in authoritarianism between northern and southern adults in the United States, or between students in this country and in the Republic of South Africa, in spite of large differences in anti-Negro attitudes. According to this study and others, there are many individuals in societies whose norms prescribe unfavorable attitudes toward Negroes who accept those norms without being authoritarian in personality. It seems clear that cultural norms alone constitute a *sufficient* condition for the development of prejudice on the part of most individuals who share the culture; thus authoritarianism is not a *necessary* condition for its development.

It could be, however, that either authoritarianism or normativeness, alone, is a sufficient condition for developing prejudice without being a necessary one. Presently available evidence suggests that some kind and degree of normativeness are *both* necessary and sufficient; if so, then authoritarianism is *neither* necessary nor sufficient but serves, rather, to make more likely or more intense the development of prejudice under the necessary conditions of normativeness. We shall now indicate just why this appears to be the case.

If any of the several characteristics of authoritarianism is central to the others, it is the combination of submissiveness to power and authority together with condescension toward weakness. Adorno *et al.* de-

Research Illustration 14.4

In an attempt to distinguish between the effects of culturally shared norms and those of authoritarian personality on unfavorable attitudes toward Negroes, Pettigrew (1958) conducted two parallel studies. The first of these was based on responses by more than 600 students (about one third of the all-white student body) at a university in the (then) Union of South Africa. As might be expected in a country that supports and legalizes a policy of apartheid, their responses showed "unusually prejudiced attitudes concerning Africans"; for example, more than 75 percent of them agreed with this statement: "Because of his immaturity, the South African native is likely to be led into all kinds of mischief and should therefore be strictly controlled in his own best interests." In addition to a list of items used to measure attitudes toward native Africans, Pettigrew obtained responses from which authoritarianism was measured.

Three important findings emerged. First, degree of prejudice was related to authoritarianism to about the same degree as repeatedly found among students in America; the correlation is about .50. Second, prejudice was particularly marked on the part of those students who identified themselves as Afrikaners (who by language, ethnic background, and political affiliation "are directly subject to the national ethos and have no conflicting national reference") as compared with students identified as "English." Third, the Afrikaners, although more prejudiced, as a group were no more authoritarian than the English students, as shown by several detailed analyses. Neither, as a matter of fact, was the total population of South African students more authoritarian than students in American colleges. In sum, *within* the South African student population, as within similar populations in America, prejudice and authoritarianism go together; but comparisons *between* South African and American students show that prejudice in one country is higher than in the other, although authoritarianism does not differ in the two countries.

Pettigrew's second study also compared groups having different cultural backgrounds: samples of adults in four southern and four northern communities in the United States were interviewed. These findings very closely paralleled those from South Africa. That is, southern respondents' attitudes toward Negroes were much less favorable than those of northern respondents, but the two populations did not differ in authoritarianism. These similar findings from two comparisons, in two remote countries, strongly support the conclusion that, although differing cultural levels of prejudice are not accompanied by different levels of authoritarianism, within a single culture prejudice and authoritarianism are positively correlated.

scribe this tendency in many ways; as applied to the problem of prejudice, the following quotation is typical:

> a political philosophy and social outlook which has no room for anything but a desperate clinging to what appears to be strong, and disdainful rejection of whatever is relegated to the bottom [and which] extends . . . to a dichotomous handling of social relationships, as manifested especially in the formation of stereotypes and of ingroup-outgroup cleavages (p. 971).

A person in whom such characteristics are pronounced needs to distinguish between strong, superior groups and weak, inferior ones, just as anti-Semites need to be sensitive to cues of Jewishness. Such a person looks to the norms of his own groups for support in making this distinction. If he lives in a society that rank-orders ethnic groups in a rather definite manner (as reported by Bogardus and many others in this country, for example), then he is familiar with norms that tell him who the "bottom" groups are. In a sense, therefore, he shares widespread prejudices within his own culture, but he does so with an intensity and a rigidity that distinguish him from his less authoritarian compatriots.

* * *

Group norms thus provide the targets for prejudice, but authoritarianism provides the dynamics of extreme intensity. This two-factor explanation accounts pretty well for all the following phenomena that have been observed.

1. Comparisons of different societies show that those which differ in degree of prejudice against the same group may not differ in general level of authoritarianism. In some societies, extremely unfavorable anti-ethnic attitudes are normative for large majorities of the population; in societies whose norms make ethnic distinctions but do not prescribe such extreme degrees of unfavorableness, it is primarily authoritarian persons who develop such extremeness. Thus levels of prejudice may differ in different societies that have about the same proportions of authoritarian individuals.

2. Comparisons of individual members of the same society whose norms do not prescribe extreme anti-ethnic attitudes show that prejudice tends to be associated with authoritarianism, for reasons just outlined.

3. Persons who are members both of majority and of minority ("target") groups share some of the majority group's norms toward their own minority group, insofar as they regard themselves as being (actually or hopefully) also members of the majority group. We would expect such attitudes (anti-Semitism among Jews, for example) to be most pronounced among the more authoritarian individuals.

4. Finally, the likelihood of being prejudiced does not vary with

degree of firsthand contact with members of the group against which prejudice is held; it varies, rather, with degree of contact with prejudiced members of groups whose norms one shares. And, within the same society (especially if its anti-ethnic norms are not extreme) the intensity of prejudice varies with authoritarianism.

Thus the two factors of norm-sharing and of authoritarianism together account rather well, at the social-psychological level, for the observed facts of ethnic prejudice.

HOSTILITY BETWEEN GROUPS

We now shift our emphasis from hostile attitudes to hostile behavior by group members toward members of other groups. Overt hostility, like most other kinds of observable behavior, usually springs from preexisting attitudes. Hence the ways in which prejudice is learned will also have a good deal to do with the ways in which it is expressed in behavior. Even when prejudice has already been acquired, however, it is more likely to lead to hostile behavior under some conditions than under others. We shall deal with the conditions under which hostile behavior occurs, and also with some of the consequences to which it leads.

Creating and Maintaining Barriers to Communication

Hostile attitudes toward a person, once they have developed, are likely to remain until further experience provides opportunities for attitude change. Suppose, for example, that two acquaintances part in anger. If the hostility of either of them is so great that they avoid each other, there is little opportunity for either of them to unlearn the hostile attitude that was responsible for their parting. This same principle (which has been labeled "autistic hostility") applies to hostile attitudes toward groups. If the members of one group share hostile attitudes toward another group, they are quite likely to take steps to reduce communication with that group. Such behavior tends to maintain the hostility, because of reduced opportunities for the kind of unlearning that is necessary if the group norms are to prescribe less rather than more hostility.

BARRIERS TO ASSOCIATION. Restricted association almost inevitably results in restricted communication, and when barriers to association are erected because of existing hostility they are likely to perpetuate or even to intensify feelings of hostility. One of the most conspicuous barriers to association between ethnic groups in our society is enforced segregation. To the extent that Jews are cut off from gentiles, or Negroes from whites, they live in different social worlds. Restrictive practices with respect to employment, recreation, housing, and church membership all constitute barriers to association.

Yet segregation is not only a matter of a system perpetuating itself because of lack of interaction with others. Group conflict must also be viewed in terms of things that people do and their reasons for doing them. One important set of reasons stems from the fact that groups that are kept apart by practices of segregation almost always differ with respect to power, privilege, and prestige. Segregation usually helps the group with the greater power and privilege to maintain its advantage. Members of the more privileged group thus feel they have something to gain by segregation and will view any lowering of the barriers to association as a threat to their preferred status. Conversely, the very presence of the barriers is threatening to the less privileged groups. Insofar as members of each group share attitudes to the effect that the other is a source of threat, they tend to shut themselves off from each other by various forms of segregation. This process is accompanied by the development of group norms that actually prescribe hostile behavior under specified conditions.

BARRIERS TO UNDERSTANDING. Communication may be restricted even when there is no segregation; if so there are, so to speak, psychological barriers to communication. The assumption that another person—a member of another group, for example—has nothing in common with oneself, or that his values are opposed to one's own, can serve as such a barrier. Research Illustration 14.5 shows how groups of students (who are probably like most other groups in this respect) tend to assume that they have less and less in common with group members from whom they feel more and more distant.

PRINCIPLES RELATED TO COMMUNICATIVE BARRIERS. One general principle emerging from these considerations, together with others previously noted in this book, has to do with the conditions that restrict communication between members of different groups. In general, the greater the degree to which members of one group perceive the behavior of members of another as being hostile, the greater the restriction of communication between them. This process is facilitated by the fact that each person's anticipations of hostility from the other group are reinforced by the shared norms of his own group. Thus the behaviors, including those producing segregation, that give rise to perceptions of hostility lead to defensiveness, mutual withdrawal, and further behaviors perceived by members of the other group as hostile. Groups between which there is less and less communication tend to become more and more distinct from each other, and as they become more distinct their respective norms diverge more and more. In such manner the cycle illustrated in Figure 14.2 is continued.

Research Illustration 14.5

Relationships between attitudes of social distance toward various groups and perceived similarity of own and others' attitudes were investigated by Muraskin and Iverson (1958). They obtained responses from four groups of college students to a modified form of the Bogardus Social Distance scale. Each student was asked to indicate the degree of social relationship that he himself would accept for twenty different minority groups. The statements ranged from "would exclude from my country," at one extreme, to "close kinship by marriage" at the other.

Some days later these students were divided into four groups and were again administered this scale. This time members of one group were asked to give the answers they thought would be made by a fellow college student who was an atheist. The other three groups gave the answers they thought would be made by a fellow student, who was a Communist, a mulatto, and a Puerto Rican, respectively. These four were selected because it had been found that they represented a range of social distance with Communists as most distant, Puerto Ricans as second, mulattoes as third, and atheists as least distant. This is illustrated in the accompanying table, which also shows that there is a relationship between the social distance one feels for a group and the attitudes that one attributes to the group in question. For example, not only is a Communist viewed as being very distant socially, but he is also perceived as one whose social perceptions differ considerably from those of the viewer (a correlation of only +.25).

Group	Average self-rating of social distance[a]	Number	Average correlation coefficient between self-ratings and attributed ratings
Atheist	4.35	25	+.66
Mulatto	4.19	17	+.59
Puerto Rican	3.77	19	+.44
Communist	2.32	26	+.25

[a] Lower scores denote greater social distance.

Finally, the subjects were asked to give the responses they thought the "ideal" American would make. An average correlation of +.82 was now obtained. If we assume that the "ideal" American is socially closer than any of the other groups, it becomes apparent that there is a direct relationship between the perceived social distance of a group and tendency to attribute to it attitudes different from one's own.

A second general principle has to do with the effects of restricted communication. The point is not that limited communication necessarily leads to hostility, nor that frequent communication will necessarily change attitudes of hostility; everyday observation provides plentiful

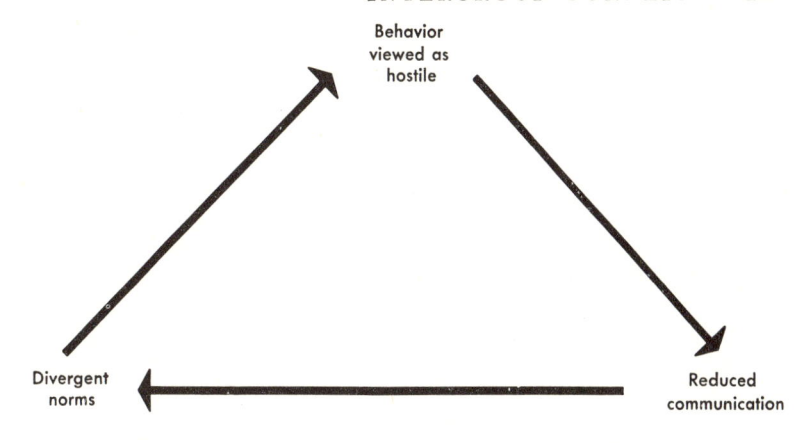

FIGURE 14.2. Schematic diagram of circular relationships among behavior, communication, and group norms

illustrations to the contrary. Our point, rather, is that if hostile attitudes already exist they are not likely to be changed without intergroup communication, which is a necessary but not a sufficient condition. Insofar as reduced communication is a consequence of hostile attitudes (as expressed, among other ways, in enforced segregation), there are certain conditions under which those attitudes may be changed through increased communication. In the final section of this chapter we shall examine some of those conditions.

Violence as an Outcome of Mutual Prejudice

When divergent norms support prejudice between two groups, overt incidents sometimes occur and bring the conflict to public attention. If Negroes use public swimming facilities usually reserved for whites, or if Puerto Ricans buy a house in a "white district," group loyalties on both sides may be aroused with such possible consequences as riots. Most violent episodes are preceded by more or less minor incidents that are the basis for rumors and further misunderstanding.

Cantril's analysis (1941) of a Negro lynching remains one of the best illustrations of violent conflict between ethnic groups. He points out that "the statistically average lynching is one that occurs in the South, has a Negro for a victim and native whites as mob members, none of whom is arrested or punished for his actions." Although the number of such lynchings has dropped in recent years, the 1950s saw several lynchings that were quite similar to the one reported in the following excerpt.

A Black-Belt Lynching

On July 18, 1930, a seven-year-old white girl, the daughter of a tobacco farmer, came home crying because Oliver Moore, a Negro house boy, had hurt her while playing a game with her and her younger sister in the barn. Because of the condition of the girl's clothes, the parents concluded that the Negro's game had been attempted rape. Moore ran away while the farmer and his wife were consulting. The county sheriff with a posse of excited citizens and a brace of bloodhounds set out in search of the Negro. The search was fruitless, but Moore was at last apprehended by a single white man on August 16. A preliminary trial was held on August 19. The father and the girls told their story. The Negro was not allowed to say anything and no lawyers volunteered their services to defend Moore, who was then lodged in the county jail to await appearance in the superior court. Since no unusual excitement had accompanied the preliminary trial, both the sheriff and the judge felt the prisoner would be quite safe in the local jail.

About one o'clock the next morning, however, a deputy sheriff in charge of the jail opened the door when he heard a knock. A number of people were outside. Some of them were masked. The sheriff was quickly covered by guns, the keys to the jail were taken by a mob member, the Negro taken out and tied in one of about twenty cars waiting outside. The whole abduction was efficiently handled and the orders of the mob leader quietly carried out. The mob was obviously well organized. Some time later the county sheriff was notified. He organized a posse to pursue the mob but did not know which way to go. About dawn the Negro's body was found hanging to a tree "riddled with bullets and buckshot." The lynching was staged as near as possible to the barn where the alleged crime had occurred. . . .

Although many of the larger papers in the state severely condemned the lynching, the smaller papers in the vicinity were not unduly perturbed. The local *Telegram* stated editorially that it did not condone the action of the masked men but added, "That the feeling of a people should be aroused is natural and we find ourselves, despite our views on lynching, not too greatly disturbed. . . . We find ourselves calmly accepting the crime last night as inevitable." Local ministers and school teachers did not dare say anything against the lynching. A court official said, "From the standpoint of state and legality it is regrettable but, personally, I think it was a good thing." A newspaper man stated, "In principle, I'm against lynching, but this crime was so horrible. I think it was all right." A policeman's reaction was, "The black son of a b⎯⎯ got what he deserved. If the crime had been committed against the lowest white woman in the world he should have been killed; if I had been there I would not have interfered, for them folks would a-killed a good man to get that nigger."

Unfortunately, no information is available concerning the personnel of the mob. However, the fact that the lynching was so efficiently conducted indicates that it had been well planned ahead of time. The judge in the preliminary trial was quite sure that many local citizens were involved. (Adapted from Raper [1933] by Cantril [1941], pp. 94–96.)

GROUP NORMS AS A KEY FACTOR IN VIOLENCE. In the episode just described, there was no necessary reason for interpreting the crying of the seven-year-old girl as a response to attempted rape. And even if the evidence of rape had been unmistakable, there was nothing inherent in the crime that made death by lynching inevitable. Such interpretations became inevitable only within a fixed set of norms that determined them. The quick, concerted action on the part of many persons, following the rumor of rape, suggests that the norms were generally shared among the white population: they provided ready-made interpretations of behavior reported on the part of Negroes.

Every set of norms involving violence has its own set of historical determinants that justify punishment in terms of shared norms. In the early days of our country such norms grew up in our western states concerning the punishment of cattle or horse thieves, regardless of their racial membership. Without shared understandings both as to the enormity of the crime and as to its appropriate punishment, Americans, who consider themselves to be law-abiding and God-fearing, would hardly participate in such violence.

THE BASIS FOR PARTICIPATING IN ACTION. The actual participants in a lynching are not a representative sampling of those who share these norms. In fact, the excesses of behavior characteristic of a lynching mob are largely a result of the fact that its participants are selected in special ways.

The fact that not all persons participate has made it possible to distinguish between two extreme "types" of lynching. The "Bourbon type," of which the foregoing incident is an example, is described by Cantril (1941) as being relatively exclusive and well regulated. It generally occurs in a Black Belt area where there is a rigid demarcation between blacks and whites and where the leaders of a community believe it is their duty to enforce community standards. Such lynchings are therefore often engineered by leading citizens with the knowledge of law-enforcement officers. The object is to punish a specific person for a specific crime. Other Negroes are protected. The mob is small and does not seem to get out of hand. The fundamental motive is to assure white supremacy and maintain the accepted mores.

The "proletariat type" of lynching generally occurs in areas where Negroes are distinctly in the minority, where competition is keen between Negroes and poor whites, and where the object is to persecute the race rather than an individual. Such lynchings are more brutal, more publicized. They are led by members of the poorer, less established classes and disapproved by the better citizens of the community. There is little interest in proving the guilt of the alleged victim or even getting the right victim. After the lynching, the mob frequently persecutes other Negroes by destroying their property or beating or killing them.

In these two different types of lynching it is apparent that different types of persons participate. In the "Bourbon" lynchings the "solid citizens" and in the "proletariat" lynchings the less "responsible" ones were primarily involved. It is easier to obtain information on the participants in a "proletariat" lynching because they do not take pains to go about it quietly, as do the "Bourbon" lynchers. Cantril described one "proletariat" lynching in which it was found that approximately 70 percent of the participants were either unemployed, common laborers, or farm workers. Approximately one fifth had police records and the leader of the mob was a man who could neither read nor write.

Not all "solid citizens" in a community participate in a "Bourbon" lynching mob, nor do all "irresponsible" ones engage in a "proletariat" one. The "Bourbon" lynchers are picked out by the leader as having the qualities needed to carry out their assignment. The "proletarian" lynchers pick themselves out on the basis of their own qualities of recklessness, excitability, and capacity for violence. In neither case would a truly representative sample of the community possess the qualities needed for such violent excesses.

THE FACILITATION OF VIOLENCE. Lynchers seldom go about their business with cool detachment as they might if they were setting out to track down someone who had escaped from the state penitentiary. It seems necessary to work up to some sort of climax that justifies the usual brutality. The steps by which mob members work themselves up to the necessary fever of excitement may be partially reconstructed from statements made by participants in lynchings, riots, and panics. Two parallel kinds of process occur. Together, they make it possible for participants to indulge in behavior that would ordinarily be abhorrent to them.

The first of these processes is *mounting tension*. There is the spiraling form of social interaction in the sense that each mob member is subjected to more and more stimulation from other mob members, which we have referred to as social facilitation. Each member of the mob is stimulated by the behavior of many others as they shout insults, call encouragement to their fellows, fire guns into the air, brandish knives, and move in unison with others toward a goal. Under such heightened stimulation, the more venturesome members of the mob take the first steps of violence while others watch the victim as he yields or fights back. Individuals reinforce each other's aggressive behavior with verbal approval or through cooperation. This provides still more stimulation until even the least impulsive members of the mob have had their turn at vengeance—often long after the victim is dead.

Accompanying this mounting tension is a second process of *narrowing perception*, without which the brutality would not occur. Mutilating a human being is not permissible by everyday standards of decent behavior. But another set of temporary standards dominates the scene. This set of standards is not a newly created one, since the mob includes primarily those who already regard lynching as proper under certain conditions. In the lynching situation the only influences brought to bear are those that accentuate the lynching standards. Thus, individuals who participate because they share prolynching norms now find themselves interacting intensely with others in a situation where everyone is bent on brutality. For them, diverging norms about the legality or morality of lynching do not constitute a source of conflict, since any individual concerned with these matters is usually afraid to speak out and thus is not heard. The daily norms permit brutality for violating the code of white supremacy; the momentary norms of the mob require it.

Under certain conditions, in sum, there is a lowering of individuals' thresholds for violent behavior of kinds that are far more extreme than are condoned by the norms that ordinarily govern their everyday lives. These conditions include (1) a preexisting state of shared prejudice against the group of which the victim of violence is a member; (2) an immediate situation that serves to heighten the existing sense of threat presented by the other group; (3) the definition of the immediate situation as one that justifies the application of a set of norms that does condone violence (norms already shared and held in readiness for such occasions); and (4) heightened excitability that finds its behavioral expression in ways that are governed, narrowly and exclusively, by a violence-condoning set of norms. The first two of these conditions precede the outbreak of violence. The latter two arise during processes of interaction, especially those of social facilitation and group reinforcement.

THE REDUCTION OF GROUP CONFLICT

Although we have stressed the circular relationships that help to perpetuate hostility, such processes are not necessarily irreversible. In fact, the very study of the ways in which these processes develop suggests that there may be points of entry at which it is possible to "break up the vicious circle." This is not an easy task, however, especially because prejudice is usually rooted in the solid ground of loyalty to one's own groups. An effective program must recognize the roots of prejudice and be far-reaching in seeking to deal with them.

Reducing Personal Susceptibility to Hostility

At the psychological level, individuals who are frustrated by a sense of deprivation and who are looking for someone to blame are likely candidates to become prejudiced persons. If they share in a set of norms according to which some groups are strong and some weak, some superior and some inferior, or some good and some bad, it would not be surprising if they chose the latter kinds of group as targets to be blamed, and if so these become perceived sources of threat.

Insofar as such processes contribute to the development of prejudice, any program that could reduce the general level of deprivation within a society should help to alleviate this source of prejudice. One such possibility might be through the improvement of economic conditions, especially as they impinge on the relatively underprivileged. There is, in fact, some evidence of a relationship between economic deprivation and prejudice, particularly in its more extreme forms. During an early period when the southern economy in the United States depended largely on the cotton crop, it was found that, for several decades, lynchings were more frequent when the price of cotton was lowest and less frequent when it was highest (Hovland and Sears, 1938; see also Mintz, 1946, for an alternative interpretation). To give another example, the Chinese were welcomed to California during the period of the gold rush because of a labor shortage. Americans later found themselves in competition with these same Chinese immigrants for jobs. Although the Chinese had been regarded with great respect when their services were needed, they were now the object of considerable resentment, and prejudice ran high. In the elections of 1867 both political parties adopted a pledge to enact legislation protecting Californians against Mongolian competition.

Although the foregoing illustrations point to the probable influence of economic factors on intergroup conflicts, a more direct examination of the relationship is provided by an analysis of Bettelheim and Janowitz (1950). They asked a number of veterans of World War II to indicate their occupational situation as it was just prior to entry into the armed services and as it was just after the war. Some had found better jobs (upward mobility), some had found jobs similar to those previously held (no change), and some were unable to find jobs that were as good (downward mobility). As Figure 14.3 indicates, the degree of anti-Semitism expressed was strikingly different for the three groups. Those veterans who were descending the vocational ladder were far more anti-Semitic than those who were rising. The same trend was found in connection with anti-Negro prejudice. This evidence that personal frustration is associated with prejudice does not show that the former is "the cause" of the latter. Indeed, other evidence obtained by Bettelheim and Janowitz shows that the downward-mobile veterans, as a group, had had histories of being previously "embittered" whereas the upward-mobile ones had not. Such personal characteristics of the former doubtless contributed to their downward mobility.

It does seem likely, nevertheless, that a person is less susceptible to the development of prejudice if the changes in his economic status are in a favorable direction. This would suggest, in turn, that if the

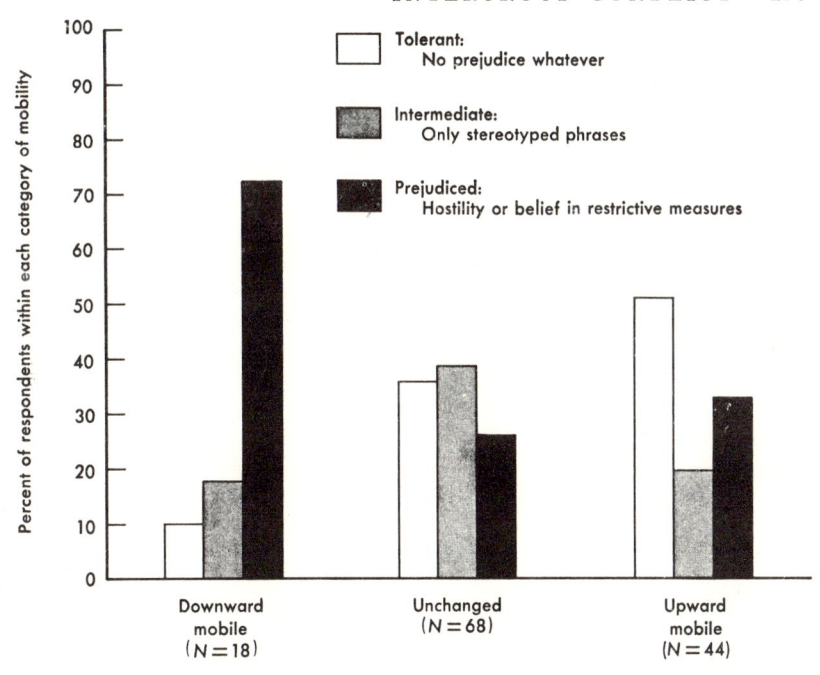

FIGURE 14.3. Attitudes toward Jews on the part of veterans in three categories of occupational mobility (adapted from Bettelheim and Janowitz, 1949)

level of prosperity of both whites and Negroes of the South were considerably increased, acts of extreme hostility would in the long run decrease. There is some evidence that a slowly rising standard of living in the South has already had a modest effect in this direction. To be sure, the recent problems over school integration have prevented a clear view of the picture, but lynchings have declined sharply and gradual acceptance of more nearly equal status appears to be in the making. The progressive industrialization of the South and the further development of the region's natural resources indicate that a trend will probably continue in this direction. The economic factor is, of course, not the only one at work here; the political, legal, and educational aspects of this problem are also of importance, as we shall note.

Changing Practices That Maintain Prejudice

Among the interactional processes by which existing prejudice is maintained are practices of discriminating against selected groups, together with the everyday observation that such practices are supported by group norms. We shall now examine some concrete instances in which such practices have been modified, with the consequence that at least some attitude change has occurred.

A Case History of Fluctuating Adherence to Ingroup Norms

Clinton, Tennessee, is a small town of approximately 4000 persons, including about 200 Negroes, in eastern Tennessee. Following the Supreme Court decision banning public school segregation, the district judge for this region ordered Clinton High School desegregated no later than the fall of 1956. Although the majority of citizens were opposed to integration, most of them were in favor of abiding by the law. Thus it can be said that a norm of acquiescence to the law had developed and grown to such an extent that things went quite smoothly in the initial stages of integration. Twelve Negro students went to the high school without incident and a Negro girl was elected vice-president of her integrated homeroom.

It is probable that tolerance of this new situation would have continued to be supported by community norms had it not been for the arrival of John Kasper. This northern segregationist was exceedingly active in drumming up racial antagonism. He talked to persons in their homes, at work, and at meetings. He warned that if people didn't want their daughter to "marry a nigger" they should do something about school integration. As a result of his activity and the attendant publicity, the only group that came to have a highly visible norm in the community was the group of extremists who now came out openly against integration. As a result of interaction with Kasper and with one another, there developed a progressively more intense anti-integration norm among these persons. Since others who may have had contrary views were not active, the members of the group came to view their norm as prevalent in the community, and they were emboldened by this belief. Negroes were stoned and a minister was attacked for trying to escort the Negro students to the school. The new norm of hostility appeared to be dominant in the community.

Then a different group of persons suddenly became active and highly visible. Clinton's mayor and the sheriff appealed for help. Moderate leaders in town organized posses to stop the mob. The Governor ordered 600 National Guardsmen to Clinton to keep order and enforce the law. In addition, the federal judge of the region issued a sweeping injunction forbidding interference with school integration. Kasper was arrested and charged with violating a federal injunction; he was also charged by state authorities with sedition and incitement to riot. Within a week Clinton was calm. The extremists found that norms which condoned violence against Negroes were not accepted by many of their acquaintances and by many persons who occupied positions of considerable importance in the community and in the state. The perception of the fact that their norms were not shared by many other persons apparently had a sobering effect on the members of the group. School was resumed on an integrated basis.

In the meantime, however, Kasper was released on bail and was then tried on the state offenses. A jury of twelve men found him innocent of these charges. Failure to find Kasper guilty of wrongdoing provided a new impetus for the extremists. They now had reason to believe that their aggressive norm was not only a reasonable one but one that was protected by law. Strengthened by what may have appeared to be legal sanctions for such behavior, violence once again flared up. White youngsters and their parents hurled stones and eggs at Negro children. The Negro students were virtually forced to leave school for their own safety.

The school board sent a letter to the Attorney General of the United States asking for federal help. It came in several ways. The F.B.I. and the Justice Department made a detailed study of interference with the federal injunction to integrate the school. Then the Justice Department arrested sixteen persons in Clinton on charges of contempt of court. An all-white jury convicted seven of these citizens and sentenced Kasper to a term in federal prison. Once again, the extremists had reason to doubt that their norm was as universally approved as they had thought. A local election in which the extremist candidates lost to the moderate candidates also undoubtedly played a considerable part in showing that aggressive hostility was approved by only a minority of persons in Clinton. Once again a moderate or tolerant norm was perceived as shared by a majority of citizens, and the Negro children returned to school without incident. This norm has prevailed since that time in Clinton.

Evidence that the "tolerance of integration" norm was increasingly accepted appeared in the form of reactions by Clinton citizens when dynamite later destroyed a portion of the high school. The outcry of disapproval served to smother this event as a possible rallying point for the extremists. Similarly, the unity demonstrated by 200 citizens who donated considerable labor to make an empty building into a temporary substitute for the high school was a highly visible activity that implied agreement with the proposition that "school must go on." This appears to have been the last straw in breaking the back of organized efforts to prevent integration. Tolerance of integration now seems to be a widely shared norm and is apparently recognized as such even by those who previously thought they had the approval of most citizens when they engaged in acts of violence; integrated public school education has since then proceeded without further incident. The Clinton story illustrates the principle that the degree to which individuals perceive different norms to be shared among persons who "count" influences public adherence to these norms. (Adapted from the *New York Times*, December 9, 1956)

LEGISLATION AS A MEANS OF CHANGING NORMS. Many years ago Sumner (1906), a sociologist, declared that "stateways" (laws) cannot change folkways, and that legislation is futile in changing basic social patterns. Although it is of course true that a law declaring that prejudiced attitudes are henceforth forbidden would not be effective, Sumner's dictum appears to ignore the very important fact that such behavioral practices as segregation are sources as well as outcomes of prejudice. This fact suggests that although the vicious circle of *prejudiced attitudes–reduced communication–further prejudice* cannot be broken in any direct way by legislation, the vicious circle of *discriminative behavior–reduced communication–further discrimination* can be broken. One of the ways in which white children acquire attitudes of prejudice is by observing that Chinese or Negroes, for example, are kept apart from whites, under less privileged circumstances, with the approval or at least the acquiescence of their families and other membership groups. Insofar as legislation is effective in eliminating clearly observable forms of discrimination, it begins to break up the circle on which continued prejudice depends. Thus the modification of behavior, through legislation, can serve to reduce the likelihood that succeeding generations of children will acquire attitudes of prejudice.

The very existence of antidiscriminative legislation may also affect the attitudes of adults over fairly brief periods of time. It has been reported, for example, that many employers have found some unforeseen and beneficial consequences of laws against discrimination in employment. Three years after the passage of the New York State law against discrimination in employment, the New York State Commission against Discrimination reported (1952) that disapproval of this law was expressed by only 5 percent of the businessmen polled. Although members of this group had been fearful of the law at its inception, they found that the effect of the law was to open up a larger labor force that could be drawn on as more workers were needed. Furthermore, employers had previously found themselves caught in the cross fire between those insisting on discriminatory employment practices and those insisting on nondiscrimination. The law forbidding discrimination now removed them from this conflict and gave them a clear course of action that had legal backing. These factors help to account for the overwhelming approval given to the law against discrimination by this business group.

Though it deals with a decision by management rather than with legislation, a study by Saenger and Gilbert (1950), suggests similar consequences of an enforced change. Certain department stores in New York City suddenly confronted the public with a *fait accompli* by hiring Negro salesclerks, with no prior announcement. Persons with known prejudices against Negro clerks accepted their presence and their services as frequently as did those who approved of Negro clerks. The fact that other customers in the store were obviously accepting the new situation without protest was apparently taken as indicating the proper standards of conduct. It is the general history of such events that if decisions by legislative or other authorities result in a change that is apparently being generally accepted, most people tend to "go along," whatever their attitudes or their behaviors may have been under previous conditions. Acceptance of such a *fait accompli* presumably occurs most readily on the part of those who have had little or no previous prejudice, and those who prefer not to be nonconformists (the latter perhaps including some highly prejudiced individuals with authoritarian tendencies). In any case, many people's attitudes of prejudice become less pronounced or even disappear with the decline of observable practices of discrimination that have previously served to remind them of ethnic distinctions, while at the same time maintaining and supporting their prejudice.

The psychological processes of attitude change on the part of persons who conform, however passively, when they observe that "the rules have changed" may often include those described by Festinger (1957) as dissonance-reducing. One way of minimizing the discomfort that a person experiences when he finds himself doing something opposed to his own attitudes is to modify those attitudes. The experiment by Janis and King (page 236) is a case in point, and the attitude changes on the part of Scott's debaters (Research Illustration 8.3, page 237) might also be interpreted in such ways.

Legislation and other forms of force are by no means always necessary, desirable, or effective. Under most conditions legislation cannot be enforced unless there already exists considerable popular support for it in the larger community or society. The introduction of unenforceable legislation is not, of course, an effective way to change attitudes; the failure of the Eighteenth Amendment, legislating prohibition, is a classic example of such a failure. Force is effective in changing attitudes to the degree that it is successful in changing practices that provide group-shared support for attitudes.

Changing Group Norms through Joint Participation

Any program for the reduction of group prejudice must be based on the recognition that prejudice is supported by group norms. Those who are interested in such a program must remember, furthermore, that at least two sets of group norms are involved. No matter how fully such a program takes into account the norms of one group—say those of non-Mexican whites in southwestern United States concerning Mexicans—it could not be very successful unless it also recognized that people of Mexican ancestry in this area also have norms of their own. These two sets of norms do not exist independently of each other. Each group's norms include ways of perceiving, feeling, thinking, and acting in relation to the other group. And each group's norms are, in part at least, a reaction to the ways in which it is treated by the other group. Hence there cannot be any very great change on the part of one set of norms if the other set is not changing at all. Thus if prejudice between two groups is to be effectively reduced, *all* the following conditions must be met:

1. The norms of Group A concerning Group B must be changed.
2. The norms of Group B concerning Group A must be changed.
3. The members of Group A must perceive that Group B's norms concerning Group A are changing.
4. Members of Group B must perceive that Group A's norms concerning Group B are changing.

Research Illustration 14.6 (Sherif *et al.*, 1961) describes, within a single experiment, nearly all the essential steps by which conflict between two groups typically arises and by which, occasionally at least, it gives way to cordial relationships. Because both the arousal and the resolution of the conflict occurred exactly under the conditions that had been created by the experimenters to make them occur, we can learn more confidently from this experiment about such conditions than from mere observation of similar changes under "natural" or uncontrolled circumstances. We shall therefore use this experiment to illustrate the conditions under which we may expect to find the four kinds of change that we have just listed as necessary for the reduction of group conflict.

The norms of the Rattlers and of the Eagles concerning each other changed, in the first place, as a result of the experimenters' lifting of barriers to association between the two groups. With the change from exclusive communication within each group to free communication between groups, individual members were presented with opportunities to discover that some of their previously group-supported impressions of the other group were wrong. Furthermore, they showed by their behavior that their attitudes toward the other group were changing. As the members of either group observed their fellow members' increasing cordiality to members of the other group, each of them discovered that his own changing attitudes were shared by others. This is precisely what is meant by changing norms.

Mere removal of barriers to communication, however, is not enough; there must also be motivation to associate and to communicate with individuals against whom there is existing prejudice. The experimental manipulations at stage 3 were planned for exactly this purpose. By providing the boys with interesting and exciting things to do, but which could not be successfully achieved without cooperation between members of both groups, individual motivation was aroused. Through joint participation in activities directed toward shared goals, members of each group interacted with members of the other one in ways that were reciprocally rewarding. Thus interpersonal relationships of hostility gave way to interpersonal attraction that represented not just personal-liking-

Research Illustration 14.6

Sherif and his associates (1961) in an experiment related to the one described in Research Illustration 15.5 (page 487), succeeded in creating at a summer camp two groups of boys, each of which developed norms of its own that included hostility to the other group. Then, through further experimental arrangements, they succeeded in overcoming both groups' hostility. The several stages of their experiment were as follows.

1. During the first six days of the boys' stay in camp the aim was to develop two separate groups, each having high cohesiveness and each being unaware of the other's existence. Each group was made up of eleven boys of about eleven years of age, of very homogeneous backgrounds but all strangers to one another. Although the two campsites were not far apart, they were out of sight and earshot of each other; each had its own facilities for swimming, boating, making campfires, and so on. They used the same mess hall, but never at the same time, and apparently did not discover each other's existence until about the fifth day. The principal methods used for creating group cohesiveness consisted of "common and interdependent activities prompted by goals integral to the actual situations"—cookouts, preparing campfires, improving the swimming facilities, treasure hunts, and so on. Before the end of stage 1 each group had adopted a name (Eagles and Rattlers); each had developed a recognized status structure among its members; individual role assignments had been developed, recognized, and accepted; and various kinds of norms had been established (concerning "toughness" and cursing, for example).

2. The second six days, designated as stage 2, were so planned as to create friction between Rattlers and Eagles. The groups were brought into contact with each other through competitive activities, including tournaments in which cumulative scores were kept for each group (not for individuals). In addition, situations were devised in ways designed to be frustrating to one group and perceived by it as caused by the other group. For example, a ball field considered by the Rattlers to belong to them was preempted by the Eagles (as arranged by the experimenters, of course). One group burned the flag of the other (without provocation by the experimenters). A tug-of-war was won by the Eagles with the aid, as the Rattlers felt, of unfair tactics; a little later the Rattlers raided the Eagles' cabin, overturning beds, generally disarranging things, and "stealing" prized knives and medals. Such conflicts were increasingly accompanied by invectives and insults from both sides toward the other group.

3. The third six-day period was planned as an "integration phase." The experimenters' strategy was the creation of "superordinate goals . . . in the sense that the resources and energies of any single group will be inadequate for the attainment of the goals, thus creating a state of real and/or perceived interdependence." The first part

of this strategy was to arrange brief "contact situations" during which all the boys participated in the same activity at the same time and place—for example, engaging in a psychological experiment, attending a movie, having a meal together. Such merely parallel activities did little, however, by way of reducing intergroup feelings of hostility. The superordinate-goal activities were then introduced. One of these followed the shutting off of the common water supply by the experimenters, who also placed "two large boulders" above one of the valves controlling the flow of water; the experimenters took pains to attribute the trouble to "vandals," so that neither group would blame the other. A plan was announced whereby the damage might be repaired, and that required a good deal of work on everyone's part. As more and more boys began to complain of thirst, Eagles and Rattlers found themselves working side by side, and even engaging in good-natured conversation. At the following meal intergroup hostilities had by no means subsided, but the experimenters soon introduced another superordinate goal. Boys were told that it would be possible to show the film *Treasure Island*, but that it would cost more money than the camp budget could afford. After a good deal of discussion it was decided that each Eagle would contribute 39¢ and each Rattler 31¢, to make up $3.50 from each group; this amount was supplemented by the counselors, and the movie was shown that evening. Later all camp members joined forces to chop down a large tree, and a long trip was planned. During this trip things were so arranged that tent-pitching and food preparation had to be done jointly; the camp truck stalled (according to plan) and everyone helped to get it started. That day boys mingled together for meals and for a good-natured water fight, without regard to their status as Rattlers or as Eagles. Final preparations for leaving camp—including general insistence on going "all in the same bus"—were made with almost no attention to previous group membership.

At the end of stage 2 sociometric preferences were made strictly within each group rather than between groups. At the end of stage 3, however, about one third of all choices were by Eagles for Rattlers, or vice versa. Similar changes are indicated by the boys' ratings of each other's characteristics, as follows:

Percent of all ratings by Eagles of Rattlers, and of Rattlers by Eagles, that were

	Favorable	Neutral	Unfavorable	Total
End of stage 2	27	10	63	100
End of stage 3	78	9	13	100

in-a-vacuum; attraction was also anchored in shared attitudes toward worthwhile activities. Both opportunity for interaction and the experience of joint participation were necessary conditions for the modification of each group's norms.

At the same time members of each group had opportunities to observe that the norms of the other group were changing. During stage 2 the Eagles' norms had included (quite correctly) the attribution to the Rattlers of hostile attitudes toward them, and the Rattlers' norms included the corresponding attributions to the Eagles. During stage 3 members of each group could freely observe that, no matter how correct their previous attributions of hostility to the other group, those attributions were no longer correct. Each boy's cordial behavior toward a member of the other group advertised, to members of the other group as well as to his own fellow members, that things had changed. As Rattlers, for example, observed that cordial behavior by an Eagle member toward a Rattler member was approved by other Eagles, it became apparent to Rattlers that Eagles' norms had changed. Thus each group's change of norms was paralleled by observations showing that the other's norms were also changing. Both kinds of changes were made possible by joint participation.

The crucial aspect of all these changes, from the point of view of reduced conflict, lies not merely in the fact that norms and perceptions of others' norms had changed, but rather in the direction of change. Two sets of norms had converged into one. Where there had been only within-group sharing, there was now between-group sharing—even to the extent that the two groups had now merged into a single one. This, at least, appeared to be the boys' own view of the matter, for groups are viewed by their own members as distinctive insofar as they see their own shared norms as distinctive.

OVERVIEW

Because the experiment described in Research Illustration 14.6 points to so many factors that contribute both to the origins and to the reduction of intergroup conflict, we have used it as a basis for drawing together the principles that have emerged in this chapter. The conditions of this experiment are not, of course, typical of those that apply to long-established ethnic groups. What Eagles and Rattlers have in common with, for example, whites and Negroes in a rural southern community is a set of principles that govern their relationships, and not a set of common "real-life" situations. The same principles apply in both cases, but their application must take immediate circumstances into account—just as engineers apply their general principles by building bridges in different ways, according to the local circumstances. It was, of course, more difficult in Clinton, Tennessee, to reduce barriers to communication and to arrange for joint participation in activities of shared importance than in a summer camp for boys of similar backgrounds, who came as strangers to one another. No attempt to reduce long-established ethnic conflicts is likely to achieve easy success, but the likelihood of its eventual success will be governed by such principles as those we have outlined.

Any successful program for reducing ethnic conflict must be far-reaching and many-sided. It must attempt to provide social conditions that reduce personal susceptibility to prejudice, it must manage to lower barriers to communication, and it must provide opportunities for joint participation on the part of many members of opposing groups. These are not separate and distinct paths to the same goal; they are interdependent approaches, all of which are necessary.

CHAPTER 15

Achieving Group Goals

THE PURPOSE OF THIS CHAPTER IS TO SHOW INTERACTION PROCESSES AT work in groups whose members interact for the purpose of achieving some shared goal. Even the most informal group, provided only that its members continue to interact for more than brief periods, occasionally acts in a goal-oriented manner—if, for example, it is only necessary to reach as simple a decision as when and where to meet again. It is particularly enlightening to study interaction in groups that are, for the moment at least, goal-oriented, because we can be pretty sure that under such conditions group members are acting *as* group members, and not merely as individuals who happen to be in the same place at the same time.

We shall begin by comparing the ways in which group members proceed in achieving shared goals with the ways in which individuals direct their activities to individual goals. These differences, whatever they turn out to be, are associated with the presence and the absence of interaction among group members. Then we shall examine the differentiated contributions that various members make to goal achievement as they interact, with special attention to the phenomena of leadership. And, finally, we shall inquire about certain characteristics of the group as a whole that are bound to affect the processes of goal achievement, just as an individual's personal characteristics will affect his modes of achieving his own goals. We shall show how group cohesiveness, as a group property of general importance, both affects and is affected by the interaction processes involved in the goal-directed activities of groups.

INTERACTION PROCESSES IN GROUP PROBLEM SOLVING

It happens that, almost from the beginnings of social psychology (cf. Triplett, 1897, pp. 5–6), experimental studies have been made concerning the relative effectiveness of individuals and of groups at work on the same or comparable problems. Some of these—like Triplett's early study, for example, or Dashiell's later one (Research Illustration 9.3, page 279)—compared individuals working alone and working in close proximity at the same tasks, with individual rather than group goals. Others, of which Shaw's experiment (Research Illustration 12.1, page 361) is one of the first examples, made comparisons of individuals' solutions with those of group members trying jointly to solve the same or similar problems. Because they make explicit provisions for group goals, we shall draw primarily from the latter type of experiments.

It is easy to think of reasons why some kinds of problem are better solved by several persons who work together than by a single one. Some tasks are so complex that they are most efficiently performed by assigning specialized tasks to different persons; others demand more information or more different points of view than a single person is likely to have; groups provide greater resource input, as noted in Chapter 9. And it is equally clear that other kinds of problems can best be attacked by single individuals—perhaps because two or more persons would get in each other's way, or because the solution, once it has occurred to any one member, is so obvious that it is immediately accepted by the others. Neither individual nor group problem solving has any over-all superiority; there are certain conditions under which each of them has special advantages. Our concern is not to evaluate group problem solving, but to see the place of social interaction in it.[1]

It is possible, as shown in Research Illustration 15.1, for interaction to take place without making any contribution to the solution of the problem that one or more group members could not have made alone. In the case of this particular study, solutions to one set of problems, dealing with spatial arrangements, required only that a single member contribute the correct "insight"; whereupon its correctness became evident to others. Thus the only kinds of interaction required were that the correct suggestion be made by someone and that the others indicate

[1] Our treatment of this problem has been greatly enriched by the comprehensive and insightful review provided by Kelley and Thibaut (1954), from which we have drawn freely.

Research Illustration 15.1

Faust (1959) designed an experiment to compare two kinds of tasks with respect to the contribution of social interaction to their solution. His subjects were students in introductory courses in psychology in two colleges, labeled A and B. At each campus students were assigned to one of fifteen groups of four persons each, or assigned to be one of forty-one individuals who worked alone. Each individual and each group of four worked for one hour on seven problems. Four of these were spatial problems. Example: Sixteen matches were laid out to make five squares, and three were to be moved to different positions to make four squares. The other three were anagram problems. Example: A sentence composed of seven words was presented; the words were in the correct sentence order but the letters of each word were scrambled. Instructions to groups and to individuals were similar except that group members were instructed to cooperate, to talk freely, and to work simultaneously on the same problem.

In the figure on page 466, comparisons of the white and black bars show that, on the average, more problems were solved in groups than by individuals working alone; all these differences are statistically significant. Since the average difference is less than 4 to 1, this superiority does not, of course, refer to efficiency in using manpower; it refers only to absolute numbers of problems solved.

Can this superiority be attributed, in part, to interactions between members of the group? To obtain an answer to this question, the data obtained from those who had actually worked alone were combined at random into nominal "groups" of the same size as the real groups, four members to a group. Then the performance of these "groups" was scored just as though the individuals had actually worked together; that is, if any individual in these artificial groups solved the problem, the group was scored as having solved it. (The problems had been carefully chosen so that when an individual discovered the right answer, it could be quickly demonstrated to the satisfaction of other group members and would be accepted by them.) The scores of these artificial "groups" thus provided a measure of the improvement in performance that could be expected by bringing individuals into groups of four even when there was no effective interaction between these individuals.

If an artificial "group" of four persons exhibits performance virtually identical with that shown by real (actually interacting) groups, we would have to conclude that there had been no improvement in the real group as a result of members' interaction with one another. We would conclude, rather, that its superiority over individuals, working alone, was due only to the presence of more than one person, any one of whom might discover the solution independently of the others. In that case, the group's superiority would be a direct effect of increased resource input, exclusively, and not at all of interaction among members.

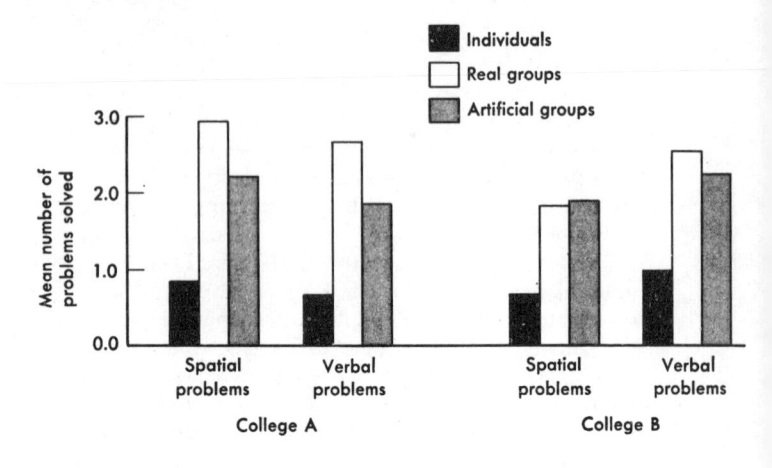

The differences that were actually found between real and artificial groups can be seen in the accompanying figure by comparing the white bars with the shaded ones. Real groups showed a superiority over artificial groups in three of four comparisons. On verbal problems, real groups did better than artificial ones in both colleges, the differences being significant or nearly so. In neither college, however, were the differences significant for the spatial problems. Thus it is reasonable to conclude that more effective interaction occurred in solving the verbal than the spatial problems. Two other findings about the group solutions are illuminating: (1) the spatial problems were essentially one-step problems, requiring only a single insight; and (2) there was little interpersonal behavior in the groups working on these problems. The verbal problems, on the other hand, involved several steps, so that the tasks of discovering these steps and fitting them together in the right order invited a good deal more interpersonal behavior.

their acceptance. Other kinds of problems require more continued or more varied kinds of interaction, the most essential of which we shall now consider.

The solution of any but the very simplest problems, whether by individuals or by groups, requires that at least two kinds of activities occur. (1) Relevant information (in the form of ideas, facts, considerations, suggestions, proposals, and so on) must be made available; typically these include alternative considerations, some of which will be accepted, tentatively at least, and others sooner or later rejected. (2) Processes of selection and combination among the recognized alternatives must occur. Thus the interactional processes involved in group problem solving will include exchanges of information by offering suggestions; by accepting, modifying, or rejecting them; and by combining into a solution one or more of those that are accepted. Our questions, in short, are these: In what ways do interactional processes determine what goes into the hopper (input), and the solutions that come out of it (output)?

Eliciting Members' Contributions

INTERACTION EFFECTS ON MEMBERS' MOTIVATION. Interactional processes affect the essential first step of making members' contributions available for group consideration by affecting members' motivations to offer contributions. Interactional events may serve either to facilitate or to inhibit the flow of contributions, and also, in selective ways, to encourage certain kinds of contributions while discouraging others. We shall therefore begin by considering various ways in which facilitative, inhibitory, and selective processes are influenced by interaction among members.

We have already seen (pages 281 ff.) that F. H. Allport found, as did Dashiell, that a majority of subjects worked faster working in each other's presence, in parallel fashion, and showed other characteristics suggesting increased energy output, as compared with individuals who were working alone. Their findings suggest that the continuing sights and sounds of others at work on the same problem, especially if combined with competitiveness, commonly have energizing effects, which Allport referred to as social facilitation. But both he and Dashiell found a minority of subjects whose productivity was reduced in the group situation; these individuals apparently found the group situation distracting. These different reactions were presumably associated with individual differences in personality, which are not our present concern; both reactions, of course, are interactional in nature.

The kinds of interaction that typically go on in cooperating groups tend also to be facilitative, though not necessarily so. The experiment by Deutsch (described in Research Illustration 11.4, page 353) showed a clear superiority of individual motivation to complete the task in cooperative as compared with competitive groups. With respect to social facilitation we may therefore conclude that under either competitive or cooperative conditions group members working on a common problem communicate to one another a sense of urgency that tends to heighten their mobilization of energy, and thus their motivation. Even those minimal forms of communication that occur merely in working side by side, with little or no competition or cooperation, often produce similar effects.

In the case of cooperation there are also motivational effects associated with group reinforcement, because of shared goals. What is rewarding to one is rewarding to all, and vice versa, and any group member can count on being rewarded by the approbation, expressed or implied, of other members for any contribution that he makes toward the group goal. Thus group members' contributions are motivated by anticipated rewards; because group norms call for problem-solving contributions, the group reinforces the kinds of behavior prescribed by its norms. These effects are peculiar to norm-sharing groups, and are thus distinct from social facilitation, the effects of which are simply those of energizing as a result of similar activities on the part of others.

Group reinforcement may, in a sense, have inhibitory as well as facilitative effects. In an experiment by Schachter *et al.* (1951), for example, it was shown that cohesive groups, whose members were presumably eager to be rewarded by one another, *depressed* their levels of productivity when their norms called for low production, whereas noncohesive groups were little affected by the same kind of norms. Norm-supported behaviors, whether in the direction of inhibiting or facilitating members' responses, are those that receive group reinforcement. In either case, individuals' motivations to make problem-solving contributions are affected either by ongoing or by anticipated responses of others.

CONDITIONS UNDER WHICH INTERACTION AFFECTS MOTIVATION. Individuals' motivations to offer problem-solving contributions are affected by several characteristics of the group. One of these is the state of *interpersonal relationships* within the group. Contributions are apt to be inhibited among a group of strangers; especially at first, members are apt to show various indications of restraint—for example, by cautiously "feeling each other out." Insofar as group members have friendly relations, they tend to communicate freely with one another—as shown, for example, by the spread of various kinds of information in the housing project described in Research Illustration 6.2. Lowered barriers to communication tend, if other things are equal, to facilitate contributions to problem solving. But friendly relationships can also serve to distract group members' attention to the task at hand. The experiment reported by Bos on page 470 illustrates this point. We would expect such distracting effects to be minimal, however, when motivation to attain a group-shared goal is strong. We may conclude, therefore, that relationships of positive attraction among group members tend to facilitate the offering of contributions insofar as they share a sense of urgency to solve the problem, and to minimize relevant contributions insofar as such a sense of urgency is lacking. In short, friendly relationships tend to exaggerate the effects of whatever sense of urgency is shared by group members.

Group size, among other properties described in Chapter 12, also affects the eliciting of members' contributions. It has been shown (cf. Bales, Strodtbeck, Mills, and Roseborough, 1951; Stephan and Mishler,

1952) that the larger a group the more of its members there are who contribute little or nothing—not only in terms of absolute numbers but even in terms of proportions. Bales *et al.*, working with groups of every size between three and eight, found that the amount of participation was fairly evenly distributed in groups of three or four persons, but participation became increasingly concentrated among smaller proportions of members as groups increased from five to eight persons. Depending on various personal characteristics and individuals' previous histories of success and failure in similar situations, increasing group size serves to facilitate the making of contributions by some individuals (the relatively rare overcontributors) but to inhibit it in most people.

Marked *status differentiation* within a group tends to inhibit contributions on the part of the lower-status members, as we noted in Chapter 11 (cf. Research Illustration 11.2, page 338). Insofar as higher-status members are abler or better informed than others, the quality of contributions made may not be affected much by the failure of others to contribute. But if the group's problem is one with which lower-status members are most familiar (for example, a grievance on the part of a work group), then any tendency of higher-status members to monopolize the conversation may have the consequence that the group does not really come to grips with some crucial aspects of the problem. There is also evidence (cf. Heinicke and Bales, 1953) that when status differences are recognized and accepted as legitimate by all or most members, better solutions are produced than in groups whose members disagree about the status hierarchy within the group—in part, perhaps, because in the latter groups there is some vying among members for position. In general, contributions, though not necessarily the most useful ones, are likely to be inhibited by marked differentiation unless group norms countering this tendency have evolved.

A group's *normativeness* refers to its power over its members with respect to the content of its norms, and this property affects not only the volume but also the content of its members' contributions. Norms may result in preselection of contributions, so that members readily make certain kinds of contributions but not other kinds. For example, the existence of a set of norms according to which members do not criticize one another may inhibit contributions (perhaps necessary ones for problem solution) that might appear to be critical of other members. Insofar as a group's norms are powerful and restrictive, they are likely to interfere with the making of original or creative contributions—for conformity is invariably the enemy of creativity. It is equally possible, however, though perhaps less frequent, that a group's norms may prescribe freedom to make unconventional, deviant, and unpopular kinds of contributions, and even provide rewards for making them.

Group Reactions to Members' Contributions

All the interactional processes and group properties that are related to the eliciting of contributions are also involved as members react to contributions that have already been made. Processes of social facilitation and group reinforcement, in particular, are likely to be intensified as members applaud, criticize, reject, or revise each other's proposals. As Bales (1955) has shown, problem-solving groups tend to move from an emphasis on eliciting ideas for consideration to an emphasis on reacting to them. Such "phase movement" is typically accompanied by a speedup in tempo: not only are there more ideas "before the house" to be reacted to, but motivation to participate becomes enhanced through social facilitation and group reinforcement. These processes are not very actively at work at the outset of a group problem-solving session; they emerge with members' interchange of ideas.

In this section we shall be less concerned with the motivational question of how interaction facilitates or inhibits members' participation than with the content of their contributions. That is, how do interactional processes affect the shaping of individuals' initial contributions into solutions that are acceptable to the group as a whole? This shaping process has to do not only with the acceptance or rejection of contributions but also with their revision and combination, and with the achievement of consensus concerning a solution.

INCREASING THE CLARITY OF CONTRIBUTIONS. Initial contributions are not always clear to others; very often, indeed, they are offered so hastily or so tentatively that their implications are not very clear to the contributors themselves. In any case, contributions cannot very well be included in a consensual solution unless they are understood in the same way by others and by their authors. The exchanges that often follow a contribution which seems to have interesting possibilities typically include questions and statements like "What do you mean by that?" or "Yes, but I don't get this part of your idea," followed by restatements, amplifications, or clarifications on the part of the original contributor. Not only do such exchanges often lead to consensual understandings; they may also lead to actual improvements by the contributor of his own idea, as the demands of clear communication force him to be clear to others as well as to himself.

An experiment by Maria Bos (1937) explores the possibility that when two or more persons work together the necessity of communicating to each other tends to clarify and sharpen the contributions of each. She used children at the age levels of 6–9 and 11–13 as subjects; the sixty-eight older children worked both individually and in pairs on the same tasks, half of them working first alone and then, several weeks later, together, while the other half reversed this order. The older children's problem was to choose from a large selection of paintings those that had been painted by the same person. The forty-three younger children, under similar but not identical conditions, were assigned the task of arranging five sets of pictures so that each sequence of pictures would tell a story. All pairs of children were encouraged to converse freely, and to work together in any way they chose, while the experimenter observed what they were doing.

In both age groups the experimenter found that the group products were superior to the individual ones. She concluded that this superiority had a good deal to do with the fact that in many instances a child's proposal was considered vague or puzzling by his partner, who by his subsequent questions forced the proposer to be more clear and specific about what he had in mind. According to her records, a child who made a suggestion often came to improve it because of such interchanges with his partner. Irrelevancies tend, by such processes, to get shorn off during the communicative exchange, so that the essentials of the contribution stand out in ways that are apparent to others as pointing toward a solution.

Bos also reports some interesting consequences of different degrees of preexperimental friendliness among her paired subjects. In her own words, "The fact of being intimate as playmates or friends did not affect either the working contact or the quality of the work. . . . It even seemed to us that a too lively personal interest of the children in each other was a stumbling block . . . the fact being that the contact which stimulates mental activity and intensity must be rooted in the *task in hand* and not in the *person*. If personal interest dominates, the attitude necessary for the work is interfered with."

ABANDONING FALSE LEADS. The more diffcult a problem, the more ambiguous it is, in the sense that there is no immediately clear path toward its solution. In the face of such ambiguity, an individual who thinks he perceives a possible path becomes motivated to pursue it, and probably to continue in that direction longer than seems profitable to other group members who are less motivated to follow it. Shaw's experiment on individual and group solving of very difficult problems (Research Illustration 12.1, page 361) illustrates the fact that individuals are more likely than groups to continue false leads for protracted periods of time: it was found that initiators rejected only one third as many of their own incorrect suggestions as were rejected by other group members. Our concern is not with who rejects the inappropriate suggestions, but simply with whether or not and how soon they get rejected; both common sense and empirical evidence indicate that they are more l ;ly to get rejected early in the game by groups than by individuals. ɪhis fact shows one important way in which interaction contributes to problem solving, especially in the case of difficult problems.

THE ACHIEVEMENT OF GROUP CONSENSUS. Let us assume that at the outset of a group's search for a solution to a problem no single individual has a solution that is immediately acceptable to all. Let us further assume that, even though the eventual solution may be self-evidently correct, on rational grounds, once it has been arrived at, the intermediate steps are not self-evident. Under these conditions the achievement of a consensual solution requires that during the course of their interaction many members are influenced to accept ideas they had not previously accepted. Some of the factors involved in such influence processes are noted in the following excerpt from a treatise on group problem solving:

> When the problem at issue requires opinions and judgments which cannot be validated by logic or empirical tests, people tend to seek support for their opinions through agreement with their associates. There appear to be at least two general types of relationship between the initiator and the recipient of a suggestion that can function to determine the degree to which the recipient agrees with and accepts the suggestion. In certain instances, the initiator may be viewed instrumentally as a "mediator of fact" by virtue of his perceived expertness, credibility, and trustworthiness. In other instances, the recipient may be motivated to agree with the initiator without regard for his "correctness"; agreement may become an independent motive. The strength of this motive seems to depend partly on the strength of positive attachment to and affection for the initiator. Thus A can produce a change in B's opinions if he is liked by B or provides the means whereby B satisfies important [motives]. When the group member has a strong positive attachment to his group and its members, he will tend to conform to the modal opinion expressed in the group. In such instances the opinion change resulting from discussion may produce a convergence upon the opinion initially held by the majority, as noted by Thorndike (1938). (Majority opinion may also be effective in the absence of positive feelings for the group. Where no expert opinion is available, the opinion held by most persons may be perceived as "the safest bet.") (Kelley and Thibaut, 1954, II, p. 743)

The effects of majority influence or of attributed expertness are not necessarily in the direction of "best" or "correct" solutions. Some of Shaw's groups, for example, rather rapidly reached consensual solutions, all of which were wrong. Insofar as unsatisfactory group solutions result from undue reliance on majority opinion or on the supposed expertness, the personal attractiveness, or the status positions of certain members, it is because either or both of two kinds of advantages of group problem solving, as summarized below, have been sacrificed.

* * *

The interaction processes that occur during group problem solving, regardless of whether they result in better or more efficient solutions than those produced by individuals working alone, produce their effects primarily in the following ways: (1) They influence members' motivation to produce ideas designed to lead toward a solution; such effects are often facilitating, but sometimes inhibiting. Insofar as social interaction and group reinforcement result in eliciting the maximum number and range of usable ideas that members are capable of contributing, solutions are facilitated. (2) Interaction processes commonly, though not necessarily, result in the clarification of individuals' contributions, in the abandonment of false leads, and in the combination of ideas proposed by different individuals, as members react to one another's contributions. Insofar as these effects occur, group solutions are different from and, especially in the case of difficult problems, often superior to solutions of which any single member is capable.

LEADERSHIP ROLES IN GOAL ACHIEVEMENT

As groups proceed with their various kinds of activities, it is easy to observe that different members make different contributions to whatever their group's objectives are. Their contributions differ both in degree and in nature; that is, some members make contributions that are more important or more indispensable than those of other members; and some of them facilitate goal achievement in one way and some in other ways. Insofar as any member's contributions are particularly indispensable, they may be regarded as leaderlike; and insofar as any member is recognized by others as a dependable source of such contributions, he is leaderlike. To be so recognized is equivalent to having a role relationship to other members, since (as we reasoned at the beginning of Chapter 11) it is not necessarily any specific behaviors on the part of a leaderlike person that make his contributions of special importance, but rather his relationship to other members. His end of such a role relationship is well described as that of a facilitator toward group goals.

This way of looking at leadership is quite different from several more conventional points of view, and sometimes in outright opposition to them. For example, a person who holds a high-status position of power or authority may or may not be a particularly valuable or indispensable facilitator, and even if he is he may not be generally recognized as such by those who work with and under him. Merely to hold a leaderlike position does not necessarily mean that one's role relationships with other group members are leaderlike. For similar reasons, leadership, if viewed as a facilitative role relationship, cannot very well be defined in terms of specific kinds of behavior. For example, the mere giving of orders is not necessarily facilitative, nor is a commanding air or a domineering manner. As noted in Research Illustration 15.3, there appear to be at least two very broad categories of behavior, one or both of which often characterize persons recognized as special facilitators, but the specific forms of their contributions may vary widely.

It is often assumed that individuals recognized as leaders must have certain kinds of personal characteristics in common. With comparatively few exceptions, however, the facts are solidly against this assumption. In a review of twenty different investigations of the traits of individuals regarded as leaders in various kinds of groups (Bird, 1940), altogether seventy-nine different traits were mentioned. Less than half of these seventy-nine traits appeared on more than one of the twenty lists, even allowing for near synonyms. Only one trait, intelligence, was included in as many as ten of the twenty lists. Not only was there little agreement among these lists; there was actually a good deal of contradiction: some included aggressiveness, ascendance, and decisiveness, whereas adaptability, tactfulness, mildness, and suggestibility appeared in others. It is not hard to see what lies behind such diversity. Different kinds of groups, existing for different purposes, are likely to find that different kinds of persons best serve as facilitators; even the same group, as a matter of fact, may find that quite different sorts of persons are equally good facilitators. Thus we cannot learn much about the nature of leadership by studying the personal characteristics of persons who are regarded as leaders.

Viewing leadership as a facilitative role relationship forces us to question another common assumption: that for each single group there is a single leader. We would not need to question this assumption if it were true that in most groups there is just one person who is recognized as *the* special facilitator in *all* ways that are important to goal achievement. Very often, however, this is simply not the case. Bales and others have shown, as in Research Illustration 15.3, that many groups distinguish between persons who are particularly good facilitators with respect to task achievement, and others whose distinctive contribution is toward the personal satisfaction of group members, both in relation to the task and to each other. It may commonly be observed, moreover, that during the course of one or more group sessions the role of principal facilitator shifts back and forth between two or more persons. It is often impossible, even with respect to one particular kind of contribution, to assert that any single person is *the* special facilitator. Such considerations suggest that it may be more harmful than helpful to think of leadership as necessarily concentrated in a single person.

Finally, the definition of leadership as a facilitative role relationship is not consistent with the rather common view that "the leader is the man who exerts the most influence." It is often the case that actual influence, in the sense of affecting the course of events, may be exercised in ways that are hardly recognized at all by other group members. Tremendous influence may stem from a person who works behind the scenes; examples from recent American history are Edward M. "Colonel" House in President Woodrow Wilson's administration, or Harry Hopkins, to whom President Franklin D. Roosevelt delegated so many crucial responsibilities. It can also happen that a titular leader who, because he works inconspicuously, is considered weak and ineffective by his associates, is in fact the controlling source of crucial decisions. Group members whose facilitative effects are not recognized by others do not thereby cease to be facilitators, but it is more accurate to say that their contributions are leaderlike than that they themselves are leaderlike. Other members cannot take their parts in a role relationship to a leader whose facilitative contributions they do not recognize. The interactional aspects of leadership (which we shall discuss further at the end of this section) depend, as do other role relationships, on the sharing of attitudes and expectations by role participants.

Hence we shall think of leadership as a matter of degree and kind of facilitation, rather than as an all-or-none affair; and as a role relationship in which the distinctive contributions of the various participants are commonly recognized, and expectations concerning one another's contributions are shared.

Modes of Facilitation

It is to be expected that the ways in which different forms of leader facilitation can most readily be distinguished will correspond to the kinds of facilitation that groups typically need. Most of this section is devoted to an examination of three kinds of group requisites, and of the ways in which interaction between leaders and other group members contributes to providing these requisites. Although they are all very common ones, it is not necessarily true that they apply to every group, nor to any group at any particular moment.

Research Illustration 15.2 presents one way of showing that group members tend to be valued by each other for different kinds of contributions. As shown in the figure that accompanies this report, the persons who (on the average, for forty-eight sessions held by four groups) were best liked were not the most active members, but the second and third most active members. The most active members typically received the most "dislike" ratings, and also the third most "like" ratings, together with the highest rating for their ideas. These and other similar findings have led Bales to propose "the hypothesis of two complementary leaders," labeled "task specialist" and "social-emotional specialist." These specialized kinds of facilitation correspond to group requisites that have to do with efficiency and with member satisfaction, respectively. We shall now examine each of these kinds of role relationships.

Research Illustration 15.2

Using the Interaction Process Recorder that is described in Appendix C, Bales observed the frequencies of each of the twelve categories of behavior on the part of each member of four five-man groups that met for twelve sessions (1958). The task assigned to each group was "to decide what should be recommended as action" in order to solve a "human-relations case." Each member, individually, was first given a five-page presentation of a problem facing an organization administrator; although all read the same material, in order to stimulate discussion they were left uncertain as to whether all had been given exactly the same information. Members were allowed to take notes, but not to consult the printed material after reading it through. Each group was allowed forty minutes, the last one or two of which were used to dictate the group's solution of the problem. There follows a brief excerpt describing a sequence of interaction on the part of one of the groups, together with the category assigned to each response in parentheses.

MEMBER 1: I wonder if we have the same facts about the problem? (*Asks for opinion.*) Perhaps we could take some time in the beginning to find out. (*Gives suggestion.*)

MEMBER 2: Yes, we may be able to fill in some gaps in our information. (*Gives opinion.*) Let's go around the table and each tell what the report said in his case. (*Gives suggestion.*)

MEMBER 3: Oh, let's get going. (*Shows antagonism.*) We've all got the same facts. (*Gives opinion.*)

MEMBER 2 (*Blushing and showing tension*): . . .

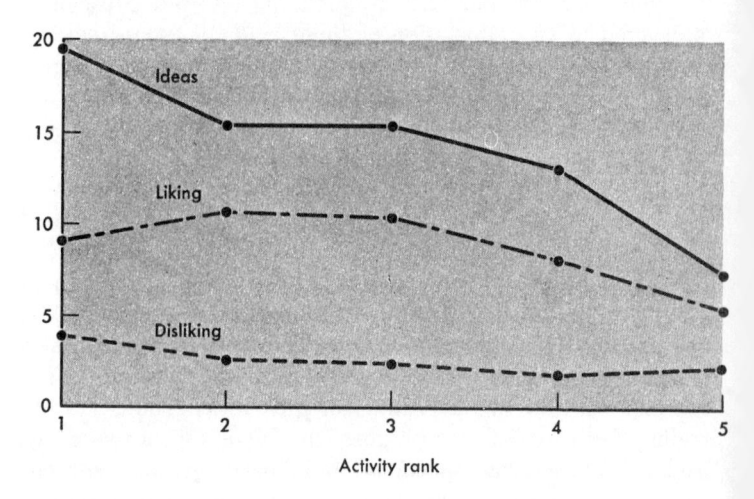

Average ratings received on ideas, liking, and disliking by men of each activity rank

At the end of each session every member was asked to rank each of the other members as to liking for him, disliking for him, and as to the value of his ideas. These rankings were later averaged for all forty-eight group sessions in order to relate them to indices of total activity on the part of each man—that is, "the total interaction initiated" by each man. In the accompanying figure, which summarizes the findings concerning this relationship, the "activity rank" refers not to any particular person in each group, but to whatever man was most active in each of the forty-eight sessions. Thus the values at the left of the figure, above Rank 1, are averages of the ratings received for whatever men happened to be most active in each session, whether or not the same individual. The figure shows that, typically, the most active man was thought to have the best ideas, but not to be the best liked.

Bales's data also show that this inverse relationship between having good ideas and being liked is characteristic of all sessions except the first one. In the first session (according to later data based on a larger number of groups), the top man in idea rank was also the top man in liking rank in more than half of the groups, but this occurred far less often during second sessions, and less than 10 percent of the time by the fourth session. Bales's own interpretation of such findings is stated, in part, as follows:

> Could it be that there was something about arriving in a top-status position, owing to technical contributions to the task problems of the group, that tended to "lose friends and alienate people"? If so, was another man likely to arise who paid more attention to the social-emotional problems of the group and so tended to collect more liking? The idea that this happens with sufficient frequency that it can be viewed as typical may be called "the hypothesis of two complementary leaders." (1958, p. 441)

FACILITATING TASK ACHIEVEMENT. Insofar as a group is task-oriented, its achievement depends not only on working out solutions and plans but also, very often, on carrying them to completion. In groups that have had a history of experience in working together toward their goals, one or more members are likely to become recognized as dependable facilitators because they are perceived as having some or possibly all of such resources as these:

they are knowledgeable about matters related to the task
they are imaginative, innovative
they are hard-headed, realistic
they are persuasive, convincing in obtaining group consensus
they are good at formulating problems or summarizing discussions
they are skilled in planning, organizing, coordinating
they can be depended on to carry through

Research Illustration 15.3

For a period of many years the Survey Research Center of The University of Michigan has studied relationships between working groups and their supervisors in varied settings. The results here reported are from section gangs on a railroad, work groups in a tractor factory, and clerical workers in an insurance company; about 2500 workers in some 400 different groups, together with supervisors in all groups, responded to interviews or questionnaires. Kahn and Katz (1960), the authors of the report, have this to say about their data-gathering procedures:

> . . . methodological emphasis was placed upon checks and controls in the field studies undertaken. Unquantified anthropological observation was replaced by standardized interviews with carefully defined samples of respondents. Impressionistic accounts of attitude and morale . . . were replaced with measures of workers' psychological responses. Effects of supervisory practices were not judged on the basis of what management assumed the results to be. Independently derived measures were employed in testing relationships. For example, supervisory behavior was measured independently of its effects upon productivity and morale of workers (p. 555).

Kahn and Katz report four ways in which high-producing groups differ from low-producing ones. The first of these is *role differentiation*: supervisors in high-producing groups typically do not perform the same tasks as do rank-and-file workers; in particular, they spend more time in planning, as reported both by themselves and by their supervisees. For example, 72 foremen in high- and in low-producing railroad groups replied as follows to the question, "How much of your time do you usually spend in supervising, and how much in straight production work?"

Production level	50% or more time spent in supervising	Less than 50% of time spent in supervising	Response not obtained	Total
higher	20	11	5	36
lower	9	22	5	36

(The differences between higher and lower production levels, in this table and in the two that follow, are highly significant: the probabilities that they are due to chance are less than .01.) Kahn and Katz regard the effects of supervising as being of two kinds: coordination and organization of tasks make for efficiency, and at the same time increases workers' motivation to produce.

A second difference between supervisors of high- and low-producing groups was that the former exercised *less close supervision* and delegated more authority. According to coders' assessments of lengthy interviews about their own jobs as supervisors of clerical workers in an insurance company, the two groups of supervisors differed as follows:

Production level	Close supervision	General supervision	Not ascertained	Total
higher	6	5	1	12
lower	11	1	0	12

Workers' own responses showed very similar differences. Close supervision (frequent checkups, detailed and frequent instructions, limitations upon employees' freedom to work in their own way) is generally intended either to keep men on the job or to make sure that their work is done in a specified manner. But it may also reduce a worker's sense of independence, and thus his motivation. According to Kahn and Katz's data, the latter effect tended to be predominant.

High-production supervisors tended, in the third place, to be more *"employee-oriented"* than other supervisors. In contrast to "production-oriented" supervisors, they give serious attention to matters of employee motivation, as reported by employees as well as by themselves. Examples of supervisors' employee-orientation include "understanding" rather than punitiveness when mistakes are made; helping employees to qualify for promotion; taking a personal interest in employees—even including their off-the-job problems. High-production supervisors were generally felt to be supportive.

As a fourth factor, though one that is less directly related to leadership, the high-production group members showed greater *cohesiveness* and pride in their jobs than the members of other groups. In the railroad study, both foremen and men in high-producing groups believed that their groups' production was "better than most," even when they had no means of knowing that this was in fact true. Clerical workers in an insurance company showed the following differences, with respect to pride in their own groups:

Production level	High pride	Medium pride	Low pride	Total
higher	47	53	43	143
lower	14	58	70	142

Typical comments by men in high-production groups include these: "I really feel a part of this group"; and "I'd rather have my job in this group than an identical one in another group." Such comments are particularly impressive in view of the fact that the men who made them did not believe that their own groups were superior in respect to skill, know-how, or education.

Finally, Kahn and Katz remind their readers that productivity is by no means perfectly correlated with supervisors' role differentiation, their not-too-close supervision, or their employee-orientation, nor with group cohesiveness; high productivity can occur in the absence of some or perhaps all of these conditions. They note that this is to be explained, in part at least, by the fact that a supervisor can increase productivity in *either* of two ways: through his technical skill or through his ability to motivate his men.

Some of these resources enable persons who possess them to make particularly useful contributions themselves, directly. Others refer to less direct forms of facilitation: insofar as any member can stimulate others to use *their* resources more fully, he has, so to speak, a multiplying effect, and this may be more significant than his own direct contributions. Some of the skills, habits, and practices on the part of supervisors of work groups that have such multiplying effects are described in Research Illustration 15.3. The more productive groups, according to these and other findings, were facilitated in either or both of these ways: (1) They were *enabled* to be effective because their supervisors provided technical know-how, planning, and coordination; (2) their members were *motivated* to be effective because their supervisors were generally supportive, and because they were proud of belonging to a successful work group. It is probable that comparatively few of the supervisors studied by Kahn and Katz combined both unusual enabling and unusual motivating skills, just as Bales found that "idea men" in his problem-solving groups were usually not "social-emotional" leaders also. Work groups are fortunate, apparently, if their appointed supervisors are particularly skillful either as enabling or as motivating facilitators. In either case, the achievement of high productivity as a group goal is dependent on those interactional processes by which group members respond to facilitating behaviors on the part of their supervisors.

The findings reported by Kahn and Katz do not necessarily mean that supervisors were influencers without themselves being influenced by interaction processes. For example, the supervisor of a group that is already a productive one sees little need of doing "straight production work," or of providing close supervision. Circular rather than one-way effects are probably the rule: an effective supervisor contributes to productivity, and is thereby encouraged to continue his effective procedures. We shall later note other instances of such circularity in interaction.

MAINTAINING SATISFYING INTERPERSONAL RELATIONSHIPS. Some groups exist, ostensibly at least, solely for the purpose of accomplishing certain tasks, but the achievement of such goals is likely to be aided or hindered by members' interpersonal satisfactions or dissatisfactions, as the studies by Bales and by Kahn and Katz have shown. Other groups have few or no objectives other than the satisfactions that members find in interacting with one another. Most if not all groups whose members continue to interact share, briefly and episodically at least, both kinds of concerns. Regardless of the nature of a group's dominant goals, therefore, their achievement can be facilitated by any member insofar as he contributes to making intermember relationships satisfying. Leaderlike behaviors that are directly facilitative in such ways include the following:

> providing warmth, friendliness
> conciliating, resolving conflict, relieving tension
> providing personal help, counsel, encouragement
> showing understanding, tolerance of different points of view
> showing fairness, impartiality

The would-be facilitator of satisfying interpersonal relationships faces a special dilemma, however: How can he, especially if he occupies a formal position of leadership, show warmth and supportiveness in an impartial manner and at the same time let both effective participators and ineffective or disturbing ones know how he assesses their work? Fiedler's studies, as summarized in Research Illustration 15.4, point to what appear to be common practices on the part of accepted leaders of effective groups, as they confront this dilemma. They tend to depersonalize their relationships to group members; that is, they are task-oriented rather than person-oriented even in their personal relationships. But Fiedler's findings, as he carefully notes, apply only to groups in which "the leader is sociometrically endorsed by the men on whom his authority depends. . . . Where his subordinates will not 'listen' to him, his attitudes cannot affect the group's behavior." All this suggests that in at least some task-oriented groups of men, a leader who discriminates between effective and ineffective workers is not regarded as unfair. When task goals are shared, personal warmth can be made subsidiary to task accomplishment, and under such conditions discrimination is facilitative; a discriminating leader is not only accepted but also, apparently, respected.

Fiedler's findings, like those of Kahn and Katz, point to ways in which through facilitative behavior a person can multiply his own effectiveness by making the group as a whole an effective one.

These findings and those of Katz and Kahn do not, however, suggest exactly the same conclusions. The importance of psychological distance in Fiedler's studies has a good deal to do with two facts: most if not all of his groups were rather small; and his "leaders" were sociometrically chosen individuals, and not necessarily official ones. Under these conditions group members can accept discrimination on the part of a leader whom they know and trust, and can profit by his somewhat cold-blooded supervision. But in larger groups, whose leaders are considered to be official supervisors who are not necessarily sociometrically preferred or even particularly trusted, the characteristics of employee-orientation and supportiveness on the part of supervisors may be fully as important as the maintaining of psychological distance.

Research Illustration 15.4

Fiedler (1960) has made a number of studies of one aspect of relations between leaders and other members of a wide variety of natural groups. His work began with discoveries that are consistent with principles of balanced interpersonal systems: most members of a college fraternity, for example, were found to see more similarity between themselves and their most preferred associates than between themselves and their least preferred ones. Such tendencies were not universal, however, and so he began to study group leaders in terms of the degree to which they did or did not perceive most and least preferred co-workers as being different; this variable he labeled *assumed similarity of opposites* (ASo). His rationale for applying this variable to group leaders was as follows: Those who discriminate sharply between the characteristics of their most and their least preferred co-workers are, in effect, rejecting the latter, whereas those who do not so discriminate are persons who prefer to keep close relationships with as many people as possible, whether or not they are desirable co-workers. Assumed *dis*similarity of opposites is thus, hypothetically, an index of interpersonal distance, in the sense of revealing more concern with work relationships than with personal involvement; assumed similarity of opposites reveals the opposite tendency.

One of the first kinds of groups that Fiedler studied was a league of fourteen high school basketball teams; the measure of a team's effectiveness was simply the proportion of games won during a season. The informal leader of each team (not necessarily the same as its captain) was designated as whatever man was most preferred by his teammates as a player, according to sociometric responses. Contrary to what you might expect, the more successful teams had chosen as their informal leader not the persons who made few discriminations among team members but those characterized by dissimilarity of opposites. In Fiedler's words,

> . . . we expected that members of good teams would have relatively close interpersonal relations with each other . . . that members of teams [whose members] accepted one another and felt close to others on the team would also feel more secure, and that this security would allow them to devote proportionally greater efforts to the task than to activities designed to consolidate their own status within the team. While this was a beautiful hypothesis, it failed to be supported. Much to our surprise, we found that the the good teams had . . . chosen as their informal leaders the low ASo persons [perceiving much dissimilarity], while the poorer teams had selected the warmer, more accepting, high ASo persons as informal leaders. The correlation between the informal leader's ASo score and the proportion of games the team had won . . . was −.69, a very high relationship for studies of this nature.

A comparable study of a second set of basketball teams yielded similar results. Later studies of student surveying teams, bomber crews, Army tank crews, shift workers in open-hearth steel mills, and staffs of consumer cooperatives provided general support for the original investigations of basketball teams, and in some cases even stronger support. Fiedler's interpretations of these findings are offered, in part, in response to the question, Why is psychological distance relevant to team performance?

> . . . we cannot adequately control and discipline people to whom we have strong emotional ties. If a man is emotionally dependent on another, he cannot afford to antagonize him since this might deprive him of the other man's support. Similarly, we can evaluate only those people, objectively, and we can control only those on whose good will we do not want to depend.

Whatever the leaderlike behaviors that contribute to satisfying interpersonal relationships, they will be most facilitative if (as in the case of task achievement) they enable a group member to multiply his own effectiveness through others. Insofar as one of Fiedler's informal leaders facilitates the arousal of a group norm of impersonality, according to which task achievement is rewarded and laxity is not, then he has multiplied his own effectiveness because group members themselves enforce the norm. Insofar as one of Kahn and Katz's supervisors contributes to the creation of cohesiveness and consensual pride in their group, he too is multiplying his effectiveness. Satisfying interpersonal relations, like task achievement, are outcomes of interaction within the group as a whole; it is the facilitative effects on members' interaction that are the essence of leadership.

Sources of Individuals' Potential for Facilitation

It is obvious that no one can be an effective facilitator in ways that are beyond his capacities or that are personally repugnant to him. But attempts to identify leaders merely in terms of their personal characteristics have not, as we indicated at the outset of this chapter, been very fruitful. Our concern is with the social sources, not the intrapersonal ones, of individuals' potential for facilitating the achievement of group goals. More specifically, our present questions are of this kind: What are the social conditions that tend to elicit whatever abilities group members have to become facilitators?

Since we have already considered some motivational aspects of this question (in Chapter 9), we shall concentrate on group-structural considerations. Certain kinds of positions make it possible for their occupants to be particularly facilitative—and equally possible, of course, for them to provide obstacles to goal achievement. We shall consider two general ways in which recognized positions—especially formal ones, like those of a president, a manager, or a foreman—carry with them a potential for facilitation.

FACILITATION THROUGH POWER. An individual's social power refers to the resources that he can muster by way of bringing influence to bear on one or more others. It is his potential to exert influence, with or without the willing consent of anyone who is the object of influence. Such power may or may not be resisted; it refers to influence potential, not to effectiveness in any particular instance.

Many formal positions confer power, in this sense, on their occupants, and this may also be true of informal positions, as in the case of some of Fiedler's more effective leaders. Two somewhat different bases of position-associated power may be distinguished: authority, and control of resources. *Authority* refers to consensually supported power; that is, the power behind a position of authority lies in the probability that others will support attempts by the position holder to exert influence, and if necessary help make his attempts successful. Consensual support for authority may be internal (on the part of group members themselves) or external (on the part of outsiders, as in the case of a group of managers who support a foreman's attempts to influence his workers). Group members may accept the authority of a position holder (that is, submit to his influence) either out of respect for his personal characteristics or out of deference to the position, regardless of who occupies it, or for some combination of these. The essence of authority is that its strength lies in group norms; members share acceptance of rules according to which authority is granted to someone.

There are many forms of *resource control*. A foreman, for example, has it in his power to make equipment or materials available to his men, and a corporation president can allocate financial resources in various ways. Control over information is a particularly effective form of exerting influence that is often available to officials. As indicated in Leavitt's experiment (Research Illustration 11.3, page 342), persons who occupy key positions in communication networks tend to be thought of as leaders. Top officials of groups or organizations often owe a great deal of their power to the fact that they have both internal and external communicative access—that is, both to their subordinates and to outsiders. Members at lower-status levels usually have less access to internal sources of information, and little or none externally.

FACILITATION THROUGH VISIBILITY. Insofar as special facilitators, whether or not they hold formal positions, are consensually recognized as such, they are generally visible to other group members. This fact in itself adds to their facilitative potential, in either or both of two ways. Their visibility, in the first place, makes them *symbols* of the group, both internally and externally. As personified symbols, both group members and outsiders tend to bring problems to them, rely on their advice, or seek their influence. Recognition as a facilitator results in acceptance as a symbol, which in turn results in increased opportunities for facilitation. Their visibility may also result in their being accepted as *models* for others to follow. Insofar as this occurs, their effectiveness may be multiplied in many ways; ineffectiveness, too, may have multiplying effects.

Leadership as a Role Relationship

It is possible for an interaction group to continue to exist, and even attain its goals quite successfully, in the absence of any particularly facilitative contributions on the part of any members; there would be no leaders in such a group. But the reverse is not true: there could be no leader apart from a group. In this sense a group is more essential to a leader than a leader to a group, and this fact alone makes clear the interactional nature of leadership, which depends quite as much on what group members do to, for, and with a leader as on anything that he does. Facilitation, after all, requires persons to be facilitated, and shared recognition of a facilitator is a matter of response by members not only to him but also to one another.

It is for such reasons that we have described leadership as a role relationship. Once a group member has become recognized by others as particularly facilitative in certain ways, those ways are likely to become habitual on his part as others develop habits of responding to his facilitative ways; thus role relationships develop that are, quite literally, two halves of the same habit.

*　　*　　*

Leadership is best understood as a role relationship in which one or more members are recognized as special facilitators toward group goals. All continuing interaction groups are confronted, briefly and occasionally at least, with problems of task achievement and of maintaining interpersonal relations that are satisfying to members. It often happens that one or more members are especially facilitative toward solving one of these kinds of problems but not the other, so that two or more persons are equally leaderlike, but in different ways. Solutions to either of these kinds of problem, moreover, may be facilitated in different ways, depending especially on the nature of the group's goals, the size of the group, the personal characteristics of leaders, and their acceptance by other group members. Leaders may or may not hold official positions, but in either case they are aided in their facilitative behavior by the visibility that comes with being recognized as facilitators, and by the power that goes with positions of leadership. Leaders' contributions are most effective when they result in increased effectiveness on the part of other members; thus their own contributions are multiplied. Effective leaderlike behavior is constantly dependent on the behavior of other members, and is thus interactional in nature, just as all role relationships are.

GROUP COHESIVENESS AND GOAL ACHIEVEMENT

In the experiment described in Research Illustration 14.6 (page 459), goal achievement was one of the conditions under which group cohesiveness arose. We shall now inquire into the reasons why this should be so, as well as the reasons for the converse relationship, according to which cohesiveness facilitates goal achievement.

Cohesiveness Contributes to Goal Achievement through Group Power

A highly cohesive group, as we noted in pages 380–386, has some or all of the following characteristics:

1. a high level of mutual attraction among its members—not necessarily in the form of personal liking, but in the general sense that members attribute reward value to each other;
2. shared attitudes, including shared acceptance of rules (normativeness), concerning group-relevant matters;
3. well-developed structural integration; members' role relationships, including those of leadership, are understood, accepted, and smoothly coordinated.

Since it is group properties like these that make up cohesiveness, our first question becomes this: Just how do these properties on the part of a group contribute to its success in goal achievement? Let us first present our answer, and then go on to justify it: Each of these properties confers power on the group over its members. The term "power" is not an explanation, but only a label for the effects that we must account for; it is the interactional processes behind the label that provide the necessary explanations. These processes may all be seen in Research Illustration 15.5, describing an experiment in which these several aspects of cohesiveness were observed as they developed and changed.

Interpersonal attraction, in the first place, confers power on the attractive person over the one to whom he is attractive. Insofar as you like someone, or trust him, or respect him, you have ceded to him power over yourself in the sense that you are influenceable by him. You have, so to speak, already decided that he is a person who does not have to

Research Illustration 15.5

In an experiment reported by Sherif and Sherif (1953), twenty-four twelve-year-old boys in an isolated summer camp served as subjects. All were from settled, Protestant families in the lower-middle income group, and none was regarded as a "behavior problem"; no boy had a previous history of friendship with any of the others. The boys did not know that an experiment was being conducted or that systematic observations were being recorded by observers who acted as counselors.

Stage 1 of the experiment consisted of a three-day period designed to permit the formation of spontaneous, informal groupings among the boys. All activities were camp-wide, with maximum freedom allowed in choosing bunks, seats, buddies, and athletic teams. At the end of this period, sociometric responses showed that the boys were already clustering into friendship groups.

Stage 2, lasting five days, then began. The twenty-four boys were then split into two groups of twelve each, in such manner that the friendship groups already formed were split up: typically, each boy found that about two thirds of his friendship choices were now in the other group, and only one third in his own new group. Each new group chose a bunkhouse, and the two groups then left immediately, in opposite directions, for hikes and cook-outs. These activities, previously chosen as particularly attractive, succeeded fairly well in minimizing the boys' resistance to their group assignments. During the five-day period each group, separately, participated in activities like preparing their own meals when they were very hungry, making preparations for overnight camping when they were tired, and selecting and improving "secret hideouts"—activities known to be appealing to the boys and that required participation by each of them. Staff members left the planning of these activities to the boys themselves, even though many of the situations were new to them.

The following table shows that at the end of stage 2 nearly all friendship choices were given to members of the stage 2 groups, even though these groups had, at the end of stage 1, included only about one third of the boys' choices. Exact percentages of friendship choices were as follows:

	Received by Red Devils		*Received by Bull Dogs*	
	from Red Devils	*from Bull Dogs*	*from Red Devils*	*from Bull Dogs*
Beginning of stage 2	35.1	64.9	65.0	35.0
End of stage 2	95.0	5.0	12.3	87.7

Although it is possible that some of these shifts in friendship choices might have occurred during the same five-day period even without experimental changes in group composition, it is much more

> plausible to attribute them to the group members' common experiences as they worked together toward common goals of importance. This interpretation is supported by other evidence indicating that each group developed a distinctive set of norms regulating the behavior of its members in specified situations. For example, deviation from prescribed norms was handled in the Bull Dog group by assigning varying numbers of stones to be removed by the offender from their swimming pond. Each group had its own ways of making lanyards, and distinctive procedures for selecting secret meeting places.

be avoided, mistrusted, or looked down on, and you are therefore relatively open to his influence—which you have, in effect, invited. Your influenceability may, of course, be limited to those areas on which your attraction is based; you might not, for example, be influenceable by your philosophy professor concerning financial matters even though you respect his mind and his character. The essence of attraction is interpersonal rewardingness, and by inviting from an attractive person further acts that are rewarding one exposes oneself to his influence.

Under conditions of continued interaction, attraction tends, in the second place, to become mutual; it is usually rewarding to O to discover that P finds him rewarding. This tendency may, of course, be offset by stronger countertendencies: it is not very rewarding to find oneself rewarding to someone for whom one has only contempt. The bases for P's attraction toward O may, moreover, be quite different from the bases for O's toward P; they are rewarded by different qualities that they find in each other. Typically, attraction that is totally unrequited tends not to persist. It is maintained by continuing interaction such that both (or all) group members continue to be rewarded; each grants to the other power over himself. Personal attraction (P to O) is an individual affair, but mutual attraction (P to O together with O to P) is a group characteristic. Thus it is not only true that attraction toward a person involves yielding power to him; it is also true, insofar as attraction is mutual, that it involves yielding power to the group of which he is a member. The latter statement is true because the power that is given is dependent on the group characteristics of mutuality and reciprocally rewarding behavior. It is the total set of interpersonal relationships characterizing the group as a whole that is the source of power over each of its members. Each group member contributes to that power, even though it may be exerted over himself. Thus the power over any member derives from all members, and is a group property.

A group also acquires power over its members insofar as they have consensual and especially *shared attitudes*. Even if attitudes are not fully shared—that is, if it is not true that all members know that all members are in agreement—a group that is perceived to be consensual by any of its members is likely to have the power to influence those members (Research Illustration 8.4, page 239). Insofar as attitudes are shared, the group's power is even more effective—not only because sharing presupposes agreement but also, more importantly, because of group reinforcement (each member's attitudes are supported by the fact of being shared), and because of internalization (each member's attitudes are his own, and no longer need the reinforcement of rewards by others). *Normativeness* is the example par excellence of the power exerted by way of shared attitudes. By sharing in the acceptance of a rule, each member contributes to and thus helps to create the group's power over all its members, including himself.

A particularly important way in which normativeness can be expressed is in *structural integration,* which refers to interdependent role relationships among group members such that their activities are coordinated and the group is like a single unit, behaviorally (cf. pages 368–372). Integration may, in fact, be considered as the outcome of shared acceptance of rules for interdependent role relationships. Any relationship of interdependence involves some loss of autonomy by the parties to the relationship, but integrated interdependence—as in the cooperation of team members, for example—often brings the more than compensating gains of sharing in the rewards of joint activity. Integration, which is a property of the group as a whole, means that the group makes behavioral demands on its members, who comply with them. Thus the group is the source of the power that regulates role relationships, which in turn make integration possible.

What mutual attraction, shared attitudes, and structural integration have in common, then, is that they are all outcomes of interaction that result in conferring power on a group over its members. These interaction processes correspond, respectively, to the providing of mutual rewards, the expression and the perception of similar attitudes, and integrated role participation. Since groups are cohesive to the extent that they are characterized by such forms of interaction, it follows that cohesive groups should have power over their members. Thus cohesiveness contributes to goal achievement insofar as a group's power is mobilized and directed toward its goal.

Goal Achievement Enhances Cohesive Power

The Sherifs' study (Research Illustration 15.5) is especially useful in showing by experimental procedures, rather than merely by the observation of groups in natural settings, that successful goal achievement can be an important determinant of group cohesiveness. Like any other good experiment, this one has the advantage of being unambiguous concerning dependent and independent relationships. We know that goal achievement preceded cohesiveness in this case because the experiment was arranged that way; and we know that there was a change in cohesiveness because at least one of its components (interpersonal attraction) was actually reversed, and thus could not have been merely the result of continued acquaintance. As we examine the processes by which this occurs we shall, as in accounting for the converse relationship, examine each of the main components of cohesiveness.

It seems self-evident that group members' success in jointly achieving a goal is likely to increase their attraction toward one another, particularly as coparticipants in that same kind of activity. Such an outcome is directly predictable on theoretical grounds, since attraction toward a person is conceptually equivalent to attributing reward value to him, and since it is rewarding to be helped in achieving a desired goal. Everyday experience supports the observation that winners stick together and losers fall apart. A great deal of research evidence also supports the prediction; thus McGrath (1965), in a detailed, quantitative analysis of some 250 experiments, reports that effectively performing groups tend to have these characteristics, among others: "little hostility and disagreement within the group; perceptions of successful outcomes . . . ; interpersonal attraction for some but not all types of operational tasks." He then goes on to conclude that "the nature of these variables makes it necessary to consider them as consequences or concomitants of task success rather than as antecedents of task success." Although we have reasoned, in the preceding section, that attraction may also be an antecedent condition, in the sense of contributing to the group's potential for task success, presently available evidence for this position is less plentiful than for attraction as a consequence of goal achievement.

Group members' success in previous goal achievement tends also to enhance the sharing of task-relevant attitudes. Shared pride in performance is a good example, as in the case of Kahn and Katz's more productive groups, whose members were aware of their high performance (Research Illustration 15.3). Shared acceptance of rules, insofar as their observance is considered responsible for previous success, tends to increase with success. Thus normativeness is reinforced by successful goal achievement.

For similar reasons, goal achievement is likely to contribute to *structural* integration. Interdependent role relationships that appear to have worked successfully are thereby reinforced, and with repeated successes they become more smoothly developed—as illustrated by a winning football team at the end of the season. As formal or informal leaders discover the ways in which they can be facilitative, their fellow members both adapt to those ways and exert influence on them. Thus role relationships between one or more special facilitators and those who are helped by them become more closely integrated, and team members come to perform more and more as a unit.

The effects of goal achievement on mutual attraction, shared attitudes, and structural integration take place through processes of interaction that follow the rewards associated with group success. Insofar as each member is motivated to achieve the goal, he is rewarded by any indication of progress toward it, and any of his own behaviors contributing to that step are reinforced. And insofar as progress depends on coordinated behavior of two or more members—either simultaneously or in sequence—each member's participation in that coordination becomes reinforced; the result is that they learn to respond to each other in coordinated fashion. Such, in principle, are the individual psychological processes that lie behind the interactional processes. The latter consist essentially of social facilitation (reciprocal heightening of motivation) and group reinforcement (the establishment or strengthening of shared norms through rewarding interaction), as outlined in Chapter 9. Because joint goal achievement is typically rewarding, it gives rise to these interactional processes that in turn strengthen a group's cohesive power.

Circular Relationships between Cohesiveness and Goal Achievement

This somewhat idealized account indicates the general nature of the relationships between goal achievement, either as dependent or as independent, and some of the components of cohesiveness; it is not intended as a literal description of invariable sequences of events. These relationships may be summarized as follows: Insofar as a group has previously made use of whatever cohesive power it has had over its members, by way of mutual attraction, shared attitudes, and structural integration, it has achieved its goals with some measure of success. And the greater its history of success the more likely it is that the group's power has been enhanced. By the same token, the less fully a group exploits its existing power, the less likely its success in goal achievement; and such failure, in turn, tends to reduce its cohesive power.

Such circularity—continuing cycles either of successful use of power, increasing power, and further success, or of unsuccessful use of power, decreasing power, and further failure—is not, however, inevitable. Each step in these cycles is merely a statement of what is most likely to happen *if* all other things remain the same. General principles must necessarily be stated in this fashion, even though in everyday experience it is rarely true that all other things remain the same. It often happens, for example, that shared awareness of failure leads group members to reexamine things; if so, the very task of reexamination sets a problem the successful solution of which may reverse the cycle, perhaps by discovering improved methods of ensuring structural integration. In analogous fashion, excessive pride in previous accomplishment may result in laxity, as if continued success were automatically guaranteed; thus the successful cycle may be reversed, as when a winning streak is broken through overconfidence. Cycles may be reversed in various ways: through changed patterns of interaction within the existing group; through actual changes in the group (such as losing some members or gaining new ones); or through external influences of many possible kinds. The reversal of cycles through such changes does not imply, however, that the general principles by which cohesiveness and goal achievement are related have been changed. On the contrary, general principles must take account of relevant conditions that may change; a general principle is embedded in a theory that accounts for varying effects by taking account of changing conditions under which the principle operates.

One of our main objectives, as we noted in Chapter 1, has been to formulate just such principles, that is, in such form that outcomes are predictable in terms of conditions included in the principle. Social psychology has only recently come to the stage where it is possible to formulate and to interrelate some of the necessary principles, in rather tentative form, on the basis of still incomplete evidence. In the long run, as the late Professor Kurt Lewin was fond of saying, there is nothing as practical as a good theory (that is, a set of interrelated principles). Social psychology's "good theory" is still far from complete. You are therefore invited to share in the task of extending and improving it.

OVERVIEW: INTERACTION AT WORK

Group members, as they work jointly to solve a problem, influence one another by affecting not only the ways in which they offer, criticize, revise, and combine proposed solutions but also their motivation to make such contributions. One or more members of continuing interaction groups are often special facilitators toward goal achievement, and insofar as they are so recognized by others they are leaderlike. There are many ways in which members can assume leadership roles of facilitation, even within the same group. Since most if not all continuing groups face problems both of task solution and of maintaining satisfying interpersonal relations, group effectiveness is likely to be increased by members' interaction with one or more leaders who are special facilitators in solving both kinds of problems.

The basic interactional processes through which groups effectively achieve their goals—social facilitation and group reinforcement, in particular—tend to enhance a group's cohesive power. Insofar as a group's power is directed toward the achievement of its goals, through such interaction, its goals are likely to be reached. The converse is also true: a history of successful goal achievement makes more likely those interactional processes by which a group's cohesive power is increased. Continuing cycles of goal achievement, increased power, repeated goal achievement, and so on, characterize effective groups.

APPENDIXES AND REFERENCES

APPENDIX A

The Measurement of Attitudes

SYSTEMATIC INQUIRY INTO ANY SUBJECT MATTER IS LIMITED BY EXISTING capacities to measure with some precision the critical variables in the area. Social psychology has been no exception. Although the concept of *attitude* has in one form or another been central to the field from the start, attitude is by definition a mental state. Within the limits of our current knowledge of physiological psychology, such states are not subject to any direct "physical" measurement. This fact, along with a prevalent suspicion that "merely verbal" responses to questions concerning an individual's mental states were fundamentally untrustworthy, greatly impeded the development of social psychology in the early decades of this century. It was not until the 1920s that any very systematic attempts were made to differentiate individuals according to verbal indications of social attitudes. And it was only as it became clear that these efforts at measurement, crude though they might be, still permitted useful inferences about attitudes and behavior to be drawn that social psychology came to flower as a self-conscious and experimental body of inquiry.

ATTITUDE ITEMS AND ATTITUDE SCALES: EARLY EFFORTS

THE LIKERT SCALE. Although it was not the earliest technique in point of time, the mode of attitude measurement that may come closest to our intuitive ideas concerning the location of individuals on a positive-negative attitude continuum is represented by the type of attitude item devised by Likert (1932). The Likert item requires the subject to indicate the direction and degree of affect he feels concerning an object, event, or possible state of affairs. Responses are made within a five-category continuum, in the following manner:

> Encircle *one* of the symbols preceding each of the following statements. *A* stands for "Agree," *SA* for "Strongly Agree," *D* for "Disagree," *SD* for "Strongly Disagree," and *?* for "Uncertain."
>
> SA A ? D SD   If the same preparation is required, the Negro teacher should receive the same salary as the White.
>
> SA A ? D SD   Negro homes should be segregated from those of White people.

Hence each such item serves to classify the respondent at a point on a simple positive-negative continuum with respect to some relatively narrow and specific state of affairs. Typically investigators have wished to deal in batteries of such items, in order to assess reliably a more generalized reaction to some complex object. Thus the Likert items used in the example are but two from a lengthier set, all of which might be expected in view of their content to reflect more general attitudes (in this case toward the Negro). It was assumed furthermore that some reasonable method of combining or summing up an individual's responses toward specific aspects of the same object (what we called in Chapter 3 "subattitudes") would provide a reliable indication of the individual's generalized attitude toward that common object. In the Negro case, for example, a white individual who responded that he strongly disagreed with items suggesting Negro-white contact or equality, and strongly agreed with items proposing segregation and invidious distinction between the races, would reasonably be rated as having an extremely negative attitude toward Negroes. Mixed or uncertain responses would by the same token suggest indifference or ambivalence, and would tend to locate the individual at some middle position on the summarized attitude continuum.

Such a combining of responses to a number of items into a single summary produces what is called an *attitude scale*. One of the most straightforward modes of combination is that suggested by Likert for turning a set of his items into a *Likert scale*. This method calls for the assignment of a sequence of integer scores such as 1, 2, 3, 4, and 5 to the five ordered categories of response, taking care that the "1" response is consistently assigned to either the positive or the negative extreme (since a "strongly disagree" may mean a negative reaction to the object for some items, whereas a "strongly agree" may have that meaning for other propositions) and then prescribes a simple summation of these scores for the individual across the whole battery. As a result, a five-item

Likert scale with such scoring would give total scores ranging from a minimum of 5 (5 × 1) to a maximum of 25 (5 × 5).

The Likert scale may seem to be such a natural way of drawing attitude measurements and combining them that other alternatives are not apparent. Yet social psychologists rapidly became aware of the many assumptions required by any technique of attitude measurement, assumptions both as to the nature of attitudes and the nature of measurement itself. This recognition has touched off much exploration of alternative techniques of attitude measurement, with differing measurement properties and based on different assumptions about attitudes. Before examining the kinds of assumptions that any measurement makes, let us consider an example of a slightly different early strategy of attitude measurement.

THE BOGARDUS SOCIAL DISTANCE SCALE. One of the first landmarks in the history of attitude measurement was the scale of "social distance" devised by Bogardus in 1925 (certain applications of which are discussed on pages 429 ff. and 446 ff.). He was interested in measuring degrees to which individual representatives of various racial and national groups were accepted or rejected. Instead of making a distinction between favorable and unfavorable attitudes, he conceived the problem in terms of degrees of "distance" that his subjects wished to keep between themselves and members of other groups. If the social distance between two intimate friends is represented by zero, at the other extreme the attitude of a rabid anti-Semite toward Jews would represent maximum social distance. Directions for responses to this scale are as follows:

> According to my first feeling reactions I would willingly admit members of each race (as a class, and not the best I have known, nor the worst members) to one or more of the classifications which I have circled.

In the original form of the scale, the names of various ethnic groups are listed at the left of the page, and across the top of the page appear verbal statements of seven steps of social distance, any one or more of which may be accepted by each respondent for each group. These seven steps are indicated in Figure A.1.

You will notice in this figure that at every step along the scale the social distance expressed for Canadians is very much less than for Greeks and Serbo-Croats and, except at the fifth step of the scale, considerably less than for Spanish. In general, the percentages increase from the first through the fifth step. And if the sixth and seventh steps had been stated in negative form—indicating *un*willingness to exclude—then the percentages would increase steadily from the first through the seventh step in most cases. This suggests a certain ordering of the social distance steps: If a person rejects the idea of a particular foreign national being em-

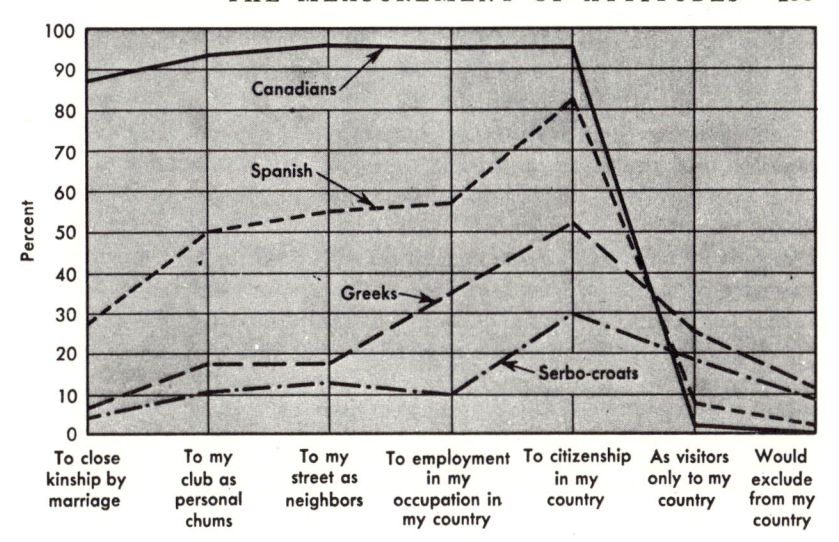

FIGURE A.1. Percentages of 1725 native Americans expressing each of seven degrees of social distance toward selected nationality groups (adapted from Bogardus, 1928)

ployed in the same occupation in his country, it is unlikely that he would admit this foreign national to close kinship by marriage.

Such an ordering of items, as we shall see, can be considered an important property of an attitude scale. In the case of the Bogardus scale, the fact that most respondents would tend to accept persons of a given nationality up to a certain degree of social proximity, and then reject them in any more intimate contact, gives us a very natural means of placing individuals in single locations on the social distance scale. That is, we would want to characterize the amount of social distance an individual feels toward a group by that point at which his acceptance turns to rejection. This single score, as a means of summarizing an individual's attitude after observing his response to a number of stimuli (in this case, seven), is analogous to the summed score for an individual on a Likert scale, although the tactics employed to arrive at such a description are quite different in the two cases.

If we were interested in measuring attitudes toward an ethnic or a racial group in terms of some generalized positive-negative continuum, what difference would it make which of these two kinds of attitude scales we decided to use? For some gross purposes, such as locating in a population those individuals who are relatively hostile to that group, and distinguishing them roughly from those more favorably disposed, it is likely that the two methods would give fairly comparable results. On the other hand, if we are conducting an experiment inducing change in ethnic group attitudes, we might not expect to be able to move many if any persons from a generally unfavorable to a generally favorable position, but would be satisfied if we could demonstrate that a significant portion of our subjects had been moved some detectable distance along the attitude continuum. For finer purposes such as these, we are likely to become much more concerned with both the accuracy and the meaning of our scale scores, as well as the kinds of units and distances that different attitude scales presume. To understand the issues involved here, we must first make some general observations about the nature of the measurement process itself.

GENERAL CHARACTERISTICS OF MEASUREMENT

The purpose of any scale is to measure something. Any object has various characteristics or dimensions that can be measured. A sample of some unknown solid, for example, may be measured in terms of its weight, its volume, its melting point, its resistance to an electrical current, and so on. In each case a different scale must be used to measure the dimension in question and each scale must be calibrated in units appropriate to the dimension being measured—pounds, cubic inches, degrees of temperature, ohms, and so on. The size of the units are matters of established convention, and originally were rather arbitrary. Instead of dividing the time continuum according to rotations of the earth into twenty-four equal parts to make hours, and subdividing this unit into sixtieths to make minutes, man might have tied his time units to the rotation of the moon around the earth and subdivided in tenths or hundredths to form smaller units. What is important is that definitions of the working units are known and have the same meaning for all who use them.

In many respects an attitude scale is like some of these other scales. It is a kind of yardstick used to assign values (usually numerical) to persons in terms of units that are defined in as exact a fashion as possible. However, it is obvious that our clarity as to the nature of the units being employed, and hence the meaning of any numbers assigned, is less than in the cases of familiar physical measurement. That is, if Subject A lifts a 50-pound weight to a certain height, while Subject B lifts a 100-pound weight and Subject C a 150-pound weight to the same height, we would not hesitate to say "B has lifted twice as much weight as A"; or "the weight C lifted is as much greater than B's as B's weight is greater than A's." If, however, on a five-item Likert scale dealing with attitudes toward Negroes, Subject A receives a score of 20, B a score of 30, and C a score of 40, we might not want to proclaim that "A is twice as hostile toward Negroes as C"; or that "C is more favorable than B by just the same amount as B is more favorable than A." In the latter case, although we may have confidence in the discriminating power of the attitude items, we are much less sure just what the units (and scale values) mean.

Levels of Measurement

Measurement is a kind of classification process, and students of these problems have found it useful to divide classification procedures into "levels of measurement" according to the number and stringency of requirements that any given measurement procedure may be said to satisfy, and hence the number and precision of statements that may be made about elements so measured. Four such levels are commonly distinguished: in ascending order, they are the nominal, ordinal, interval, and ratio levels. These levels can be ordered in the sense that measurement satisfying the requirements of each "higher" level automatically satisfies all of the requirements of the levels "below" it.

NOMINAL CLASSIFICATION. One form of classification so crude that we would not think of it as measurement at all involves the sorting of elements into classes, with no specification as to the relationship of one class to another. In such a classification procedure, we might use numbers to label the classes we establish, but the numbers have no significance relative to one another save as discriminable symbols. A good example is the numbers worn on sports uniforms, particularly when the first digit of two numbers used may have the limited meaning of designating a particular position on the team. However, if all guards on a football team wear jerseys with numbers in the 60s, and all fullbacks have numbers in the 30s, we do not thereby conclude that the guards are twice as big, tall, rough, or sure-handed as the fullbacks, or even that they are *more* of anything than the fullbacks. Numbers in this case are simply being used as symbols to mark off nominal classes of objects, and any other set of symbols less suggestive of a natural order—colors or different leaf shapes—could designate the classes as well.

What distinguishes classification at this level from higher forms of measurement is the simple fact that the symbols chosen to label the classes are not intended to indicate any particular relationship between those classes. The higher forms of measurement have in common the fact that some kinds of relation between the classes are specified by numerical labels; these higher forms differ from one another in the precision with which these relations are specified.

ORDINAL MEASUREMENT. The first thing that we might want to specify about relations between classes of objects is that one class is greater or less than some of the other classes with respect to some property. Ideally, we would want to be able to put all our classes into an order of hierarchy of "more than" and "less than" relationships, much as physical scientists can organize substances into a hierarchy with respect to the property "hardness" by observing which substances can scratch which other substances. To feel successful in establishing such an ordering, we would certainly require that if category B is greater than category A, and category C is greater than category B with respect to the same property, then certainly category C must be greater than category A with respect to that property. If a diamond scratches iron, and iron scratches lead, then it must be true that the diamond will scratch lead, or we will be forced to conclude that these substances are not suited to measurement with respect to hardness at the ordinal level.

Two crucial observations are to be drawn about measurement at this level. The first is that by the time we reach the ordinal level, we are beginning to assume some underlying *dimension* of variability along which objects are being compared. To say that one object or class of objects is greater than another is meaningless save with respect to some specified property or dimension. Many problems of attitude measurement come to hinge on the isolation of a particular dimension of variability along which these psychological states may be ordered.

The second observation is that ordinal measurement provides a means of organizing observations about objects even where we cannot establish clear units marking off even divisions of the dimension being measured, in the sense that the lines representing inches make even divisions on a foot ruler. There are, for example, no such units of hardness, although substances can be ordered by relative hardness with great reliability, and the information turns out to be tremendously important in many contexts. This fact is very useful for us, since units pertaining to the properties of psychological states that most interest us are notoriously difficult to establish. At the same time, this absence of clarity about units limits the kinds of statements we can make about the objects we have ordered. We still cannot make any assertions which presume that we know the distances between our ordered classes or, more especially, that the distances are equal. To make such assertions, we need to have measurable units.

INTERVAL AND RATIO MEASUREMENT. When we do have clear units, as is the case in much familiar physical measurement, we can begin to make more powerful statements. Knowing only that as heat increases, first silver, then gold, and then iron will melt, serves to locate the melting point of these elements ordinally but no more precisely. Although we might rank these elements 1, 2, and 3 with respect to melting point, we would not be justified in expecting that the additional heat required to melt iron as opposed to gold would be the same as that required to melt gold by comparison with silver, simply because we have located each element one rank apart. Examining the elements with actual units of temperature, however, would show their melting points to occur at 960°, 1063° and 1535° C, respectively, and would imply that gold and silver are much more similar with respect to melting point than iron is to either of them.

Even with such units (and hence what is called interval or equal-interval measurement) we are not equipped to make statements about our objects that consider their measures as ratios. It would not be meaningful to say, for example, that it takes half again as much heat to melt iron as it does to melt silver or gold, for such a proposition assumes that 0° C is a point at which there is no heat at all, a matter we know to be untrue. Such statements presume measurement at a ratio level, for which the prime requirement, in addition to the presence of equal units, is the existence of a zero point, or state of total absence of whatever property is being measured. Centigrade measures of temperature are not based on a zero point that is meaningful in this sense.

Attitude Scales and Levels of Measurement

Much of the early history of attitude measurement was marked by efforts to ensure that measurement was at least ordinal, while attempting to strive toward interval measurement. It should be clear that ordinal measurement is a minimal requirement for attitude measurement of any scientific value. We must certainly be sure that 5 units of favoring a certain thing, such as one's political party, really represent a greater degree of favoring than do 4 units, and a lesser degree of favoring than 6 units.

It may appear surprising that attitude scales have not always been satisfactory in this respect. Examples can be found of scales for which the position labeled "8 units" represents a more favorable position than "7 units" for some people but a less favorable position than "7 units" for others. Most often, these difficulties arise when the tactics employed for obtaining a summary score across a number of stimulus items is unfortunately chosen relative to the mixture of items expected to make the total scale. Suppose, for example, a scale of attitudes toward juvenile delinquents has been designed by the simple method of scoring one unit for each "favorable" response to any 1 of 20 items about juvenile delinquents. Such scores could run from 0 to 20. Suppose, furthermore, that some of the items dealt with basic matters related to attitudes toward juvenile delinquents: "Delinquents require not just punishment alone but the care and understanding we give invalids." And suppose that other items represent only superficial aspects of the issue such as: "Juvenile delinquents need better medical care." If a person accepted seven of the first kind of items, and no others, he would receive a score of 7, while a person who accepted nine of the latter kind of items, and no others, would get a summary score of 9. Under these conditions we might not feel that the score of 9 really represented a more favorable attitude than the score of 7. There are other ways in which the same mistake can be made in measuring the correct order of positions on the attitude scale.

THE RANK-ORDER METHOD OF SCALING. A primary difficulty in many of these cases is the simple addition of scores across a set of items that may not be of equal importance or of equal efficacy in tapping the dimension that the investigator originally had in mind. One way of avoiding the summation of scores is involved in the rank order method of scaling. This method hinges on the use of judges to aid in scale construction. For the simplest version of this approach we might first draw up a number of statements that we assume to represent all shades of opinion toward religion, from very unfavorable, through neutral, to very favorable. These would be placed in random order and given to a number of judges with the request that they work independently and place these in rank order from very unfavorable (on the left) to very favorable (on the right). They would be asked to make sure that each statement expresses an attitude more favorable than all statements placed to the left of it. If certain statements are placed in somewhat different positions by the judges, they are revised or discarded until all judges rank the statements in exactly the same order. We would have a crude attitude scale if we then asked subjects to consider all the statements and indicate which one fell closest to their own position. Measuring the attitudes of three people, we might find, for example, that individual A agrees most with the statement that our judges placed in position 4. Individuals B and C may agree most with statements in positions 8 and 9, respectively. We would probably be correct in inferring that A has the most unfavorable attitude toward religion, that C has the most favorable attitude, and that B's attitude is intermediate. This is clearly an ordinal scale, as we have no idea of the distance between each of the positions on our scale.

Our simplified example differs from frequent practice, since items are often kept even if judges do not agree exactly. In this case the mean, or preferably the median position given the items by the judges, is taken to be the scale value. Guilford (1954) and others have suggested an extension of this and even more elaborate means for trying to convert rank order judgments into more precise scales, as we shall see below.

Where a number of items have been responded to separately by each subject and some kind of addition of scores is required, a customary check against mislocation is to perform one or another type of analysis of the "internal consistency" of responses to the items that are expected to

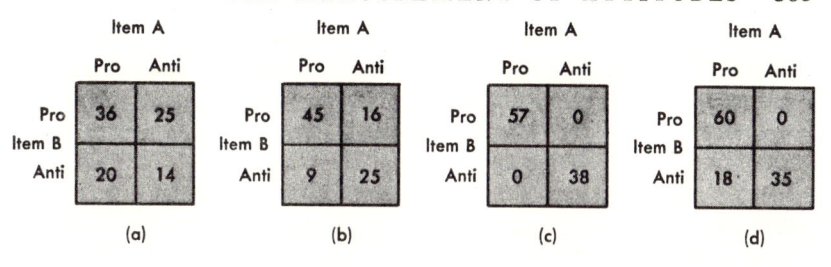

	Item A			Item A			Item A			Item A	
	Pro	Anti		Pro	Anti		Pro	Anti		Pro	Anti
Pro Item B	36	25	Pro Item B	45	16	Pro Item B	57	0	Pro Item B	60	0
Anti	20	14	Anti	9	25	Anti	0	38	Anti	18	35
	(a)			(b)			(c)			(d)	

FIGURE A.2. Some possible relations between two items involving dichotomous responses

be combined into a final attitude scale. This analysis often involves a study of the way in which responses to each item are related either to each other item, or to the expected summary scale score. A statistical device known as the *coefficient of correlation* provides one handy measure of the degree to which responses to one item relate to those made on another. Some possible patterns of relations between items in simplified (dichotomous) form are presented in Figure A.2. In the first pairing of items (a) there is no relationship, for persons "pro" on item A are no more likely to be "pro" on item B than are persons "anti" on item A. This absence of relationship is expressed as a correlation coefficient of 0.0. In (c), however, responses to the two items are perfectly related (a correlation of 1.0), for all people "pro" on item A are "pro" on item B as well, whereas the remainder are "anti" on both items. In (b) an intermediate case is presented, where there is some relationship, although scarcely a perfect one. The actual correlation coefficient for (b) would lie somewhere between 0.0 and 1.0 (such as .4), the exact location being determined by the type of coefficient employed.

Expectations of internal consistency in evaluation of attitude items for scales require at least intermediate if not quite strong relations between items, or between each item and the total scale score. If, for example, one or two items relate very poorly to all others in a prospective scale, the investigator is likely to decide either of two things: the items were so poorly worded or in some other sense defective that responses were laden with error; or, if they were measuring some real state or dimension, it was some dimension or dimensions unrelated to the investigator's original intent. In either case, the items are likely to be discarded.

Such analyses of internal consistency have been commonly expected in dealing with Likert attitude scales. You will recall, however, that a measure such as the Bogardus social distance scale used a slightly different rationale for combining items, as it tended to presume a very special kind of internal consistency such that an individual would "go just so far" in letting a person of another group near him, but would go no farther. This breaking point defined his location on the social distance scale. However, such an assumption may actually be violated by the data collected, where we might discover, for example, that substantial proportions of the Americans depicted in Figure A.1 might accept Spanish people as personal chums at a club, but reject the notion of their moving onto their streets as neighbors. Once again, these responses might be considered "error" or the result of the intrusion of other dimensions of consideration than pure social distance.

GUTTMAN SCALING. In the early days of attitude measurement, if such apparently irregular responses to a scale like the Bogardus measure were not too frequent, the investigator might simply assign an "average" location to these irregular subjects. In a most interesting approach to problems of scaling attitudes, however, Guttman (1950) began to examine items apparently ordered on the basis of "difficulty" or relative extremity to determine whether the attitude domain covered by the items was sufficiently unidimensional to warrant placing the items in a single scale, or was instead cluttered with other sufficiently potent dimensions (or sheer error) that no unidimensional scale could reasonably be constructed. For the sake of clarity, good measurement usually proceeds one dimension at a time, since even with dimensions that have some relationship to one another, there is likely to be ambiguity about the ordering of intermediate cases where more than one dimension is involved. If you were asked to employ a scale of "bigness," taking into account both the dimensions of height and weight at the same time, you would have no trouble with people both extremely tall and extremely heavy ("extremely big"), or those both short and light in weight ("extremely small"). But in-between them a tall, thin man who weighs 190 pounds bigger than a short, fat man who weighs 210 pounds? It is easy to rank people on either dimension by itself, but the situation becomes confused when we try to compress both on a single scale.

The basic idea of Guttman scaling (also called "cumulative scaling") as a test of unidimensionality is readily conveyed with an illustration suggested by Stouffer (1955). Imagine a spelling test consisting of three words:

Catastrophe
Cattle
Cat

Since these items differ quite markedly in difficulty, there is a particular kind of consistency we would expect in the responses. If an individual can spell the hardest word, it is likely that he can also spell the easier words. If he can spell only two words, we know *which* two words they are. If he can spell only one, we know *which* one that is. The kind of interrelation of items necessary to produce a good Guttman scale looks more like Figure A.2(d) than like Figure A.2(b), as you can see if you consider item A to be the spelling of "cattle" and item B the spelling of "catastrophe." Eighteen people who can spell "cattle" cannot spell "catastrophe"; but nobody represents the reverse situation. A little further thought may suggest to you why, in principle, items conforming to the Guttman criteria avoid ambiguity in their combination. That is, for a pair of items like those in Figure A.2(b) it is clear that people falling in the "pro-pro" cell and in the "anti-anti" cell are clearly most "pro" and most "anti," respectively, with the "anti-pro" and "pro-anti" people falling somewhere in between. The ambiguity is present because it is not clear which of these mixed responses is more "pro" than the other. The Guttman configuration in effect sidesteps this problem by requiring that only one intermediate cell be occupied.

The Guttman reasoning can readily be extended to many more than two items, and indeed for technical reasons a demonstration of Guttman properties becomes increasingly impressive the more items satisfy the criteria. Suppose you had six statements of known degrees of favorability toward Communism that you wanted to test for dimensionality. These statements are given to a number of subjects with the instructions to place a plus sign beside those attitudes with which they personally agree and a minus sign beside those with which they disagree. A hypothetically perfect outcome in the Guttman sense involving seven subjects is shown in Table A.1. The numbers across the top indicate that the items are placed in position from item 1 (least favorable) on the left to item 6 (most favorable) on the right.

TABLE A.1. Favorable (+) and unfavorable (−) responses of seven subjects to six statements on Communism arranged in order from the least to the most favorable statement

Subject	Least favorable 1	2	3	4	5	Most favorable 6
A	+	+	+	+	+	+
B	+	+	+	+	+	−
C	+	+	+	+	−	−
D	+	+	+	−	−	−
E	+	+	−	−	−	−
F	+	−	−	−	−	−
G	−	−	−	−	−	−

In this ideal example, a subject who agrees with any one item also agrees with all items that express less extremely favorable attitudes. There is no disruption in the internal order of the responses. In a looser scale construction, it would be possible for a person to get a score of 3 by agreeing with *any* three items. But in a perfect Guttman configuration, anyone with a score of 3 (as subject D) must have agreed with items 1, 2, and 3 rather than any other combination of three items. In other words, to know the total score of *any* subject is to know exactly the items with which he agreed and disagreed.

Such an outcome is one criterion of unidimensionality. In actual practice, one seldom finds the ideal outcome described. But the closer the responses approach this ideal, the more likely it is that the scale is not simultaneously tapping several different attitude dimensions. In order to calculate the degree to which responses to an attempted scale conform to this ideal, Guttman has devised a *coefficient of reproducibility*. This measure indicates the percentage of accuracy with which responses to the various statements can be reproduced (or predicted) from knowledge of the total scores. In our illustration, the coefficient of reproducibility would be 100 percent. For an excellent discussion of this technique, White and Saltz (1957) may be consulted.

Other methods are sometimes employed for assurance that subjects are being placed on the scale at locations that are at least reasonably ordered. Over and above the examination of patterns of internal consistency, for example, corroborating information can sometimes be imported from outside to show that the more favorable a score obtained on a scale, the more favorable are those persons' attitudes or behaviors with respect to the external evidence. Suppose we had a five-point scale of attitudes toward the importance of public education in American society. And suppose the percentages of those possessing equal summary scores who voted for a local school bond issue were as shown in Table A.2. If we can assume that general attitudes toward the importance of education would weigh heavily in voting on the bond issue, then these results would certainly encourage us to believe that *at least for the group as a whole,* an attitude score of 5 represents a more favorable attitude than a score of 4, and so on down the attitude scale. This is not by itself any assurance that the attitude of every *individual* with a score of 5 is more favorable than that of every individual with a score of 4, but simply shows that the general or majority trend is in this direction. The goal remains to make this true for as many individuals as possible. To the extent that this goal is reached, one has attained relatively clean measurement at the ordinal level.

Although measurement even at this level has great utility, there are often pressing practical reasons for attempting to design attitude scales that approach the interval level by having their units as nearly equal as possible. Suppose you were asked to direct a "crash program" to help avoid a catastrophic war by reducing attitudes of mistrust and suspicion on the part of various national groups. Assume, further, that it is your job to make a preliminary study of the effectiveness of various methods

TABLE A.2. The percentage voting favorably on the local school bond issue for each of five groups having different attitudes toward education (hypothetical data)

Score on attitude toward education	Percentage voting for the local school bond issue
5	88
4	72
3	60
2	49
1	34

of changing attitudes of mistrust and suspicion. The only way to determine what constitutes an effective method is to try different procedures with samples of various groups of persons and measure the attitude change produced. You find that a certain method, when applied to a group whose average score at the start was 6.0, raises the score to 9.0 on a scale ranging from 0 to 10. But suppose the same method, applied to another group whose initial score averages 3.0, raises it only one point, to 4.0. You can correctly conclude that the method is more effective for the former than for the latter group *only if you are sure* that the units of the scale are virtually equal at these different zones in the scale. Otherwise, no conclusion can be drawn about the relative effectiveness of the method for the two different groups. For this purpose, then, a merely ordinal scale would not be adequate.

Later in this section we shall describe attempts to construct attitude scales with a claim to approximations of equal units. First, however, it will be useful to consider one or two other aspects of measurement. Thus far, in discussing the differing levels to which measurement may aspire, we have been talking about general strategies of measurement. We need also be concerned with ways in which our success may be evaluated after the fact, whatever the level of measurement at which we have attempted to operate.

The Accuracy of Measurement

Measurement, even physical measurement, is accurate only within certain tolerances. If you were given a stick a meter long, subdivided into centimeters, and were told to measure the length of a table to hundredths of a centimeter, you would tend to get slightly differing results on each fresh trial. Over many trials, the results would tend to cluster within a specifiable range, and location of the most frequent measures would tend to fall toward the middle of this range. You would have fair assurance that the average of your results over many trials might be your best estimate as to the "true" length of the table. Nevertheless, it would be wise to keep in mind that even easy and unambiguous physical measurement inevitably suffers some margin of error.

Error, although something to be well sensitized to, cannot therefore be considered frightening. How concerned one must be about a certain amount of known error in a set of measurements has less to do with the magnitude of the error in an absolute sense than with the magnitude of the error relative to the purposes to which the measurements will be put. Error that may be disastrously large for some purposes—ordering a drafting device that must snugly grip the ends of the table—may be trivial for other purposes, such as ordering a new table of "matching" size. This presupposes, however, that we are able to equip ourselves with fairly precise information as to the accuracy of our measurements in any given case.

A great deal of effort has gone into the devising of ways to evaluate the accuracy of psychological measurements. In the process, it has become clear that "accuracy" is in some ways too gross a term, for there are several senses in which a measurement can be inaccurate. We have noted above, for example, that when an investigator finds patterns of responses to attitude items that are puzzlingly inconsistent, he may conclude that they have been distorted by error (boxes carelessly checked by the subject, for example), *or* that other dimensions than the one intended are intruding to distort the responses. These two kinds of possibility correspond roughly to two of the principal kinds of accuracy with which an investigator must be concerned—the reliability of his measurement and its validity.

THE RELIABILITY OF AN ATTITUDE SCALE. We would have great trouble making effective use of a yardstick made of highly elastic rubber. A number of persons measuring the same object with it would get different measurements, depending on how much the yardstick was stretched in the process. It would not be a *reliable* measuring instrument; that is, it would not give consistent results. Such reliability, like other desirable characteristics of attitude scales, is not easy to obtain.

Since the margin of error or unreliability in an instrument can be gauged by the consistency of results it generates when applied over and over again to the same object(s), the most straightforward way to get an estimate of the reliability of an attitude scale would be to have the same individuals respond to the items twice or more. This is known as the *test-retest technique*. The more nearly everyone gets the same score each time he responds to it, the greater the reliability of the scale is said to be. Typically, estimates of reliability are expressed by coefficients of correlation (see above), where a correlation of 1.0 would indicate perfect reliability, in the sense that each person taking the test a second time would keep the same position, relative to others retaking the test, which he held on the first trial. Many attitude scales have been found to have reliabilities in the neighborhood of .95. This is sufficiently close to 1.0 to be considered highly reliable.

There are weaknesses in this test of reliability, however. If the retest is administered after only a short interval, subjects may remember their responses and try to be consistent with their former performance. This would produce a spuriously high coefficient of reliability. Yet if the retest is postponed for any substantial interval, the possibility increases that the estimate of reliability may turn out to be spuriously low, since some individuals may have experiences that actually change their attitudes between tests. Kelly's study (1955) of engaged couples who were retested, sixteen to eighteen years later, shows that this problem of change can be quite serious when the time interval is large. Retests of values and vocational interests showed the greatest stability. Self-ratings and other personality variables were next in stability. The lowest consistency of all was found for a series of attitude scales that registered a "test-retest" reliability of .10, hardly above chance.

Ideally, the concept of reliability and the possibility of real change as time passes suggest that we should reduce to zero the time interval between taking the two scales. The method most commonly used for measuring reliability succeeds in doing this in one limited sense. A scale with at least twice as many items as are wanted for the final version is prepared. This long scale is then treated as being composed of two halves, each of which is regarded as a separate but equivalent scale, given simultaneously. To make the scales more truly simultaneous, as opposed to successive, it is a good precaution to split the items into two groups by some means other than dividing them into first and last half. One method is to regard the even-numbered items as one half of the scale and the odd-numbered items as the other half. This is known as the *split-half technique* for measuring reliability. As in other measures of reliability, the more nearly the coefficient of correlation between two scales approaches 1.0, the more reliable the scale. Each method of testing reliability has its advantages and drawbacks. For an excellent, detailed consideration of these methods see Guilford (1954).

There are two general ways of increasing the reliability of a scale. The first involves simply increasing the number of items in the scale. It it easy to see that the shortest of all possible scales—a one-item scale—is not a very reliable one. An individual may not have a clear-cut attitude toward an occasional item and could answer "Agree" or "Disagree" about equally well. His decision is a toss-up, and the next time he answers this item he may give just the opposite response. The more items a scale contains, the greater the chance that there will be a number of items to which an individual can respond decisively. Thus, other things being equal, the longer an attitude scale, the more reliable it should be. In practice, increasing the length of a scale almost always increases its reliability. There are highly useful mathematical formulas that can tell us in advance how much the reliability of a scale will be improved if its length is increased by a specified amount.

The second way of increasing the reliability of an attitude scale is to increase the certainty that each item "taps" the same attitude—to make sure that all items measure the same state of readiness rather than different ones. The goal here is to make the scale unidimensional in the sense described several pages ago. The following item taps more than one dimension: "Atomic warfare is a serious threat and we should provide underground shelters for all citizens." Whether a person answers "Agree" or "Disagree" might depend on the way he perceives the question. At one moment he might agree because he believes that atomic warfare is a genuine threat. But at another moment he may disagree because he may not believe that underground shelters constitute an answer to this problem. The question, an ambiguous one, is subject to the fluctuations of ambiguous stimuli referred to in Chapter 2. The more items of this type a scale contains, the lower its reliability is likely to be.

VALIDITY OF THE SCALE. Any measurement is said to be valid to the extent that it taps the dimension we are trying to measure, uninfluenced by anything else. In short, a scale is valid if it measures what it is supposed to measure and only what it is supposed to measure. Edwards (1958) has provided an excellent illustration of poor validity in a number of personality scales that ask a person to rate himself on various characteristics. He has repeatedly found that whether a person answers "True" or "False" (meaning that the person feels the statement does or does not apply to him as an individual) is not primarily determined by whether the statement actually "fits" that person. Rather, it appears to depend largely on whether the statement is a socially acceptable one in the eyes of the person taking the scale. Many personality tests based on self-ratings thus seem to be measuring one's knowledge of what is socially desirable. Since they measure imperfectly what they are supposed to measure, and measure more accurately something they are not designed to measure, their validity is low.

The validity of a scale may be low for another reason. If we have not been careful to check the reliability of our instrument, we may find that it has low validity because it is a very unreliable or inconsistent instrument. A scale cannot be expected to measure accurately what it is supposed to measure if it is so unreliable that it gives quite different results each time it is administered. For this reason the practice is to give a scale a reliability test first. If it does not have high reliability, there is no point in testing its validity since we already know that it will be low. In this sense, the reliability of a test sets a limit on its validity.

It should be obvious from the foregoing that a valid scale must be a reliable one. It is not true, however, that a reliable measure is necessarily valid. An experiment conducted by a consumers' testing organization will make this clear. To test the comparative merits of different brands of fingernail polish, pieces of ivory were coated with the products of different companies and then mechanically tumbled in hot, soapy water. This treatment was used because it was believed that the greatest wear and tear on fingernail polish was the result of placing the hands in dish water. When the pieces of ivory were removed it was found, as anticipated, that there were large differences in durability from brand to brand. The test was repeated several times. The brand found to be most durable on the first test was the most durable on the second test; and so on. The test was *highly* reliable. To test the validity of this method of measurement, the investigators enlisted the help of a number of housewives and repeated the test under "real-life" conditions. When the outcome of this test was compared with the mechanical test, it was found that there was very little agreement in the durability rankings of the various brands. The mechanical testing device did not provide a valid measure of durability under normal wearing conditions —presumably because wear is due to more than just the impact of soap and water. High reliability is no guarantee of high validity. A very reliable attitude scale may not measure what it is designed to measure. Its "face validity" (what it appears to measure "on the face of it") may be excellent but it needs to be confirmed by methods to be described.

Once we are sure we are dealing with a reliable scale, how can we be sure that it is also a valid one? One method consists in testing for internal consistency, to which reference has already been made. Careful item analysis sometimes reveals that there are two or three "clusters" of items in a scale. The items in such a cluster are very closely related to one another (that is, people who respond favorably to one item are quite apt to respond favorably to each of the others in that cluster), but they are less closely related to items in different clusters. This is just what was found in a study of "radicalism-conservatism" reported by Williams and Wright (1955). An analysis showed that the original scale, designed to measure the dimension "radicalism-conservatism," was actually composed of two subscales which were virtually independent of one another. One of the subscales measured "threat orientation," that is, the fears people were responding to. The other measured "group identification," that is, similarity to groups of persons with whom they believed they had common interests and goals. Since these two subscales are quite distinct, the total scale is of uncertain validity because it measures two quite different attitudes simultaneously. This test does not meet the criterion of internal consistency or unidimensionality. The statistical technique known as *factor analysis,* which examines the pattern of intercorrelation between all items, is often used to determine whether there are several factors being measured.

Another useful method of validating attitude scales consists in checking the responses made to attitude scales against some other type of behavior. If the attitudes that can be inferred from other forms of behavior (verbal or nonverbal) correspond to whose that are inferred from verbal responses to attitude scales, then the validity of the scale has been given partial confirmation. In Table A.2 (page 509) we have in effect illustrated the method of testing the correspondence between verbal responses on an attitude scale and behavior with which it ought to be related if the test actually measures what it is supposed to measure.

Reliability and Validity of Specific Attitude Scales

The accuracy of attitude scales as measuring instruments depends both on the content of the scales (which may be taken to include the general measurement technique and the specific item-by-item content) and on the population to which the scale is applied. Statements of reliability or validity for a given approach to attitude measurement thus must be seen as specific to both content and population. This signifies in turn that we cannot meaningfully say, for example, that Likert scales in general have a certain reliability. What the reliability might be for a specific version of a Likert scale would be affected by the content of the scale and the population to which it had been applied.

SCALE CONTENT. Generally, when one speaks of broad techniques such as the Likert or the Guttman scaling, the scale content goes unspecified. However, in the case of one scale discussed above—the Bogardus social distance scale—the content is largely specified, with only the identity of the ethnic group to be judged varying from application to application. Hence we may consider what is known of the reliability and validity of this scale in its traditional form to demonstrate the significance as well as the complexity of considerations that estimates of scale accuracy may entail.

The first observation of interest is that the Bogardus scale has proved highly reliable as a measure of *general* social distance, as distinguished from distance in regard to a *specific* racial or national group. Split-half reliability coefficients of .90 and higher have repeatedly been obtained. These coefficients are extracted by calculating each individual's total score of social distance expressed toward a random half of the groups responded to, and correlating these scores with comparable ones for the other half of the groups judged. Hence we can be quite certain that if we know an individual's social-distance score as expressed, for example, toward the French, Mexicans, Syrians, Japanese, and so on, we can predict with great accuracy his score expressed toward a different set of groups—say Irish, Italians, Jews, and Hindus. This information has substantive implications to the effect that individuals differ in the amount of social distance they desire from "outsiders," in addition to the commentary on the reliability of the scale as an instrument for measurement of this general tendency.

The group reliability of the Bogardus scale has also been shown to be very high when another method of measuring reliability is used. Many groups of white American subjects over several decades have continued to show about the same order of preference on this scale, as noted on pages 428 ff. A scale that had poor reliability could not continue to show such consistent group results. Additional support for this view comes from the work of Prothro and Miles, who administered a revised Bogardus scale of social distance in the South and found that the scale ranks correlated .84 with the original ranks obtained by Bogardus a quarter of a century ago (see Research Illustration 14.1, page 429).

For purposes of measuring order of preference among various ethnic groups, the validity as well as the reliability of the Bogardus scale seems satisfactory, at least as the validity can be checked by examining the correspondence of Bogardus results with those from other scales employing different strategies of measurement. For example, the order of preference expressed by a single individual for various ethnic groups is in most cases about the same regardless of whether we use the Bogardus scale or the method of paired comparisons (to be described below). It has also been found that scores from scales of a Bogardus type relate closely to scores from a scale measuring an intensity dimension of the attitudes involved. Dodd and Griffiths (1958) obtained the social distance responses of a cross section of adults toward several ethnic groups. They then asked, "Do you feel strongly about liking or not liking any of these groups as equals in . . ." (here the various social distance situations were inserted—"marriage," "as equals on a job," and so on). They found that the mean intensity of expression was greatest for those individuals at the hostile end of the social distance scale and was least at the least hostile position of the scale.

Very little is known about the reliability or validity of Bogardus scores made by any one individual in respect to any one ethnic group. Such specific attitudes are measured on this scale by single responses which, as we have already noted, are necessarily somewhat unreliable. But for two other purposes—measuring an individual's *general* social distance, and measuring his order of preference among ethnic groups—both its reliability and validity seem satisfactory.

THE POPULATION MEASURED. It is easy to overlook the possibility that a coefficient of reliability or a statement of validity obtained for a given attitude scale on one specific population may itself be a misleading estimate of the reliability of the same scale as applied to some other rather dissimilar population. This kind of problem has been encountered very frequently, for example, with Guttman scaling. Originally the technique was seen as a means of determining whether a particular content domain was "scalable"—that is, was susceptible to unidimensional measurement, quite apart from population differences. However, it was soon discovered that a set of items generating a very clean cumulative scale when applied to one population might not produce a scale satisfying standard criteria when applied to some quite different population. Hence the success of a particular set of items in producing unidimensional response patterns is not an absolute property of the items by themselves, but rather a property of the interaction between the item meanings and the response dispositions of the particular population. It is likely that much the same observation can be drawn concerning the reliability and validity of particular scales.

There seem to be two kinds of reasons why measurement accuracy is to some degree relative to the populations being measured. The first set of reasons springs from the fact that any attitude items are verbal propositions and depend on verbal and hence cultural meanings. To the degree that there are subcultural variations in the meaning of words or the aspects of a problem area that are most salient, one can expect variations in response patterns across cultural and subcultural groups. For the mainstream of American culture, for example, admitting foreigners to one's occupation is a less sensitive matter than admitting them to residence on one's street as neighbors. However, it is easy to imagine subcultural islands in which a particular ethnic group in a given geographic area has a monopoly on a given occupational specialty, so that the specialty is ethnically homogeneous. For individuals in such an occupation, the admission of some other ethnic group to the occupation may have quite a different meaning from what such admission would have for people employed in some broad and already heterogeneous occupational specialty. Hence the apparent "order" of the Bogardus items might depart from the standard order in systematic ways for this population group.

This kind of problem is most severe, of course, for investigators wishing to employ attitude scales on populations that are culturally somewhat distinct from those on which scale accuracy was originally evaluated, and for investigators dealing directly with large and heterogeneous populations. Campbell *et al.* (1960), after applying a version of the authoritarianism scale to a national sample of adults, have noted that predictions from differences in authoritarianism to other kinds of attitudes which fit the original theory (see Research Illustration 5.1, page 122), and demonstrated many times in research with college student populations, seem to be quite successful as well when tested on college-educated portions of the adult population. However, these predictive successes are almost completely obliterated within poorly educated strata of the population. The authors conclude that either the measure declines in reliability as one moves to less well-educated portions of the population, or that poorly educated people respond to the items in terms of somewhat different dimensions from those that characterize the responses of relatively well-educated subjects.

A second type of reason why the measurement accuracy of an attitude scale may vary by the population studied has to do less with the differential meanings attributable to attitude statements than with the fact that for any given attitude domain (religion, aspects of politics, ethnic prejudice, and so on), populations may vary grossly in their proportions of members who have sharply crystallized attitudes on the items. A well-prepared attitude scale gauging reactions to one or another national political issue, if applied to a sample of subjects who are engrossed in national political issues (dues-paying members of political parties, for example), may well show high reliability. However, the same scale applied to a sample of sharecroppers in the South who rarely hear any national political news, who have never thought about the issue at stake, and who are quite indifferent to the outcome, would be likely to show a very low reliability. The reliability coefficient for the same scale could be expected to fall at some intermediate point for less extreme groups, according to the proportions in each population that had some interest in the dimension covered.

RESPONSE SET. A related problem affecting measurement accuracy is the fact that subjects responding to certain kinds of attitude scales may be as much influenced by the mere form in which the items or their alternatives are cast as they are by the item content. Of several different response sets that have been demonstrated to affect attitude measurement, the most pervasive and damaging is frequently referred to as the tendency toward *acquiescence*, or "yea-saying." This problem bedevils the many kinds of attitude scales based on individual items requiring "yes-no" or "agree-disagree" responses. It refers to a tendency on the part of respondents faced with such items to agree more often than the content or consistency with other responses would lead one to expect. In the limiting case, we might imagine an assertion and its direct negation imbedded in a long list of attitude propositions; the normal expectation would be that a person agreeing with one would disagree with the other. The acquiescent respondent would agree with both. Occasionally a tendency in the opposite direction—toward overgeneralized disagreement or "nay-saying"—can be detected, although it seems less prevalent. In both cases, the question form seems more important in determining the response than its content.

Following a suggestion by Christie and Cook (1958), Campbell *et al.* (1960) applied to a national adult sample five of the items measuring authoritarianism (cf. Research Illustration 5.1, page 122), in each of which an "agree" response was supposed to be authoritarian, but also included another five items based on the original items, yet revised slightly so that "disagree" became the authoritarian response. It was found that scores on the two halves not only failed to meet expectations of a positive correlation in content terms, but actually in content terms were *negatively* correlated in slight degree (persons "authoritarian" on one half appearing relatively "nonauthoritarian" on the other). In other words, for this total administration, there was more "consistency" in giving "yes" or "no" answers than in choosing authoritarian or nonauthoritarian responses.

Of course, where authoritarianism is being directly measured, it can be argued that the tendency to agree with what are usually flat and sweeping propositions coming from some "authoritative" source, such as an experimenter or an interviewer, is itself evidence of the exaggerated subservience characteristic of the authoritarian syndrome. This kind of subservience is indeed one of the accepted interpretations of the acquiescence phenomenon, although, as we have seen above, Edwards (1958) has for some kinds of measurement linked these response sets to perceptions on the part of the subjects as to the socially desirable response. Other observers, noting the fact that acquiescence is far more common among less-educated subjects (and nay-saying, when it occurs, seems more characteristic of high education), have suggested that acquiescence is characteristic of uncritical judgment. The most comprehensive recent review of interpretations is given by Christie and Lindauer (1963). Whatever the nature of the acquiescent tendency, it seems clear that we may be disturbed by the problem, even in the measurement of dimensions like authoritarianism, insofar as mechanical response to question form dwarfs any reaction to question content; and, of course, for dimensions where willingness to agree is quite irrelevant, such a response set poses grave difficulties indeed.

Recognition of these problems has led some investigators to an increased interest in approaches to attitude measurement that do not rest on simple agree-disagree items, but demand instead other kinds of operations, such as indication of a choice or preference order between a set of substantive alternatives. These developments may help a good deal in reducing some of the uncertainties posed by acquiescence.

Nevertheless, acquiescence is not the only kind of response set that can adulterate attitude measures, and for any form in which attitude measurement is cast, there may well be some discernible biases traceable to the form of the question. We cannot cover all possibilities here. However, another that has drawn a good deal of attention affects those instruments requiring the subject to locate himself on some continuum or within a multiple set of categories (for example, the Likert item as well as several techniques to be discussed below). Here there seem to be tendencies on the part of some individuals toward heavy use of extreme categories, whereas others tend to avoid the extremes in favor of the middle. Some tend to use many categories; others, few. These tendencies appear stable for individuals across enough different types of content to suggest that, quite independent of content, there is a direct interaction between some stable personality trend and the sheer form of the question.

Response sets can be insidious not only because they affect measurement accuracy (both reliability and validity), but also because they can affect in deceptive ways the investigator's estimate of how accurate his measurement has been. Consider, for example, a battery of attitude items all of which are "keyed" in such a way that an "agree" response has the same content meaning. It should be clear that insofar as acquiescent or rejecting tendencies influence responses quite independently of item content, estimates of scale reliability will be artificially inflated, whether these estimates are based on criteria of internal consistency or test-retest methods. The problem may be somewhat less where validity criteria are involved; however, if validity is estimated on the basis of correlations between the original scale and others that purport to measure the same attitudinal dimension and that also fall prey to the same response sets, then our estimates of validity may likewise be overly generous. Campbell and Fiske (1959) have suggested that some of the apparent "organization" of attitudes commonly seen in high correlations between negative feelings toward a wide variety of ethnic outgroups (Research Illustration 5.1, page 122) may result from measuring feelings toward these different groups by attitude items in the same form, so that the same response sets are activated and build intercorrelations to spuriously high levels. They argue that validity can scarcely be judged save as correlations are high between methods that differ maximally in their approach.

OTHER APPROACHES TO ATTITUDE MEASUREMENT

Up to this point we have described only two or three major strategies of attitude measurement, such as the Likert and the Guttman scaling. A very large number of schemes for attitude measurement have been proposed, some of them for quite special purposes (for example, the Bogardus social distance scale), but many of a general purpose nature. Now that we have a better sense of some of the underlying issues of methodology and measurement with which any attempt to measure attitudes must cope, we may consider some of the other approaches. Only a few of the better known and more general purpose approaches can be covered. These differ from one another considerably in terms of (a) the level of measurement aspired to, (b) unidimensional vs. multidimensional intent, and (c) direct questioning as opposed to inferences about attitudes through indirect material.

Aspirations toward Interval Measurement

THURSTONE'S METHOD OF EQUAL-APPEARING INTERVALS. Guttman scaling and the rank-order method described above produce what are quite straightforwardly ordinal scales that do not pretend to suggest relative distances between scale categories. As we have observed, scaling that would have some claim to establishing distances between discriminated categories could be valuable in many instances. One prominent effort in this direction is an extension of the rank-order method.

This method was developed first in connection with a scale of attitudes toward the church (Thurstone and Chave, 1929), although subsequently scales toward a variety of other social objects were constructed. A collection of 130 items believed to represent all degrees of favoring or opposing the church was made and each was written on a separate card. They were then independently classified by each one of 300 judges according to the following instructions:

> You are given eleven slips with letters on them, A, B, C, D, E, F, G, H, I, J, K. Please arrange these before you in regular order. On slip A put those statements which you believe express the highest *appreciation* of the value of the church. On slip F put those expressing a neutral position. On slip K put those slips which express the strongest *depreciation* of the church. On the rest of the slips arrange statements in accordance with the degree of appreciation or depreciation expressed in them.

It is important to note that only the middle and the two extreme positions on which statements were to be sorted were defined for the judges. Thurstone and Chave believed it was essential that the other cards not be defined in order that the intervals between the slips would represent *equal-appearing intervals* of favorableness or unfavorableness. If the intervals are regarded as equal by the judges, then the numbers from 1 to 11 can replace the lettered slips A to K and, in essence, each judge has rated each statement on an eleven-point scale that appears to him to have equal intervals between each point. Thurstone found that most judges agreed reasonably well in their sorting of most statements. Where there was considerable disagreement (as measured by a simple statistical device) these items were discarded as being too ambiguous to use for this purpose. The scale value assigned to each remaining statement was simply the median of the scale positions assigned by the various judges.

Scale values were thus determined for a considerable number of items ranging from one extreme end of the scale to the other. Many more items were available than needed for adequate reliability, even after the more ambiguous items had been discarded. So an ultimate selection was made in such a manner as to have items that spread out fairly evenly over the entire scale range. For most of his final scales, Thurstone has usually included about 22 items scattered at approximately half-unit distances from 1 to 11. A few items from the final scale, together with the scale values of each, are shown here:

- 1.5 I believe church membership is almost essential to living life at its best.
- 2.3 I find the services of the church both restful and inspiring.
- 4.5 I believe in what the church teaches, but with mental reservations.
- 5.6 Sometimes I feel that the church and religion are necessary, and sometimes I doubt it.
- 7.4 I believe the church is losing ground as education advances.
- 9.6 I think the church is a hindrance to religion, for it still depends upon magic, superstition and myth.

In making use of this scale for the purpose of determining the attitude of an individual, he is simply instructed to check all statements with which he agrees. The statements are printed in random order rather than in the order of their scale values as shown. The individual's scale position is readily found by obtaining the average of the scale values of all the items he has checked. For example, if a subject had checked only the first two items included on the partial list, his scale position would be 1.9, which is the sum of the values 1.5 and 2.3 divided by 2 (the number of items he checked). There are often enough items available that two comparable forms of this test can be made. When these two forms are given to the same persons, the correlation between the two attitude scores gives a check on the reliability of this instrument. This figure is typically above .85—an encouraging evidence of the stability of the instrument.

The question has been raised as to whether the scale values do not depend, to some extent, on the attitudes of the persons who originally served as judges. After all, the judges are human and have their own attitudes toward the church or whatever else they are judging. To test this possibility, one of Thurstone's associates had two groups of judges sort the same group of 114 items concerning attitudes toward Negroes (Hinckley, 1932). One group of judges consisted of southern whites, selected as being unfavorable in their attitudes; the other judges were northern whites, selected as being much more favorable. Scale values were determined independently on the basis of the two sets of judges. The correlation between these two sets of scale values was calculated and found to be .98—an almost perfect degree of agreement. A number of similar studies have shown essentially the same outcome. This led to McNemar's contention (1946) that all attempts to show that the scale values are biased by the attitudes of the judges had failed.

More recent work has again raised certain doubts on this score. Hovland and Sherif (1952) used much the same procedure as Hinckley and worked with his original statements. They obtained equal-appearing interval judgments from a group of Negro judges, a group of white judges with favorable attitudes toward the Negro, and a group of white judges with unfavorable attitudes toward the Negro. They found that for both the Negro judges and the white judges having favorable attitudes toward the Negro, the items reported to be in neutral and moderately favorable positions by Hinckley were displaced toward the unfavorable end of the scale. Similarly, for the group of anti-Negro white judges, they found a displacement of moderately unfavorable and neutral statements toward the favorable end of the scale. They were able to obtain scale values that agreed well with those reported by Hinckley if they used a group of white judges and applied the Thurstone method for eliminating careless judges—which had also been used by Hinckley. This involved eliminating all judges who placed thirty or more statements in a single category. Hovland and Sherif found that what this did was to eliminate over three fourths of the Negro judges and two thirds of the white judges who had favorable attitudes toward Negroes. This method for eliminating "careless" judges apparently has the effect of eliminating most of those judges who have attitudes that could result in scale values somewhat different from those obtained by using other judges.

For these reasons, it is at present not possible for us to be sure that scale values of statements are *completely* independent of the attitudes of the judges. The more recent work of Prothro (1955) is more reassuring.

Using the method of equal-appearing intervals, Prothro (1955) had one set of anti-Jewish Arabs judge a series of statements such as "Jews do not impress me favorably" with respect to the *degree* of favorability or unfavorability toward Jews that the proposition represented. Another set of anti-Jewish Arabs was asked to rate the same statements as they might be used to refer to *any* group, with no specific mention of Jews ("——— as a group do not impress me favorably"). In contrast to the findings of Hovland and Sherif, the amount of favorability or unfavorability that the two sets of Arab judges saw in the statements was essentially the same, whether Jews or a generalized "group" were objects of the attitude. It is apparent that additional work is needed to clarify the nature of this influence.

The method of equal-appearing intervals is not a perfect scaling method. One limitation that has been widely felt is that it does not provide for *degrees* of agreement, but demands all-or-none agreement for each item. Many have, therefore, made use of scales constructed by Thurstone's methods, but with instructions to subjects to answer the items in the Likert manner. It has been shown that even with the smaller number of items left when the "neutral" Thurstone statements are eliminated, the split-half reliability coefficients are higher when scored by Likert than by Thurstone methods (Likert, Roslow, and Murphy, 1934). This procedure is the more justifiable since the discovery that "neutral" items in Thurstone scales are a source of considerable nonvalidity, for they commonly mean different things to different subjects—ambiguity of the item, annoyance with it, conflict about it, or indifference to the issue, and so on (Edwards, 1946). Similarly, Eysenck and Crown (1949) have suggested a method of scoring that combines the weights of the Likert procedure and the scale values of Thurstone's method in the form of products. Multiplying the Thurstone scale value of each item by a Likert weight, the individual's total score is a sum of these products. These workers report a higher split-half reliability (.94) from this method than was obtained for scores from the Thurstone method alone (.83) or the Likert method alone (.90). They call this procedure the *scale-product method*.

Even with such scoring adjustments, the Thurstone method suffers conceptual ambiguities. In his scaling methods, Guttman challenged one of these by asserting that if a set of statements were truly ordered by degree of favorableness with respect to a single pure attitude dimension, then only error could result in a subject's agreeing with statements at scale values of 3 and 6, but disagreeing with items at 4 and 5. Despite such shortcomings, the Thurstone procedure has been one of the more popular ones devised to ascertain the position of a person on an attitude continuum.

THE PAIRED COMPARISONS METHOD OF SCALING. Another way of arriving at scale values for attitude statements represents quite a different technique, although it also employs judges and is based on Thurstone's law of comparative judgment (1927). To illustrate a portion of the calculations involved, we make use of material provided by Hill (1953). At the time of the Korean war, he asked ninety-four individuals to make judgments, on a comparative basis, of the relative degree of favorableness of seven statements concerning the participation of the United States in the Korean conflict:

(a) I suppose the United States had no choice but to continue the Korean war.
(b) We should be willing to give our allies in Korea more money if they need it.
(c) Withdrawing our troops from Korea at this time would only make matters worse.
(d) The Korean war might not be the best way to stop Communism, but it was the only thing we could do.
(e) Winning the Korean war is absolutely necessary whatever the cost.
(f) We are protecting the United States by fighting in Korea.
(g) The reason we are in Korea is to defend freedom.

Each of the seven statements was paired with every other statement and each of the judges was asked to state which member of each pair was believed to be a more favorable attitude toward participation in the Korean war. Table A.3 shows the frequency with which each statement was judged to be more favorable than the one paired with it. For example, item (g) was judged to be more favorable toward the participation in the war than item (a) by 88 of the 94 judges, as shown by the entry at the intersection of column (g) with row (a). Similarly, every other figure in the table shows the frequency with which each statement, indicated by letter at the top of the table, was judged more favorable than the statements indicated by letter at the left-hand side of the table. The diagonal entries (the number 47) involve a comparison of each statement with itself and are assumed to be equal to 94 divided by 2. Several additional calculations, and reference to a normal probability table, yield the scale values shown at the bottom of the table. The details of this calculation, and the rather complex assumptions on which it rests, are well described by Edwards (1957). You will note that the statements listed were already arranged in the order of their scale values. Since item (a) had the lowest scale value, it was arbitrarily made the zero point, and given a scale value of .000. Item (a) is the least favorable, and item (g) the most favorable attitude toward participation in the Korean war. Because each item has a specific scale value that represents a presumed distance above that of the first item, this is an approximation to an interval scale. We know not only that one item represents a more favorable attitude than another but we also have some idea as to how much more favorable it is. By using these items as part of an attitude scale and finding which item(s) an individual agrees with, we can assign him an attitude rating corresponding to the scale position of the item(s) that express his own personal opinion.

A disadvantage of this method is that it becomes very time consuming if many items are used. The number of comparisons that must be made if each statement is to be paired with every other is given by the formula $n(n-1)/2$ where n stands for the number of statements.

TABLE A.3. The frequency with which each of the 7 statements listed by letter at the top was judged to be more favorable than each of the statements listed by letter at the side; number of judges = 94 (adapted from Hill, 1953)

Statements	(a)	(b)	(c)	(d)	(e)	(f)	(g)
(a)	47	65	75	80	75	86	88
(b)	29	47	51	54	62	68	81
(c)	19	43	47	49	59	60	63
(d)	14	40	45	47	49	63	67
(e)	19	32	35	45	47	51	55
(f)	8	26	34	31	43	47	57
(g)	6	13	31	27	39	37	47
Derived scale values	.000	.602	.839	.904	1.058	1.243	1.457

Substituting in this formula will show that if the scale value for fifty statements is desired, the judges will be required to make 1225 comparisons! A possible advantage over the rank-order method of scaling is that it forces the judge to compare each statement with every other and thus may be conducive to greater accuracy.

Since persons who judge pairs of statements also have attitudes of their own toward these matters, it is possible that distortions in scale values might occur similar to those occasionally reported for the method of equal-appearing intervals. To check this possibility Kelley, Hovland, Schwartz, and Abelson (1955) used 20 of the Hinckley statements that had been found to show the distortion effect cited by Hovland and Sherif. They asked a group of Negro and a group of white subjects, comparable to those used in the Hovland and Sherif study, to make judgments of the 190 pairs of statements that result when the materials are scaled using the paired comparison method. They found that the scaling of the statements was quite similar for the Negro and the white judges. The distortion (or displacement) effect observed when the method of equal-appearing intervals was used tended to be eliminated. Hence it is possible that this method has an advantage over the method of equal-appearing intervals, and should be given consideration when the attitude of the judges might be a distorting factor.

THE UNFOLDING TECHNIQUE OF COOMBS. A technique of scaling suggested by Coombs (1964) bears some resemblance to both the paired comparisons method and Guttman scaling. It is similar to paired comparisons in that it strives to capture more information than a purely ordinal scale represents, and gets its leverage on the problem by dealing with the structures of judgmental orderings of objects. It differs from

526 - APPENDIX A

that technique, however, in several important respects. Like Guttman scaling, it involves no panel of judges, but restricts itself to rigorous inferences from the empirical patterns of preference orders established between items by the subjects themselves. And like Guttman scaling, it can be seen as a test of unidimensionality as well as a technique for locating subjects on an attitude continuum. In so doing, it extracts more information about distances between items than Guttman scaling, although it does not pretend to establish "units" in the sense of equal-interval scaling.

To understand how the Coombs method can produce information less powerful than interval measurement but more powerful than traditional ordinal measurement, it is necessary to grasp the key idea employed. Let us work with the seven items concerning the Korean war used above to illustrate the paired comparisons method. We start with the assumption that these items in their alphabetic order fall on a continuum of favorableness to the Korean war, although later we can test the adequacy of the assumption. What we do not know is whether the relative distances between these items are equal, or whether the differences in favorableness between some adjacent items are very large relative to the differences between other adjacent items. In other words, we cannot distinguish between any of the following arrangements, each of which maintains the ordinal relation of the seven items.

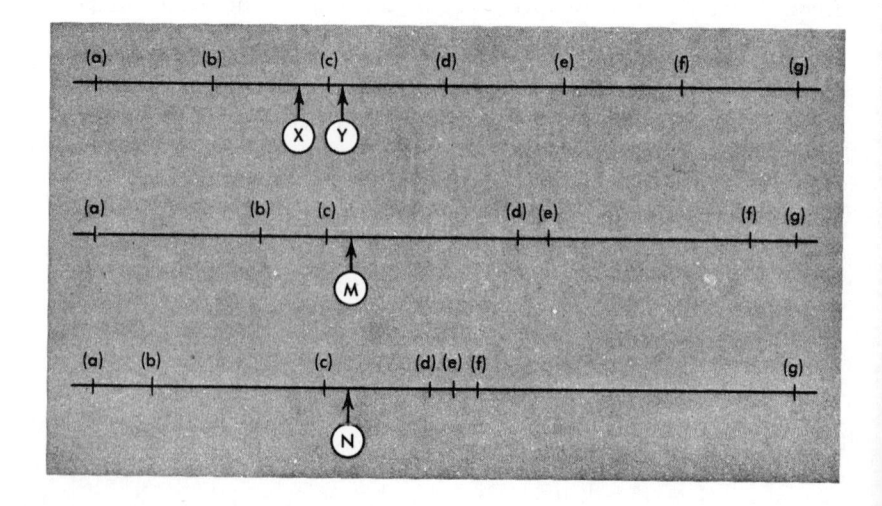

The information required of the subject is an indication of the item he feels best represents his own position, the item next closest, and so on to the item he finds most discrepant with his own position. Let us imagine that his first choice is statement (c). This locates his own position somewhat between (b) and (d), but closer to (c) than to either of them. If there were some reason to believe that the items were equally spaced, then his second choice would tell us at which side of (c) he was located. If he lies at X in the first array shown here, his second choice would be (b); but if he is at Y his second choice should be (d). This reasoning does not follow, however, save as we may assume that the items are evenly spaced, and we do not know this yet: in the second array, the subject M is on the (d) side of (c), yet given the unusual spacing of items, his second choice should be (b) nonetheless. One thing we can be certain about, however, and that is that the second choice of an individual located at or near (c) must be either (b) or (d). If it is neither, but is one of the other items, then we must conclude that our ordering of the items is incorrect or that other dimensions are affecting this individual's response in addition to the dimension with respect to which we have ordered the items (if error can be ruled out). Let us suppose that for a large number of subjects, choices *do* proceed through adjacent items to one side or the other, so that the responses pass the test of unidimensionality. (In the Coombs technique, as with Guttman scaling, how closely the data must fit the ideal model to assure us of unidimensionality within reasonable error is difficult to specify.) Then from the patterning of preferences expressed by individuals at different points we can piece together a picture of the relative distances between items. Thus individuals located closest to item (c) above should give the following order of preference if located at X: (c), (b), (d), (a), (e), (f), (g). If located at Y, the expected order would be only slightly different: (c), (d), (b), (e), (a), (f), (g). If however the subject were located at roughly the same point as Y on the continuum with respect to (c), but the spacing of items were grossly different, quite different orders would be generated. For M, the order would be (c), (b), (d), (e), (a), (f), (g); but for N the order would be (c), (d), (e), (f), (b), (a), (g). For each pattern of relative spaces the expected order can be readily visualized as the order of items moving away from the crease if the scale were folded back on itself at the point where the subject himself is located.

Assuming that from his own vantage point on the continuum each subject is gauging the variable distances between adjacent items in the same way, it is a relatively straightforward matter to convert the data to a specification of relative distances between items. It is important to understand that no absolute distances are claimed if the technique is used with minimal assumptions, nor are any units established. What *is* ascertained is simply the relative size (that is, an ordinal scaling) of the six "distances" that can separate seven ordered items.

The Coombs technique is intriguing because it is the first approach to scaling that gets beyond the simple ordinal level of measurement without dependence on the subjective judgment of the investigator or of a panel of judges. Its utility hinges on the orderliness of preference hierarchies in the human mind, and it is not clear how frequently data from attitude domains will fit the model assumed. Nonetheless, quite comparable assumptions underlie the use of judges, although they are made less explicit and verified less rigorously. Both as a device for checking the dimensionality of preferences and as a means of pinning down a sense of spacing between items, the unfolding technique may be a highly useful tool.

Multidimensional Scaling

The approaches to attitude measurement covered up to this point have all assumed that the goal of the scaling operation was to locate subjects on a unidimensional continuum, in most cases having to do with degree of affect toward some object. For the bulk of the techniques mentioned, the possibility that responses might be affected by more than one dimension of judgment has been either ignored or loosely examined through some analysis of internal consistency. It is only in the case of Guttman scaling and the Coombs unfolding technique that the development of a successful scale from multiple items must first pass through a rigorous test to assure unidimensionality.

Another strategy that has been attracting recent interest is to accept the fact that subjects may respond to even a relatively homogeneous domain of objects or situations in terms of a multiplicity of dimensions, and to carry on from that point, using relatively sophisticated techniques of statistical analysis (most often, factor analysis) to ask such questions as "What are the minimal number of dimensions necessary to account for the patterns of responses?" and "What interpretations may be given each of these dimensions?" When reasonably clear answers to questions of this sort can be made, it is possible analytically to locate the position of the subject as a point in a plane or a space of whatever number of dimensions is required to fit the data. Furthermore, by noting the projection of this point on the axes defining varying dimensions in the space, it is possible to characterize the location of the individual on any single one of the dimensions taken alone.

THE SEMANTIC DIFFERENTIAL. One of the most prominent measurement procedures embracing multiple dimensions is actually a combination of a scaling procedure and an association method. Osgood, Suci, and Tannenbaum (1957) asked their subjects to respond to a word (known as a "concept") by rating it on a series of seven-interval rating scales, each bounded by a pair of bipolar adjectives. In the example presented below, the concept being rated is "Father." Only two of the many scales are shown in this illustration. Typical instructions follow:

The purpose of this study is to measure the *meanings* of certain things to various people by having them judge them against a series of descriptive scales. In taking this test, please make your judgments on the basis of what these things mean *to you*. On each page of this booklet you will find a different concept to be judged and beneath it a set of scales. You are to rate the concept on each of these scales in order. (A number of examples and further specific instructions often accompany these instructions).

FATHER

active ___:___:___:___:___: X :___ passive

soft ___: X :___:___:___:___:___ hard

If a person checks the two scales in the manner indicated, it appears that for our subject the concept "Father" has the meaning or connotation of a submissive person. In developing this technique, Osgood, Suci, and Tannenbaum initially used 20 such concepts and rated each on the same list of 50 bipolar adjective scales. When 100 subjects had rated each of the 20 concepts on the 50 scales, a factor analysis of the ratings revealed that a number of the scales of judgment were highly interrelated. In other words, if the subject rated a concept near the good end of the good–bad scale, he also tended to rate this same concept, on the other scales of this group, as beautiful, sweet, clean, kind, nice, and fair, rather than ugly, sour, dirty, cruel, awful, or unfair. The converse of this is also true. When one asks what this cluster of scales has in common that causes them to be responded to in much the same way, it can be seen that all represent ways of evaluating things. It appears that one dimension of meaning is the *evaluation dimension* and that when we are asked what something means to us, we often think in such "evaluative terms" as good–bad, beautiful–ugly, and the rest of the words in this cluster of scales (see Research Illustration 2.4, page 41).

Factor analysis also revealed that responses to another group of scales were also correlated with each other. The following scales were among those in the second cluster that were rated in much the same way by the subjects: large–small, strong–weak, heavy–light, thick–thin, rugged–delicate. If a subject rated a concept near the small end of the large–small scale, he also tended to characterize this same concept as weak, light, thin, delicate, and so on. Inspection of this group suggests that this dimension of meaning can be called a *potency dimension*. When asked what something means to us we often think in such "potency terms" as large–small, strong–weak, and the rest of the words in this cluster of scales.

A similar analysis revealed the presence of another cluster of scales that included the following: agitated–calm, tense–relaxed, active–passive, and fast–slow. For obvious reasons this was called an *activity dimension.* Other relatively minor dimensions were also found.

Since connotative meaning seems to have three major dimensions, it should be possible to devise an instrument for the measurement of meaning by using a few scales to represent each of these three factors. Such an instrument is called a *semantic differential.* The most commonly used semantic differential consists of four scales to measure the evaluation dimension, three to measure the potency dimension, and three to measure the activity dimension. In using the semantic differential, a subject rates a word, an object, a person (or even a picture or the name of a political candidate) on these ten scales. The ratings determine what the word connotes, for that subject, along each of the three dimensions. Since these three scales can be thought of as occupying positions in three-dimensional space, one could construct a three-dimensional model containing these three scales placed at right angles to each other. This would make it possible to show the connotative meaning of any word or other concept in terms of a point within this three-dimensional "semantic space."

In practice, variations of the semantic differential are being used as attitude scales. In attitude studies it may sometimes be useful to know where a person places a concept on all three of the scales. Hence, the semantic differential may be thought of as a multiple-dimension attitude scale. The most frequent usage at present, however, involves the rating of words, persons, and objects along the dimensions of the evaluation scale alone. It has been found that this evaluation dimension is the one most frequently utilized when persons are asked what something means to them. It is also the dimension that comes closest to the positive–negative or favorable–unfavorable continuum that is usually involved in attitude studies. Even when this single dimension of the semantic differential is used in studying attitudes, we are still dealing with a multiple-dimension scale. The reason is that a person actually makes two responses in using this scale. To take the good–bad scale as an example, one must first indicate a favorable or unfavorable direction by moving to the right or the left of the neutral point on this seven-point scale. One then makes what amounts to an intensity rating by moving one, two, or three steps beyond the neutral point toward the extreme right or left end of the scale.

An excellent illustration of the usefulness of the semantic differential in attitude work can be seen by consulting the work of Nunnally and Kittross (1958). They were interested in the attitude of the public toward persons working in the mental health field. To ascertain this, they used as concepts the words "Doctor," "Nurse," "Psychiatrist," "Psychoanalyst," "Psychologist," "Social Worker," and so on. Individuals rated each of these concepts on a number of the scales of the evaluation dimension. It was found that there were more favorable evaluations for those persons that could be identified with physical medicine, such as doctor and nurse, than for those who could not be so identified. It was possible to determine the *precise nature* of the difference in favorableness of attitude toward these persons by noting *which* of the scales were most responsible for this difference. The semantic differential thus affords comparative ratings and also provides a means of analyzing the character of the differences found. It is currently being employed in many different kinds of attitude research.

Indirect Methods of Measuring Attitudes

In a very real sense, all measurements of attitude are made "indirectly." The phrase has come to be applied, however, to methods that on the surface do not appear to be getting at attitudes at all. They might, perhaps, be called "concealed" methods. Under certain conditions, subjects may express their attitudes with less distortion if they do not realize they are expressing attitudes.

Several investigators have made use of "projective" techniques for the measurement of attitudes. Such procedures, which have been widely used in the study of personality, are derived from subjects' responses to ambiguous or unstructured situations. A favorite device is the use of pictures so ambiguous that they may be interpreted in many different ways. The assumption is that when a subject makes one specific interpretation—and particularly if he does so repeatedly and rather consistently—this interpretation is determined not by something in the picture but by his own response tendencies. This assumption, as we have already seen, is justified by the known facts about the perception of ambiguous stimuli.

This method has been applied by Proshansky (1943) to the measurement of attitudes toward labor. Subjects were shown pictures, selected from various sources, that rather obviously had something to do with working people involved in some sort of conflict situation. Each subject was then asked to describe with as much detail as possible what the picture was about, in such a manner as to make a running account or "story." The following excerpts are taken from two contrasting accounts of the same picture.

Subject 1

Home of a man on relief—shabby—dresses poorly. Scene is probably of a shack down South. Also might be the home of some unemployed laborer. Horrible housing conditions. Why don't the government provide for these people. The ordinary worker is always forgotten and allowed to rot.

s

Subject 2

Picture of one room, very messy, stove in center, woman on the left, man standing next to stove, couple of children near them. This is a room of what we call "poor people." They seem to be messy, sloppy people, who seem to enjoy dwelling in their own trash.

Three qualified judges then rated each "story" as to the degree of favorable or unfavorable attitude toward labor shown. The pooled ratings for each subject were then correlated with scores made by the same subject in responses to a "direct" scale—that is, one that was quite obviously getting at attitudes toward labor. For two groups of student subjects, the resulting coefficients of correlation were .87 and .67. These correlations are high enough to indicate that the two methods were getting at the same attitude, and hence we have a good deal of confidence in the validity of each measure.

Another promising indirect method is the *Error Choice Technique* introduced by Hammond (1948). In a test of attitudes toward labor, he constructed a number of items that permitted the subject to choose one of two possible alternatives as the correct one. One of the items reads, "The number of man-days lost because of strikes from January to June was (1) 34.5 million (2) 98.6 million." Neither figure was correct. They deviated equally from the actual figure, although in opposite directions. The test was administered as if it were simply an information test. In order to make this approach plausible, a number of items with correct alternatives were distributed among the items that forced erroneous choices.

The subjects were a group of businessmen and a group of men employed in a labor union. It was found that the errors made by each group were significantly different and reflected a systematic bias on the part of the members of the two groups. Thus, the labor men tended to choose the figure favoring labor and the businessmen tended to choose the figure unfavorable to labor. In an attempt to see whether it made any difference whether the nature of the task was concealed, Hammond gave the test to two comparable groups. It was presented as an "information test" to one group but quite openly as an "attitude test" to another. He found that one third of the responses made by these two groups were significantly different from one another. It apparently can make a difference whether or not subjects are aware that their attitude is being studied.

To determine how accurately this error-choice technique distinguishes between persons with known attitudes on an issue, Kubany (1953) studied two groups: graduate students in social work, who were known to be favorable to some form of National Health Insurance, and third-year medical students, who were known to be opposed to it. The

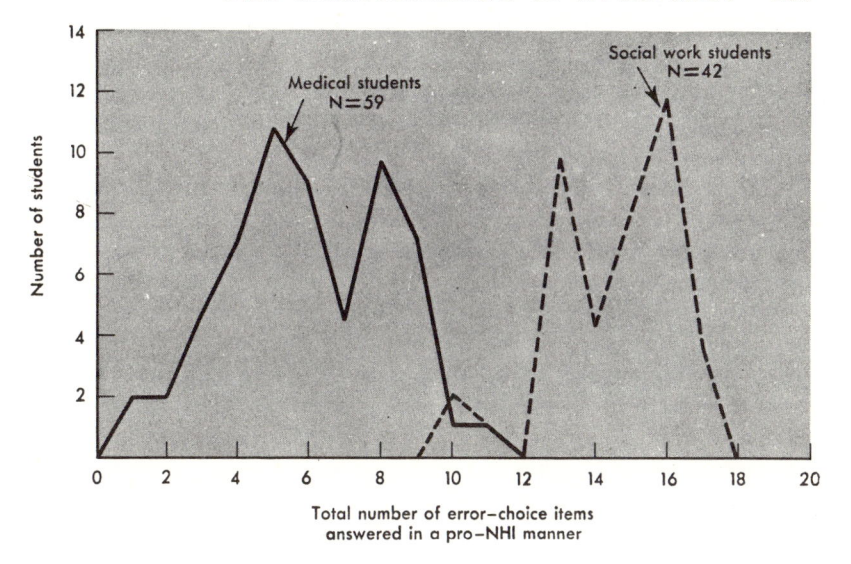

FIGURE A.3. The number of persons in each of two student populations obtaining the stated pro-NHI scores on eighteen error-choice items (adapted from Kubany, 1953)

few members of each group who did not have the attitude typical of their group were eliminated from the sample, after administration of the error-choice items, on the basis of a direct question concerning whether the subject favored or opposed NHI. Thus the members of the two groups were known to have definite and opposing attitudes.

A number of genuine information items were intermixed with the error-choice items. Using tests of internal consistency, eighteen error-choice items were chosen as the basis of computing scores for the two groups. Figure A.3 shows the number of error-choice items answered in a pro-NHI manner for each group. The average number of errors in the favorable direction for social workers was 14.64. The average in the favorable direction for medical students was only 5.93. The figure shows remarkably little overlap between the scores made by the two groups. Consequently the validity was high for this situation. It appears to be one of the better indirect methods of measuring the systematic errors often associated with attitudes. For intensive studies of individual attitudes, "indirect" methods should be combined with direct ones.

* * *

Although it may seem that finding out what people's attitudes are on a particular topic should be a simple and straightforward matter, doing so with adequate attention paid to the accuracy and greatest possible precision of measurement can lead to very complicated considerations indeed. We have attempted over the course of this section to suggest some of these considerations, and the major strategies that have been developed for coping with the problems they pose.

Thus there is not *a* way to measure attitudes. Rather, there are many ways. Each way has its liabilities as well as its assets. Perhaps for any single inquiry in the domain of social psychology, one form of attitude measurement would recommend itself over all others, and we certainly should expect to tailor our choice of measurement tools to the peculiar requirements of the measurement situation. Nevertheless, for many specific purposes it would be hard to choose on a priori grounds among several types of attitude measurement. In these cases, the existence of multiple tools is not only legitimate but welcome. For in view of the fundamental ambiguities in measurement of psychological states (as compared with physical measurement), we shall be most confident of a growing body of generalizations in social psychology if we know that they can be demonstrated and replicated quite as well with one measurement strategy as with another.

APPENDIX B

Survey Research and the Measurement of Public Opinion

MANY OF THE METHODS OF ATTITUDE MEASUREMENT SURVEYED IN APPENDIX A presuppose both the willingness and the ability of subjects to respond to fairly long lists of items, sometimes involving rather intricate instructions. It is usually easy to persuade groups of college students to make the discriminating responses required by some of these more extended approaches to attitude measurement. However, for some social-psychological phenomena we cannot be entirely confident that findings on haphazard collections of students, however often they are replicated, are exhaustive proof of the generality of our propositions. Furthermore, there are many other kinds of people—union members, Negroes, professors, the aged, congressmen—whose attitudes have a good deal of intrinsic interest for many social psychologists. Yet for such populations, only a small and unrepresentative proportion would be likely to have the time, inclination, and capacity to respond to such scales. Nor can representative samples of such populations be herded into a room and given even a brief paper-and-pencil test as a group. Typically what is required is some form of personal interviewing at the convenience of the selected respondent.

When survey research studies of attitudes in various significant populations first developed in the 1930s, they were most often concerned merely with ascertaining the division of opinion in some population over some controversial public issue. At that time, all that seemed necessary was to formulate the questions, decide who was to be questioned, ask the questions, and add up the answers.

Since that time, however, numerous changes have occurred. Although there always remains some interest in whether one or another population is 70–30 in favor or 70–30 against some topical proposition, questions of this simplicity are no longer the primary concern of academic survey research. Such work has moved on to the examination of more complex aspects of attitudes, including determinants of their structure and evolution over time within natural social contexts, as well as the study of other psychological facets of social process, such as the diffusion of information, the exertion of influence, conflicts in perceptions between groups, the acceptance of socially defined roles, and the like.

Furthermore, although it first seemed easy to locate some members of an interesting population and ask them some questions, a good deal of methodological research has made clear that all kinds of misleading results can be generated if inadequate attention is given to the nature of the questions asked, the conditions under which they are asked (including the nature of the questioner), and the selection of the respondents, among other things. This is not to say, of course, that there is no overlap between methodological problems involved in achieving good attitude measurement in a class of college sophomores and survey research on other populations. Indeed, for virtually every problem that arises in the one kind of investigation setting, there is at least some roughly analogous problem in the other setting. This is only natural, for both kinds of investigation involve the extraction of information, often subjective, from human beings. Nonetheless, the survey research setting has tended to sensitize investigators to certain kinds of problems.

Here we shall consider only a few of the broadest problems that survey research methodology has faced. For more detailed treatments, the reader might consult Hyman (1955), Moser (1958), or Selltiz, Jahoda, Deutsch, and Cook (1959).

Preparation of Questions

Social psychologists have learned in recent years how many traps there are into which they may fall if their questions have not been adequately prepared. The best way of avoiding error is to pretest the questions by asking them of a sample of respondents and then subjecting the answers to careful analysis. Some of the most common sources of error are discussed below.

AMBIGUITY IN QUESTIONS. The wording of questions is a source of possible misunderstanding and error. The following suggestions have been adapted from ideas presented by Edwards (1957) and Cantril and Fried (in Cantril, 1944):

1. Avoid questions that may be interpreted in more than one way.
2. Keep the questions simple, clear, and direct.
3. Avoid the use of double negatives.
4. Avoid questions that involve technical or unfamiliar words.
5. The number of alternative answers should not be so large as to be confusing.
6. The number of alternative answers should not be so small as to be incomplete.
7. Avoid questions that tap only surface rationalizations.
8. Avoid questions that yield only stereotyped answers.

These are only a sampling of the many things that must be carefully considered. For a check list of one hundred such matters to keep in mind when preparing questions for public opinion interviewing, see Payne (1951).

An example will show the unexpected nature of problems encountered in asking questions. In a recent survey of the reasons why persons were moving into a certain city, questions were being directed to those who had recently arrived. Preparatory to more specific questions, they were asked, "Is this city like the place you lived in before you moved here?" A considerable number of persons answered, "Oh, I like it here!" or "Oh, I don't like it here!" It finally became apparent that the word "like" in the question was being interpreted by many in the sense of "like-dislike" rather than in the intended sense of "similar-dissimilar." The question was thus an ambiguous one because it meant one thing to some persons and another thing to others.

There are many similar illustrations of pitfalls in the phrasing of questions. Although the preceding suggestions for avoiding ambiguity in wording questions can be very helpful, they cannot cover all contingencies. For this reason, it is advisable to try out questions in the form of a "pilot survey" before using them. Asking the questions of a small sample of persons to be studied will often turn up areas that need to be revised.

BIAS IN QUESTIONS. The way in which a question is worded can predispose many respondents toward one kind of answer rather than another. Here are some of the ways in which this may occur:

1. The question tailored to fit the investigator's stereotype of the respondent. Kahn and Cannell (1957) show that if a person is attempt-

ing to obtain opinions on the control of monopolies, he might be tempted to adopt the following terminology with an obviously uneducated person: "You haven't read any recent material on monopolies, I suppose?" This definitely predisposes toward a negative answer and represents a real danger in opinion measurement.

2. Stating a proposition favorably or unfavorably, rather than both or neither. Here is an example of how responses may differ when the same issue is presented differently; the responses are by two equivalent samples of the same population to whom the following different questions were put (Rugg and Cantril, in Cantril, 1944):

Because every man is entitled to safe and healthy working conditions, labor (in defense industries) should be allowed to strike for them	Agree	45%
	Disagree	45
	Don't know	10
	Total	100%
Because working conditions in this country are the best in the world, labor (in defense industries) should not be allowed to strike about them.	Agree	74%
	Disagree	17
	Don't know	9
	Total	100%

These responses make clear that the tendency toward acquiescence discussed in Appendix A (pages 517–519) is fully as much of a problem in personal interviews (if not more) as it is in printed or paper-and-pencil attitude tests. Many individuals will agree with a series of statements and later agree with them again when stated in a converse form.

3. The use of emotionally charged words or phrases. Cantril and his associates have shown, for example, that between 1939 and 1941 phrases like "go to war" invariably brought a less favorable response than phrases like "using the army and navy to aid another country."

4. The use of prestige symbols. It has repeatedly been shown that if a statement is credited to a respected public figure, it is more generally accepted than if the same statement is presented with no supporting name.

Many other sources of bias might be mentioned. A few will be mentioned in the later section on interviewing. These biases are usually introduced unwittingly, as a result of inadequate pretesting. The consequences, of course, are equally unfortunate whether the bias is deliberate or unintended.

THE DISADVANTAGES OF SINGLE QUESTIONS. It has already been noted that a single-item scale is necessarily an unreliable one. This is just as true if the item is a question asked by a doorbell ringer as it is if the item is included in a printed scale or questionnaire. In addition to this, there is no accurate method of estimating other dimensions of attitudes—

such as intensity, range, and consistency—from a brief response to a single question. These other dimensions are just as useful in survey research studies as they are in attitude scale studies. Consequently, many of the more recent public opinion studies make use of a whole battery of carefully designed questions. In such a battery, each question is carefully designed to measure a particular aspect or dimension of the total opinion profile. Thus each question tends to give information that supplements the information derived from the other questions. Where the outcomes appear to be consistent with one another, we feel we have achieved a somewhat orderly picture of how opinion grows and is sustained. Where the outcomes are not consistent with our anticipations, they indicate the areas in which further research is needed to supplement our inadequate understanding.

QUESTIONS THAT REVEAL THE RESPONDENT'S OWN COGNITIVE CONTEXT. Thus far we have considered only questions providing ready-made alternatives, such as yes–no, agree–disagree, or declarative statements. Since the respondent must select from the choices presented to him, he is sharply limited in the answers he can give. Such questions are often referred to as "structured," or "fixed-alternative" questions.

There is, however, another approach to the preparation of questions. It is based on the fundamental assumption that we can learn most about people's attitudes if we *first* ask them very broad, unstructured questions which allow them to express, freely and spontaneously, the aspects of the attitudinal area which are of most central concern to them as individuals. Such questions are referred to as *open-ended* because they do not limit the respondent to any fixed set of alternatives in replying. Interviewers using such questions are usually trained to "probe"—that is, to ask further questions, such as "Why?" or "I wonder if you'd tell me more about that"—whenever they do not feel satisfied that the respondent has described his own attitude completely. Responses to the questions are written down verbatim and later analyzed to determine the context the respondent was using and the major features of his response.

Very often the early, open-ended questions are followed, toward the end of the interview, with more specific probes using fixed-alternative questions. This device of proceeding from less structured to more structured questions is called a *funnel sequence*. A major purpose of the funnel sequence is to prevent early questions from biasing the responses to questions that come later. The following series of questions illustrates the funnel sequence. They are taken from Kahn and Cannell (1957) and are used to determine whether the respondent thinks our foreign policy toward Russia should be relaxed or restricted, and why he holds his opinion:

1. How do you think this country is getting along in its relations with other countries?
2. How do you think we are doing in our relations with Russia?
3. Do you think we ought to be dealing with Russia differently from the way we are now?
4. (If yes to question 3) What should we be doing differently?
5. Some people say we should get tougher with Russia, and others think we are too tough as it is. How do you feel about it?

The first question is very general and permits the respondent to be quite spontaneous in selecting his own mode of response. It thus tends to tap whatever judgmental dimensions and cognitive features of the attitude object are most central for the particular respondent. At the same time it avoids suggesting to the respondent how he should answer the remainder of the questions. By the time we come to question 5 the interrogation has come to focus very specifically (the narrow part of the funnel) on something more precise we want to know about. If question 5 had been placed first in this sequence it would undoubtedly have biased the answer to question 1 by prematurely suggesting a context in which that question might be answered. (For another illustration of the funnel method, see Research Illustration 3.1, page 60.) This method, when properly used, removes one source of invalidity because each response can be interpreted within the context in which it was meant to be expressed by the respondent. It provides a rich array of information from which many dimensions of attitudes may be studied.

A distinct disadvantage of the open-ended interview is that it is more time consuming and costly than the quick "polls" which use structured questions exclusively. Part of the reason is that it takes more time to conduct the interview, but a great deal of time and professional care are needed to code or classify the full, verbatim answers written down at the time of the interview as well. Answers to structured questions are essentially preclassified and need only be transcribed, while conversational answers must be examined and coded later at a much slower rate.

Nevertheless, such extra care is often well repaid. Particularly in surveying educationally heterogeneous populations with respect to public issues that are often extremely remote in a psychological sense from substantial portions of the respondents, large numbers of "agrees" and "disagrees" may be collected in response to structured questions that are hasty fabrications to conceal the fact that the respondent has never thought about the subject, much less formed an attitude about it. Converse (1964) has shown that even on structured questions prefaced by the suggestion that the respondent need not try to give an opinion unless the attitude item was something that had concerned him, large numbers of "attitudes" were expressed that showed statistically random properties over time in subsequent retests. Differences in long-term (two- and four-year) test-retest reliabilities on items for which little "topical" opinion change was expected were very great between those respondents who, in response to earlier open-ended questions, had voluntarily indicated an interest in the attitude area, and those who had failed to make such mentions spontaneously (.8, for example, as opposed to .2).

Problems of Sampling

It is almost never possible to interview all the members of a population. How, then, can we be sure that the respondents selected are truly representative of the total population that we want them to represent?

The necessity for accurate sampling methods is illustrated by the early history of polling in this country. During the presidential campaign of 1924, the *Literary Digest*, a thriving magazine, mailed out hundreds of thousands of straw ballots, a considerable proportion of which were marked and mailed back. The ballots thus returned favored the election of Calvin Coolidge, a Republican, by more than a safe margin, and in November he was elected. In 1928 and 1932, millions of ballots were again returned, out of still more millions that had been mailed, and they correctly predicted the outcomes of both elections—Republican Hoover in 1928 and Democrat Roosevelt in 1932—although by far too small a margin in the latter year.

Encouraged by their success, the *Literary Digest* pollers sent out still more millions of ballots in 1936 and confidently announced that the results consistently favored the *defeat* of President Roosevelt. Actually, Mr. Roosevelt carried every state except Maine and Vermont. Why did a procedure so successful on three previous occasions fail so dismally the fourth time? The answers now seem quite clear. The names of people to whom ballots were sent were taken from lists of telephone subscribers and automobile owners. In the 1930s such a sample gave little representation to working-class people of limited means. Prior to 1936 socio-economic differences in party voting were apparently so slight that this bias did not affect estimates of the outcome substantially. By 1936, however, the accidental exclusion of people in too straitened circumstances to own cars or telephones systematically concealed a massive amount of support for Roosevelt. Modern methods of polling gained much by the analysis of reasons for this failure.

Scientific research is dogged by some of the same sampling problems. In an attempt to study the social attitudes of leading psychologists, Keehn (1955) mailed a public opinion inventory to each of fifty-two well-known psychologists. Of these, twenty-seven were returned in usable form. Analysis of these returns led to the conclusion that this small group of well-known psychologists was quite similar with respect to several characteristics—one of which was humanitarianism. Can we conclude from this that psychologists, as a group, are characterized by humanitarian tendencies? That this would be a hazardous inference can be seen by noting that almost half of the sample did not return questionnaires. This *might* mean that returns were received only from the individuals who were humanitarian enough to reply to the questionnaire! If true, it would mean that the sample simply failed to include the large group of psychologists (almost half of the original group polled) who were the least humanitarian in their tendencies.

Good sampling is firmly based in a well-developed body of theory that derives from probability theory. The general notions of sampling theory tend to follow what one might expect on commonsense grounds, although occasionally the theory suggests surprising possibilities. As a first requirement in any sample design, for example, it is necessary to decide how accurate the results must be. This may sound absurd: of course the results should be as accurate as human effort and ingenuity can make them. But nothing short of a full census or enumeration of all members of a specified population can be sure of representing the population exactly: *any* sampling of that population contains the possibility of some error. Since many costs of research increase as a direct function of the number of interviews taken (sample size) we are unlikely to try to study all members of anything but the smallest populations. As soon as the population in question is one with thousands of members, we shall want to restrict our efforts to a sample, and we are willing to put up with a certain amount of possible error in exchange for major savings in time and money. Fortunately, if rigorous sampling methods are employed (see below) it is possible in most instances to calculate in advance the limits of likely error in estimates of population characteristics of samples of varying prospective sizes.

Although it is not commonly realized, the amount of likely error is for most practical purposes tied more closely to *absolute* sample size than to its size relative to the total population. This is not true of very small populations, where we might easily have the resources to sample as much as one quarter of the population. That is, quite as we would expect intuitively, 80 cases sampled from a population of 100 will suffer much less probable sampling error than 80 (or 100) cases drawn from a population of 300. However, for populations numbering more than several thousand elements, from which we are unlikely to draw a sample which is more than 15–20 percent of the population size, the primary determinant of the amount of likely error is the absolute size of the sample, and not its relative or proportionate size. Thus, astonishing though it may seem, under ideal sampling conditions a sample of 1000 cases drawn from the population of Peoria, Illinois, would represent that city with less precision (greater expected error) for most characteristics than would a proper sample of 1100 cases taken to represent the population of the United States.

It is for this reason that very representative samples of the American population may be based on one or two thousand cases, and this is the typical size of a national sample. Changing a sample design from 2000 to 2100 cases costs as much as changing 500 to 600. But when one is talking of samples of 2000 cases, the addition of another hundred cases reduces likely error by only a tiny fraction of the reduction achieved by adding them to an original sample of 500 cases. Thus in the range from 1000 to 2000 cases, each additional interview costs very much relative to the slight amount of error it reduces. A well-constructed national sample of 1500 cases will have average error limits of about ± 3 percent. That is, if such a sample shows 57 percent of its respondents reporting frequent church attendance, there is only 1 chance in 20 that the true value, if the same question were asked on a complete national census, would lie outside the range from 54 to 60 percent. For most purposes, this is sufficient accuracy.

All these expectations are valid, however, only if the sample has been drawn with rigorous care following the specifications of the theory. To fit the theory, the sample drawn must be such that *every person in the population has the same chance* (or, for some complex samples, a *known* chance) *of being selected in the sample*. Any hidden defect in the sample that in actuality raises the probability that certain people or certain types of people get into the sample relative to others leads to sample bias and means that the expectations based on sampling theory are no longer valid for this sample.

And, of course, once a sample fitting these specifications is selected, the whole effort is bootless unless we actually follow through and interview the specific persons selected for the sample. In other words, every possible effort must be made to interview every person designated for the sample, rather than giving up on some that are hard to find and substituting other population members who are more accessible. The people who are most difficult to find often have attitudes and other characteristics different from those of people easy to find. This was clear, for example, in a study by Maslow and Sakoda (1952), who were concerned with the possibility that Kinsey's study of human sexual behavior might be biased by the omission of data from individuals who did not readily volunteer. Their findings indicated that persons who readily assent to interviewing score higher on measures of "self-esteem" than do nonvolunteers. Since it was found that high self-esteem correlates positively with unconventional sexual behavior, it is quite unlikely that those who volunteered for this interviewing gave accurate data for the entire population.

SAMPLING METHODS. How do we draw a sample to ensure that every person has an equal chance of selection? This outcome is assured if the selection proceeds on a random basis. However, this does not mean a haphazard basis. It takes a good deal of care to select elements in a fashion that is truly random in the statistical sense. A number of methods of population sampling are possible: choice between them depends largely on the ancillary information about the population that is available.

The crucial question initially is whether or not the sampler is fortunate enough to possess a listing of all the people in the population from which he wishes to draw his sample. If he does, then the sampling problem is a relatively simple one. Suppose there are 3000 names in the total population, and suppose it has been decided that a sample of 300 will meet the requirements for accurate representativeness. Then all that need be done is to select one name out of every ten. The selection must be made, however, by some strictly random procedure. It would not do, for example, to select the first 300 names on the list, because the names might be bunched in certain ways. If the names are already arranged in some random order (for *most* purposes, an alphabetical order may be assumed to be random), then the simplest method is to take every tenth name, in order. Professional samplers always use some strictly chance method, such as use of a table of random numbers, to determine which number should be used in starting the list. This procedure, commonly known as *systematic sampling*, meets the basic requirement that every person in the total population has the same chance of being in the sample.

It is impossible to use systematic sampling for large populations where there is no list of names. Many of the large polling services, therefore, use some variant of a method known as *quota sampling*. This form of sampling, as we shall see, fails to ensure that every person in the population has the same chance of being in the sample. However, in view of its wide use, it warrants description by way of contrast with the more rigorous probability sampling methods.

In quota sampling, it is first decided that the sample shall be composed of certain proportions of men and women, of upper-, middle-, and lower-class respondents, or of Negroes and whites, and so on. Such decisions are determined by the known characteristics of the total population of which the sample is to be representative. If we desire information about a total population made up of "all adult Americans," then the ratio of men and women should be about 50–50, and the ratio of whites to Negroes should be about 9 to 1. Information about the composition of the total group is obtained from census data and other similar sources. The sample is designed to include the correct ratios of men and of Negroes, for example, if there is any reason to believe that the attitudes being studied are in any way related to factors of sex or race. It is usually not thought necessary to make sure that the sample includes the proper ratio of tall and short people because there is no reason to believe that attitudes toward most public issues are influenced by tallness or shortness.

When these figures have been decided upon, each interviewer assigned to a certain community is instructed to interview a certain number of individuals in specified ratios. His quota requirement—say of 100 respondents—may be made up of 50 percent males, 90 percent whites, 30 percent under 30 years of age, 40 percent between 30 and 50 years of age, and so on. There may be other requirements in addition to these but otherwise he is left to his own devices. He may call on people in their homes, accost them in restaurants or railroad stations or simply stop them in the streets. Interviewers are usually warned against making use of their own friends because of the possibility that these would represent a special selection rather than a random one.

The quota system is the simplest and cheapest method devised for reaching large numbers of people, but it clearly fails to meet the basic requirement that every person in the total population should have an equal chance of being included in the sample. If the interviewer does not like certain sections of town or prefers to avoid houses that do not have sidewalks leading up to the front door it may mean that certain kinds of people have little chance of being included in the sample. Other persons who are likely to be missed are those who are not often at home or who do not frequent places where the interviewers are likely to go. Thus there is considerable evidence that the quota system is subject to certain systematic biases in sampling—biases that often reflect the more common middle-class attitudes.

Limitations inherent in quota sampling are almost certainly responsible in some part for consistent errors on the part of some of the well-known polling services in their studies of popular presidential choices. As Katz has shown in a series of critical analyses of these polls (1941, 1944, 1949), many of the earlier attempts underestimated the size of the Democratic vote. One of the best-known polling services had a record of such underestimation, ranging between 2 and 6 percentage points, as compared with the actual vote cast. Those in charge of these services are well aware of this error and have tried to correct it. The "middle-class bias," to which we have just referred, probably has a good deal to do with this error. It was not entirely this factor that explained the very inaccurate poll predictions at the time of the 1948 election, when it was predicted that Dewey would beat President Truman. As has been pointed out by Campbell, Gurin, and Miller (1954), the number of voters who were still undecided a month before the 1948 election was unusually high (19 percent). The conventional assumption that these undecided voters would split their votes in the same proportions as those who had expressed preferences was one of the factors that led the poll takers into their disastrous prediction. A substantial majority of these actually cast their votes for Truman (Mosteller *et al.*, 1949).

Where no complete population listing is available, sampling methods that can avoid these biases are laborious and expensive. The most commonly used among them is known as *area sampling*, which is essentially a method of choosing places first and people only secondarily. The method is most successful if the investigator possesses accurate maps of city blocks or rural areas. The essential characteristic of the method is that the residences in which interviews are to be held are predetermined by strictly random methods. Thus, instead of being told to question so many women and so many Negroes, the interviewer is told to go to a specified place—and to go back again and again, if necessary, until the respondent in question has been found or it is clear that he cannot be found. The place may be identified by street and number, or be marked on an aerial photograph. Or the interviewer may be told to go to the first farmhouse north of a certain road intersection, or to the fourth apartment (numbered in a specified way) on the third floor of a certain apartment building. Exact procedure also demands that, once the specified residence has been located, a random method be employed for selecting which person in the household is to be interviewed.

If such methods are followed faithfully, the interviewer has no discretion at all in the choice of respondents. The reasons for not allowing him any choice are not that his honesty is suspected, but that, being human, his choices are likely to be determined by seemingly innocent preferences that may bias the outcome.

The advantages of the method lie in the fact that a sample so chosen represents a very faithful cross section of the total population. Even this method is not infallible, however. Some people are constantly moving about, or for other reasons have no place of residence, and thus are excluded from an area sample. Some people included in the sample (like those selected by other sampling methods) refuse to be interviewed. While area sampling is very expensive and time consuming, it is nevertheless the best-known method of sampling large and far-flung populations whose members occupy identifiable places of residence.

Problems of Interviewing

The crucial part of the interviewer's task is to establish relations of such a kind that the respondent will express freely the opinions that the interviewer is seeking. Even with the best personal qualifications and the best training, there are certain conditions under which the interviewer does not succeed in doing this.

THE INTERVIEWER'S OWN ATTITUDES. One way in which the attitude of the interviewer can bias the outcome of a study involves the manner in which the interviewer responds to statements made by the respondent. In one experiment in this area, Greenspoon (1951) asked college students to say nouns, aloud, just as these occurred to them. In the case of each student in the experimental group, the experimenter said "Mm-hmmm" whenever the subject voiced a plural noun. Members of a control group received no such reinforcement. The subjects who received the verbal reinforcement came to voice more plural nouns than did the control group, and this was true even for subjects who were not aware of any connection between their utterances and the response of the experimenter. (Research Illustration 7.4, page 214, is also relevant.)

Hildum and Brown (1956) believe that Greenspoon's experiment stands as a warning to the social psychologist who uses interviews to collect research data. To emphasize their point, they administered to male college students a telephone questionnaire on General Education containing fifteen statements, some representing an attitude favorable to General Education and some an unfavorable attitude. Subjects were given their choice of four responses: Agree strongly, agree slightly, disagree slightly, and disagree strongly. Some of the students were reinforced with the word "Good" for each response indicating a favorable attitude toward General Education and some were reinforced for unfavorable attitudes. The responses were significantly biased in the direction of the verbal reinforcement. It is likely that smiles, frowns, and gestures, in addition to verbal responses, should be avoided by an interviewer lest his own attitude unwittingly influence the respondent in the manner just described.

This does not mean, however, that the interviewer must remain as wooden and immobile as possible during the interview. Indeed, particularly where open-ended material is involved, he has some responsibility to make sure that the respondent's answers are sufficiently clear that they will be codable. Toward this end, he should be trained in the art of nondirective probing—a repertoire of phrases such as "I wonder if you could tell me a bit more about that," "How do you mean?" and the like—which can help to clarify responses and elicit further detail without indicating approval or disapproval of what is being said.

A second way in which the interviewer's attitude can influence interview data is through bias resulting from his own expectations. Smith and Hyman (1950) used a carefully recorded interview in which a respondent had been coached to take a strong internationalist position on foreign affairs but also, in answer to one particular question, to take an isolationist position. Only one fifth of the interviewers who listened to this recorded interview coded the inconsistent isolationist response correctly. Their expectations, based on the respondent's replies to previous questions, apparently influenced their perception of an answer given later in the interview. (This phenomenon is quite similar to the "halo effect" often found when working with rating scales; a person who has a generally favorable or unfavorable impression of another frequently tends to rate him in much the same way on a large number of specific characteristics instead of giving individual consideration to each characteristic in turn.) It is not yet clear whether the best remedial step is to eliminate interviewers who have strong attitudes in the area of investigation or to rely on training methods that would give interviewers knowledge of these sources of difficulty.

OBSERVABLE CHARACTERISTICS OF THE INTERVIEWER. A number of studies have shown that the nature of the interviewer can influence the responses given, especially when the respondents belong to some minority group or when the interviewer is thought to belong to such a group. The first of these conditions is illustrated in a study conducted by the National Opinion Research Center (cited by Cantril, 1944). A sample of Negroes in a southern city was asked by white interviewers, "Do you think it is more important to concentrate on beating the Axis or to make democracy work better here at home?" An equivalent sample of Negroes in the same city was asked the same question by Negro interviewers. To the white interviewers 62 percent of the respondents answered, "Beat the Axis," but only 39 percent of the other sample gave this answer to the Negro interviewers. Somewhat similar studies have shown that working-class respondents are more reticent about giving "pro-labor" answers to interviewers judged to be middle class than to those judged to be more like themselves. Since the training of interviewers cannot have much effect on their skin color or their manner of speech, the lesson to be learned from these studies is that interviewers should be of an appearance not likely to inhibit spontaneous answers on the part of their respondents.

CHARACTERISTICS OF BOTH THE INTERVIEWER AND THE RESPONDENT. Much of the previous discussion has dealt with bias introduced by the characteristics of the interviewer or the respondent alone. It is possible that if certain kinds of interviewers consistently interview certain kinds of respondents, a special kind of bias might emerge from their joint effects. Sheatsley (1951) studied just this possibility by analyzing the records of the National Opinion Research Center and other agencies for insight into the nature of this situation. His statement of findings is worth quoting:

> We have a condition in which the great bulk of market and opinion research interviewing today is conducted by women talking to men, by college graduates talking to the uneducated, by upper-middle-class individuals talking to those of low socio-economic status, by younger people talking to the increasingly larger older-age groups, by white persons talking to Negroes, and by city dwellers talking to rural folk.

This situation might be viewed as an interviewer-response pattern that is characteristic of many research settings. At *every point* in this pattern there is the possibility of systematic bias! It is safe to say that the magnitude of error resulting from this multiple source of bias is not known at the present time. Kahn and Cannell (1957) have attempted to depict this complex interaction in the form of a diagram that shows the background characteristics and psychological factors for both interviewer and respondent. Figure B.1 shows their "model of bias" for interview situations. The first pair of boxes, A_I and A_R (background characteristics), includes some of the major attributes that interviewer and respondent bring to the interview situation. The psychological characteristics of interviewer and respondent that are relevant to the interview appear as boxes B_I and B_R, representing perceptions, attitudes, expectations, and motives. Boxes C_I and C_R represent behavioral factors, and are viewed as the resultant of background factors and psychological forces.

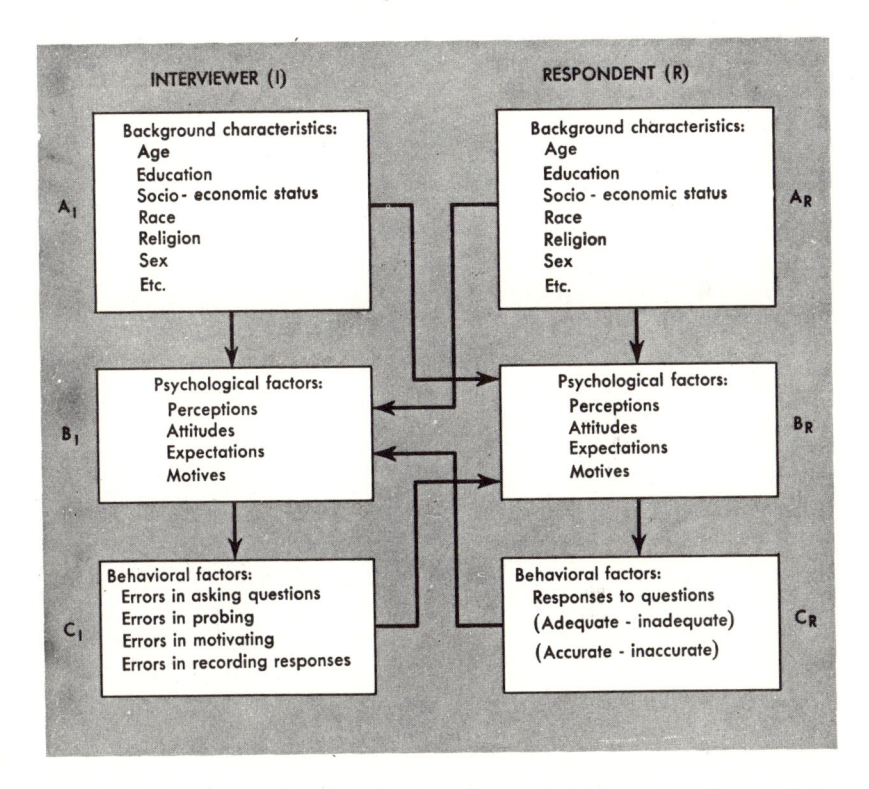

FIGURE B.1. A model of bias showing the complex interaction characteristic of interviewing situations. Arrows indicate presumed direction of influence. (Adapted from Kahn and Cannell, 1957)

The interconnecting arrows show the interview to be an interactive process in which the background characteristics, psychological attributes, and behaviors of *both* interviewer and respondent are important determinants of the bias.

Coding the Responses

An interview schedule consisting exclusively of structured questions and check-box answers poses little problem in coding. More complex problems develop whenever open-ended questions have been used, for some sort of subsequent coding process is necessary. The process is essentially one of making judgments as to the attitudes reflected by the respondent's replies.

The dependence on one further stage of human judgment means one more point at which reliability and validity can be attenuated. Good coding, particularly of open-ended material, requires coders who are well versed in the coding process itself as well as familiar with the general content area covered by the interviews and the specific aims of the study. Moreover, good coding depends on good interviewing: interviewers who are not alert or who are insufficiently trained in the purposes of the specific study and the kinds of coding it will undergo may accept fragmentary or ambiguous answers without properly probing in neutral fashion for sufficient illuminating detail. Such responses place a heavy burden on the coder, and at times are simply uncodable.

Even with well-trained coders and interviews held with the problems of coding in mind, sound coding operations use running controls to maintain the quality of coder performance. The key device here is a procedure of *check-coding*, or having a random sampling of interviews coded by two persons independently. In the early stages of coding a large number of interviews from a single study, 20 percent or more of the interviews may be doubly coded, until it is clear that frames of reference among the coders for classifying the more difficult responses have converged and stabilized (as is evidenced by high levels of agreement between independent codings). Then perhaps the check-coding rate may be progressively reduced toward one interview in twenty, enough to keep a running check against the possibility that some coders might drift out of the appropriate frame of reference. Typically, all of the check-coding data for the whole study can be accumulated and organized in ways that are useful for participants who must be concerned with reliability rates. They can be split question by question so that users of the study can be informed as to any particular questions on which intercoder reliability could not reach adequate standards. Or they can be split coder by coder so that the coding supervisor can have information about individual differences in reliability performances within the staff of coders.

In general, it is not surprising that coding reliability is highest (near perfect) where it requires simply the transcription of checked boxes, and loses some little reliability the more the material is open-ended and the code categories refer to more subtle matters about which the respondent rarely expresses himself directly. Nevertheless, in a well-controlled coding operation, even the latter kinds of codings can be carried out at sufficient levels of reliability, and sometimes it is just such codings that are most important for social-psychological purposes.

A good example of a study that was made much more informative because a nonobvious characteristic was carefully coded was reported by Campbell (1947). His problem was to discover some of the characteristics associated with anti-Semitism, and in particular to test the hypothesis that "personal dissatisfaction" was apt to be associated with it. A national sample of adult, white non-Jews was interviewed by means of open-ended questions, except for a few direct ones concerning attitudes toward Jews, near the close of the interview. No direct questions whatever were asked about the respondent's state of satisfaction. There were many questions, however, in reply to which it was easy for him to indicate either satisfaction or dissatisfaction, with economic and political conditions in particular. Because the questions were prepared with this problem in mind, and because interviewers were aware of the purposes of the study, it proved possible for them to record replies in such a way that they could be coded according to the degree of the respond-

TABLE B.1. The relationship between economic and political satisfaction and attitude toward Jews (adapted from Campbell, 1947)

Attitude toward Jews	Satisfied in both (%)	Partly satisfied, partly dissatisfied (%)	Dissatisfied in both (%)	Total (%)
Express liking	12	10	8	11
Show no dislike	73	48	25	50
Express mild dislike	8	22	30	21
Dislike, avoid them	7	14	13	13
Show active hostility	0	6	24	5
	100	100	100	100
Proportion of total sample	20	72	8	100

ent's satisfaction. Over-all codes (that is, codes based on the total interview) were also drawn up to indicate degrees of favorable or unfavorable attitude toward Jews. (A six-degree code, representing six combinations of full or partial satisfaction or dissatisfaction, both economically and politically, was actually used. For purposes of simplicity, however, we have pooled the four degrees of partial satisfaction and partial dissatisfaction in Table B.1.)

The relationship between these two characteristics, as shown in the table, is very clear. Those who are most dissatisfied are most anti-Semitic, and those who are most satisfied are least anti-Semitic. Those partly satisfied and partly dissatisfied are, almost without exception, also intermediate in attitude toward Jews. The close relationship between these two characteristics does not, in itself, tell us that either one results from the other. Judging from other evidence, the cause-and-effect relationship is a complicated one, and may in part be explained by personality traits that underlie both characteristics. Our present point, however, is that the relationship could never have been discovered at all without careful coding. And careful coding, in turn, depends on adequate planning of the study as a whole, precise formulation of questions, and skilled interviewing.

* * *

The survey research process involves a lengthy chain of human efforts, from original study design, through sampling, to interviewing, coding, and the ultimate analysis of the data gathered. At each of these stages there are possible sources of error, both of the unsystematic or random type and of the systematic error that introduces bias in the findings. Just as no chain is stronger than its weakest link, so sound survey research is dependent on great care being taken throughout the whole process. As is so often the case, accuracy is neither easy to achieve nor inexpensive.

APPENDIX C

Interaction Process Analysis (Bales)

BY FAR THE MOST HIGHLY DEVELOPED AND WIDELY USED METHOD OF describing interaction among members of small groups is that of Bales (1950). Though initially devised for use in group discussions of a problem-solving nature, and still used primarily for such purposes, it is in principle applicable to the observation of virtually any set of interacting persons. The essential ingredients of the procedure are a set of behavior categories and an instrument known as the interaction recorder, pictured in Figure C.1.

In practice, the recorder is typically used by an observer behind a one-way mirror. His task is to classify every observed act of verbal and nonverbal communication among members into one, and only one, of the twelve categories described below. The great advantage of the interaction recorder is that the observer, once he is familiar with both the category system and the apparatus, can (somewhat in the manner of a stenotypist) instantly punch in the number of the appropriate category of the behavior that he has just observed. The twelve category symbols appear, in order, at the left of the apparatus, with a recording space to the right of each of them. A record of interaction can be kept in the proper time sequence by making entries on the moving paper.

It is apparent that the twelve categories, which appear in Figure C.2, are systematically arranged, in symmetrical form. That is, there are two

FIGURE C.1. The interaction recorder used by observers of group behavior (courtesy of Robert F. Bales)

supercategories: the socio-emotional area (A and D) and the task area (B and C); the former is subdivided into positive (A) and negative (D) reactions, and the latter into answers (B) and questions (C). Within the socio-emotional area there are three dimensions (solidarity–antagonism, tension release–tension, and agreement–disagreement); and three other dimensions within the task area (giving–asking for suggestions, giving–asking for opinion, giving–asking for orientation). The symmetrical nature of the system is apparent from the arrows at the right of Figure C.2.

Bales has this to say about other features of the system:

> The set of categories is held to form a logically exhaustive classification system. Every act that occurs is classified into one of the twelve categories. All of the categories are positively defined—that is, none of them is treated as a residual or wastebasket category for "leftovers." With competent observers and hard training, correlations between observers ranging between .75 and .95 can be obtained (1952, page 150).

An examination of these categories makes it clear that interactional analysis is not interested in the specific content of communication, but rather in the kind of interpersonal behavior that occurs. Every act is seen as having some kind of functional relevance to the ongoing activity of the group. It is the identification of these functional relationships

INTERACTION PROCESS ANALYSIS (BALES) - 555

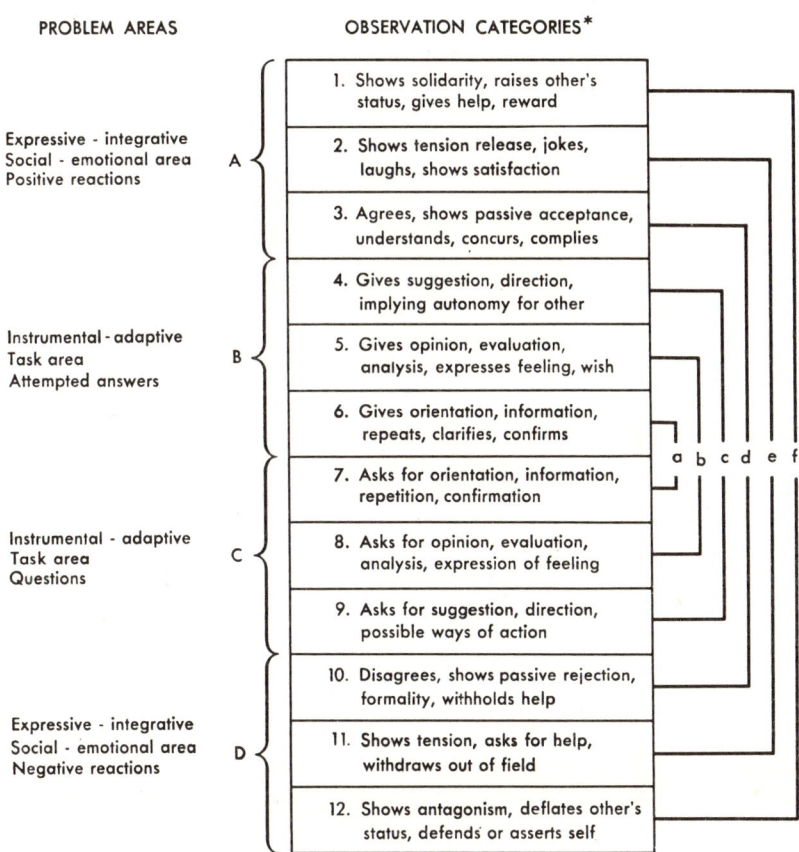

PROBLEM AREAS   **OBSERVATION CATEGORIES***

Expressive - integrative
Social - emotional area
Positive reactions
— A:
1. Shows solidarity, raises other's status, gives help, reward
2. Shows tension release, jokes, laughs, shows satisfaction
3. Agrees, shows passive acceptance, understands, concurs, complies

Instrumental - adaptive
Task area
Attempted answers
— B:
4. Gives suggestion, direction, implying autonomy for other
5. Gives opinion, evaluation, analysis, expresses feeling, wish
6. Gives orientation, information, repeats, clarifies, confirms

Instrumental - adaptive
Task area
Questions
— C:
7. Asks for orientation, information, repetition, confirmation
8. Asks for opinion, evaluation, analysis, expression of feeling
9. Asks for suggestion, direction, possible ways of action

Expressive - integrative
Social - emotional area
Negative reactions
— D:
10. Disagrees, shows passive rejection, formality, withholds help
11. Shows tension, asks for help, withdraws out of field
12. Shows antagonism, deflates other's status, defends or asserts self

a   b   c   d   e   f

*A subclassification of system problems to which each pair of categories is most relevant:

a. Problems of orientation
b. Problems of evaluation
c. Problems of control
d. Problems of decision
e. Problems of tension - management
f. Problems of integration

FIGURE C.2. Categories of interaction process analysis (Bales, 1952)

which the system is designed to facilitate and refine. Thus the *general* characteristics of interaction groups, as contrasted with their incidental and idiosyncratic features, can be studied, and so it is possible to make comparisons of different groups in comparable ways.

Profile analysis is one of the useful ways in which observations recorded in such ways can become illuminating. Figure C.3 shows the relative frequencies of the several categories that have typically been found in problem-solving discussion groups. "Gives opinion" and "shows

556. - APPENDIX C

Shows solidarity		3.4
Shows tension release		6.0
Shows agreement		16.5
Gives suggestion		8.0
Gives opinion		30.1
Gives information		17.9
Asks for information		3.5
Asks for opinion		2.4
Asks for suggestion		1..1
Shows disagreement		7.8
Shows tension		2.7
Shows antagonism		.7

Percentage of total

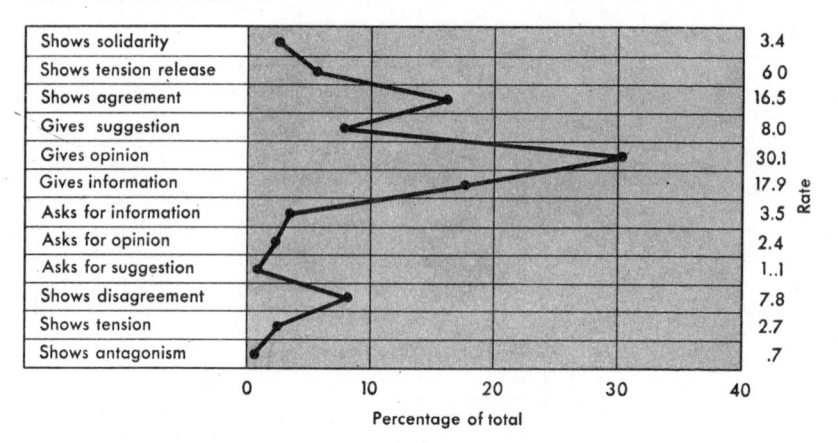

FIGURE C.3. Types of interaction and their relative frequencies. This profile of rates is the average obtained on the standard task from twenty-four different groups, four of each size from two to size seven, each group meeting four times, making a total of ninety-six sessions. The raw number of scores is 71,838. (Bales, 1955)

agreement" are relatively frequent, whereas "shows solidarity," "asks" (for orientation, opinion, suggestion) are infrequent, as are also "shows tension" and "shows antagonism." In general, groups of this kind show more positive than negative responses, and more giving than asking for opinions, information, and suggestion (though we have inadequate data from non-Western societies in this respect).

As Bales is careful to note (1952), different kinds of profiles are to be expected from different kinds of groups working under different conditions. He compares, for example, the profiles of two groups, one of them being the highest and the other the lowest of sixteen groups in satisfaction with their own solution; on a scale ranging from 0 to 12, the mean rating of the satisfied group was 10.4, and for the dissatisfied group 2.6. These two groups showed only small differences in most of the categories but the following comparisons of percentage rates are instructive, for the few categories that did differ noticeably:

Interaction category	Satisfied group	Dissatisfied group
3. Agrees	24.9	9.6
4. Gives suggestions	8.2	3.6
7. Asks for orientation	1.7	5.7
10. Disagrees	4.0	12.4

INTERACTION PROCESS ANALYSIS (BALES) - 557

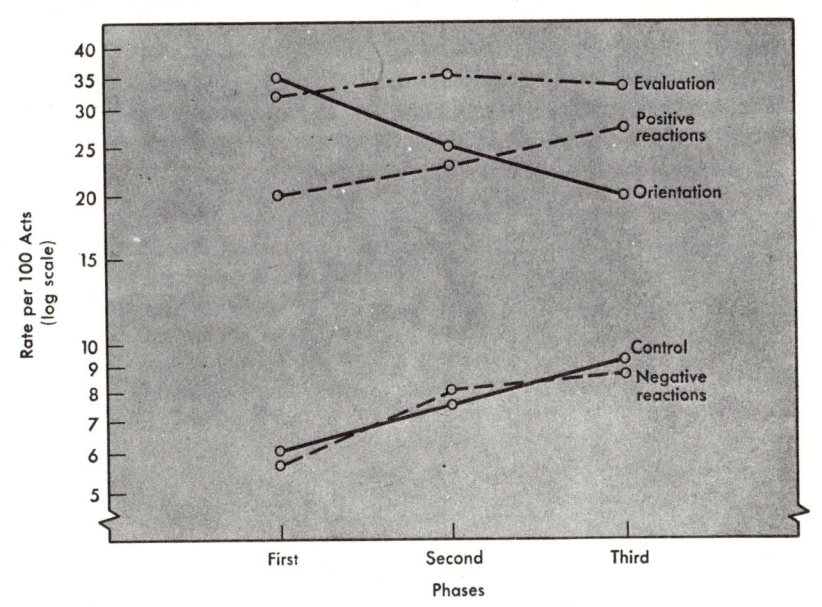

FIGURE C.4. Relative frequency of acts by type and phase, based upon twenty-two sessions (Bales, 1952)

In the group that felt itself successful, for whatever reasons, the members offered relatively many suggestions (but not opinions) that were accepted by others, and rarely needed to ask such questions as, "Where are we going?" Altogether, the "satisfied" group made about twice as many "positive reactions" (Categories 1–3) as did the "dissatisfied" group (33.5 percent as against 17.2 percent), and less than a third as many "negative reactions" (5.3 percent as compared with 17.2 percent). We do not know that the same differences would distinguish all satisfied and dissatisfied groups, nor just why these differences appeared, but the comparisons show one way in which the method may be put to use.

Bales has also been interested in *phase movement*, that is, successive stages through which problem-solving groups proceed. One of his analyses is based upon twenty-two group sessions, half of them dealing with "full-fledged problems (essentially problems of analysis and planning, with the goal of group decision), and half with more truncated or specialized types of problems." In all groups, responses were computed separately for the first, second, and last thirds of the discussion period, with results as shown in Figure C.4. Bales's summary of these findings is as follows:

> Those groups dealing with full-fledged problems tended to show a typical phase movement through the meeting: the process tended to move

qualitatively from a *relative* emphasis on attempts to solve problems of *orientation* ("what is it") to attempts to solve problems of evaluation ("how do we feel about it") and subsequently to solve problems of *control* ("what shall we do about it"). Concurrent with these transitions, the relative frequencies of both *negative reactions* . . . and *positive reactions* tends to increase (1952, page 157).

As to reasons why such phase movements should appear, Bales suggests that considerations of "control" usually presuppose group solutions of orientation and, to some degree, of evaluation; hence the decline, from early to late phases, in the prominence of "orientation" and the increase of "control." Both positive and negative reactions increase after early phases, because

> efforts to solve problems of orientation, evaluation, and control as involved in the task lead to differentiation of the roles of the participants, [and these] tend to carry status implications which may threaten or disturb the existing order or balance of status relations among the members. Disagreement and an attempt to change existing ideas and values may be necessary to solve the task problem but may lead, nevertheless, to personalized anxieties or antagonisms and impair the basic solidarity of the group (1952, page 158).

Interesting questions also arise about *individual contributions*—how much each one participates, who speaks to whom, and so on. (The identities of individuals can readily be recorded by the observer.) Bales finds, for example, that even in groups with as few as six members there is wide disparity among them in the frequency of speaking and being spoken to. Averaging eighteen such groups, he found (1952) that the most active member spoke about eight times as frequently as the least active one, and was directly spoken to nearly ten times as often. The most active man, moreover, directed far more comments to the group as a whole than to specific individuals, whereas the reverse was true for all other members. Not surprisingly, there is an almost perfect correlation between the members' frequencies of speaking and of being spoken to.

Such individual differences correspond not only to personality differences of members but also to role differentiations in the group. Bales reports (1952) that typically the rank order of members' participation, from most to least often, is the same as the order of their ratings of each other in productivity (who has the best ideas and who does the most to guide the discussion effectively). Frequency of participation is also very highly correlated with order of popularity (who is most liked or disliked)—even though, as reported in other studies (cf. Research Illustration 15.2, page 476) the *kinds* of contributions made by the best-idea man and the best-liked man tend to be quite different.

* * *

The preceding sample of findings reported by Bales and his associates is small but representative. Because his procedures, worked out after years of trial and error, are systematic, and because under proper conditions they provide reliable data, groups about which certain things are known can be compared, and things can be learned about them that were not previously known. As has so often been the case in the development of science, important relationships wait upon the development of adequate instruments and procedures. In this case the relationships in which we are interested are those between forms of interaction on the one hand, and on the other the relevant characteristics of groups, of their individual members, and of the immediate situations in which they are interacting.

References

ABELSON, R. P. 1954 A technique and a model for multidimensional attitude scaling. *Amer. Psychologist 9*, 319 (abstr.).

ABELSON, R. P., & ROSENBERG, M. J. 1958 Symbolic psycho-logic: a model of attitudinal cognition. *Behav. Sci. 3*, 1–13.

ADORNO, T. W., FRENKEL-BRUNSWIK, ELSA, LEVINSON, D., & SANFORD, R. N. 1950 *The authoritarian personality.* New York: Harper & Row.

ALLPORT, F. H. 1920 The influence of the group upon association and thought. *J. exp. Psychol. 3*, 159–182.

ALLPORT, F. H. 1924 *Social psychology.* Boston: Houghton Mifflin.

ALLPORT, G. W. 1961 *Pattern and growth in personality.* New York: Holt, Rinehart and Winston.

ALLPORT, G. W., & ODBERT, H. S. 1936 Trait names: a psycho-lexical study. *Psychol. Monogr. 47*, No. 211.

ALLPORT, G. W., VERNON, P., & LINDZEY, G. 1951 *A study of values.* Boston: Houghton Mifflin.

ALLYN, J., & FESTINGER, L. 1961 The effectiveness of unanticipated persuasive communications. *J. abnorm. soc. Psychol. 62*, 35–40.

ANGELL, R. C. 1958 *Free society and moral crisis.* Ann Arbor: Univ. of Michigan Press.

ARONSON, E., & CARLSMITH, J. M. 1962 Performance expectancy as a determinant of actual performance. *J. abnorm. soc. Psychol. 65*, 178–182.

ASCH, S. E. 1940 Studies in the principles of judgments and attitudes: II. Determination of judgments by group and ego standards. *J. soc. Psychol. 12*, 433–465.

ASCH, S. E. 1946 Forming impressions of personality. *J. abnorm. soc. Psychol. 41*, 258–290.

ASCH, S. E. 1951 Effects of group pressure upon the modification and distortion of judgment. In H. Guetzkow (Ed.), *Groups, leadership and men*. Pittsburgh: Carnegie Press.

ASCH, S. E. 1952 *Social psychology*. Englewood Cliffs, N.J.: Prentice-Hall.

ASCH, S. E. 1955 Opinions and social pressure. *Sci. Amer. 193 (5),* 31–35.

ATTNEAVE, F. 1959 *Application of information theory to psychology*. New York: Holt, Rinehart and Winston.

BACK, K. W. 1950 Communication in experimentally created hierarchies. In L. Festinger, K. Back, S. Schachter, H. H. Kelley, & J. W. Thibaut, *Theory and experiment in social communication*. Ann Arbor: Inst. for Soc. Research, Univ. of Michigan.

BACK, K. W. 1951 Influence through social communication. *J. abnorm. soc. Psychol. 46,* 190–207.

BAKER, B. O., & SARBIN, T. R. 1956 Differential mediation of social perception as a correlate of social adjustment. *Sociometry 19,* 69–83.

BALES, R. F. 1950 *Interaction process analysis: a method for the study of small groups*. Reading, Mass.: Addison–Wesley.

BALES, R. F. 1952 Some uniformities of behavior in small social systems. In G. E. Swanson, T. M. Newcomb, and E. L. Hartley (Eds.), *Readings in social psychology* (ed. 2). New York: Holt, Rinehart and Winston.

BALES, R. F. 1955 How people interact in conferences. *Sci. Amer. 192 (3),* 31–35.

BALES, R. F. 1958 Task roles and social roles in problem-solving groups. In Eleanor Maccoby, T. M. Newcomb, & E. L. Hartley (Eds.), *Readings in social psychology* (ed. 3). New York: Holt, Rinehart and Winston.

BALES, R. F., & STRODTBECK, F. L. 1951 Phases in group problem solving. *J. abnorm. soc. Psychol. 46,* 485–495.

BALES, R. F., STRODTBECK, F. L., MILLS, T. M., & ROSEBOROUGH, MARY E. 1951 Channels of communication in small groups. *Amer. sociol. Rev. 16,* 461–468.

BARRON, M. L. 1954 *The juvenile in delinquent society*. New York: Knopf.

BAVELAS, A. 1950 Communication patterns in task oriented groups. *J. acoust. Soc. Amer. 22,* 725–730.

BAYTON, J. A. 1941 The racial stereotype of Negro college students. *J. abnorm. soc. Psychol. 36,* 97–102.

BENEDICT, RUTH 1938 Continuities and discontinuities in cultural conditioning. *Psychiatry 1,* 161–167.

BERGLER, E. 1957 *The psychology of gambling*. New York: Hill & Wang.

BETTELHEIM, B., & JANOWITZ, M. 1950 *Dynamics of prejudice: a psychological and sociological study of veterans*. New York: Harper & Row.

BINET, A. 1900 *La suggestibilité*. Paris: Schleicher.

BIRD, C. 1940 *Social psychology*. New York: Appleton-Century-Crofts.

BLUM, G. S., & MILLER, D. R. 1952 Exploring the psychoanalytic theory of the "oral character." *J. Person. 20,* 287–304.

BOGARDUS, E. S. 1925 Measuring social distance. *J. appl. Sociol. 9,* 299–308.

BOGARDUS, E. S. 1928 *Immigration and race attitudes*. Boston: Heath.

BOS, MARIA 1937 Experimental study of productive collaboration. *Acta Psychol.* 3, 315–426.
BOSSOM, J., & MASLOW, A. H. 1957 Security of judges as a factor in impressions of warmth in others. *J. abnorm. soc. Psychol.* 55, 147–148.
BREHM, J. W. 1960 A dissonance analysis of attitude-discrepant behavior. In C. I. Hovland & M. J. Rosenberg (Eds.), *Attitude organization and change.* New Haven: Yale Univ. Press.
BREHM, J. W., & COHEN, A. R. 1962 *Explorations in cognitive dissonance.* New York: Wiley.
BRONFENBRENNER, U. 1958 Socialization and social class through time and space. In Eleanor Maccoby, T. M. Newcomb, & E. L. Hartley (Eds.), *Readings in social psychology* (ed. 3). New York: Holt, Rinehart and Winston.
BRONFENBRENNER, U., HARDING, J., & GALLWEY, MARY 1958 The measurement of skill in social perception. In D. C. McClelland, A. L. Baldwin, U. Bronfenbrenner, & F. L. Strodtbeck (Eds.), *Talent and society.* Princeton: Van Nostrand.
BRUNER, J. S., & TAGIURI, R. 1954 The perception of people. In G. Lindzey (Ed.), *Handbook of social psychology, II.* Reading, Mass.: Addison-Wesley.
BRUNSWIK, E. 1939 Probability as a determiner of rat behavior. *J. exp. Psychol.* 25, 175–197.
BURGESS, E. W., & COTTRELL, L. S. 1939 *Predicting success or failure in marriage.* Englewood Cliffs, N.J.: Prentice-Hall.
CAMPBELL, A. A. 1947 Factors associated with attitudes toward Jews. In T. M. Newcomb & E. L. Hartley (Eds.), *Readings in social psychology.* New York: Holt, Rinehart and Winston.
CAMPBELL, A., CONVERSE P., MILLER, W. E., & STOKES, D. 1960 *The American voter.* New York: Wiley.
CAMPBELL, A., GURIN, G., & MILLER, W. E. 1954 *The voter decides.* New York: Harper & Row.
CAMPBELL, D. T., & FISKE, D. W. 1959 Convergent and discriminant validation by the multitrait-multimethod matrix. *Psychol. Bull.* 56, 81–105.
CANTRIL, H. 1941 *The psychology of social movements.* New York: Wiley.
CANTRIL, H. 1944 In H. Cantril (Ed.), *Gauging public opinion.* Princeton: Princeton Univ. Press.
CANTRIL, H., & FRIED, E. 1944 In H. Cantril (Ed.), *Gauging public opinion.* Princeton: Princeton Univ. Press.
CARLSON, E. 1956 Attitude change through a modification of attitude structure. *J. abnorm. soc. Psychol.* 52, 256–261.
CENTERS, R. 1949 *The psychology of social classes.* Princeton: Princeton Univ. Press.
CHILD, I. 1943 *Italian or American?: the second generation in conflict.* New Haven: Yale Univ. Press.
CHRISTIE, R., & COOK, PEGGY 1958 A guide to published literature relating to the authoritarian personality through 1956. *J. Psychol.* 45, 171–199.
CHRISTIE, R., HAVEL, J., & SEIDENBERG, B. 1958 Is the F-Scale irreversible? *J. abnorm. soc. Psychol.* 56, 143–159.
CHRISTIE, R., & LINDAUER, FLORENCE 1963 Personality structure. *Annual Rev. Psychol.* 14, 201–230.

T

REFERENCES

CLARK, K. B., & CLARK, MAMIE P. 1947 Racial identification and preference in Negro children. In T. M. Newcomb & E. L. Hartley (Eds.), *Readings in social psychology*. New York: Holt, Rinehart and Winston.

CLINE, V. B., & RICHARDS, J. M., JR. 1960 Accuracy of interpersonal perception—a general trait? *J. abnorm. soc. Psychol.* 60, 1–7.

COCH, L., & FRENCH, J. R. P. 1948 Overcoming resistance to change. *Hum. Relat.* 1, 512–532.

COFFIN, T. E. 1941 Some conditions of suggestion and suggestibility. *Psychol. Monogr.* 53, No. 4, 125.

CONVERSE, P. E. 1964 The nature of belief systems in mass publics. In D. Apter (Ed.), *Ideology and discontent*. New York: Free Press.

COOLEY, C. H. 1902 *Human nature and the social order*. New York: Scribners.

COOMBS, C. H. 1964 *A theory of data*. New York: Wiley.

DASHIELL, J. 1930 An experimental analysis of some group effects. *J. abnorm. soc. Psychol.* 25, 190–199.

DASHIELL, J. 1935 Experimental studies of the influence of social situations on the behavior of the individual human adult. In C. Murchison (Ed.), *Handbook of social psychology*. Worcester, Mass.: Clark Univ. Press.

DAVIE, M. R., & REEVES, R. J. 1939 Propinquity of residence before marriage. *Amer. J. Sociol.* 44, 510–517.

DEARBORN, D. C., & SIMON, H. A. 1958 A selection prescription: a note on the departmental identification of executives. *Sociometry* 21, 140–144.

DENNIS, W. 1957 Uses of common objects as indicators of cultural orientations. *J. abnorm. soc. Psychol.* 55, 21–28.

DEUTSCH, M. 1949 Experimental study of the effects of cooperation and competition upon group processes. *Hum. Rel.* 2, 199–232.

DEUTSCH, M. 1957 *Conditions affecting cooperation:* Section I: Factors related to the initiation of cooperation; Section II: Trust and cooperation. New York: Center for Human Relations, New York University.

DEUTSCH, M., & COLLINS, MARY E. 1951 *Interracial housing and a psychological evaluation of a social experiment*. Minneapolis: Univ. of Minn. Press.

DEWEY, J. 1922 *Human nature and conduct*. New York: Holt, Rinehart and Winston.

DIMOCK, H. 1937 *Rediscovering the adolescent*. New York: Association Press.

DODD, S. C., & GRIFFITHS, K. S. 1958 The logarithmic relation of social distance and intensity. *J. soc. Psychol.* 48, 91–101.

DOLLARD, J., DOOB, L. W., MILLER, N. E., MOWRER, O. H., & SEARS, R. R. 1938 *Frustration and aggression*. New Haven: Yale Univ. Press.

DRAKE, ST. C., & CAYTON, H. R. 1945 *Black metropolis*. New York: Harcourt, Brace.

DYSON, F. J. 1958 Innovation in physics. *Sci. Amer.* 199, 74–82.

EDWARDS, A. L. 1946 A critique of "neutral" items in attitude scales constructed by the method of equal appearing intervals. *Psychol. Rev.* 53, 159–169.

EDWARDS, A. L. 1957 *Techniques of attitude scale construction*. New York: Appleton-Century-Crofts.

REFERENCES

EDWARDS, A. L. 1958 *The social desirability variable in personality assessment and research.* New York: Holt, Rinehart and Winston.

ENGEL, G. 1959 The stability of the self-concept in adolescence. *J. abnorm. soc. Psychol.* 58, 211–215.

ENGEL, M., O'SHEA, H. E., FISCHEL, M. A., & CUMMINS, G. M. 1958 An investigation of anti-Semitic feelings in two groups of college students: Jewish and non-Jewish. *J. soc. Psychol.* 48, 75–82.

ENGLISH, H. C., & ENGLISH, AVA C. 1958 *Dictionary of psychological terms.* New York: Longmans, Green.

EYSENCK, H. J., & CROWN, S. 1949 An experimental study in opinion-attitude methodology. *Int. J. Opin. Att. Res.* 3, 47–86.

FAUST, W. F. 1959 Group versus individual problem-solving. *J. abnorm. soc. Psychol.* 59, 68–72.

FESHBACH, S., & SINGER, R. D. 1957 The effects of fear arousal and suppression of fear upon social perception. *J. abnorm. soc. Psychol.* 55, 283–288.

FESTINGER, L. 1959 Informal social communication. *Psychol. Rev.* 57, 271–282.

FESTINGER, L. 1957 *The theory of cognitive dissonance.* New York: Harper & Row.

FESTINGER, L., SCHACHTER, S., & BACK, K. W. 1950 *Social pressures in informal groups: a study of human factors in housing.* New York: Harper & Row.

FESTINGER, L., & THIBAUT, J. W. 1951 Interpersonal communication in small groups. *J. abnorm. soc. Psychol.* 46, 92–99.

FIEDLER, F. 1960 The leader's psychological distance and group effectiveness. In D. Cartwright & A. Zander (Eds.), *Group dynamics: research and theory* (ed. 2). New York: Harper & Row.

FLUGEL, J. C. 1954 Humor and laughter. In G. Lindzey (Ed.), *Handbook of social psychology, II.* Reading, Mass.: Addison-Wesley.

FULCHER, J. S. 1942 Voluntary facial expression in blind and seeing children. *Arch. Psychol.* 38, No. 272.

GIROUD, A. 1911 La suggestibilité chez les enfants d'école. *Année psychologique* 8, 362–388.

GOLLIN, E. S. 1958 Organizational characteristics of social judgment: a developmental investigation. *J. Pers.* 26, 139–154.

GORDEN, R. L. 1952 Interaction between attitude and the definition of the situation in the expression of opinion. *Amer. sociol. Rev.* 17, 50–58.

GOULDNER, A. W. 1960 The norm of reciprocity: a preliminary statement. *Amer. sociol. Rev.* 25, 161–179.

GOULDNER, A. W., & GOULDNER, HELEN 1963 *Modern sociology: an introduction to the study of human interaction.* New York: Harcourt, Brace, & World.

GREENSPOON, J. 1951 The effect of verbal and non-verbal stimuli on the frequency of members of two verbal response classes. Unpublished doctoral dissertation, Indiana University.

GUILFORD, J. P. 1954 *Psychometric methods.* New York: McGraw-Hill.

GUTTMAN, L. 1950 The basis for scalogram analysis. In S. A. Stouffer *et al.*, *Measurement and prediction.* Princeton: Princeton Univ. Press.

HAIGH, G. 1949 Defensive behavior in client-centered therapy. *J. consult. Psychol. 13,* 181–189.

HAMMOND, K. R. 1948 Measuring attitudes by error choice: an indirect method. *J. abnorm. soc. Psychol. 43,* 38–48.

HARARY, F., & ROSS, I. C. 1957 A procedure for clique detection using the group matrix. *Sociometry 20,* 205–215.

HARLOW, H. F. 1953 Mice, monkeys, men and motives. *Psychol. Rev. 60,* 23–32.

HART, I. 1957 Maternal child-rearing practices and authoritarian ideology. *J. abnorm. soc. Psychol. 55,* 232–237.

HARTLEY, E. L. 1946 *Problems in prejudice.* New York: King's Crown Press.

HASTORF, A. H., & CANTRIL, H. 1954 They saw a game: a case study. *J. abnorm. soc. Psychol. 49,* 129–134.

HEIDER, F. 1946 Attitudinal and cognitive organization. *J. Psychol. 21,* 107–112.

HEIDER, F. 1958 *The psychology of interpersonal relations.* New York: Wiley.

HEINICKE, C., & BALES, R. F. 1953 Developmental trends in the structure of small groups. *Sociometry 16,* 7–38.

HELSON, H. 1948 Adaptation-level as a basis for a quantitative theory of frames of reference. *Psychol. Rev. 55,* 297–313.

HILDUM, D. C., & BROWN, R. W. 1956 Verbal reinforcement and interviewer bias. *J. abnorm. soc. Psychol. 53,* 108–111.

HILL, R. J. 1953 A note on inconsistency in paired comparison judgments. *Amer. sociol. Rev. 18,* 564–566.

HINCKLEY, E. D. 1932 The influence of individual opinion on construction of an attitude scale. *J. soc. Psychol. 3,* 283–296.

HOFFMAN, M. L. 1957 Conformity as a defense mechanism and a form of resistance to genuine group influence. *J. Person. 25,* 412–424.

HOMANS, G. C. 1950 *The human group.* New York: Harcourt, Brace.

HOMANS, G. C. 1961 *Social behavior: its elementary forms.* New York: Harcourt, Brace.

HORNEY, KAREN 1945 *Our inner conflicts.* New York: Norton.

HOROWITZ, E. L. 1936 Development of attitudes towards Negroes. *Arch. Psychol. No. 194.*

HOROWITZ, E. L., & HOROWITZ, RUTH 1938 Development of social attitudes in children. *Sociometry 1,* 301–338.

HOVLAND, C. I., HARVEY, O. J., & SHERIF, M. 1957 Assimilation and contrast effects in reaction to communication and attitude change. *J. abnorm. soc. Psychol. 55,* 244–252.

HOVLAND, C. I., JANIS, I. L., & KELLEY, H. H. 1953 *Communication and persuasion.* New Haven: Yale Univ. Press.

HOVLAND, C. I., MANDELL, W., CAMPBELL, ENID H., BROCK, T., LUCHINS, A. S., COHEN, A. R., MCGUIRE, W. J., JANIS, I. L., FEIERABEND, ROSALIND, L., & ANDERSON, N. H. 1957 *The order of presentation in persuasion.* New Haven: Yale Univ. Press.

HOVLAND, C. I., & SEARS, R. R. 1938 Minor studies of aggression: VI. Correlation of lynchings with economic indices. *J. Psychol. 19,* 301–310.

HOVLAND, C. I., & SHERIF, M. 1952 Judgmental phenomena and scales of attitude measurement: item displacement in Thurstone scales. *J. abnorm. soc. Psychol. 47*, 822–832.

HURWITZ, J., ZANDER, A., & HYMOVITCH, B. 1960 Some effects of power on the relations among group members. In D. Cartwright & A. Zander (Eds.), *Group dynamics* (ed. 2). New York: Harper & Row.

HYMAN, H. 1955 *Survey design and analysis*. New York: The Free Press.

HYMAN, H., & SHEATSLEY, P. 1947 Some reasons why information campaigns fail. *Pub. Opin. Quart. 11*, 413–423.

INDIK, B. P. 1961 Organization size and member participation. Unpublished dissertation. Univ. of Michigan.

JACKSON, J. M. 1959 Reference group processes in a formal organization. *Sociometry 22*, 307–327.

JACKSON, J. M. 1960 Structural characteristics of norms. In G. E. Jensen (Ed.), *Dynamics of instructional groups*. Chicago: Univ. of Chicago Press.

JANIS, I. L., & KING, B. T. 1954 The influence of role playing on opinion change. *J. abnorm. soc. Psychol. 49*, 211–218.

JENNINGS, HELEN 1950 *Leadership and isolation*. New York: Longmans, Green.

JONES, E. E. & THIBAUT, J. W. 1958 Interaction goals as bases of inference in interpersonal perception. In R. Tagiuri & L. Petrullo (Eds.), *Person perception and interpersonal behavior*. Stanford, Calif.: Stanford Univ. Press.

KAHN, R. L., & CANNELL, C. F. 1957 *The dynamics of interviewing*. New York: Wiley.

KAHN, R. L., & KATZ, D. 1960 Leadership practices in relation to productivity and morale. In D. Cartwright & A. Zander (Eds.), *Group dynamics: research and theory* (ed. 2). New York: Harper & Row.

KAHN, R. L., & WOLFE, D. M. 1961 Role conflict in an organization. In K. Boulding (Ed.), *Conflict management in organizations*. Ann Arbor, Mich.: Foundation for Research on Human Behavior.

KAHN, R. L., WOLFE, D. M., QUINN, R. P., SNOEK, J. D., & ROSENTHAL, R. A. 1964 *Organizational stress: studies in conflict and ambiguity*. New York: Wiley.

KATZ, D. 1941 The public opinion polls and the 1940 election. *Pub. Opin. Quart. 5*, 52–78.

KATZ, D. 1944 The polls and the 1944 election. *Pub. Opin. Quart. 8*, 468–482.

KATZ, D. 1949 Polling methods and the 1948 polling failure. *Int. J. Opin. Att. Res. 2*, No. 1, 469–480.

KATZ, D. 1960 The functional approach to the study of attitudes. *Pub. Opin. Quart. 24*, 163–204.

KATZ, D., SARNOFF, I., & MCCLINTOCK, C. 1956 Ego defense and attitude change. *Hum. Relat. 9*, 27–45.

KATZ, D., SARNOFF, I., & MCCLINTOCK, C. M. 1957 The measurement of ego-defense as related to attitude change. *J. Pers. 25*, 465–474.

KEEHN, J. D. 1955 The expressed social attitudes of leading psychologists. *Amer. Psychologist 10*, 208–210.

KELLEY, H. H., HOVLAND, C. I., SCHWARTZ, M., & ABELSON, R. P. 1955 The influence of judges' attitudes in three methods of scaling. *J. soc. Psychol.* 42, 147–158.

KELLEY, H. H., & THIBAUT, J. W. 1954 Experimental studies of group problem solving and process. In G. Lindzey (Ed.), *Handbook of social psychology, II.* Reading, Mass.: Addison-Wesley.

KELLEY, H. H., THIBAUT, J. W., RADLOFF, R., & MUNDY, D. 1962 The development of cooperation in the "minimal social situation." *Psychol. Monogr.* 76, No. 19, 1–19.

KELLEY, H. H., & WOODRUFF, CHRISTINE L. 1956 Members' reactions to apparent group approval of a counternorm communication. *J. abnorm. soc. Psychol.* 52, 67–74.

KELLY, E. L. 1955 Consistency of the adult personality. *Amer. Psychologist* 10, 659–681.

KELLY, J. G., FERSON, J. E., & HOLTZMAN, W. H. 1958 The measurement of attitudes toward the Negro in the South. *J. soc. Psychol.* 48, 305–317.

KELMAN, H. 1958 Compliance, identification and internalization. *J. Conflict Resol.* 2, 57–60.

KELMAN, H., & HOVLAN, C. I. 1953 "Reinstatement" of the communicator in delayed measurement of opinion change. *J. abnorm. soc. Psychol.* 48, 327–335.

KING, B. T., & JANIS, I. L. 1956 Comparison of the effectiveness of improvised versus non-improvised role-playing in producing opinion changes. *Hum. Relat.* 9, 177–186.

KITT, A. S., & GLEICHER, D. B. 1950 Determinants of voting behavior: a progress report on the Elmira election study. *Pub. Opin. Quart.* 14, 393–412.

KUBANY, A. J. 1953 A validation study of the error-choice technique using attitudes on national health insurance. *Educat. psychol. Measmt* 13, 157–163.

LANDIS, C. 1924 Studies of emotional reactions. II. General behavior and facial expression. *J. comp. Psychol.* 4, 447–509.

LEARY, T. F. 1957 *Interpersonal diagnosis of personality: a functional theory and methodology of personality.* New York: Ronald Press.

LEAVITT, H. J. 1951 Some effects of certain communication patterns on group performance. *J. abnorm. soc. Psychol.* 46, 38–50.

LE BON, G. 1895 *The crowd: a study of the popular mind.* London: T. Fisher Unwin.

LEUBA, C. J. 1955 Toward some integration of learning theories: the concept of optimal stimulation. *Psychol. Rep.* 1, 27–33.

LEVINE, J. M., & MURPHY, G. 1943 The learning and forgetting of controversial material. *J. abnorm. soc. Psychol.* 38, 507–517.

LEWIN, K. 1947 Group decision and social change. In T. M. Newcomb & E. L. Hartley (Eds.), *Readings in social psychology.* New York: Holt, Rinehart and Winston.

LEWIN, K. 1951 *Field theory in social science.* New York: Harper & Row.

LIBO, L. 1953 *Measuring group cohesiveness.* Ann Arbor, Michigan: Institute for Social Research, Univ. of Michigan.

LIEBERMAN, S. 1956 The effects of changes in roles on the attitudes of role occupants. *Hum. Relat.* 9, 385–402.

LIKERT, R. 1932 A technique for the measurement of attitudes. *Arch. Psychol.* 22, No. 140.

LIKERT, R., ROSLOW, S., & MURPHY, G. 1934 A simple and reliable method of scoring the Thurstone attitude scales. *J. soc. Psychol.* 5, 228–238.

LINDZEY, G., & ROGOLSKY, S. 1950 Prejudice and identification of minority group membership. *J. abnorm. soc. Psychol.* 45, 37–53.

LINTON, R. 1945 *The cultural background of personality.* New York: Appleton-Century-Crofts.

LIPPITT, R., WATSON, JEAN, KALLEN, D., & ZIPF, S. 1959 *Evaluation of a human relations laboratory program.* New York: National Training Laboratories Monograph #3. New York Univ. Press.

LIPPITT, R., & WHITE, R. K. 1943 The "social climate" of children's groups. In R. G. Barker, J. Kounin, & H. Wrights (Eds.), *Child behavior and development.* New York: McGraw-Hill.

LOOMIS, J. L. 1959 Communication, the development of trust and cooperative behavior. *Hum. Relat.* 12, 305–315.

LUCHINS, A. S. 1957 Experimental attempts to minimize the impact of first impressions. In C. Hovland *et al.* (Ed.), *The order of presentation in persuasion.* New Haven: Yale Univ. Press.

MACCOBY, ELEANOR E. 1959 Role-taking in childhood and its consequences for social learning. *Child Devel.* 30, 239–252.

MACCOBY, ELEANOR E., MACCOBY, N., ROMNEY, A. K., & ADAMS, J. S. 1961 Social reinforcement in attitude change. *J. abnorm. soc. Psychol.* 63, 109–115.

MCCORD, J., & MCCORD, W. 1958 The effects of parental role model on criminology. *J. soc. Issues* 14, 66–75.

MCDOUGALL, W. 1908 *Introduction to social psychology.* London: Methuen.

MCGRATH, J. E., & ALTMAN, I. 1965 *Small group research: a synthesis and critique of the field.* New York: Holt, Rinehart and Winston.

MCGUIRE, W. J. 1960 A syllogistic analysis of cognitive relationships. In M. Rosenberg *et al., Attitude, organization, and change: an analysis of consistency among attitude components.* New Haven: Yale Univ. Press.

MCGUIRE, W. J. 1961 The effectiveness of supportive and refutational defenses in immunizing and restoring beliefs against persuasion. *Sociometry* 24, 184–197.

MCNEMAR, Q. 1946 Opinion-attitude methodology. *Psychol Bull.* 43, 289–374

MANN, F., & BAUMGARTEL, H. 1952 *Absences and employee attitudes in an electric power company.* Ann Arbor: Institute of Social Research, Univ. of Michigan.

MASLOW, A. H., & SAKODA, J. M. 1952 Volunteer-error in the Kinsey study. *J. abnorm. soc. Psychol.* 47, 259–262.

MAUSS, M. 1954 *The gift.* New York: Free Press.

MEREI, F. 1949 Group leadership and institutionalization. Translated and prepared by Mrs. David Rapaport for *Hum. Relat.* 2, 23–39.

MERTON, R. K. 1949 Discrimination and the American creed. In R. M. MacIver (Ed.), *Discrimination and national welfare.* New York: Inst. Relig. & Soc. Stud.

MERTON, R. K. 1957 *Social theory and social structure.* New York: Free Press.

MILES, M. B. 1959 *Learning to work in groups.* New York: Bureau of Publications, Teachers College, Columbia University.

MILLER, G. A. 1951 *Language and communication.* New York: McGraw-Hill.

MILLER, G. A. 1956 The magical number seven, plus or minus two: some limits on our capacity for processing information. *Psychol. Rev.* 63, 81–97.

MILLER, N. E., & DOLLARD, J. 1941 *Social learning and imitation.* New Haven: Yale Univ. Press.

MINTZ, A. 1946 A reexamination of correlations between lynchings and economic indices. *J. abnorm. soc. Psychol.* 41, 154–160.

MOSER, C. A. 1958 *Survey methods in social investigation.* New York: Macmillan.

MOSTELLER, F., HYMAN, H., MCCARTHY, P., MARKS, E., & TRUMAN, D. B. 1949 *The pre-election polls of 1948.* Bulletin 60 of the Social Science Research Council. New York: Social Science Research Council.

MURASKIN, J., & IVERSON, M. A. 1958 Social expectancy as a function of judging social distance. *J. soc. Psychol.* 48, 11–14.

MURPHY, G. 1947 *Personality: a bio-social approach to origins and structure.* New York: Harper & Row.

NEWCOMB, T. M. 1943 *Personality and social change.* New York: Holt, Rinehart and Winston.

NEWCOMB, T. M. 1961 *The acquaintance process.* New York: Holt, Rinehart and Winston.

NEWCOMB, T. M. 1963 Stabilities underlying changes in interpersonal attraction. *J. abnorm. soc. Psychol.* 66, 376–386.

NORMAN, R. D. 1953 The interrelationships among acceptance-rejection, self-other identity, insight into self, and realistic perception of others. *J. soc. Psychol.* 37, 205–235.

NUNNALLY, J., & KITTROSS, J. M. 1958 Public attitudes toward mental health professions. *Amer. Psychologist* 13, 589–594.

OSGOOD, C. E. 1953 *Method and theory in experimental psychology.* New York: Oxford University Press.

OSGOOD, C. E., SUCI, G. J., & TANNENBAUM, P. H. 1957 *The measurement of meaning.* Urbana, Ill.: Univ. of Illinois Press.

OSGOOD, C. E. 1962 Studies on the generality of effective meaning systems. *Amer. Psychologist* 17, 10–28.

PAYNE, S. L. 1951 *The art of asking questions.* Princeton: Princeton Univ. Press.

PETTIGREW, T. F. 1958 Personality and socio-cultural factors in intergroup attitudes; a cross-national comparison. *J. Conflict Resol.* 2, 29–42.

PILISUK, M. 1962 Cognitive balance and self-relevant attitudes. *J. abnorm. soc. Psychol.* 65, 95–103.

PROSHANSKY, H. M. 1943 A projective method for the study of attitudes. *J. abnorm. soc. Psychol.* 38, 393–395.

PROTHRO, E. T. 1955 The effect of strong negative attitudes on the placement of items in a Thurstone scale. *J. soc. Psychol. 41*, 11–18.

PROTHRO, E. T., & MILES, O. K. 1953 Social distance in the deep South as measured by a revised Bogardus scale. *J. soc. Psychol. 37*, 171–174.

RAPER, A. 1933 *The tragedy of lynching*. Chapel Hill: Univ. of North Carolina Press.

ROETHLISBERGER, F. J., & DICKSON, W. J. 1939 *Management and the worker*. Cambridge: Harvard Univ. Press.

ROGERS, C. R. 1958 A process conception of psychotherapy. *Amer. Psychologist 13*, 142–149.

ROMMETVEIT, R. 1955 *Social norms and roles: explorations in the psychology of enduring pressures*. Minneapolis: Univ. of Minnesota Press.

ROSENBERG, M. J. 1960 Cognitive reorganization in response to the hypnotic reversal of attitudinal affect. *J. Person. 28*, 39–63.

ROSENBERG, M. J., HOVLAND, C. I., MCGUIRE, W. J., ABELSON, R. P., & BREHM, J. W. 1960 *Attitude, organization and change: an analysis of consistency among attitude components*. New Haven: Yale Univ. Press.

ROSS, E. A. 1908 *Social psychology: an outline and source book*. New York: Macmillan.

ROTTER, J. B. 1954 *Social learning and clinical psychology*. Englewood Cliffs, N.J.: Prentice-Hall.

RUGG, D., & CANTRIL, H. 1944 In H. Cantril (Ed.), *Gauging public opinion*. Princeton: Princeton Univ. Press.

RUNKEL, P. J. 1956 Cognitive similarity in facilitating communication. *Sociometry 19*, 178–191.

SAENGER, G., & GILBERT, E. 1950 Customer reactions to the integration of Negro sales personnel. *Int. J. Opin. Res. 4*, 57–76.

SANFORD, R. N. 1936 The effect of abstinence from food upon imaginal processes: a preliminary experiment. *J. Psychol. 2*, 129–136.

SCHACHTER, S. 1951 Deviation, rejection and communication. *J. abnorm. soc. Psychol. 46*, 190–207.

SCHACHTER, S., ELLERTSON, N., MCBRIDE, DOROTHY, & GREGORY, DORIS 1951 An experimental study of cohesiveness and productivity. *Hum. Relat. 4*, 229–238.

SCHANCK, R. L. 1932 A study of a community and its groups and institutions conceived of as behaviors of individuals. *Psychol. Monogr. 43*, No. 2.

SCHEIN, E. P., with SCHNEIER, INGE, & BARKER, G. H. 1961 *Coercive persuasion: a socio-psychological analysis of the "brainwashing" of American prisoners by the Chinese communists*. New York: Norton.

SCODEL, A., & MUSSEN, P. H. 1953 Social perceptions of authoritarians and non-authoritarians. *J. abnorm. soc. Psychol. 48*, 181–184.

SCOTT, W. A. 1957 Attitude change through reward of verbal behavior. *J. abnorm. soc. Psychol. 55*, 72–75.

SECORD, P. F., BEVAN, W., & KATZ, B. 1956 The Negro stereotype and perceptual accentuation. *J. abnorm. soc. Psychol. 53*, 78–83.

SELLTIZ, CLAIRE, JAHODA, MARIE, DEUTSCH, M., & COOK, S. W. 1959 *Research methods in social relations*. New York: Holt, Rinehart and Winston.

SHANNON, C. E., & WEAVER, W. 1949 *The mathematical theory of communication*. Urbana, Ill.: Univ. of Illinois Press.

572 · REFERENCES

SHAW, C. R. 1938 *Brothers in crime.* Chicago, Ill.: Chicago Univ. Press.
SHAW, MARJORIE E. 1932 A comparison of individuals and small groups in the rational solution of complex problems. *Amer. J. Psychol.* 44, 491–504.
SHAW, MARJORIE E., & PENROD, W. T. 1962 Does more information, available to a group, always improve group performance? *Sociometry* 25, 377–390.
SHEATSLEY, P. B. 1951 An analysis of interviewer characteristics and their relationship to performance. II. *Int. J. Opin. Att. Res.* 5, 79–94.
SHERIF, M. 1935 A study of some social factors in perception. *Arch. Psychol.* 27, No. 187.
SHERIF, M. 1936 *The psychology of social norms.* New York: Harper & Row.
SHERIF, M., & SHERIF, CAROLYN 1953 *Groups in harmony and tension.* New York: Harper & Row.
SHERIF, M., HARVEY, O. J., WHITE, B. J., HOOD, W. R., & SHERIF, CAROLYN 1961 *Intergroup conflict and cooperation.* Norman, Oklahoma: Univ. of Oklahoma Book Exchange.
SIDOWSKI, J. B. 1957 Reward and punishment in a minimal social situation. *J. exp. Psychol.* 54, 318–326.
SIDOWSKI, J. B., WYCKOFF, L. B., & TABORY, L. 1956 The effect of reinforcement and punishment in a minimal social situation. *J. abnorm. soc. Psychol.* 52, 115–119.
SIMMEL, G. 1950 *The sociology of Georg Simmel* (translated and edited by K. H. Wolf). New York: Free Press.
SKINNER, B. F. 1953 *Science and human behavior.* New York: Macmillan.
SLATER, P. E. 1958 Contrasting correlates of group size. *Sociometry* 21, 129–139.
SMELSER, W. T. 1961 Dominance as a factor in achievement and perception in cooperative problem-solving interaction. *J. abnorm. soc. Psychol.* 62, 353–542.
SMITH, H. L., & HYMAN, H. 1950 The biasing effect of interviewer expectations on survey results. *Pub. Opin. Quart.* 14, 491–506.
SPRANGER, E. 1928 *Types of men* (trans. by P. J. W. Pigors). Halle: Niemy.
STEPHAN, F. F., & MISHLER, E. G. 1952 The distribution of participation in small groups: an exponential approximation. *Amer. sociol. Rev.* 17, 598–608.
STOUFFER, S. A. 1955 *Communism, conformity and civil liberties.* New York: Doubleday.
STOUFFER, S. A., GUTTMAN, L., SCHUMAN, E. A., LAZARSFELD, P. F., STAR, SHIRLEY A., & CLAUSEN, J. A. 1950 *Measurement and Prediction.* Princeton, N.J.: Princeton Univ. Press.
SUCHMAN, E. A. 1950 The intensity component in attitude and opinion research. In S. A. Stouffer *et al., Measurement and prediction.* Princeton: Princeton Univ. Press.
SUMNER, W. G. 1906 *Folkways.* Boston: Ginn.
SUTHERLAND, E. H. (Ed.) 1937 *The professional thief.* Chicago: Univ. of Chicago Press. Copyright 1937 by the University of Chicago.
TAGIURI, R. 1958 In R. Tagiuri & L. Petrullo (Eds.), *Person perception and interpersonal behavior.* Stanford, Calif.: Stanford Univ. Press.

TAGIURI, R., BLAKE, R. R., & BRUNER, J. S. 1953 Some determinants of the perception of positive and negative feelings in others. *J. abnorm. soc. Psychol. 48*, 585–592.

TANNENBAUM, P. H. 1956 Initial attitude toward source and concept as factors in attitude change through communication. *Pub. Opin. Quart. 20*, 413–425.

TARDE, G. 1890 *The laws of imitation* (translated by E. C. Parsons, 1903). New York: Holt.

TEAHAN, J. E. 1958 Future time perspective, optimism, and academic achievement. *J. abnorm. soc. Psychol. 57*, 379–380.

THIBAUT, J. W., & KELLEY, H. H. 1959 *The social psychology of groups.* New York: Wiley.

THOMAS, E. J., & FINK, C. F. 1963 Group size. *Psychol. Bull. 60*, 371–384.

THORNDIKE, R. L. 1938 The effect of discussion upon the correctness of group decisions when the factor of majority influence is allowed for. *J. soc. Psychol. 9*, 343–362.

THURSTONE, L. L. 1927 A law of comparative judgment. *Psychol. Rev. 34*, 273–286.

THURSTONE, L. L. 1938 *Primary mental abilities.* Chicago: Univ. of Chicago Press.

THURSTONE, L. L., & CHAVE, E. J. 1929 *The measurement of attitudes.* Chicago: Univ. of Chicago Press.

TRIPLETT, N. 1897 The dynamogenic factors in pacemaking and competition. *Amer. J. Psychol. 9*, 507–533.

TUDDENHAM, R. D., & MCBRIDE, P. D. 1959 The yielding experiment from the subject's point of view. *J. Person. 27*, 259–271.

TURNER, R. H., & VANDERLIPPE, R. H. 1958 Self-ideal congruence as an index of adjustment. *J. abnorm. soc. Psychol. 57*, 202–206.

VERPLANCK, W. S. 1955 The control of content of conversation: reinforcement of statements of opinion. *J. abnorm. soc. Psychol. 51*, 668–676.

VIDULICH, R. N., & KAIMAN, I. P. 1961 The effects of information source status and dogmatism upon conformity behavior. *J. abnorm. soc. Psychol. 63*, 639–642.

WALLER, W. W., & HILL, RUTH 1951 *The family: a dynamic interpretation.* New York: Holt, Rinehart and Winston.

WALSTER, E., & FESTINGER, L. 1962 The effectiveness of "overheard" persuasive communications. *J. abnorm. soc. Psychol. 65*, 395–402.

WARNER, W. L., & LUNT, P. S. 1941 *The social life of a modern community.* New Haven: Yale Univ. Press.

WARNER, W. L., MEEKER, M., & EELLS, K. 1949 *Social class in America.* Chicago: Social Science Research Assoc.

WEISS, W. 1957 Opinion congruence with a negative source on one issue as a factor influencing agreement on another issue. *J. abnorm. soc. Psychol. 54*, 180–186.

WHITE, B. W., & SALTZ, E. 1957 Measurement of reproducibility. *Psychol. Bull 54*, 81–99.

WHITE, R., & LIPPITT, R. 1960 Leader behavior and member reaction in three "social climates." In D. Cartwright & A. Zander (Eds.), *Group dynamics: research and theory* (ed. 2). New York: Harper & Row.

WHITE, W. A. 1938 *Puritan in Babylon: the story of Calvin Coolidge.* New York: Macmillan.

WHYTE, W. H. 1956 *The organization man.* New York: Simon and Schuster.

WIENER, N. 1954 *The human use of human beings.* Garden City, N.Y.: Doubleday.

WILKINS, E. J., & DE CHARMS, R. 1962 Authoritarianism and the response to power cues. *J. Person.* 30, 439–457.

WILLIAMS, R. J., & WRIGHT, C. R. 1955 Opinion organization in a heterogeneous adult population. *J. abnorm. soc. Psychol.* 51, 559–564.

WINCH, R. F. 1958 *Mate-selection: a study of complementary needs.* New York: Harper & Row.

WINCH, R. F., KTSANES, T., & KTSANES, VIRGINIA 1954 The theory of complementary needs in mate selection: an analytic and descriptive study. *Amer. sociol. Rev.* 19, 241–249.

WOLFE, D. M., & SNOEK, J. D. 1962 A study of tensions and adjustment under role conflict. *J. soc. Issues* 18, 102–121.

WOODWORTH, R. S. 1938 *Experimental psychology.* New York: Holt, Rinehart and Winston.

ZANDER, A., COHEN, A. R., & STOTLAND, E. 1957 *Role relations in the mental health professions.* Ann Arbor, Michigan: Institute for Social Research, Univ. of Michigan.

INDEXES

INDEX OF NAMES

Abelson, R. P., 51, 121, 122, 131, 525
Adorno, T. W., 2, 121, 174, 440, 441
Allport, F. H., 6, 281, 282, 283, 422, 467
Allport, G. W., 12, 139, 140, 153, 178, 179, 303
Allyn, J., 101
Angell, R. C., 248
Aronson, E., 141
Asch, S. E., 82, 166, 182, 238, 239, 241, 253, 282
Attneave, F., 187

Back, K. W., 313, 316, 381, 382, 383, 385
Baker, B. O., 416
Bales, R. F., 468, 469, 470, 474, 475, 476, 477, 480, 553–559
Barron, M. L., 412
Baumgartel, H., 386
Bavelas, A., 343
Bayton, J. A., 435
Benedict, Ruth, 418
Bergler, E., 32
Bettelheim, B., 452, 453
Bevan, W., 74
Binet, A., 279
Bird, C., 474
Blake, W., 256
Blum, G. S., 26
Bogardus, E. S., 429, 435, 443, 496, 499, 505, 515
Bos, Maria, 468, 470, 471
Bossom, J., 166
Brehm, J. W., 105, 106
Bronfenbrenner, U., 175, 426
Brown, R. W., 547
Bruner, J. S., 163, 168, 258
Brunswik, E., 32
Burgess, E. W., 329

Campbell, A., 26, 116, 117, 516, 517, 545
Campbell, A. A., 551
Campbell, D. T., 519
Cannell, C. F., 537, 539, 549
Cantril, H., 74, 447, 448, 449, 450, 537, 538, 548
Carlsmith, J. M., 141
Carlson, E., 97, 110
Cayton, H. R., 408
Chave, E. J., 520
Child, I. L., 407, 416
Christie, R., 172, 517, 518
Clark, K. B., 432
Clark, Mamie P., 432
Cline, V. B., 175, 176
Coch, L., 6, 385
Coffin, T. E., 278, 279
Cohen, A. R., 105
Collins, Mary E., 87, 94
Converse, P. E., 540
Cook, Peggy, 172, 517
Cook, S. W., 536
Cooley, C. H., 142
Coombs, C. H., 192, 525, 526, 527, 528
Cottrell, L. S., 329
Crown, S., 523

Dashiell, J. F., 6, 282, 283, 464, 467
Dearborn, D. C., 35
De Charms, R., 164
Dennis, W., 64
Deutsch, M., 87, 94, 247, 352, 353, 467, 534
Dewey, J., 264
Dickson, W. J., 313
Dimock, H., 385
Dollard, J., 4, 258, 274, 275, 277
Dodd, S. C., 515

577

578 - INDEX OF NAMES

Drake, St. C., 515
Dyson, F. J., 115

Edwards, A. L., 512, 518, 523, 524, 537
Engel, G., 143
Engel, M., 435
English, Ava C., 257
English, H. C., 257
Eysenck, H. J., 523

Faust, W. F., 465
Ferson, J. E., 421
Festinger, L., 101, 102, 105, 106, 129, 137, 146, 311, 313, 316, 385, 457
Fiedler, F., 481, 482, 483, 484
Fink, C. F., 359
Fiske, D. W., 519
Flugel, J. C., 262
French, J. R. P., Jr., 6, 385
Fried, E., 537
Fulcher, J. S., 170

Gallway, M., 175
Gilbert, E., 456
Giroud, A., 279
Gleicher, D. B., 251
Gollin, E. S., 177, 178
Gorden, R. L., 108
Gouldner, A. W., 263, 316
Gouldner, Helen, 316
Greenspoon, J., 547
Griffiths, K. S., 515
Guilford, J. P., 504, 511
Gurin, G., 545
Guttman, L., 506, 507, 508, 514, 516, 519, 520, 523, 525, 526, 527, 528

Haigh, G., 145
Hammond, K. B., 532
Harary, F., 304
Harding, J., 175
Harlow, H. F., 24, 25
Hart, I., 440, 441
Harvey, O. J., 101
Hastorf, A. H., 74
Hebb, D. O., 25
Heider, F., 31, 159, 167, 168, 171, 189, 213
Heinicke, C., 469
Helson, H., 162
Hildum, D. C., 547

Hill, R. J., 523, 525
Hill, Ruth, 249
Hinckley, E. D., 521, 522, 525
Hoffman, M. L., 252
Holtzman, W. H., 421
Homans, G. C., 219, 262, 310, 313, 316
Horney, Karen, 295, 296
Horowitz, E. L., 432, 437, 438, 439, 440
Horowitz, Ruth, 432
Hovland, C. I., 95, 99, 101, 102, 162, 452, 522, 525
Hurwitz, J., 338
Hyman, H. H., 78, 110, 536, 547
Hymovitch, B., 338

Indik, B. P., 364
Iverson, M. A., 446

Jackson, J. M., 376, 377, 395
Jahoda, Marie, 536
Janis, I. L., 102, 108, 236, 457
Janowitz, M., 452, 453
Jennings, Helen, 363
Jones, E. E., 257

Kahn, R. L., 368, 402, 478, 479, 480, 481, 483, 490, 537, 539, 549
Kaiman, I. P., 233
Katz, D., 43, 59, 74, 97, 145, 478, 479, 480, 481, 483, 490, 545
Keehn, J. D., 541
Kelley, H. H., 102, 103, 229, 249, 259, 260, 261, 270, 272, 464, 472, 535
Kelly, E. L., 511
Kelly, J. G., 421
Kelman, H. C., 95, 99, 102, 241
King, B. T., 108, 236, 457
Kitross, J. M., 530
Kitt, Alice S., 251
Ktsanes, T., 301
Ktsanes, Virginia, 301
Kubany, A. J., 532, 533

Landis, C., 170
Leary, T. F., 297, 298
Leavitt, H. J., 342, 343, 484
Le Bon, G., 5, 274
Leuba, C. J., 25
Levine, J. M., 76, 163
Lewin, K., 104, 408, 409, 410, 492
Libo, L., 385

INDEX OF NAMES - 579

Lieberman, S., 333, 334
Likert, R., 497, 498, 499, 505, 514, 519, 523
Lindauer, Florence, 518
Lindzey, G., 139, 140, 434, 436
Linton, R., 326, 337
Lippitt, R., 385
Loomis, J. L., 247
Luchins, A. S., 161

McBride, P. D., 253
McClintock, C., 97, 145
Maccoby, Eleanor E., 7, 235
McCord, J., 413
McCord, W., 413
McDougall, W., 4, 273, 274, 277
McGrath, J. E., 490
McGuire, W. J., 98, 134
McNemar, Q., 522
Mann, F., 386
Maslow, A. H., 166, 541
Mauss, M., 263
Maxwell, J. C., 115
Merei, F., 223, 224, 282
Merton, R. K., 47, 67, 416
Miles, O. K., 429, 515
Miller, D. R., 26
Miller, G. A., 188
Miller, N. E., 4, 274, 275, 277
Miller, W. E., 555
Mills, J. M., 468
Mintz, A., 452
Mishler, E. G., 468
Moser, C. A., 536
Mosteller, F., 546
Muraskin, J., 446
Murphy, G., 76, 141, 163, 523
Mussen, P. H., 180

Newcomb, T. M., 54, 72, 172, 173, 267, 268, 269, 304, 319, 339, 340, 348, 379
Norman, R. D., 179
Nunnally, J., 530

Odbert, H. S., 12
Osgood, C. E., 34, 41, 157, 161, 528, 529

Payne, S. L., 537
Penrod, W. T., 208
Pettigrew, T. F., 441, 442

Pilisuk, M., 150
Proshansky, H. M., 531
Prothro, E. T., 429, 515, 522

Raper, A., 448
Richards, J. M., Jr., 175, 176
Roethlisberger, F. J., 313
Rogers, C., 145
Rogolsky, S., 434, 436
Rommetveit, R., 285, 332
Roseborough, Mary E., 468
Rosenberg, M. J., 83, 84, 120, 131
Roslow, S., 523
Ross, E. A., 4, 273, 274, 277
Ross, I. C., 304
Rotter, J. B., 31
Rugg, D., 538
Runkel, P. J., 190, 191, 192

Saenger, G., 456
Sakoda, J. M., 543
Saltz, E., 508
Sanford, R. N., 163
Sarbin, T. R., 416
Sarnoff, I., 97, 145
Schachter, S., 202, 313, 316, 384, 385, 468
Schanck, R. L., 225, 282, 378, 422
Schein, E. H., 114
Schwartz, M., 525
Scodel, A., 180
Scott, W. A., 108, 237, 457
Sears, R. R., 452
Secord, P. F., 74
Selltiz, Claire, 536
Shannon, C., 36
Shaw, C. R., 412
Shaw, Marjorie E., 208, 361, 464, 471, 472
Sheatsley, P. B., 78, 110, 548
Sherif, Carolyn, 487, 489
Sherif, M., 101, 230, 231, 232, 233, 241, 282, 459, 487, 489, 522, 525
Sidowsky, J. B., 260, 261
Simmel, G., 309
Simon, H. A., 35
Skinner, B. F., 24, 258
Slater, P. E., 362
Smelser, W. T., 398
Smith, H. L., 547
Snoek, J. D., 401, 403
Spranger, E., 139, 173, 300, 318

Stephan, F. F., 468
Stouffer, S. A., 59, 60
Strodtbeck, F. L., 468
Suchman, E. A., 49
Suci, G. J., 528, 529
Sumner, W. G., 455
Sutherland, E. H., 412, 414, 416

Tagiuri, R., 163, 168, 258, 299
Tannenbaum, P. H., 90, 91, 528, 529
Tarde, G., 274
Teahan, J. E., 33
Thibaut, J. W., 201, 229, 249, 257, 270, 272, 464, 472
Thomas, E. J., 359
Thorndike, R. L., 472
Thurstone, L. L., 381, 520, 521, 522, 523
Triplett, N., 5, 6, 464
Tuddenham, R. D., 253
Turner, R. H., 144

Vanderlippe, R. H., 144
Vernon, P. E., 139, 140

Verplanck, W. S., 213, 214, 266
Vidulich, R. N., 233

Waller, W. W., 249
Walster, E., 102
Warner, W. L., 340, 423, 424, 425
Weaver, W., 36
Weiss, W., 101, 110
Westermarck, E., 263
White, B. W., 508
White, R. K., 385
White, W. A., 136
Whyte, W. H., 313, 315
Wiener, N., 212
Wilkins, E. J., 164
Williams, R. J., 513
Winch, R. F., 301
Wolfe, D. M., 368, 401, 402, 403
Woodruff, Christine L., 103
Woodworth, R. S., 169
Wright, C. R., 513

Zander, A., 559

INDEX OF SUBJECTS

Abilities, 395–396
Absenteeism, 386
Absolute judgments, 29
Accessibility, communicative, relationships of, 341–345
Acquisitiveness, 25
Adaptation
 individual, to environment, 44
 mutual, 7–10
Adaptation, interpersonal, 264–273
 individual, 265–269
 to others' attitudes, 269–270
 reciprocal, 270–272
 as triple confrontation, 273
Adaptability, 153
Adolescents
 delinquent, 412–416
 marginality of, 408–410, 417, 419, 426
 see also Juvenile delinquency
Aggressiveness, 25, 296
Ambiguity, figure–ground, 36–37
Analysis (Bales), interaction process, 553–559
Animals, communication with, 30
Anti-Semitism, 2, 122, 123, 432–434, 551–552
Apperception test, thematic, 33, 38
Association
 barriers to, 444
 frequency of, 340, 347, 423
 selective, 420–423
Attitude
 definition of, 40, 46
 direction of, 48
 functions of, 43–44
 and motives, difference between, 42
 prejudice, an acquired, 431–434
Attitude change, 15, 80–114, 152, 397
 attitude properties and, 89–94

balance affected by, 130
persuasion and, 94–104
primary conditions for, 82–89
principles of, 109–110
resistance to, 117–118, 136–138, 143–145
strategies of, 110–114
Attitude concept, 40, 41, 45
Attitude continuum, 50, 54, 55, 63
 zero point of, 62
Attitude object
 centrality of, 92–94
 characteristics of, 50–66, 79
Attitude organization, 152
 focal objects of, 138–139
 and object-belongingness, 121–124
 see also Attitudes, organization and stability of
Attitude scales, *see* Scales, attitude
Attitude stability, 92, 114, 136, 152
 correlation between, and age, 118
 time and, 138
 see also Attitudes, organization and stability of
Attitude structures, incorporating information into, 207–211
Attitudes
 anchors for, 146
 attribution of, to others, 5, 6
 common, but unshared, 12
 competitive, 6
 congruence of own and others', 125–129
 consensual and shared, within groups, 222–226
 different persons', toward the same things, 5
 discrepant, 12
 toward ethnic groups, 428–429, 433–436, 440–441

581

582 - INDEX OF SUBJECTS

Attitudes (Continued)
formal properties of, 48–66
formation of, 43–45
group members', 317–319
individuals', 17–18
of interacting persons toward one another, 5
interconnected, 151–152
interdependence of, 124
interpersonal, as basis of group structuring, 320–321
judging others', 171–174
and learning, 75–78
manipulators of, 110–112
measurement of, 496–534
message senders', 194–203
and motives, 42–43
multiple, behavior a function of, 69–70
nature of, 47–79
organization and stability of, 115–153
and overt behavior, 67–73
perceived, 5
and perception, 74–75
person as system of, 71, 72
preexisting, 14
shared, 11–12, 428, 488–489
systems of, 132–133, 135, 138–139, 150, 151, 152
Attitudes and situations, variations in behavior a function of, 67–69
Attraction, 66, 125
bases of, 298–302
dyadic, as basis for group structure, 302–309
interpersonal, 280, 281, 292–295, 298–302, 349, 486–488
mutual, see Attraction, reciprocal
of opposites, 301
reciprocal, 218, 246, 267–270, 280, 284, 293–294
among sharers, 227–228, 255
Attraction relationships, subgroup structuring of, 309–321
Authoritarianism, 2, 174, 179, 180, 422–423
measuring, 517–518
relationships of, to prejudice, 440–443
Authority, 484

Autokinetic phenomenon, 231–232, 233
Autonomy, self-perceptions of conformity and, 253–254
Aversion, 125, 219, 295, 298
among gang members, 292
mutual, 294
and stable dyads, 305–306

Balance, principle of, 129–136, 150, 152, 153
Balance and reality, 250–253
BaThonga, 327
Behavior
categories (Bales), 553–559
circular, 276
communicative, 185–220
compliant, 277–280, 296
a function of multiple attitudes, 69–70
highly organized, 21, 27
interpersonal, 21, 256, 264, 297–298, 304
motivated, 21–22, 26, 31–32, 35, 39, 40
observed, 10, 20
overt, 47–48, 67–73, 78, 79
predicting, 48
see also Predictability
role prescriptions and, 330–335
standard, 285
Behavioral distance, relation of, to status distance, 340–341
Behavioral interdependence, coordinated, 369
Behaviors
observable, 3
repertoire of, 394
sequence of, 3
Belongingness, see Object-belongingness
Bias, 38
coder, 75
Bogardus social distance scale, see Scales
Brainwashing, 112, 114

Causality, 31–32
and instrumentality, 124
Centrality
of attitude objects, 66, 79, 150

Centrality (*Continued*)
  communicative, 341–344
  object, 127, 135, 141
  psychological, of object for individual, 58–65
  structural, of groups, 319–320
Characteristics
  group, 289–291
  personal, relationship of, to grouping, 319–320
Choice, occupational, 395
Circularity, between cohesiveness and goal achievement, 491–493
Classes, social, barriers between, 423–427
Clique structure, 317–319
  propinquity as determinant of, 310–315
Cliques, 309–310
Codes, shared, necessity of, in communication, 10
Cognitive context, causality a, 31
Cognitive dissonance, theory of, 105–106, 129, 137, 236
Cognitive elements, interdependence between, 120
Cognitive organization, 27–33, 121
Cognized object, dimensionality of, 51–53
Cohesiveness, group, 246, 380–386, 463
  and goal achievement, 486–492
Commitment, participation and, 104–110
Communication
  with animals, 30
  barriers to, 444–447, 458
  as common to all forms of interaction, 10–12
  continuing, some effects of, 216–218
  effects of group size mediated by, 363–364
  a form of interaction, 156
  on a given topic, 213–216
  mass, 78
  meaning of, 184
  place of, in human interaction, 66, 189–190
  rational basis for occurrence of, 190–194

  rewardingness of, 218–219
  see also Behavior, communicative
Communicative accessibility, 341–345, 349–350
Communicative structure, of groups, 346–348
Communism, 60–61, 76
Compartmentalizing, 131
Competition, cooperation and, role relationships of, 351–356
Competitiveness, 6, 282–284
Compliance, *see* Behavior, compliant
Computers, 37
Concept formation studies, 30
Conditioning, instrumental, 24
Conflict, 9
  ethnic, 462
  intergroup, 391–392, 428–462
    reduction of, 451–462
  role, 394, 404–427
Conformity, 241–242, 246, 248
  and autonomy, self-perception of, 253–254
Congruence, attitudinal, 125–129
"Connectedness," 120
Consensus, 373–375, 380
  communication that implies, 284–285
  consequence of, 222–228, 230
  group, achievement of, 471–472
Consistency, 73
Consonance, 129
Contradictions, attitude–behavior, 47, 67
Contributions, group members'
  group reactions to, 470–473
  to problem solving, 467–469
Coolidge, Calvin, attitudes of, 136
Cooperation, and competition, role relationships of, 351–356
Costs, rewards and, *see* Rewards
Crowds, 5
Cues
  awareness of, 168
  internal, 178
  interpreting, 169, 170, 179
  selection of, 161–166
Curiosity-manipulation, 24–25

Daydreaming, 32
Decoding of information, 35–38, 74, 75

584 · INDEX OF SUBJECTS

Demand input, interaction affected by, 362–363
Demographic variables, 316–317
Detached persons, 296
Differences, group, 12–13
Differential, semantic, 41, 528–531
Differentiation, structural, and integration, 364–373
Dimensionality of cognized object, 51–53
Discrimination, racial, 47
 laws against, 71
 see also Anti-Semitism; Ethnic groups; Negroes; Prejudice
Discriminators, unprejudiced, 47, 67
Dispositional properties, 159–160, 161
Dispositions, stored, 67, 68, 78
 see also Attitudes
Dissonance, cognitive, see Cognitive dissonance
Distance, social, measurement of, 423, 434–435, 436
 see also Scales, Bogardus
Dreams, Freud's theory concerning, 32
Drive states, satisfaction of, 38
Drives
 definition of, 23, 24
 distinguished from motives and goals, 24
 hunger, 23–25, 26
 learning process and, 23–25
 primary, 25–26
Dyads
 characteristics of three basic kinds of, 304–307
 mutually attractive, 307–309
Dynamics, 129, 135

Economic factors in group conflicts, 440, 452–453
Ego-involvement, and resistance of attitudes to change, 143–145
Eisenhower, Dwight D., attitudes toward, 70
Elaboration, of group structure, 364–368
Elements, cognitive, interdependence between, 120
Emotional states, recognizing others', 169–170

Emotions, discrimination between, 48
Energizing effects, of interaction, 6
Energy
 drives as sources of, 23–24
 mobilization of, 22
Environment, individual adaptation to, 44
Ethnic groups, attitudes toward, 428–429, 433–436, 440–441
 see also Anti-Semitism; Discrimination; Negroes; Prejudice
Ethnic origin, marginality due to, 405–408
Ethnocentrism, 122, 123
Evaluation factors, 41
Evaluations of oneself, feedback concerning others', 266–269, 286
Expectations, role, 8, 9, 31–32, 37
 contradictory, 405, 417
 shared, 418–420

Facilitation
 modes of, 475–485
 social, 281–282, 284, 286
Fantasy, 32
Feedback of information, 11, 204
 concerning others' evaluations of oneself, 266–269, 286
 nature of, 211–213
Figure–ground ambiguity, 36–37
First impressions, basis of, 302–303
Focal objects
 of attitude organization, 138–139
 intercommunication between, 151
 other persons and groups as, 145–147
 self as, 141–145
Food motive, 22, 24, 25, 26
Forgetting, 75–77, 136
Friendships, development of, 8–9, 22
Frustration
 adolescent group, 415
 basis for, 9
 personal, 415
 prejudice associated with, 451–452
Function, of a social position, 325–328
Function, of attitudes
 adjustment, 43
 ego-defensive, 43
 knowledge, 44
 value-expressive, 44

INDEX OF SUBJECTS - 585

Goal
  cohesive power enhanced by, 489–493
  definition of, 24
Goal achievement
  through collective efforts, 26
  group cohesiveness and, 486–493
Goal orientation, motivation and, 21–24
Goals, 21–24, 31, 39, 46
  distinguished from drives, 24
  group, achieving, 463–493
Group, attraction structure of, 282
Group cohesiveness, and goal achievement, 486–493
Group conflict, economic factors in, 440, 452–453
Group consensus, achievement of, 471–472
Group death, 351
Group decisions, 103–104, 105
Group differences, 12–13
Group formation, spontaneous, 311–313, 487–488
Group goals, achieving, 463–493
Group norms
  formation of, 221–255
  function of, 240–241
  nature of, 228–230
  psychological processes affected by, 230–240
  and the sharing process, 242–255
Group productivity, 14
Group properties, 357–388
  classification of, 358–359
  definition of, 357
  interaction mediating between individual and, 12–15
Group-relevant attitudes, 224–225, 238, 250
Group settings, interaction in, 391–392, 553–559
Group size, 468–469
  effects of, mediated by communication, 363–364
Group solidarity, 14, 227–228
Group structures and properties, 289–291
Group structuring
  dyadic attraction a base for, 302–309
  forms of, 348
  interpersonal attitudes as basis of, 320–321
  see also Structuring, subgroup
Groups
  conflict in, 17
  human, identifying, 289–291
  interaction, see Interaction groups
  minority, see Minority groups
  as multidimensional systems of roles, 346–356
  nonconforming, membership in, 412–416, 427
  prejudice against, an acquired attitude, 431–434
Habit
  joint, 9
  multiperson, 8
  "two halves of the same," 7
Habits, traditions developed from, 223
Hamilton, A., ego-involved attitude of, toward dueling, 143
Hemingway, E., interpretation of luck by, 36–37
Hostility
  autistic, 305, 444
  toward ethnic minorities, 47, 122, 123
  between groups, 441, 444–451, 458–462
  within groups, 219
  reducing personal susceptibility to, 451–453
  see also Conflict, intergroup; Prejudice
Hunger drive, 23, 24, 25, 26
Hypnosis, 83, 84
Hysteria, national, concerning Communism, 61
  see also Communism

Identification, 280
Imbalance
  conditions governing degree of discomfort at, 131–136, 138
  outcomes of, 149–152
Imitation
  a form of interpersonal behavior, 274–277
  within group, 223–224

INDEX OF SUBJECTS

Imitation (*Continued*)
  of self, 276
  a unilateral influence process, 3–5, 280
  see also Leaders
Immigrants
  Italian-American, 407–408
  marginality of, 405–406
Inclusiveness
  of attitude object, 53, 79
  difference between centrality and, 63
Individuals
  attitudes of, 17–18
  interdependence of, 27
Influence
  reciprocal, 5–7, 257, 281–287
  unilateral, 3–5, 257, 273–281, 286
Influenceability, reciprocal, 284
Information
  acceptance of, 118
  ambiguous incoming, 35, 73, 78, 86–88
  common but unshared, 11
  contradictory, 88, 89, 92, 94
  decoding incoming, 35–36, 38
  discrepant, 11
  equalizing, 196–198
  feedback of, 11, 204
  incomplete, 73–74, 79
  incorporating, into attitude structures, 207–211
  about objects, changes in, 86–89
  organizing, 28–29
  persuasive, 94
  redundant, 35
  resistance to, 120
  shared, 11
  socially mediated, 111, 118
  sources of, 32, 33
  stimulus, ambiguity in, 75
  stored, 11, 27–28, 31, 37–38, 39, 40, 60, 63, 91–92, 118–119, 120, 136, 138
  threatening, 136, 138
  and uncertainty, 187–188
  unorganized, 27–28
Information costs, 60–61
Ingenuity, 27
Input, 73, 78, 79
Insecurity, 400
Insight, 108

Instrumentality, causality and, 31, 124
Insulation, social, 420–426, 427
Integration
  as dependent variable, 369–372
  group, 368–373
  as independent variable, 372–373
  racial, 87
  structural differentiation and, 364–373
Interaction
  between-person processes of, 20
  communication a form of, 10–12, 156, 184, 189–190
  and congruence, 127–128
  demand input effect on, 362–363
  energizing effects of, 6
  goals achieved by, 26
  group properties related to, 368–388
  in group settings, 391–392, 553–559
  individual contribution to, 45–46
  networks of interpersonal relationships and, 363
  observing and understanding, 1–15, 17–18
  problems concerning, 183–184, 185
  process analysis, 553–559
  processes of, 155–156
  spatial arrangements, effect of on, 310–316
  within-person processes affected by, 20
  see also Behavior; Communication
Interaction groups, 156, 291, 292, 553–559
  characteristics of, 14, 221–222, 322
  goal-oriented, 463
  size of, 359
  stability of, 321
  structure of, 346–349
  at work, 492–493
Interdependence
  behavioral, 8
  between cognitive elements, 120
Interpersonal relationships
  interaction affected by networks of, 363
  maintaining satisfying, 480–483
  structures of, 292–321
Intervals, equal-appearing, Thurstone's method of, 520–523

INDEX OF SUBJECTS - 587

Interviewing
  open-ended, 539–540
  problems of, 547–550
  structured questions used in, 539–540
  see also Responses
Interviewers
  characteristics of, respondents and, 548–550
  respondents influenced by, 546–548
Isolates, 310, 319, 321, 347
Italian-Americans, 407–408

Job description, 395
Judging others, 171–181
Juvenile delinquency, 412–416, 427, 503–504

Kasper, John, 454–455
Kwakiutl Indians, 327

Language
  a distinctive human capacity, 27
  dolphin, 30
  evaluative factor in, 41
  symbols of, 30, 32
  translation problems in, 64
  use of, 36, 63
Leaders, 12, 223–224, 342–343
Leadership, 463
  role of, in group goal achievement, 473–486
Learning, 20
  attitudes and, 75–80
  drive-reduction theory of, 25
  future, 42
  human capacity for, 26
  instrumental, 24
  part of, in prejudice, 432–433
  possibilities of, 27
  tension-reduction theory of, 24
Learning process
  drives and the, 23–25
  motivated behavior and, 40
Legislation
  a means of changing norms, 455–457
  against racial discrimination, 71
Likert scale, *see* Scales
Liking, reciprocal, basis of group formation, 9
Lynching, 447–451

Marginal man, 405–410, 417, 419, 426–427
Marginality in role relations, 400
Mass communication, 78
Meaning, 35
Means–end relationships, 31, 39, 124
Measurement, attitude, 496–534, 535
  accuracy of, 509–514
  general characteristics of, 500–519
  indirect method of, 531–533
  interval and ratio, 502–503
  levels of, 501–509
Memory, 27, 29, 32, 37, 75, 77, 78
Message receiving, psychological processes in, 204–211
Message sending, psychological processes in, 190–203
Messages, nature of, 186–190
Minority groups
  hostility toward, 47
  prejudice against, 97–98, 121
Models, 4, 5
Mohave Indians, 418–419
Morale, 372
Motivated behavior, *see* Behavior, motivated
Motivation, 9
  complex, and the organization of psychological processes, 27–40
  as goal orientation, 21–22
  individual, to conform, 241–242
  nature of, 20–21
Motive arousal, 40, 42
Motives
  acquisition of, 23–27
  attitudes and, 42–43
  definition of, 22
  distinguished from drives, 24
  message senders', 194–203
  number and variety of human, 25–27
Multidimensionality, 51–53
Multiple attitudes, individual the possessor of, 102

Negroes
  attitudes toward, 84, 86, 87–88, 421–422, 497
  prejudice against, 2, 432–433, 435, 438–442, 454–456
  role conflict of, 406–408, 410–412, 417, 427

588 - INDEX OF SUBJECTS

Negroes (*Continued*)
   traits attributed to, 74–75
   see also Lynching
Neurotics, 295
Norm-sending, 285
Normativeness, 376–380, 384, 441, 469
   structural integration an expression of, 489
Norms, group, 15, 221–255
   behavioral, 238–240
   changing, by legislation, 455–457
   changing, through joint participation, 457–461
   cognitive, 233–235
   common elements among different kinds of, 248–250
   evaluative, 235–238
   imperfect sharing of, 250–253
   perceptual, 230–233

Object, attitudinal, 43–44
Object change, attitudes affected by, 83–86
Object generalization, 28–31, 121–124
Object-belongingness, 28, 31, 109, 128
   attitude organization and, 121–124
Objects, valenced, 40
Observer, characteristics of, as affecting cue selection, 161–168
Opinions, public expression of, 108
Organization
   and learning, 38–40
   meaning of, 46
   and perception, 33–38
   see also Psychological activities, organization of
Output, 73, 78, 79
   group, quantity and quality of, 6
Overload, role, 394, 401–404
Overt behavior, *see* Behavior, overt

Parkinson's law, 367
Participation and commitment, 104–110
Perceived person, 158–160
Perceiver, psychological processes of, 160–168
Perception
   attitudes and, 74–75

organization and, 33–38
phenomena of, 34
reciprocal, by interacting persons, 182–184
social, 34
Perception, interpersonal, 3, 157–184
   accuracy in, 168–181
   psychological processes in, 158–168
Perceptual selectivity of information, 34–35
Peripherality, 341–344
Persuasion, 125, 126
   attitude change and, 94–104, 109, 111
Phase movement (Bales), 557–558
Pluralistic ignorance, 371
Politics, 70, 71, 75, 115–117, 128, 130–131, 132–133
Poll-taking methods, 541–546
   area sampling, 546
   quota system, 544–545
Popularity
   individual, status structure in terms of, 348
   relation of, to group structure, 319–320, 558
Popularity status, 337–341, 365–366
Positional distance, and role relationships, 336–346
Positions, attractiveness of, and associated roles, 395–398
Positions, social
   achieved, 326
   ascribed, 326
   assignment of individuals to, 326–327
   functions of a, 325–328
   prestige, 326
   and role prescriptions, 324–336
Power
   conveyed by information, 12
   interpersonal attraction and, 486–488
Practitioner vs. social psychologist, 110–111
Predictability, 8, 19, 48, 72–73, 77, 240–243
Prejudice, 428–458
   against groups, 2, 86, 97–98, 121, 428
   age relationship to, 438–439
   bases of, 430–444

INDEX OF SUBJECTS · 589

Prejudice (*Continued*)
 and discrimination, distinction between, 47
 frustration associated with, 451–452
 generalized, 2
 part of learning in, 432–433
 personality factors in, 440–444
 specialized, 2
 susceptibility to, 440–441
 violence resulting from, 447–451
 see also Anti-Semitism; Negroes
Prejudiced nondiscriminator, 47, 67
Pressure, *see* Role overload
Prestige, professional, 337
Problem-solving groups, 12, 359–362, 363
 interaction processes in, 464–473, 553–559
Profile analysis (Bales), 555–557
Propaganda, 110
Properties
 dispositional, 159–160, 161
 group, 358
 group structures and, 289–291
 individual and group, interaction as mediating between, 12–15, 18
Propinquity, as determinant of clique structure, 310–316
"Psycho-logic," 120
Psychological activities, organization of, 19–46
Psychological processes
 influence of attitudes on, 73–78
 organization of, 27–40
Public opinion, survey research and the measurement of, 535–551

Reality
 balance and, 133–136, 250–253
 social, 234, 244
Recorder (Bales), interaction, 553, 554
Reference group, 109–110, 145–147, 253
Referents, 198, 209–211
 definition of, 186
 primary, 205–207
 receivers' selection of, 205–207
 secondary, 188
Reflexes, interpersonal, 257–259
Regularities, 228–229
 descriptive, 3

explanatory, 3
individual, 18
Reinforcement, group, 282–287
Relationships
 basic forms of, 297
 facilitative, 474
 instrumental, 124
 parent-child, 8, 397, 418–419
 task-relevant, 321
Research, survey, and measurement of public opinion, 535–551
Residues, 54
Resistance, to attitude change, 117–118, 136–138, 143–145
Resource input, interaction affected by, 359–362
Respondent, characteristics of interviewer and, 548–550
Response, interpersonal, 256–287
Response interference, 272
Responses
 coding, 550–552
 emotional, 258
 perceiving and repeating, 276–277
 smiling, 259
 survey, conditioned by form of question, 538
Reward values, 38
 primary, 39
 secondary, 39
Rewardingness of communication, 218–219
Rewards, 24, 106, 108
 and costs, individual, 271–272
 in the dyad, 271–273
Rivalry, 6
Role, occupational, compatibility of, 396–398
Role conflict, minimizing, 417–426
Role demands, complex, 393–427
Role differentiation, in problem-solving groups, 558
Role expectations, 8, 9, 31–32, 37
 contradictory, 405, 417
 shared, 418–420
Role overload, 394, 401–404
Role partners, 264, 280
Role prescriptions
 ambiguous, 399–401, 404
 gains and pains in, 394–404
 inadequate, 398–408
 prejudice included in, 437–440

590 - INDEX OF SUBJECTS

Role prescriptions (*Continued*)
 and role behavior, 330–335
 social positions and, 324–336
Role relations
 marginality in, 400
 variety in, 395
Role relationships, 8–10, 291, 322–356
 dimensional descriptions of, 345–346
 leadership as, 473–475, 485–486
 positional distance and, 336–346
 rewarding, 395
Role structure, 348–349
Role support, 301–302
Role-playing, and attitude change, 107–109
Roles
 acceptability of, 395
 groups as multidimensional systems of, 346–356
 interlocking, 329
Rorschach test, 38
Rules
 accepting, 243–246, 249, 254
 recognizing existence of, 242–243
 shared acceptance of, 489–490
Russians, attitudes toward, 84–85, 88

Saliency, 37–38, 58–59
Sampling, problems of, in poll-taking, 541–546
Sanctions, 230
Scales
 attitude, 56, 497, 499–500, 503–509, 510–519
 Bogardus, 429–430, 446, 498–500, 505, 514–515, 516, 519
 Guttman, 506–509, 514, 516, 519, 520, 523, 525–526, 527, 528
 Likert, 496–499, 500, 505, 514, 518, 519
 Prothro and Miles, 429, 515
 social distance, *see* Scales, Bogardus
Scaling
 Coombs technique of, 525–528
 cumulative, 506–509
 equal-appearing interval method of, 520–528
 multidimensional, 528–531
 paired-comparison method of, 523–525
 rank-order method of, 504–509

Secondary values, compatibility of, 396–398
Segregation, 87, 445–447, 456
 school, 454
 see also Negroes
Selectivity, perceptual, of information, 34–35
Self
 and attitude organization, 143
 as focal object, 141–144
 ideal, 144
 social nature of, 142–143
Self-image, 43–44
Self-other congruence principle, 141, 152
Self-perceptions, of conformity and autonomy, 253–254
Semantic differential, 41, 528–531
Sequence
 behavior, 39, 264
 distress–distress, 263–264
 interpersonal, 257–264
 response, 259
 response–response, 286
 reward–reward, 259–263, 264
 smile–smile, 258–259, 261–263, 264
 thought–action, 32
Sharers, attraction among, 227–228, 255
Sharing, 11, 375–376, 384
Sharing process, group norms and, 242–255
Similarity of attitudes, 373
Situations, 67–68, 69, 71, 79
 minimal social, 259–261, 263
Size, group, 359–364
Social distance, measurement of, 423, 434–435, 436
 see also Scales, Bogardus
Social facilitation, 6–7, 281–282, 284, 286, 467, 468, 470, 491
Social object, 65–66
Social positions
 nature of, 324–326
 significance of, 327
Social psychologist, 20, 51, 498
 vs. practitioner, 110–111
Social psychology, 2–3, 4–7, 21, 24, 75, 273, 492, 496
Social reality, 234, 244
Societies, positions common to all, 326
Solidarity, group, 227, 228, 246

Source credibility, 100, 118
Spatial arrangements, effect of, on interaction, 310–316
Stability, 24
  of dyadic relationships, 304–307
  group, 286, 321
  organization and, of attitudes, 115–153
Status
  differential, 340–341, 469
  hierarchical, 336–341
  popularity, 337–341, 365–366
  in problem-solving groups, 558
Status distance, relation of, to behavioral distance, 340–341
Status structure in terms of individual popularity, 348
Stevenson, Adlai, attitudes toward, 70
Stimulation, 6, 25
Stimuli, judging, 29
Stimulus objects, 51
"Stop thinking," 131, 135, 136
Structural differentiation and integration, 364–373
Structural integration
  goal-achievement contribution to, 490–491
  normativeness an expression of, 489
Structures
  group, and properties, 289–291
  of interpersonal relationships, 292–321
Structuring, subgroup, of attraction relationships, 309–321
Subattitudes, 120–121
Substitutability, 244–248, 249, 418
Suggestibility, 274, 278, 279
Survey research studies
  and measurement of public opinion, 535–552
  preparation of questions for, 536–541
Symbols, 10
  formation and manipulation of, 30
System, definition of, 132
Systems of roles, groups as multidimensional, 346–356

Tension-reduction theory of learning, 24
Thematic apperception test, 33, 38
Thieves, professional, 412–414
Thinking machines, 37
Thought, problem-solving vs. autistic, 32–33
Total group, role structure of, 346–349
Traditions, fixed, 223
Trait names, 12
Triads, 303, 307–310
Trust, mutual, 9, 246–247

Uncertainty, information and, 187–188
Unidimensionality, 51–58
Uniformity, attitudinal, 373–380
Unprejudiced discriminator, 47, 67

Valence implications, 77, 82, 92, 100, 111, 112, 113, 120
Values, as inclusive attitudes, 44–45
Values, inclusive
  types of, 139
  profile of, 140
Values, secondary, compatibility of, 396–398
Variable
  dependent, elaboration as, 366–367
  integration as, 369–370
  group property a, 358
  independent, elaboration as, 367–368
  integration as, 372–373
Variables, demographic, 316–317
Violence, 447–451
  group norms a key factor in, 448–449
Voters, 70, 71, 72
  changing attitudes of, 80–81
  see also Politics

Win-stay, lose-change, 259, 261
Wishing, 33
Work groups, 6